"The editors' stated purpose for the *Handbook* was to present technically sound, research-based assessment procedures that engage the full spectrum of individual assessment objectives that organizations face when attempting to maximize their human talent. They succeeded. The coverage is broad, deep, and accessible to a wide audience. It examines our most fundamental assessment issues from a variety of perspectives and in a variety of contexts. It covers the landscape, and the differences across perspectives are informative, even for a hard-core academic. *Read* it."

—*John Campbell*, professor of Psychology and Industrial Relations, University of Minnesota

Handbook of Workplace Assessment

The Professional Practice Series

The Professional Practice Series is sponsored by The Society for Industrial and Organizational Psychology, Inc. (SIOP). The series was launched in 1988 to provide industrial and organizational psychologists, organizational scientists and practitioners, human resources professionals, managers, executives, and those interested in organizational behavior and performance with volumes that are insightful, current, informative, and relevant to *organizational practice*. The volumes in the Professional Practice Series are guided by five tenets designed to enhance future organizational practice:

1. Focus on practice, but grounded in science
2. Translate organizational science into practice by generating guidelines, principles, and lessons learned that can shape and guide practice
3. Showcase the application of industrial and organizational psychology to solve problems
4. Document and demonstrate best industrial and organizational-based practices
5. Stimulate research needed to guide future organizational practice

The volumes seek to inform those interested in practice with guidance, insights, and advice on how to apply the concepts, findings, methods, and tools derived from industrial and organizational psychology to solve human-related organizational problems.

Previous Professional Practice Series volumes include:

Published by Jossey-Bass

Implementing Organizational Interventions
Jerry W. Hedge, Elaine D. Pulakos, Editors

Organization Development
Janine Waclawski, Allan H. Church, Editors

Creating, Implementing, and Managing Effective Training and Development
Kurt Kraiger, Editor

The 21st Century Executive: Innovative Practices for Building Leadership at the Top
Rob Silzer, Editor

Managing Selection in Changing Organizations
Jerard F. Kehoe, Editor

Evolving Practices in Human Resource Management
Allen I. Kraut, Abraham K. Korman, Editors

Individual Psychological Assessment: Predicting Behavior in Organizational Settings
Richard Jeanneret, Rob Silzer, Editors

Performance Appraisal
James W. Smither, Editor

Organizational Surveys
Allen I. Kraut, Editor

Employees, Careers, and Job Creating
Manuel London, Editor

Published by Guilford Press

Diagnosis for Organizational Change
Ann Howard and Associates

Human Dilemmas in Work Organizations
Abraham K. Korman and Associates

Diversity in the Workplace
Susan E. Jackson and Associates

Working with Organizations and Their People
Douglas W. Bray and Associates

Handbook of Workplace Assessment

The Professional Practice Series

Handbook of Workplace Assessment

Evidence-Based Practices for Selecting and Developing Organizational Talent

John C. Scott
Douglas H. Reynolds, Editors

Foreword by Allan H. Church and Janine Waclawski

JOSSEY-BASS
A Wiley Imprint
www.josseybass.com

Published by Jossey-Bass
A Wiley Imprint
989 Market Street, San Francisco, CA 94103-1741—www.josseybass.com

Jossey-Bass books and products are available through most bookstores. To contact Jossey-Bass directly call our Customer Care Department within the U.S. at 800-956-7739, outside the U.S. at 317-572-3986, or fax 317-572-4002.

Jossey-Bass also publishes its books in a variety of electronic formats. Some content that appears in print may not be available in electronic books.

Library of Congress Cataloging-in-Publication Data

Handbook of workplace assessment : evidence-based practices for selecting and developing organizational talent / John C. Scott, Douglas H. Reynolds, editors ; foreword by Allan H. Church. — 1st ed.
    p. cm. — (The professional practice series)
    Includes bibliographical references and index.
    ISBN 978-0-470-40131-6
  1. Employees—Rating of. 2. Needs assessment. 3. Organizational change. 4. Personnel management. I. Scott, John C. (John Carlson), 1955– II. Reynolds, Douglas H.
    HF5549.5.R3H28 2010
    658.3'124—dc22

                                                   2010003886

Printed in the United States of America
FIRST EDITION
HB Printing   10 9 8 7 6 5 4 3 2 1

Contents

Figures, Tables, and Exhibits

Figures

Tables

Exhibits

Foreword

Welcome to the newest volume in the Professional Practice book series of the Society for Industrial and Organizational Psychology (SIOP). We are very excited about this volume and the contribution that we believe it will make not only to the series overall but also to the field in general.

The idea for this book came out of one of our first editorial board meetings at an annual SIOP meeting about six or seven years ago. The approach during our years as series coeditors was to call our board together (since we typically had a quorum at the annual conference) to meet and discuss the trends and practices we were seeing in the field. We talked about sessions we had seen at the conference that were good, bad, or ugly and used these thoughts as fodder to brainstorm ideas for what we hoped would be great future volumes for this series. For the most part, the output of those brainstorming sessions came to fruition in the form of several volumes of which we are very proud. This book is one that we have had a lot of passion and anticipation for since those early days. However, we also recognized that completing this task would require a lot of effort, insight, and dedication to put together under the right volume editors. Luckily for us, it all fell into place under the editorship of John Scott and Doug Reynolds. They have done a fantastic job of surveying the simultaneously broad and deep field of assessment and putting it all together in one place under a simple yet elegant framework.

Talent identification and assessment is one of the most critical issues facing organizations today. From our vantage point as practitioners (one of us as an organization development specialist and the other as a human resource generalist), we see this as a major challenge. A good or bad hire in isolation can have a long-lasting organizational impact (think about your personal experiences here), and in the aggregate, its impact is profound: it determines not only the organizational culture but also ultimately its success or failure. In this way, assessment is key to our practice as I-O professionals. The concept behind this volume is to provide internal and external practitioners with a much-needed compendium of tools and techniques for effective and accurate assessment.

Our previous volume examined talent management. This time the focus is on the assessment itself and truly understanding what works and for whom. We believe this book will be helpful not only to I-O practitioners working in the assessment arena but also to other professionals who are engaged in assessing or hiring activities in corporations. As with previous volumes, our aim is to provide practical solutions grounded in research and applied experience. We believe this volume does just that. The Appendix alone is a gold mine of information for anyone interested in assessment—not to mention the main content of the volume. In our opinion, John and Doug have made a major contribution to the field with their efforts. We sincerely appreciate their dedication to making this edition a reality. Thanks, guys!

Pound Ridge, New York   Janine Waclawski
May 2010   Allan H. Church

Preface

There has been a marked trend over the past few years for organizations of all sizes to streamline their workforces and focus on selecting and retaining only the "best and the brightest" employees. Couple this with the skills gap that will soon emerge due to the magnitude of baby boomer retirements, and it is no surprise that organizational priorities have been steadily shifting toward talent acquisition and retention. As organizational consultants, we are continually engaged in dialogue about how assessments can best be leveraged to achieve a company's talent management objectives. Specifically, human resource (HR) and line leaders want to know if assessments should be used and, if so, what specific instruments would be applicable, whether they can be administered online, whether they need to be proctored, what the costs are, whether there are specific legal constraints, whether they can be implemented in multiple languages in multiple countries, how an assessment program should be managed, how to know if the process is working, and what the expected return on investment is. And these are just a few of the questions that need to be answered to ensure that an assessment program meets stakeholder needs, achieves the organization's goals, and has a positive impact on its bottom line.

The field of assessment has advanced rapidly over the past decade due in part to advancements in computer technology. By leveraging technology, organizations can reach across the boundaries of language, literacy, and geography to reliably assess a vast catalogue of candidate skills and abilities. Organizations can now harness the capabilities of sophisticated, Web-based assessment tools to simulate actual work environments—effectively measuring candidates' ability to perform under real-life conditions. Technological advances have also fostered a number of assessment methodologies such as adaptive testing that have led to significant improvements in measurement precision and efficiency.

Despite these advances, there remain some fundamental questions and decisions that each organization must grapple with to ensure it is maximizing the potential of its assessment program and taking advantage of well-researched theories and state-of-the-art practice. This book presents sound, practical guidelines that are steeped in empirical research for implementing an assessment process that will effectively drive an organization's critical talent decisions.

The Audience

This book is designed for a broad readership, from HR professionals who are tasked with implementing an assessment program to assessment professionals and practitioners of industrial-organizational (I-O) psychology, who advise, build, validate, and implement assessments. In addition, this book is intended for the users of assessments, including hiring managers and organizational leaders, who are looking for direction on what to assess, what it will take, and how to realize the benefits. This book is also intended for assessment researchers as well as instructors and graduate students in disciplines such as I-O psychology, HR management and organizational behavior, consulting psychology, and organizational development.

Overview of the Book

This book is divided into four parts: it examines frameworks for organizational assessment; assessment for selection, promotion, and development; strategic assessment programs; and advances, trends and issues. The Appendix provides examples of the types of tests and assessments currently available for use in the workplace.

The foundational chapters contained in Part One are designed to provide readers with a thorough understanding of what should be assessed and why and how to ensure that assessment programs are of the highest quality and reflect the latest thinking and practice in the field. Part Two is devoted to the specific applications of workplace assessment and covers a variety of positions where high-volume or high-stakes decisions need to be made. The chapters in this part emphasize examples of current best practices in assessment to help practitioners understand, apply, and evaluate the success of these practices in their own work contexts. The focus is on assessment systems in place today and that are needed in the future as business needs change. The chapters address the application of assessments to clerical, professional, technical, sales, supervisory and early leadership, and managerial and executive positions. In addition, a chapter addresses the special case of police and firefighter selection.

Part Three highlights some of the key strategic applications of assessment that organizations rely on to boost their competitive edge. The chapters focus on succession management, staffing for organizational change (downsizing, mergers, and reorganizations), assessing for potential, and global selection. The chapters in Part Four cover a wide range of advances, trends, and issues: technology-based delivery of assessment, the legal environment, alternative validation strategies, addressing flaws in assessment decisions, and the strategic use of evaluation to link assessment to bottom-line organizational priorities.

A brief description of each of the chapters follows.

Part One: Framework for Organizational Assessment

Kevin Murphy sets the stage in Chapter One by discussing broad dimensions of individual differences that are likely to be relevant for understanding performance effectiveness and development in the workplace and delineates two general strategies for determining what to assess in organizations. In Chapter Two, Fritz Drasgow, Christopher Nye, and Louis Tay outline the characteristics and features that differentiate outstanding assessment programs from mediocre systems and provide information that practitioners can use to move toward state-of-the-art measurement in their organizations. The next six chapters examine the most commonly assessed characteristics in the workplace: cognitive ability, personality, background and experience, knowledge and skill, physical performance, and competencies. These chapters highlight the challenges faced in accurately and fairly assessing these characteristics and detail advances in the field and the state of practice for their measurement.

Michael McDaniel and George Banks kick off these topics in Chapter Three with a review of the research and practice in the use of general cognitive ability tests in workplace assessment. They trace the history of intelligence testing from its roots to modern applications and detail the merits of cognitive ability assessment for selecting and developing top talent. In Chapter Four Robert Hogan and Robert Kaiser provide a compelling look at the use of personality assessment, why it is so misunderstood, and how it can be leveraged to predict significant outcomes. Leaetta Hough follows in Chapter Five on the assessment of background and experience; she addresses factors affecting this tool's validity and provides empirically based recommendations for improving its accuracy in predicting behavior. In Chapter Six Teresa Russell highlights the different types of knowledge and skill measures and offers some innovative ideas for measuring both declarative and procedural knowledge and skills.

Deborah Gebhardt and Todd Baker focus in Chapter Seven on assessments used for selecting candidates for strenuous jobs. There are many critical applications of these assessments in both the public and private sectors where failure to meet physical demands can have a significant impact on job performance and safety. Finally, Jeffery Schippmann rounds out Part One with a groundbreaking and forthright portrayal of the evolution of the role of competencies in assessment programs.

Part Two: Assessment for Selection, Promotion, and Development

Judith Komaki opens this part with a fictional but very realistic account of an HR manager who is asked to produce a valid test of managerial skills on a shoestring budget. The frustrations and complexities of finding an off-the-shelf test that maps onto the required skills are brought to light in this engaging and perceptive chronicle. Wanda Campbell follows in Chapter Nine by drawing on her experience leading nationwide testing consortia to detail the use of assessment procedures for selecting, promoting, and developing individuals across a variety of technical roles. In Chapter Ten, Lia Reed, Rodney McCloy, and Deborah Whetzel describe the evolution of responsibilities in both clerical and professional jobs over the past twenty years and provide an insightful analysis of the resulting impact on assessment decisions associated with these typically high-volume hiring jobs. Steven Brown focuses in Chapter Eleven on practical techniques and unique challenges associated with sales assessment (for example, dispersed locations and unproctored testing). He provides particularly valuable recommendations for how to properly define success criteria for salespersons and ensure that the assessment tools are validated. In Chapter Twelve, Mark Schmit and Jill Strange show how assessments can be leveraged to stem the tide of supervisory derailment in organizations and demonstrate how these assessments are important to the bottom line.

Ann Howard and James Thomas delve into the arena of high-stakes decision making in Chapter Thirteen on executive and managerial assessment. They address the unique characteristics and challenges associated with working at this level and show how the effective design and implementation of managerial and executive assessment programs can provide significant benefits to organizations. Chapter Fourteen by Gerald Barrett, Dennis Doverspike and Candice Young describes the special case of public sector assessment, with a specific focus on police and firefighter selection. The authors detail the challenges and outline strategies for successfully navigating in this highly contentious and heavily litigated area.

Part Three: Strategic Assessment Programs

In Chapter Fifteen, Matthew Paese outlines six fundamental actions required for organizations to shift from a traditional replacement-focused succession management system to a more contemporary growth-focused system, which is required to close the ever-widening leadership capability gaps. Rob Silzer and Sandra Davis follow with an incisive chapter that leverages a new integrated model of potential for making long-term predictions of performance. They describe a variety of assessment strategies and tools in the context of this model for assessing potential and fit and show how the proper measurement of these critical elements links to an organization's competitive edge and bottom line.

In Chapter Seventeen, John Scott and Kenneth Pearlman outline the strategies necessary to build a legally defensible staffing model under various reduction-in-force (RIF) conditions, including mergers and acquisitions, restructuring, and targeted or across-the-board RIFs. Ann Marie Ryan and Nancy Tippins close Part Three with an astute analysis of issues faced by practitioners who must refine the methods used for single-country assessment and confront issues of validation, cultural differences, country-specific legal issues, consistency of use, measurement equivalence, and the impact of culture on design and implementation.

Part Four: Advances, Trends, and Issues

Douglas Reynolds and Deborah Rupp begin Part Four with Chapter Nineteen on technology-based delivery of assessment. They examine the conditions that have enabled the growth of technology-facilitated assessment, as well as the applicable professional standards, guidelines, and legal considerations that are specific to technology-based assessments. They emphasize the context for system deployment, options for system design, and the major issues that arise as these systems are implemented in organizations. In Chapter Twenty, Lawrence Ashe and Kathleen Lundquist focus on the legal environment in which workplace assessments operate, highlighting not only relevant government regulations and case law but also the current priorities of agencies enforcing federal equal employment opportunity law. They explore the future of employment litigation and provide a comprehensive approach for building legal defensibility into the workplace assessment process.

Morton McPhail and Damian Stelly in Chapter Twenty-One provide a summary of the alternative approaches for validating workplace assessments and cover the development of new validity evidence where traditional techniques are not applicable. In Chapter Twenty-Two James Outtz explores how the common flaws in deciding what to assess can have a major impact on both the organization and its employees and candidates, particularly in high-stakes testing situations. He provides a number of solutions for consideration, including the use of an evidence-based approach and broadening the range of assessments under consideration.

In Chapter Twenty-Three, Jane Davidson helps readers understand how to leverage the evaluation of workplace assessment as a strategic tool for driving business success and achieving competitive advantage. Finally, in Chapter Twenty-Four, Paul Sackett offers concluding thoughts and future directions for the assessment field.

Appendix

The Appendix offers practical suggestions for assessments across the full range of applications that are covered in this book. It is designed as a user-friendly resource to help readers make decisions about which assessments they should consider for their needs. The Appendix, organized into sections related to four types of assessments—construct targeted, position targeted, management and leadership targeted, and job analysis support—provides test and publisher names of popular or commonly used instruments, along with a brief description of each.

Orientation

The chapters in this book provide a range of perspectives on how best to apply the science of people assessment to the workplace. The gracious experts who have contributed to this book were asked to blend the best of the common base of scientific knowledge with the unique demands of the workplace applications with which they are most familiar.

A tour of these topics could be considered in a similar light to a tasting tour across a wide range of cuisine. Just as different chefs draw selectively from the available ingredients and techniques to meet the tastes and expectations of their local culture, the experts here focus on the use of human characteristics and proven measurement techniques to meet the demands of a wide range of workplace environments. By understanding the ingredients (Part One), how they are combined in different contexts (Parts Two and Three), and new techniques and emergent issues (Part Four), readers should be better prepared to assemble their own unique recipe. We hope the tour is both informative and enjoyable.

■ ■ ■

Darien, Connecticut   John C. Scott
Pittsburgh, Pennsylvania   Douglas H. Reynolds
May 2010

Acknowledgments

We are pleased to have had such a renowned group of globally recognized authors agree to devote their knowledge, experience, and time to the creation of this handbook. Their contributions reflect cutting-edge theory and practice, and it is clear why they are at the pinnacle of their profession. We greatly appreciate all of the effort and commitment that went into bringing these chapters to life. Without the dedication of the chapter authors, this book would not have been possible.

In addition, we express our sincere gratitude to a second set of authoritative experts who provided in-depth chapter reviews and astute feedback. Their contributions significantly improved this handbook, and we are extremely thankful for their efforts. These reviewers were Seymour Adler, Herman Aguinis, Ronald Ash, Dave Bartram, Milton Blood, Joan Brannick, Eric Dunleavy, Charlotte Gerstner, Arthur Guttman, Monica Hemmingway, Cal Hoffman, Joyce Hogan, Lawrence James, Jerard Kehoe, Rich Klimoski, Deirdre Knapp, Elizabeth Kolmstetter, Manny London, Joyce Martin, Jennifer Martineau, James Outtz, Neal Schmitt, Jeffery Stanton, Garnett Stokes, George Thornton, and Mike Zickar.

We also thank Janine Waclawski and Allan Church, the editors of Jossey-Bass's Professional Practice Series, for their invaluable guidance throughout the preparation of this book. Special thanks go out as well to Matt Davis and Lindsay Morton and the editorial staff at Jossey-Bass for keeping us on track.

Of course, we are particularly grateful to our respective families: Kimberly, Justin, and Jeremy Scott, and Jennifer Cooney, Sam, and Caleb Reynolds. Through their love, patience, tolerance, and generosity, each contributed mightily to this project.

The Editors

John C. Scott is chief operating officer and cofounder of APT *Metrics*, Inc., a global human resource consulting firm that designs sophisticated talent management solutions for Fortune 100 companies and market innovators. He has more than twenty-five years of experience designing and implementing human resource systems across a variety of high-stakes global settings. For the past fifteen years, he has directed APT's talent management practice areas to serve a broad range of client sectors: retail, pharmaceutical, telecommunications, entertainment, insurance, technology, hospitality, aerospace, utilities, and financial services.

John is coeditor of *The Human Resources Program-Evaluation Handbook* and coauthor of *Evaluating Human Resources Programs: A Six-Phase Approach for Optimizing Performance*. He has also authored numerous chapters and articles in the areas of assessment, selection, and organizational surveys and serves on the editorial board of Wiley-Blackwell's Talent Management Essentials series.

John was the 2009 conference program chair for the Society for Industrial and Organizational Psychology (SIOP) and was recently appointed as SIOP's representative to the United Nations. He received his Ph.D. in industrial-organizational psychology from the Illinois Institute of Technology.

■ ■ ■

Douglas H. Reynolds is vice president of assessment technology at Development Dimensions International, where he leads the development and deployment of assessment and testing products. His work has been implemented in many Fortune 500 companies and several federal agencies. In the 1990s, he designed some of the first Internet-based assessments used for large-scale corporate recruiting. More recently, his work has focused on the use of computer-delivered simulations for executive and leadership evaluation. He is also an expert witness on personnel selection practices, and his articles, book chapters, and presentations often focus on the intersection of technology and assessment.

Recently Doug coauthored *Online Recruiting and Selection*, a book on the integration of technology with personnel selection practices. He also serves on the editorial boards of the *Journal of Management* and Wiley-Blackwell's Talent Management Essentials series.

Doug is active in SIOP leadership, currently serving on the executive board as the communications officer and in the past as chair of the Visibility and Professional Practice committees. In prior roles, he was a senior scientist at the Human Resources Research Organization and adjunct faculty at George Washington University. He earned his Ph.D. in industrial-organizational psychology from Colorado State University.

The Contributors

R. Lawrence Ashe Jr., the chair of Ashe, Rafuse & Hill in Atlanta, Georgia, is in his forty-third year of advising on and litigating employment law, test validity, and civil rights issues. He is nationally recognized for his class action and test validation expertise and experience. He has tried more employment selection class actions to judgment than any other management lawyer in the country, including some of the largest cases tried to date. His civil rights practice is 10 to 15 percent representation of plaintiffs with the balance defendants. Test validity and other employment selection issues are over one-third of his practice. Lawrence is a founding board member of Atlanta's Center for Civil and Human Rights and a board and executive committee member of the National Council for Research on Women. He is a Fellow in the American College of Trial Lawyers and the College of Labor and Employment Lawyers. He graduated from Princeton University and Harvard Law School.

■ ■ ■

Todd A. Baker is a senior research scientist at Human Performance Systems, Inc. and has twenty years of experience developing and validating physical performance and cognitive assessments for public, private, and military organizations. He has conducted job analyses for hundreds of physically demanding jobs and developed and validated numerous physical performance and cognitive test batteries for evaluation of applicant and incumbent personnel for public safety and private sector positions. In 2006, Todd was part of a team that was awarded the Society for Industrial and Organizational Psychology M. Scott Myers Award for Applied Research in the Workplace for developing and validating the assessments and medical guidelines used for selecting transportation security officers. In 2003, he was part of a team that was awarded the International Public Management Association–Assessment Council Innovations Award. Todd has litigation experience, providing testimony in the areas of job analysis, physical performance tests, promotional tests, and the Fair Labor Standards Act.

■ ■ ■

George C. Banks holds an M.A. in industrial-organizational psychology from the University of New Haven and is pursuing a Ph.D. at Virginia Commonwealth University. His research focuses on employment testing, applicant attraction, and team development. George is a member of the Academy of Management and the Society for Industrial and Organizational Psychology.

■ ■ ■

Gerald V. Barrett, president of Barrett and Associates since 1973, has been involved in the development and validation of employment tests for numerous jobs, including firefighter and police officer. He has consulted with numerous public and private organizations and has been engaged as an expert witness in over 160 court cases, usually dealing with issues of alleged age, race, national origin, or sex discrimination in selection, promotion, termination, reduction in force, or compensation. Gerald received his Ph.D. in industrial psychology from Case Western Reserve University and his J.D. from the University of Akron's School of Law. He is both a licensed psychologist and a licensed attorney in the State of Ohio. He is a Fellow of the American Psychological Association and the American Psychological Society. The Society for Industrial and Organizational Psychology presented him with the Distinguished Professional Contributions Award in 1992 in recognition of his outstanding contributions to the practice of industrial-organizational psychology. He also received the Life Time Achievement Award from the Industrial Organizational Behavior Group.

■ ■ ■

Steven H. Brown is president of SHB Selection Consulting and senior consultant, assessment solutions, for LIMRA International. He consults internationally in the areas of selection and assessment. Previously he was vice president and director of LIMRA International's Assessment Solution Group, a professional staff engaged in human resource research, selection product development, and recruiting and selection process consultation. Steve holds a B.A. from DePauw University and a Ph.D. in industrial-organizational psychology from the University of Minnesota. He is a Fellow of the American Psychological Association, the Society for Industrial and Organizational Psychology (SIOP), and the American Psychological Society. He has published numerous articles in professional journals about personnel and sales selection. He has served on the editorial board of *Personnel Psychology* and was a member of the task force that wrote SIOP's *Principles for the Validation and Use of Personnel Selection Procedures.*

■ ■ ■

Wanda J. Campbell is the senior director of employment testing for Edison Electric Institute, the trade association of investor-owned electric utility companies. She manages a nationwide testing program that includes nine employee selection test batteries, seven of which are for technical jobs, as well as a career assessment and diagnostic instrument. EEI tests have become the industry standard for the electric utility industry. She is a member of the Society for Industrial and Organizational Psychology (SIOP), the Society of Consulting Psychology, the American Psychological Association, and the Maryland Psychological Association. She served on the committee responsible for the 2003 revision of the SIOP *Principles for the Validation and Use of Personnel Selection Procedures* and is currently serving on the SIOP Workshop Committee. She has made over thirty presentations at professional conferences and coauthored four book chapters. She is licensed as a psychologist in the State of Maryland and is currently serving as the treasurer for the Maryland Psychological Association. She earned her Ph.D. in industrial-organizational psychology from Old Dominion University. Prior to becoming a psychologist, Wanda worked for five years as an equal opportunity specialist for the Equal Employment Opportunity Commission.

■ ■ ■

E. Jane Davidson runs an evaluation consulting business (Real Evaluation Ltd.), working across a range of domains including leadership development, human resources, health, education, and social policy. Her work includes evaluation training and development, facilitated self-evaluation and capacity building, independent evaluation, and formative and summative meta-evaluation (advice, support, and critical reviews of evaluations). Previously she served as associate director of the Evaluation Center at Western Michigan University. There, she launched and directed the world's first fully interdisciplinary Ph.D. in evaluation. She has presented numerous keynote addresses and professional development workshops internationally. Jane is the author of *Evaluation Methodology Basics: The Nuts and Bolts of Sound Evaluation* (2004). She was the 2005 recipient of the American Evaluation Association's Marcia Guttentag Award, awarded to a promising new evaluator within five years of completing the doctorate. She received her Ph.D. from Claremont Graduate University in organizational behavior, with substantial emphasis on evaluation.

■ ■ ■

Sandra L. Davis is chief executive officer of MDA Leadership Consulting, a talent management and leadership development firm. She cofounded the company in 1981 and currently focuses her consulting work on senior executive talent evaluation. She is widely known as an executive coach and thought leader in the industry, counting numerous Fortune 500 companies among her clients. She has contributed chapters and articles to professional books and journals related to assessment, leadership development, coaching, and succession. She served on the Strong Interest Inventory Advisory panel for Consulting Psychologists Press; her book *Reinventing Yourself* was based on her work in the practical use of tests. She is a member of the American Psychological Association and the Society for Industrial and Organizational Psychology. Prior to founding MDA, she served on the faculty of the University of Minnesota and worked for Personnel Decisions. Sandra earned her B.S. from Iowa State University and her Ph.D. in counseling psychology with an emphasis in industrial-organizational psychology from the University of Minnesota.

■ ■ ■

Dennis Doverspike is a professor of psychology at the University of Akron, senior fellow of the Institute for Life-Span Development and Gerontology, and director of the Center for Organizational Research. He holds a Diplomate in industrial-organizational psychology and in organizational and business consulting from the American Board of Professional Psychology (ABPP) and is a licensed psychologist in the State of Ohio. Dennis has over thirty years of experience working with consulting firms and with public and private sector organizations, including as executive vice president of Barrett & Associates. He is the author of two books and over one hundred refereed journal publications. Current major additional positions include president of the ABPP specialty board in organizational and business consulting. He received his Ph.D. in psychology in 1983 from the University of Akron. His M.S. in psychology is from the University of Wisconsin–Oshkosh and his B.S. is from John Carroll University. His areas of specialization include job analysis, testing, and compensation.

■ ■ ■

Fritz Drasgow is a professor of psychology and labor and industrial relations at the University of Illinois at Urbana-Champaign. Previously he was an assistant professor at Yale University's School of Organization and Management. He has also provided consultation on testing and measurement issues to a variety of organizations in the private and nonprofit sectors. Drasgow's research focuses on psychological measurement, computerized testing, and the antecedents and outcomes of sexual harassment. He is a former chairperson of the American Psychological Association's Committee on Psychological Tests and Assessments, the U.S. Department of Defense's Advisory Committee on Military

Personnel Testing, the Department of Defense and Department of Labor's Armed Services Vocational Aptitude Battery Norming Advisory Group, the American Psychological Association's Taskforce on Internet Testing, and the American Institute of Certified Public Accountants' Psychometric Oversight Committee. Drasgow is a member of the editorial review board of eight journals, including *Applied Psychological Measurement, Journal of Applied Psychology,* and the *International Journal of Selection and Assessment.* He is a former president of the Society for Industrial and Organizational Psychology and received its Distinguished Scientific Contributions Award. He received his Ph.D. from the University of Illinois at Urbana-Champaign.

■ ■ ■

Deborah L. Gebhardt is president of Human Performance Systems, Inc., and has over twenty-five years of experience developing and validating physical performance tests, fitness programs, and medical guidelines and standards for public, private, and military organizations. She holds Fellow status in the Society for Industrial and Organizational Psychology (SIOP) and the American College of Sports Medicine (ACSM). She has published research in the areas of job analysis, physical test development and standards, medical guidelines, injury analysis, and biomechanics. She has conducted over one hundred physical performance test development and validation projects in the federal, public, private, and military sectors. In 2006, Gebhardt was part of a team that was awarded the SIOP M. Scott Myers Award for Applied Research in the Workplace for developing and validating the assessments and medical guidelines used for selecting transportation security officers. In 2003, she was part of a team that was awarded the International Public Management Association–Assessment Council Innovations Award. She has served as an expert witness in class action (Title VII) and Americans with Disabilities Act litigation, and arbitrations regarding the physical performance tests, job analysis, validation, and medical guidelines used in the selection and retention of workers.

■ ■ ■

Robert Hogan, president of Hogan Assessment Systems, is an international authority on personality assessment, leadership, and organizational effectiveness. He was McFarlin Professor and chair of the Department of Psychology at the University of Tulsa for fourteen years. Prior to that, he was professor of psychology and social relations at The Johns Hopkins University. He has received a number of research and teaching awards, is the author of *Personality and the Fate of Organizations* and the Hogan Personality Inventory, and is the editor of the *Handbook of Personality Psychology* (1997). Robert received his Ph.D. from the University of California, Berkeley, specializing in personality assessment. He is the author of more than three hundred journal articles, chapters, and books. He is widely credited with demonstrating how careful attention to personality factors can influence organizational effectiveness in a variety of areas—ranging from organizational climate and leadership to selection and effective team performance. Robert is a Fellow of the American Psychological Association and the Society for Industrial and Organizational Psychology.

■ ■ ■

Leaetta M. Hough is founder and president of the Dunnette Group, an adjunct professor in the psychology department at the University of Minnesota, past president of the Society for Industrial and Organizational Psychology (SIOP), and past president of the Federation of Associations in Behavioral and Brain Sciences, a coalition of twenty-two scientific societies. She is coeditor of the four-volume *Handbook of I-O Psychology*, lead author of chapters in the *Annual Review of Psychology*, the *International Handbook of Work and Organizational Psychology*, the I-O volume of the *Comprehensive Handbook of Psychology*, the *Handbook of Personnel Selection*, and the *Biodata Handbook*, as well as dozens of articles in refereed journals. She has developed new methods of work analysis, performance appraisal systems, and selection methods, including hundreds of valid and defensible personnel selection and performance measures, many of which are innovative, nontraditional measures that have minimal, if any, adverse impact against protected groups. She is an internationally recognized expert in the measurement of personality, creativity, and global mind-set.

■ ■ ■

Ann Howard is chief scientist for Development Dimensions International (DDI), a global talent management company. She leads the Center for Applied Behavioral Research (CABER), DDI's hub for research to support evidence-based talent management. She directs research that measures the effectiveness and organizational impact of DDI interventions and investigates global workplace practices and issues. Previously, as DDI's manager of assessment technology integrity, she designed, implemented, and evaluated assessment center platforms and set quality standards for DDI's assessment technologies. During twelve years at AT&T she codirected two longitudinal studies of the lives and careers of managers. She is the senior author (with Douglas W. Bray) of *Managerial Lives in Transition: Advancing Age and Changing Times*, which received the George R. Terry Award of Excellence from the Academy of Management. She has written more than one hundred book chapters, monographs, and papers on topics such as assessment centers, executive selection, managerial careers, and leadership development. She has also edited several books on the changing workplace, including *The Changing Nature of Work* and *Diagnosis for Organizational Change: Methods and Models*. She is a Fellow and past president of the Society for Industrial and Organizational Psychology.

■ ■ ■

Robert B. Kaiser is a partner with Kaplan DeVries, an executive development firm, and was previously at the Center for Creative Leadership. He has written over one hundred publications and presentations, including three books. His work on leadership, development, and assessment has appeared in *Harvard Business Review* and *Sloan Management Review*, as well as top-tier scholarly journals. He is the coauthor, along with Bob Kaplan, of the Leadership Versatility Index, a 360-degree feedback tool that received three U.S. patents. Rob also has a consulting practice in which he grooms high potentials for the executive suite, and in his talent management work for global corporations, he provides research-based services that include developing custom leadership models and assessment tools as well as statistical analysis of performance data to inform talent management strategy. He has an M.S. in industrial-organizational psychology from Illinois State University.

■ ■ ■

Michael R. Kemp works in Development Dimensions International's Assessment and Selection Analytics Group, where he designs, develops, and ensures the ongoing effectiveness of DDI's screening, testing, and assessment solutions worldwide. His major areas of focus are test and assessment content design, validation and documentation, development of local and global norms, and the analysis of operational data. He is also a Ph.D. candidate in industrial-organizational psychology at Central Michigan University. For his doctoral work, his research focuses on leadership development and multisource feedback. Other research interests are applicant assessment and selection, employee engagement, occupational stress, and leadership derailment. He is an affiliate member of the Society for Industrial and Organizational Psychology and has presented research on leadership theory at past conferences.

■ ■ ■

Judith L. Komaki, a former professor of industrial-organizational psychology at Purdue University and City University of New York's Baruch College, initially set up motivational programs. But she quickly learned that without proper management support, the program, no matter how well designed, would be doomed to failure. Hence, she shifted to leadership, identifying what effective leaders did aboard racing sailboats and in darkened theaters. While watching stage directors in connection with an Army Research Institute contract, she noticed what was onstage and what was missing. Rarely did she find characters resembling herself—a professional woman of color—so she began writing plays.

One play forced her to come to terms with the insidious effects of race, something she had assiduously avoided. But realizing her arsenal of professional skills, she began using them to pursue social and economic justice, taking to heart the management adage "We treasure what we measure." She is the author of a leadership book (*Leadership from an Operant Perspective*, Routledge, 1998), an off-off Broadway play, and an article about pursuing the dreams of Martin Luther King Jr. ("Daring to Dream: Promoting Social and Economic Justice at Work," 2007).

■ ■ ■

Kathleen K. Lundquist is CEO and cofounder of APT Metrics, a global human resource consulting firm that designs talent management solutions for Fortune 100 clients. An organizational psychologist, she testifies frequently as an expert witness in employment discrimination class action lawsuits on behalf of both defendants and plaintiffs and has provided invited testimony before the U.S. Equal Employment Opportunity Commission. Following settlements of high-profile class actions, the courts have appointed her to design and implement revised HR processes for organizations such as the Coca-Cola Company, Morgan Stanley, Abercrombie & Fitch, Ford Motor Company, and the Federal Bureau of Investigation. In consulting with clients ranging from multinational corporations to government and nonprofit employers, she designs proactive measures to improve the fairness, validity, and legal defensibility of HR processes before they are challenged. She is a former research associate with the National Academy of Sciences, a fellow in psychometrics with the Psychological Corporation, and a summer research fellow with the Educational Testing Service. Kathleen is a member of the corporate advisory board of the National Council for Research on Women.

■ ■ ■

Rodney A. McCloy is a principal staff scientist at the Human Resources Research Organization (HumRRO), serving as an in-house technical expert and a mentor to junior staff. He is well versed in several multivariate analytical techniques and has applied them to numerous research questions, particularly those involving personnel selection and classification, job performance measurement and modeling, and attrition and turnover. His assessment and testing experience has spanned both cognitive and noncognitive domains and has involved several large-scale assessment programs, including the Armed Services Vocational Aptitude Battery, National Assessment of Educational Progress, and General Aptitude Test Battery. He directs HumRRO's internal research and development program and is active in the academic community, having served as an adjunct faculty member of the psychology departments at George Mason University and the George Washington University. He currently serves on the advisory board for the Masters of I-O Psychology Program at Northern Kentucky University and is a Fellow of the American Psychological Association and the Society for Industrial and Organizational Psychology. He received his B.S. in psychology from Duke University and his Ph.D. in industrial-organizational psychology from the University of Minnesota.

■ ■ ■

Michael A. McDaniel is a professor of management and research professor of psychology at Virginia Commonwealth University. He is internationally recognized for his research and practice in personnel selection system development and validation. He is also known for his applications of meta-analysis in employment testing, management, and other fields. McDaniel has published in several major journals, including the *Journal of Applied Psychology, Personnel Psychology, International Journal of Selection Assessment,* and *Intelligence.* He is a member of the Academy of Management and a Fellow of the Society for Industrial and Organizational Psychology, the American Psychological Association, and the Association for Psychological Science. He received his Ph.D. in industrial-organizational psychology from George Washington University.

■ ■ ■

S. Morton McPhail, a senior vice president and managing principal with Valtera Corporation, received his master's and doctoral degrees in industrial-organizational psychology from Colorado State University. He has served as a consultant for over thirty years to a wide variety of public and private sector clients on issues including employee selection and promotion, test validation, training and development, performance assessment, and termination. He has served as an expert in litigation involving such diverse issues as job analysis, test development and validation, violence in the workplace, equal employment opportunities, compensation, and reductions in force. He has published in professional journals and presented on numerous topics at professional meetings. Mort serves as adjunct faculty for both the University of Houston and Rice University and is on the editorial board of *Personnel Psychology*. A Fellow of the Society for Industrial and Organizational Psychology, Mort is currently its financial officer/secretary. He is a licensed psychologist and serves on a committee of the Texas Psychology Board regarding development and validation of the state's jurisprudence and ethics examination for licensure.

■ ■ ■

Kevin R. Murphy is a professor of psychology and information sciences and technology at Pennsylvania State University. He is a Fellow of the American Psychological Association, American Psychological Society, and the Society for Industrial and Organizational Psychology (SIOP). He has served as president of SIOP (1997–1998) and as associate editor and then editor of the *Journal of Applied Psychology* (1991–2002), as well as a member of the editorial boards of *Human Performance, Personnel Psychology, Human Resource Management Review, International Journal of Management Reviews, Journal of Industrial Psychology*, and *International Journal of Selection and Assessment*. He is the recipient of the SIOP's 2004 Distinguished Scientific Contribution Award. He is the author of over 150 articles and book chapters, and author or editor of eleven books, in areas ranging from psychometrics and statistical analysis to individual differences, performance assessment, gender, and honesty in the workplace.

Kevin's main areas of research are personnel selection and placement, performance appraisal, and psychological measurement. His current work focuses on understanding the validation process.

■ ■ ■

Christopher D. Nye is a Ph.D. candidate at the University of Illinois at Urbana-Champaign. His research primarily involves personnel selection and assessment, organizational research methods, and workplace deviance. His master's thesis examined the prevalence of cheating in multistage testing programs and was later published in the *International Journal of Selection and Assessment*. His dissertation is focused on developing new methods for interpreting the results of studies examining bias in psychological measures. He has also conducted psychometric research for several large organizations, including the Department of Defense, the College Board, and the National Council of State Boards of Nursing.

■ ■ ■

James L. Outtz is president of Outtz and Associates, a consulting firm in Washington, D.C. He develops selection procedures for a wide variety of organizations, from Alcoa to the Federal Deposit Insurance Corporation. His interests include selection, training, performance management, job analysis and work design, workforce diversity, and equal employment opportunity. His professional service includes membership on the Ad Hoc Committee on Revision of the Principles for the Validation and Use of Personnel Selection Procedures. In addition, he has served as consulting editor to the *Journal of Applied Psychology*. He is nationally recognized for his work in the area of adverse impact and alternative selection procedures, subjects about which he has written extensively. He is the editor of *Adverse Impact: Implications for Organizational Staffing and High Stakes Selection* (2010). He received his Ph.D. in industrial-organizational psychology from the University of Maryland. He is a Fellow in the Society for Industrial and Organizational

Psychology, the American Psychological Association, and the American Educational Research Association.

■ ■ ■

Matthew J. Paese is vice president of executive succession management at Development Dimensions International (DDI) and holds his Ph.D. in industrial-organizational psychology from the University of Missouri–St. Louis. Coauthor of *Grow Your Own Leaders* (2002) and numerous articles in the areas of talent management, executive assessment, succession, and development, he has spent more than fifteen years consulting with CEOs and senior teams from leading organizations around the world. His work includes the design and implementation of strategic talent initiatives, including organizational talent strategy, succession management, CEO succession, executive assessment, executive coaching, and executive team building. Paese has consulted extensively with executives from many organizations including Wal-Mart, Microsoft, and BP. Prior to joining DDI in 1994, he worked for Anheuser-Busch, where he was responsible for executive assessment and selection initiatives.

■ ■ ■

Kenneth Pearlman is in independent consulting practice following a twenty-seven-year career employed in both the public and private sectors, including the U.S. Office of Personnel Management, AT&T, and Lucent Technologies. He has specialized in research and applications in the areas of personnel selection and assessment, work and skill analysis, organizational and employee survey development, leadership assessment and development, and productivity measurement and enhancement. He has authored or coauthored over one hundred journal articles, technical reports, book chapters, papers, and presentations in these areas. He is a Fellow of the American Psychological Association, the Association for Psychological Science, and the Society for Industrial and Organizational Psychology (SIOP). He is on the editorial boards of *Personnel Psychology, Industrial and Organizational Psychology,* and the *International Journal of Selection* *and Assessment,* and served for eight years on the editorial board of SIOP's Professional Practice book series. He is coholder of a U.S. patent on a work analysis software tool. He has served as a member of the National Research Council's Board on Testing and Assessment. He received his B.A. in psychology from the Catholic University of America and his Ph.D. in industrial-organizational psychology from the George Washington University.

■ ■ ■

Lia M. Reed is an industrial-organizational psychologist in the Selection, Evaluation and Recognition Department of the U.S. Postal Service. She helps manage over twenty preemployment tests for the Postal Service, covering over two hundred job titles across four unions. Previously she worked for consulting firms where she assisted clients in developing, validating, and administering a variety of assessments. For the past ten years, Lia's work has focused primarily on the development and validation of preemployment and promotional tests for public, private, and government organizations, and she has worked on a wide variety of assessments. She received her M.A. and Ph.D. from DePaul University in Chicago. She is a member of the Society for Industrial and Organizational Psychology, the American Psychological Association, and the Society for Human Resource Management and has served as a board member of the Personnel Testing Council of Metropolitan Washington.

■ ■ ■

Deborah E. Rupp is an associate professor of labor/employment relations, psychology, and law at the University of Illinois at Urbana-Champaign. Her research related to assessment focuses on assessment center validity, the use of the method to foster professional development, and the use of technology to enhance assessment and development. She has coauthored the new edition of *Assessment Centers in Human Resource Management* with George C. Thornton and was the first recipient of the Douglas W. Bray and Ann Howard Award (for research on leadership assessment and development). She also conducts research on organizational justice, corporate social responsibility, and emotions at work, and has published over fifty scholarly papers. She is currently an associate editor at *Journal of Management*, recently cochaired the International Congress on Assessment Center Methods, and co-led the International Taskforce on Assessment Center Guidelines in publishing a revision to the *Guidelines and Ethical Considerations for Assessment Center Operations*. Her assessment center research was also cited by U.S. Supreme Court Justice J. Ginsburg in proceedings surrounding the decision of the employment discrimination case *Ricci* v. *DeStefano et al.*

■ ■ ■

Teresa L. Russell is a principal staff scientist at the Human Resources Research Organization and has more than twenty-five years of experience in personnel selection and classification. Early in her career, she gained a broad base of experience as a part of the U.S. Army's Project A research team, developing spatial and perceptual tests, content-analyzing critical incidents, developing performance rating scales, and collecting and analyzing data. Since that time, she has been involved in the development and validation of predictor measures for a wide variety of military and civilian organizations. She is currently the project director for a series of projects to develop and validate a measure of information and communication technology literacy for inclusion on the Armed Services Vocational Aptitude Battery. She has authored book chapters on cognitive ability measurement, measurement plans and specifications, experimental test battery psychometrics, and career planning, as well as dozens of technical reports and conference papers.

■ ■ ■

Ann Marie Ryan is a professor of organizational psychology at Michigan State University. Her major research interests are improving the quality and fairness of employee selection methods and topics related to diversity and justice in the workplace. In addition to publishing extensively in these areas, she regularly consults with organizations on improving assessment processes. She is a past president of the Society for Industrial and Organizational Psychology and past editor of the journal *Personnel Psychology*. She received her B.S. with a double major in psychology and management from Xavier University and her M.A. and Ph.D. in psychology from the University of Illinois at Chicago.

■ ■ ■

Paul R. Sackett is the Beverly and Richard Fink Distinguished Professor of Psychology and Liberal Arts at the University of Minnesota. He received his Ph.D. in industrial-organizational psychology at the Ohio State University in 1979. His research interests revolve around various aspects of testing and assessment in workplace, educational, and military settings. He has served as editor of the journals *Industrial and Organizational Psychology Perspectives on Science and Practice* and *Personnel Psychology*. He has also served as president of the Society for Industrial and Organizational Psychology, cochair of the committee producing the Standards for Educational and Psychological Testing, a member of the National Research Council's Board on Testing and Assessment, and chair of the American Psychological Association's Committee on Psychological Tests and Assessments and its Board of Scientific Affairs.

■ ■ ■

Jeffery S. Schippmann is the senior vice president of human resources and chief talent officer for Balfour Beatty Construction in Dallas, Texas. Previously he was vice president of global talent management for the Hess Corporation, where he was responsible for succession planning, performance management, talent assessment, and management development and training activities. Previously, he was the director of Organization and Management Development for PepsiCo. In this role he was responsible for a broad range of talent management programs and initiatives over a six-year period, including significant work to refocus managers on people development activities and restructuring the Pepsi "employment deal." Before Pepsi, Jeff was in consulting with Personnel Decisions International in a variety of roles focusing on selection and staffing solutions, executive assessment and development, assessment centers, and competency modeling for a broad range of clients including Texas Instruments, Bank One, Memorial Sloan-Kettering, American Express, Boeing, and Ford. He received his Ph.D. in industrial-organizational psychology at the University of Memphis in 1987 and is the author of two books and numerous book chapters and articles, including work appearing in the *Journal of Applied Psychology* and *Personnel Psychology*.

■ ■ ■

Mark J. Schmit is the western regional vice president for APT, with an office in Denver. He has more than twenty years of experience in the field of human resources (HR). He has spent time as an HR generalist, academic, applied researcher, and internal and external consultant to both public and private organizations. He has developed recruitment, selection, promotion, performance management, organizational effectiveness, and development tools and systems for numerous organizations. Most recently he has been involved in employment discrimination litigation, serving as an expert witness and consultant from the field of industrial-organizational psychology. Schmit earned a Ph.D. in industrial-organizational psychology from Bowling Green State University in 1994. He has published more than twenty-five professional journal articles and book chapters and delivered more than forty-five presentations at professional meetings on HR and industrial-organizational psychology topics. He is an active member of the American Psychological Association, Society for Industrial and Organizational Psychology, and Society for Human Resource Management.

■ ■ ■

Rob Silzer is managing director of HR Assessment and Development, a corporate consulting firm, and is on the I-O psychology doctoral faculty at Baruch College and Graduate Center, City University of New York. He has consulted with leaders in over 150 organizations, focusing on leadership assessment, selection, succession, development, coaching, and talent management. Rob is also a fellow of the American Psychological Association, the Association for Psychological Science, the Society for Industrial and Organizational Psychology, and the Society of Consulting Psychology. After receiving his Ph.D. in industrial-organizational psychology and counseling psychology from the University of Minnesota, he served as director of personnel research at Fieldcrest-Cannon and president of PDI–New York. He has taught doctoral courses at the University of Minnesota, New York University, and Baruch–CUNY. Rob has served on the editorial boards of *Personnel Psychology, Industrial and Organizational Psychology,* and *The Industrial-Organizational Psychologist* and as president of the Metropolitan New York Association of Applied Psychology. Rob has edited several books, including *Strategy-Driven Talent Management* (with Ben Dowell), *The 21st Century Executive,* and *Individual Psychological Assessment* (with Dick Jeanneret). He has authored over one hundred articles, book chapters, professional workshops, and presentations. He enjoys global adventure travel, mountain trekking, alpine skiing, and scuba diving.

■ ■ ■

Damian J. Stelly, organization development director at JCPenney, leads the company's performance management and employee selection programs and consults with leaders regarding organizational development and research initiatives. As an internal and external consultant, he has also held positions at Anheuser-Busch and Valtera Corporation. Damian has managed a broad range of projects, including the development of selection and placement systems, survey programs, performance management programs, organizational development initiatives, and employee development programs. He has presented or published on a variety of topics, including validation methods, test development, and leadership behavior. He is a member of the American Psychological Association and the Society for Industrial and Organizational Psychology. Damian holds a B.A. in psychology from Louisiana State University and received his M.A. and Ph.D.

in industrial-organizational psychology from the University of Missouri–St. Louis. He is licensed as a psychologist in Texas.

■ ■ ■

Jill M. Strange, a project manager at APT with ten years of experience in the field of industrial-organizational psychology, specializes in the design, development, and implementation of competency models and competency-based tools and provides consulting services in the areas of job analysis, employee selection development and validation, and litigation support. She has led several large-scale efforts in the areas of competency modeling, job analysis, and selection assessment design for industry, government, and military clients. In addition, she worked with several clients to design and validate selection assessments as well as performance assessment systems and workforce planning strategies. Strange is the author of over fifteen peer-reviewed articles and book chapters on the subjects of leadership, assessment, and competency modeling and frequently presents at professional meetings and conferences on these areas. She earned her Ph.D. in industrial-organizational psychology from the University of Oklahoma and is Senior Professional in Human Resources (SPHR) certified. She is a member of the American Psychological Association and the Society for Industrial and Organizational Psychology.

■ ■ ■

Louis Tay is a doctoral student in industrial-organizational psychology at the University of Illinois at Urbana-Champaign. His research interests include subjective well-being, emotions, and culture. He is actively working on conceptual and methodological advances in psychological measurement, encompassing the synthesis of item-response theory, latent class modeling, and hierarchical linear modeling. He has conducted research with several large organizations, including the American Dental Association, the College Board, and the Gallup Organization. He has published in several journals, including *International Journal of Testing*, *Journal of Applied Psychology*, and *Organizational Research Methods*.

■ ■ ■

James N. Thomas, vice president of consulting services at Development Dimensions International, heads its Northeastern Regional Consulting Group headquartered in New York City. Previously he led its Southeastern Regional Consulting team located in Atlanta. Thomas has developed and deployed talent management solutions for many Fortune 500 companies and public sector entities in the Americas, Europe, Asia, and Australia. He has recognized expertise in recruitment, selection, assessment, and executive development and has published on topics ranging from job analysis, and behavioral interviewing to psychological assessment. He has also presented at numerous national and international human resource conferences.

■ ■ ■

Nancy T. Tippins is a senior vice president and managing principal of Valtera Corporation, where she is responsible for the development and execution of firm strategies related to employee selection and assessment. She has extensive experience in the development and validation of tests and other forms of assessment that are designed for purposes of selection, promotion, development, and certification and used for all levels of management and for hourly employees. She has designed and implemented global test and assessment programs, as well as designed performance management programs and leadership development programs. Prior to joining Valtera, she worked as an internal consultant in large Fortune 100 companies managing the development, validation, and implementation of selection and assessment tools. She is active in professional affairs and is a past president of the Society for Industrial and Organizational Psychology (SIOP). She is a Fellow of SIOP, the American Psychological Association, and the Association for Psychological Science. Nancy received M.S. and Ph.D. degrees in industrial-organizational psychology from the Georgia Institute of Technology.

■ ■ ■

Deborah L. Whetzel is a program manager of the Personnel Selection and Development program at the Human Resources Research Organization. She has over twenty years of experience in personnel selection research and development in both the public and private sectors. Her areas of expertise include job analysis, leadership competency models, performance appraisal systems, development of structured interviews and situational judgment tests, and developing and validating assessment processes. She has conducted several meta-analyses; most recently she analyzed the validity of various measures (cognitive ability and personality) for predicting performance in clerical occupations. She has coedited two books, *Applied Measurement: Industrial Psychology in Human Resources Management* and *Applied Measurement Methods in Industrial Psychology*. Deborah has served as an adjunct professor in the graduate program at George Mason University and in the undergraduate program at Virginia Commonwealth University. She earned her Ph.D. at George Washington University specializing in industrial-organizational psychology.

■ ■ ■

Candice M. Young holds an M.A. in industrial-organizational psychology (I-O) and is a senior associate in human resource consulting with Barrett and Associates. Young has extensively studied the content areas of personnel selection, training, and performance appraisal, as well as organizational behavior and motivation. Furthermore, she has been trained in psychometrics, advanced research methods, and statistics. She has provided litigation support for race, sex, and age discrimination lawsuits and has performed test development activities for selection and promotional purposes in the public and private sector. Candice is a doctoral candidate at the University of Akron. She received her M.A. in industrial-organizational psychology from Xavier University and her B.A. in psychology from Spelman College.

Handbook of Workplace Assessment

Part One

Framework for Organizational Assessment

CHAPTER 1

INDIVIDUAL DIFFERENCES THAT INFLUENCE PERFORMANCE AND EFFECTIVENESS

What Should We Assess?

Kevin R. Murphy

Assessment in organizations can be carried out for a variety of purposes, many with high stakes for both individuals and organizations. The stakes can be particularly high when assessments are used to make decisions about personnel selection and placement or about advancement and development of individuals once they have been hired. If assessments focus on traits, attributes, or outcomes that are not relevant to success and effectiveness, both organizations and individuals may end up making poor decisions about the fit between people and jobs. If assessments are appropriately focused but poorly executed (perhaps the right attributes are measured, but they are measured with very low levels of reliability and precision), these assessments may lead to poor decisions on the parts of both organizations and individuals.

In this chapter, I focus on broad questions about the content of assessments (for example, What sorts of human attributes should assessments attempt to measure?) and say very little about the execution of assessments (the choice of specific tests or assessment methods, for example) or even the use of assessment data. My discussion is general rather than specific, focusing on general dimensions of assessment (whether to assess cognitive abilities or broad versus narrow abilities, for example) rather than on the specifics of assessment for a particular job (say, the best set of assessments for selecting among applicants for a job as a firefighter).

This chapter provides a general foundation for many of the chapters that follow. It sets the stage by discussing broad dimensions of individual differences that are likely to be relevant for understanding performance, effectiveness, and development in the workplace. The remaining chapters in Part One start addressing more specific questions that arise when attempting to assess these dimensions. Chapter Two reviews the range of methods that can be used to assess the quality of measures, and Chapters Three through Eight provide a more detailed examination of specific domains: cognitive abilities, personality, background and experience, knowledge and skill, physical and psychomotor skills and abilities, and competencies.

Part Two of this book discusses assessment for selection, promotion, and development, and Parts Three and Four deal with strategic assessment programs and with emerging trends and issues.

I begin this chapter by noting two general strategies for determining what to assess in organizations: one that focuses on the work and the other that focuses on the person. The person-oriented approaches are likely to provide the most useful guidance in determining what to assess for the purpose of selection and placement in entry-level jobs, and work-oriented assessments might prove more useful for identifying opportunities for and challenges to development and advancement.

Two Perspectives for Determining What to Assess

A number of important decisions must be made in determining what to assess, but the first is to determine whether the focus should be on the person or the work. That is, it is possible to build assessment strategies around the things people do in organizations in carrying out their work roles (work oriented) or around the characteristics of individuals that influence what they do and how well they do it in the workplace (person oriented). For example, it is common to start the process of selecting and deciding how to use assessments with a careful job analysis on the assumption that a detailed examination of what people do, how they do it, and how their work relates to the work of others will shed light on the knowledge, skills, abilities, and other attributes (KSAOs) required to perform the job well. An alternative strategy is to start by examining the individual difference domains that underlie most assessments and to use knowledge about the structure and content of those domains to drive choices about what to assess.

The choice of specific assessments is a three-step process that starts with choosing between a broadly person-oriented or work-oriented approach, then making choices about the domains within each approach to emphasize (for example, whether to focus on cognitive ability or on personality), and finally narrowing down the choice of specific attributes (say, spatial ability) and assessment methods (perhaps computerized tests). As I noted earlier, this chapter focuses on the first two of these steps.

Work-Oriented Strategies

Different jobs involve very different tasks and duties and may call on very different sorts of knowledge or skill, but it is possible to describe the domain of work in general terms that are relevant across a wide range of jobs and organizations; such a wide-ranging description provides the basis for worker-oriented strategies for determining what to assess. Starting in the late 1960s, considerable progress was made in the development of structured questionnaires and inventories for analyzing jobs (for example, the Position Analysis Questionnaire; McCormick, Jeanneret, & Mecham, 1972). These analysis instruments in turn helped to define the contents and structure of the O*NET (Occupational Information Network; Peterson, Mumford, Borman, Jeanneret, & Fleishman, 1999) Generalized Work Activities Taxonomy, arguably the most comprehensive attempt to describe the content and nature of work. Table 1.1 lists the major dimensions of this taxonomy.

Table 1.1. O*NET Generalized Work Activities

Information input	Looking for and receiving job-related information
	Identifying and evaluating job-relevant information
Mental processes	Information and data processing
	Reasoning and decision making
Work output	Performing physical and manual work activities
	Performing complex and technical activities
Interacting with others	Communicating and interacting
	Coordinating, developing, managing, and advising
	Administering

If you were to ask, "What do people do when they work?" Table 1.1 suggests that the answer would be that they gather information, process and make sense of that information, make decisions, perform physical and technical tasks, and interact with others. The specifics might vary across jobs, but it is reasonable to argue that Table 1.1 provides a general structure for describing jobs of all sorts and for describing, in particular, what it is that people do at work. Each of these major dimensions can be broken down into subdimensions (which are shown in this table), most of which can be broken down even further (for example, administering can be broken down into performing administrative activities, staffing organizational units, and monitoring and controlling resources) to provide a more detailed picture of the activities that make up most jobs.

In the field of human resource (HR) management, the detailed analysis of jobs has largely been replaced with assessments of competencies. The term *competency* refers to an individual's demonstrated knowledge, skills, or abilities (Shippmann et al., 2000). The precise definition of competencies and the similarities and differences between traditional job analysis and competency modeling are matters that have been sharply debated (Shippmann et al., 2000), and it is not clear whether competency modeling is really anything other than unstructured and informal job analysis. Nevertheless, the business world has adopted the language of competencies, and competency-based descriptions of work are becoming increasingly common.

Some competency models are based on careful analysis and compelling data, most notably the Great Eight model (Bartram, 2005):

Great Eight Competency Model

- Leading and deciding
- Supporting and cooperating
- Interacting and presenting
- Analyzing and interpreting
- Creating and conceptualizing
- Organizing and executing
- Adapting and coping
- Enterprising and performing

Bartram summarizes evidence of the validity of a range of individual difference measures for predicting the Great Eight. Unlike some other competency models, assessment of these particular competencies is often done on the basis of psychometrically sound measurement instruments.

Drilling Deeper

Work can be described in general terms such as the competencies detailed in the previous section. A more detailed analysis of what people do at work is likely to lead to an assessment of more specific skills and an evaluation of background and experience factors that are likely to be related to these skills. In this context, *skill* has a specific meaning: the consistent performance of complex tasks with a high level of accuracy, effectiveness, or efficiency. Skills are distinct from abilities in three ways: (1) they involve the performance of specific tasks, (2) they involve automatic rather than controlled performance, and (3) they are the result of practice. These last two features of skills are especially critical. The acquisition and mastery of skills usually requires a substantial amount of practice or rehearsal, which suggests a link between assessment of skills and assessments of background and experience. In the past two decades, considerable progress has been made in assessments of background and experience (Mael, 1991), but it is fair to say that there are not well-established taxonomies of job-related skills or of background and experience factors, making it difficult to describe these domains in a great deal of detail.

Inferring Job Requirements

One of the most difficult challenges that proponents of worker-oriented approaches face is to convincingly translate information about what people do at work into judgments about the KSAOs required for performing well in particular jobs. This is sometimes done on an empirical basis (for example, the Position Analysis Questionnaire provides data that can be used to determine the predicted validity of a range of ability and skill tests), but it is most often done on the basis of subjective judgments. Virtually all methods of job analysis and competency modeling involve inferences about the attributes required for successful performance, but these judgments are rarely themselves validated. Indeed, there is little scientific evidence that given a good description of the job, analysts can make valid inferences about what attributes are required for successful performance beyond a handful of obvious prerequisites; knowing that electricians work with wires that are often color-coded, it is not hard to infer that color vision is required for this job, for example. Usually inferences of this sort are based on the assumption that if the content of the test matches the content of the assessments, those tests will be valid predictors of performance on the job.

Murphy, Dzieweczynski, and Yang (2009) reviewed a large number of studies testing the hypothesis that the match between job content and test content influences the validity of tests and found little support for this hypothesis. Nevertheless, an analysis of the job, whether it is done in terms of competencies, generalized work activities, or detailed questionnaires, is often the first step in making a decision about the content and the focus of workplace assessments.

Work-oriented approaches to assessment are likely to be particularly useful as part of the process of making decisions about placement and development. In particular, comparisons between the content of previous and current jobs and the content of future jobs are useful for identifying developmental needs and gaps between the knowledge, skills, and experiences developed in previous jobs and those required in future assignments.

Person-Oriented Analyses

A very different strategy for making decisions about what attributes should or should not be included in assessments starts from the perspective of differential psychology: using what we know about individual differences to drive what we assess. In particular, this approach takes our knowledge of the dimensions and structure of human cognitive ability, normal personality, and interests and value orientations as a starting point for determining what to assess.

Cognitive Ability

There are enduring and stable individual differences in performance on virtually all tasks that involve the active processing of information; these individual differences form the core of the domain we refer to as cognitive ability.

The key to understanding the structure of human cognitive abilities is the fact that scores on almost any reliable measure that calls for active information processing will be positively correlated with any other reliable measure that also involves cognitive activity. That is, scores on virtually all cognitively demanding tasks exhibit positive manifold (Carroll, 1993). Thus, scores on paragraph comprehension measures will be correlated with scores on numerical problem solving, which will be correlated with scores on spatial relations tests and so on. The existence of positive manifold virtually guarantees that the structure of human abilities will be hierarchically arranged, with virtually all specific abilities (or groups of abilities) positively correlated with more general ability factors. Theories of cognitive ability that give little emphasis to *g* or deny the utility of a general factor do not seem to provide any convincing explanation for positive manifold.

Carroll's (1993) three-stratum model of cognitive ability (based on the results of a large number of factor-analytic studies) nicely illustrates the nature of modern hierarchical models. The essential features of this model are shown in Figure 1.1. At the most general level, there is a *g* factor, which implies stable differences in performance on a wide range of cognitively demanding tasks. At the next level (the broad stratum) are a number of areas of ability, which imply that the rank ordering of individuals' task performance will not be exactly the same across all cognitive tasks, but rather will show some clustering. Finally, each of these broad ability areas can be characterized in terms of a number of more specific abilities (the narrow stratum) that are more homogeneous still than those at the next highest level.

The hierarchical structure of the domain of cognitive abilities has important implications for understanding three key aspects of cognitive ability tests: (1) the validity of these tests as predictors of job performance and effectiveness, (2) the relationships among abilities and the relative importance of general versus specific abilities for predicting performance, and (3) adverse impact. First, abundant evidence shows that cognitive ability is highly relevant in a wide range of jobs and settings and that measures of general cognitive ability represent perhaps the best predictors of performance (Schmidt & Hunter, 1998). The validity of measures of general cognitive ability has been established in all sorts of jobs and settings, and it is reasonable to believe that a good ability test will be a valid predictor of performance in virtually any application of testing.

The hierarchical structure of the cognitive domain is almost certainly a key to the widespread evidence of the validity of cognitive tests. All jobs require active information processing (such as retrieving and processing information, making judgments), and

Figure 1.1. The Cognitive Domain

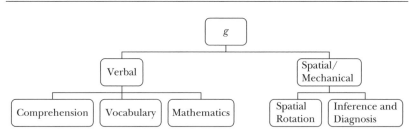

even when the content of the job focuses on very specific tasks or types of ability (a job might require spatial visualization abilities, for example), the strong intercorrelations among abilities virtually guarantee that measures of general ability will predict performance. This intercorrelation among cognitive abilities also has important implications for evaluating the importance of general versus specific abilities.

A good deal of evidence exists that the incremental contribution of specific abilities (over and above general ability) to the prediction of performance or training outcomes is often minimal (Ree, Earles, & Teachout, 1994). Because of the correlation among measures of general and specific abilities, payoff for the specific abilities required in a job is usually small. Measures of general ability will usually be as good as, and often better than, measures of specific abilities as a predictor of performance and effectiveness.

The strong pattern of intercorrelation among cognitive abilities poses a strong challenge to the hypotheses that many types of intelligence exist (Gardner, 1999) or that important abilities have not yet been fully uncovered. In particular, the overwhelming evidence of positive correlations among virtually all abilities raises important questions about the nature of emotional intelligence.

Organizations have shown considerable interest in the concept of emotional intelligence (EI: Murphy, 2006). There are many different definitions and models of EI, but the claim that it is a distinct type of intelligence is at the heart of the debate over its meaning and value. On the whole, little evidence exists that emotional intelligence is related to other cognitive abilities, casting doubts on its status as an "intelligence." Some evidence suggests that EI is related to a variety of organizationally relevant criteria, but on the whole, the claim that EI is a distinct type of intelligence and an important predictor of performance and effectiveness does not hold up to close scrutiny (Murphy, 2006). More generally, the idea that there are distinct types of intelligence does not square with the evidence.

Finally, the hierarchical structure of the cognitive domain has important implications for the likelihood that ability measures will lead to different outcomes for members of different ethnic and racial groups. Black (and, to a lesser extent, Hispanic) examinees consistently receive lower scores on cognitive ability tests than white examinees, and the use of cognitive ability tests in personnel selection or placement will normally lead to adverse impact against black and Hispanic examinees (Schmitt, Rogers, Chan, Sheppard, & Jennings, 1997). Some differences in the amount of racial disparity are expected with measures of different specific abilities (in general, the stronger the correlation of specific abilities with g, the larger the racial disparities), but one consequence of the positive manifold among measures of various abilities is that adverse impact will be expected almost regardless of what specific abilities are measured. The hierarchical structure of the cognitive ability domain has several implications for research and practice in personnel assessment, including:

- General abilities have broad relevance in most settings.
- Identifying the right specific abilities is not necessarily important.
- The faults of general abilities will be shared with specific ones.
- The belief in multiple types of intelligence or newly discovered intelligences is not consistent with the data.

First, the hierarchical structure of cognitive abilities means that general abilities are more likely to be useful for predicting and understanding behavior in organizations than more narrowly defined specific abilities. This structure guarantees that even if it is the specific ability that is important, general abilities will also turn out to be good predictors in most settings. Because general abilities are usually measured with more reliability and more precision, making the case for focusing on specific rather than on general abilities is often hard.

Second, if the goal is predicting future performance and effectiveness, this structure suggests a diminishing payoff for getting it exactly right when drawing inferences about the abilities required by a job. For example, the spatial-perceptual branch of most hierarchical models of cognitive ability includes a number of specific abilities (say, three-dimensional spatial visualization versus the ability to estimate distance and range). The further down the chain of related abilities one goes (from general to spatial to three-dimensional spatial visualization), the less difference choices among branches of the ability tree are likely to make in determining the eventual value and criterion-related validity of ability tests.

Third, the use of ability tests in making decisions about people in organizations such as personnel selection or placement will lead to adverse impact against members of a number of racial and ethnic groups, and the use of specific rather than general ability measures will rarely change this fundamentally. Specific ability measures do show slightly lower levels of adverse impact than general ones, but they also typically show lower levels of criterion-related validity. The decision to use cognitive ability tests in organizations is necessarily also a decision to accept a certain level of adverse impact; the decision to refrain from using such tests is almost always also a decision to sacrifice validity.

Finally, the long-standing assumption and hope of many researchers and practitioners (especially in educational settings) that we can identify many separate types of intelligence is exactly that: an assumption and an aspiration. Models that posit multiple intelligences or suggest that specific types of content such as emotional information require their own type of intelligence are popular but not well supported. In the case of emotional intelligence, which has attracted a great deal of attention in both educational and organizational settings, improvements in the models and measures of this construct may eventually lead to the acceptance of EI as a distinct and important domain of human cognitive ability, but there are few data on the immediate horizon to lead us to believe that current conclusions about the structure and nature of human cognitive ability will need to be radically changed to accommodate separate intelligences such as EI.

Personality

The link between personality and behavior in organizations has a long history of interest. In a highly influential review, Guion and Gottier (1965) cast considerable doubt on the value of personality measures, especially as predictors of job performance. They concluded that "there is no generalizable evidence that personality measures can be recommended as good or practical tools for employee selection" (p. 159) and that "it is difficult to advocate, with a clear conscience, the use of personality measures in most

situations as a basis for making employment decisions about people" (p. 160). This review led to a long period of skepticism about
the relevance of personality in understanding performance and
effectiveness in the workplace. Not until the 1990s did personality
reemerge as a viable tool for understanding and predicting performance and effectiveness (Barrick & Mount, 1991). It is now widely
accepted that measures of normal personality have some value as
predictors of performance, but the validities of these measures are
often low. Nevertheless, they are also viewed as useful measures
for helping to structure and manage development and placement
programs.

As with cognitive ability, one of the keys to understanding
the relevance and value of personality measures is to examine the structure and the contents of this domain. The Five
Factor Model, often referred to as the "Big Five," has emerged
as a dominant model for describing normal personality. This
model has been replicated across a number of methods, settings, and cultures, and it provides a good starting point for
describing what exactly *personality* means. This model suggests
that normal personality can be described largely in terms of
five broad factors that are at best weakly related to one another
and (with the exception of Openness to Experience) with cognitive abilities:

- Neuroticism: emotional instability, tendency to experience
  negative emotions easily
- Extraversion: outgoing, energetic, tending toward positive
  emotions
- Agreeableness: cooperates with, is compassionate and consid-
  erate toward others
- Conscientiousness: reliability, self-discipline, achievement oriented, planfulness
- Openness to Experience: curiosity, imagination, appreciation
  for new ideas and experiences, appreciation of art, emotion,
  adventure

The two structural aspects of the domain of normal personality that are most important for understanding the ways broad personality dimensions might be used in assessment are the relatively

weak correlations among the dimensions of normal personality and the relatively weak relationships between personality and cognitive ability. The weak correlations among the Big Five mean that different dimensions of personality really do convey different information and that all sorts of personality profiles are possible. The weak correlations between personality and cognitive ability have three very different and very important implications. First, personality measures will contribute unique information not captured by cognitive ability. That is, whatever variance in performance, behavior, or effectiveness is explained by personality will almost certainly be distinct from variance explained by cognitive ability. Second, personality measures will not share some of the characteristics common to ability measures. In particular, measures of normal personality are typically unrelated to the respondent's race, ethnicity, or gender.

Whereas the use of cognitive ability tests is a major cause of adverse impact in personnel selection, the use of personality measures can reduce adverse impact. Unfortunately, the reduction in adverse impact when ability and personality measures are combined is not as large as one might expect; the combination of ability tests (which have adverse impact) and personality inventories (which do not) leads to some reduction in adverse impact, but it will not cut it in half (Ryan, Ployhart, & Friedel, 1998). Third, the weak relationships between personality and cognitive ability are consistent with one of the most contentious issues in research on personality assessment in organizations: the validity of broad personality dimensions as predictors of performance and effectiveness. Although there is considerable interest in the use of personality assessments in organizations, studies of the validity of personality measures as predictors of performance have consistently shown that the correlations between personality and performance are small (Morgeson et al., 2007). If the goal is to predict performance and effectiveness, it is unlikely that measures of broad personality dimensions will help very much.

The two alternatives to using broad personality dimensions in assessment might yield higher levels of validity. First, it is possible to use finely grained measures. For example, measures of the Big Five often provide separate assessments of multiple facets of each major dimension. For example, the NEO-PI (Costa & McCrae, 1995) yields scores on the Big Five and on several facets of each dimension; these are shown in Table 1.2. For example, Conscientiousness can be broken down into Competence, Order, Dutifulness, Achievement-striving, Self-discipline, and Deliberation. It is possible that different facets are relevant in different jobs or situations and from assessment of specific facets will yield different levels of validity from those that have been exhibited by measures of the Big Five.

An alternative to the use of finely grained measures is the use of composite measures. For example, there is evidence that

Table 1.2. Facets of the Big Five

Neuroticism	Extraversion
Anxiety	Warmth
Hostility	Gregariousness
Depression	Assertiveness
Self-consciousness	Activity
Impulsiveness	Excitement seeking
Vulnerability	Positive emotions
Conscientiousness	Agreeableness
Competence	Trust
Order	Straightforwardness
Dutifulness	Altruism
Achievement-striving	Compliance
Self-discipline	Modesty
Deliberation	Tender-mindedness
Openness	
Fantasy	
Aesthetics	
Feelings	
Actions	
Ideas	
Values	

integrity tests capture aspects of Conscientiousness, Neuroticism, and Agreeableness (Ones, Viswesvaran, & Schmidt, 1993); the breadth of the domain these tests cover may help to explain their validity as a predictor of a fairly wide range of criteria. In principle, there might be no effective limit to the types of composite personality tests that might be created, and some of these might plausibly show very respectable levels of validity. However, this strategy almost certainly involves a trade-off between the potential for validity and interpretability.

The use of personality assessments to make high-stakes decisions about individuals is controversial (Morgeson et al., 2007), in large part because most personality inventories are self-reports that are potentially vulnerable to faking. The research literature examining faking in personality assessment is broad and complex (Ones, Viswesvaran, & Reiss, 1996), but there is consensus about a few key points. First, people can fake, in the sense that they can often identify test responses that will paint them in the most favorable light. Second, while faking can influence the outcomes of testing, it often does not greatly affect the validity of tests. This is because positive self-presentation biases are often in play when job applicants and incumbents respond to personality inventories, meaning that everyone's scores might be inflated. Although faking is a legitimate concern, it is probably more realistic to be worried about the possibility of differential faking. That is, if some people inflate their scores more than others, faking could change both the mean score and the rank order of respondents. In other words, if everyone fakes, it might not be a big problem, but if some people fake more or better than others, faking could seriously affect the decisions based on personality inventories.

As with cognitive ability, the structure and nature of the domain of normal personality have important implications for research and practice in organizational assessment:

- The relative independence of major personality dimensions puts a greater premium on identifying the right dimensions and the right rules for combining information from separate dimensions.

- Personality measures provide information that is distinct from that provided by ability measures.
- The relatively low correlations with ability suggest that personality measures will be poor predictors of performance and effectiveness; the available evidence seems to confirm this prediction.
- Narrow dimensions of personality are easiest to interpret, but are often similarly narrow in terms of what they predict. The broadest dimensions show more predictive power but are hard to sensibly interpret.

First, the broad dimensions that characterize the Big Five are relatively distinct, which poses both opportunities and challenges. On the opportunity side, it is more likely that the complex models (for example, configural models, in which the meaning of a score on one dimension depends on a person's score on other dimensions) will pay off in the domain of personality than in the domain of cognitive ability. In the ability domain, the pervasive pattern of positive correlations among virtually all ability measures means it is hard to go too far wrong. Even if you fail to identify the exact set of abilities that is most important, you can be pretty certain of capturing relevant variance with measures of general abilities. In the personality domain, choices of which dimensions to assess and how to combine them are likely to matter. This also means that identifying the best way to use personality information is likely to be a much more difficult challenge than identifying the best way to use information about abilities.

Second, personality and ability seem to be largely independent domains. There are some broad personality dimensions that may be related to *g*, but most are not. This means that potential exists for personality measures to contribute to the prediction of performance and effectiveness above and beyond the contributions of ability measures. Unfortunately, as noted in our third point, this often does not happen. The validities of personality measures are statistically different from zero but are often not much greater than zero (Morgeson et al., 2007).

Finally, personality assessment often poses trade-offs. One trade-off is often between predictive power and interpretability and another between ease of use and trustworthiness. Personality measures are usually self-reports, and they are not necessarily hard to develop. They are, however, vulnerable to faking. Ability tests have many defects, but at least it is hard to "fake smart." A personality inventory that shows an applicant to be high on Conscientiousness and Agreeableness might mean exactly what it appears to mean—or it might mean that the respondent knows that high scores on these dimensions are viewed favorably, and is faking.

Interests and Value Orientations

Organizational assessments are used not only to predict performance and efficiency but also to evaluate the fit between people and environments or jobs. Ability and personality measures can be very useful in assessing fit, but many discussions of fit focus on interests and value orientation, based on the argument that the congruence between the interests and the values of an individual and the environment in which he or she functions is an important determinant of long-term success and satisfaction. There are important questions about the extent to which fit can be adequately measured and about the importance of person-environment fit (Tinsley, 2000), but the idea of congruence between individuals and environments is widely accepted in areas such as career development and counseling. Numerous models have been used to describe the congruence between individuals and environments; Lofquist and Dawis's (1969) Theory of Work Adjustment represents the most comprehensive and influential model of fit. The theory examines the links between the worker's needs and values and the job's ability to satisfy those needs, and it also considers the match between the skills an individual brings to the job and the skills required for effective performance in that job.

Assessments of interests have long been an important part of matching individuals with jobs. Strong (1943) defined an interest as "a response of liking" (p. 6). It is a learned affective response to an object or activity. Things in which we are interested elicit positive feelings, things in which we have little interest elicit little affect, and things in which we are totally disinterested elicit apathy or even feelings of aversion. Interest measures are widely used to help individuals identify vocations and jobs that are likely to satisfy and engage them.

The dominant theory of vocational choice was developed by Holland (1973), who suggested that vocational interests can be broken down into six basic types: realistic (interest in things), investigative (interest in ideas), artistic (interest in creating), social (interest in people), enterprising (interest in getting ahead), and conventional (interest in order and predictability). The Holland RIASEC model is shown in Figure 1.2.

The hexagonal structure of Figure 1.2 reflects one of the key aspects of the Holland model. Interests that are close together on the Holland hexagon, such as Realistic and Investigative, are more likely to co-occur than interests that are far apart such as Realistic and Social. The great majority of measures of vocational interests and theories of vocational choice are based on the Holland model.

Unlike the field of interest measurement, there is no single dominant model of work-related values. Probably the best-researched

Figure 1.2. Holland Taxonomy of Vocational Interests

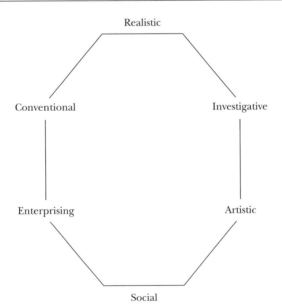

Realistic

Conventional   Investigative

Enterprising   Artistic

Social

model is that proposed by Lofquist and Dawis (1969). Their taxonomy of work-related values, shown in Table 1.3, was adopted by O*NET as a way of characterizing the values most relevant to various occupations.

Like many other taxonomies, the O*NET Work Value Taxonomy is hierarchically structured. At the highest level of abstraction, jobs can be characterized in terms of the extent to which they are likely to satisfy value related to opportunities for achievement, favorable working conditions, opportunities for recognition, emphasis on relationships, support, and opportunities for independence. One of the many uses of O*NET is to match jobs to people's values. For example, individuals who value achievement and recognition can use O*NET to identify jobs that are likely to satisfy those preferences. The lower level of the taxonomy helps to clarify the meaning of each of the higher-order values and provides a basis

Table 1.3. O*NET Work Value Taxonomy

Achievement	Relationships
Ability utilization	Coworkers
Achievement	Social service
	Moral values
Working conditions	**Support**
Activity	Company policies and practices
Independence	Supervision, human relations
Variety	Supervision, technical
Compensation	
Security	
Working conditions	
Recognition	**Independence**
Advancement	Creativity
Recognition	Responsibility
Authority	Autonomy
Social status	

for a more finely grained assessment of person-job fit. For example, good working conditions might refer to almost any combination of opportunities for activity, independence, variety, compensation, or job security.

Assessments of cognitive abilities and personality traits are often used to predict criteria such as performance and effectiveness. Assessments of interests and values are not likely to reveal as much about performance, but are related to criteria such as satisfaction, burnout, and retention. Good person-job fit is thought to enhance the attractiveness and the motivational potential of a job, and in theory these assessments can be used for both individual counseling and placement. In practice, systematic placement (hiring an individual first and deciding afterward what job or even what occupational family to assign that person to) is rarely practiced outside the armed services. However, interest measures might be quite useful for career planning activities at both the individual and the organizational levels. For example, executive development programs often involve a sequence of jobs or assignments, and the use of interest and value assessments might help in fine-tuning the sequence of assignments that is most likely to lead to successful development.

Implications for Assessment in Organizations

Individual differences in cognitive ability, personality, values, and interests are likely to affect the performance, effectiveness, motivation, and long-term success of workers at all levels in an organization. A general familiarity with the structure and the content of each of these domains provides a good starting point for designing organizational assessments.

The essential feature of cognitive abilities is their interrelatedness. This presents both opportunities and challenges when using ability tests in organizations. Because virtually all abilities are correlated (often substantially) with general abilities, it is hard to go seriously wrong with the choice of ability measures; jobs that require one ability also tend to require the constellation of other related abilities. Because virtually all jobs require and involve the core activities that define cognitive ability (the acquisition, manipulation, and use of information), it is generally a safe bet that ability measures will turn out to be valid predictors of performance. Unfortunately, the interconnectedness of abilities also implies that any of the shortcomings of general cognitive ability as a predictor will be broadly shared by more specific measures. In particular, ability measures of all sorts are likely to show substantial adverse impact on the employment opportunities of black and Hispanic applicants and employees, and this impact has both legal and ethical implications. Depending on the weight you give to predictive validity versus the social impact of using ability tests to make high-stakes decisions, you might come to very different conclusions about whether including these measures in organizational assessments makes sense (Murphy, 2010).

The domain of normal personality has a much different structure. The Big Five personality factors are interrelated, but the correlations among dimensions are generally quite weak, and no general factor describes human personality. Like many other taxonomic structures, the Big Five can be broken down into facets, or they can be combined into composites, but moving from the level of the Big Five to either higher (composite) or lower (facet) levels of abstraction often involves trade-offs between interpretability and predictive value.

Two issues seem especially important when using personality measures as part of assessment in organizations. First, these are usually self-reports and are vulnerable to manipulation and misrepresentation. There are important debates about the actual effects of faking on validity and the outcomes of selection (Morgeson et al., 2007), but the possibility that respondents might be able to consciously inflate their scores on high-stakes assessments is likely to be a realistic barrier to their use in many settings. More important, the validity of these measures as predictors of criteria such as performance or effectiveness is often disappointing, and the value of obtaining these assessments is not always clear.

Vocational interests are well understood and are captured nicely by Holland's hexagonal model. This model posits relationships among interests that can be captured by the distance between any pair of interests on the hexagon; this model has been applied with considerable success in vocational counseling. However, it is not always clear how to use assessments of interests or values to make more detailed predictions of judgments. There are many models of person-job fit, and different models often depend on different sets of values. No single agreed-on taxonomy adequately captures the universe of organizationally relevant values. Nevertheless, the general proposition that some jobs are more likely than others to fit an individual's values and that some individuals are more likely than others to fit any specific job seems well established, and the measurement of work-related values has potential for both research and practice.

This chapter has been intentionally broad in its focus, and the implications for assessment laid out in the preceding paragraphs are similarly broad. Chapters Two through Eight examine more specific issues in assessments of domains ranging from abilities to personality to background and experience. Chapters Nine through Fourteen show how assessments of these domains are used in making decisions in occupations ranging from hourly or skilled work to executive and managerial positions. Chapters Fifteen through Twenty-Four discuss a wide range of questions encountered when developing and using assessments in a range of organizational contexts.

References

Barrick, M. R., & Mount, M. K. (1991). The Big Five personality dimensions and job performance: A meta-analysis. *Personnel Psychology, 44*, 1–26.

Bartram, D. (2005). The great eight competencies: A criterion-centric approach to validation. *Journal of Applied Psychology, 90*, 1185–1203.

Carroll, J. B. (1993). *Human cognitive abilities: A survey of factor-analytic studies.* New York: Cambridge University Press.

Costa, P. T., & McCrae, R. R. (1995). Domains and facets: Hierarchical personality assessment using the Revised NEO Personality Inventory. *Journal of Personality Assessment, 64*, 21–50.

Gardner, H. (1999). *Intelligence reframed: Multiple intelligences for the 21st century.* New York: Basic Books.

Guion, R. M., & Gottier, R. F. (1965). Validity of personality measures in personnel selection. *Personnel Psychology, 18*, 135–164.

Holland, J. L. (1973). *Making vocational choices: A theory of careers.* Upper Saddle River, NJ: Prentice Hall.

Lofquist, L. H., & Dawis, R. V. (1969). *Adjustment to work.* New York: Appleton–Century–Crofts.

Mael, F. A. (1991). A conceptual rationale for the domain of attributes of biodata items. *Personnel Psychology, 44,* 763–792.

McCormick, E. J., Jeanneret, P. R., & Mecham, R. C. (1972). A study of job characteristics and job dimensions as based on the Position Analysis Questionnaire (PAQ). *Journal of Applied Psychology, 56,* 347–368.

Morgeson, F. P., Campion, M. A., Dipboye, R. L., Hollenbeck, J. R., Murphy, K., & Schmitt, N. (2007). Reconsidering the use of personality tests in personnel selection contexts. *Personnel Psychology, 60,* 683–729.

Murphy, K. R. (2000). What constructs underlie measures of honesty or integrity? In R. Goffin & E. Helmes (Eds.), *Problems and solutions in human assessment: A festschrift to Douglas N. Jackson at seventy* (pp. 265–284). Norwell, MA: Kluwer.

Murphy, K. R. (2006). *A critique of emotional intelligence.* Mahwah, NJ: Erlbaum.

Murphy, K. (2010). How a broader definition of the criterion domain changes our thinking about adverse impact. In J. Outtz (Ed.), *Adverse impact* (pp. 137–160). San Francisco: Jossey-Bass.

Murphy, K. R., Dzieweczynski, J. L., & Yang, Z. (2009). Positive manifold limits the relevance of content-matching strategies for validating selection test batteries. *Journal of Applied Psychology, 94,* 1018–1031.

Ones, D. S., Viswesvaran, C., & Reiss, A. D. (1996). Role of social desirability in personality testing for personnel selection: The red herring. *Journal of Applied Psychology, 81,* 660–679.

Ones, D. S., Viswesvaran, C., & Schmidt, F. L (1993). Comprehensive meta-analysis of integrity test validities. *Journal of Applied Psychology, 78,* 679–703.

Peterson, N. G., Mumford, M. D., Borman, W. C., Jeanneret, P. R., & Fleishman, E. A. (1999). *An occupational information system for the 21st century: The development of O*NET.* Washington, DC: American Psychological Association.

Ree, M. J., Earles, J. A., & Teachout, M. S. (1994). Predicting job performance: Not much more than g. *Journal of Applied Psychology, 79,* 518–524.

Ryan, A. M., Ployhart, R. E., & Friedel, L. A. (1998). Using personality testing to reduce adverse impact: A cautionary note. *Journal of Applied Psychology, 83,* 298–307.

Schippmann, J. S., Ash, R. A., Carr, L., Hesketh, B., Pearlman, K., Battista, M. et al. (2000). The practice of competency modeling. *Personnel Psychology, 53*, 703–740.

Schmidt, F. L., & Hunter, J. E. (1998). The validity and utility of selection methods in personnel psychology: Practical and theoretical implications of 85 years of research findings. *Psychological Bulletin, 124*, 262–274.

Schmitt, N., Rogers, W., Chan, D., Sheppard, L., & Jennings, D. (1997). Adverse impact and predictive efficiency of various predictor combinations. *Journal of Applied Psychology, 82*, 719–730.

Strong, E. K. (1943). *Vocational interests of men and women.* Stanford, CA: Stanford University Press.

Tinsley, H. E. (2000). The congruence myth: An analysis of the efficacy of the person-environment fit model. *Journal of Vocational Behavior, 56*, 147–179.

CHAPTER 2

INDICATORS OF QUALITY ASSESSMENT

Fritz Drasgow, Christopher D. Nye,
Louis Tay

Assessment, whether for selection or development, can play a critical role in elevating an organization from mediocrity to excellence. However, this is true only if the assessment is excellent. In this chapter, we describe the characteristics and features that differentiate outstanding assessment programs from mediocre systems. With this information, organizational practitioners can thoughtfully consider how assessments can be implemented in their organizations, evaluate any current uses of tests and assessments, and move toward state-of-the-art measurement.

When an organization decides to begin an assessment program, its first decision concerns whether to purchase a test from a test publisher or consulting firm or develop the assessment tool in-house. We begin the chapter by reviewing the issues to consider when making this important decision. We next discuss the test construction process, which begins with the question, "What should the test measure?" and addresses item writing, pretesting, and psychometric analyses. The next two sections examine the critical quality issues of reliability and validity. Obviously organizations want their assessments to be reliable and valid, but there are some subtleties that test users should understand in order to make informed judgments; we summarize these issues.

We then discuss operational models for assessment programs. With advances in computer technology and the Internet, organizations have a dizzying array of choices. Some of the topics discussed include testing platform (paper-and-pencil versus computer), unproctored Internet testing, cheating, and score reporting.

The next section of the chapter addresses quality control, a topic that receives little attention in many testing programs. There have been several highly publicized fiascos in high-profile testing programs in recent years and undoubtedly many other problems that were kept under wraps. Consequently, we discuss issues to consider and steps organizations can take to ensure high quality. Finally, we end with a few brief conclusions.

We expect that people with diverse backgrounds will read this chapter. We encourage those with psychometric training, including classical test theory (CTT) and item response theory (IRT), to dig into the technical details that are needed to fully address the quality of a testing program. To this end, the equations that are referenced throughout the chapter are in Table 2.1 for convenience. For those who do not have this background, we encourage looking at the big picture to gain an understanding of critical issues. We have attempted to give conceptual descriptions of each topic so that all readers can understand important problems; a flowchart of the key processes related to quality assessment is shown in Figure 2.1. Organizational leaders can then consult with either internal or external measurement professionals for guidance on technical concerns.

Buy Versus Build

If a decision is made to implement an assessment program, the organization must decide whether to purchase a commercially available test or develop a measure in-house. To make this decision, organizations need to weigh the costs and benefits of each approach to determine which will be more appropriate, and a number of questions must be addressed. First, do any currently available tests meet the needs of the organization? Specifically, do the commercially available tests validly measure the requisite knowledge, skills, and abilities (KSAs) and have rigorous empirical support for their validity? Commercial tests frequently assess constructs that are broadly focused and applicable across a wide range of jobs. Although the predictive validity of many general

Figure 2.1. Flowchart of Key Processes in Quality Assessment

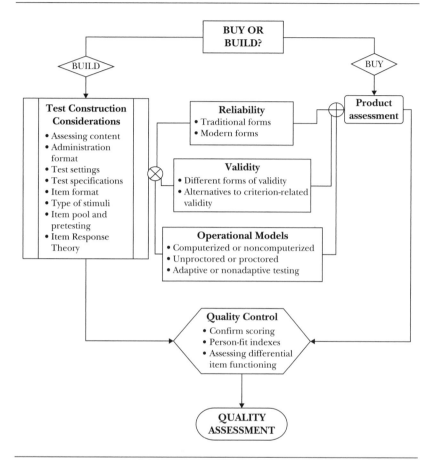

Note: ⊗ represents the confluence of decision factors associated with test construction; ⊕ represents the confluence of decision factors associated with product assessment.

constructs such as general cognitive ability has been established by meta-analytic research, these tests may be criticized for their apparent lack of job relevance and face validity. In contrast, a homegrown test can be developed to measure the specific knowledge, skills, or ability obviously required in the target job.

A related concern involves the empirical evidence supporting the validity of a measure. Although most practitioners are aware of legal and professional guidelines stressing the importance of validity, organizations might not employ a sufficient number of people in a particular job category to obtain an accurate estimate of the correlation between a predictor and an outcome. As a result, irrelevant characteristics of the available sample (known as sampling error) may severely affect the magnitude of the observed relationship. This effect is largely responsible for the variation in the size of the relationship between predictor and criterion across organizational settings (Schmidt & Hunter, 1977). In contrast, the best commercial tests have substantial empirical evidence about validity; an evaluation of the extent and rigor of validity evidence is a key consideration in choosing which commercial test to purchase. Thus, in situations where organizations lack the sample size for appropriate validation studies, commercially available tests may be the only viable alternative.

Another consideration in the buy-versus-build decision concerns whether an organization seeking to develop a test in-house has the necessary skills and resources to do so. Expertise in test development, test administration, and statistical analysis may not be available. Test development, for example, requires carefully defining the KSAs to be assessed, developing a test blueprint that specifies the content areas to be measured and the number of items from each content area to be included, and then writing a sufficient number of items for each content area. Thus, a specialized knowledge of the subject matter is required, and a substantial review of relevant literature will frequently be necessary. Even if a sufficient understanding of the construct can be obtained, it may still be difficult to write discriminating items at the appropriate difficulty levels.

Once the items have been written, psychometric knowledge is required to ensure that the test has appropriate measurement properties. For example, statistical analysis using IRT is often used for this purpose. Briefly, IRT is a psychometric method that can be used to predict an individual's performance on a test item by relating characteristics of the item to the ability of the person on the latent trait being measured (here, the term *latent* is used to reference a characteristic such as intelligence or personality that is not directly observable). However, many organizations do not have expertise in IRT. Additional difficulties may be encountered when using computerized or computer-adaptive tests (CATs). (See Drasgow, Luecht, & Bennett, 2006, for a description of the complexities of a technologically sophisticated testing program.)

Other decision factors are the time lines and the breadth of the assessment program. Organizations with an immediate need may benefit from purchasing a commercially available test because test development and validation can be time-consuming. An organization should also consider how frequently the test will be used. For example, if a brief unproctored Internet test is used as an initial screening for tens of thousands of job applicants, a commercially available test may become very expensive as costs accrue with each administration. In contrast, organizations that use assessments only intermittently may not recoup the cost of developing the test in-house.

Finally, test security should also be considered. Are cheating conspiracies likely? Test security is enhanced by using multiple forms of paper-and-pencil tests. Even more effective is the use of a CAT with a large item pool and an effective item exposure control algorithm. To illustrate the significance of this problem, note that there have been significant cheating conspiracies involving college entrance and licensure exams. Even multiple conventional forms and CATs can be susceptible to large-scale cheating conspiracies, such as online sharing sites and companies devoted to cracking the tests. One benefit of commercially developed assessments is that the developers are well positioned to ensure the security of the exam because their business success is severely affected by cheating conspiracies. Some professional test developers may even employ individuals with the sole responsibility of searching for and eliminating item-sharing sites and companies.

In sum, the buy-versus-build decision involves considerations of availability, feasibility, timeliness, in-house expertise, cost, and so forth. Clearly this is a critical and complex choice. Regardless of the buy-versus-build decision, a quality assessment must be created by a careful process. In the remainder of this chapter, we provide more details about this process and note criteria for evaluating quality. Before deciding to build a test, an organization should evaluate whether it has the resources necessary to perform the steps we describe. And before buying, the organization should examine documentation from the test publisher to ascertain whether the criteria we describe next are satisfied.

Test Construction Considerations

Several steps in the development process have a critical impact on the quality of an assessment. Integrating these steps provides a systematic approach to test development and ensures a high-quality result. A less-systematic approach may produce a test that misses important aspects of the KSAs to be assessed, which is likely to reduce the effectiveness of the assessment.

The first step in test development lies in identifying what a test is intended to measure. Here, test developers establish the content that will be assessed. In an employment setting, this is most frequently done with a thorough job analysis. Test developers may survey or interview subject matter experts, examine critical incidents, or rely on expert judgment. Because it is usually impossible to assess all important KSAs for a particular job or job family, the criteria for including content should be based on information provided by the job analysis regarding the importance of each dimension. For psychological phenomena such as intelligence, personality, and attitudes, inclusion criteria should also be based on a careful definition of the trait to be assessed, followed by a thorough review of the literature on the topic.

The second step is to determine the testing format that is most appropriate for the purposes of the test. With the large number of administration formats now available for psychological testing, this issue is fundamental to the test construction process. In addition to the traditional paper-and-pencil format, a conventional test (one in which all examinees are administered the same set of items) may also be administered by stand-alone computers or using the Internet. In contrast to fixed conventional tests, CATs select items to be appropriately difficult for each examinee. This format is increasing in importance, particularly for licensing and credentialing exams. Another choice is the setting for test administration. In contrast to the traditional proctored environment, unproctored Internet testing allows unsupervised examinees to take the exam at a time and place of their convenience.

Each of these testing formats has implications for the type and number of items used. In a computerized format, novel item stimuli may be presented interactively as audio, video, pictures, or some combination of media. For CATs to operate effectively, a large pool of items is required to ensure accurate ability estimates and increase test security. Similar security issues are salient for unproctored tests. As a result, it is often advisable to administer both an unproctored selection test and, later, a proctored confirmation test to verify results. Here, the proctored confirmation test may be a parallel form of the unproctored exam.

The choice between administration methods may also affect the third step in test construction where test specifications are formulated. These guidelines should be used as a road map for item writers. For example, test specifications would detail the number of items assessing verbal, quantitative, and spatial abilities in a measure of cognitive ability. In addition, these plans may specify the item difficulty and discrimination levels required for accurate ability estimates. These criteria are particularly important for CATs, where the quality of ability estimates improves when the item pool contains items with a wide range of difficulties.

The test specifications give the appropriate number and content of items as well as the format for the test. The number of items should be chosen based on considerations for reliability, content coverage, and test security. However, workplace assessments must effectively balance content sampling with space and time limitations. Assessments with too few items may not adequately measure the entire domain of the trait (content validity) or provide consistent results (reliability). And assessments with too many items may result in test-taker fatigue or negative reactions and may not be appropriate for situations with strict time constraints.

The choice of the item format may mitigate some of the disadvantages traditionally associated with measurement. For example, forced-choice response formats, where respondents must choose between two or more items matched on social desirability, may reduce the prevalence of faking on personality items. Other novel stimuli may also be appropriate. Video- or computer-simulation tests may provide an effective means for measuring context-based phenomena such as emotional intelligence or situational judgment.

The next step is to create an item pool. Ensuring content and construct validity through the generation of appropriate items is one of the most difficult and important tasks of the test developer. Content validity addresses the appropriateness of the content covered by the test, whereas construct validity examines whether the test assesses the trait it is designed to measure (see the section on validity below and Chapter Twenty for further discussion). Without these forms of validity, the interpretation of results may be difficult. Developing content-valid items will be easier if the domain is well defined and the test specifications ensure adequate content coverage. However, generating construct-valid items can be more complex. It is surprisingly difficult to develop items that assess a single construct; other traits may be substantially correlated with an item because of common underlying antecedents.

Issues with the validity of items in the pool illustrate the importance of the next step in test development: item pretesting. Few test developers would put a new item on an operational test without first evaluating its measurement properties in a pretest sample. Ideally a large and representative sample is used for pretesting. Perhaps the best situation is one in which new pretest items are embedded in operational test forms and administered to job applicants; this is what is done to pretest items for the Armed Services Vocational Aptitude Battery (ASVAB). Then items can be evaluated statistically with classical test theory (CTT) statistics such as the proportion right, $\hat{p}$, the item-total point-biserial correlation, and the item-total biserial correlation. These analyses are often used as a first step in the evaluation process.

Many testing programs also use IRT to conduct item-level analyses. Although IRT techniques are mathematically complex, there are several important benefits to using them in addition to the traditional CTT methods. First, IRT item parameters are invariant across samples of test takers. Thus, in contrast to CTT statistics that are affected by the ability distribution of the sample, IRT parameters will be equivalent across groups. For example, items on a job knowledge test may appear difficult for a sample of novices (a low-ability sample) while simultaneously appearing easy for more experienced workers (a high-ability sample) when CTT statistics are used. This is especially important when the sample used to pretest items (say, current employees who are experienced) differs from the sample for which the test will be used (job applicants who are likely to be novices). Second, IRT methods can be used to ensure that a test adequately assesses ability or skill at key points on the latent trait continuum (for example, at important cut scores). Finally, ability estimates are invariant across items. Whereas the number-right score of CTT is affected by the difficulty of the items (it is harder to obtain a high score on a test with more difficult items), IRT ability estimates take into account item characteristics such as difficulty; this is the key reason IRT is needed for CAT. Given these important characteristics, we discuss IRT methodology as well as traditional methods throughout the rest of this chapter.

The basic building block of IRT is the item response function (IRF), which describes the relationship between the probability of correctly answering an item and an individual's latent trait level. Figure 2.2 shows the proportion correct on an item for respondents who answered different numbers of items correctly on a thirty-item test. Clearly the proportion correct increases for individuals with higher test scores. Replacing the number-correct score with θ, the latent trait of IRT, leads to the IRF illustrated in Figure 2.3. This IRF can be represented for item i by equation 1 in Table 2.1. Here $u_i = 1$ indicates a correct response was made to item i and $P(u_i = 1|\theta)$ is the probability of that positive response given an examinee trait level θ. In equation 1, a_i represents the item discrimination or the steepness of the IRF, b_i represents the item difficulty, and c_i represents the guessing parameter.

After items have been selected, the final step in the development process is to evaluate the quality of the test as a whole. The primary criteria for this evaluation are the reliability and validity of the assessment. In the following sections, we address each of these issues.

Figure 2.2. Proportion Correct on an Item by Individuals with Different Total Test Scores

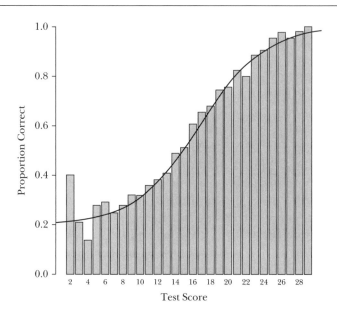

Figure 2.3. Three-Parameter Logistic Item Response Function for a Hypothetical Job Knowledge Test

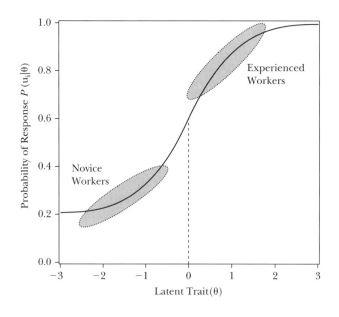

Table 2.1. IRT and CTT Equations for Evaluating Quality Assessments

Description	Equations	
Item response function	$P(u_i = 1 \mid \theta) = c_i + \dfrac{1 - c_i}{1 + \exp[-1.702a_i(\theta - b_i)]}$	Equation 1
Standard error of measurement in CTT	$SE(X) = \hat{\sigma}_x \sqrt{1 - r_{xx}}$	Equation 2
Number right score	$X = \sum\limits_{i=1}^{n} u_i$	Equation 3
Relationship between τ and θ	$\tau = E(X) = \sum\limits_{i=1}^{n} P_i(\theta)$	Equation 4
Conditional standard error of measurement in IRT	$SE(X \mid \tau) = SE(X \mid \theta_\tau) = \sqrt{\sum\limits_{i=1}^{n} P_i(\theta_\tau)[1 - P_i(\theta_\tau)]}$	Equation 5

Reliability

Reliability refers to the extent to which test scores are consistent or free from random error. It is a crucial property because no test can be valid unless it is reliable. Just as a test can be valid for one purpose but not another, a test can be reliable in one context but not in another. The *Standards for Educational and Psychological Testing* (American Educational Research Association, American Psychological Association, & National Council on Measurement in Education, 1999) state that test users have the responsibility of determining whether a measure of reliability is relevant to their intended use and interpretation. If the reliability estimate is not relevant, test users have the obligation to obtain the necessary reliability evidence.

Although it is difficult to draw a line in the sand, reliability should be in the neighborhood of .90 (or greater) for high-stakes decisions (such as hiring versus not hiring) based on one test score. If a measure is used in a selection composite or as one of several pieces of information considered when making a high-stakes decision, reliability should be at least .80. A measure that does not reach an adequate level of reliability should be revised.

Traditional Forms of Reliability

In this section we review traditional measures of reliability and their limitations. These reliability indexes all range from 0 to 1, with 1 indicating perfect reliability.

Test-retest reliability is estimated by administering a test or scale to a sample at two points in time and then correlating the scores. It is an important index for characteristics that should be stable across time. For example, intelligence is a highly stable trait, and consequently a minimal requirement for an intelligence test is to have substantial test-retest reliability.

Internal consistency reliability includes split-half reliability, the Kuder-Richardson KR20 and KR21 reliabilities, and Cronbach's coefficient alpha. All of these measures are functions of the intercorrelations of the items constituting a test. Thus, for a fixed test length, internal consistency reliability is higher when the test's items are more strongly correlated.

Reliability coefficients can be manipulated and artificially inflated. Therefore, it is important to consider several factors when interpreting a reliability coefficient, including test content, interitem correlations, test length, and the sample used to estimate reliability.

By incorporating highly redundant items, it is possible to manipulate reliability (and particularly internal consistency reliability) to produce substantially inflated values. Therefore, before giving credibility to a measure of reliability, it is important to examine the content of the measure for substantive richness and breadth. A narrow and excessively redundant measure may have an internal consistency reliability in excess of .95 but nonetheless be lacking in regard to other important properties, such as construct validity, which would reduce its correlation with job performance and other important variables.

For many types of measures, the average interitem correlation should fall in the range of .15 to .50. Having several items that are highly correlated (for example, .80) indicates excessive redundancy. For example, when assessing conscientiousness, two items might be, "I am careful in my work" and "I am meticulous in my work." Or in assessing math ability, two items could be restatements of the same problem but employ different numbers. Because variants of the same item will be answered by applicants in similar ways, such redundant items should be excluded because they ostensibly increase reliability but do not truly add new information.

Classical test theory shows that reliability can be increased by adding more items. Some high-stakes licensing exams, for example, consist of several hundred items. If a test has a long form and a short form, the reliability of the long form should be larger than the reliability of the short form, and it is important not to confuse the two. Unfortunately, high reliabilities of long tests are sometimes mistaken as indicating unidimensionality.

Reliability also depends on the characteristics of the sample. Range restriction, which occurs when the selection process has resulted in a sample that displays a truncated range of test scores, lowers inter-item correlations and results in lower reliability. Conversely, an artificially broad sample for example, using a sample of third-, fourth-, and fifth-grade students to estimate the reliability of a math achievement test designed for fourth graders, will inflate reliability. Because estimates of test reliability are sample dependent, it is important to ask whether the sample that was used to estimate test reliability is similar to the sample used for a specific organizational assessment purpose. If it is not, then the reliability estimate will be less informative for the organization.

Perhaps the greatest limitation on test-retest reliability results from the fact that reliability is sample dependent. Test-retest reliability is often estimated in a small, experimental study because it is difficult to administer the same test twice to a random sample under operational conditions. Thus, the question arises of whether results from the sample in the small research study can be generalized to other groups of test takers. Answering this question can be difficult or impossible.

Because reliability is subgroup dependent, it is inappropriate to say, "The reliability of test X is .92." Instead, a statement about reliability should include information about the group for which it was computed.

Additional concerns can be seen by looking at the technical definition of *reliability* as defined with classical test theory (the squared correlation between true scores, that is, the hypothetical scores people would receive if assessed with a perfect test, and observed scores). For example, the traditional reliability index is uninformative as to test precision at different score levels; one value of reliability is given for the test. Similarly, the standard error of measurement (the standard deviation of observed scores around the examinee's true score) of a test score X is given by equation 2 in Table 2.1, where $\hat{\sigma}_x$ is the standard deviation of test scores, and r_{xx} is the test's reliability; no differentiation is made between high, low, or moderate values of X. In many situations, it is critical to determine the test's precision at important cut scores where high-stakes decisions are made (AERA/APA/NCME, 1999).

Although CTT provides only a single standard error of measurement for a test, the standard error in IRT is conditional on the level of the latent trait. Thus, we denote the conditional standard error of measurement at a given true score τ by $SE(X|\tau)$ and the conditional standard error at a given latent trait score θ by $SE(X|\theta)$. These values, computed using IRT, allow test users to understand the magnitude of measurement error at critical score ranges.

Modern Forms of Reliability

A modern perspective on reliability is grounded in IRT, so the details are more complicated.

If number-right scoring is used on a test, the total test score is determined by counting the number of items answered correctly. Mathematically, the number-right score can be defined by equation 3 in Table 2.1, where X is the total score on the n item test and the score on item i is coded $u_i = 1$ if correct and 0 if incorrect. It can be shown that there is a one-to-one correspondence between the true score τ of classical test theory and the θ of IRT when the assumptions of IRT hold (see equation 4 in Table 2.1). Using θ_τ to indicate the value of θ corresponding to a particular true score τ, the conditional standard error of measurement is given in equation 5 in Table 2.1.

An alternative process can be used to compute the standard error of the estimate $\hat{\theta}$ of θ. This begins with the item information curve, as shown in Figure 2.4, which can be constructed for each item by using its item parameters a_i, b_i, and c_i. Notice that the peak of each item information function is close to the difficulty (b_i) of the item. Moreover, items with greater discrimination (larger a_i values) yield more information.

The test information curve (TIC), denoted as $I(\theta)$, is the sum of the item information curves. The TIC is important because it is inversely related to the conditional standard error of $\hat{\theta}$, specifically, $SE(\hat{\theta}|\theta) = \left(1/\sqrt{I(\theta)}\right)$. Note that IRT formalizes the intuition that items that discriminate at specific ability levels are most informative at those ability levels but much less informative at other levels.

Item information curves play a critical role in test development. One can examine the item information curves of all the items that have been pretested and then select the items that yield the most information at trait levels corresponding to important cut scores. In this way, test length can be minimized while providing highly precise measurement at the cut scores.

Figure 2.4. Example of Three-Item Information Curves for Items with Varying Levels of Difficulty and Discrimination

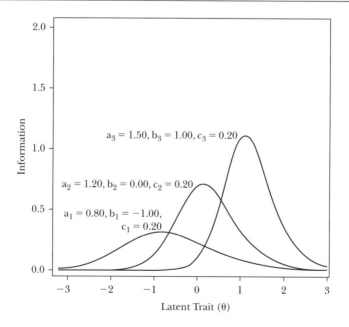

A much shorter test can be more informative than a longer test at a specific point on the trait continuum (for example, the cut score for determining passing on a licensing exam). Consider a shorter test formed by selecting items that are most informative at the specific trait level and a longer test constructed using a traditional approach where items are selected with varying levels of difficulty. An IRT analysis could show that the standard error of measurement at the cut score was smaller for the shorter test. If a test is built to be precise at only one cut score, it can be much shorter than a test built by traditional means, perhaps a third or a quarter as long.

Validity

When evaluating the quality of a test, it is important to assess both reliability and validity. Whereas reliability reflects the consistency with which the latent trait is measured, validity provides the justification for the inferences drawn from scores on the test. Although both factors play an active role in high-quality assessments, the 1985 *Test Standards* stated clearly and unambiguously that "validity is the most important consideration in test evaluation" (AERA/APA/NCME, 1985, p. 9).

Although organizational psychologists ordinarily use the term *validity coefficient* to refer to the correlation between a test *X* and a measure of job performance *Y*, *validity* is actually a much broader term. The 1999 *Test Standards* stated, "Validity refers to the degree to which evidence and theory support the interpretations of test scores" (AERA/APA/NCME, 1999, p. 9). There are a multitude of sources of evidence, including test content, the internal structure of the test, convergent and discriminant validity, test-criterion relationships, and validity generalization (see Chapter Twenty-One for a full description of these concepts).

Before purchasing a test, an organization should consider the evidence in relation to these aspects of validity. Alternatively, if an organization decides to create its own test, it should begin to accumulate these types of evidence to support its test use. In the remainder of this section, we review the various types of validity evidence and comment on challenges that may be encountered.

At the beginning of the test development process, the developer should carefully define the KSAs or other characteristics to be assessed by the test. Then the test blueprint should specify the content areas to be tested and how many items to include from each area. A first question is therefore, "Was the test actually built according to the original trait definition and test blueprint?" Yogi Berra is credited as saying, "You can see a lot by just looking," and the obvious implication is that test users should examine a test's content to ascertain whether it matches the test blueprint. For employee selection and development, the organization should ask whether the test assesses KSAs or some other characteristic that a job analysis indicated is critical for individuals in a particular job.

Factor analysis is frequently used to examine the internal structure of a test. If, for example, the trait definition states that a unitary characteristic is evaluated by the test, then a dominant first factor should appear. If a measure of emotional stability has facets of No Anxiety, Even Tempered, and Well-Being, a three-factor structure should be obtained.

Convergent and discriminant validity evidence is also important. Convergent validity is obtained when the test is positively and substantially correlated with another measure that it should correlate with. Discriminant validity is obtained when the test is not correlated with measures of theoretically distinct traits. Measures of emotional intelligence, for example, have been criticized as not exhibiting discriminant validity because they are excessively correlated with measures of other well-established traits (Davies, Stankov, & Roberts, 1998).

For good reasons, organizational psychologists have historically emphasized criterion-related validity, and consequently the most often used measure of the test-criterion relationship is the correlation coefficient. In fact, the massive quantity of such correlations enabled Schmidt and Hunter (1977) to create the validity generalization (VG) paradigm as a means of integrating findings across multiple studies. Central to VG are steps designed to overcome problems commonly encountered in criterion-related studies.

A first problem results from unreliability. If we could measure, say, mechanical aptitude and job performance perfectly for a sample of mechanical maintenance workers, we would obtain a higher test-performance correlation than we ordinarily find when mechanical aptitude and job performance are measured with error. Let τ_X denote a true score on a test X and τ_Y denote the true score on a job performance measure Y. Then the correlation $r(\tau_X, \tau_Y)$ between true scores τ_X and τ_Y is related to the correlation $r(X,Y)$ between observed scores X and Y by the equation

$$r(X,Y) = r(\tau_X, \tau_Y)\sqrt{r_{XX} r_{YY}}$$

where r_{XX} and r_{YY} are the reliabilities of X and Y. Consequently, unreliability in X and Y attenuates the correlation. For example, if the correlation between true scores for a test and job performance was .50, the reliability of the test was .81, and the reliability of the job performance measure was .49, then the correlation between the two observed measures would be $.50 \times \sqrt{.49 \times .81} = .315$.

The VG analysis corrects for unreliability in the criterion measure, but not unreliability in the test because unreliability in the test degrades the quality of selection decisions. Therefore, Schmidt and Hunter (1977) did not correct for less-than-perfect r_{XX}. In evaluating a test, it is very important to remember that test reliability affects the quality of decisions, and consequently reliability should be of the magnitude previously described (and computed from a relevant sample).

Another problem encountered in criterion-related validity studies results from restriction of range. Organizations obviously prefer applicants who do well on selection tests to applicants who do poorly, and thus the full range of scores on the selection test is not typically observed for the group that is hired and therefore has criterion data available. The significance of this problem is illustrated by a study of U.S. Army Air Force pilot trainees conducted during World War II (Thorndike, 1949). A group of 1,036 completed pilot training because of the need for pilots during the war; only 136 would have been selected for training on the basis of a composite selection index under normal conditions. The correlation of the selection composite with performance in training was .64 for the total group, but only .18 for the 136 individuals with the highest composite scores.

Lord and Novick (1968, p. 143) provide the rather complicated formula that can be used to correct an observed correlation for range restriction. In evaluating the criterion-related validity evidence of a test, it is very important to know whether correlations have been corrected for range restriction and unreliability in the criterion. If such correlations have not been corrected, the validity evidence is biased (and often substantially biased) in the direction of no relationship.

As suggested in the section on test development, the use of small samples has a strong impact on the sampling error of validity coefficients. This variability led many to believe that the relationship between a test and job performance was context specific and that local validity studies were required to justify the use of predictors in each organization. VG research has shown that this belief is clearly false. Nonetheless, any observed correlation of a test with job performance based on a sample of less than several hundred is highly suspect: sample error has an inescapable effect. VG is the best solution to this problem, but an adequate number of studies needs to be included in the analysis. For example, in their original paper, Schmidt and Hunter (1977) used data from $k = 114$ studies to demonstrate that tests of mechanical principles were highly effective in predicting the job performance of mechanical repairmen. It is very important to note that results of a VG analysis of $k = 4$ or 5 studies should be given little credibility.

Another issue to consider when interpreting the results of any criterion-related validity study or VG study concerns the conditions under which the data were collected. Were they collected in an actual operational setting where applicants knew that their scores would affect the likelihood of their being hired? Or were they told that scores were collected "for research purposes only"? Results from studies that ask participants to participate for research purposes may not generalize to the operational context of an assessment. A particularly striking example was provided by White, Young, Hunter, and Rumsey (2008). These authors described the substantial differences between validity coefficients obtained from a large military concurrent validation study using job incumbents (people who were told their participation was for research purposes only) and longitudinal research on applicant samples responding to operational exams. Although the concurrent validation study showed that socially desirable responding did not affect the validity of a personality measure, validity was severely attenuated in the operational sample. The lesson learned from White et al. is that generalizing research findings to operational contexts is difficult, particularly for measures where test takers can deliberately manipulate their scores by "faking good."

Although test-criterion relationships are typically reported in terms of correlations, other approaches are possible. Utility analysis, for example, links the validity of an assessment to its impact on performance. Taylor and Russell (1939) defined *utility* as the increased accuracy in the prediction of a dichotomous job performance measure (one that classifies people into "successful" and "unsuccessful" categories, for example) obtained from using a particular selection measure. Their conceptualization incorporates the correlation between a test and job performance, the selection ratio (the proportion of applicants who are hired), and the base rate of successful employees (the proportion of new employees who would be successful if the test were not used). The Taylor-Russell tables provide the improvement in success rate (the proportion of selected applicants who are subsequently determined to be successful) that can result from various combinations of these factors.

Cascio (1991) described several disadvantages of this conceptualization of utility. First, the Taylor-Russell tables assess utility only relative to the success rate rather than a monetary outcome. Second, this approach defines success as a dichotomous variable and therefore does not quantify the magnitude of success. In other words, the dichotomous success variable may underestimate the true utility of a measure.

Another popular method of assessing utility was developed by Naylor and Shine (1965). These authors conceptualized utility in terms of the increase in the average job performance score that can be obtained by using an assessment. The disadvantages of this method are that it does not account for the administration costs of the assessments and does not reflect the economic impact of using a particular predictor (Cascio, 1991).

Brogden (1949) and Cronbach and Gleser (1965) proposed a utility estimate that is assessed as the dollar value of work output rather than the expected improvement in job performance. This method defines the net dollar gain, ΔU, as

$$\Delta U = N \times \bar{T} \times SD_Y \times r_{XY} \times \bar{Z}_X - C$$

where N is the number of people hired in a year, $\bar{T}$ is the average tenure for new employees, SD_Y is the standard deviation of job performance expressed in dollars, r_{XY} is the validity of the test, $\bar{Z}_X$ is the average standardized score of the selected applicants on the test, and C is the total cost of administrating the test.

Although the above equation is widely known, it appears to have had limited impact. For example, in the late 1980s, military researchers (Automated Sciences Group & CACI, 1988) conducted this type of utility analysis in an attempt to justify the implementation of the computer-adaptive version of the ASVAB, known as CAT-ASVAB. Military leaders were not impressed with "utility dollars" and did not order implementation of CAT-ASVAB. A few years later, a financial analysis was conducted (Hogan, McBride, & Curran, 1995) that compared the total cost (in actual dollars, not utility dollars) of continuing to administer the paper-and-pencil ASVAB in the Military Enlistment Processing Stations (MEPS) versus the cost of buying computers and implementing CAT-ASVAB in the MEPS. It turned out that the Department of Defense could save millions of dollars per year by implementing CAT-ASVAB, and consequently military leaders decided to implement it. (The principal source of savings was reduced processing time, so fewer applicants needed hotel accommodations for an overnight stay.) In sum, actual dollars were compelling to the Department of Defense leadership, but utility dollars were not.

Finally, another method of characterizing test-criterion relationships has been figuratively called a return-on-investment (ROI) study. Here the organization assesses some important aspect of job performance and then compares this type of performance for people who are high, medium, and low on the selection measure. For example, the U.S. Army is very concerned about attrition during the first term of enlistment, particularly for individuals who do not have a high school diploma. Young, Heggestad, Rumsey, and White (2000) developed the Assessment of Individual Motivation (AIM) to identify military applicants who are likely to complete their first term. The AIM was administered to a sample of 11,848 GED holders, scores on the AIM composite were stratified into ten decile groups, and attrition rates were computed after nine months in the Army. Figure 2.5 shows that accessions in the top 40 percent on the AIM composite had attrition rates very close to the rate of high school diploma holders (this latter group had a 16.3 percent attrition rate), but attrition rates were much higher for individuals with lower composite scores.

The ROI plot clearly shows the value of the AIM composite; this approach appears to be gaining traction with organizational leaders. Ironically, the correlation of the AIM composite with nine-month attrition was a seemingly trivial $-.114$. Although statistically significant (the sample size was over eleven thousand), a correlation of $-.114$ would be likely to elicit the reaction that the selection tool accounted for just 1 percent of the variance in attrition and was therefore virtually useless. Figure 2.5 demonstrates that individuals with as high as 30 percent attrition rates can be screened out, and individuals with a 16 or 17 percent attrition rate screened in. Obviously this is not a trivial difference, and it

Figure 2.5. ROI Plot Depicting Attrition Rates Across Levels of the Army's AIM Composite

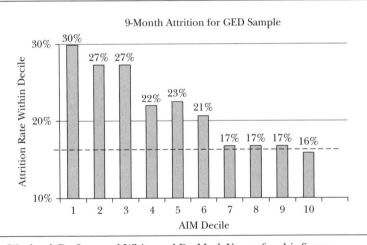

Note: We thank Dr. Leonard White and Dr. Mark Young for this figure.

clearly demonstrates that the AIM can make an important contribution to enlistment screening.

Operational Models for Assessment

The proliferation of technology in the workplace has allowed organizations to increase efficiency at lower costs. Similarly, new test systems have also been developed to tap advantages of technological advances. Chief among them are computerized tests delivered over the Internet or an intranet. Such tests can be administered either adaptively (CAT) or nonadaptively (with computerized page turners); they may also be administered in proctored or unproctored settings.

To help organizations decide whether computerized testing adds value or whether unproctored testing should be implemented, we discuss the advantages and disadvantages of these delivery options. Next, we examine the related issue of test security. In the final subsection, we review best practices for test score reporting.

Computer-Administered Tests

Compared to paper-and-pencil tests, computerized tests can be easier to administer and score, and potentially they have lower costs. Because computerized tests usually provide several screens of instructions and are self-timed, they may require fewer proctors, which lowers cost. Furthermore, examinee responses are recorded automatically, allowing instantaneous scoring with minimal error. Tests can also be updated much more easily. For example, the system stores the operational test solely on a central server; when an examinee begins a test session, the exam is downloaded to his or her personal computer. In this situation, any change in the test can be made easily and implemented instantly. In contrast, months may be required to print and distribute a revised paper-and-pencil form. For all of these reasons, computerized tests are increasing in popularity.

Another advantage of computer-administered tests is that multimedia capabilities can be used. For example, a situational judgment test may use video clips depicting common workplace situations instead of text-based descriptions. The value of multimedia cannot be overstated because research shows that video-based situational judgment tests are less correlated with cognitive ability than paper-and-pencil versions of the same test and therefore yield incremental validity above cognitive ability and less adverse impact (Olson-Buchanan et al., 1998). Multimedia is also particularly important when one attempts to assess other skills, such as negotiation or conflict resolution, not easily tested with a paper-and-pencil format. Moreover, well-constructed, multimedia assessment usually has a more positive response from test takers. Richman, Olson-Buchanan, and Drasgow (2000) found that managers completing a multimedia assessment perceived the assessment as more face valid and had more positive attitudes as compared to managers who were administered nonmultimedia assessments with equivalent content.

Adaptivity, which is conveniently implemented in a computerized setting, has important advantages. Specifically, CAT results in shorter tests with higher measurement precision. The general idea behind CAT is that items are selected adaptively so that their difficulty matches a test taker's ability. The prototypical algorithm involves computing a provisional estimate of ability ($\hat{\theta}$) based on the responses to items previously administered, selecting the next item from the item pool that is maximally informative, and administering this item to the examinee. This process is repeated until the ability estimate is sufficiently precise or a fixed test length is reached. Thus, each test is tailored to the individual test taker. This is unlike conventional tests where all test takers answer the same items regardless of whether they are too hard or too easy, which may result in boredom, random responding, or guessing. Most important, time savings associated with CAT can be converted into cost savings.

There are challenges that organizations must face if they wish to implement a CAT. First, it is costly to implement CAT because developing and pretesting a large item pool is time consuming and expensive. Furthermore, continued technical and psychometric expertise is necessary to support a CAT testing program.

Internet Testing: Unproctored and Proctored Testing

With its exponential growth, companies are turning to the Internet as a medium for testing. In fact, the United States alone has about 223 million Internet users, with another 795 million users worldwide (*CIA Fact Book*, 2008). Within the United States, about 80 percent of adults go online (Pew Internet & American Life Project, April 2009). At such high levels of use, it is likely that job applicants will have little problem accessing tests using the Internet.

Organizations that adopt Internet testing enjoy scalability, speed, and convenience benefits. First, Internet testing is scalable in that increased volume of testing, even if the number of applicants doubles, results in very little additional cost. Second, the speed at which tests can be distributed and scored is unparalleled. New or updated test forms can be uploaded onto a server and implemented immediately. After tests are completed, scores can be instantaneously delivered online to companies and applicants. Third, it is more convenient and less costly for companies to prescreen applicants over the Internet because it incurs lower overhead. For example, applicants can take a test in the convenience of their homes with no travel costs for the company.

Despite the convenience, flexibility, and reduced cost of unproctored Internet testing, this format is not without problems, including questions about standardization of test administration conditions, test-taker integrity, and test security.

Test-taking conditions can differ substantially across locations. This may affect reliability and validity due to the type of instrumentation (for example, computer interface or speed of Internet connection), the degree of noise and other distractions, and even the temperature, lighting, and ventilation in the room where the test is administered. To circumvent such variability, some organizations use proctored Internet testing at a specific location to ensure that test conditions are equivalent for all test takers. Given the additional costs, it is important to ask if test standardization is necessary. There are three main considerations: test purpose, test content, and testing stage (Tippins et al., 2006). First, tests that are mainly used for career assessment and personal development purposes may not require such stringent standards as high-stakes tests. Second, whether proctored and unproctored tests are equivalent may depend on the test content. For example, a recent meta-analysis found that noncognitive assessments (personality and biodata) have equivalent validity across proctored and unproctored conditions (Beaty et al., 2009), whereas cognitive tests are thought to have a greater potential for being nonequivalent. Third, it is less important to standardize tests that are used for an initial screen-out procedure as compared to tests in later stages focused on selecting-in applicants.

The benefits of proctored tests are that they address not only the problem of test-client integrity and test security but also variability in test conditions. Test-client integrity concerns whether a test taker is the actual applicant or some confederate whom the applicant believes can obtain a high test score. Verification procedures can be implemented to ensure a correspondence between the actual and alleged test taker (for example, the use of a driver's license or passport). In contrast, it is difficult or impossible to ensure test-client integrity in unproctored environments. However, when initial tests are unproctored, it is possible to require a short follow-up test in a proctored environment for test takers who make the initial cut. Test scores that are substantially lower in the proctored environment are indicative of cheating.

Proctored environments have another advantage in terms of test security: individuals cannot easily harvest test items when they are under close supervision. In unproctored environments, it is difficult to prevent the copying of items even after disabling copying and printing functions from browsers because other forms of recording, such as analog recording, video recording, or manually copying of test items, can still be used.

It should be noted that proctored testing is only one component determining end-user test security. In the next section, we discuss how different test systems can be made more secure with respect to large-scale or small-scale cheating.

Test Security and Types of Cheating

Test security is important in two ways. First, when test security is high, the likelihood that test items are disclosed to potential test takers is low, and thus the validity of the test can be maintained. If items are revealed to test takers beforehand, test scores are contaminated by the degree of item preknowledge. With substantial item preknowledge, it is unlikely that test scores will be related to job performance, and therefore the test will be invalid. Second, ensuring test security protects costs invested in item development, especially if the test is developed in-house. The total cost of item writing, editing, pretesting, calibrating, and so forth is often said to cost on the order of a thousand dollars per item, and therefore organizations can have a considerable investment in their tests.

Test compromise can occur through large-scale cheating conspiracies or small-scale cheating (Chuah, 2005). Large-scale cheating refers to organized cheating efforts where an organizational entity, usually a test preparation company, systematically harvests and discloses items from a testing program to potential test takers. In large-scale cheating, legal and statistical interventions are available. For example, a recent court ruling in a copyright-infringement lawsuit ordered ScoreTop.com, a Web site disclosing stolen Graduate Management Admission Test (GMAT) items, to pay $2.3 million plus legal costs and to disclose its clientele so their scores could be revoked ("Graduate Exam Publisher Wins Suit Against Web Site," 2008). It appears likely that such organized cheating conspiracies will generally be targeted at large testing programs such as the GMAT, the Graduate Record Examination, and the Multi-State Bar Exam, all of which have had large-scale cheating problems.

Small-scale cheating occurs when initial test takers (conspirators) share information with future test takers (beneficiaries) in an ad hoc fashion. For example, surveys on college students show that a substantial proportion of people admit to cheating, including asking for test items, copying answers, or sharing answers with others (Cizek, 1999). These behaviors continue to be apparent with postgraduate students and professionals (Cizek, 1999). Because of the random nature of information sharing, it is difficult to take appropriate legal action or use statistical procedures to identify cheating. Hence, it is important to consider the use of appropriate test systems in forestalling the effects of cheating.

CATs are much more robust with regard to small-scale cheating than conventional tests, even when multiple forms of the conventional test are used (Guo, Tay, & Drasgow, 2009). This is true because CATs administer an individualized test to each person; if the item pool is large and an exposure control algorithm is used, different examinees will see different items. Even if many items have been given to beneficiaries, they are still likely to be administered a largely unique set of items, making item preknowledge less useful. Thus, to reduce the impact of small-scale cheating, CAT is advised. Otherwise it is important to use multiple forms of conventional tests.

Test Score Reporting

While test scores may not be reported to job applicants, they are reported to incumbents for career assessment purposes or training and to individuals taking tests for higher education, accreditation, or licensing. As such, reported scores can help identify strengths and weaknesses in different professional areas. Many testing programs provide subscale scores based on item content for score reports. However, subscales have fewer items (sometimes as few as three or four) and are therefore much less reliable. More important, there may not be a unique factor (or subdimension) underlying the subscale, implying that the main factor accounts for almost all of the nonerror variance on the test. Consequently there may be little psychometric justification for reporting subtest scores.

Quality Control

In the past decade, there have been many incidents of incorrectly scored tests. For example:

- Between October 2004 and December 2005, a professional association mistakenly failed 1,882 examinees taking its credentialing exam, resulting in hundreds of people losing their jobs (http://www.iht.com/articles/2006/11/05/bloomberg/bxexam.php).
- Thousands of October 8, 2005, SAT answer sheets were not scanned accurately by an educational testing company, and consequently incorrect scores were issued (http://www.nytimes.com/2006/03/23/education/23sat.html).
- In 2002, an educational testing company misscored almost 8,000 Minnesota high school Basic Standards Tests in math, causing several hundred students to be denied a high school diploma (http://news.minnesota.publicradio.org/features/200211/25_pugmiret_testsettle).

It is very likely that many more undisclosed problems have occurred. In this section, we provide some suggestions about how to avoid testing mistakes.

First, it is a good idea to score each exam twice, using completely independent systems. For a paper-and-pencil exam, this would mean scanning each answer sheet twice on different scanners. Then the scanned answers should be scored twice on different computer systems that use different files containing the answer keys. Then a psychometric analysis should be conducted to ensure that item difficulties ($\hat{p}$ values) and item-total correlations are close to the pretest values or values obtained previously from operational test forms. For a computerized test, test administrators should, on a regular basis, key in specified answer patterns, which can then be compared to what is saved by the computer and uploaded to the central server; any discrepancy indicates a problem. Then the psychometric analysis described above should be performed.

Person-fit analysis (Levine & Drasgow, 1982) uses IRT to compute a goodness-of-fit measure for each examinee. The problems listed above could have been caught before scores were reported if Drasgow, Levine, and Williams's (1985) standardized person index for polytomously scored responses (responses with three or more scoring categories) had been computed. This measure has a mean of 0 and a standard deviation of 1 when examinees respond normally; anomalous responses produce large negative person-fit values. If the testing organizations listed above had computed the standardized person index, they would have observed many aberrant values in the range of -3, -4, or even larger negative values. This would have clearly raised a red flag.

Another concern about test scoring asks whether all groups are assessed equivalently. This can be examined by IRT by comparing the IRFs estimated for different groups. Suppose an item yielded the IRFs shown in Figure 2.6 for men and women for some item. Assuming that reasonably large sample sizes were used for both men and women, then any of the many differential item functioning (DIF) analysis methods would find that these two IRFs are significantly different. DIF, in the IRT framework, occurs when individuals from different groups, but with the same standing on the latent trait assessed by the test, have unequal chances

Figure 2.6. Hypothetical IRFs for Men and Women

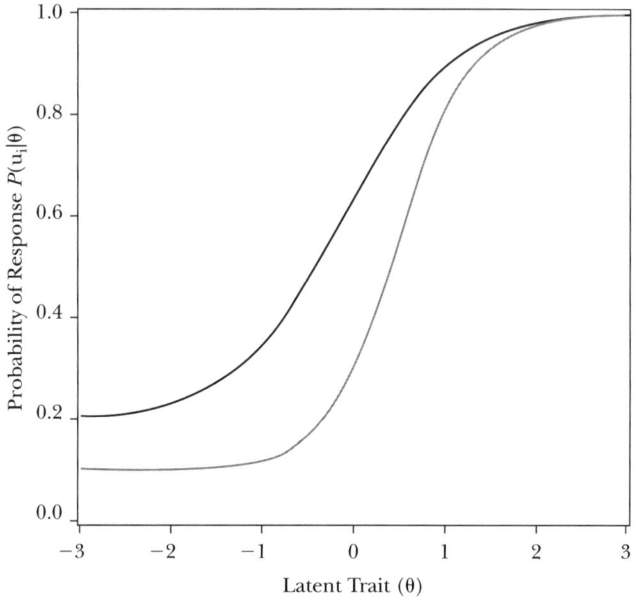

Note: Black and grey lines represent hypothetical IRFs for men and women respectively.

of responding correctly. Measurement equivalence occurs when individuals with the same standing on the latent trait have equal chances of responding correctly, regardless of their group. Thus, establishing measurement equivalence is an important prerequisite to producing accurate scores across subgroups.

Conclusion

We have outlined many exemplary testing practices as well as numerous pitfalls. Of course, no testing program should be evaluated with a checklist mentality, where strong features and weaknesses are simply added up. But as the 1985 *Test Standards* (AERA/APA/NMCE, 1985) said, "Validity is the most important consideration," and it is crucial to examine whether a test is being used in a valid way.

Tests should be reliable for their intended use. By this we do not mean that coefficient alpha should be large for some unspecified sample. Instead, tests should consistently classify test takers into meaningful groupings such as "recommended for hiring" versus "not recommended for hiring," "high potential" versus "not high potential" for development, "recommended for a training program" versus "not recommended for training," and so forth. A small conditional standard error of measurement at the cut score for the categories is needed for consistent classification. More generally, small conditional standard errors of measurement are needed at all important cut scores for a test to validly fulfill its intended function.

Modern views describe validity as a unitary construct. We have described how the test content and its internal structure, convergent and discriminant validity, and test-criterion relationships are all important facets of validity. We urge test users and judges of test use to look beyond the statistical significance and magnitude of a test-criterion correlation when evaluating validity. The U.S. Army example in Figure 2.5 clearly demonstrates that focusing on a small correlation can obscure an important and powerful relationship.

A reliable and valid test constitutes one of the most extraordinary returns on investment available to organizations. For example, a thirty-minute test of sales skills, purchased for perhaps $10 per test taker, may increase revenue per salesperson by $100,000 per year. In this era of growing domestic and international competition, organizations cannot forgo this competitive advantage.

References

American Educational Research Association, American Psychological Association, & National Council on Measurement in Education. (1985). *Standards for educational and psychological testing.* Washington, DC: American Psychological Association.

American Educational Research Association, American Psychological Association, & National Council on Measurement in Education. (1999). *Standards for educational and psychological testing.* Washington, DC: American Psychological Association.

Automated Sciences Group & CACI, Inc.-Federal. (1988). *CAT-ASVAB program: Concept of operation and cost/benefit analysis.* Fairfax, VA: Author.

Beaty, J. C., Nye, C. D., Borneman, M. J., Drasgow, F., Kantrowitz, T. M., & Grauer, E. (2009). *Proctored versus unproctored Internet tests: Are unproctored tests as predictive of job performance?* Manuscript submitted for publication.

Brogden, H. E. (1949). When testing pays off. *Personnel Psychology, 2,* 171–185.

Cascio, W. F. (1991). *Costing human resources: The financial impact of behavior in organizations.* Florence, KY: Cengage.

Chuah, S. C. (2005). *Conspiracy theory: An empirical study of cheating in a continuous testing environment.* Unpublished doctoral dissertation, University of Illinois at Urbana-Champaign.

CIA Factbook. (2008). *Field listing—Internet users.* Retrieved from https://www.cia.gov/library/publications/the-world-factbook/rankorder/2153rank.html.

Cizek, G. J. (1999). *Cheating on tests: How to do it, detect it, and prevent it.* Mahwah, NJ: Erlbaum.

Cronbach, L. J., & Gleser, G. C. (1965). *Psychological tests and personnel decisions* (2nd ed.). Urbana: University of Illinois Press.

Davies, M., Stankov, L., & Roberts, R. D. (1998). Emotional intelligence: In search of an elusive construct. *Journal of Personality and Social Psychology, 75,* 989–1015.

Drasgow, F., Levine, M. V., & Williams, E. (1985). Appropriateness measurement with polychotomous item response models and standardized indices. *British Journal of Mathematical and Statistical Psychology, 38,* 67–86.

Drasgow, F., Luecht, R., & Bennett, R. (2006). Technology and testing. In R. L. Brennan (Ed.), *Educational measurement* (4th ed., pp. 471–515). Westport, CT: American Council on Education/Praeger.

Graduate exam publisher wins suit against Web site. (2008, July 3). *Wall Street Journal,* p. A2.

Guo, J., Tay, L., & Drasgow, F. (2009). Conspiracies and test compromise: An evaluation of the resistance to test systems to small-scale cheating. *International Journal of Testing, 9,* 283–309.

Hogan, P. F., McBride, J. R., & Curran, L. T. (1995). *An evaluation of alternate concepts for administering the Armed Services Vocational Aptitude Battery to applicants for enlistment.* Monterey, CA: Personnel Testing Division, Defense Manpower Data Center.

Levine, M. V., & Drasgow, F. (1982). Appropriateness measurement: Review, critique and validating studies. *British Journal of Mathematical and Statistical Psychology, 35,* 42–56.

Lord, F. M., & Novick, M. R. (1968). *Statistical theories of mental test scores.* Reading, MA: Addison-Wesley.

Naylor, J. C., & Shine, L. C. (1965). A table for determining the increase in mean criterion score obtained by using a selection device. *Journal of Industrial Psychology, 3,* 33–42.

Olson-Buchanan, J. B., Drasgow, F., Moberg, P. J., Mead, A. D., Keenan, P. A., & Donovan, M. A. (1998). Interactive video assessment of conflict resolution skills. *Personnel Psychology, 51,* 1–24.

Pew Internet & American Life Project. (2009). *Internet adoption.* Retrieved February 10, 2010, from http://www.pewinternet.org/Static-Pages/Trend-Data/Internet-Adoption.aspx.

Richman, W. L., Olson-Buchanan, J. B., & Drasgow, F. (2000). Examining the impact of administration medium on examinee perceptions and attitudes. *Journal of Applied Psychology, 85,* 880–887.

Schmidt, F. L., & Hunter, J. E. (1977). Development of a general solution to the problem of validity generalization. *Journal of Applied Psychology, 62,* 529–540.

Taylor, H. C., & Russell, J. T. (1939). The relationship of validity coefficients to the practical effectiveness of tests in selection. *Journal of Applied Psychology, 23,* 565–578.

Thorndike, R. L. (1949). *Personnel selection.* Hoboken, NJ: Wiley.

Tippins, N. T., Beaty, J., Drasgow, F., Gibson, W. M., Pearlman, K., Segall, D. O. et al. (2006). Unproctored Internet testing in employment settings. *Personnel Psychology, 59,* 189–225.

White, L. A., Young, M. C., Hunter, A. E., & Rumsey, M. G. (2008). Lessons learned in transitioning personality measures from research to operational settings. *Industrial and Organizational Psychology: Perspectives on Science and Practice, 1,* 291–295.

Young, M. C., Heggestad, E. D., Rumsey, M. G., & White, L. A. (2000, August). *Army pre-implementation research findings on the assessment of individual motivation (AIM).* Paper presented at the American Psychological Association, Washington, DC.

CHAPTER 3

GENERAL COGNITIVE ABILITY

Michael A. McDaniel, George C. Banks

The success of an organization depends on the effective performance of its employees. For this reason, managers, supervisors, and other organizational leaders have a vested interest in the human capital that comprises their organization. Thus, leadership within an organization should strive to select and develop the most talented individuals. One way in which talented individuals can be identified is through the evaluation of their general cognitive ability. In this chapter, we review the research on cognitive ability that is of relevance to applied human resource researchers and practitioners.

General cognitive ability is the ability that consistently differentiates individuals on mental abilities regardless of the cognitive task or test (Jensen, 1998). Thus, general cognitive ability can be measured in a variety of ways with a variety of tests. For the purpose of this review, general cognitive ability is synonymous with traditional conceptions of intelligence such as IQ and Charles Spearman's general intelligence factor (*g*). This review is restricted to cognitive ability conceptions of intelligence and does not review other assessments that have adopted the word *intelligence*, such as emotional intelligence and practical intelligence. We also exclude measures and models of intelligence for which there is little research support.

Many well-known tests measure general cognitive ability for workplace assessment. Some general cognitive ability tests that are commonly used in workplace assessment are presented in the Appendix. Some of the many vendors of such tests are better than others. We list a few test publishers whose cognitive ability tests are well constructed, widely used, and for which there is excellent documentation.

Dominant Models of General Cognitive Ability

Multiple models describe the nature of general cognitive ability, but for the purposes of this overview, we focus on the most widely recognized and accepted models in the field. We begin with a review of Spearman's general intelligence factor, or g. We then summarize Cattell's model of crystallized and fluid intelligence and John Carroll's three-stratum model of cognitive ability.

General Intelligence Factor Model

Spearman (1904) presented a model of intelligence explained by two factors, the general cognitive ability factor (g) and the specific factor, abbreviated as s (Carroll, 1993; Jensen, 1998). The s allows an individual to be more effective at one cognitive ability test than another one when there is task- or domain-specific knowledge. Thus, s is unique from g, which is responsible for an individual's effectiveness on all tests of cognitive ability. Spearman was able to derive his model of the g factor from a method known as factor analysis (which he also invented). Through factor analysis, a researcher can determine correlations between specific variables in a cognitive test and a common variable that is present throughout tests (Jensen, 1998). Spearman named the common variable in this case g. Through factor analysis, he concluded that g is the common factor that differentiates individuals on all tests of cognitive ability. The primary reason that Spearman's model has prevailed as one of the dominant models of cognitive ability is that empirical research has produced strong results demonstrating the importance of the g factor in all cognitive ability tests (Jensen, 1998).

Cattell's Crystallized and Fluid Intelligences

Raymond Cattell, a student of Charles Spearman, proposed that crystallized and fluid intelligence are two underlying components of the *g* factor (Cattell, 1943; Jensen, 1998). Cattell's model, like Spearman's, also has substantial research support. Fluid intelligence is the ability to solve novel problems through reasoning. Crystallized intelligence is the ability to rely on prior experience and knowledge to solve problems. Individual differences in fluid intelligence contribute to individual differences in crystallized intelligence. Thus, it is not surprising that fluid and crystallized intelligence measures are highly correlated. Fluid intelligence tends to peak in early adulthood and then declines with age.

Jensen (1998, p. 123) offered the following two items:

1. Temperature is to cold as height is to: (a) hot (b) inches (c) size (d) tall (e) weight.
2. Bizet is to Carmen as Verdi is to: (a) Aïda (b) Elektra (c) Lakmé (d) Manon (e) Tosca.

The first item primarily places demands on fluid intelligence to see the logical relationships (d is the answer). The second item primarily places demands on crystallized intelligence, particularly on knowledge related to opera (a is the answer).

Carroll's Three-Stratum Theory

Carroll's three-stratum theory (Carroll, 1993) complements the other two models of cognitive ability. In extensive series of factor analyses, Carroll offered evidence for three layers, or strata, of cognitive ability that attempt to explain a narrow, broad, and more general level of cognitive ability (Jensen, 1998). Carroll devised his model to describe Spearman's *g* factor as his stratum III or more general level. Carroll's broad level, stratum II, incorporates Cattell's fluid and crystallized intelligence, as well as six other factors. The third level Carroll proposed is the narrow level, or stratum I. In Carroll's model, this lowest level addresses sixty-nine abilities (Jensen, 1998). Figure 3.1 graphically displays this model. Note the space gap in stratum II between crystallized intelligence and general memory and learning. This gap was intentional to show the relative importance of the stratum 2 abilities

Figure 3.1. Carroll's Three-Stratum Theory of Cognitive Ability

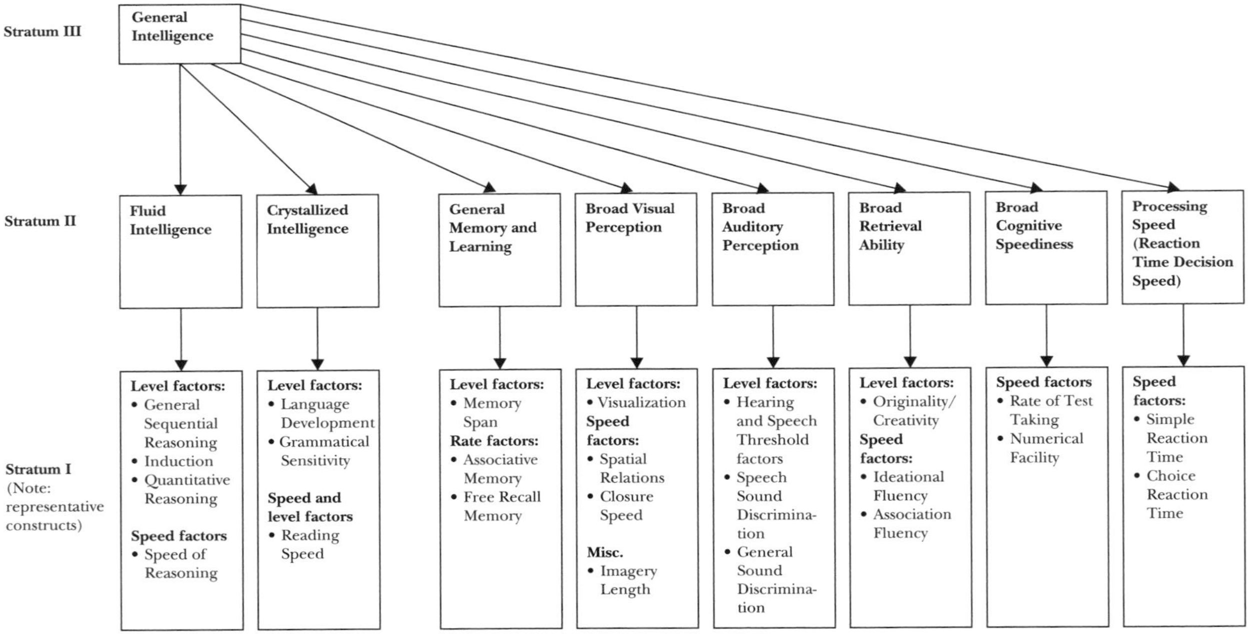

Source: Adapted with permission from Carroll (1993), Figure 15.1 (p. 627). Copyright Cambridge University Press.

to general intelligence. Fluid and crystallized intelligence are the most highly related factors to general intelligence. The other factors are related, but to a lesser degree. The order of the lesser contributors is also important and reflects their contribution to general intelligence. For example, memory contributes more to general intelligence than does broad visual perception.

Cognitive Ability and the World of Work

Cognitive ability and the world of work spans several topics. The knowledge base on cognitive ability is intricately tied to a body of knowledge called validity generalization, which we examine first in this section. Next, we examine the value of cognitive ability in the prediction of training performance and job performance. We then address two issues relevant to the use of cognitive ability tests: the linearity of prediction and the relative value of general versus specific abilities in prediction. We follow this with a discussion of evidence relevant to three demographic subgroup issues: race/demographic mean differences in cognitive ability, validity for different subgroups, and the failure of efforts to reduce subgroup mean differences by altering items.

Validity Generalization

Beginning in the 1920s, it was observed that different applications of the same general cognitive ability test yielded different validity results, that is, the magnitude of the relationship between the test and job performance varied (Schmidt & Hunter, 1998). This caused some to speculate that there were some unknown characteristics of the situation in which the test was used that caused the general cognitive ability test to be predictive of job performance in one situation (for example, a teller job in a bank on Oak Street), but not predictive or less predictive in a different situation (a teller job in a bank on Elm Street). This speculation became known as the situational specificity hypothesis (Schmidt & Hunter, 1998). Because the situational characteristics presumably causing these validity differences were not identified through job analysis, it became the custom that the validity of a general cognitive ability test was examined in each setting in which the test was used.

In the late 1970s, Schmidt and Hunter questioned the legitimacy of the situational specificity hypothesis. They demonstrated that random sampling error, and not some unknown situational moderator, was the primary reason that the validity of general cognitive ability tests varied across applications (Schmidt & Hunter, 1977). In addition, they documented how measurement error made general cognitive ability tests appear less valid than they were. Also, differences across studies in the extent of measurement error, in addition to random sampling error, caused predictive validity of general cognitive ability tests to vary across situations. Similarly, they documented how range restriction made general cognitive ability tests appear to be less valid than they were and that differences across studies in the degree of range restriction caused the predictive validity of general cognitive ability tests to vary across situations.

In brief, the seminal work of Schmidt and Hunter demonstrated that the validity of general cognitive ability tests was quite stable across settings once one adjusted the data for random sampling error and differences across studies in measurement error and range restriction. Schmidt and Hunter also demonstrated that the true predictive validity of general cognitive ability tests had been substantially underestimated due to a failure to consider the effects of measurement error and range restriction.

Prediction of Training Performance

No one can perform successfully in a job without the necessary job knowledge and job skills. Although an organization can select applicants who have the needed knowledge and skills, many jobs require that new employees be trained after they are hired. These jobs include entry jobs in the police and fire services and jobs in the military. The acquisition of skill and knowledge depends on learning, and the rate of learning is related to general cognitive ability (Jensen, 1998). It should not be surprising that general cognitive ability tests are excellent predictors of success in training programs for newly hired employees. Two types of studies are most useful for summarizing the value of general cognitive ability tests in the prediction of training performance.

The first type of particularly valuable studies are validity generalization studies that have examined the value of general cognitive ability in the prediction of training performance in specific job families. For example, Barrett, Polomsky, and McDaniel (1999) reported a validity of .77 for general cognitive ability tests and firefighter training performance. Pearlman, Schmidt, and Hunter (1980) reported a validity of .71 for general cognitive ability tests and clerical training performance. Hirsh, Northrop, and Schmidt (1986) reported a validity of .71 for a general cognitive ability composite for police and detective training performance. There are many additional studies, including ones that that have examined semiprofessional occupations (Trattner, 1985) and blue-collar jobs where apprenticeship training was common (Northrop, 1988). Lilienthal and Pearlman (1983) reported general cognitive ability validities for training performance in entry-level aid and technician occupations in the health, science, and engineering fields. Hunter and Hunter (1984) reported training validities for a large number of jobs grouped by job complexity (the cognitive demands of the jobs). These validities varied from .50 to .65.

The second type of valuable studies are primary validity studies that use military data. Such studies are of particular value because they use well-developed tests of general cognitive ability, everyone who enters the military receives some job training, and the sample sizes are huge. Olea and Ree (1994) reported validities for general cognitive ability tests and pilot and navigator training in the U.S. Air Force. General cognitive ability predicted training performance (validity = .31) for the pilots and .46 for the navigators. Earles and Ree (1992) examined the validity of general cognitive ability in 150 military training programs using data from 88,724 U.S. Air Force recruits. The general cognitive ability test showed impressive validities across all 150 training programs.

Prediction of Job Performance

Schmidt and Hunter (1998), in their review of eighty-five years of employment testing research, offered .51 as the validity of general cognitive ability and job performance. This value corresponds to the validity of general cognitive ability for medium complexity jobs as reported by Hunter and Hunter (1984), who documented that the validity of cognitive ability tests increases as the complexity (cognitive demands) of the jobs increases. The validity for the most complex jobs is .56, and for the least complex jobs the validity is .23. Ree, Earles, and Teachout (1994) documented the validity of general cognitive ability for seven diverse U.S. Air Force jobs, reporting an average validity across jobs of .42. Many additional studies evaluate the validity of general cognitive ability for the prediction of job performance (see McDaniel, 2007). Without any doubt, general cognitive ability is a large-magnitude, robust predictor of job performance.

Prediction Linearity

A common misperception is that beyond a certain level, general mental ability has no practical importance in the prediction of training and job performance. This is simply untrue. The relationship between general cognitive ability and both training and job performance is linear (Coward & Sackett, 1990). This means that on average, higher-scoring applicants will have better job performance than lower-scoring applicants. Thus, to maximize the productivity of those hired, applicants can be rank-ordered from high to low on test scores and hired in that order.

General Versus Specific Cognitive Abilities

Although this chapter concerns general cognitive ability measures, it is useful to understand the relations between general cognitive ability and specific cognitive abilities in the prediction of training performance. Examples of specific cognitive ability tests are arithmetic reasoning, reading comprehension, and word knowledge. Two lines of evidence are useful in examining the contribution of specific abilities relative to general cognitive ability in the prediction of training and job performance. One line of evidence concerns the relationship between the validity of a specific cognitive ability test and its relationship with general cognitive ability (the loading of the specific cognitive ability test on the general cognitive ability factor). Two large U.S. military studies have examined this with respect to training performance validity (Ree & Earles, 1992, 1994). These studies clearly showed that the validity of a specific cognitive ability test increases to the extent that the test has a large loading on the general cognitive ability factor. That is, the larger the general cognitive ability loading of the specific cognitive ability measures, the larger the validity of the specific cognitive ability. A second line of evidence is the extent to which specific cognitive abilities predict training and job performance over and above general cognitive ability. Ree and Earles (1994) and Ree et al. (1994) showed that specific cognitive abilities do little in the prediction of training and job performance over and above general cognitive ability. In summary, with respect to validity in the prediction of training and job performance, prediction is a function of general cognitive ability and specific abilities have little to no additional value.

Differences on Cognitive Ability Among Ethnic/Race Demographic Groups

There are large differences (about one standard deviation difference) between mean levels of general cognitive ability for whites and blacks in the U.S. population (Jensen, 1998). Although smaller than the black-white differences in mean levels of cognitive ability, the mean differences between Hispanics and whites are also large. Asian-white mean differences in cognitive ability are usually small and often favor Asians. Unfortunately, the mean race differences between blacks and whites have remained fairly constant for at least ninety years (Jensen, 1998). Although some researchers argue that the black-white mean gap is narrowing, others argue that such claims are incorrect. Regardless of whether the gap is constant or somewhat narrowing, the black-white and Hispanic-white mean differences are currently large enough to result in disparate hiring rates (for example, hiring a larger proportion of the white applicants than the black or Hispanic applicants).

For at least two reasons, the differences between whites and blacks in job-applicant settings are smaller than the one standard deviation difference in the population. One reason is that those at the lowest levels of general cognitive ability are not job applicants. Second, jobs often have educational or experience requirements. Job applicants who meet the educational and experience requirements will be more equal in general cognitive ability than a random sample of the population. Thus, one would expect large mean ethnic differences for jobs with low educational and experience requirements and smaller mean ethnic differences for jobs with extensive educational and experience requirements. Thus, for example, mean ethnic differences should be smaller for those whose highest educational credential was a four-year college degree than for those who did not graduate from high school. Roth, BeVier, Bobko, Switzer, and Tyler (2001) provided the best estimates of mean ethnic differences in general mental ability among applicant groups. The mean difference is expressed as standardized mean differences (d) in a standard deviation metric. Thus, if $d = 1$, the white mean on general cognitive ability is one standard deviation higher than the black mean. Based on 125,654 applicants, the mean d for low-complexity jobs was .86. For medium-complexity jobs (31,990 applicants), the mean d was .72. Based on 4,884 applicants, the mean d for high-complexity jobs was .63. This pattern of larger mean differences for lower-complexity jobs is consistent with the expected mean differences varying as a function of educational and experience requirements. At all complexity levels, these differences are large and will cause disparate hiring rates by race if hiring is solely based on scores on general cognitive ability tests in a race-blind manner. Adding other predictors to a cognitive ability test battery may reduce the disparate hiring rates.

Single-Group Validity, Differential Validity, and Differential Prediction

The large mean differences between whites and blacks in general cognitive ability raise the possibility that general cognitive ability tests are biased against blacks. The hypothesis of single-group validity holds that a general cognitive ability test has validity for one group (for example, whites) but zero validity for another group (for example, blacks). The hypothesis of differential validity holds that a test has validity for one group but a substantially different validity for another group. After substantial research examined this issue, the National Academy of

Sciences concluded that single group and differential validity is very uncommon (Wigdor & Garner, 1982).

Over time researchers realized that the critical issue was differential prediction because it is possible to have a test with equal validity for two groups, but the optimal regression line to predict job performance might not be the same. Differential prediction may occur in two ways: the regression slopes might be different, or the regression intercepts might be different. The conclusion from the literature is that different slopes by race do not occur (Bartlett, Bobko, Mosier, & Hannan, 1978).

The finding of different intercepts by race is more common. However, the error in prediction favors minority groups. That is, when a common regression line is used to predict job performance for all races, the job performance of Hispanics and blacks is overpredicted on average (Hartigan & Wigdor, 1989). Therefore, when differential prediction occurs in employment tests, it is to the advantage of black and Hispanic applicants and the disadvantage of white applicants. One could obtain accurate prediction for all groups by using different regression lines for each group, but that would be a violation of the 1991 Civil Rights Act for U.S. employers.

Altering Item Types to Reduce Mean Ethnic Differences

Some speculate that mean ethnic differences may be reduced in employment tests by altering the tests in some way. Outside of cognitive ability testing, one can reduce the mean ethnic differences by reducing the extent to which the test correlates with general cognitive ability. For example, Whetzel, McDaniel, and Nguyen (2008) showed that the magnitude of ethnic differences in situational judgment tests was largest for those tests most highly correlated with cognitive ability. Video is often used to reduce the cognitive loading of employment tests because it reduces the reading demands of the test.

For cognitive ability tests, the issue of test format and mean ethnic score differences is typically discussed as an issue of cultural loading. The idea is that test items may reflect the culture and experience of majority group applicants more so than those of minority groups, and the resulting score differences are functions of the cultural loading and not differences in general cognitive ability. Jensen (1990) reviewed efforts to build culture-reduced measures of general cognitive ability. One such effort was the Davis-Eells Games measure. The authors of the measure sought to remove verbal, abstract, and academic content from their test items. Their items consisted of one-frame cartoons that displayed pictures of people in familiar situations. The test examiner would ask a question about the cartoon, and the correct answer would be based on a reasonable inference about the situation displayed in the cartoon. Jensen noted that the test did not result in smaller mean ethnic differences. The same conclusion was drawn for all of the culturally reduced tests reviewed. Thus, there is no evidence that one can alter the magnitude of mean ethnic differences in general cognitive ability tests by changing item types.

Guiding Practice

In this section we address issues related to guiding practice. We focus on the diversity-validity dilemma, content validity considerations in selection measures, and validity generalization in the context of the *Uniform Guidelines, Principles,* and *Standards.*

The Diversity-Validity Dilemma

Most employers seek to simultaneously obtain a diverse workplace and hire the best available applicants (Pyburn, Ployhart, & Kravitz, 2008) because both goals can potentially improve organizational effectiveness. When attempting to address a diversity-validity dilemma, an organization must begin by evaluating underlying assumptions of effectiveness. Once it establishes a set of criteria, it can proceed to operationalize practices and procedures linked to effective hiring (Banks, 2008).

Merit selection is the hiring of the best available applicants. General cognitive ability is the best single predictor of training and effective job performance. It also has the largest white-black mean differences. This potentially causes racial diversity and merit selection to be competing goals. Pyburn et al. (2008) referred to this as the *diversity-validity dilemma.* Employers respond to this dilemma in various ways. Some use predictors with lower validity and lower adverse impact than general cognitive ability tests to reduce ethnic mean differences in hiring rates. Although this promotes diversity, it can make the organization less effective because the lower validity tests are not as efficient in identifying the best employees. Other employers use general cognitive ability tests and accept the social and legal consequences of hiring fewer minorities. Pyburn et al. (2008) reviewed the legal issues facing employers due to the diversity-validity dilemma.

Ployhart and Holtz (2008) reviewed sixteen approaches for reducing demographic subgroup differences. The two most relevant to cognitive ability are using a predictor other than cognitive ability and manipulating the scoring of tests. Both approaches involve reducing the influence of general cognitive ability in the selection process, and most conclude that validity will or may suffer when compared to that of general cognitive ability. Concerning the first approach, one can use something other than general cognitive ability (say, a personality test); however, such predictors typically have lower validity, and often much lower validity.

An example of the second approach is to add other predictors to a selection system already containing general cognitive ability. Ployhart and Holtz (2008) noted that this strategy may reduce mean race differences and yield validity higher than general cognitive ability alone. For example, McDaniel, Hartman, Whetzel, and Grubb (2007) showed that adding a situational judgment test or a Big Five personality assessment to a measure of general cognitive ability could yield a larger validity than general cognitive ability alone. Another example of the second approach concerns banding where tests are grouped into categories (for example, well qualified, qualified, not qualified) and it is asserted, incorrectly, that all applicants in the same category are equally qualified. We note that any banding should serve to reduce the validity of the general cognitive ability test on average, because it obscures real score differences among applicants. Ployhart and Holtz noted that banding does little to reduce subgroup differences unless preferences are given to the subgroup (for example, the hiring manager is forced or influenced to hire the minority in the band before hiring any of the majority group members in the band). A final example of the second approach concerns manipulating the weighting of predictors to minimize subgroup differences. For example, in a selection battery to screen police officers, the reading examination was scored pass-fail, and the passing score was set at the score corresponding to the bottom 1 percent of the incumbent officers. This effectively stripped all cognitive ability variance from the test battery (Gottfredson, 1996).

In summary, the diversity-validity dilemma is a serious one with no ready solution. A general cognitive ability test is typically the best predictor of job performance. Typically it is also the predictor with the largest mean ethnic group differences. In general, strategies that serve to reduce the magnitude of the mean group differences in general cognitive ability reduce the validity of the test battery. One exception to this observation is the supplementing of a general cognitive ability test with a measure with lower mean subgroup differences, such as a measure of personality or of situational judgment. When the general cognitive ability measures and these other measures are optimally weighted in a selection composite, the validity will likely exceed that of the general cognitive ability measure alone, and the mean subgroup difference may be somewhat smaller. However, Potosky, Bobko, and Roth (2005) noted that the reductions in mean ethnic differences are often minimal.

Because there appears to be no magic bullet to reduce mean race differences in tests of general cognitive ability, employers who use these tests may wish to consider some forms of affirmative action to promote diversity without sacrificing the integrity of their selection system. Kravitz (2008) reviewed a variety of affirmative action efforts to increase diversity and recommended efforts that do not entail preferences for minorities in hiring.

Content-Validity Considerations in the Selection of Measures

Content validity concerns the extent to which the content of the test represents the content of the job. General cognitive ability can be measured with a variety of tests. From the perspective of applicant acceptance, it may be useful to identify cognitive ability tests that reflect job content. For example, logic-based measurement approaches for measuring verbal ability (Colberg, 1985) are offered as methods to measure cognitive ability in a manner to reflect job content. Such measures likely have a positive effect on an applicant's reactions to the test. Likewise, reading comprehension items can be based on material that is typically read on the job.

The key to building a general cognitive ability measure from a set of content-valid specific abilities is to use a diverse set of such tests so that they have sufficient breadth of coverage to yield a composite measuring general cognitive ability. If specific ability tests such as memory or spatial ability are given, it is preferable to combine several of them so that the resulting test battery will be a good assessment of general cognitive ability. The use of a single specific ability test is likely to yield lower validity because it does not fully assess general cognitive ability.

Validity Generalization and the *Uniform Guidelines, Principles,* and *Standards*

Substantial research has shown that cognitive ability tests predict job performance at some level for all jobs. This conclusion is primarily based on validity generalization studies. Landy (2003) and McDaniel (2007) reviewed the status of the validity generalization with respect to the *Uniform Guidelines on Employee Selection Procedures* (Equal Employment Opportunity Commission, Civil Service Commission, Department of Labor, & Department of Justice, 1978). One notable issue is that validity generalization is not addressed in the *Uniform Guidelines.* In part, this oversight is due to the bulk of the validity generalization research being published after the propagation of the *Uniform Guidelines.* However, with a careful reading of the *Uniform Guidelines,* one might have hope that this oversight would be resolved because the *Uniform Guidelines* state:

> The provisions of these guidelines relating to validation of selection procedures are intended to be consistent with generally accepted professional standards for evaluating standardized tests and other selection procedures, such as those described in the Standards for Educational and Psychological Tests prepared by a joint committee of the American Psychological Association, the American Educational

Research Association, and the National Council on Measurement in Education. . . . and standard textbooks and journals in the field of personnel selection [section 5C].

As McDaniel (2007) noted, the Society of Industrial and Organization Psychology (SIOP) contacted the agencies that authored the *Uniform Guidelines* shortly after their release to detail the ways in which the guidelines were inconsistent with professional practice and guidance. Unfortunately, the letter did not result in a revision of the *Uniform Guidelines*. Thus, although the *Uniform Guidelines* state that they are intended to be consistent with professional standards, the federal agencies that are responsible for them have not called for their revision during the past thirty years.

Professional organizations with relevance to employment testing have acknowledged the significant scientific status of validity generalization analyses (McDaniel, 2007). One set of testing guidelines, the *Standards for Educational and Psychological Testing* is published jointly by three professional organizations (American Educational Research Association, the American Psychological Association, & the National Council on Measurement in Education, 1999). The other major set of testing guidelines, the *Principles for the Validation and Use of Personnel Selection Procedures*, is published by SIOP (2003). Both sets of guidelines comment favorably on the use of validity generalization as a means for establishing the validity of an employment test. The *Principles* state that validity generalization findings for cognitive ability tests are "particularly well established" (p. 28). Thus, although the *Uniform Guidelines* are mute with respect to validity generalization, the professional guidelines support the value of validity generalization in documenting the validity of general cognitive ability tests and other personnel selection tests.

Copus (2006) provided a critique of employment discrimination enforcement efforts of the U.S. Office of Federal Contract Compliance Programs (OFCCP) that rely on the *Uniform Guidelines* and provided compelling arguments for greater acceptance of validity generalization results in the enforcement field. Copus argued that OFCCP's perspective on test validation is inconsistent with professional standards in two key ways. First, Copus criticized the OFCCP for requiring that an employer conduct a validation study when the use of the test results in a disparate hiring rate for women or minorities. Second, Copus asserted that OFCCP inappropriately requires fairness studies to determine if tests have the same degree of job relatedness for majority and minority applicants. Copus noted that the validity generalization evidence for the validity of cognitive ability tests is so overwhelming that local validation studies, even in the presence of disparate impact, are unneeded. He wrote that "validity generalization research in lieu of local studies fully satisfies the professional standards set forth in both the APA *Standards* and SIOP *Principles*" (p. 6). Copus then reviewed the research literature on validity generalization and discredits OFCCP's requirement for fairness studies by reviewing the literature on differential validity and prediction.

McDaniel (2007) speculated on why the *Uniform Guidelines* have not been revised to reflect current scientific knowledge as expressed in professional documents such as the *Principles* and *Standards*:

> A primary use of the *Uniform Guidelines* is to pressure employers into using suboptimal selection methods in order to hire minorities and Whites at approximately the same rates. If employers do not hire minorities at about the same rates as Whites, the *Uniform Guidelines* are invoked by enforcement agencies and plaintiffs to require the employer to prepare substantial validity documentation. . . . In other areas of federal regulations and guidelines, such regulations and guidelines are often updated to reflect scientific knowledge and professional practice. It is well past the time for the *Uniform Guidelines* to be revised [pp. 168–169].

Conclusion

This chapter has reviewed research and practice in the use of general cognitive ability tests in workplace assessment. We examined models of general cognitive ability and detailed research and applied issues in the use of general cognitive ability tests in workplace assessment. Cognitive ability tests show substantial validity for all jobs and exceed the validity of other tests. These tests are not biased against minorities in the prediction of job performance, although one can expect blacks and Hispanics on average to score lower than whites and Asians. The mean differences occur because the tests accurately measure the mean differences in cognitive ability in the population. There are many inexpensive, commercially available cognitive ability tests. Any merit-based selection system should include such tests.

References

American Educational Research Association, American Psychological Association, & National Council on Measurement in Education. (1999). *Standards for educational and psychological testing*. Washington, DC: American Educational Research Association.

Banks, G. P. (2008). *The issue of race: A resolution for the 21st century*. New York: Seabury Press.

Barrett, G. V., Polomsky, M. D., & McDaniel, M. A. (1999). Selection tests for firefighters: A comprehensive review and meta-analysis. *Journal of Business and Psychology, 13*, 507–514.

Bartlett, C. J., Bobko, P., Mosier, S. B., & Hannan, R. (1978). Testing for fairness with a moderated multiple regression strategy: An alternative to differential analysis. *Personnel Psychology, 31*, 233–241.

Carroll, J. B. (1993). *Human cognitive abilities: A survey of factor-analytic studies*. Cambridge: Cambridge University Press.

Cattell, R. (1943). The measurement of adult intelligence: Present practice in adult intelligence testing. *Psychological Bulletin, 40*, 153–193.

Colberg, M. (1985). Logic-based measurement of verbal reasoning: A key to increased validity and economy. *Personnel Psychology, 38*, 347–359.

Copus, D. (2006, March 27). *Validation of cognitive ability tests*. Letter to Charles James, Office of Federal Contract Compliance Programs. Morristown, NJ: Ogletree Deakins.

Coward, W. M., & Sackett, P. R. (1990). Linearity of ability-performance relationships: A reconfirmation. *Journal of Applied Psychology, 75*, 297–300.

Earles, J. A., & Ree, M. J. (1992). The predictive validity of the ASVAB for training grades. *Educational and Psychological Measurement, 52*, 721–725.

Equal Employment Opportunity Commission, Civil Service Commission, Department of Labor, & Department of Justice. (1978). *Uniform guidelines on employee selection procedures. Federal Register, 43*(166), 38290–39315.

Gottfredson, L. S. (1996). Racially gerrymandering the content of police tests to satisfy the U.S. Justice Department: A case study. *Psychology, Public Policy, and Law, 2*, 418–446.

Hartigan, J. A., & Wigdor, A. K. (Eds.). (1989). *Fairness in employment testing: Validity generalization, minority issues, and the General Aptitude Test Battery.* Washington, DC: National Academy Press.

Hirsh, H. R., Northrop, L. C., & Schmidt, F. L. (1986). Validity generalization results for law enforcement occupations. *Personnel Psychology, 39,* 399–420.

Hunter, J. E., & Hunter, R. F. (1984). Validity and utility of alternative predictors of job performance. *Psychological Bulletin, 96,* 72–98.

Jensen, A. R. (1990). *Bias in mental testing.* New York: Free Press.

Jensen, A. R. (1998). *The g factor: The science of mental ability.* Westport, CT: Praeger.

Kravitz, D. A. (2008). The diversity-validity dilemma: Beyond selection: The role of affirmative action. *Personnel Psychology, 61,* 173–193.

Landy, F. J. (2003). Validity generalization: Then and now. In K. R. Murphy (Ed.), *Validity generalization: A critical review* (pp. 155–195). Mahwah, NJ: Erlbaum.

Lilienthal, R. A., & Pearlman, K. (1983). *Validity of federal selection tests for aide/technicians in the health, science, and engineering fields.* Washington, DC: National Technical Information Service. (NTIS no. PB83202051).

McDaniel, M. A. (2007). Validity generalization as a test validation approach. In S. M. McPhail (Ed.), *Alternative validation strategies* (pp. 159–180). San Francisco: Jossey Bass.

McDaniel, M. A., Hartman, N. S., Whetzel, D. L., & Grubb. W. L. III. (2007). Situational judgment tests, response instructions and validity: A meta-analysis. *Personnel Psychology, 60,* 63–91.

Northrop, L. C. (1988). *Situational specificity and validity generalization results for apprentice occupations.* Washington, DC: U.S. Office of Personnel Management.(NTIS no. PB88213608).

Olea, M. M., & Ree, M. J. (1994). Predicting pilot and navigator criteria: Not much more than g. *Journal of Applied Psychology, 79,* 845–851.

Pearlman, K., Schmidt, F. L., & Hunter, J. E. (1980). Validity generalization results for tests used to predict job proficiency and training criteria in clerical occupations. *Journal of Applied Psychology, 65,* 373–406.

Ployhart, R. E., & Holtz, B. C. (2008). The diversity-validity dilemma: Strategies for reducing racioethnic and sex subgroup differences and adverse impact in selection. *Personnel Psychology, 61,* 153–172.

Potosky, D., Bobko, P., & Roth, P. L. (2005). Forming composites of cognitive ability and alternative measures to predict job performance and reduce adverse impact: Corrected estimates and realistic expectations. *International Journal of Selection and Assessment, 13,* 304–315.

Pyburn, K. M. Jr., Ployhart, R. E., & Kravitz, D. A. (2008). The diversity-validity dilemma: Overview and legal context. *Personnel Psychology, 61*, 143–151.

Ree, M. J., & Earles, J. A. (1992). Intelligence is the best predictor of job performance. *Current Directions in Psychological Science, 1*, 86–89.

Ree, M. J., & Earles, J. A. (1994). The ubiquitous predictiveness of *g*. In M. G. Rumsey, C. B. Walker, & J. H. Harris (Eds.), *Personnel selection and classification* (pp. 127–135). Mahwah, NJ: Erlbaum.

Ree, M. J., Earles, J. A., & Teachout, M. S. (1994). Predicting job performance: Not much more than *g*. *Journal of Applied Psychology, 79*, 518–524.

Roth, P. L., BeVier, C. A., Bobko, P., Switzer, F. S. III, & Tyler, P. (2001). Ethnic group differences in cognitive ability in employment and educational settings: A meta-analysis. *Personnel Psychology, 54*, 297–330.

Schmidt, F. L., & Hunter, J. E. (1977). Development of a general solution to the problem of validity generalization. *Journal of Applied Psychology, 62*, 529–540.

Schmidt, F. L., & Hunter, J. E. (1998). The validity and utility of selection methods in personnel psychology: Practical and theoretical implications of 85 years of research findings. *Psychological Bulletin, 124*, 262–274.

Society for Industrial and Organizational Psychology. (2003). *Principles for the validation and use of personnel selection procedures* (4th ed.). Bowling Green, OH: Author.

Spearman, C. (1904). "General intelligence," objectively determined and measured. *American Journal of Psychology, 15*, 201–293.

Trattner, M. H. (1985). *Estimating the validity of aptitude and ability tests for semiprofessional occupations using the Schmidt-Hunter interactive validity generalization procedure*. Washington, DC: U.S. Office of Personnel Management. (NTIS no. PB86169463).

Whetzel, D. L., McDaniel, M. A., & Nguyen, N. T. (2008). Subgroup differences in situational judgment test performance: A meta-analysis. *Human Performance, 21*, 291–309.

Wigdor, A. K., & Garner, W. R. (Eds.). (1982). *Ability testing: Use, consequences, and controversies*. Washington, DC: National Academy Press.

CHAPTER 4

PERSONALITY

Robert Hogan, Robert B. Kaiser

This chapter provides an overview of personality psychology as it applies to business practices. It begins with the definition of *personality*, a topic that is often discussed but seldom defined; the lack of agreed-on definitions is responsible for considerable unnecessary confusion. It then examines the kinds of personality assessments available to be used by business, evaluates the pragmatics of personality assessment, reviews the inevitable criticisms of personality assessment, and speculates on future directions for personality assessment.

Defining Personality

Personality psychology consists of three related activities. The first involves efforts to conceptualize human nature—how people are alike. These discussions primarily concern motivation. A simple example would be the debate about Theory X (employees are lazy and need direction and discipline) versus Theory Y (employees are motivated by needs for self-fulfillment that are often frustrated by bad management). To the degree that management practices take motivation into account, these discussions are enormously important. Maslow's theory of self-actualization is the core of Theory Y and has been vastly popular over the years, despite lacking empirical support. Recent work in evolutionary psychology suggests that biologically grounded motives such as needs for social acceptance, status, and a sense of meaning and purpose are important in the workplace; these survival-relevant motives are easy to measure and are empirically linked to behavior.

The second major activity in personality psychology is identifying the most important ways in which people differ from one another and then developing measures of those differences. Scores on these measures can then be used to make decisions about, for example, employee selection and promotion. Thousands of published personality measures are available, each concerning dimensions that interest the test authors but may not be relevant to the world of work (an example is androgyny). This bewildering variety of personality measures also creates much of the confusion surrounding the use of personality to predict occupational performance.

The third major activity in personality psychology concerns determining how individual differences in personality develop. Results from this line of research have important implications for career coaching and guidance; they provide suggestions regarding how to assist and encourage others in ways that are informed by data as opposed to personal opinion.

As for the definition of the term *personality* itself, we prefer to draw on MacKinnon's important (1944) observation that personality should be defined in two ways. On the one hand, personality refers to factors inside people that explain their behavior. Different writers prefer different internal factors—egos, temperaments, schemas, and so on—and we call this *personality from the perspective of the actor.* Personality also refers to the distinctive impressions that people make on others, which are captured in trait words used to describe others (*friendly, energetic,* and so on)—and we call this *personality from the perspective of the observer.* We find it useful to summarize the first definition of personality in terms of identity (how people think about themselves) and the second definition in terms of reputation (how others think about them). Reputation tells us how people typically behave; identity tells us why they behave that way. Much confusion in the literature results from not keeping these two definitions distinct.

To the degree that success in business involves getting the people issues right, personality psychology is an indispensable tool.

The early giants of industrial-organizational (I-O) psychology— Mark May, Ross Stagner, and Edwin Ghiselli—made exactly this argument. Somewhere along the way, though, doubts arose.

Business Applications of Personality Assessment

This section concerns how personality measurement is used in business applications. It describes the kinds of measures that are available, the kinds of jobs for which they are best suited, how the measures are developed, and the purposes for which they are best suited.

What Kinds of Measures Are Available?

In business, personality is assessed in one of four standard ways. By far the most common and most problematic method of assessment is the interview. In the typical case, the interviewer asks the interviewee questions and then rates the answers using a private and intuitive coding method. From time to time, organizations try to standardize interviews by requiring interviewers to ask each interviewee the same questions and rate their responses in a standard manner. The problem is that interviewers quickly become bored with standardized lists of questions, and what happens next is called "interview creep"—the standardization steadily melts away. Despite the subjective and unsystematic nature of interviews, it is a fact of nature that organizations refuse to give them up; virtually every hiring process will include some sort of interview, and the interview results often override the results of more standardized assessment processes.

A second and less frequently used assessment method involves questionnaires containing statements to which people respond; the responses to the statements are aggregated and used to form scores on the dimensions covered by the questionnaire such as extraversion. Some of these questionnaires, such as the well-known California Psychological Inventory and the Myers-Briggs Type Indicator, are commercially published, professionally reviewed, Internet enabled, and available in multiple languages. Other personality measures are home grown. There are thousands of ad hoc personality questionnaires available; each is scored in terms of idiosyncratic dimensions, most are of questionable quality, and it is impossible to review them here. Potential users of any personality measure should demand to see the technical manual supporting the use of the test. Tests should be compared and evaluated in terms of the validity data contained in the technical manuals.

Beginning in the early 1990s, substantial consensus emerged among researchers regarding the appropriate structure (dimensionality) for personality questionnaires. This agreed-on structure is called the Five Factor Model (FFM: Wiggins, 1996); it suggests that all existing inventories of normal personality measure the same five broad dimensions with more or less efficiency. Table 4.1 presents the Five Factor Model.

The third way in which business organizations measure personality is with observer rating forms: observers are asked to rate or describe target persons using a defined set of performance dimensions. The best known of these procedures is the 360-degree evaluation, where target persons are rated by superiors, peers, and subordinates using a standardized rating form. Virtually every consulting firm in the developed world has a proprietary 360 rating scheme. Despite their popularity, these instruments generally have very poor measurement properties. The dimensions are often so highly intercorrelated that the ratings do not distinguish distinct aspects of performance, and ratings are typically averaged across dimensions to create an overall score. These overall scores are primarily a function of how well the raters like the person being rated. Furthermore, there is no agreed-on structure or content to 360-degree rating forms (however, see Bartram, 2005, for suggestions about how to standardize them).

The fourth common way in which personality is measured is by means of performance on unstructured tasks. The key assumption for this kind of assessment is that because the tasks are unstructured, the manner in which people respond to them will indicate how they typically respond in ambiguous situations, and in this way, they will reveal their "personalities" and performance capabilities. Projective tests such as the Rorschach ink blots and the Thematic Apperception Test are two well-known and widely used measures of this type, of which there are many and most of which lack adequate reliability and validity.

Table 4.1. The Five Factor Model of Personality

Factor	Definition	Low Standing	High Standing
Extraversion	Combines ambition, which concerns taking initiative, being competitive, and seeking leadership roles, and sociability, which concerns seeming outgoing, energetic, and entertaining	Complacent and unassertive; withdrawn, reserved, and quiet	Proactive and assertive; talkative and socially engaged
Agreeableness	Concerns being sensitive, considerate, and skilled at maintaining relationships	Tough-minded, frank, and direct	Friendly, warm, and pleasant
Conscientiousness	Concerns being reliable, dependable, and rule abiding	Nonconforming, impulsive, and flexible	Organized, dependable, and hard working
Emotional Stability	Concerns self-confidence, composure, optimism, and stable moods	Tense, irritable, and negative	Confident, resilient, and optimistic
Openness	Concerns being curious, imaginative, visionary, and intellectually engaged	Focused and pragmatic	Creative and curious

Note: *Emotional Stability* is sometimes referred to as *Neuroticism* and *Openness* is sometimes referred to as *Openness to Experience* by other writers.

For What Jobs Is Personality Assessment Most Valuable?

Every job in every organization has a distinctive set of psychological demands. For example, long-distance truck drivers need to work alone, remain vigilant over long periods of time, follow rules closely, and be impervious to boredom; in contrast, bomb disposal technicians must enjoy taking risks but be willing to follow standardized procedures exactly. In principle, personality assessment is valuable for selecting people into every job in every organization (J. Hogan & Holland, 2003).

In reality, it is not technically feasible to use personality to select people into every job in every organization. This is because every organization considers itself to be unique, and every organization has many specialized jobs with unique titles. To develop personality-based selection procedures for all these jobs, and to do so correctly, would require more time and money than most organizations are willing to expend. It is therefore necessary to simplify the problem.

Our approach to simplifying this problem begins with the perceptive and heuristic Holland model (Holland, 1973). Holland proposes that all occupations can be sorted into one of six ideal types (Realistic, Investigative, Artistic, Social, Enterprising, and Conventional) and that each occupational type is also a distinctive personality type; there is a characteristic personality "profile" associated with each type. Gottfredson and Holland (1996) showed that the Holland model can classify every job in the *Dictionary of Occupational Titles*. This then provides links between personality and most major jobs in the real world.

Hogan and Hogan (2007) build on this important finding. Their test, the Hogan Personality Inventory (HPI), is a measure of normal personality based on the FFM and designed to predict occupational performance. They have data comparing scores on the HPI with performance for every major job category in the U.S. economy. Using the principles of validity generalization (meta-analysis, synthetic validity, and job component validity) and the Department of Labor Standard Occupational Classification System, they provide estimates for the validity of the FFM dimensions of personality for predicting performance across all major job categories.

In principle, then, personality measures can be used to forecast performance in all jobs in every organization. In practice, however, entry-level employees are typically screened using short and inexpensive measures of integrity/reliability, resilience/stress tolerance, and service orientation. Applicants for more senior positions in sales and management are more often screened with more extensive batteries.

How Are These Measures Developed?

The best-known personality inventories (CPI, 16PF, HPI) were developed following accepted professional standards and guidelines. But the scoring systems for interview questions, observer rating forms (including 360-degree appraisals), and the various projective tests are typically ad hoc, and the measures are often used with little concern for reliability and validity.

For What Purposes Are These Measures Used?

In the workplace, personality assessment is used for three purposes. First, assessment is frequently used to provide individuals with feedback that is intended to increase their self-awareness and improve their ability to work as part of a team. The Myers-Briggs Type Indicator in particular is widely used for these purposes; it tells people how they tend to perceive the world, as compared with how others see the world, and how these perceptual differences can lead to unintended misunderstandings and conflict. The so-called 360-feedback process is also used to enhance self-awareness. A target person is described by subordinates, peers, and superiors using a standardized rating form. The results are summarized and reported back to the target person, a process that is as often disheartening as it is enlightening—because most people think more highly of themselves than others actually do.

Second, and related to the preceding point, assessment results are often used for career guidance. Suppose a person wants a career in the entertainment industry, perhaps as a script writer. Script writers need to be verbally fluent, hard working, persistent, imaginative, and able to meet deadlines. The person will be assessed for these characteristics, and his or her fit with the profile can be evaluated in terms of potential strengths and developmental needs. Management and leadership development programs rely heavily on assessment for career guidance. The relevant profile for effective performance in managerial or leadership roles is reasonably well understood; in addition, a vast armada of leadership assessment material is commercially available. Leadership development is a $50 billion a year industry in the United States alone, and it is increasing with worldwide demand.

Finally, personality assessment is used for personnel selection. As noted above, we can profile the psychological requirements of every job in the U.S. economy. We can then match the assessment profile of an applicant to the required profile of any job and determine the likelihood of the person succeeding in the job. Employment interviews are an informal way of doing personality-based personnel selection; assessment centers and standardized psychometric batteries are a more formal way of doing it.

How Well Does Personality Assessment Work?

The question of how well personality assessment works is, of course, the bottom-line issue for this chapter. A naive reader might think this is a straightforward empirical question, but in academic life, few important questions seem capable of being answered in a straightforward manner. Especially on this question, opinion is bitterly divided.

Framing the Question

Some writers (like the authors) are enthusiastic advocates of personality assessment. Others doubt that personality assessment works and vigorously criticize its use for selection purposes (Morgeson et al., 2007). As always, conceptual confusions cloud these discussions. Persons new to this field need three pieces of background information in order to understand the debate.

The Measurement Problem

First, the accepted method for determining the validity of psychometric tests is a statistical procedure called meta-analysis, and the preferred version of meta-analysis is validity generalization

(Hunter & Schmidt, 2004). The correlation between test scores and performance criteria in any single research study is regarded as one data point, and that data point is assumed to be contaminated by a variety of statistical artifacts. The process of meta-analysis collects as many studies as are available on the relationship between a type of test (or measurement dimension) and performance criteria. The results of all the studies are combined and then corrected for statistical artifacts, such as the degree of measurement error and range restriction in the test and in the outcome measure. These "corrected" results are assumed to provide the best possible estimate of the "true" relationship between a type of test (or measurement dimension) and a class of outcomes (or criteria). To summarize, meta-analysis is used to answer the question of how well a test works in predicting occupational performance.

Second, meta-analysis is well suited for estimating the validity of measures of cognitive ability, popularly known as intelligence quotient (IQ). The reason meta-analysis works well for measures of intelligence is that the various measures are all highly intercorrelated, which means that collectively, they represent the same large general factor. Because measures of intelligence are so statistically similar, one can compare the results from different studies with little regard for the particular measure that the researchers use.

In the case of personality, however, it is essentially impossible to combine measures across studies. The number of scales or dimensions on the best-known personality inventories varies widely, from three on the Eysenck Personality Inventory to twenty-one on the California Psychological Inventory. Furthermore, scales with the same names on different inventories (for example, Agreeableness) are not highly correlated—unlike the different measures of intelligence—and they predict different outcomes differently. This fact makes it virtually impossible to combine studies across different personality inventories; consequently, standard meta-analytic studies of the validity of personality for predicting occupational performance underestimate that validity (Barrick & Mount, 1991). A solution to this problem is to do the meta-analyses using one inventory at a time (J. Hogan & Holland, 2003).

The third problem concerns how to define job performance—more specifically, how to assign numbers to individual differences in performance—in a way that is comparable across organizations. Job performance is typically defined in one of three ways. In the first case, it is defined in terms of performance in training. When performance is defined this way, intelligence always outperforms personality in terms of validity because intelligence is the best single predictor of training performance. In the second case, performance is defined in terms of supervisors' ratings of overall job performance. In our view, this is problematic because overall ratings of performance tend to be political judgments; they reflect how much a supervisor likes an employee rather than how well he or she is performing. In the third and ideal case, performance is defined in terms of the relevant components of the job (for example, showing effort, maintaining personal discipline, facilitating team performance), which can be identified statistically (Campbell, McCloy, Oppler, & Sager, 1993). Once the relevant dimensions of performance have been defined and measured, the predictors should be aligned with these dimensions in ways that make conceptual sense. For example, one would not use a measure of intelligence to predict ethical behavior because many smart people have problems with integrity (financial managers, for example). However, a measure of Conscientiousness would be expected to predict ethical behavior because following rules is a key element of Conscientiousness.

The Comparative Validity of Personality

When the performance dimensions have been defined explicitly and the predictors have been aligned with the performance dimensions, it becomes possible to evaluate how well personality assessment works. As always, these judgments are relative. Consider Table 4.2, which presents meta-analytic estimates for the uncorrected validity coefficients for seven commonly used predictors of occupational performance. These validity coefficients vary between .11 and .28, and these values should be considered when evaluating the validity of personality measures.

Consider next the finding by Judge, Colbert, and Ilies (2004) that the fully corrected, meta-analytically derived validity for predicting leadership with measures of intelligence is .27. These data

Table 4.2. Validity of Assessments for Predicting Job Performance

Predictor	r_{obs}	Study
Conscientiousness tests	.18	Barrick & Mount (1991)
Integrity tests	.21	Ones, Viswesveran, & Schmidt (1993)
Structured interviews	.18	McDaniel, Whetzel, Schmidt, & Maurer (1994)
Unstructured interviews	.11	McDaniel, Whetzel, Schmidt, & Maurer (1994)
Situational judgment tests	.20	McDaniel, Hartman, Whetzel, & Grubb (2007)
Biodata	.22	Bliesener (1996)
Intelligence	.21	Pearlman, Schmidt, & Hunter (1980)
Assessment centers	.28	Arthur, Day, McNelly, & Edens (2003)

Note: r_{obs} = mean observed validity.

suggest that validity coefficients above .30 are unusual for any single predictor of job performance, leadership, or other occupational criteria. Our point is that when evaluating the validity of personality measures for predicting occupational performance, one should bear in mind the size of the validity coefficients that can normally be expected for any class of measurement variables, and that number is somewhere between .11 and .30.

As a second example of how well personality measures work, consider Table 4.3, which presents the results of a careful meta-analytic study of the links between personality (defined in terms of the FFM) and leadership (Judge, Bono, Ilies, & Gerhardt, 2002). The correlations are consistent with the best results in Table 4.2; they show that good leaders seem self-confident (Emotional Stability), socially poised (Extraversion), visionary (Openness), trustworthy (Conscientiousness), and not necessarily nice (Agreeableness). The fully corrected multiple correlation, using all five dimensions in Table 4.3, is .48.

**Table 4.3. Relation Between Five Factor Model of
Personality and Leadership**

Dimension	k	N	r_{obs}	ρ
Extraversion	60	11,705	.22	.31
Agreeableness	42	9,801	.06	.08
Conscientiousness	35	7,510	.20	.28
Emotional Stability	48	8,025	.17	.24
Openness	37	7,221	.16	.24

Note: k = number of correlations; r_{obs} = mean observed validity; ρ = corrected
correlation.
Source: Judge, Bono, Ilies, & Gerhardt (2002).

In the best meta-analytic study of personality and job performance in the published literature, J. Hogan and Holland
(2003) focused on one inventory, and aligned the personality
dimensions with the relevant criteria—they did not try to predict training with Adjustment (a measure of FFM Emotional
Stability) or sales performance with Prudence (a measure of FFM
Conscientiousness). As shown in Table 4.4, the observed validity
coefficients (*r*) for personality compare favorably with those in
Table 4.2 for other predictors of job performance.

Predicting Job Performance and More

These tables show that personality reliably predicts job performance. For those who care about social justice, it is also
important to note that unlike intelligence measures, personality measures are race and gender neutral so that, on average, minorities and women get the same scores as white males.
Furthermore, personality predicts a wide range of important
workplace outcomes in addition to job performance. Table 4.5
provides a summary of these personality-related outcomes,
which range from job performance, leadership, and teamwork
to counterproductive job behavior and absenteeism, as well as
job and career satisfaction, health behavior, and even life expectancy. (For an extended discussion of the validity issue, see
Hogan, 2005.)

Table 4.4. Summary of J. Hogan and Holland (2003) Results

HPI Scale	k	N	r_{obs}	ρ
Adjustment	24	2,573	.25	.43
Ambition	28	3,698	.20	.34
Sociability	NA	NA	NA	NA
Likeability	17	2,500	.18	.36
Prudence	26	3,379	.22	.36
Inquisitive	7	1,190	.20	.34
Learning Approach	9	1,366	.15	NA

Note: HPI = Hogan Personality Inventory; k = number of correlations; r_{obs} = mean observed validity; ρ = corrected correlation. HPI Adjustment corresponds to FFM Emotional Stability; HPI Ambition and Sociability represent the two major components of FFM Extraversion; HPI Likeability corresponds to FFM Agreeableness; HPI Prudence corresponds to FFM Conscientiousness; and HPI Inquisitive and Learning Approach correspond to two components of FFM Openness.

Table 4.5. Organizationally Significant Outcomes Predicted by Personality Assessment

Outcome	Research Support
Job performance	Barrick & Mount (1991); Hogan & Holland (2003)
Leadership	Judge, Bono, Illies, & Gerhardt (2002)
Teamwork and team performance	J. Hogan & Holland (2003); Peeters, Van Tuijl, Rutte, & Raymen (2006)
Absenteeism	Ones, Viswesvaran, & Schmidt (2003)
Counterproductive work behavior	Berry, Ones, & Sackett (2007)
Job and career satisfaction	Judge, Heller, & Mount (2002)
Health behaviors and life expectancy	Roberts, Kuncel, Shiner, Caspi, & Goldberg (2007)

Standard Criticisms of Personality Assessment

The standard criticisms of personality assessment can be reduced to three fundamental claims: (1) the tests have minimal or trivial validity for predicting real-world outcomes, (2) scores on the tests are contaminated by social desirability response bias, and (3) scores on the tests can be altered by deliberate faking (for an energetic presentation of these criticisms, see Morgeson et al. 2007).

Validity

Concerning the claim that personality measures lack validity for predicting occupational performance, readers should consult the prior section on validity and form their own opinions. The real-world significance of validity coefficients is not obvious. However, consider the fact that top performers in every job are more productive than bottom performers; these differences range from 38 percent in unskilled positions to 98 percent for managerial and professional positions (Hunter, Schmidt, & Judiesch, 1990). Next, consider that hiring employees using a test with a validity of .20 improves the odds of hiring a good performer to 60 percent and reduces the odds of hiring a bad performer to 40 percent, which means you are 50 percent more likely to make a good hiring decision (Rosenthal & Rubin, 1982). With a validity of .30, the odds are 65 percent to 35 percent, which is 86 percent more likely to lead to a good decision. Organizations can significantly improve the productivity of their employees by using selection procedures with validities in the .20 to .30 range.

Social Desirability

The second criticism of personality assessment—that scores are contaminated by social desirability response bias—has been around for over fifty years; it has been extensively studied and consistently rejected. The criticism is based on the assumption that when people read items on a personality inventory, they are primarily motivated to respond in a way that presents themselves in the best possible light—that is, respond to the items in ways that are socially desirable rather than in ways that reflect their true selves. The claim is that people's natural bias toward socially desirable responding invalidates personality measures.

A fundamental insight of personality psychology is that individual differences are associated with every generalization we make about people. This is true for the statement that people are motivated to make good impressions on others. Some people are and some are not, and these differences can be assessed using measures of social desirability, of which many are available. It then becomes a straightforward task to determine the degree to which socially desirable responding affects the validity of personality assessment. There is a substantial and convergent literature on this point; a paper by Ones, Viswesvaran, and Reiss (1996) is among the best. These papers show that socially desirable responding is a reliable dimension of personality related to the FFM dimensions of Emotional Stability and Conscientiousness and correcting personality test scores for socially desirable responding does not improve validity.

Faking

The third claim, that faking invalidates the use of personality measures for employee selection, is a more general statement of the second claim. In a nutshell, the argument is that when employees complete a personality measure as part of the preemployment screening process, they "fake"—distort their scores so as to improve their chances of being hired—and this tendency invalidates the use of personality measures for hiring purposes. The empirical literature on the faking issue is enormous, complex, tedious, and largely beside the point. The research shows that after completing a personality measure, people can alter their scores on the second trial. The research also shows that on average, job applicants tend to get "better" scores than job incumbents (Ellingson, Sackett, & Connelly, 2007). However, only one study in this literature uses actual job applicants in an effort to determine the degree to which faking occurs in the selection process.

Hogan, Barrett, and Hogan (2007) tested a large group of applicants for a government job with the HPI. Over five thousand of these people were denied employment; six months later, they reapplied for the same job and completed the HPI a second time. It is reasonable to assume that these people were motivated to improve their scores on the second occasion. The data indicated that 95 percent of the scores across more than five thousand people and seven scales remained the same. Of the 5 percent of scores that changed, 2.5 percent became worse, and 2.5 percent became better. The authors conclude that in real employment settings, faking is not a problem.

In a concurrent validity study, assessment data and criterion or performance data are gathered at roughly the same time. In a predictive validity study, assessment data are gathered but not used for selection; then at some later time, criterion data are recorded. A common finding is that validity coefficients in concurrent validity studies tend to be higher than validity coefficients in predictive studies, and some people see this as problematic. We disagree. We believe that these differences are the result of measurement error. In a concurrent study, the supervisors know all the incumbents whom they are evaluating. In a predictive study, by the time the criterion data are gathered, some of the incumbents and supervisors will have left, the job performance of the newly hired incumbents will not have stabilized, and as a result, the validity coefficients will be attenuated.

Future Directions

The development of the Five Factor Model (FFM) in the 1980s triggered a wave of meta-analytic studies of the links between personality and job performance. These efforts rejuvenated personality research in applied psychology. However, future development requires moving beyond the FFM, exploring alternative measurement methods, becoming clearer about the agenda for personality measurement, and developing better theory to guide empirical research.

Beyond the FFM

The evidence is clear that personality, framed in terms of the FFM, predicts performance in virtually every job from entry level to leadership positions, as well as job satisfaction and career success. But most people understand that there is more to personality than the FFM. Two recent developments suggest ways to expand the personality domain.

Judge and colleagues propose a higher-order personality dimension of core self-evaluations (Judge, Locke, & Durham, 1997), defined as a broad judgment that people make about their basic worth and ability to influence events. Judge argues that this higher-order dimension is composed of four narrower themes: self-esteem, generalized self-efficacy, locus of control, and emotional stability. Research shows that these four themes do indeed form a single higher-order factor. Moreover, this higher-order factor, core self-evaluations, is a better predictor of job performance and job satisfaction than any of the four component variables. Most important, core self-evaluations add incremental validity over the FFM, indicating that they reflect unique work-related variance (Judge, Erez, Bono, & Thoresen, 2003). This research is important because it demonstrates that by thinking big, we can identify broad, integrative dispositions that enhance our ability to predict important outcomes at work.

Recent research has focused on understanding ineffectiveness, counterproductivity (Berry et al., 2007), and managerial incompetence (Hogan, Hogan, & Kaiser, 2010). This has led to an interest in dysfunctional aspects of personality, based on the notion that undesirable tendencies such as arrogance, passive-aggression, eccentricity, paranoia, and perfectionism are functionally distinct from the FFM. There are three published inventories of dysfunctional personality designed to assess extreme variations in normal personality that are appropriate for use in the workplace (Hogan & Hogan, 2008; Moscosco & Salgado, 2004; Schmit, Kilm, & Robie, 2000). This is in contrast with measures of psychopathology such as the Minnesota Multiphasic Personality Inventory, which are inappropriate for selection purposes.

This new research on dysfunctional dispositions is promising for two reasons. First, it provides insight into such phenomena as employee deviance, career failure, and bad leadership. Second, although the dimensions of dysfunctional personality are related to the FFM, they predict different outcomes and add incremental validity over the FFM in predicting workplace criteria (Hogan & Hogan,

2008; Schmit et al., 2000). Thus, the links between dysfunctional personality tendencies and occupational performance are a promising topic for future research.

Alternative Measurement Methods

The questionnaire method of assessing personality is well accepted in organizational research. However, certain trends suggest it is time to consider alternatives. On the one hand, persistent concerns about faking have led to a search for alternatives to standard personality questionnaires. On the other hand, advances in understanding the cognitive processes underlying personality make alternative assessment strategies more feasible. Thus, we believe future methods of personality assessment may be influenced by advanced projective techniques and theory-driven interview techniques.

Projective Techniques

Projective tests are designed to assess covert belief systems by presenting test takers with ambiguous stimuli into which they project their assumptions and expectations. These methods, such as the Rorschach and the Thematic Apperception Test, are characterized by subjective scoring systems with notoriously low reliabilities. However, two recent methods combine the goal of assessing covert motives and beliefs with the standardized scoring procedures of traditional inventory methods.

James's (1998) conditional reasoning approach assumes that people's personalities reflect the way they think. Most people believe that their own behavior is logical, and they develop beliefs and biases that justify their actions; for example, aggressive people assume other people want to harm them. Individuals who think differently also behave differently, and these differences can be captured with inductive reasoning problems that elicit test takers' beliefs and assumptions.

James and colleagues have developed conditional reasoning measures of achievement motivation and aggression. These tests are standardized, can be administered in groups, and produce reliable scores. Moreover, these scores are essentially uncorrelated with traditional inventory measures of achievement motivation and aggression (Bing et al., 2007; James, 1998). However, these scores correlate quite well with organizational criteria. These findings have prompted researchers to distinguish between the explicit components of personality (consciously accessible self-perceptions that can be assessed with traditional inventories) and the implicit components of personality (covert factors that require indirect assessment). Research indicates that the explicit and implicit components have both unique and interactive effects in predicting such outcomes as persistence, task performance, and counterproductive behavior, with multiple correlations in the .40 to .60 range (Bing et al., 2007).

Greenwald and Banaji's (1995) implicit attitude test (IAT) is another new method for measuring subconscious thoughts. Although originally designed to assess racist and sexist attitudes, the method has recently been used to measure personality. IATs are administered by computer, require respondents to indicate whether two paired words or phrases are similar or different, and then use reaction time to measure the strength of association. For instance, respondents who quickly associate "me" with "industrious" are thought to be more conscientious than those who take longer to make the association.

Preliminary evidence suggests that IAT-based measures of the FFM are unrelated to traditional inventory-based measures of the FFM and may add incremental validity in predicting behavioral outcomes (Steffens & König, 2006). However, this new area of research has not been extended to the workplace. Furthermore, IATs require a large number of trials to produce reliable scores, which ultimately may make this approach impractical for assessing the full range of personality dimensions (the FFM) in organizational applications.

Interviews

The employment interview is the most popular method of personality assessment and personnel selection (Huffcut, Conway, Roth, & Stone, 2001). However, most interviews are unstructured and assess the characteristics needed for job performance in a haphazard manner. Nonetheless, there is evidence that observer ratings add incremental validity beyond traditional personality inventories in predicting performance (Mount, Barrick, & Strauss,

1994), which suggests that interview-based assessments are potentially valuable. Research indicates how interviews might be better designed to assess personality.

Binning, LeBreton, and Adorno (1999) note that employment interviews are high-fidelity settings for personality assessment because, like much of job performance, they occur in contexts involving spontaneous social interaction. But the potential of this method depends on interviews that are carefully designed to measure job-related personality characteristics. This requires interviews to be designed around a personality-based job analysis and focused on certain personality dimensions but also to allow interviewer discretion to probe responses. For example, interviewers may need to probe for counterproductive personality tendencies. Huffcutt et al. (2001) provide evidence that systematic but flexible interviews designed to evaluate job-related personality attributes can yield criterion-related validities that compare favorably with inventory-based measures.

Employment interviews can also be used to elaborate inventory-based personality data from earlier phases of the selection process. Binning et al. (1999) suggested integrating these two types of assessment to increase predictive validity. In a subsequent selection study in a call center, they showed that combining personality scores with ratings from an interview designed to probe the inventory results added incremental validity in predicting turnover, and reduced turnover rates by more than 50 percent.

Remembering the Goals of Assessment

When psychological assessment was invented in the late nineteenth century, Alfred Binet and other pioneers were quite clear that the tests were intended to predict useful outcomes—in Binet's case, academic performance. Charles Spearman's early research changed the focus of measurement in a way that many people found appealing but that, in our judgment, has proved to be a dead end. Spearman shifted the emphasis from predicting outcomes to measuring entities. And with the emphasis on measuring entities such as g and traits, the concern with predicting outcomes gradually faded. By the 1950s, Binet's pragmatic approach to assessment was seen as an example of "dustbowl empiricism"—a term of derision applied to empirically keyed instruments whose focus was prediction, such as the MMPI and CPI.

We believe that future progress in personality assessment depends on improving the ability to predict organizational outcomes: productivity, turnover, theft, and so on. Currently researchers seem concerned with measuring personality constructs for their own sake. For example, the research on using interviews to assess personality primarily concerns how well interview ratings converge with other measures of personality, not how this research enhances validity. Similarly, most research on the FFM concerns interpreting, replicating, and generalizing the FFM structure. This work has been useful in providing a robust taxonomy for classifying the dimensions of personality, but it has almost nothing to do with predicting outcomes that matter in the workplace.

A related problem has been the emphasis on increasingly sophisticated statistical methodologies that yield no real gain in validity. For example, Cherneyshenko, Stark, Drasgow, and Roberts (2007) examined the use of item-response theory and ideal-point latent variable theory for personality scale construction. They report that personality items fit ideal-point models of nonlinear item-construct relationships better than more traditional and much simpler linear models. However, there were no differences in the two procedures in terms of the ability to predict observed outcomes. Despite the difficulty of using the complex ideal-point approach, the authors recommended it as a more flexible and advantageous solution.

Current research uses increasingly complex methodological designs, measurement methods, and data-analytical techniques. However, these methods—structural equation modeling, item-response theory, and multilevel and longitudinal latent variable models—have not improved the ability to predict important criteria. The goal of assessment is not to measure entities but to predict outcomes; the former matters only if it enhances the latter.

Better Theory

Clearer thinking, not more sophisticated statistical methods, will improve the prediction of workplace outcomes. Two examples support this view.

Predictor-Criterion Alignment

Critics of personality assessment for employee selection base their criticism on the modest validity coefficients reported in meta-analyses (Morgeson et al., 2007). For example, Schneider (2007) estimates the overall validity for measures of conscientiousness to be in the .20s. We have discussed how validities of this magnitude can lead to significant gains in employee productivity. We add that meta-analytical research often underestimates validity because it rarely distinguishes among different kinds of job performance criteria. For example, the positive correlations between Conscientiousness and rule following are simply added to the negative correlations between Conscientiousness and creativity, which cancel each other and underestimate the "true" validity of Conscientiousness. In addition, the Conscientiousness dimension has two components: responsibility and achievement orientation. These components correlate in opposite directions with criteria such as persistence on a futile task, and when they are combined in a global measure of Conscientiousness, they yield a zero correlation (Moon, 2001). However, when they are correlated separately with the criterion, they yield significant but opposite validity coefficients: responsible people persist at problems that cannot be solved, and achievement-oriented people move on to those that can be solved.

Poor criterion measurement is widespread in applied research (Murphy, 2008). When supervisors' ratings of employee performance reflect how much they like the employees, the correlations between these ratings and the relevant personality dimensions underestimate the personality-performance relationship. Future research should pay closer attention to the adequacy of performance criteria and use theory to align criterion measures with relevant personality dimensions.

All Personality Measures Are Not Created Equal

Meta-analyses assume that personality scales from different inventories with similar names are equivalent and measure the same thing. However, this assumption is not justified conceptually or empirically. For example, Grucza and Goldberg (2007) compared the validity of eleven different personality inventories for predicting three types of behavioral criteria. Overall the average validities were similar across instruments; however, scales from some inventories predicted certain criteria better than scales with similar names from other inventories. The researchers called for more comparative studies of the ability of different inventories to predict specific classes of behavior. Such research would be invaluable for organizational practitioners who must choose among overtly similar inventories.

One implication of the Gruzca and Goldberg (2007) paper is that meta-analysts should code different inventories and scales as potential moderator variables. That is, variations in validity coefficients for a particular personality dimension-criterion relationship may be attributed to differences in the scales used in the primary studies. An alternative is to conduct meta-analyses using measures from only one inventory (J. Hogan & Holland, 2003).

Other Opportunities

Few organizational researchers have studied nonlinear and interactive effects between two or more personality dimensions. However, a small number of studies of these effects support the contention that these more complex relationships yield incremental predictive validity (Benson & Campbell, 2007).

Prediction methods that consider entire personality profiles are also an interesting research topic. Such multivariate approaches are potentially useful because single personality dimensions may yield relatively small relationships with a criterion, but when considered together, they often yield sizable multiple correlations. For example, the combined FFM predicts leadership with a corrected multiple correlation of .48 (Judge et al., 2002).

Holistic methods can also put the person back in *person*ality by using individuals rather than variables as the unit of analysis. It would be useful to study how configurations of personality characteristics predict outcomes because historically, we have studied how single personality variables are related to criteria, but in practice we make decisions about people, who are constellations of personality characteristics. Unfortunately, we know much more about variables than we do about persons.

Last Thoughts

People new to the field may be surprised to learn that academic psychology is rather hostile to personality psychology. It all started in the late nineteenth century. The original pioneers such as Francis Galton maintained that personality is largely innate, under genetic control, and very hard to change. This view supported a racially biased, politically conservative philosophy, and it generated a furious liberal backlash led by Franz Boas, the father of cultural anthropology. Boas devoted his career to promoting the idea that human behavior should be explained in terms of culture. American social scientists, responding to Boas's call, argued that social, historical, economic, and situational factors explain what people do, which makes their behavior changeable in principle. Behaviorism, the guiding metaphysic of American psychology for perhaps eighty years, is the logical extension of this view: what people do depends on where they are (situations), not who they are (personality). This view is consistent with a liberal political philosophy and the spirit of democracy—and by definition, it is rooted in ideology.

By attending to two important distinctions, much of the historical antipathy to personality psychology should go away. First, consider the distinction between identity—how people think and talk about themselves—and reputation—how other people think and talk about those persons. The study of identity has not been very productive, but the study of reputation has been immensely productive. This is so because the best predictor of future behavior is past behavior, reputation is a summary of a person's past behavior, and by definition it is the best data source we have about that person's future behavioral tendencies. So if we direct personality research to the study of reputation, we are on strong empirical grounds and can avoid issues of political ideology.

Second, consider the distinction between defining the goals of assessment as measuring psychological entities (traits, intelligence, and so forth) versus predicting significant outcomes. We believe that applied assessment has a job to do, and that job is to predict behaviors that matter in the workplace. By focusing on prediction and not worrying about the entities that may have been measured, it becomes a relatively simple matter to evaluate the merits of personality assessment. It is far from perfect, but better than any other single alternative. Test users (organizations) are usually happy to be able to forecast stable trends in behavior (reputation) and are unconcerned about how well entities have been measured. Obviously, prudent researchers would combine assessment methods to maximize prediction, but that is not our point here. Our point is that the antipathy toward personality psychology is unfounded based on the available data.

References

Arthur, W., Jr., Day, E. A., McNelly, T. L., & Edens, P. S. (2003). A meta-analysis of the criterion-related validity of assessment center dimensions. *Personnel Psychology, 56*, 125–154.

Barrick, M. R., & Mount, M. K. (1991). The Big Five personality dimensions and job performance: A meta-analysis. *Personnel Psychology, 44*, 1–26.

Bartram, D. (2005). The great eight competencies: A criterion-centric approach to validation. *Journal of Applied Psychology, 90*, 1185–1203.

Benson, M. J., & Campbell, J. P. (2007). To be, or not to be, linear: An expanded representation of personality and its relationship to leadership performance. *International Journal of Selection and Assessment, 15*, 232–249.

Berry, C. M., Ones, D. S., & Sackett, P. R. (2007). Interpersonal deviance, organizational deviance, and their correlates. *Journal of Applied Psychology, 92*, 410–424.

Bing, M. N., Stewart, S. M., Davison, H. K., Green, P. D., McIntyre, M. D., & James, L. R. (2007). An integrative typology of personality assessment for aggression: Implications for predicting counterproductive workplace behavior. *Journal of Applied Psychology, 92*, 722–744.

Binning, J. F., LeBreton, J. M., & Adorno, A. J. (1999). Assessing personality. In R. W. Eder & M. M. Harris (Eds.), *The employment interview handbook* (pp. 105–123). Thousand Oaks, CA: Sage.

Bliesener, T. (1996). Methodological moderators in validating biographical data in personnel selection. *Journal of Occupational and Organizational Psychology, 69*, 107–120.

Campbell, J. P., McCloy, R. A., Oppler, S. H., & Sager, C. E. (1993). A theory of performance. In N. Schmitt & W. C. Borman (Eds.), *Personnel selection in organizations* (pp. 35–70). San Francisco: Jossey-Bass.

Cherneyshenko, O. S., Stark, S., Drasgow, F., & Roberts, B. W. (2007). Constructing personality scales under the assumption of an ideal point response process: Toward increasing the flexibility of personality measures. *Psychological Assessment, 19*, 88–106.

Ellingson, J. E., Sackett, P. R., & Connelly, B. S. (2007). Personality assessment across selection and development contexts. *Journal of Applied Psychology, 92*, 386–395.

Gottfredson, G., & Holland, J. L. (1996). *Dictionary of Holland occupational codes* (3rd ed.). Odessa, FL: Psychological Assessment Resources.

Greenwald, A. G., & Banaji, M. R. (1995). Implicit social cognition: Attitudes, self-esteem, and stereotypes. *Psychological Review, 102*, 4–27.

Grucza, R. A., & Goldberg, L. R. (2007). The comparative validity of 11 modern personality inventories: Predictions of behavioral acts, informant reports, and clinical indicators. *Journal of Personality Assessment, 89*, 167–187.

Hogan, J., Barrett, P., & Hogan, R. (2007). Personality measurement, faking, and employment selection. *Journal of Applied Psychology, 92*, 1270–1285.

Hogan, J., Hogan, R., & Kaiser, R. B. (2010). Management derailment: Personality assessment and mitigation. In S. Zedeck (Ed.), *American Psychological Association handbook of industrial and organizational psychology.* Washington, DC: American Psychological Association.

Hogan, J., & Holland, B. (2003). Using theory to evaluate personality and job-performance relations. *Journal of Applied Psychology, 88*, 100–112.

Hogan, R. (2005). In defense of personality measurement: New wine for old whiners. *Human Performance, 18*, 331–341.

Hogan, R., & Hogan, J. (2007). *Validity of the Hogan Personality Inventory for job family selection.* Tulsa, OK: Hogan Assessment Systems.

Hogan, R., & Hogan, J. (2008). *Hogan Development Survey manual* (2nd ed.). Tulsa, OK: Hogan Assessment Systems.

Holland, J. L. (1973). *Making vocational choices: A theory of careers.* Upper Saddle River, NJ: Prentice Hall.

Huffcutt, A. I., Conway, J. M., Roth, P. L., & Stone, N. J. (2001). Identification and meta-analytic assessment of psychological constructs measured in employment interviews. *Journal of Applied Psychology, 86*, 897–913.

Hunter, J. E., & Schmidt, F. L. (2004). *Methods of meta-analysis: Correcting error and bias in research findings* (2nd ed.). Thousand Oaks, CA: Sage.

Hunter, J. E., Schmidt, F. L., & Judiesch, M. K. (1990). Individual differences in output variability as a function of job complexity. *Journal of Applied Psychology, 75,* 28–42.

James, L. R. (1998). Measurement of personality via conditional reasoning. *Organizational Research Methods, 1,* 131–163.

Judge, T. A., Bono, J. E., Ilies, R., & Gerhardt, M. W. (2002). Personality and leadership: A qualitative and quantitative review. *Journal of Applied Psychology, 87,* 765–780.

Judge, T. A., Colbert, A. E., & Ilies, R. (2004). Intelligence and leadership: A quantitative review and test of theoretical propositions. *Journal of Applied Psychology, 89,* 542–555.

Judge, T. A., Erez, A., Bono, J. E., & Thoresen, C. J. (2003). The Core Self-Evaluations Scale (CSES): Development of a measure. *Personnel Psychology, 56,* 303–331.

Judge, T. A., Heller, D., & Mount, M. K. (2002). Five-Factor Model of personality and job satisfaction: A meta-analysis. *Journal of Applied Psychology, 87,* 530–541.

Judge, T. A., Locke, E. A., & Durham, C. C. (1997). The dispositional causes of job satisfaction: A core evaluations approach. *Research in Organizational Behavior, 19,* 151–188.

MacKinnon, D. W. (1944). The structure of personality. In J. McVicker Hunt (Ed.), *Personality and the behavior disorders* (Vol. 1, pp. 3–48). New York: Ronald Press.

McDaniel, M. A., Hartman, N. S., Whetzel, D. L., & Grubb, W. L. (2007). Situational judgment test, response instructions, and validity: A meta-analysis. *Personnel Psychology, 60,* 63–91.

McDaniel, M. A., Whetzel, D. L., Schmidt, F. L., & Maurer, S. D. (1994). The validity of employment interviews: A comprehensive review and meta-analysis. *Journal of Applied Psychology, 79,* 599–616.

Moon, H. (2001). The two faces of conscientiousness: Duty and achievement striving in escalation of commitment dilemmas. *Journal of Applied Psychology, 86,* 533–540.

Morgeson, F. P., Campion, M. A., Dipboye, R. L., Hollenbeck, J. R., Murphy, K., & Schmitt, N. (2007). Reconsidering the use of personality tests in personnel selection contexts. *Personnel Psychology, 60,* 683–729.

Moscoso, S., & Salgado, J. F. (2004). "Dark side" personality styles as predictors of task, contextual, and job performance. *International Journal of Selection and Assessment, 12,* 356–362.

Mount, M. K., Barrick, M. R., & Strauss, J. P. (1994). Validity of observer ratings of the Big Five personality factors. *Journal of Applied Psychology, 79,* 272–280.

Murphy, K. R. (2008). Explaining the weak relationship between job performance and ratings of job performance. *Industrial and Organizational Psychology, 1*, 148–160.

Ones, D. S., Viswesvaran, C., & Reiss, A. D. (1996). Role of social desirability in personality testing for personnel selection: The red herring. *Journal of Applied Psychology, 81*, 660–679.

Ones, D. S., Viswesvaran, C., & Schmidt, F. L. (1993). Comprehensive meta-analysis of integrity test validation. *Journal of Applied Psychology, 78*, 679–703.

Ones, D. S., Viswesvaran, C., & Schmidt, F. L. (2003). Personality and absenteeism. *European Journal of Personality, 17*(Suppl.), 519–538.

Pearlman, K., Schmidt, F. L., & Hunter, J. E. (1980). Validity generalization results for tests used to predict job proficiency and training success in clerical occupations. *Journal of Applied Psychology, 65*, 373–406.

Peeters, H., Van Tuijl, H.F.J., Rutte, C. G., & Raymen, J. M. (2006). Personality and team performance. *European Journal of Personality, 20*, 377–396.

Roberts, B. R., Kuncel, N. R., Shiner, R., Caspi, A., & Goldberg, L. R. (2007). The power of personality: The comparative validity of personality traits, socio-economic status, and cognitive ability for predicting important life outcomes. *Perspectives on Psychological Science, 2*, 313–345.

Rosenthal, R., & Rubin, D. B. (1982). A simple, general purpose display of magnitude of experimental effect. *Journal of Educational Psychology, 74*, 166–169.

Schmit, M. J., Kilm, J. A., & Robie, C. A. (2000). Development of a global measure of personality. *Personnel Psychology, 53*, 153–193.

Schneider, B. (2007). Evolution of the study and practice of personality at work. *Human Resource Management, 46*, 583–610.

Steffens, M. C., & König, S. S. (2006). Predicting spontaneous big five behavior with implicit association tests. *European Journal of Psychological Assessment, 22*, 13–20.

Wiggins, J. S. (1996). *The Five-Factor Model of personality.* New York: Guilford Press.

CHAPTER 5

ASSESSMENT OF BACKGROUND AND LIFE EXPERIENCE
The Past as Prologue
Leaetta M. Hough

Virtually everyone—the general public, scientists, practitioners, young, and old—accepts past behavior as a powerful predictor of future behavior. Even if the motivations behind a person's behavior are unknown, it is understood that when placed in a similar situation, the person is likely to do what he or she did before. Behavioral consistency is readily accepted as a real phenomenon applicable to almost all living things. Human beings in the work setting are no exception. Biodata (past behavior and experiences, background, biographical or autobiographical data) are an excellent source of information for understanding the person and predicting likely future behavior.

It seems so simple. Yet assessing people by measuring their past is complicated, with a myriad issues to consider. An important goal of this chapter is to provide a set of questions that researchers, practitioners, and decision makers should ask when developing or evaluating biodata measures. Topics addressed in this chapter include validity of biodata measures, factors that affect their validity, and the implications of the findings for developing and evaluating biodata measures. First, a definition of *biodata* is needed.

Definition of Biodata

Biodata are information about an individual's past behavior and experience. The motives for industrial-organizational (I-O) psychologists who have studied biodata are at least twofold. Bill Owens and his colleagues, especially Michael Mumford and Garnett Stokes, sought to understand individual development by discovering patterns of differential development through subgrouping people according to biographical information and profiles (Mumford, Stokes, & Owens, 1990). Their goal was to understand how past behavior influences or sets the stage for future behavior. This theoretical orientation used empirical data to induce the patterns of individual development and principles underlying why and how past behavior influences future behavior. Other researchers were more applied, focusing primarily on predicting an outcome such as job performance, training performance, success in school, and turnover. Both research streams contribute enormously to our knowledge base, and while in pursuit of their goals, researchers in both research streams developed biodata measures.

Biodata measures are data-gathering devices that gather more (or less) structured information and score the information in a more (or less) structured way. The measures differ substantially from each other. The variations and combinations on who, what, when, where, and how are almost endless. In short, biodata are the individual's life history, and biodata measures gather that information and score it. This chapter sets out information about all of these different permutations of biodata measures, with special emphasis on the more frequently used biodata measures.

Biodata measures vary in terms of:

- Whether quantitative or qualitative information is gathered—for example, number of times something was done ("How often have you performed this task?") or reactions to situations ("Describe a time when a supervisor gave you negative feedback. How did you react?").
- Whether typical behavior or maximal behavior is sought—for example, "How often do you exercise at least thirty minutes a day?" versus "What are your most significant accomplishments?"

- Whether self-evaluative or factual information is gathered.
- The amount of structure provided in the response format. For example, "Describe a time when . . ." allows an open-ended response, whereas, "How often have you performed a specific task?" is typically followed by multiple-choice response options."
- Whether the response options are continuous—for example, "most" to "least"—or categorical—for example, terminated from employment, retired, employed, or volunteer.
- The source of the information. Questions might be asked of the individual (self-report) or of some other person (other report). Or the data might be archival.
- How the information is scored. Scoring procedures might be empirically developed, resulting in algorithms that generate scores or rationally developed by experts.
- The response mode. Responses might be provided in written form or orally in an interview.

Validity of Biodata Measures

The ways in which the information is gathered and scored and the purposes for which the scores are used are evaluated by amassing validity evidence—criterion-related, construct, and content—as well as other information, such as applicant reaction, cost, and mean score differences between groups. The fundamental validity issue is the degree to which the interpretations of scores are appropriate for their intended or actual use. This chapter examines validity and research evidence for biodata measures with a focus on what we can learn from the research and how we can put that knowledge to use. The research findings provided the foundation for a set of questions that appear at the end of the chapter. The questions are intended to be used when evaluating biodata measures that assess an individual's past behavior and experience.

The evidence is clear: biodata predict valued organizational criteria as well as other criteria, such as life expectancy, divorce, and illness. This conclusion is true across virtually all kinds of biodata measures, scale development methods, criteria, criterion constructs, criterion measurement methods, validation study designs, and populations studied (quantitative summaries are found in Bliesener, 1996; Huffcutt & Arthur, 1994; Hunter & Hunter, 1984; McDaniel, Schmidt, & Hunter, 1988a, 1988b; Ng, Eby, Sorensen, & Feldman, 2005; Quiñones, Ford, & Teachout, 1995; Schmitt, Gooding, Noe, & Kirsch, 1984). The expected criterion-related validity (observed validity) of a well-developed biodata measure is in the mid-.20s to low .30s. When compared with other predictor measures, the criterion-related validity of biodata measures ranks among the best, rivaling the validity of general cognitive ability measures, considered by many to be the best predictor of overall job performance. The cumulative evidence is that biodata predicts virtually all criteria that I-O psychologists have examined.

Of course, aggregating correlation coefficients across so many different studies, types of biodata measures, predictor and criterion variables, and scale construction methods ignores all the variables that are known or thought to moderate the validity of biodata measures. For example, research informs us that:

- Validity study design affects validity. Concurrent validity studies result in higher criterion-related validities than predictive validity designs.
- Population studied affects validity. Studies involving job incumbents result in higher criterion-related validities than studies involving job applicants.
- Type of criterion affects validity. Criterion-related validities are higher for training criteria than job performance criteria.

Nonetheless, biodata measures predict valued organizational criteria even when summaries report results from studies that included research designs, populations, and so forth known to result in lower criterion-related validities. Importantly, research also indicates that certain scale development features and item characteristics can enhance the validity of biodata measures.

Item-Generation Methods: Advantages and Disadvantages

A variety of item-generation strategies exist. The better ones include an analysis of the characteristic to be measured or criterion to be predicted. If, for example, the purpose is to measure leadership, an analysis of what is meant by leadership is needed. Is it charismatic leadership, thought leadership, ethical leadership, and so forth? What precisely is to be measured? A good definition of the characteristic is required. It is a first step in developing a measure that has construct validity. If, however, the purpose is to predict turnover, an analysis of the causes or reasons for turnover in the particular setting should be examined. If the purpose is to predict job performance, an analysis of the job (work) and the context within which the work is performed is required. An analysis of the criterion is a first step in developing a measure that has criterion-related validity. If both construct and criterion-related validity are desired, the individual difference characteristic and the criterion, such as job performance, need to be carefully defined. An analysis of the characteristic to be measured and criterion to be predicted informs the test developer (or test user) of the content to be included in the item pool for the measure (scale)—a critically important initial step. Good theories, good job and work analyses, good definitions, and good thinking are needed. The sections that follow provide examples of item generation strategies that are likely to generate valid biodata measures.

Functional Job Analysis Approach

This method of job analysis produced the occupational classification system in later editions of the *Dictionary of Occupational Titles* (DOT; U.S. Department of Labor). It results in task-, attribute-, and behavior-based information very helpful for generating job-relevant biodata items (and scales). The task-based component includes work functions (what gets done) and working conditions. The attribute-based component focuses on individual difference characteristics needed to perform the job effectively, and the behavior-based component focuses on what workers do with things, data, and people. An important part of the functional job analysis approach is the information generated about levels of skill needed in each of three types of skills:

- *Adaptive skills*—behavioral styles and competencies that enable a person to cope with the requirements of conformity and change related to physical, interpersonal, organizational, and working conditions

- *Functional skills*—mental, interpersonal, and physical capacities related to data, people, and things
- *Specific content skills*—competencies that enable a person to perform the specific job tasks, including environmental and work conditions that relate to procedures, standard operating procedures, machines, and equipment

This approach brings into focus the context of the task or work and the adaptive skills that include working conditions, effort, and responsibility. (For more information about this method, see Fine & Cronshaw, 1994.)

Each task statement in a functional job analysis contains information about the behavior, knowledge, skills, and abilities needed for effective job performance. That information, in conjunction with the context of the job, results in biodata items such as these:

- When given a work assignment, you prefer to have:
  a. discretion to do the work on your own
  b. direction from a supervisor or others
- As a student, you preferred homework assignments that:
  a. were detailed and explicit
  b. allowed you to define what to do and how to do it

Functional task statements can lead directly to biodata items such as, "How many times have you repaired the starter on an automobile?" or "How many years have you worked in a job in which you repaired the starter on an automobile?" that yield observed criterion-related validities in the .20s and sometimes higher (meta-analysis; Quiñones et al., 1995). Such biodata items appear to be very good for predictors of task performance but less good for predictors of organizational citizenship behavior or contextual performance. An important consideration in writing response options for such items is that experience beyond five years is unlikely to add much accuracy in predicting performance (Schmidt, Hunter, Outerbridge, & Goff, 1988). For example, five years may be too many years for some jobs (such as unskilled assembly line jobs) but not enough for others (surgeons). The amount of time beyond which more experience is helpful in predicting performance undoubtedly depends on the complexity of the task and job in question, with less time required for routine tasks and jobs.

The functional job analysis approach is excellent for developing content- and criterion-valid biodata scales for predicting job performance criteria. It is both job focused and worker focused; it produces information about individual difference characteristics required for effective job performance and thus helpful information about the content of biodata items to measure the worker or individual difference characteristic. In the absence of a job to analyze, the method is less helpful for developing construct-valid biodata measures of individual difference characteristics.

Mumford and Stokes Item-Generation Method

This method is based on traditional procedures used in differential psychology to develop construct-valid measures of individual difference variables in which initial item generation is based on a theory of the individual difference variable. The theory defines the construct and specifies the elements to be included in the measure. In this case the interactional model of development (Mumford et al., 1990; Mumford, Reiter-Palmon, & Snell, 1994) is the guiding theory—a theory that assumes that adult development is an ongoing, dynamic interaction between the individual and situations to which the person is exposed. Biodata items generated using the interactional model include the context or situation.

When the purpose of the measurement is prediction of job performance, this method of item development relies on job analysis to identify the knowledge, skills, abilities, and other personal characteristics (KSAOs) that affect performance. Then the job analysis results and the interactional model of development are used to identify life experiences, circumstances, and situations in which people might have acquired or demonstrated the needed KSAOs. Items are then written to capture or reflect individuals' differential experiences and expressions of the KSAOs. Again, the biodata items generated are likely to include the context or situation.

The item-writing procedures are labor intensive. As Mumford, Costanza, Connelly, and Johnson (1996) noted, item-writing training alone requires eighty hours of instruction and hands-on training. During training, item writers learn about the logic of using biodata to measure an underlying disposition, how prior behaviors and experiences reflect underlying dispositions, and how the behaviors and experiences are manifestations of the underlying disposition or construct. The interactional model of adult development with its resulting individual differences is explained. Training includes instruction in item writing, important item characteristics (such as verifiability, need for escape clauses, and appropriateness of content), and item review procedures.

Actual item writing includes or requires:

- Operational definitions of the constructs
- Individual item writer review of each construct
- Discussion of the implications for and manifestations of the construct in people's lives
- Description of the target population that is expected to complete the biodata items as well as a description or discussion of life experiences likely to be common to the target population
- Identification of situations in which manifestations of the construct might occur, with an emphasis on psychologically meaningful situations to ensure meaningful items and response options
- Discussion of differences in behaviors, reactions, outcomes, and so forth that people exposed to the situation might experience
- Use of these differences to generate items and item-response options that include frequency or intensity of the behaviors, reactions, outcomes, and other experiences that might occur in the situation

Once the response options are chosen or identified (often a five-point, continuous response option), the item writers engage in a panel discussion during which each biodata item is examined for:

- Construct relevance
- Relation to other constructs being measured
- Extent to which respondents have control over their behavior and experience in the situation
- Likelihood that most or all target respondents have had exposure to the situation
- Social desirability or ease of intentional distortion
- Intrusiveness and acceptability of the item to respondents
- Clarity

After all the items have been examined and discussed, the panel reaches a consensus about the fifteen to twenty-five best items for each construct. These items form the scale designed to measure the construct. Items in the scale include a range of situations that are considered likely to measure an underlying disposition (construct) that generalizes across situations.

Some sample items designed to measure prior leadership experiences are:

- During high school, how many times were you elected to be an officer of an organization?
  5 or more times
  3 or 4 times
  1 or 2 times
  Never
  I didn't go to high school.
- In the past three years, when you have been in a group situation, how often did the others look to you for direction?
  Much more often than others
  More often than others
  About as often as others
  Less often than others
  Much less often than others

Critical Incident Technique

The critical incident technique is a behavioral analysis of a phenomenon and is often used in job analysis to identify behavioral components of the job. People who are directly involved in the phenomenon (a job incumbent, for example) or affected by the behavior (a supervisor, peer, or subordinate) provide the behavioral information. Data can be gathered in interviews or workshops, individually, or in groups. The first step is to explain to the participants the purpose of the effort, why they specifically have been asked to provide the information, how the information will be used, as well as to assure them that the information they provide is both confidential and anonymous. Then participants are trained in writing useful performance examples (critical incidents). They are asked to think about times when someone in the job did something indicative of how he or she performed the job. Sometimes participants need greater specificity than "the job," and in such cases specifying an outcome, such as "affecting productivity," "affecting quality," and "affecting satisfaction" can be helpful. For each incident the participant is then asked to describe:

- The circumstances leading up to the incident
- Exactly what the person did that was helpful or unhelpful
- Why the behavior was helpful or unhelpful
- An approximate time period when the incident occurred

Additional helpful information the participant can provide is:

- A preliminary job performance category the behavior represents
- An estimate of the level of effectiveness of the behavior

After gathering the critical incidents (behavioral examples), the incidents are categorized into groups of similar content, often an iterative process and involving more than one person. The critical incident technique, when used in combination with a "retranslation" procedure that involves others' sorting the incidents into tentative categories, yields categories of behaviorally defined and agreed-on homogeneous dimensions.

This approach to job analysis and identification of homogeneous constructs provides an excellent basis for biodata item development. It provides a thorough analysis of behavior and definition of the construct to be measured. For example, the critical incident method of job analysis provides clear definitions of the constructs and examples of behaviors to guide item development in the Mumford and Stokes method of item generation. Incidents that are categorized in the dimensions are used even more directly in developing questions for what has been referred to as the "behavior description interview" (Janz, Hellervik, & Gilmore, 1986). Questions generated for a behavior description interview ask the person, "What would you do if . . . ," and then provide a description of the situation.

Perhaps the most direct application of the critical incident method for biodata item development is the Accomplishment Record (Hough, 1984), which uses a critical-incident-generated construct and its definition as the stem for each biodata item and asks the respondent to provide an example of his or her most significant or meritorious accomplishment relevant to the construct, thus ensuring content validity. The following Accomplishment Record item is in the category of assertive advocacy:

> The following is a definition of "assertive advocacy." It is not an exhaustive definition. Your report of an accomplishment or experience should *relate* to this category but does not need to address all of the specific bullet points listed below:
>
> - Being assertive, forceful, and competitive in promoting the appropriate viewpoint, whether it is your independent idea, another person's, or the result of a team effort
> - Challenging others to defend or support their positions
> - Quickly adapting and persuasively responding to counterarguments
>
> *(continued)*

- Date (approximately) of accomplishment:

- General statement of the situation or circumstances surrounding what you accomplished:

- Description of exactly what you did (how you did it, actions you took, outcomes of actions):

- Name of person who can verify your accomplishment/experience:

- His or her contact information:

Scoring procedures for the Accomplishment Record method rely on experts and expert judgment for development of scoring guidelines. (Scoring procedures are described in a later section in this chapter.)

Retrospective Life Experience Essay and Interview Technique

In this method, people in the target population are asked to provide written essays about generic life experiences: disappointing situations, stressful situations, individual accomplishments, and group accomplishments, among others. A subset of the people is interviewed to learn more in-depth information about the life experiences. The objective is to gather information that might lead to insights into experiences that shape current behavior and provide content for generating biodata items. It is a method of generating rich, developmentally important past experiences and is aligned with the interactional model of development (Russell, Mattson, Devlin, & Atwater, 1990).

Criteria to be predicted are identified and defined using sources such as performance appraisal forms that delineate components of success for the job: leadership, stress response, goal setting, and achievement. Then the autobiographical life history essays are content-analyzed to identify experiences that might relate to the success components. Once relevant prior experiences are identified, biodata items are written.

An example of an item generated using this method is:

> How often has someone gotten credit for work you did?
> a. Very often
> b. Often
> c. Sometimes
> d. Rarely
> e. Never

Scale Development Methods: Advantages, Disadvantages, and New Developments

There are three main types of scale construction strategies. In their pure form, they are known as *inductive*, *deductive*, and *external*.

Inductive (Internal) Strategy of Scale Construction

The inductive strategy, also known as the internal scale construction method, assumes an underlying set of individual difference characteristics that can be discovered through factor or cluster analysis of respondents' answers to a set of questions. In this method, the primary, if not sole, determinant of quality is the internal structure of the scale: its internal consistency. It is data driven (factor analyses of item responses, internal reliability estimates, and item-total scale correlations), but the focus is internal rather than external. Items that do not correlate adequately with the other items in the scale are considered poor items that should be removed. The objective is homogeneous scales, which typically means a reduction in the complexity of the scale and a reduction in variance accounted for in the original item pool. It also potentially eliminates items that correlate highly with valued external criteria. This strategy has been favored by many researchers interested in construct validity, but it is an unnecessary, perhaps mistaken, allegiance; homogeneity of item content, especially as determined in this manner, is not synonymous with construct validity.

The inductive method produces good measurement of individuals' standing on a variable but only within a relatively narrow range of the distribution of possible scores. People at the extremes of the distribution are not well measured. Items that effectively measure and differentiate those people would have been deleted during scale development because their infrequency of endorsement would have resulted in low item-total scale correlations and hence deletion. Thus, the error of measurement is typically greater at the extremes of the distribution, the part of the distribution that may be of most interest in many applied settings. This measurement phenomenon is an important negative feature of the inductive or internal method of scale construction.

External (Empirical) Strategy of Scale Construction

The external strategy, also known as the empirical scale construction method, seeks to predict a criterion and typically produces heterogeneous scales with low alpha reliabilities and low item-total scale correlations. Whereas both the inductive and deductive strategies are construct oriented, the pure form of the external strategy is not. It is atheoretical. It produces scales that are heterogeneous, that is, scales that lack a coherent theme.

Similar to the inductive (internal) strategy of scale construction, this is a data-driven method; it differs from the inductive method in its focus on external criteria. An important shortcoming of this method is that it capitalizes on sample-specific variance, or chance. Large samples and cross-validation are requirements of this method of scale construction. Even when cross-validation has been undertaken, generalizability of the results to other settings, populations, or applications is typically unknown. Moreover, it is difficult, if not impossible, to create a truly equivalent or alternate form with the external scale construction strategy, although if the biodata scale consists of factual biographical questions and verification is possible, the need for an equivalent or alternate form may be unnecessary.

Empirical weighting strategies generate a composite score based on item or item-option weights identified through statistical analyses. Items or item-response options that are statistically related to a criterion are retained and weighted according to the magnitude of their relationship with the criterion. Empirical weighting strategies require administration of the biodata measure to a carefully identified group of people (called the developmental sample) for whom high-quality criterion data can also be obtained.

The effectiveness of empirically developed keys depends on several factors, one of which is the identification and measurement of the criterion. An empirically developed key for predicting a criterion can be only as good as the effectiveness with which the criterion measure differentiates people on the criterion, whatever the criterion might be. If, for example, the criterion is task performance, the criterion measure needs to differentiate better from less good performers on the task reliably and accurately.

Another important factor is the sample size of the group (called the developmental sample) on which the weights of the items or response options are determined. As a rule of thumb, the number of people needed in the development sample is five to ten times the number of items or predictors included in the initial item pool. This large a number is important because empirical approaches capitalize on chance variation in the developmental sample. Empirical methods identify responses to biodata items and response options that maximally differentiate higher- from lower-scoring people in the same sample on a second variable, the criterion. However, the maximization procedures capitalize on chance variation—variation that is specific to the people in the developmental sample—resulting in an overestimate of the real relationship between biodata responses and the criterion.

Another important factor that affects the quality of the resulting key is the appropriateness of the people in the developmental sample: the more similar they are to the people who will complete the biodata measure and about whom decisions will be made, the more likely the validity of the measure will remain intact. Thus, if the biodata measure is to be administered as part of a personnel selection process, the developmental sample should be as similar as possible to the job applicant pool (Stokes & Cooper, 2004).

At least three factors affect the practical usefulness of the bio-data measure:

- Quality of criterion and its measurement
- Number of people in the developmental sample
- Similarity of the people in the developmental sample to the people for whom the biodata measure will be used

In short, the scoring key needs to predict the criterion in a group of people who were not in the developmental sample but are similar to the people in the applicant pool.

A correlation coefficient is often the index of relationship that is computed to express the relationship between scores on the bio-data and a criterion. If the index of relationship is computed on the people included in the developmental sample, it is a fold-back correlation and is inflated because of capitalization on chance variation in the development sample. Cross-validation of empirical scoring keys is essential. A variety of cross-validation strategies exist, one of which is gathering predictor and criterion scores on an independent sample (people not included in the development sample). Another approach is to apply a shrinkage formula to the fold-back coefficient obtained in the development sample. When a comparison is made of the effectiveness of an empirically developed scoring key with a rationally developed (or expert-developed) scoring key, only the cross-validity of the empirically developed key is appropriate. Rationally developed keys do not require cross-validation because they do not capitalize on sample-specific variance.

Empirical keying approaches have evolved over the years. Two basic differences between the models are whether weighting occurs at the item-response-option level or the item level as a whole and whether the criterion is a continuous variable or a dichotomous (or dichotomized) variable. Some of the more commonly used ones follow:

Item-Level Weighting Approaches

- Correlational method
  - This is a least-squares solution that maximizes the relation between the items and the criterion in the developmental sample.
  - Response options are typically continuous (for example, "most" to "least").

- Item-criterion relationships are linear; more of the item is associated with more of the criterion or less of the item is associated with less of the criterion.
- Item weights are based on the magnitude and direction (correlation) of the relationship of the item with the criterion.
- Sometimes values such as integer weights that approximate the correlation are used to reduce the shrinkage in cross-validity.
- Differential regression methods
  - The first three items of the correlational method apply.
  - This is a step-wise regression analysis procedure that weights items based on the increment in criterion variance accounted for by the addition of the item over and above the items already included.
  - Very large developmental samples (thousands of people) are needed to produce stable results. Otherwise cross-validities will shrink substantially, possibly entirely.

Item-Response-Level Weighting Approaches

- Horizontal percentage method (also known as the contrasting group method)
  - This approach is appropriate for items whose response options are not linearly related to the criterion.
  - The criterion is dichotomous (naturally occurring discrete groups such as "terminated" versus "not terminated").
  - If the criterion is dichotomized (artificially formed "extreme" groups), the two groups need to be approximately equal. Ideally, a top third and a bottom third of the total group are formed.
  - The number of people in the high-scoring group endorsing an option is tallied, divided by the total number of people in both high- and low-scoring groups, and converted to a percentage. The same procedure is applied to all items and response options and then repeated for the low-scoring group.
  - For more variations on this method, see Guion (1965).
- Vertical percentage method (also known as the contrasting group method)
  - The first three items for the horizontal percentage method apply to this method as well.

- The number of people in the high-scoring group endorsing an option is tallied, divided by the number of high-scoring people responding to the item, and converted to a percentage. The same procedure is applied to all the items and response options, and the same procedure repeated for the low-scoring group.
- For more variations on this method see Devlin, Abrahams, and Edwards (1992).

A comparison of empirical item and item-response-option scoring approaches reveals that no one empirical method of item and item-response-option scoring emerges as better than the others in all circumstances. When empirical scoring strategies are used, the recommendation that sample sizes from five to ten times greater than the number of items (or response options) be used is time-proven advice. Importantly, simple unit weights appear robust. When sample sizes are smaller than recommended and if simple unit weights are not used, the vertical percentage method is generally recommended over other empirical scoring methods (Devlin et al., 1992). Whatever method is used, the test developer and test user need to be cognizant of the problems of capitalizing on chance, especially when the number of people in the developmental sample is not significantly larger than the number of predictors to be weighted.

A somewhat more refined recommendation is:

- With developmental sample sizes fewer than 150, unit weights are likely to produce the most stable results.
- With developmental sample sizes between 150 and 250, zero-order correlations are probably okay.
- With developmental sample sizes of more than 250, multiple regression analyses are probably okay (Campbell, 1974).
- With developmental sample sizes in the thousands, differential regression analyses are probably okay (Steinhaus & Waters, 1991).

Deductive (Rational) Strategy of Scale Construction

The deductive strategy, also known as the rational scale construction method, is based on a researcher's theory or intuitive skills that guide item development and selection to measure an individual difference characteristic. Although sometimes the theory leads to items that are not obvious in their measurement of a particular construct, this strategy typically results in transparent items—items for which test takers can readily identify the underlying construct measured. An important criticism of this strategy is its reliance on expert judgment. In its pure form, this method of scale construction is only as good as the theory or an expert's insight. Another important criticism is that items are easily faked, with or without coaching. However, with factual biodata items, faking is lying, and as we will see later, there are effective deterrents to faking (and lying).

In contrast with empirical scoring procedures that capitalize on differences between how higher and lower performers on a criterion variable respond to a biodata measure (or any other predictor measure), rational scoring procedures do not require developmental samples, nor are estimates of their criterion-related validity subject to shrinkage. They do not involve capitalizing on chance. Instead, rational scoring procedures capitalize on the expertise and insight of the test developer or theorist. Rational methods require high-quality definitions of the construct to be measured or criterion to be predicted.

Following are examples of rationally or expert-developed measures and scoring procedures of biographical information:

Point Method

- Requires a task or functional job analysis that subject matter experts (SMEs) review to understand the work and the requirements of the work.
- SMEs specify type and length of education, specific experiences, and so forth that they think provide applicants with the skills and experiences to perform the work as indicated by the job analysis.
- SMEs assign points (weights) to each item (experience, training class, and so forth) identified in the previous step to reflect its relevance to the work. This process yields a rating schedule specifying points (weights) associated with possible applicant background experiences.
- Trained analysts examine an applicant's biographical information and, using the rating schedule, assign points to the applicant's experiences, knowledge, and skills.

Equal or Unit Weighting of Items and Item-Options Method

- Biodata items are generated using, for example, the Mumford and Stokes item-generation method.
- Response options are assigned weights. For example, if there are three response options, such as "more often," "about as often," and "less often," the weights are often 1, 2, 3 or 3, 2, 1 depending on the positive or negative relationship expected between the option and the construct measured or criterion to be predicted.

Accomplishment Record Method

- The critical incident method of job analysis provides the constructs and definitions for the stem of each item.
- Rating principles and scales are developed for each construct or item by (an example of the rating principles and an accomplishment-anchored scale for one construct is shown in Exhibits 5.1 and 5.2, respectively):
  - Gathering a sample of accomplishments from people similar to the applicant pool for each construct (item)

Exhibit 5.1. Rating Principles for the Assertive Advocacy Construct of an Accomplishment Record for Economists

Assertive Advocacy

General definition: Being assertive, forceful, and competitive in promoting the appropriate viewpoint, whether it is an independent idea, another economist's, or the result of a team effort; challenging others to defend or support their positions.

Guidelines for ratings: In assertive advocacy, accomplishments at the lower levels represent a straightforward presentation of position in a situation where forceful assertion is not required. At higher levels, accomplishments are of two types: attempts to resolve conceptual disagreement with other professionals and attempts to influence the general orientation of working groups. Persuasive efforts are often successful. At the highest levels, accomplishments focus on affecting the outcome of major cases and projects. This may occur in a formal setting, for example, while serving as an expert witness or participating in settlement negotiations or in less formal presentations to other staff members.

- Having SMEs rate the accomplishments
- Inducing the principles underlying the rating process
- Selecting benchmarks for points on the rating continuum
- Respondents provide written autobiographical descriptions of what they have done that demonstrates their most significant achievement or accomplishment relevant to the construct (item).

Exhibit 5.2. Rating Scale for the Assertive Advocacy Construct of an Accomplishment Record for Economists

ASSERTIVE ADVOCACY

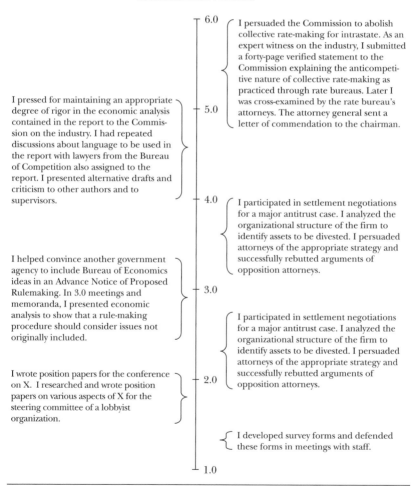

6.0   I persuaded the Commission to abolish collective rate-making for intrastate. As an expert witness on the industry, I submitted a forty-page verified statement to the Commission explaining the anticompetitive nature of collective rate-making as practiced through rate bureaus. Later I was cross-examined by the rate bureau's attorneys. The attorney general sent a letter of commendation to the chairman.

I pressed for maintaining an appropriate degree of rigor in the economic analysis contained in the report to the Commission on the industry. I had repeated discussions about language to be used in the report with lawyers from the Bureau of Competition also assigned to the report. I presented alternative drafts and criticism to other authors and to supervisors.

5.0

4.0   I participated in settlement negotiations for a major antitrust case. I analyzed the organizational structure of the firm to identify assets to be divested. I persuaded attorneys of the appropriate strategy and successfully rebutted arguments of opposition attorneys.

I helped convince another government agency to include Bureau of Economics ideas in an Advance Notice of Proposed Rulemaking. In 3.0 meetings and memoranda, I presented economic analysis to show that a rule-making procedure should consider issues not originally included.

3.0

I participated in settlement negotiations for a major antitrust case. I analyzed the organizational structure of the firm to identify assets to be divested. I persuaded attorneys of the appropriate strategy and successfully rebutted arguments of opposition attorneys.

I wrote position papers for the conference on X. I researched and wrote position papers on various aspects of X for the steering committee of a lobbyist organization.

2.0

I developed survey forms and defended these forms in meetings with staff.

1.0

- Respondents provide outcome information and the name and contact information of a person who can verify the autobiographical description.
- Applicant autobiographical descriptions are scored using the rating principles and scales either by trained experts or a computerized scoring algorithm.

Behavior-Based Interview and Rating Scales Method

- Questions are often derived from a behavioral analysis of work.
- Rating scales are developed by identifying possible responses to the questions and assigning points to the answers.
- An interviewer asks the applicant the questions (for example, "What did you do when . . . ?") and then scores the responses using the behavior-based rating scales.

A comparison of rational/construct-oriented scoring approaches indicates that all but the traditional point method have criterion-related validity comparable to empirically generated scoring approaches. The traditional point method is included in this review because of its popularity. It is not, however, a recommended approach. The other methods do demonstrate good criterion-related validity and have advantages and disadvantages that the test developer and test user should evaluate and choose depending upon their circumstances.

One of the advantages of the Accomplishment Record method (Hough, 1984) is the use of raters to score the accomplishments and experiences. In many situations, a process that is devoid of human judgment is considered a negative. Although the rating process is more subjective than using a mathematical formula, the rating principles and guidelines enable highly job-relevant, unique autobiographical information to be scored reliably. Interrater agreement indexes indicate good reliability for the ratings—approximately .80. Computerized scoring of text or open-ended responses is possible. Computerized scoring of text is in its infancy but is likely to become more common with advances in technology. An algorithm is developed that captures the policy of the expert raters and rating principles, guidelines, and scales.

The effectiveness of the algorithm can be evaluated by examining the relationship of the computer-generated scores with expert-generated scores, as well as the relationship of the computer-generated scores with valued external criteria such as job performance. At this time, development costs and the validity of computerized scoring of text are still hurdles, although they are becoming less so. Meta-analysis of the relationship between scores on the Accomplishment Record (sometimes called the behavioral consistency method) and job performance indicates observed criterion-related validities are in the mid-.20s (McDaniel et al., 1988a).

The behavior-based interview method is similar to the Accomplishment Record method. The important difference is, of course, that a person asks the question and the respondent typically responds orally rather than in written form. Multiple meta-analyses indicate that the more structured the interview questions and rating process are, the higher the criterion-related validity is. Given that the interview questions are job relevant and the questions and rating process are structured, observed criterion-related validities can be expected to be in the .20s and even higher. As with the Accomplishment Record, the process involves human judgment. The interview, however, takes significantly more human time than the Accomplishment Record.

Comparison of Inductive, Deductive, and External Strategies

The purpose and circumstances of the assessment are important when comparing and evaluating scale construction methods. Depending on the purpose and circumstances of the assessment, one method may be better than the others. If, for example, construct validity is important, the external (empirical) scale construction method is not a good choice. The internal or rational scale construction methods are more appropriate. Frequently the purpose of measurement is to predict some future outcome. Thus, the expected level of accuracy with which each of the three scale construction methods predicts valued outcomes is of vital importance. An obvious example is personnel selection, where accuracy of prediction is critically important to the organization and individuals involved. Unlike the inductive or deductive (rational) methods, which seek to understand and measure a construct, a presumed strength of the external method is its focus on predicting an external criterion of interest such as job performance, training performance, turnover, or satisfaction.

Hough and Paullin (1994) gathered criterion-related validities for each of the three scale development methods and compared the results. Their conclusion was that the three scale construction strategies produce reasonably similar levels of criterion-related validity for predicting external criteria, although the internal construction technique fared somewhat less well than the others. The criterion-related validities of the rational method were, on average, slightly higher (.01) than the cross-validities of the empirical method and about .06 higher than the validities of the internal method.

Yet even when the purpose is selection and criterion-related validity is of paramount importance, construct validity is also important. An important goal of science is to understand and predict phenomena. Meta-analyses of validities of construct-oriented scales for predicting specific criteria are more likely to lead to useful generalizations than are meta-analyses of heterogeneous scales that lack a coherent theme. Construct-oriented scales are building blocks in the development of scientific knowledge. Although both science and practice benefit from the development and use of construct-oriented scales, no one scale construction method is inherently better than the others.

All three approaches have advantages and disadvantages and are more or less appropriate depending on the purpose of the assessment. There is no clearly right or wrong approach, and scale developers often blend features of the three strategies, producing hybrid scale construction methods.

New Developments in Scale Construction Methods

A hybrid approach that appears to solve some of the problems associated with the traditional inductive, deductive, and external scale development methods is the ideal point response scale development method. A data-driven, construct-oriented approach, it assumes that people endorse items that are closer to their true trait level than items that are further away. Thus, even if items and item response options are infrequently endorsed, they are retained if they effectively measure and differentiate people at the ends of the continuum. Scale construction strategies that rely on factor analysis to identify high-quality items discard items that are infrequently endorsed because of their resulting low item-total scale correlations. Instead of using factor analysis, factor loadings, item-total scale correlations, and alpha coefficients to determine the usefulness of an item for a scale, ideal point response methods rely on item-response theory analyses to evaluate items. Scales developed using this approach more accurately measure people high and low on the construct and without sacrificing criterion-related validity (Chernyshenko, Stark, Drasgow, & Roberts, 2007). Although the correlation coefficient (an index of criterion-related validity) is insensitive to minor changes in the rank order of people, the effect of deleting items at the extremes of the continuum, such as with the traditional internal method of scale construction, may be one reason the internal method has, in the past, produced somewhat lower criterion-related validities (on average) than the rational or external methods.

It is important to understand the basic methods, their differences, and when each approach or elements of each approach contribute to quality measurement aligned with the purpose of the assessment. The key is attention to the purpose of the assessment, along with careful attention to activities that affect the quality of the assessment, regardless of the scale development method.

Characteristics of Criterion-Valid Items

Research that investigates the validity of items regardless of item-generation method and scoring development method indicates that item-level validity is associated with certain item-level characteristics. Analyses of the characteristics of items that demonstrate validity indicate that the following item characteristics are associated with higher criterion-related validity (Barge, 1987; Lefkowitz, Gebbia, Balsam, & Dunn, 1999; Mabe & West, 1982):

* Verifiability
* Indirectness (opinions of others about the respondent)
* Relevance to the job or criterion of interest

The importance of the third characteristic, relevance to the job or criterion of interest, is obvious and requires no further explanation. However, the process through which the first two characteristics, verifiability and indirectness, affect validity is unknown. One hypothesis is that the extent to which responses are intentionally distorted is reduced when the responses are verifiable (as well as when respondents are informed that the information might be verified or that they will be asked to elaborate on their responses in an interview). Similarly, responses obtained from persons other than the target person are likely to suffer less from intentional distortion than information provided by the target person. Test developers are well advised to incorporate these characteristics into their test items.

Validity Generalization and Other Factors That Affect Usefulness of Biodata Measures

Generalizability of validity is probably the most important issue when evaluating the usefulness of biodata measures. It goes far beyond whether the validity of an empirically developed scoring key generalizes to the holdout sample. The issue of validity generalization considers the stability of biodata validities across organizations, national boundaries, and ethnic and cultural groups, as well as testing situations in which people are motivated to respond with less-than-accurate and honest answers. For example, do criterion-related validities obtained in testing settings with respondents who have little or no motivation to distort their responses (such as in no-consequences settings) compare favorably with criterion-related validities obtained in high-stakes applicant testing situations in which people are motivated to distort and even lie about their backgrounds and experiences? Are validities stable across ethnic and cultural groups? Are validities similar across jobs, organizations, and industries? These are important questions for empirically developed as well as rationally developed scales.

All of the considerations and factors discussed above are relevant. For example, well-defined constructs and high-quality job analyses are critically important. When empirically based construction methods are used, high-quality criterion measurement or carefully formed criterion groups are also critically important, as is a high ratio of respondents in the developmental sample to number of predictors, as high as 5 or 10 to 1. If the validity does not generalize to the holdout sample, a group of people highly similar to those in the developmental sample, the validity is certainly not likely to generalize to people who are different—for example, people of different ethnic or cultural backgrounds, nationalities, gender, age, or different motivations, jobs, and organizations.

In general, research indicates that if all the considerations and factors are properly addressed during the initial development of the measure, validities do generalize. This does mean that the different circumstances and populations in which the measure will be used need to be adequately represented in the initial development of the measure.

In the situation of high-stakes testing, additional considerations are important. Research indicates that all biodata measures can be distorted. However, distortion and lying can be minimized in these ways:

- Verifiable items are included in the biodata measure.
- Respondents are warned that their responses might be verified, and some responses are verified.
- Respondents are informed that they might be asked to explain some of their responses in an interview, and some respondents are interviewed about some of their responses.
- Consequences occur when distortion or lying is detected.

In practice, all of these efforts need to be examined for unintended consequences. For example, overly negative or severe consequences can have a chilling effect on the respondent group, perhaps resulting in complaints and an undesired reduction in the applicant pool. If the detection strategy triggers a negative consequence, the detection strategy must be highly accurate. Unjustly accusing people of distorting their responses or lying is not good, and the consequences for having done so can be time-consuming and costly. A policy of following up or checking some answers of all respondents or a random sample of respondents is less likely to engender negative reaction and animosity.

Questions to Ask When Evaluating Biodata Measures

1. What is the purpose of the measurement? How will the scores be interpreted and used? With whom will the measure be used? What are the situations in which the scores will be used?
2. What kind of validity evidence is presented? Is the validation evidence appropriate for the way the scores will be used? Is the validity estimate likely to generalize to ways in which and the populations to whom the instrument will be used? Have circumstances changed? Is the evidence reasonably current?
3. What scale development strategy was used? Is it appropriate for the purpose of the measurements and their intended use? Is it based on theory, hypotheses, or empirical differences in a criterion or criterion groups?
4. What item-generation method was used? How was the domain of behavior to be measured defined?
   • Is the construct definition high quality? Does it provide adequate information about what is to be measured?
   • Does it lend itself to the generation of biodata items that measure that specific construct or domain of behavior?
   • Are equivalent forms needed? If yes, is the scale development strategy amenable to generating them?
   • Are respondents able to answer each item? Is there an escape clause? Is there at least one response option that every respondent can endorse?
5. What kind of item or item-response scoring method was used during scale development?
   • If scoring was empirically developed to differentiate people on a criterion, was the criterion well measured? Were the criteria groups well formed on the basis of their differences on the criteria? Or are there differences that are likely to be extraneous to the criterion of interest?
   • Does the strategy capitalize on chance in the developmental sample? If yes, was the number of people in the developmental sample large enough to justify its use for the

present purpose? If yes, was cross-validity calculated? How much shrinkage occurred? Does the evidence support the use of the measure for the population and situation intended?

6. What information is provided about accuracy of measurement and reliability? What reliability estimates are provided? If they are indexes of homogeneity of items in the measure, is that the appropriate type of reliability? Are test-retest reliabilities provided and adequate? If expert judgment is part of the scoring, what is the interrater reliability? Are the levels of reliability and accuracy of measurement appropriate for the intended use of the measurements?

7. Is the population for which and the setting in which the measure will be used similar to the developmental sample? What information is provided to indicate that the measure will generalize to populations and settings not included in the development of the measure?

8. Is the measure fair for protected groups? Are mean scores for different ethnic and age groups similar?

9. How costly is the measure to develop? How costly is the measure to administer once developed?

10. What are respondents' reactions to the biodata measure likely to be?
   - Are they likely to distort their responses? If yes, are deterrents in place?
   - Are they likely to withdraw from the testing situation? If yes, what changes can be implemented that might alleviate the problem?

Conclusion

The old adage that past behavior is the best predictor of future behavior may be true, but analyzing past behavior to predict future behavior is not a simple undertaking. Many factors interfere with the success of such an undertaking. Nonetheless, we know a number of scale-development activities that improve the accuracy of predicting an individual's future behavior, the most basic of which is to understand both what is to be predicted and what in the past is relevant.

References

Barge, B. N. (1987). Characteristics of biodata items and their relationship to validity. In S. D. Ashworth (Chair), *Biodata in the 80s and beyond*. Symposium conducted at the 95th annual meeting of the American Psychological Association, New York.

Bliesener, T. (1996). Methodological moderators in validating biographical data in personnel selection. *Journal of Occupational and Organizational Psychology, 69*, 107–120.

Campbell, J. P. (1974). *Psychometric theory in industrial and organizational psychology* (Rep. No. 2001). Arlington, VA: Personnel and Training Research Programs, Office of Naval Research.

Chernyshenko, O. S., Stark, S., Drasgow, F., & Roberts, B. W. (2007). Constructing personality scales under the assumptions of an ideal point response process: Toward increasing the flexibility of personality measures. *Psychological Assessment, 19*, 88–106.

Devlin, S. E., Abrahams, N. M., & Edwards, J. E. (1992). Empirical keying of biographical data: Cross-validity as a function of scaling procedure and sample size. *Military Psychology, 4*, 119–136.

Fine, S. A., & Cronshaw, S. (1994). The role of job analysis in establishing the validity of biodata. In G. S. Stokes, M. D. Mumford, & W. A. Owens (Eds.), *The biodata handbook: Theory, research, and application* (pp. 39–64). Palo Alto, CA: Consulting Psychologists Press.

Guion, R. M. (1965). *Personnel testing*. New York: McGraw-Hill.

Hough, L. M. (1984). Development and evaluation of the "Accomplishment Record" method of selecting and promoting professionals. *Journal of Applied Psychology, 69*, 135–146.

Hough, L. M., & Paullin, C. (1994). Construct-oriented scale construction: The rational approach. In G. S. Stokes, M. D. Mumford, & W. A. Owens (Eds.), *The biodata handbook: Theory, research, and application* (pp. 109–146). Palo Alto, CA: Consulting Psychologists Press.

Huffcutt, A. I., & Arthur, W. Jr. (1994). Hunter and Hunter (1984) revisited: Interview validity for entry-level jobs. *Journal of Applied Psychology, 79*, 184–190.

Hunter, J. E., & Hunter, R. F. (1984). Validity and utility of alternative predictors of job performance. *Psychological Bulletin, 96*(1), 72–98.

Janz, T., Hellervik, L., & Gilmore, D. C. (1986). *Behavior description interviewing: New, accurate, cost effective*. Needham Heights, MA: Allyn & Bacon.

Lefkowitz, J., Gebbia, M. I., Balsam, T., & Dunn, L. (1999). Dimensions of biodata items and their relationships to item validity. *Journal of Occupational and Organizational Psychology, 72*, 331–350.

Mabe, P. A. III, & West, S. G. (1982). Validity of self-evaluation of ability: A review and meta-analysis. *Journal of Applied Psychology, 67,* 280–296.

McDaniel, M. A., Schmidt, F. L., & Hunter, J. E. (1988a). A meta-analysis of the validity of methods for rating training and experience in personnel selection. *Personnel Psychology, 41,* 283–314.

McDaniel, M. A., Schmidt, F. L., & Hunter, J. E. (1988b). Job experience correlates of job performance. *Journal of Applied Psychology, 73,* 327–330.

Mumford, M. D., Costanza, D. P., Connelly, M. S., & Johnson, J. F. (1996). Item generation procedures and background data scales: Implications for construct and criterion-related validity. *Personnel Psychology, 49,* 361–398.

Mumford, M. D., Reiter-Palmon, R., & Snell, A. F. (1994). Background data and development: Structural issues in the application of life history measures. In G. S. Stokes, M. D. Mumford, & W. A. Owens (Eds.), *The biodata handbook: Theory, research, and application* (pp. 555–581). Palo Alto, CA: Consulting Psychologists Press.

Mumford, M. D., Stokes, G. S., & Owens, W. A. (1990). *Patterns of life history: The ecology of human individuality.* Mahwah, NJ: Erlbaum.

Ng, T.W.H., Eby, L. T., Sorensen, K. L., & Feldman, D. C. (2005). Predictors of objective and subjective career success: A meta-analysis. *Personnel Psychology, 58,* 367–408.

Quiñones, M. A., Ford, J. K., & Teachout, M. S. (1995). The relationship between work experience and job performance: A conceptual and meta-analytic review. *Personnel Psychology, 48,* 887–910.

Russell, C. J., Mattson, J., Devlin, S. E., & Atwater, D. (1990). Predictive validity of biodata items generated from retrospective life experience essays. *Journal of Applied Psychology, 75,* 569–580.

Schmidt, F. L., Hunter, J. E., Outerbridge, A. N., & Goff, S. (1988). Joint relation of experience and ability with job performance: Test of three hypotheses. *Journal of Applied Psychology, 73,* 46–57.

Schmitt, N., Gooding, R. Z., Noe, R. A., & Kirsch, M. (1984). Meta-analyses of validity studies published between 1964 and 1982 and the investigation of study characteristics. *Personnel Psychology, 37,* 407–422.

Steinhaus, S. D., & Waters, B. K. (1991). Biodata and the application of a psychometric perspective. *Military Psychology, 3,* 1–23.

Stokes, G. S., & Cooper, L. A. (2004). Biodata. In M. Hersen (Ed.-in-Chief) & J. C. Thomas (Vol. Ed.), *Comprehensive handbook of psychological assessment: Vol. 4. Industrial and organizational assessment* (pp. 243–268). Hoboken, NJ: John Wiley.

CHAPTER 6

KNOWLEDGE AND SKILL

Teresa L. Russell

When people think about tests, they probably best remember academic achievement tests they took in school or to get into college. While achievement testing is high-stakes and big business, there are many other important uses of knowledge and skill measures. Licensure and certification tests serve the purpose of protecting the public from incompetent or unsafe practice. Hundreds of occupations across a variety of industries, such as health care, finance, and construction, require knowledge or skill testing to ensure a basic level of competence. Knowledge and skill testing, using work samples, for example, is commonly used for selection or promotion. These assessments can also serve as criterion measures in research projects to validate entry-level selection tests. In the military, scores on information tests such as general science and electronics information facilitate the assignment of new recruits to military occupations where they can best build on existing knowledge and skill. Clearly knowledge and skill tests play an important role in academic and career choices as well as job opportunities for most Americans.

This chapter defines *knowledge* and *skill* and describes different types of knowledge and skill measures, measure development, psychometric and operational considerations, and measurement challenges.

Knowledge and Skill Definitions

A general theory of performance (Campbell, McCloy, Oppler, & Sager, 1993) offers useful definitions of knowledge and skill. According to that theory, individual differences in performance are a function of three determinants: declarative knowledge (DK), procedural knowledge and skill (PKS), and motivation (M). DK is knowledge about facts, such as knowledge of physiology or computer technology. PKS refers to knowing what to do and how to do it—for example, knowing how to install a wireless network, how to plan and manage one's own time, and how to communicate with others. Motivation reflects choices about whether to expend effort engaging in the behavior, how much effort to expend, and how long to persist with that level of effort. Individual differences in general cognitive ability, personality traits, interests, education, training, experience, commitment, and values are determinants or predictors of DK, PKS, and M.

The idea that interests and abilities are determinants of knowledge and skill is not new. When World War II researchers needed to quickly build tests to classify tens of thousands of recruits into military jobs, they theorized that topical information tests (general knowledge of aviation and knowledge of tools, for example) would be objective measures of the recruits' interests and abilities related to the topic (Fruchter, 1947). Regardless of whether information tests were direct measures of achievement or surrogate measures of interests, information tests served them well, proving to be highly valid for predicting training success and improving the classification of recruits into occupations.

Declarative Knowledge

Declarative knowledge is more than a simple memory for facts. It requires an understanding of facts and principles and how they fit together. Declarative knowledge test items, often in multiple-choice or other objective test formats, can be thought of as lying on a continuum of application, where items at one end elicit only a comprehension of facts. Further along the continuum, items require analysis and synthesis—more complex levels of cognition. Six levels of cognition that are widely used to categorize items used in academic testing are knowledge, comprehension, application, analysis, synthesis, and evaluation (Bloom, Engelhart, Furst, Hill, & Krathwohl, 1956).

Measure Development

The first step in DK measure development is to develop a test plan, shown in Table 6.1, that compares worker characteristics to be measured against possible measurement methods. Worker characteristics to be measured, listed along the rows, should result from a job analysis. Possible measurement methods, derived from review of the research literature, are listed in the columns. Judgments about the quality with which different measurement methods are likely to measure the worker characteristics appear in the cells of the matrix. Table 6.1 shows an example test plan for an information technology (IT) job at Firm XYZ. As shown, the plan is to use a technology knowledge test to measure three areas of knowledge identified in a job analysis as being important for the IT job, reading and mathematics tests to measure those abilities, and a situational judgment test and a work sample test to get at other skills needed for the job.

Once the decision has been made to develop a knowledge test, it is important to create a blueprint for the test indicating the allocation of items across particular content domains. Table 6.2 provides an example test blueprint for the technology knowledge test for the IT job at Firm XYZ. Content allocations can be computed using quantitative data from job analysis survey ratings or from subject matter experts' (SME) holistic allocations of items to content domains. One useful approach is to combine both strategies. This involves collecting job analysis ratings of importance for specific knowledge statements, using the job analysis data to create preliminary weights for the knowledge domains, and asking experienced SMEs to make adjustments in the final weighting plan. These adjustments are often needed because survey knowledge statements are typically correlated with each other and varied in their level of specificity. When job analysis ratings are combined empirically, the results may overemphasize domains that contain numerous specific statements or highly correlated knowledge. Other operational issues, such as whether the knowledge or skill is testable given constraints on testing methods and testing time, are also important to consider. This makes it difficult to use job analysis ratings alone in creating the test blueprint. Raymond and Neustel (2006) provide a useful

Table 6.1. Hypothetical Test Plan

	Measures				
Worker Characteristics	Technology Knowledge Test	Reading Comprehension Test	Mathematics Test	Situational Judgment Test	Work Sample Test
1. Knowledge of network security concepts and procedures [examples given]	X				
2. Knowledge of network configuration including hardware and software [examples given]	X				
3. Knowledge of the function and operation of typical personal computer hardware and software [examples given]	X				
4. Skill in helping customers solve computer problems				X	
5. Skill in using the general features of office software including [examples given]					X
6. Ability to perform mathematical operations using binary and hexadecimal numbers			X		
7. Ability to read and comprehend technical documents		X			

Table 6.2. Hypothetical Technology Knowledge Test Blueprint

	Weighting		
Knowledge Domains and Subdomains	Domain Weight (%)	Within-Domain Weight (%)	Overall Test Weights (%)
1. Network security concepts and procedures	20%		
Malware (trojans, viruses, worms) concepts and operations		60%	12%
Firewall strengths and weaknesses		30	6
Wireless security		10	2
2. Network configuration	30		
Network protocols		20	6
Network architecture		30	9
Network hardware		50	15
3. Function and operation of PC hardware and software	50		
Basic computer concepts (e.g., memory, bytes)		50	25
Workstation assembly (with peripherals)		20	10
Operating system fundamentals		30	15
	100%		100%

discussion of approaches for using job analysis information to establish weights in a test blueprint.

Types of Declarative Knowledge Items

Another aspect of the test specification process is to determine what types of item formats will be used and in what proportions. Everyone knows what a multiple-choice item looks like. It has a stem and usually three to five possible response options. There are several kinds of other objective test formats such as open-ended, true-false, multiple mark, and matching—for example:

MULTIPLE CHOICE

- Which of the following devices links two networks together and controls how packets are exchanged?
  a. Bridge
  b. Hub
  c. Router
  d. Switch

OPEN-ENDED

- A _____connects computers to the network, sending packets to all ports.

MULTIPLE MARK

Which of the following describes the functioning of a hub? Select all that apply.
- Extends the range of network signals traveling through cable
- Links two networks together
- Connects computers to the network
- Combines two networks or partitions in a single network
- Controls how packets are exchanged
- Sends packets to all ports
- Sends packets only to the recipient's ports

As these examples show, the same content can be written for different formats. Open-ended items require a computer or a human to match the examinee's response to a scoring key. The open-ended format has become popular for discrete entries such as numerical responses to mathematical items since numerical responses can typically be computer scored. Matching narra-tive, open-ended responses from an examinee to a key is a more sophisticated problem. In multiple-mark items, the examinee selects one or more procedures that are appropriate from a separate listing of procedures. True-false items suffer from the problem that there is a 50 percent probability of guessing the item correctly. Multiple-mark items use a multiple-choice format, but ask examinees to mark the correct answers and leave incorrect ones blank. This format suffers from a few problems, in particular, the inability to distinguish missing responses from ones intentionally left blank.

The choice of item format can affect weighting and scaling decisions. Multiple-choice and true-false items are usually dichotomously scored. Multiple-mark and matching items are polytomous. For example, the matching item in the previous examples could yield a maximum of four points if the examinee made all matches correctly. Or the examinee might receive partial credit for one, two, or three correct matches. So would this item count as four items toward the test blueprint? One concern has to do with attributing too much of the blueprint to one concept—in this case, to network hardware in our example blueprint, particularly if the total number of items on the test is to be small. Since longer items take more response time, fewer can be included, making adequate coverage of the desired content more difficult.

Another issue has to do with the psychometric model to be used in analyzing the data. Classical test statistics were designed for dichotomously scored tests and do not conform well to polytomous items. There are item-response theory (IRT) models that are appropriate for analyzing partial credit or polytomously scored items. However, the IRT models for polytomous items involve estimating numerous parameters and, in turn, require very large sample sizes to estimate those parameters adequately. In many situations, the test developer will not have samples large enough for the IRT-based methods.

Operational Considerations

Operationally, MC and other objective format items have many advantages. Items are relatively easy to develop and replace, and they can be machine scored. Development, administration, and maintenance costs are low relative to other formats. Since most tests of DK are developed to contain many items, individual items are not thought to be highly memorable. Therefore, outside of outright attempts to cheat or steal the test, multiple-choice items are thought to be fairly resistant to compromise.

Multiple-choice tests, in particular, are desirable because a century or so of research with this item type has cumulated in well-regarded methods. Classical test statistics and IRT methods for MC tests have received substantial research and are mature technologies. Procedures for setting passing scores on MC tests, while never perfect, have been studied and refined for many years. For these reasons, MC tests of DK are appropriate for most operational situations.

Psychometric Properties

One main advantage of multiple-choice tests lies in their proven psychometric quality. These tests typically yield highly reliable scores (with observed reliabilities commonly in the .80 to .90 range). There is strong evidence of the validity of multiple-choice tests of job knowledge for many occupations (Hunter, 1986). On the downside, objective job knowledge tests yield a white-black subgroup difference of about three-quarters of a standard deviation between the two means (Ford, Kraiger, & Schechtman, 1986).

Measurement Challenges

The two measurement challenges in DK testing are enhancing authenticity and minimizing obsolescence. Multiple-choice tests have been criticized in recent years for their perceived lack of authenticity—a failure to reflect real-world application of knowledge and skill. The argument is that simple declarative knowledge items may not adequately reflect the complexity of the work environment. However, multiple-choice knowledge test items can be made more authentic by writing items that require the examinee to apply knowledge. Enhancing authenticity may also have the added advantage of enhancing applicants' perceptions of fairness. Test items that have a strong relationship to job content are more likely to be perceived as fair (Rynes, 1993).

Perceptions of one's own performance are also important determinants of how a measure will be viewed. Not surprisingly, applicants tend to dislike tests on which they perform poorly and like ones on which they do well. Even so, research suggests that applicants give more weight to the credibility of the instrument and its scoring than their own performance on it.

Minimizing obsolescence might be a more difficult problem, depending on the content area of the test. In high-technology settings, test items can quickly become outdated due to technological change. Some software certification programs revise their test items continuously; that would clearly be impracticable for many testing programs. In a recent effort to develop a measure of information and communications technology literacy, we adopted a policy of avoiding reference to specific software and versions of software because those versions change rapidly. We chose to focus on understanding the use and functioning of types of software. We also asked subject matter experts to rate the rapidity of change for job-relevant technology knowledge areas and flag test items having content likely to change. In doing so, we found that certain domains in our test blueprint were more dynamic, and we revised the blueprint to emphasize stable areas.

Obsolescence can also be a result of changes in the applicant pool. For example, in an information and communications technology literacy project, we found that high school curricula are continuously moving toward better technology education. This means that test items that are difficult for job applicants today might be easier for the job applicants of tomorrow. Therefore, there is no way to avoid the need to track item parameter drift shifts in item characteristics over time. Assessing drift is computationally identical to using IRT methods to detect differential item functioning (DIF) or item bias. Such methods compare the test item parameters for groups of people (such as whites and black or males and females). An item would be biased if individuals from different groups who have the same standing on the trait measured by the test have unequal chances of responding correctly. In item parameter drift analysis, groups of subjects are defined by administrative time periods instead of demographic variables.

Applications

Declarative knowledge testing is useful in situations where the candidates for a job, professional licensure, or an academic program need to have a basic understanding of particular topics to perform well in their job, profession, or school. These applications include educational testing, licensure and certification testing, promotion testing, and selection testing for occupations where knowledge will be required on entry to the job. Knowledge tests are also appropriate for identifying occupations in which candidates may perform well, such as in classification into military occupations. DK measures are not useful for entry-level occupations that do not require knowledge or skill on entering the job.

Another factor to consider is the DK construct to be measured. Some constructs may be less testable than others. Testing knowledge areas that are undergoing rapid change should be undertaken with awareness that tests of rapidly changing areas require frequent maintenance and analysis to identify item parameter drift.

Procedural Knowledge and Skill

Measures of PKS require examinees to demonstrate what should be done and have the skill to do it. A host of measures can be thought of as assessing PKS, including work samples or simulations, situational interviews, performance tests, and situational judgment tests (SJTs). They vary in the extent to which they emphasize knowledge or skill and exhibit fidelity to the work environment. For example, work samples require examinees to perform a task, and in doing so, examinees must demonstrate procedural knowledge and skill, often in a simulation or scenario intended to mirror the job. In contrast, SJTs and situational interviews are abstractions of the work environment. They present scenarios and ask the examinee how he or she would perform (or has performed) in the situation. The emphasis is on procedural knowledge because the test does not require the examinee to demonstrate the skill. SJTs and situational interviews might be thought of as low-fidelity measures, while work samples are high-fidelity simulations.

Types of Procedural Knowledge and Skill Measures

This section focuses on the two ends of the fidelity spectrum: SJTs and work samples, where work samples can include very high-fidelity simulations.

Situational Judgment Tests

SJTs provide a verbal or written description of a scenario and a list of potential actions that could be taken. There are two main types of response instructions: behavioral tendency and knowledge based. Behavioral tendency instructions ask the respondent to indicate what he or she would be most and least likely to do in the situation (Motowidlo, Hanson, & Crafts, 1997). Knowledge-based instructions require the respondent to draw on prior knowledge in making responses. They ask the respondent to rate the effectiveness of the actions or indicate which actions are most and least effective—for example:

You work in IT operations at Firm XYZ, and today it is your turn to work on the help line. An employee in marketing calls you. He is steaming mad because his computer went down, and he fears he lost his work. He begins by yelling at you about how the new technology is always failing. You think that you might be able to retrieve his work, depending on the specific problem. Rate the effectiveness of each of the following actions you could take using this 1 to 7 scale:

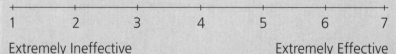

| 1 | 2 | 3 | 4 | 5 | 6 | 7 |

Extremely Ineffective   Extremely Effective

A. Tell the customer that you will talk to your boss and get back to him.
B. Ask the customer to check to ensure his computer is plugged in correctly.
C. Tell the customer that you can't fix it unless he shuts up and answers some questions for you.
D. Allow the customer to vent for a moment. Then begin asking questions to diagnose the problem.
E. Reassure the customer that you can fix the problem.

There are trade-offs with the two types of instructions. Knowledge-based instructions tend to result in greater resistance to faking and somewhat higher correlations with general cognitive ability (McDaniel, Hartman, Whetzel, & Grubb, 2007). SJTs using the behavioral tendency instructions tend to be more strongly related to personality variables. Even so, the criterion-related validities for tests using the two types of instructions are comparable (McDaniel et al., 2007).

Work Samples

"A work sample test requires examinees to perform a task or an essential part of a task . . . under conditions similar to those in which the task is performed on the job" (Felker, Curtin, & Rose, 2007). Work samples, also referred to as performance tests and simulations, have no one format; they are as varied as the plethora of tasks in the world of work itself. Typically a work sample measures performance on a task or a cluster of tasks that go together or measure the same skill.

Figure 6.1. A Performance-Based Item

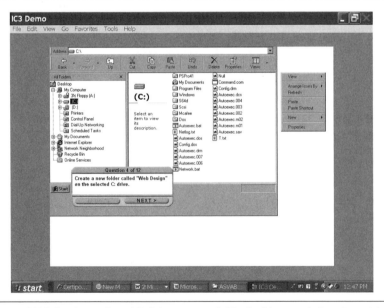

Work samples vary greatly in their complexity. In recent years, computer-administered testing has facilitated the development of short performance-based items, like the one shown in Figure 6.1. It asks the examinee to perform a very narrow task of creating a folder called "Web Design." A work sample that is moderate in complexity appears in Figure 6.2. It provides a scenario and asks the examinee to perform a database search in response to a customer's question. Even more complex work samples can simulate the work environment, such as flying an aircraft, controlling air traffic, or monitoring refinery equipment to ensure safe operation. Figure 6.3 shows a screen shot from the Console Operator Basic Requirements Assessment (COBRA), which simulates a refinery process. The exam takes four hours: two hours for training, one hour of practice, and one hour for four scored test scenarios.

Figure 6.2. A Moderately Complex Work Sample

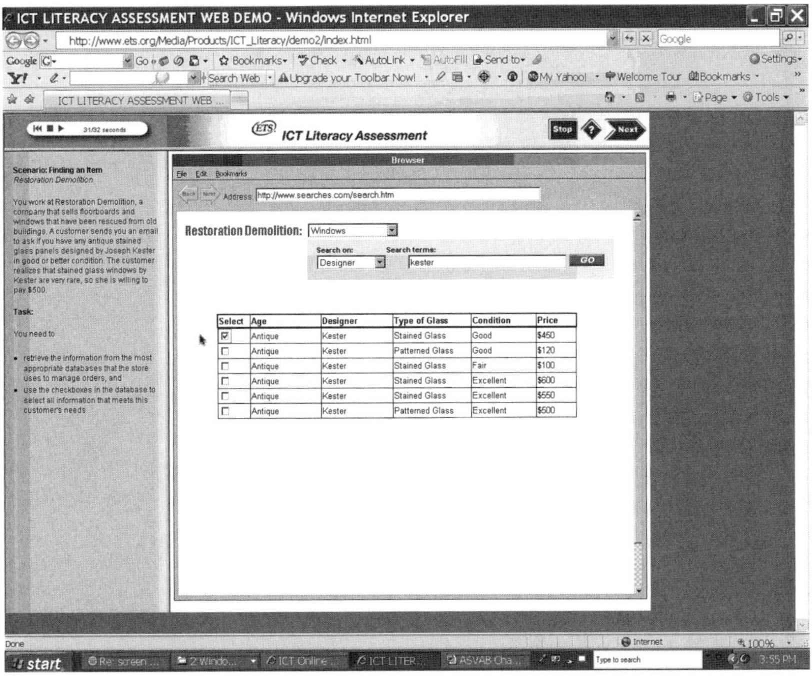

Source: © 2009 Educational Testing Service. All rights reserved. Used with permission. http://www.ets.org.

Figure 6.3. A Highly Complex Work Sample or Simulation

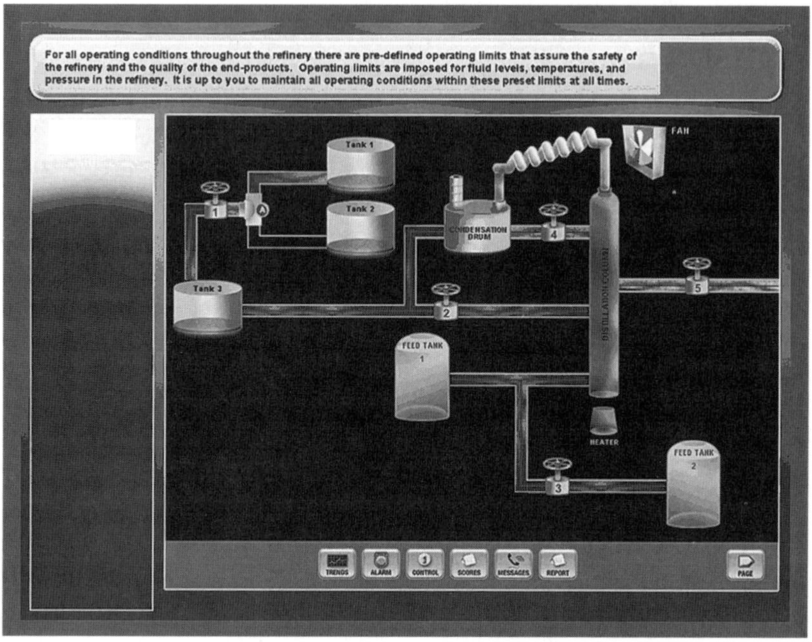

Source: © 2009 Job Performance Systems, Inc. All rights reserved. Used with permission. http://www.getcobra.com.

Measure Development

Developers must consider a number of factors when creating knowledge and skill measures. These measures typically require some level of subject matter expert (SME) input, and developers must determine who has the expertise to serve as an SME. For example, instructors often serve as SMEs for licensure exam development. Job incumbents may be the appropriate SMEs for the development of SJT or other job skill measures. Other development decisions have to do with variations in procedures, format, and scoring methods.

Situational Judgment Tests

SJT developers must make a number of decisions about the content of items, response options, response instructions, and the scoring key. Weekley, Ployhardt, and Holtz (2006) lay out and discuss the many decisions SJT developers must make and the pros and cons of different approaches.

The two primary methods of developing content are the subject matter expert–based (SME-based) approach (Motowidlo et al., 1997) and the construct-oriented approach—based on professional judgment and construct definitions from the research literature (Weekley et al., 2006). The advantages of the SME-based approach are enhanced content validity and greater realism of the response options (actions). On the downside, involving SMEs is more laborious than constructing items based on professional judgment and, perhaps, less generalizable outside the development sample. A construct-oriented approach is also useful if the test is intended to measure constructs from a particular theory. Such instruments have been developed to measure agreeableness and teamwork knowledge and skill.

Motowidlo et al. (1997) provide a step-by-step guide for developing SME-based SJTs. In this approach, the stem for the test question is extracted from situations described in critical incidents or scenarios. The next step is to develop response options. Here, job incumbents and supervisors (SMEs) are asked to write short statements describing actions that could be taken in each situation. This helps ensure that the response options are viable responses to the situation. Researchers analyze the content of the written statements to form the response options. Once the options are developed, a separate group of experienced or high-performing individuals provides responses to the test questions. Their responses provide the basis for the scoring key.

Work Samples

While some developers identify the skill to be measured and then the tasks that require the skill, it is also common to select tasks for measurement based on job analysis data. Linkages between the tasks and the knowledge and skills made during a job analysis can help to identify tasks to test in order to get at particular knowledge and skills.

Selection of which tasks and how many tasks to test is not as straightforward as it may seem. Important, frequently performed, or difficult tasks are candidates for measurement with work samples. If there are distinct domains of work activities, tasks should be sampled within domains. Another consideration is the degree to which the processes and products of the task are measurable. Tasks with distinct, observable steps and products that can be scored are the best candidates for measurement. (Felker et al., 2007, offer a useful overview of methods to select tasks.) The number of tasks to test is also a critical concern; testing few tasks results in greater measurement error. In sum, identifying which and how many tasks to test requires balancing task criticality, feasibility of measurement, and overall coverage of the content specifications.

Scoring protocols must be embedded in the task during development of the work sample. Work sample tests traditionally have required human scorers—people who either observed and rated the performance of a task or evaluated the quality of the product against a rubric. With the move to computer-administered testing, the development of automated scoring schemes for work samples or simulations has become one of the hottest topics in computer-based testing (CBT). The following are several suggestions for the development of scoring schemes (Felker et al., 2007):

- *Score the product.* The process used to perform a task such as setting up a firewall may not matter, but the product is very important.
- *Score process when it matters.* For some tasks, the step-by-step sequence of activities performed is important. Even so, scoring processes is much more difficult than scoring products. Here are some tips:
  - *Avoid scoring processes just because they are convenient* (for example, the number of mouse clicks on a help button). Processes should be theoretically important for accomplishing the task.
  - *Make processes observable.* If processes are to be scored, they must be made observable. For example, unobservable behaviors such as "reviewing," "checking," or "reading" could be tested by having the examinee report about materials reviewed, checked, or read.
  - *Use objective standards for scoring processes.* The performance standards for processes must be as objective as possible.

Standards that rely on the scorer's judgment should be avoided. For example, the standard, "Completes Form X adequately," is too vague; a better standard would articulate how thoroughly and legibly the form must be completed.

- *Query or interview the examinee during the work sample.* The military services have a long tradition of work sample testing. They have found that work samples can be unfeasible for any number of reasons, such as excessive administration time, processes that are unobservable, or performing the task is physically dangerous or requires expensive equipment. This has led the services to supplement work samples in the following ways:

  - *Fold questions for the examinee into the work sample.* Military observers often ask examinees questions about a task as they perform it. With a CBT, for example, a hypothetical coworker could call or e-mail the examinee with a technical question. It might even be a multiple-choice question, for example, "Here's the situation . . . Which software installation preference should I pick: a, b, c, or d?"

  - *Ask examinees to verbalize their work.* In some military testing, examinees have been asked to report the steps they are taking (for example, "I am checking the oil gauge"); this is particularly useful for scoring important processes that are difficult to observe. One way this could manifest itself in IT work, for example, would be to create a scenario where examinees must keep a detailed log or journal of their actions and observations.

- *Incorporate task features that affect difficulty and complexity into the scoring system.* This involves identifying features that make tasks more difficult or complex and, in turn, manipulating the features experimentally to produce progressively more difficult test items or components. For example, a gauge-monitoring task might become increasingly difficult with the number and type (digital or analog) of gauges that must be monitored. These features of the task can be systematically altered across items; for example, easy items might have two digital gauges, and difficult items might have multiple analog and digital gauges. Separate scores could be computed for different levels of the task.

- *Use constrained, constructed-response items.* This approach presents the task in a way that limits the range of possible answers. For example, asking examinees to write a computer program is a free-response or open-ended task. Asking students to correct the bugs in a computer program is a way to constrain the responses. The advantage of this format is that it can be objectively machine-scored.
- *Use policy capturing to identify the holistic scoring rules and weights of expert human raters.* A number of test developers have attempted to create scoring algorithms that reproduce the scores given by human judges. This usually follows one of two approaches: regression or rule (policy) based. The regression approach breaks a task down into essential features that can be counted or measured by the computer; examples are co-occurrences of words or numbers of commas in an essay, positioning of buildings in drawings, and the number of medical tests ordered by doctors. Experts also score the performance using a holistic approach. Numerical values for the features are placed in a regression equation to predict experts' ratings. Individuals' scores on the exercise are based on the final regression weights, which must be cross-validated. The rule-based approach is to attempt to capture the policy of experts in specific scoring rules. The rule-based approach assigns points to specific performances. If the person does X, then he or she receives a certain number of points. The score on the exercise is the total number of points received.

Operational Considerations

Even the most valid and reliable test may not be useful in a particular setting. Operational concerns such as test development, administration, cost, the potential for coaching, and the need to develop parallel forms are important to consider in selecting a measurement method.

Situational Judgment Tests

Accumulating evidence of their validity for predicting job performance with less adverse impact than cognitive measures makes SJTs desirable. In addition, they appear to be less vulnerable to faking than personality measures (Hooper, Cullen, & Sackett, 2006), and their job relevance makes them more likely to be acceptable to applicants. However, the SJT format creates some challenges for selection testing programs. Because SJTs are typically multidimensional, internal consistency estimates are not high, but they are not expected to be. The appropriate reliability estimate is a test-retest estimate, but few organizations commit the resources needed to obtain it. Multidimensionality also makes it difficult to construct parallel forms with sufficient between-form reliability without essentially cloning the items (that is, replicating items with minor changes to insignificant content). Does item cloning achieve the goal of greater test security? To the extent that SJT items are more highly memorable and coachable than simpler items typically found on cognitive tests, cloning may be an insufficient form development method. This is of particular concern for organizations that test and retest a large volume of applicants.

Work Samples

Work samples are widely thought to be highly credible to examinees because their work relevance is direct. One concern about work samples is that they could be easily recollected by the examinees, who might discuss them with others. For example, a work sample that involves maintaining e-mails (say, deleting and storing) might be one that an examinee with foreknowledge might practice and learn. This makes construction of alternate forms and equating of forms highly important. Even so, it can be argued that alternate forms are not necessary for some work samples, particularly if they are not product-scored or require demonstration of a skill that cannot be faked just because the examinee knows the setup details (for example, changing a tire).

A related concern is coachability. A test is coachable if general rules can be used to respond successfully to items. For example, if a research task were scored by counting the number of materials researched, examinees could be coached to look at as many materials as possible to improve their scores.

Scoring with human judges can be expensive. If the work sample is administered and scored by computer, clearly consistency of administration and scoring would be high. Although the costs of administration and scoring might be fairly low for a CBT work sample, the costs of software development for the test are typically high, and the development of a computer-administered scoring algorithm could require a series of research projects.

Psychometric Characteristics

Empirical validity and reliability of the measurement method are also critical considerations for test developers. Several researchers have studied these characteristics in the context of knowledge and skill measures.

Situational Judgment Tasks

SJTs have become increasingly popular in employment testing because they address knowledge and skills that are difficult to measure with traditional multiple-choice test formats; yield reasonably high estimated validities for predicting job performance (average $r = .34$ uncorrected) and add incremental validity over general cognitive ability ($\Delta r = .08$ corrected) (McDaniel et al., 2007); and typically yield small to moderate subgroup differences, albeit the magnitude of the race difference varies with the cognitive load of the SJT (Whetzel, McDaniel, & Nguyen, 2008).

Work Samples

Work sample scores are generally less reliable than those from multiple-choice tests. One reason is error due to human judgment—error that can be reduced by clear scoring rubrics and rigorous scorer training. Another reason has to do with the complexity of the scoring task. As test complexity increases, it becomes more difficult to quantify performance or specify scoring rules in detail. Complex simulations sometimes have very few data points on which to base estimation of reliability. Error can also result from how tasks were sampled for testing. That is, work samples can be expensive to develop and score. Therefore, developers typically select tasks to test with a work sample. Error will be greater if the tasks selected for testing are not highly representative of the major parts of the job.

Work samples often rely on content validity as their primary source of validation evidence. Even so, work samples have been used as predictors in criterion-related validity studies, particularly for skilled technical and clerical jobs. A meta-analysis of validity studies conducted over eighty-five years (Schmidt & Hunter, 1998) reported a mean validity of .54, uncorrected for range restriction, for work sample tests.

Subgroup differences in scores from work sample tests tend to be a little lower than those from traditional cognitive ability measures, although this is sometimes due to the lower reliability of work sample scores. A recent meta-analysis reported an average white-black difference of .73 standard deviations (Roth, Bobko, McFarland, & Buster, 2008), which compares favorably to the often reported difference of one standard deviation for cognitive ability measures.

Measurement Challenges

Although measures of procedural knowledge and skill have the advantage of greater authenticity to the work environment, there are several challenges for these measurement methods.

Situational Judgment Tasks: What Do They Measure?

Tests using an SJT format have been around for more than a hundred years. One of the first widely researched SJTs was the Judgment in Social Situations subtest of the George Washington Social Intelligence Test (Moss & Hunt, 1926), consisting of "questions requiring judgment in typical problems and appreciation of human motives" (p. 4). Moss and Hunt's work with the Social Intelligence Test initiated a debate in the literature about what the test measures. Based on factor-analytic work with the test and measures of cognitive ability, Thorndike (1936) concluded that the Judgment in Social Situations subtest primarily measured abstract intelligence, though it "may tap slightly some unique field of ability" (p. 233).

The debate about what SJTs measure and why they work continues today. One point of agreement is that an SJT is a measurement method—a format of a test. What it measures is a function of content choices made by developers. Even so, the method itself puts constraints on the types of constructs likely to be measured. That is, the characteristics of the SJT make it particularly suitable for measuring some constructs and unsuitable for measuring others. At the highest level, SJTs simply measure judgment. Virtually all SJTs have a strong interpersonal component, and some have a positive relationship with cognitive ability.

Perhaps the most notable trend regarding SJTs is toward theory development. Weekley and Ployhart's *Situational Judgment Tests* (2006) contains five chapters on theory development for SJTs. For example, Motowidlo, Hooper, and Jackson (2006) present a model whereby traits, such as personality characteristics, indirectly influence choices made on SJTs. More specifically, people's traits influence their experiences, and experiences and traits together influence their implicit beliefs about the effectiveness of courses of action that express particular traits (for example, how effective a very agreeable action is in a situation). In turn, those implicit trait policies influence decisions made on an SJT. Other theorists have drawn on literature from cognitive psychology or decision making to explain why SJTs work.

Work Samples: How to Obtain Reliable Scores Within Practical Constraints on Time

Work samples vary in complexity and fidelity. As complexity increases, testing time usually increases, and development of human or computer scoring algorithms becomes more challenging. Other score-related issues can also be difficult to resolve, such as equating test forms, setting the passing score, and developing adequate diagnostic feedback for examinees.

Applications

Because of their ease of administration and strong psychometric track record, SJTs are highly versatile across situations. Work samples can be difficult and expensive to develop and costly to administer. This makes them best suited to situations where candidates must come to the job with a particular skill or must be able to learn that skill in a short period of time. Because of their direct relationship with job content, work samples are also often a method of choice if the selection system must rely on content validity.

Conclusion

Knowledge and skill assessment play an important role in our lives. Assessment scores determine what schools we can attend and what occupations we may hold. Assessment of DK is, for the most part, based on multiple-choice test scores, which are well supported by psychometric research. Measurement challenges for DK assessment stem from the need to enhance test credibility through greater authenticity and ensure the currency and accuracy of test items written for highly dynamic knowledge domains. PKS measures vary greatly in terms of fidelity and complexity. SJTs, which are low-fidelity PKS measures, are a reasonably mature methodology, although the debate about what SJTs measure continues. Complex, high-fidelity PKS assessments present a host of measurement challenges regarding content coverage, scoring, alternate forms assessment, and standard setting. These are important areas of future research.

References

Bloom, B. S., Engelhart, M. D., Furst, E. J., Hill, W. H., & Krathwohl, D. R. (1956). *Taxonomy of educational objectives: The classification of educational goals. Handbook I: Cognitive domain.* New York: McKay.

Campbell, J. P., McCloy, R. A., Oppler, S. H., & Sager, C. E. (1993). A theory of performance. In N. Schmitt & W. C. Borman (Eds.), *Personnel selection in organizations* (pp. 35–70). San Francisco: Jossey-Bass.

Felker, D. B., Curtin, P. J. & Rose, A. M. (2007). Tests of job performance. In D. L. Whetzel & G. R. Wheaton (Eds.), *Applied measurement: Industrial psychology in human resources management* (pp. 319 – 348). Mahwah, NJ: Erlbaum.

Ford, J. K., Kraiger, K., & Schechtman, S. L. (1986). Study of race effects in objective indices and subjective evaluations of performance: A meta-analysis of performance criteria. *Psychological Bulletin, 99*(3), 330–337.

Fruchter, B. (1947). Information tests. In J. P. Guilford & J. I. Lacey (Eds.), *Army Air Forces Aviation Psychology Program research reports: Printed classification tests* (pp. 341–370). Washington, DC: U.S. Government Printing Office.

Hooper, A. C., Cullen, M. J., & Sackett, P. R. (2006). Operational threats to the use of SJTs: Faking, coaching, and retesting issues. In J. A. Weekley & R. E. Ployhart (Eds.), *Situational judgment tests: Theory, measurement and application* (pp. 205–232). Mahwah, NJ: Erlbaum.

Hunter, J. E. (1986). Cognitive ability, cognitive aptitudes, job knowledge, and job performance. *Journal of Vocational Behavior, 29*, 340–362.

McDaniel, M. A., Hartman, N. S., Whetzel, D. L., & Grubb, W. L. (2007). Situational judgment tests, response instructions, and validity: A meta-analysis. *Personnel Psychology, 60*, 63–91.

Moss, F. A., & Hunt, T. (1926, March). Ability to get along with others. *Industrial Psychology*, 170–178.

Motowidlo, S. J., Hanson, M. A., & Crafts, J. L. (1997). Low-fidelity simulations. In D. L. Whetzel & G. R. Wheaton (Eds.), *Applied measurement methods in industrial psychology* (pp. 241–260). Palo Alto, CA: Davies-Black.

Motowidlo, S. J., Hooper, A. C., & Jackson, H. L. (2006). A theoretical basis for situational judgment tests. In J. A. Weekley & R. E. Ployhart (Eds.), *Situational judgment tests: Theory, measurement and application* (pp. 57–82). Mahwah, NJ: Erlbaum.

Raymond, M., & Neustel, S. (2006). Determining the content of credentialing examinations. In S. M. Downing & T. M. Haladyna (Eds.), *Handbook of test development* (pp. 181–254). Mahwah, NJ: Erlbaum.

Roth, P., Bobko, P., McFarland, L., & Buster, M. (2008). Work sample tests in personnel selection: A meta-analysis of black-white differences in overall and exercise scores. *Personnel Psychology, 61*, 637–662.

Rynes, S. L. (1993). Who's selecting whom? Effects of selection practices on applicant attitudes and behavior. In N. Schmitt & W. C. Borman (Eds.), *Personnel selection in organizations* (pp. 240–274). San Francisco: Jossey-Bass.

Schmidt, F. L., & Hunter, J. E. (1998). The validity and utility of selection methods in personnel psychology: Practical and theoretical implications of 85 years of research findings. *Psychological Bulletin, 124*(2), 262–274.

Thorndike, R. L. (1936). Factor analysis of social and abstract intelligence. *Journal of Educational Psychology, 27*, 231–233.

Weekley, J. A., & Ployhart, R. E. (Eds.) (2006). *Situational judgment tests: Theory, measurement and application*. Mahwah, NJ: Erlbaum.

Weekley, J. A., Ployhart, R. E., & Holtz, B. C. (2006). On the development of situational judgment tests: Issues in item development, scaling, and scoring. In J. A. Weekley & R. E. Ployhart (Eds.), *Situational judgment tests: Theory, measurement and application* (pp. 157–182). Mahwah, NJ: Erlbaum.

Whetzel, D. L., McDaniel, M. A., & Nguyen, N. T. (2008). Subgroup differences in situational judgment test performance: A meta-analysis. *Human Performance, 21*, 291–309.

CHAPTER 7

PHYSICAL PERFORMANCE

Deborah L. Gebhardt, Todd A. Baker

Physical ability assessment encompasses many fields of study, ranging from physiology and biomechanics to applied psychology and medicine. Organizations with physically demanding jobs use physical assessments for selection and classification purposes. The military has a long history of evaluating the physical demands of the tasks performed by soldiers. Similarly, public safety agencies need to ensure that their personnel are capable of meeting physical job demands due to the critical nature of their mission. In many jobs in the private sector, failure to meet the physical demands may result in injury and low productivity (for example, natural gas and electric industries).

A historical background of physical testing by Hogan (1991) highlighted the events that lead to the types of physical testing used today. This overview includes research related to physical ability domains and the underlying physiological and neuromuscular constructs. The overview demonstrates how the fields of physiology, industrial engineering, biomechanics, and industrial-organizational psychology (I-O) contribute to the development of physical testing.

In the mid-1970s, women began to seek nontraditional jobs that were physically demanding, such as those of firefighter or plant mechanic. This resulted in litigation due to the differential passing rates for men and women. Court rulings struck down testing procedures due to the lack of relationship between the preemployment evaluation and job requirements. This litigation had a positive effect that resulted in greater attention being placed on the procedures used for selection into these jobs. Job analysis procedures and test validation became scrutinized not only by the courts but also by organizations that implemented selection procedures.

Physical performance tests are used for selecting candidates into jobs, retaining and promoting incumbents, and evaluating physical fitness. Organizations implement these tests for reasons such as reducing injuries and related costs, decreasing turnover, and identifying individuals with the capabilities to perform the job successfully. Employers are faced with determining whether a job has adequate physical demand to require an assessment of candidates. Several parameters indicate that a job has substantial physical demand:

- Lifting objects that weigh fifty pounds or greater
- Repetitive lifting of lighter objects (for example fifteen pounds) continuously over a shift
- Lifting objects overhead that weigh forty pounds or greater
- Moving continuously while carrying lighter objects (for example a walking mail carrier)
- Wearing equipment that weighs fifteen pounds or more when performing job tasks
- Running

These criteria can be used to identify jobs that may require a physical screening assessment. For the general public, a substantial number of adults would be unable to perform job tasks on a daily basis that contain any of these parameters. Therefore, the goal of physical testing is to ensure that the individuals in these jobs can perform strenuous tasks safely and effectively.

Performance of physical tasks can be affected by a medical disease or condition. Although physical performance and health status can be interrelated (pneumonia results in decreased aerobic capacity, for example), this chapter deals only with physical performance. Information related to medical health status and its relationship to job performance can be found in the medical guidelines development literature (Marchese et al., 2007).

Identifying Physical Job Requirements

The accurate identification of physical job requirements is needed to design effective physical performance tests. These requirements are identified through a job analysis. A thorough job analysis provides the information to (1) identify the physical tasks and working conditions that are important to successful job performance, (2) develop tests that assess essential tasks and required abilities, (3) assist in establishing job-related passing scores, and (4) defend the use of the tests during litigation.

Successful performance of arduous jobs depends on the demands of the tasks, the environment in which they are performed, and the capabilities of the worker. Therefore, parameters beyond cognitive job factors must be addressed. It is important to consider not only the tasks performed, but also the environment and ergonomic parameters that affect task performance (for example, wearing protective gear). A multidisciplinary approach using techniques from I-O psychology, physiology, and biomechanics is used to identify the essential job tasks and quantify the physical work demands. This approach provides the foundation for setting occupational standards.

Identification of Essential Tasks

Identification of the physical demands of a job or activity requires (1) observations and interviews, (2) task statements that reflect physical demand, (3) rating scales (frequency, time spent) that provide discrete levels linked to physiological parameters, and (4) questions that address ergonomic and environmental parameters. Observation of the techniques workers use to complete tasks successfully is important to defining the physical demand. The observations are enhanced by interviews with supervisors and incumbents who supply the details as to the sequence of activities and the environmental parameters that affect performance.

A task statement should address one activity, such as "climb telephone pole." Task statements that contain multiple tasks lead to an inability to assess task demands accurately. For example, "repair air-conditioning unit" may mean carrying fifty-pound parts to the unit or using a small screwdriver to adjust the air flow.

When rating scales are used to identify the essential job tasks, the frequency and time spent scales should contain discrete anchors (for example, "one to three times per week"), as opposed to relative anchors ("some of the time"). The frequency and time spent data, combined with an importance rating, can form an algorithm to define the essential job tasks. Furthermore, the discrete frequency and time spent data (for example, "1 minute" or "8 to 20 minutes") obtained in the job analysis can be used to classify tasks by physical demand. For jobs with tasks that have a low probability of occurrence but a high consequence if inadequately performed, an expected-to-perform scale can be used. In addition, a physical effort rating scale can be used to obtain an initial assessment of the physical demand of a job. This scale provides anchors with known physiological demand, such as kilocalories. The number of tasks with mean physical effort ratings at specified levels can be used as an initial method to classify multiple jobs. In the physical arena, incumbents who perform the job should be used to provide the frequency and time spent task ratings because supervisors (e.g., paramedic commander) may not be located at the job site and therefore have no direct knowledge of task frequency or time spent.

Numerous decision rules or algorithms have been used to identify essential tasks from task ratings. Although no one algorithm is associated with physically oriented job analysis, the nature of the job may dictate the type used. In the public safety jobs such as law enforcement, a specified level for an importance or frequency rating mean is identified because many highly important tasks (for example, "discharge weapon on the job") are performed infrequently. For jobs with repetitive tasks, such as those of a factory assembly worker, importance, frequency, and time-spent ratings can be normalized (z-score) and summed to yield a criticality value. This quantity is compared to a predetermined cutoff number and tasks with values meeting or exceeding the cutoff being essential. Regardless of the method or algorithm used to identify the essential tasks, the essential tasks should be reviewed to ensure they capture the operational characteristics and mission of the job.

Classification of Physical Demand

Classifying the physical demand of a job in terms of ability requirements necessitates a methodology that links essential tasks and physical abilities. Over the years, researchers in the fields of exercise physiology and I-O psychology have identified a variety of physical ability combinations to describe physical performance (Fleishman, 1964; Hogan, 1991; Jackson, 1971; Myers, Gebhardt, Crump, & Fleishman, 1993). Although there is agreement across studies related to many of the abilities, the results of studies that used factor analysis to identify physical abilities were dependent on the types of assessments used in the study. A review of these studies found seven abilities that describe physical performance:

- Muscular strength (static strength)
- Muscular endurance (dynamic strength)
- Aerobic capacity (cardiovascular endurance)
- Anaerobic power
- Equilibrium
- Flexibility
- Coordination and agility

These seven abilities form the foundation for identifying and designing tests that assess the physical abilities of work activities. Table 7.1 contains a listing of these abilities, along with their definitions.

The level of physical abilities required to perform job tasks may range from minimal to extreme. For example, writing a memo requires a minimum level of muscular strength, while dragging a fire hose into a burning building requires a high level of strength. To determine whether the physical demand of a job warrants evaluation, physical ability rating scales with behavioral anchors that define the level of the ability required for task performance can be used. The physical ability rating scales are used by incumbents, supervisors, or job analysts to yield a profile of

Table 7.1. Physical Abilities and Definitions

Ability	Definition
Muscular strength	Ability of the muscles to exert force to lift, push, pull, or hold objects. The magnitude of the force depends on the size of the muscles (cross-section).
Muscular endurance	Ability to exert force continuously over moderate to long time periods. The length of time a muscle can contract depends on the size of the muscles involved, the chemical composition of the muscle tissue, and the muscle fiber type (e.g., slow twitch).
Aerobic capacity or cardiovascular endurance	Ability of the respiratory and cardiovascular systems to provide oxygen continuously for medium- to high-intensity activities performed over a moderate time period (e.g., > 5 minutes).
Anaerobic power	Ability to perform high-intensity short-duration activities (e.g., 5–90 sec.) using stored energy (e.g., adenosine triphosphate).
Equilibrium	Ability to maintain the body's center of mass over the base of support (e.g., feet) in the presence of outside forces (e.g., gravity, slipping on ice). Equilibrium involves maintaining and recovering a balanced position.
Flexibility	Ability to bend, stoop, rotate, and reach in all directions with the arms and legs through the range of motion at the joints (e.g., knee, shoulders). Flexibility is dependent on the extensibility of the ligaments, tendons, muscles, and skin.
Coordination and agility	Ability to perform motor activities in a proficient sequential pattern by using neurosensory cues such as change of direction.

physical demand. The physical ability profiles allow one to determine the level of physical abilities required for the job, the need for physical testing, the similarity of demand across jobs, and the tests that are relevant for the job.

Impact of Environment on Physical Demand of Job Tasks

The environmental conditions of the workplace can vary due to temperature and climate, as well as the clothing worn by a worker. Research has shown that working in heated environments decreases work productivity and can result in a higher body core temperature. To offset this problem, researchers found that individuals with higher aerobic capacity acclimatize to a heated environment and have higher productivity than do individuals with lower aerobic capacity (Astrand, Rodahl, Dahl, & Stromme, 2003). Data related to the environmental conditions in the workplace can be gathered from an organization's operating procedures, past weather data, job analysis questionnaires, and incumbent focus groups.

Methods to Quantify Physical Demand

In addition to rating scales, methodologies exist for directly measuring the physical demand of essential tasks. An initial approach involves gathering measures such as distance walked, weights of objects, and heights of shelves to provide important information that, when linked to the frequency and time spent rating data, can yield measures of work performed (work = force × distance). Forces required to perform tasks such as turning a valve or pushing carts can be gathered with a load cell or a dynamometer. A second method, biomechanical analysis, uses physics and anatomy principles to assess movement patterns when performing work tasks and compares different techniques and conditions for performing work tasks, such as forces generated by an individual. Data derived from these methods are used to determine passing scores for physical selection tests, as well as to identify task performance techniques or ergonomic settings that lead to injury.

The National Institute for Occupational Safety and Health has used biomechanical analysis to investigate manual materials handling. Its research has resulted in a sophisticated mathematical model used to calculate the load limit for lifting (Walters, Putz-Anderson, Garg, & Fine, 1993). A less complex biomechanical model was designed to determine the force exerted to lift the ends of a patient-loaded stretcher (Gebhardt & Crump, 1984). The resulting value from this model was used as the selection test passing score. Finally, biomechanical analysis can be used to identify risks for injury. For example, analysis of pole climbing in the telecommunications and electric utility industries found that use of a straight leg descent resulted in higher forces at the knee joint than a slightly flexed knee descent (Gebhardt, 1984).

A third approach requires measuring physiological response to work by assessing heart rate response, oxygen uptake rate, rise in core body temperature, or lactate buildup. Heart rate provides a measure of cardiovascular strain and is related to the intensity of an activity, as well as environmental conditions. Peak and average heart rates can be used to compare activities performed in the same environment. This approach was used in a manual materials handling study to determine the peak and average heart rates of food industry product selectors when they are "picking orders" and the heart rate response of a physical simulation (Gebhardt, Baker, & Thune, 2006). These data, coupled with validation data, were used to identify the passing score for the entry-level test.

Energy costs of work activities can be determined by direct measurement of oxygen uptake (VO_2) during task performance. A select number of jobs contain tasks requiring levels of aerobic capacity that warrant testing of the ability (Bilzon, Scarpello, Smith, Ravenhill, & Rayson, 2001; Sothmann, Gebhardt, Baker, Kastello, & Sheppard, 2004). This research found that the energy expenditure (VO_2) requirements for firefighters ranged from 33.5 to 45.0 milliliters of oxygen per kilogram of body weight per minute ($ml \cdot kg^{-1} \cdot min^{-1}$) for urban, forest, and shipboard firefighters (Gledhill & Jamnik, 1992; Sothmann, Saupe, Jasenof, Blaney, Donahue-Furman et al., 1990). These measures of heart rate and oxygen uptake form the basis for identifying physical tests and passing scores for selection and retention purposes.

In summary, ergonomic, biomechanical, and physiological data provide information that is important to defining the physical demand of a job. These data help define job demands, the nature of the assessments, and the passing scores.

Physical Performance Test Design and Selection

After establishing that a job is physically demanding, there are several reasons for assessing individuals prior to hire. Research has shown that there are consequences when a worker is incapable of meeting job demands: (1) increases in injuries, (2) days lost from work, (3) worker compensation costs, and (4) decrease in productivity. Two types of physical performance tests are used to reduce these consequences. The first type is basic ability tests based on the physiological components of the individual physical abilities. These tests assess a single ability (muscular strength, aerobic capacity, for example) and require an examinee to perform uncomplicated movements. Basic ability tests are completed in a controlled setting and have low potential for causing injury. Furthermore, these tests can be used for multiple jobs requiring the same abilities. Informative reviews of basic ability tests were completed in the 1990s (Hogan, 1991; Landy et al., 1992).

The second type, job simulations, requires completion of actual or simulated job tasks, such as lifting and carrying containers. Typically job simulations are designed for a single job and are not applicable across multiple jobs. The simulations can be developed from the essential job tasks but may not include skills that are learned in job training or on the job (Equal Employment Opportunity Commission, 1978). Although job simulations have face validity, developing simulations that do not include learned skills and have meaningful scoring protocols can be difficult.

Basic Ability Tests

Three types of tests are used to assess muscular strength: isometric, isotonic, and isokinetic. Isometric or static strength tests are used frequently in a selection setting because of their ease of administration and transport across test locations. These tests require generating a maximal effort while maintaining a static position (for example, elbow flexed to ninety degrees) in which there is no change in the length of the muscle (Astrand et al., 2003; McArdle, Katch, & Katch, 2007). For example, the leg lift test involves standing in a lifting position (hips and knees flexed), grasping a bar at knee level, and exerting a vertical force by attempting to lift the bar upward. Isometric tests are used to evaluate shoulder, arm, torso, and leg strength and are valid predictors of job performance ($r = .39$ to $.87$) for industrial and public safety jobs (Baumgartner & Jackson, 1999; Blakely, Quiñones, Crawford, & Jago, 1994).

Isotonic tests involve movement at a joint and result in muscle contraction or shortening (McArdle et al., 2007). These tests typically require one movement such as lifting, say, a sixty-pound box from floor to waist height. Research found these tests to be valid predictors of public safety job performance (Gebhardt, Baker, & Sheppard, 1999).

Isokinetic testing assesses the torque (τ) or angular force produced at the torso, shoulders, elbow, or knees. The torque is generated by rotating a limb about an axis such as moving the forearm toward the shoulder by flexing the elbow, which in turn produces a torque curve (McGinnis, 2007). Isokinetic tests are used primarily for manual materials handling jobs and require computerized equipment that controls the speed at which an individual can flex or extend a joint. Scores are produced for each joint assessed and summed to form a strength index. Research has indicated that isokinetic test scores are related to injury reduction (Gilliam & Lund, 2000; Karwowski & Mital, 1986). Furthermore, isokinetic test scores have been found to be highly related ($r = 0.91$ to 0.94) to isometric and isotonic test scores (Elmhandi, Feasson, Camdessanche, Calmels, & Gautheron, 2004; Karwowski & Mital, 1986).

Resistance to muscle fatigue is assessed by muscular endurance tests of varying duration and workload that are based on the level of muscular endurance required by the job. Muscular endurance tests require performing a movement multiple times for a specified duration or to exhaustion, such as push-ups, arm endurance, or lifting a fifty-pound container. For example, the arm endurance test involves pedaling an arm ergometer for a specific time period at a set workload. The test score is the number of revolutions completed in a specified time frame or the time at which the person can no longer maintain a specific cadence.

Aerobic capacity tests measure the cardiovascular response to a specific workload. The tests require movement at a specified cadence for a set time frame (submaximal) or to exhaustion (maximal). A treadmill or bicycle ergometer is used to evaluate maximum aerobic capacity ($VO_{2\,max}$) by increasing the workload in defined increments using speed, resistance, or incline. The test score is generated by analyzing expired gases (say, carbon dioxide), yielding an oxygen uptake value in milliliters of oxygen per kilogram of body weight ($ml \cdot kg^{-1} \cdot min^{-1}$). Submaximal tests typically employ heart rate response to exercise to predict aerobic capacity. Step tests and bicycle ergometer tests use heart rate response to obtain an estimate of $VO_{2\,sub\,max}$ (Astrand et al., 2003). The Americans with Disabilities Act of 1990 (ADA) considers these tests to be medical evaluations because heart rate and other physiological variables are assessed. However, other submaximal aerobic tests such as the 1.5-mile run and 1-mile walk are scored based on the time to complete the activity and thus are not considered medical tests. Therefore, they can be administered prior to the conditional offer of employment.

Equilibrium and flexibility tests have shown limited validity in the employment setting with correlations with job performance typically ranging from 0.00 to 0.18 (Baumgartner & Jackson, 1999). Although equilibrium and flexibility have been shown to be required for a variety of jobs, the lack of relationship to job performance may be due to the specificity of the movements requiring these abilities. However, when high levels of these abilities are required, such as working at heights of forty feet to secure containers to ship decks, significant correlations with job performance were found (Gebhardt, Schemmer, & Crump, 1985).

Although basic ability tests are practical and each allows for the assessment of one ability, they typically lack resemblance to job tasks (face validity). Table 7.2 provides examples of basic ability tests for each physical ability. The validity of these tests is discussed in the test validity section. An additional listing of tests can be found in Hogan (1991).

Table 7.2. Basic Ability Test Examples and Their Validity

	Muscular Strength		Muscular Endurance		
	Ratings	*Work Samples*		*Ratings*	*Work Samples*
Arm lift	.08 to .56	.20 to .74	Arm endurance	.21 to .71	.25 to .72
Chest pull	.47	.50	Leg endurance	.19 to .62	.48 to .75
Dynamic lift	.55	—	Push-ups	.38 to .79	.34 to .81
Handgrip	.02 to .51	.21 to .63	Sit-ups	.14 to .59	.01 to .68
Leg lift	.20 to .75	.52 to .77	Trigger pull	.28 to .47	.47
Leg press	.40	.35			
Shoulder lift	−.08 to .37	.32 to .66			
Trunk pull	−.03 to .29	.26 to .57			

	Aerobic Capacity		Anaerobic Power		
	Ratings	*Work Samples*		*Ratings*	*Work Samples*
Bicycle ergometer	.10 to .37	.15 to .53	Arm ergometer (10 s)	.21 to .57	.40 to .75
Modified stair climb	.14 to .43	.38 to .62	100-yard run	.25	.21 to .41
Step test	.03 to .32	.22 to .37	300-meter run	.37 to .46	.46 to .75
1-mile walk	.41	.53			
1.5-mile run	.23 to .62	.41 to .50			

	Equilibrium			Flexibility	
	Ratings	*Work Samples*		*Ratings*	*Work Samples*
Stabilometer	.09 to .20	.31 to .33	Sit and reach	−.02 to .30	.01 to .24
			Twist and touch	.04 to .14	—

	Coordination	
	Ratings	*Work Samples*
Side step	.21 to .57	.10 to .56
Illinois agility run	.48	.65
Shuttle run	.53	.67

Job simulations must contain only critical job parameters that can be scored in a manner that reflect individual differences (American Educational Research Association, American Psychological Association, & National Council on Measurement in Education, 1999). Furthermore, the fact that there are fewer movement constraints in job simulations may lead to a higher risk for injury when applicants exert themselves beyond their physical capabilities. When job simulations are constructed using essential tasks and relevant ergonomic parameters such as duration or intensity, they typically possess content validity. The challenge is duplicating job tasks without required skills learned on the job or in training.

Job simulations are frequently used to evaluate applicants for public safety jobs. For example, a law enforcement simulation may include (1) quickly exiting a vehicle, (2) running in pursuit, (3) climbing a fence, (4) restraining a suspect, and (5) performing simulated handcuffing. The duration and distance of this event should correspond to actual officer pursuit incidents. The simulation should also be completed using movement patterns found on the job. For example, a firefighter or blue-collar trade test should not require applicants to run during the test. Furthermore, when job simulations consist of a series of tasks, the sequence of performance should replicate the job as closely as possible.

Job simulations used in industrial settings primarily address manual materials handling jobs. Manual materials simulations require lifting and carrying objects of varying weight and are scored by determining the time to complete the test or the number of objects moved in a specified time. Another approach to assessment of manual materials handling capabilities is isoinertial testing, which requires lifting predetermined weights at a defined pace (such as every five seconds) to multiple heights (waist or shoulder, for example). The weight of the objects lifted is increased until the subject achieves maximum capacity or the maximum weight identified by the job analysis is completed. These tests are an inexpensive method to assess applicants and were found predictive of job performance and injury occurrence (Gebhardt et al., 2006; Mayer et al., 1988).

Physical Test Reliability

Researchers have demonstrated that both basic ability and job simulation tests are reliable when properly set up and administered. Test-retest reliabilities ranged from 0.65 to 0.95 for over twenty basic ability tests (Myers et al., 1993) and from 0.50 to 0.88 for job simulations (Gebhardt & Baker, 2010; Jackson, Laughery, & Vaubel, 1992b).

Validity of Physical Tests

Physical tests have a demonstrated history of validity in the employment arena as demonstrated by the relationship between test scores and job performance (Gebhardt & Baker, 2010; Hogan, 1991; Jackson et al., 1992). These studies typically followed models found in the *Uniform Guidelines* (Equal Employment Opportunity Commission et al., 1978), which defined three types of validity (content, construct, and criterion related), as well as approaches delineated in more recent publications (American Educational Research Association et al., 1999; Society for Industrial and Organizational Psychology, 2003).

Many research studies used a criterion-related validity model to establish test validity and identify effective passing scores. Common criterion measures used were supervisor and peer ratings of essential tasks and physical abilities, productivity measures, and work samples (Blakely et al., 1994; Gebhardt et al., 2006). Regardless of the criterion type selected, the key is to ensure that individual differences can be identified.

Reviews of published studies, meta-analyses, and technical reports in which empirical data were gathered demonstrated that physical test results are significantly related to both supervisor and peer ratings, as well as productivity data and days lost from work (Blakely et al., 1994; Arvey, Landon, Nutting, & Maxwell, 1992; Gebhardt, 2000). Individual basic ability tests have been found to be significantly related to supervisor and peer ratings of job performance ($r = .14$ to $.63$) in the public safety and blue-collar sectors such as police officer and maintenance mechanic. When basic ability test scores are correlated with work sample criterion measures, the magnitude of the simple validities increases to as high as 0.75 (Baker, Gebhardt, Billerbeck, & Volpe, 2009).

Table 7.2 shows the range of the simple validities across basic ability tests and job performance in industrial and public safety settings. The criterion measures related directly to physical job performance and included supervisor and peer ratings, work samples, and direct measures of job productivity. The range of the validity coefficients across the basic ability tests occurred due to varying physical demands across jobs. For example, the sit-and-reach test may have a high validity coefficient for jobs where work is performed in awkward positions. Conversely, this test will have a low validity coefficient for jobs requiring standing to operate equipment.

Similar to basic ability tests, job simulations have demonstrated validity from two perspectives: job content and criterion-related validity. Sothmann and associates (Sothmann et al., 1990; Sothmann, Gebhardt, Baker, Kastello, & Sheppard, 2004) used basic ability tests and a firefighter simulation criterion measure to identify a firefighter selection test. The individual correlations of the firefighter simulation with measures of strength and aerobic capacity ranged from 0.37 to 0.58. Similarly, simulations of law enforcement scenarios have yielded substantial validity coefficients ($r =.40$ to .63) when supervisor and peer ratings of job performance were used (Anderson, 2003; Gebhardt, Baker, Billerbeck, & Volpe, 2009). In addition, a study for a warehouse selector job found an isoinertial job simulation test to be a valid predictor ($r = .63$) of job performance (Gebhardt et al., 2006).

Although the job simulations have content validity when constructed using essential tasks and ergonomic parameters, content validity alone may not provide adequate support, as seen in litigation (*United States* v. *City of Erie*, 2005; *EEOC* v. *Dial Corporation*, 2006). One of the difficulties with content validity is determining a passing score that reflects acceptable job performance. If a job simulation is matched to on-the-job criteria such as time to complete a specified segment of work or specific force levels such as a lift of a patient-loaded gurney by a paramedic, the passing score may be obtained from job analysis, physiological data (Sothmann et al., 1990), or biomechanical data (Gebhardt & Crump, 1984).

Test Scoring and Setting Passing Scores

Although validity is paramount to the effectiveness of a test, it is only one of the needed components when developing a test. The generation of a passing score that defines the minimum capabilities is also necessary.

Types of Scoring

Similar to cognitive tests, physical performance test batteries are scored using a multiple hurdle or compensatory model. The multiple hurdle model requires that a passing score be achieved on each test in the battery. The compensatory model combines the score achieved for each test in the battery into a composite score that is compared to an overall passing score. Use of the compensatory model allows for a higher score on one test in the battery to offset a lower score on another test. In some instances, a combination of the two scoring models is used.

When a compensatory model is used, physical tests are usually weighted to offset the differences in scoring metrics. For example, one test may have a scoring range of 10 to 20, while another may have a range of 40 to 150. Combining the raw scores allows tests with the higher score magnitudes to overshadow performance on a test with a lower value range. Therefore, regression weights, unit weighting, or assigning point values for specific test score ranges (for example, stanine) are the most common methods to alleviate this issue. The unit weighting method allows each test to provide an equal contribution to the composite score. Use of regression weights results in tests that are more predictive of job performance being given greater weight than tests that are less predictive.

The point-value approach involves converting a test score or range of scores to a corresponding point value. If the point-value scoring approach is used, a point value for each test score or a range of test scores is established based on the distribution of test scores, such as percentiles, stanine scores, or standard error of the difference (Cascio, Outtz, Zedeck, & Goldstein, 1991).

Multiple hurdle and compensatory models have been used in combination when a two-tiered approach is needed. A two-tiered model is used when one test involves use of a medical measure such as heart rate, a submaximal VO_2 bicycle test, or is highly critical to job performance. A two-tiered system, in which one set of tests (arm endurance, arm lift, and hose drag) was scored with a compensatory model followed by an aerobic capacity test, after a job offer, was used to select firefighters (Sothmann et al., 2004). Thus, applicants had to pass the three-test battery and then the aerobic capacity test.

The compensatory scoring model generally results in less adverse impact by sex than the multiple hurdle model (Gebhardt, 2000). However, this advantage can be a drawback when an individual scores extremely low on one test but passes the test battery because of an extremely high score on another test. This occurs when men perform well on muscular strength tests and poorly on aerobic, anaerobic, and flexibility tests. Passing the test battery with this combination of scores is undesirable because the individual would perform poorly in a job that requires abilities besides strength. A method to eliminate this is to construct point-value ranges for each test in which an applicant must achieve a minimum point value on each test.

Passing Score Determination

Physical test passing scores should be reasonable and consistent with the demands of the job. Due to differences in physiological makeup, women may perform physical tasks differently than men do while achieving successful job performance. The key is to determine the test scores at which an individual will not perform effectively and safely. Criterion-referenced and norm-referenced passing scores have been used for physical tests (Landy & Conte, 2007; Safrit & Wood, 1989). Criterion-referenced passing scores use test and job performance data to arrive at a passing score. Norm-referenced passing scores use tables of established test-score performance from archive data to arrive at a passing score.

When available, ergonomic and physiological data can provide defined levels for passing scores. A prime example is the identification of the levels of aerobic capacity required to perform job tasks (Gebhardt et al., 2006; Gledhill & Jamnik, 1992; Sothmann et al., 2004). Once established for a job, this value serves as the passing score for the aerobic test bicycle ergometer or treadmill, for example. However, these defined levels are not uniformly applicable to another job title that may vary in physical demand. Therefore, these types of data must be established for the specific job under study.

Similarly, biomechanical and ergonomic data have been used to set passing scores. The forces required to tighten and loosen valves and turnbuckles were measured in an oil refinery and longshore industries, respectively, and served as the point for identifying test passing scores (Gebhardt et al., 1985; Jackson et al., 1992). When a selection test mimics a key critical task, biomechanical modeling can be used to identify the passing score. Gebhardt and Crump (1984) used job analysis, gurney specifications, and paramedic log data to construct a model that identified the force required to complete the task of lifting the head end of a patient-loaded gurney. The required force generated from the model was used as the passing score for the selection test.

Similar to ergonomic measures, the pace with which job tasks are performed can provide information needed to establish passing scores. The use of pacing data in establishing passing scores is most effective for jobs in which the time to complete a task is important to performance effectiveness, but where faster task completion is not always prudent. Pacing data were used to help identify a passing score for a firefighter selection test due to the dangers of moving too quickly when performing fire suppression (Sothmann et al., 2004).

The second type of passing score, norm referenced, occurs when an individual's test scores are compared to the scores of a known population or sample of individuals who have taken the test, or the normative group. In this type of scoring, a particular percentile level for a normative cohort is selected as the passing score. Some law enforcement agencies use this type of passing score to select new officers. Typically multiple passing scores by sex or age, or both, are set at the same percentile. Using sit-ups as an example, the passing score for men twenty to twenty-nine years old would be 38 at the 40th percentile. Men in the age groups thirty to thirty-nine and forty to forty-nine would have passing scores of 35 and 29, respectively. For women in these three age groups, the passing scores would be 32, 25, and 20, respectively. The premise for this scoring approach is that regardless of the group (for example, men and women) the passing score is set at the same percentile.

The Civil Rights Act of 1991 states that passing scores cannot vary on the basis of sex, race and national origin (RNO), or age, but some law enforcement agencies continue to use this approach. Two reasons given for using multiple passing scores are that the tests being used measure physical fitness, not job performance, and the scores are the same because they represent the same percentile rank. However, if the purpose of the test is to measure job performance or make employment decisions, such as selection, retention, or promotion, compliance with statutes such as the Civil Rights Act of 1991 is required. In addition, the different scores associated with the percentile selected as the passing score do not correspond to acceptable or unacceptable job performance. In order for multiple passing scores to correspond to minimally acceptable job performance, it must be demonstrated that each passing score represents minimally acceptable job performance. Sex-normed passing scores were recommended by the plaintiffs for the 1.5-mile run in *Lanning* v. *Southeastern Pennsylvania Transit Authority* (1999). The court rejected this recommendation and stated that in order to validate different passing scores, the job relatedness of each passing score would need to be established.

In summary, effective passing scores should maximize correct decisions (pass acceptable individuals, fail unacceptable individuals) and minimize incorrect decisions (fail acceptable performers, pass unacceptable performers). To arrive at passing scores that represent the minimum acceptable job performance, organizations should use various sources of information.

Physical Test Adverse Impact and Test Fairness

Physiological parameters such as height, weight, percentage of body fat, and lean body mass contribute to significant differences between men and women on physical tests (basic ability, job simulation). The effect sizes for these differences range from 0.6 to 1.6, with the greatest disparity for muscular strength and anaerobic power tests (Blakely et al., 1994; Gebhardt et al., 2005;

Baker, 2007; Gebhardt, 2007). The magnitude of these test score differences has been found between incumbent men and women with acceptable job performance. The effect of the physiological sex differences on test performance was corroborated in a study that found fewer test score differences by sex when hierarchical regression analysis was used to control for percentage of body fat and lean body mass (Arvey et al., 1992). Furthermore, the magnitude of sex differences is less for tests that do not predominately measure strength, such as sit-ups and a maze crawl. Nevertheless, almost all physically demanding jobs require muscular strength, muscular endurance, or both. Thus, physical tests that have utility will also have adverse impact.

Physical test score differences have been found for age and, in some cases, RNO. Age differences have occurred for both basic ability and job simulation tests, with the performance of individuals fifty years of age and older being less than those under forty years old (Arvey et al., 1992; Blakely et al., 1994). Test score differences by RNO occur infrequently, and when present, they are primarily due to a predominance of women in one of the subgroups.

To investigate RNO differences using large samples of minorities not usually found in validation studies, Baker (2007) analyzed over fifty thousand male subjects from the African American, Hispanic, and white subgroups. The study found that whites performed significantly better than African Americans on basic ability and job simulation tests requiring moderate levels of rapid or continuous movement (for example, 1.5-mile run, firefighter evolution), with the effect sizes ranging from 0.29 to 0.52. Conversely, African American and white men performed significantly better than Hispanics on tests of muscular strength (Baker, 2007; Blakely et al., 1994).

There are several approaches to reducing adverse impact while maintaining test utility:

- Examine previous research to select tests with lower sex mean differences that accurately assess individual differences.
- Use targeted recruitment of individuals who possess the abilities required on the job such as those who participate in health club activities.

- Provide practice of test skills when a job simulation is used as the test.
- Provide a preemployment fitness program for candidates.
- Provide an on-site presentation of the job demands by having an employee perform selected demanding job tasks.
- Use statistical analyses such as multiple regression that identify the tests that have unique and significant contributions to the prediction of job performance. Identification of tests that significantly contribute to the prediction of job performance reduces test redundancy that can occur when using all tests with significant correlations with a criterion measure.
- Use a compensatory scoring model, which typically results in less adverse impact by sex than the multiple-hurdle model (Gebhardt, 2000; Sothmann et al., 2004).

In summary, both basic ability and job simulation tests can have adverse impact on protected groups (sex, age). Although past research has shown that the tests are fair to protected groups, efforts to reduce adverse impact as listed above should be used.

Implementation of Physical Tests

During the test implementation phase, several factors must be addressed to ensure the effective use of the test battery. First, the placement of the test battery in the selection process must be determined. Typically physical tests are administered prior to conditional offer of employment, because physical tests are one of the less expensive selection tools. Tests that require a measure of medical data such as heart rate must be given after a conditional offer of employment to comply with ADA (1990). Second, the order of the tests should take into account the physiological system being evaluated in each test to ensure that performance of one test does not adversely affect performance on the next test. For example, if a 1.5-mile run is completed, the next test in the battery should measure a component that does not involve the lower extremities. Third, a retest policy should be developed that takes into account the time needed to improve one's physical capabilities and organizational issues such as turnover and the size of the applicant pool. If a sustained exercise program is used, a minimum of two to three months is required for strength and aerobic gains (McArdle et al., 2007). Conversely, the test scores for candidates passing the test have a "shelf life" since an individual's fitness level is affected by inactivity, injury, or aging.

The fourth and fifth factors, verification of safe participation and test administration, pose dilemmas for employers. Because of inherent risks to individuals participating in strenuous activities, several organizations, such as the American College of Sports Medicine, have published guidelines for screening individuals prior to exercise testing (Thompson, Gordon, & Pescatello, 2009). At a minimum, assessing blood pressure and heart rate is recommended to determine whether an individual is at risk for testing, which is a violation of ADA if it is performed prior to conditional offer of a job. Employers have used waiver forms and medical clearance by a physician to address this issue when administering physical tests prior to a conditional job offer. The medical clearance provides no medical information to the employer and indicates only whether the individual can safely perform the physical tests.

Finally, employers must determine whether the tests will be administered by the employer or a third-party provider. To make this decision, employers should consider the cost and complexity of testing, availability and qualifications of in-house staff, number of applicants, availability and location of applicant pool, and the need for immediate results to support a job offer.

Litigation Related to Physical Testing

Due to physiological differences between men and women, physical test score differences on measures of muscular strength, muscular endurance, anaerobic power, and aerobic capacity are expected. These test score differences lead to differential hiring rates between men and women. In most instances, the women's passing rate is less than 80 percent of the men's passing rate, thus violating the four-fifths rule-of-thumb that defines adverse impact (Equal Employment Opportunity Commission et al., 1978). However, researchers have found similar differences by sex for measures of physical job performance (Blakely et al., 1994; Hogan, 1991). Thus, there are not only test score differences by sex but also physical job performance differences.

The *Uniform Guidelines* (Equal Employment Opportunity Commission et al., 1978) indicate that adverse impact is permissible if the validity, test fairness, and business necessity have been established. The courts have upheld physical tests that have adverse impact when validity and test fairness evidence across protected groups such as sex and age have been established (*Porch* v. *Union Pacific Railroad*, 1997) and rejected tests that did not provide adequate evidence (*Varden* v. *City of Alabaster, Alabama and John Cochran*, 2005). Reviews of physical testing from the 1970s to the 1990s found litigation to be filed under the Civil Rights Act of 1964 and 1991 and the ADA.

Title VII of the 1964 Civil Rights Act

Most early litigation was related to issues not directly associated with physical testing, such as sex as a bona fide occupational qualification, height, and weight. A review of Title VII physical performance test cases found a poor record in which seven of ten court decisions ruled in favor of the plaintiffs (Hogan & Quigley, 1986). These court rulings struck down tests on the basis of no or inadequate job analyses and validation procedures.

The courts have also addressed issues related to passing scores and the business necessity of physical tests. The *Lanning* v. *SEPTA* cases (1999, 2002) addressed both issues during the evaluation of the need for transit officer candidates to complete the 1.5-mile run in twelve minutes. This passing score was regarded as too stringent by plaintiffs and resulted in a passing rate of 55.6 percent for men and 6.7 percent for women. At the conclusion of the trials, the district court found that the test was job related and met the burden of business necessity. This decision demonstrated that identifying a job-related passing score is as important as establishing the test's validity and business necessity. Further, this decision demonstrated that employers have the right to improve the capabilities of their workforce, thereby negating the capabilities of the incumbent personnel.

The lack of a defined job analysis and inability to demonstrate the relationship of the passing score to minimally acceptable job performance were at the heart of *United States* v. *City of Erie* (2005) and *EEOC* v. *Dial Corp* (2006). The police department in Erie, Pennsylvania, developed a selection test and used the mean incumbent time to complete the test as the passing score. After implementation, it was found that the test had an adverse impact on women. Similarly, Dial Corp. implemented a lifting test to reduce injuries that not only had disparate impact on women but was more difficult than the job required. Furthermore, some women who passed the test were rejected for hire based on subjective judgments of their test performance. In both cases, the courts found for the plaintiff, indicating that no systematic job analysis or validity evidence was present to support test validity and business necessity.

A testing issue not typically seen in the cognitive testing arena is the use of physical tests for job retention. Law enforcement agencies and fire departments have instituted incumbent physical assessment as a means to maintain or improve incumbent physical job performance. In response to incumbent testing, challenges regarding the use of these tests for employee retention or promotion have evolved. The courts have ruled that an employer can implement these tests, but the tests must meet the same legal standards as candidate selection tests (*Smith v. Des Moines*, 1997; *UWUA Local 223 & The Detroit Edison Co.*, 1991).

In two cases heard by the courts regarding use of physical testing and mandatory retirement age for state troopers, the courts have ruled for and against a mandatory retirement age. In the first case, state troopers brought suit under the Age Discrimination in Employment Act of 1967 to eliminate the mandatory retirement age of fifty-five. The court ruled that troopers age fifty-five or older could remain with the department (*Gately v. Massachusetts*, 1996). However, all troopers must demonstrate that they are capable of performing the physical aspects of the job by completing and passing an annual physical performance test. In the second case (*Whitney and Badgley v. Kerry Sleeper Commissioner Vermont State Police and Vermont Department of Public Safety*, 2008), troopers challenged the mandatory retirement age of fifty-five because they had passed their annual physical test each year. The court ruled in favor of the mandatory retirement age of fifty-five, stating that decrements in physical as well as cognitive and psychomotor (reaction time) capabilities occur as individuals age. Furthermore, the incumbent physical test was age and gender normed, so the passing scores did not correspond to minimum physical job requirements.

Americans with Disabilities Act of 1990

The ADA and its federal sector companion, the Rehabilitation Act of 1973, seek to protect individuals with physical and mental disabilities. Title I of ADA states that a conditional offer of employment must be given before medical status inquires can be made [42 U.S.C. § 12112 (b) (5–6) (d) (2–4)]. It states that physical tests may be administered prior to conditional offer of employment if no medical data are gathered. Medical data in the physical test setting include blood pressure, heart rate, and body temperature. Therefore, tests of aerobic capacity that use heart rate response to generate a measure of VO_2, such as the step test, stationary bicycle, or treadmill, cannot be administered until after conditional offer of a job.

Although most ADA litigation cases pertain to medical issues, a few physical testing cases have been filed under ADA (Rothstein, Carver, Schroeder, & Shoben, 1999). In the private sector, a disabled plaintiff was denied transfer from a sedentary position to a physically demanding job (*Belk* v. *Southwestern Bell Telephone Company*, 1999). The court ruled in favor of the plaintiff for reasons unrelated to the physical test battery, so the battery was not struck down. In two public sector cases involving incumbent personnel who filed suit after being unable to meet the required incumbent physical standard (*Andrews* v. *State of Ohio*, 1997; *Smith* v. *Des Moines*, 1996), the courts ruled in favor of the defendants in both cases, stating that the incumbents were not disabled as defined by the ADA.

Reduction in Injuries and Lost Time from Work

Organizations have implemented physical tests as a means to reduce injuries, worker compensation costs, lost time from work, and turnover, as well as increase productivity. The military has a long history of investigating the impact of various training regimes on the injury rate of personnel and their ability to continue with the mission. Physical testing and remedial programs in the U.S. Army were shown to reduce injuries and identified the physiological parameters that lead to injury (Knapik et al., 2004).

Studies by Baker and Gebhardt in the railroad industry found cost savings and reduction in days lost from work when physical selection assessments were used. In a study using injury data, higher physical test scores were found to be significantly related to reduction in injuries and lost work days for railroad track laborers (Baker & Gebhardt, 1994). The utility analysis of the track laborers who passed and failed the physical test battery found that the 20 percent of the incumbents who would have failed the test accounted for 67 percent of the injury costs (Baker & Gebhardt, 1994). The utility analysis found the annual savings to be $3.1 million. In the second railroad study, train service employees such as conductors and brakemen who were tested and hired were compared to employees who were not tested but were hired during the same time period (Gebhardt & Baker, 2001). The study found that the tested and hired group's average injury costs of $15,315 were statistically lower than the $66,148 for the untested and hired group when controlling for age and job tenure. Furthermore, the tested group had a statistically lower injury rate and days lost resulting from injury per person with and without controlling for age, job tenure, and years injured.

In the freight industry, a physical selection test resulted in a reduction in injuries for truck drivers and dockworkers (Gilliam & Lund, 2000). Baker and colleagues found that freight industry employees who were tested prior to hire had 1.7 to 2.2 times less likelihood of incurring an injury than their untested counterparts (Baker, Gebhardt, & Koeneke, 2001). Further, the tested group had significantly fewer lost days due to injury than the untested group. In another freight industry study involving manual materials handling, higher scores on physical tests were found to be significantly related to fewer on-the-job injuries (Craig, Congleton, Kerk, Amendola, & Gaines, 2006).

The impact of physical testing in injury reduction and lost time from work is evident. The cost savings are substantial when one considers payment for injuries and lost time from work, along with replacing the injured worker. Review of the research showed that both basic ability and job simulations result in injury reduction. In most instances, tests involving muscular strength are most related to reductions in injury and lost time from work.

Conclusion

Both basic ability and job simulation tests have been shown to be valid predictors of job performance and result in reductions in injuries, lost work time, and worker compensation costs, coupled with increases in productivity. Although physical tests typically have an adverse impact on women, litigation in this area has demonstrated that the tests will be upheld or struck down based on the quality of the job analysis and validity evidence. Therefore, it is critical when selecting or designing physical tests that the potential level of test adverse impact be considered, along with the physiological and ergonomic demands of the job. Use of a criterion-related validity model provides the most information for setting test passing scores, and content validity provides limited information for making these decisions unless physiological or ergonomic data, or both, are present. During the test implementation phase, employers should consider who will administer the tests, location of the applicant pool, and number of test locations. Finally, mechanization has reduced the physical demands of some jobs, but until robotics sophistication improves, there will always be physically demanding jobs.

References

American Educational Research Association, American Psychological Association, & National Council on Measurement in Education. (1999). *Standards for educational and psychological testing.* Washington, DC: American Educational Research Association.

Anderson, C. K. (2003). Physical ability testing for employment decision purposes. In W. Karwowski & W. S. Marras (Eds.), *Occupational ergonomics: Engineering and administrative controls* (pp. 1–8). New York: Routledge.

Andrews v. *State of Ohio,* 104 F.3d 803 (6th Cir., 1997).

Arvey, R. D., Landon, T. E., Nutting, S. M., & Maxwell, S. E. (1992). Development of physical ability tests for police officers: A construct validation approach. *Journal of Applied Psychology, 77,* 996–1009.

Astrand, P., Rodahl, K., Dahl, H. A., & Stromme, S. G. (2003). *Textbook of work physiology* (4th ed.). Champaign, IL: Human Kinetics.

Baker, T. A. (2007). *Physical performance test results across ethnic groups: Does the type of test have an impact?* Paper presented at the Society for Industrial and Organizational Psychology, New York.

Baker, T. A., & Gebhardt, D. L. (1994). *Cost effectiveness of the Trackman Physical Performance Test and injury reduction.* Hyattsville, MD: Human Performance Systems.

Baker, T. A., Gebhardt, D. L., & Koeneke, K. (2001). *Injury and physical performance tests score analysis of Yellow Freight System dockworker, driver, hostler, and mechanic positions.* Beltsville, MD: Human Performance Systems, Inc.

Baumgartner, T. A., & Jackson, A. S. (1999). *Measurement for evaluation in physical education and exercise science* (6th ed.). Dubuque, IA: William C. Brown.

Belk v. *Southwestern Bell Telephone Company,* 194 F.3d 946 (8th Cir. 1999).

Bilzon, J. L., Scarpello, E. G., Smith, C. V., Ravenhill, N. A., & Rayson, M. P. (2001). Characterization of the metabolic demands of simulated shipboard Royal Navy fire-fighting tasks. *Ergonomics, 44,* 766–780.

Blakely, B. R., Quiñones, M. A., Crawford, M. S., & Jago, I. A. (1994). The validity of isometric strength tests. *Personnel Psychology, 47,* 247–274.

Cascio, W. F., Outtz, J. L., Zedeck, S., & Goldstein, I. L. (1991). Statistical implications of six methods of test score use in personnel selection. *Human Performance, 4,* 233–264.

Craig, B. N., Congleton, J. J., Kerk, C. J., Amendola, A. A., & Gaines, W. G. (2006). Personal non-occupational risk factors and occupational injury/illness. *American Journal of Industrial Medicine, 49,* 249–260.

EEOC v. *Dial Corp,* No. 05–4183/4311 (8th Cir. 2006).

Elmhandi, L., Feasson, L., Camdessanche, J. P., Calmels, P., & Gautheron, V. (2004). Isokinetic assessment of muscular strength in subjects with acute inflammatory demyelinating polyradiculoneuropathy. *Annales de Readaptation et de Medecine Physique, 47,* 209–216.

Fleishman, E. A. (1964). *Structure and measurement of physical fitness.* Upper Saddle River, NJ: Prentice Hall.

Gately v. *Massachusetts,* No. 92–13018 (D. Mass. Sept. 26, 1996).

Gebhardt, D. L. (1984). Center of mass displacement for linemen in the electric industry. In D. Winter, R. Norman, R. Wells, K. Hayes, & A. Patla (Eds.), *Biomechanics, IX-A.* Champaign, IL: Human Kinetics.

Gebhardt, D. L. (2000). Establishing performance standards. In S. Constable & B. Palmer (Eds.), *The process of physical fitness standards development.* Wright-Patterson AFB, OH: Human Systems Information Analysis Center.

Gebhardt, D. L. (2007). *Physical performance testing: What is the true impact?* Paper presented at the Society for Industrial and Organizational Psychology, New York.

Gebhardt, D. L., & Baker, T. A. (2001). Reduction of worker compensation costs through the use of pre-employment physical testing. *Medicine Science in Sports and Exercise, 33,* 111.

Gebhardt, D. L., & Baker, T. A. (2010). Physical performance testing. In J. Farr & N. Tippins (Eds.), *Handbook of employee selection.* New York: Routledge Academic.

Gebhardt, D. L., Baker, T. A., Billerbeck, K. T., & Volpe, E. K. (2009). *Development and validation of physical performance tests of Los Angeles County Police Department SWAT and Metro Personnel.* Beltsville, MD: Human Performance Systems.

Gebhardt, D. L., Baker, T. A., & Sheppard, V. A. (1999). *Development and validation of a physical performance test for the selection of City of Chicago paramedics.* Hyattsville, MD: Human Performance Systems.

Gebhardt, D. L., Baker, T. A., & Thune, A. (2006). *Development and validation of physical performance, cognitive, and personality assessments for selectors and delivery drivers.* Beltsville, MD: Human Performance Systems.

Gebhardt, D. L., & Crump, C. E. (1984). *Validation of physical performance selection tests for paramedics.* Bethesda, MD: Advanced Research Resources Organization.

Gebhardt, D. L., Schemmer, F. M., & Crump, C. E. (1985). *Development and validation of selection tests for longshoremen and marine clerks.* Bethesda, MD: Advanced Research Resources Organization.

Gilliam, T., & Lund, S. J. (2000). Injury reduction in truck driver/dock workers through physical capability new hire screening. *Medicine Science in Sports and Exercise, 32,* S126.

Gledhill, N., & Jamnik, V. K. (1992). Characterization of the physical demands of firefighting. *Canadian Journal of Sport Science, 17,* 207–213.

Hogan, J. C. (1991). Physical abilities. In M. D. Dunnette & L. M. Hough (Eds.), *Handbook of industrial and organizational psychology* (Vol. 2, pp. 753–831). Palo Alto, CA: Consulting Psychologists Press.

Hogan, J. C., & Quigley, A. M. (1986). Physical standards for employment and the courts. *American Psychologist, 41,* 1193–1217.

Jackson, A. S. (1971). Factor analysis of selected muscular strength and motor performance tests. *Research Quarterly, 42,* 164–172.

Jackson, A. S., Laughery, K. R., & Vaubel, K. P. (1992). Validity of isometric tests for predicting the capacity to crack, open and close industrial valves. In *Proceedings of the Human Factors Society 36th Annual Meeting* (pp. 688–691). Santa Monica, CA: Human Factors.

Karwowski, W., & Mital, A. (1986). Isometric and isokinetic testing of lifting strength of males in teamwork. *Ergonomics, 29,* 869–878.

Knapik, J. J., Bullock, S. H., Canada, S., Toney, E., Hoedebecke, E., Jones, B. et al. (2004). Influence of an injury reduction program on injury rate and fitness outcomes among soldiers. *Injury Prevention, 10,* 37–42.

Landy, F., Bland, R., Buskirk, E., Daly, R. E., Debusk, R. F., Donovan, E. et al. (1992). *Alternatives to chronological age in determining standards of suitability for public safety jobs.* Center for Applied Behavioral Sciences. State College: The Pennsylvania State University.

Landy, F. J., & Conte, J. M. (2007). *Work in the 21st century: An introduction to industrial and organizational psychology.* Malden, MA: Blackwell Publishing.

Lanning v. *Southeastern Pennsylvania Transportation Authority,* 181 F.3d 478, 482–484 (3rd Cir. 1999).

Lanning v. *Southeastern Pennsylvania Transportation Authority,* 308 F.3d 286 (3rd Cir. 2002).

Marchese, V. G., Connolly, B. H., Able, C., Booton, A. R., Bowen, P., Porter, B. N. et al. (2007). Relationships among severity of osteo-necrosis, pain, range of motion, and functional mobility in children, adolescents, and young adults with acute lymphoblastic leukemia. *Physical Therapy, 8,* 341–350.

Mayer, T. G., Barnes, D., Nichols, G., Kishino, N. D., Coval, K., Piel, B. et al. (1988). Progressive isoinertial lifting evaluation. II. A comparison with isokinetic lifting in a disabled chronic low-back pain industrial population. *Spine, 13,* 998–1002.

McArdle, W. D., Katch, F. I., & Katch, V. L. (2007). *Exercise physiology: Energy, nutrition, and human performance* (5th ed.). Baltimore, MD: Lippincott Williams & Wilkins.

McGinnis, P. M. (2007). *Biomechanics of sport and exercise* (2nd ed.). Champaign, IL: Human Kinetics.

Myers, D. C., Gebhardt, D. L., Crump, C. E., & Fleishman, E. A. (1993). The dimensions of human physical performance: Factor analyses of strength, stamina, flexibility, and body composition measures. *Human Performance, 6,* 309–344.

Porch v. *Union Pacific Railroad,* Administrative Law Proceeding, State of Utah. 2003.

Rothstein, M. A., Carver, C. B., Schroeder, E. P., & Shoben, E. W. (1999). *Employment law* (2nd ed.). St. Paul, MN: West Group.

Safrit, M. J., & Wood, T. M. (1989). *Measurement concepts in physical education and exercise science.* Champaign, IL: Human Kinetics Books.

Smith v. *City of Des Moines, Iowa*, #95-3802, 99 F.3d 1466, 1996 U.S. App. Lexis 29340, 72 FEP Cases (BNA) 628, 6 AD Cases (BNA) 14 (8th Cir. 1996). [1997 FP 11]

Society for Industrial and Organizational Psychology. (2003). *Principles for the validation and use of personnel selection procedures* (4th ed.). Bowling Green, OH: Author.

Sothmann, M. S., Gebhardt, D. L., Baker, T. A., Kastello, G. M., & Sheppard, V. A. (2004). Performance requirements of physically strenuous occupations: Validating minimum standards for muscular strength and endurance. *Ergonomics, 47,* 864–875.

Sothmann, M. S., Saupe, K., Jasenof, D., Blaney, J., Donahue-Fuhrman, S., Woulfe, T. et al. (1990). Advancing age and the cardiovascular stress of fire suppression: Determining the minimum standard for aerobic fitness. *Human Performance, 3,* 217–236.

Thompson, W. R., Gordon, N. F., & Pescatello, L. S. (2009). *ACSM's guidelines for exercise testing and prescription* (8th ed.). Philadelphia: Wolters Kluwer/Lippincott Williams & Wilkins.

United States v. *City of Erie, Pennsylvania*, #04–4, 352 F. Supp. 2d 1105 (W.D. Pa. 2005).

UWUA Local 223 & The Detroit Edison Co., AAA Case No. 54–30–1746–87 (Apr. 17, 1991).

Varden v. *City of Alabaster, Alabama and John Cochran*, U.S. District Court, Northern District of Alabama, Southern Division; 2:04-CV-0689-AR.

Walters, T. R., Putz-Anderson, V., Garg, A., & Fine, L. J. (1993). Revised NIOSH equation for the design and evaluation of manual lifting tasks. *Ergonomics, 36,* 749–776.

Whitney and Badgley v. *Kerry Sleeper, Commissioner VT State Police and VT Department of Public Safety*, 2008.

Federal Laws

Age Discrimination in Employment Act of 1967, 29 U.S.C. Sec. 621 et seq. (1967).

Americans with Disabilities Act of 1990, 42 U.S.C.A.

Civil Rights Act of 1964 (Title VII), 42 U.S.C. §2000e-2 et seq. (1964).

Civil Rights Act of 1991, S. 1745, 102nd Congress. (1991).

Equal Employment Opportunity Commission, Civil Service Commission, Department of Labor, and Department of Justice (1978). *Uniform guidelines on employee selection procedures.* Washington, DC: Bureau of National Affairs.

Rehabilitation Act of 1973, 29 U.S.C. 701 et. seq. (1973).

CHAPTER 8

COMPETENCIES, JOB ANALYSIS, AND THE NEXT GENERATION OF MODELING

Jeffery S. Schippmann

Whether you love the concept of competencies, hate the concept, or are unsure what they are and question if they even rise to the status of a viable concept, the fact is they have become so fully embedded in the language and practice of business and the world of work they are here to stay. It therefore makes sense to put competencies, and competency modeling, into context to help bring the concept and the approach into focus with reference to the broader frame of work analysis practices used to build platforms for assessment.

Despite what may appear to be the case, competencies and competency modeling did not just appear out of the ethereal mist. There is an extensive history of research and practice concerning the architecture of work. In providing a brief review of

I benefited from discussion and review from a number of colleagues during the preparation of this chapter, including Bill Cunningham, Ed Fleishman, Dick Jeanneret, Felix E. Lopez, and Erich Prien. Although they may not agree with all of my conclusions or displays, their suggestions along the way certainly resulted in a better finished product. Two anonymous reviewers also provided a number of helpful suggestions on an early draft. Finally, thanks are extended to the Forsyth County Sheriff's Department of Winston-Salem, North Carolina, for access to space and room to write.

this history, my intent is to provide some necessary background and grounding in terms of terminology and a structure for thinking about the important decision points in research and practice. I begin by defining two key terms.

Competencies are the measurable, organizationally relevant, and behaviorally based capabilities of people. In this respect, they can be thought of as reflecting the evolution of knowledge, skills, abilities, and other characteristics (KSAOs) to descriptors that have become more specific, behavioral, and useful (Barrett, 1996). This said, the state of practice was so diffuse and poorly understood twenty-five years ago that many experts in the field of applied psychology, when asked to define *competencies,* would have defaulted to a statement along the lines of, "It depends on who you are talking to" (Zemke, 1982). In fact, it is not hard to find prominent human resource (HR) researchers who say virtually the same thing today. This kind of response, however, is unacceptable. It is time for some of us in the field to get our elitist noses out of the air and embrace what is good, sharpen up and supplement what is dull or missing, thoughtfully integrate with existing methods, and move forward to a higher playing field of research and practice. We must not forget the derisive comments about "floundering in a morass of semantic confusion" (see Kershner, as cited in McCormick, 1976), and worse (Prien, 1977), that were frequently directed at those in the job analysis ranks not that many years ago.

Competency modeling is the research procedure used for arriving at a definition and structure of the requirements for individual success for a given target of jobs (for example, managerial jobs or protective service officer jobs). In competency modeling, the job target may also be the overall organization, such as companywide leadership competencies, or all jobs in a broad job class, such as sales jobs across the organization. The defining features of competency modeling projects (versus job analysis) frequently include these practices:

- A focus on the individual capabilities required for success (versus a focus on tasks or the components of the job or the work environment)
- An emphasis on broadly applicable individual characteristic capabilities (versus a focus on the position, or a narrow job group, or technical requirements)

- A clear link to broad business strategy (versus a focus on job success without much consideration of business strategy or broad business initiatives)
- A coherent organization development and change emphasis (versus a number of loosely linked tactical research projects)

More on each of these defining features follows as we progress through the chapter. For now, though, in order to further define competency modeling as currently practiced and lay a foundation for the future, it is important to understand some of the historical confluence of thinking between job analysis and competency modeling.

Historical Links Between Competency Modeling and Job Analysis

Most HR interventions, such as assessment, development, and performance review, involve making decisions about people based on knowing something about the work being (or to be) performed and something about the people performing the work. In short, the equation has a work component and a people component. The investigative procedures used to capture facts about work, or the people who perform the work, have often been described as job analysis. Furthermore, different job analytic procedures may emphasize one side of the equation more than the other. The early focus of job analysis procedures, such as those used by Flanagan (1954), Fine (1955), and Hemphill (1960), was on the work itself. These methods were generally referred to as work oriented and examined tasks, activities, responsibilities, or other job characteristics or work outcomes.

Evolving somewhat later was a second broad class of job analysis methods, where the focus was primarily on the people side of the equation. These methods, often referred to as worker-oriented methods, focused on the knowledge, skills, abilities, experiences, personality traits, or other individual difference characteristics of the job incumbents. The work of McCormick, Jeanneret and Mecham (1972), Primoff (1975), and Fleishman (see Fleishman & Quaintance, 1984) are examples of this methodological focus.

The hybrid job analysis methods, which made a distinct effort to jointly look at both types of information, started appearing in the mid-1970s. At this point, researchers and practitioners such as Prien (see Prien & Ronan, 1971), Lopez (1986), Levine (1983), and Cunningham, Boese, Neeb, and Pass (1983) entered the picture. However, in none of the work mentioned up to this point (work oriented, worker oriented, hybrid, or otherwise) is there any reference to competencies. What can be found, however, is a confluence of thought and practice that, when combined with some other tributaries of thought and practice, can help explain how we got to where we are.

Figure 8.1 presents a streams-of-the-story pictorial history of job analysis and competency modeling and illustrates the evolving streams of thought. (Only material mentioned in the body of the text is included in the chapter references; a complete reference list for Figure 8.1 may be obtained by contacting the author.) So in terms of deep or upstream history, Figure 8.1 depicts the work-oriented job analysis methods growing out of the atomistic scientific management procedures of Taylor (1911). These methodologies continued to run their course through the 1950s, 1960s, and 1970s and are presented along the bottom of this figure. The worker-oriented methods, which are somewhat tenuous extensions of the generic "therblig" elements of analysis used by Gilbreth and Gilbreth (1917) and the job psychograph methodology proposed by Viteles (1923), run their course along the top half of the streams-of-the-story depicted in Figure 8.1.

So where do competencies fit into the picture? While the attempt to point to the true beginning of an idea or concept is difficult and seldom less than perfectly satisfying, a case can be made that McClelland's seminal paper, "Testing for Competence" (1973), provided much of the consolidated thinking and impetus (Barrett, 1996). As Figure 8.1 illustrates, McClelland's ideas helped guide the work of Boyatzis (1982) and others at Hay-McBer in their efforts to analyze the critical competencies of successful managers. Thus, the first competency dictionary was created, comprising broad competency dimensions like initiative, teamwork, and adaptability. This work then fed into the prominent competency assessment methodology described by Spencer, McClelland, and Spencer (1994).

It is worth noting that Primoff's worker-oriented job element method of job analysis (1975) may be thought of as something of a precursor to the significant contributions made by the Hay-McBer approach to modeling. The individual difference characteristics like initiative, teamwork, and adaptability at the core of the job element method are not unlike the competency dimensions with the same names (see Spencer & Spencer, 1993). Also, the approach used by Primoff and associates at the U.S. Office of Personnel Management involved targeting job requirements that differentiated high from low performers (Primoff & Eyde, 1988). This methodology was a defining feature of many of the early competency modeling approaches. Of course, the critical incident interviewing approach that Flanagan (1954) developed was also influential in the formulation of early competency modeling methods (Goleman, 1981). However, between Flanagan and the later competency modeling approaches, there were some less-well-known bridging efforts (as an example, see Williams, 1956).

Though not built into the representation of Figure 8.1, it probably makes sense to consider the job analysis work behind the creation of the great assessment center programs of the late 1960s and early 1970s. In many ways, the broad, generic individual difference dimensions at the measurement core of these centers were a harbinger of things to come in terms of competency modeling (Schippmann, Hughes, & Prien, 1987; Schippmann et al., 2000). Assessment center dimensions like drive or energy or creativity and so forth, defined as they were by behavioral statements in the centers at AT&T (Bray & Grant, 1966), IBM (Hinrichs, 1969), and Sohio (Thompson, 1970), look a lot like the competency modeling dimensions with the same names found in the generic models of providers of competency modeling services like Hay-McBer (Spencer & Spencer, 1993), PDI (Davis, Hellervik, Skube, Gebelein, & Sheared, 1996), Lominger (Lombardo & Eichinger, 1998), and DDI (Byham & Moyer, 2005).

However, as influential as the original Hay-McBer approach has been (and subsequent extensions by firms like Lominger), by far the biggest push to competency modeling came from a *Harvard Business Review* article by Prahalad and Hamel (1990) describing core competencies as an integral part of business strategy. Despite being a distinct concept (competencies in this discourse are more design components of an organization's business strategy than individual-level attributes), the huge popularity

Figure 8.1. Job Analysis and Competency Modeling: Streams-of-the-Story History

With thanks and input from Bill Cunningham, Ed Fleishman, Dick Jenneret, Felix Lopez, and Erich Prien.

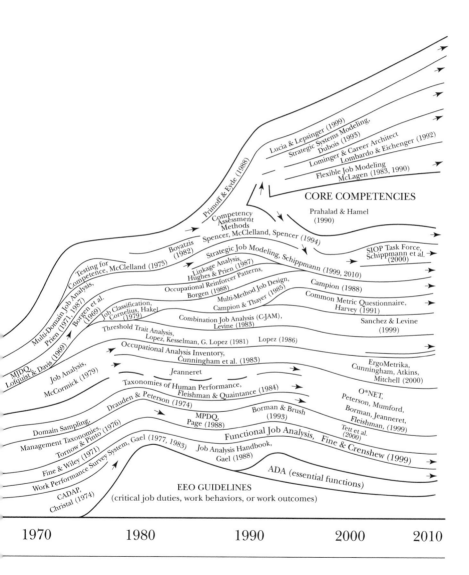

Lucia & Lepsinger (1999)
Strategic Systems Modeling, Dubois (1993)
Lominger & Career Architect
Lombardo & Eichenger (1992)
Flexible Job Modeling
McLagen (1983, 1990)

Primoff & Eyde (1988)

Competency Assessment Methods

CORE COMPETENCIES

Prahalad & Hamel (1990)

Spencer, McClelland, Spencer (1994)

Boyatzis (1982)

Strategic Job Modeling, Schippmann (1999, 2010)

SIOP Task Force, Schippmann et al. (2000)

Testing for Competence, McClelland (1973)

Linkage Analysis, Hughes & Prien (1987)

Multi-Domain Job Analysis, Prien (1971, 1987)

Borgen et al. (1969)

Occupational Reinforcer Patterns, Borgen (1988)

Campion (1988)

Job Classification, Cornelius, Hakel (1979)

Multi-Method Job Design, Campion & Thayer (1985)

Common Metric Questionnaire, Harvey (1991)

MJDQ, Lofquist & Davis (1969)

Threshold Trait Analysis, Lopez, Kesselman, G. Lopez (1981)

Combination Job Analysis (C-JAM), Levine (1983)

Lopez (1986)

Sanchez & Levine (1999)

Job Analysis, McCormick (1979)

Occupational Analysis Inventory, Cunningham et al. (1983)

Jeanneret

ErgoMetrika, Cunningham, Atkins, Mitchell (2000)

Taxonomies of Human Performance, Fleishman & Quaintance (1984)

Drauden & Peterson (1974)

O*NET, Peterson, Mumford, Borman, Jeanneret, Fleishman, (1999)

MPDQ, Page (1988)

Borman & Brush (1993)

Tett et al. (2000)

Domain Sampling, Management Taxonomies, Tornow & Pinto (1976)

Functional Job Analysis, Fine & Crenshew (1999)

Fine & Wiley (1971)

Work Performance Survey System, Gael (1977, 1983)

Job Analysis Handbook, Gael (1988)

CADAP, Christal (1974)

ADA (essential functions)

EEO GUIDELINES
(critical job duties, work behaviors, or work outcomes)

1970   1980   1990   2000   2010

of this article galvanized interest among business leaders around the world in the idea of core leadership or people-related skills.

At this point, there ceased to be a need by organizational researchers and practitioners to push efforts to study worker characteristics, and there was a tremendous pull by businesspeople and HR specialists to adapt and extend the ideas proffered by Prahalad and Hamel and make them fit-for-purpose in their own organizations. Influential chapters and books by McLagan (1990), Dubois (1993), and Lucia and Lepsinger (1999) certainly helped move matters along. Huge competency modeling conferences sponsored by firms like Linkage (1996) were also important in creating converts and disciples. The net effect was that within the span of several years after Prahalad and Hamel's article, a competency modeling tsunami washed over the global business landscape. Concurrently the job analysis professionals who had been toiling in this research space for many years simply lost all control of terms, definitions, measurement best practices, and everything else. By the mid-1990s, practice and application had outstripped research and reporting by such a huge margin that nobody had a clear sense of what was going on.

Into this information breach, the Society for Industrial and Organizational Psychology commissioned a task force from its Professional Practice Committee and the Scientific Affairs Committee and charged the team to build a framework for understanding, develop standards for practice, and report back to members. The resulting framework, standards, and report were published in 2000 (Schippmann et al., 2000). An important part of this report included the ten-dimension Level of Rigor scale. It is worth explaining the components of this scale in some detail in the next section.

Building a Basis for Assessment: Comparing and Contrasting Competency Modeling and Job Analysis

The results of a competency modeling or job analysis effort are seldom viewed as an end product. Instead they provide an intermediate product used to select (or develop or modify) a selection system, a multirater feedback instrument, an assessment center, a coaching and development program, and so on. Consequently the fit between the applications that are selected (or developed or modified) will be no better than the quality of the information produced by this essential first step. Furthermore, there is a widespread operating assumption among HR professionals that the front-end modeling or analysis activities must meet some minimal standards of acceptability so that inferences from the "results" can be confidently drawn (Schippmann et al., 2000). The ten dimensions in the Level of Rigor scale represent a way to measure the extent to which potential sources of confusion have been managed and controlled for as part of the analysis or modeling effort. The ten dimensions are listed below and, for illustrative purposes, the complete definitions and levels for the first four dimensions are presented in Table 8.1:

1. Method of investigation
2. Type of descriptor content collected
3. Procedures for developing descriptor content
4. Detail of descriptor content
5. Link to business goals and strategies
6. Content review
7. Prioritizing descriptor content
8. Assessment of reliability
9. Item or category retention criteria
10. Documentation

The full set of Level of Rigor scale dimensions is essentially a high-level road map for how to do it right. It also provides a framework for practitioners and researchers to use for reporting on their work efforts and for making comparisons across projects. While the Level of Rigor framework has received only limited attention since it was published, it has slowly been gaining acceptance and reference in appropriate places, as in the SIOP *Principles for the Validation and Use of Personnel Selection Procedures* (2003).

The SIOP task force took the additional step of comparing and contrasting typical competency modeling efforts from typical job analysis efforts, all part of trying to come to grips with the question, "What is competency modeling?" Based on a review of

206

Table 8.1. Level of Rigor Scale

Variable	1 Low Rigor	2 Low/Medium Rigor	3 Medium Rigor	4 Medium/High Rigor	5 High Rigor
Method of investigation	Same method for collecting information (for example, focus group, observation, interview, or fixed-content questionnaire) is employed, regardless of setting or target population.	Same two methods used every time regardless of the research setting and intended application.	Variable combination of two methods used depending on some effort to consider the constraints of the research setting.	Variable combination of two or three methods used, depending on the research setting, target population, and intended application.	Variable combination and logically selected mix of multiple methods used to obtain information (focus group, observation, interview, or questionnaire) depending on the research setting, target population, and intended application.
Type of descriptor content collected	Same type of information (for example, competencies, work activities, KSAOs, or performance standards) collected every time, regardless of intended applications.	Same two types of information collected every time, regardless of intended applications.	Variable combination of two types of information collected, depending on the intended applications.	Variable combination of two or three types of information collected, depending on the intended applications.	Variable combination of multiple types of information (for example, competencies, work activities, KSAOs, or performance standards) collected, depending on the intended applications.

Procedures for developing descriptor content	No effort to gather information from content experts; instead the researcher or analyst serves as sole content expert.	Information is gathered from convenient samples of content experts using ad hoc or unstructured procedures. No qualification criteria (such as time on the job, top performers) are used to identify individuals in the best position to serve as content experts.	Information is collected from a large number of content experts using a semistructured protocol. Some effort is made to identify individuals most qualified to serve as content experts.	Information collected from content experts using a structured protocol and with reference to a fairly well-thought-out sampling plan. Content experts meet some qualification criteria (for example, time on job, top performers based on appraisals).	Information collected from content experts using a structured protocol and following a logically developed sampling plan, with a comprehensive and representative sample. Content experts meet some qualification criteria (for example, time on job, top performers).
Detail of descriptor content	Handful of broad labels representing categories of content, with no associated definitions.	Broad labels with narrative definitions or small sample of descriptor items serving as the operational definition.	Moderately specific labels representing different categories or content and a mix of descriptor items helping to operationally define each category.	Fairly precise labels representing different categories of content that subsume fairly comprehensive sets of item-level descriptors that operationally define each category.	A number of precise labels representing discrete categories of content that subsume very comprehensive and crisply defined sets of item-level descriptors that operationally define each category and leave no room for misinterpretation.

the literature and thirty-seven subject matter expert (SME) interviews with leading academics and practitioners, the eleven members of the task force completed a rating task using the Level of
Rigor scale applied to both competency modeling and job analysis. While certainly not perfect, and in full recognition that there
is no such thing as a typical modeling or analysis effort, the two
resulting profiles of practice nevertheless seemed to be appropriate representations of describing practice differences at that
point in time (Schippmann et al., 2000). Generally the results
indicated that job analysis methods were viewed as being more
rigorous, particularly in terms of selecting descriptor content,
assessing the reliability of compiled judgments, final documentation, and so forth. In terms of linking the results to business
goals and longer-term business strategies, however, competency
modeling efforts were seen as more rigorous. Nevertheless, several common features of competency modeling warrant further exploration. Going a bit deeper with each of the defining
features of competency modeling noted at the beginning of the
chapter will provide a means for presenting the evolving thinking
and research directions in the field. This thinking and research
are important because the resulting descriptions or models guide
the development, selection, and evaluation of relevant predictor
instruments in an assessment context and the identification and
creation of meaningful learning experiences and development
opportunities and tools in a development context, for example.

Competency Modeling: A Focus on Individual Characteristics Required for Success

Perhaps the most prominent defining feature of the original approach to competency modeling was a focus on the individual
characteristics required for success—concepts like judgment, initiative, dependability, and decisiveness. Of course, this focus by
itself is not a make-or-break differentiator because a number of the
worker-oriented approaches to job analysis had a similar emphasis. That said, Goleman's (1981) article in *Psychology Today* certainly
helped popularize a frequently cited definition: "Competencies are
defined not as aspects of a given job, but as special characteristics
of people who do the job best" (p. 39).

This definition requires some expansion. Clearly some people perform certain work activities better than others, and it can be argued that this varying degree of possession of specific competencies explains different levels of task performance. It can make some sense to think of competencies as being composed of three broad classes of individual characteristics: abilities; traits; and interests, values, and motivations (Schippmann, 1999). These three classes of individual difference characteristics constitute the deep structure, or foundation, on which education or training and experience opportunities are laid. In this scheme, opportunities comprise the middle structure that rests on the foundation. Competencies, then, constitute the occupationally relevant surface structure and represent the capstone to the people pyramid illustrated in the top left of Figure 8.2 (the measurable, organizationally relevant, and behaviorally based capabilities of people described in terms of actions or what people do to succeed).

However, it can also be useful to think of competencies from the work-being-performed perspective too. The work pyramid (top right in Figure 8.2) is also capped off with a competency block. These competencies are the same kind of individual difference capabilities described on the people side of the equation, but with one difference: the competencies referred to here are those required to perform a job, role, or function or serve as a leader in a particular organization, versus those possessed by or available on the part of an individual. So rather than reiterate the components that comprise competencies from an individual perspective, the focus here is to describe the underlying drivers that highlight certain competencies being more or less important in a given context. As the top right of Figure 8.2 illustrates, work activities and work context determine competency requirements, and the organization's vision, strategic objectives, and initiatives form the basis for the work context and associated work activities. A more detailed discussion of this approach may be found elsewhere (Schippmann, 1999), though for purposes of this discussion, it is necessary to cover a couple of additional points.

To be clear, the people side of the modeling equation views competencies as a constellation of knowledge, skills, abilities, traits, interests, values, motivations, education and training, and experience

Figure 8.2. The Competency Pyramids

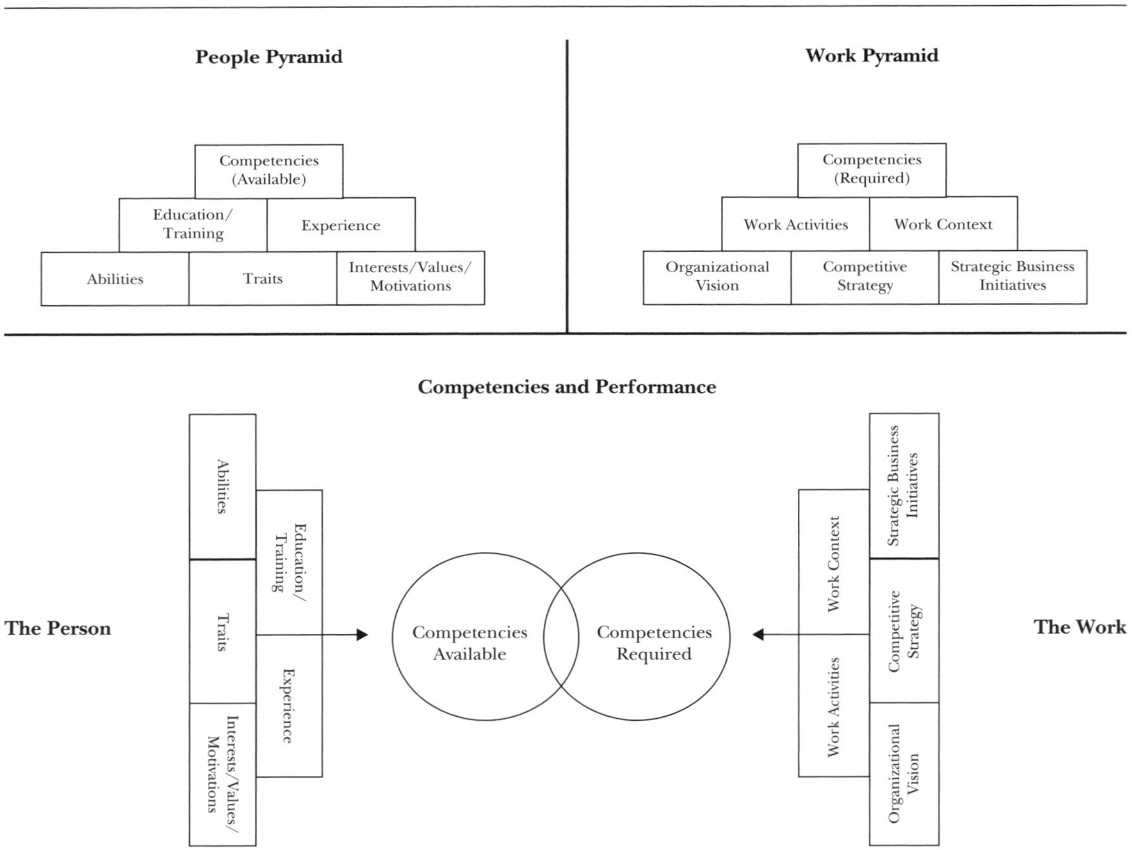

People Pyramid

Work Pyramid

The Work

	Competencies (Available)	
Education/ Training		Experience
Abilities	Traits	Interests/Values/ Motivations

	Competencies (Required)	
Work Activities		Work Context
Organizational Vision	Competitive Strategy	Strategic Business Initiatives

Competencies and Performance

Organizational Vision	Competitive Strategy	Strategic Business Initiatives
	Work Activities	Work Context

Competencies Required

Competencies Available

	Education/ Training	Experience
Abilities	Traits	Interests/Values/ Motivations

The Person

210

components that give rise to the competencies that are available. The work side of the modeling equation takes into account the organization direction, strategies, business initiatives, work context, and activities that give rise to the competencies required. The bottom half of Figure 8.2 extends the ideas of the people and work pyramids a little further by showing how these two perspectives work together in an assessment context. In this example, the amount of overlap between the individual competencies available and the work competencies required is minimal. Obviously this degree of overlap has performance implications for the person performing the work. If the available competencies are significantly less than what is required, the performance implications are negative. To the extent they match, or match in the most important areas, the performance implications are positive.

It should be noted that at least historically, a common methodological approach for identifying competencies to include in the final model was to focus on those capabilities that differentiated high performers from average performers. In other words, what competencies do high performers demonstrate that average performers in the target group do not? From the perspective of building an assessment protocol, this tactic may result in overlooking or undervaluing the basic competencies that are foundational for success in the target job. For example, strong analytical and problem-solving capabilities were fundamentally important to software engineers with a global technology company, although other competencies such as teamwork and collaboration were among those that characterized and differentiated top performers in the company. A preemployment assessment protocol that in any way undervalued the importance of the analytical and problem-solving capabilities required for job success (which, because of the high level of capability across employees, were not useful as a differentiator between high and average employees) would have inappropriately limited the value of the screening process. My sense is that the tactic of focusing only on the competencies that differentiate high from average employees is not the defining feature of mainstream competency modeling approaches it once was, perhaps due to the expansion of competency modeling beyond supporting primarily developmental tools into broader HR applications such as selection.

In terms of measurement issues, a central feature of a competency modeling or job analysis effort is a determination of the most important aspects for a given context or application. Typically this involves having incumbents, SMEs, or modeling or analyst experts evaluate (rate or rank) content to determine the most important (or some other judgment, such as "most difficult to learn") components. As such, one should expect that the judgments made by these experts would agree, although there are certainly limitations to consider (Morgeson & Campion, 1997).

Interest in this area has been growing, and progress is being made in understanding the factors that influence the quality of these judgments and the subsequent inferences (Sanchez & Levine, 1994; Lievens, Sanchez, & De Corte, 2004; Dierdorff & Wilson, 2003). In summary, as one might expect, when the descriptor material being evaluated (a competency or task, for example) is more general (low in specificity) and less observable, variability due to rater differences increases and reliability decreases (Dierdorff & Morgeson, 2008).

Similar results were found in a range of job modeling research projects and associated content libraries where the composition of work activity statements and competency statements was graded in terms of specificity using the four-step Statement Detail Scale (Schippmann, 1999). An old truism in the work analysis field has been that the same level of specificity is not required for all types of information or to support all possible HR applications. Despite this broadly accepted belief, no specific rules have guided practice. The work with the Statement Detail Scale was an initial effort to provide some broad practice guidelines, and the application of the scale as a way to evaluate the potential quality of inferences from different inventories was, in all honesty, an afterthought.

Not surprisingly, given the more general nature of the early competency modeling descriptors, the reliability of judgments made with reference to this content has been found to be quite low (Lievens et al., 2004). However, these authors also found that by including a focus on the work side of the equation and adding task statements, the interrater reliability of the competency modeling effort was improved. Similarly, Catano, Darr, and Campbell (2007) supplemented core competencies used in a performance appraisal system with task information from a functional job analysis, and thereby increased the reliability and validity of the performance ratings. In sum, the early yet emerging point of view is that blending traditional competency measurement with some complementary focus on the work side of the equation may enhance the inferences that can be drawn from the results of a competency modeling effort.

Competency Modeling: A Focus on Broadly Applicable Individual Characteristic Dimensions

The second key defining feature of competency modeling is that the descriptions of individual-level capabilities that are provided are typically core, or common, for very broad groups of employees in an organization—all executives, for example, or even all employees in the company (Schippmann et al., 2000). In other words, the focus of the early competency modeling efforts was on broad applicability and leveraging what is common. As a result, the descriptive material produced by these efforts was at a fairly high level and general in nature. Because of this companywide emphasis, competencies were the natural choice of descriptive material to be built into human resource management (HRM) software solutions that were beginning to capture attention in the business marketplace in the 1990s.

Although the first-generation HRM systems were primarily focused on administrative aspects of HR, such as employee and applicant tracking, payroll, and benefit information, the second generation of HRM tools has become much more useful and integrative. Schuler and Jackson (2005) note that horizontal integration is now a hallmark of HRM systems and that many HR practices that were previously considered distinct activities (screening and selection, performance appraisal, succession planning, individual development, and others) now must be integrated for the system solution to be fully used. These second-generation tools are now being broadly used across the business landscape (Hollincheck, 2007), and one need only look at the underlying descriptive content and HR architecture of offerings by SuccessFactors, Authoria, Oracle-PeopleSoft, SAP, Pilat HR Solutions, Saba, and others, to see how the broad, companywide nature of competencies is being used to knit the HR components together.

The historical emphasis of the job analytic approaches, of course, has been description at a granular level, with a focus on highlighting what is distinct and different across jobs, occupational groups, and levels in an organization—a poor philosophical and practical fit for the needs of the second-generation HRM systems. However, the system-driven HRM march and evolution will continue, and the best is yet to come. For these systems to be truly valuable as integrating and delivery platforms for best-in-class HR programs and processes, they now need to build vertical scalability, and not just broad horizontal applicability, into the content architecture. Just as Schippmann et al. (2000) called for a next-generation work modeling approach that blends the best of competency modeling with job analysis, the call here is for third-generation HRM tools to accommodate the vertical scalability of descriptor content. (The same level of detail is not needed to support all types of HR applications.)

As an example, consider the detailed map of competencies of a retail consumer electronics company presented by Schippmann (1999). In brief, the work described covered the four primary business units of a Global 1000 organization. Furthermore, the organization's competency dictionary was segmented into four broad classes of competencies:

- *Core or organizationwide*—competencies that cut across all business units, job levels, and job functions, such as analytical thinking and innovation
- *Business-unit specific*—competencies that supported the strategies of particular business groups, such as customer orientation and risk taking
- *Job-level specific*—competencies that defined the expectations of vertically arranged job groups, such as "provide direction" or "coach others" from the management area
- *Functionally specific*—competencies that defined the technical knowledge and skills required to perform in different functional areas of the business, such as financial statements and analysis from the accounting area, database management from the IT area, international marketing from the marketing area, and microelectronic fabrication from the engineering area

Thus, any one "job" in the organization is a mix of core, business-unit-specific, job-level-specific, and functionally specific competencies. A singular focus in any one area, core, function, or otherwise would overlook important aspects of what it takes to succeed. Stated somewhat differently, descriptive models should consist of both organizational and job-specific success factors (see Chapter Seventeen). Again, not all HR interventions require information at the same level of detail to achieve maximum utility. Too little detail for one kind of HR application (say, selection) could create exposure from a legal defensibility standpoint. And too much detail or descriptive content can obscure the payoff of a different application (such as broad career planning and the creation of career ladders). The ability to package, scale, and prioritize the most useful content for an intended purpose will be a defining step forward from second- to third-generation HRM systems. Neither competency modeling nor job analysis alone has shown the ability to get us there. However, a blended, next-generation work modeling approach could do just that.

Competency Modeling: A Clear Link to Strategy

As mentioned in the review provided by the SIOP Task Force (Schippmann, 1999), making an attempt to build the strategic and future-oriented needs of the organization into the results is another distinguishing feature of the competency modeling approach. On the job analysis side of the fence, this hugely important focus was, with few exceptions (see Schneider & Kronz, 1989), simply ignored over the years. Although today there is a significant amount, and range, of practice, there is, sadly, little research or formal description of practice (Schippmann, 1999, and Olesen, White, & Lemmer, 2007, are a couple of exceptions). An example of how the strategic link can be made will be useful here.

Company ABC is the disguised name of a major U.S. player in the vertical construction space. In this instance, the HR team partnered with the corporate strategy team to distill the strategic plans and the annual operating plans from the past several years into a clear picture of where the organization currently sat in terms of the macro, micro, and organization environment (Schippmann, 2008). Similarly, a reasonably clear view of the aspirational future organization was built based on the same set of strategic plans and additional planning discussions with the executive leadership of the organization. This future look was an articulation of the organization's destination—its goals and aspirations based on what was known about the business environment and speculations about the future, filtered through a lens of what was considered valuable, worthwhile, and reasonably attainable. A high-level summary of the current organization and the envisioned future organization is presented in Figure 8.3.

The key, though, is how to get from the current business definition on the left side of the figure to the hoped-for future state on the right side. In the project described here, the intent was to identify the challenges standing in the way (the brick wall in Figure 8.3). To do this, a series of one-on-one interviews was conducted with the top thirty-one executives in the company. In independent interviews, these executives were presented with the current and future parts of the picture and simply asked, "How do we get there?" Prompts during the interviews included, "What does the company need to do differently?" "What does the company need to fix or get better at?" and "What does the company need to start, or stop, doing?" The responses were captured and thematically analyzed to create a report that grouped similar conclusions and inputs into homogeneous categories. (A slightly modified and disguised version of this report is available from the author on request.) A histogram summarizing the frequency with which similar challenges and issues were independently offered by these executives was part of this report (Figure 8.4). The top ideas generated in these individual discussions then formed the basis for further discussions by the executive team, and the prioritized challenges and issues are represented as the brick wall in Figure 8.3.

The components of how Company ABC was going to forge a path to the future then served as the reference point for evaluating the existing leadership competency model for the organization. With reference to the strategic direction and key issues described, the seventeen dimensions and sixty items of the

Figure 8.3. Strategic Direction and Challenges for Company ABC

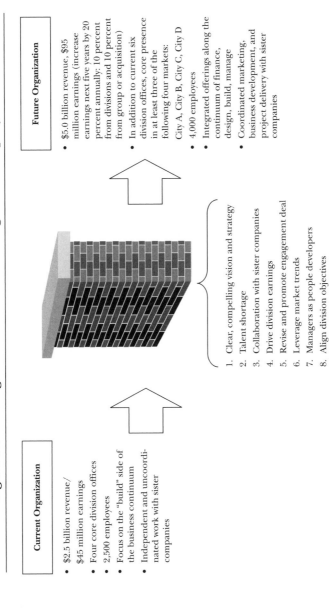

Current Organization

- $2.5 billion revenue/ $45 million earnings
- Four core division offices
- 2,500 employees
- Focus on the "build" side of the business continuum
- Independent and uncoordinated work with sister companies

1. Clear, compelling vision and strategy
2. Talent shortage
3. Collaboration with sister companies
4. Drive division earnings
5. Revise and promote engagement deal
6. Leverage market trends
7. Managers as people developers
8. Align division objectives

Future Organization

- $5.0 billion revenue, $95 million earnings (increase earnings next five years by 20 percent annually: 10 percent from divisions and 10 percent from group or acquisition)
- In addition to current six division offices, core presence in at least three of the following four markets: City A, City B, City C, City D
- 4,000 employees
- Integrated offerings along the continuum of finance, design, build, manage
- Coordinated marketing, business development, and project delivery with sister companies

Figure 8.4. Strategic Challenges for Company ABC

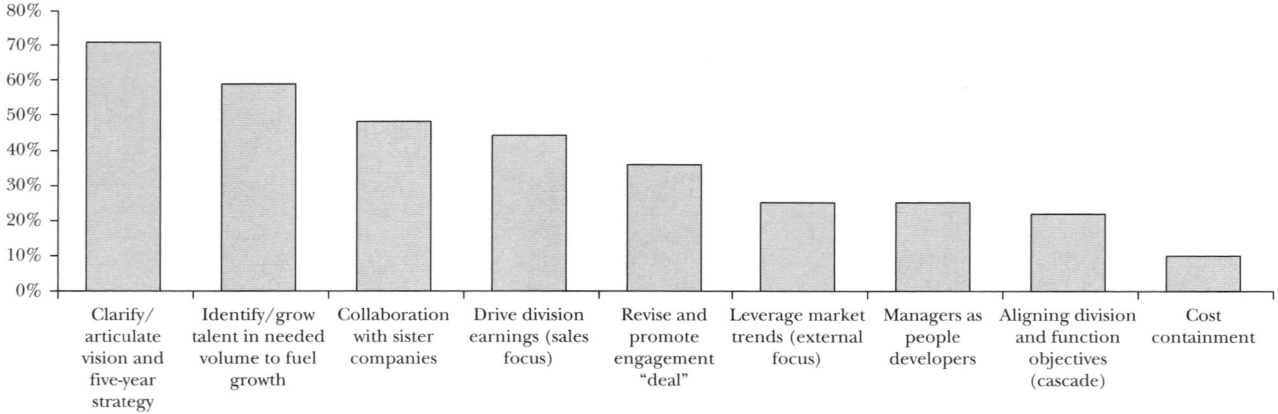

existing model were then evaluated by SMEs using a simple three-point scale:

1. Essential and directly relevant for accomplishing strategic business objectives
2. Useful and indirectly relevant for accomplishing strategic business objectives
3. Incidental and/or not particularly relevant for accomplishing strategic business objectives

In a manner very similar to (and really just an extension of) Lawshe's content validity ratio (1975), a novel strategic relevance ratio (SRR) methodology was employed. The SRR for the existing model was .68, which was barely significant. The process was useful for identifying items that were, in relative terms, much less important for achieving strategic objectives in the current construction business environment. At the same time, glaring gaps in the existing model were exposed, and currently work is underway to close these gaps. Once the model is enhanced, it will be reevaluated using the SRR methodology as a way to evaluate and track the relevance of the content on an ongoing basis as an extension of the existing business strategic planning process.

In sum, the competency modeling approach, which encourages greater consideration of an organization's strategic needs (Schuler & Jackson, 2005), is an important step forward in the work analysis field. Incorporating some of the methodological rigor from traditional job analysis into this strategic linkage work creates the basis for an even more powerful approach. Blending the strengths of both will be necessary to build assessment protocols for the sophisticated, scalable, and future-oriented assessment applications described in the remaining chapters of this book.

Competency Modeling: A Coherent Organization Development and Change Emphasis

In part because of competency modeling's focus on broadly applicable characteristics and in part due to the effort to link to broad business strategy, these projects often become highly visible organizational development or organizational change interventions

(Schippmann, 1999; Campion, Fink, & Ruggeberg, 2008). Anytime the organization's senior teams are involved in talking about strategy, anytime the vision and core values of the firm get examined, reshaped, and written down, anytime there are broad discussions about how a company wants people to behave and work together, the visibility and potential impact of a particular intervention go way up. This is very different from the tenor of the conversations and level of interest that typically accompany the mind-numbingly arcane, grindingly difficult, and what-difference-can-it-make level of detail found with many traditional job analysis projects.

Think about it. Organizational development and change efforts have been incredibly hot topics over the past twenty-five years for several fundamental reasons. In addition to the pace of change and the wild swings of the world's economic markets, there has been a focus on globalization, mergers, acquisitions, the impact of interrelated customers, and many other changes. In one way or another, this is all about taking a broad view, piecing things together, and figuring out how to work better in interrelated environments. While the traditional job analysis approaches could have much to offer here, we simply have not delivered; instead we have been content to focus primarily on how things are different at an atomistic level.

However, what we have done in the past does not have to be the case going forward. A number of interesting efforts to develop approaches for leading and driving change have been made over these past twenty-five years, and the gulf between what they propose and what traditional job analysis practitioners and researchers are trying to do is not as great as one might initially imagine. One of the more prominent change approaches is Kotter's (1996) eight-step change model, which I think is particularly useful. Because of the prominence (business leaders recognize the name and they know the books) and practicality of the approach, I typically use a six-step variant (see Schippmann & Newson, 2008) as a basis for structuring and driving modeling interventions:

- Establish value and urgency.
- Build the coalition.

- Refine the vision and strategy.
- Communicate for buy-in.
- Create short-term wins.
- Assimilate the change.

In the main, this is about making sure the change introduced to the organization, whether modeling or a subsequent intervention based on modeling work, is meaningful and accepted. The competency modeling contingent got us knocking on the OD door. Combining the creative competency modeling ideas and efforts in this area with some of the rigor and power of job analysis methodology, and supported by basic change principles as described above, get us to the point where we can break down the door and move right in and take residence.

Strategic Competency Modeling and Assessment

Few organizations operating in today's complex business environment can be successful without talented people working together to implement the strategies of their respective organizations. Furthermore, few would question that the level of success attained by individuals and work teams in an organization is directly influenced by the quality and success of the HR programs and processes designed to support the organization's people. The challenge is how to do this and how to integrate these HR applications so they work together in a complementary manner.

Unfortunately the creative, forward-looking, and model-building component involved in this constellation of HR research activities often seems to get overlooked in traditional approaches to job analysis. And the logic, precision, and rigor needed to generate fundamentally sound information that can be used to guide improved decision making have often been in short supply in some traditional approaches to competency modeling. What has been called for is a blending of the two approaches into a next-generation fact-gathering approach that is appropriately rigorous and specific (where rigor and specificity are required, and without going overboard), strategic, integrative and platform friendly, and overall more of an organization development change effort than a collection of singular, microfocused, and tactical projects (Schippmann, 1999; Schippmann et al., 2000; Schuler & Jackson, 2005).

Schippmann (1999) presented a blended approach referred to as strategic job modeling. Barney (2000) presented a variant blend approach called strategic work modeling. Campion et al. (2008) have presented a blend of best practices and refer to the practice simply as "doing competencies well." Regardless of the name, the directional path forward is reasonably clear. It is not an either-or proposition any more than traditional competency modeling or traditional job analysis is. The strengths and flexibility of both are required. As a proposal, from a purely marketing perspective, it might make sense to embrace strategic competency modeling to leverage the positive brand equity that has developed in the business marketplace around the word *competency*.

Regardless of name, the purpose of this blended approach will be to provide a scalable platform for the broad range of assessment, development, performance review, and change management tools and approaches, among many others, that will be required to guide and elevate the people-related capabilities of organizations operating in today's increasingly competitive business environment. In an era where good decision-making information is more important than ever before, there should be significant focus on the science and judgment that go into building the soundness of the research yielding the model or descriptive framework. What is meant by soundness? The answer is multifaceted and brings us back to the Level of Rigor scale. Is the resulting framework and descriptive material:

- At the appropriate detail to drive the intended applications?
- Appropriately linked to business goals and strategies?
- Meaningful, relevant, and reliably interpretable?

All of the characteristics noted in the Level of Rigor scale, taken together, determine the strength of the evidence we have that the model is fairly and accurately describing the right stuff. To the extent a model is fairly and accurately describing the right stuff in a comprehensive and robust manner, it is relevant. Note my use of the word *relevant*, and not *valid*. It is not appropriate to describe a competency model as valid or not valid any more than a taxonomy from a job analysis effort would be considered valid or not valid.

For example, a preemployment test can be designed to measure a particular competency and predict a particular performance outcome. To the extent that this test delivers on this expectation, the inferences about future performance from the test scores are valid. In the same manner, an individual coaching program can be created to measure and develop a specific set of competencies. If the program produces the expected outcome, it may be thought of as being truly effective. Thus, in the HR realm, validity can be defined as the best approximation of the truth or falsity of the inferences and predictions based on some HR intervention or application.

In contrast to validity, relevance addresses the question of whether the result produced by the intervention focuses on the right set of criteria and has a meaningful relationship to the higher-order objectives of an organization's success and goal attainment. For example, the preemployment testing program for the individual banking department of a former client focused entirely on basic administrative competencies, and the program was producing adequate validities. Therefore, in one sense, it could be construed to be working and the resulting inferences from the test scores to be valid. However, after conducting an SRR analysis of the macroenvironment and strategic context, several looming changes were highlighted and used to modify the program. In short, to compete in an increasingly deregulated and unprotected market with a host of new competitors entering the business space, the strategy of the bank was shifting from a passive service orientation to a very proactive sales orientation. In turn, the front-end individual banking jobs were becoming less focused on basic administration and much more focused on sales and upselling. At that time, the current testing program, although in one sense valid and working, was not particularly relevant when juxtaposed with the organization's strategic needs, which were, out of necessity, dramatically changing in order to meet the future. The SRR analysis was used to evaluate the relevance of the competency framework and guide necessary enhancements.

Figure 8.5 presents the concepts of validity and relevance within the context of the strategic competency modeling enterprise.

In this representation, criterion-related validity examines the close-in relationship between final outcomes or results and the expectations or inferences derived from specific HR applications, such as scores from an assessment program. Content validity refers to the connection between the important components of the job (or job class or broad organizational role, for example; as the assessment target becomes broader, the definition of success broadens as well) and the appropriate sampling and translation of those components into the specific HR application. Construct validity is the overarching evidentiary approach that includes both content and criterion-related research as well as broader research strategies (see the description in Chapter Twenty-One for elaboration).

In sum, within the context of strategic competency modeling, relevance examines the distal relationship between results and the organization's needs associated with upstream superordinate goals (Schippmann, 1999). Without yielding any quality in terms of establishing the job relatedness, the assessment protocols for the next era of HR applications will need to maximize the link and payoff associated with these broader ultimate objectives.

A relevant and well-supported competency model or taxonomy can be expected to go a long way toward furthering the assessment or other objectives of a researcher or practitioner. While well beyond the scope of this chapter to describe how to conduct a strategic competency modeling effort, it is possible to make some suggestions that may be built on by the remaining chapters in this book.

First and foremost, it is important to be clear about the objectives of one's particular assessment enterprise. What are you trying to do? The mix of answers to this question will guide the thinking and emphases in the competency modeling effort. Will the modeling work be used to build a platform of information that can be used to support a particular assessment application, a cluster of applications, or all of the applications in an HR system? There is an investigative and creative aspect to modeling. In this light, it can be appropriate to think of the modeling enterprise as a series of questions whose answers guide you where to go in terms of the next step in building a meaningful

Figure 8.5. Visual Representation of Relevance and Validity

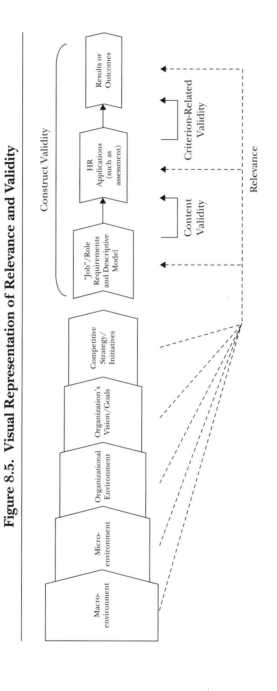

225

information path to support the intended applications—for example (paraphrasing from Schippmann, 1999):

- What is the organization's vision and competitive strategy, and what are the corresponding strategic initiatives already in play? Within this context, what are the desired business outcomes?
- What HR applications are required to achieve the desired outcomes? Given these applications, what type of information needs to be built into the information platform, and what degree of detail is required in the descriptor content?
- Who is the target population? Given the scope of the target population, how is existing descriptive information leveraged? How are existing models or descriptive information collected and integrated to create a rationally derived model?
- If the research context and the target applications require following up on the rationally derived model and the collection of data to create an empirically evaluated model, then which questions are asked, and of whom? How many respondents are needed?
- How should the results from the modeling exercise be analyzed and then displayed to best support the applications? What kinds of decision rules should be applied to guide the final components of the model, and what degree of research documentation is required?

Of course, each modeling situation is unique and has its own requirements and variables to consider, and making specific recommendations is difficult. However, using a question set such as this one to spur thinking, push the consideration options, and encourage time spent evaluating the logic and implications of decisions is valuable.

Finally, when building a model to support an assessment platform, it seldom makes sense to start from scratch; there is simply too much starting material that can be used to jump-start this part of the project. Certainly proprietary models are available for the domain of management work from vendors like Lominger and Personnel Decisions International (see Tett, Guterman, Bleier, &

Murphy, 2000, for an overview of the competency dimensions). In addition, Bartram (2005) presents 112 discrete competency items that roll up into 20 competency dimensions, which then are subsumed under 8 competency factors (all part of the SHL competency framework). Nonproprietary models for managers and executives may also be found in the literature from authors such as Tett et al. (2000), who identified 53 competency dimensions from 12 published and practitioner models, and Schippmann (1999), who presented a 156-item, 25-dimension, 6-factor competency model (and corresponding work activity taxonomy) based on an analysis of 32 published and unpublished research efforts.

Adapting (versus simply adopting) these starting-point descriptive frameworks can jump-start efforts to identify important predictor constructs, provide a basis for identifying training needs or coaching targets, and so forth. However, a caution is in order when using descriptive information from existing models: it can be tempting to assume a particular framework is complete and sufficient without critically examining the structure and descriptive content to ensure appropriate and comprehensive coverage for the target applications in the target organizations (for guidance, refer to the Level of Rigor scale; see Schippmann et al., 2000).

Conclusion

These are interesting times for those of us working in HR. The need for speed and simplicity has become greater, while the HR applications we work with have become more varied, sophisticated, and interrelated. Concurrently the information platforms required to support the creation, selection, and modification of these applications are also being driven by the need for speed, simplicity, variety and flexibility, sophistication, and interrelatedness. The ideal approach for developing the information models to support these applications is not traditional job analysis. Neither is it traditional competency modeling. Instead, a blended approach is called for. The next era of HR applications (assessment based and otherwise) will be best supported by the more sophisticated and flexible information platforms created by these next-generation blended approaches.

References

Barney, M. (2000). Interdisciplinary contributions to strategic work modeling. *Ergometrika, 1*, 24–37.

Barrett, R. S. (1996). *Fair employment strategies in human resource management.* Westport, CT: Quorum Books.

Bartram, D. (2005). The great eight competencies: A criterion approach to validation. *Journal of Applied Psychology, 90*, 1185–1203.

Boyatzis, R. E. (1982). *The competent manager: A model for effective performance.* Hoboken, NJ: Wiley.

Bray, D. W., & Grant, D. L. (1966). The assessment center in the measurement of potential for business management. *Psychological Monographs, 80*(17).

Byham, W. C., & Moyer, R. P. (2005). *Using competencies to build a successful organization.* Pittsburgh, PA: Development Dimensions International.

Campion, M. A., Fink, A. A., & Ruggeberg, B. J. (2008). *Doing competencies well in applied settings.* SIOP preconference workshop, San Francisco.

Catano, V. M., Darr, W., & Campbell, C. A. (2007). Performance appraisal of behavior-based competencies: A reliable and valid procedure. *Personnel Psychology, 60*, 201–230.

Cunningham, J. W., Boese, R. R., Neeb, R. W., & Pass, J. J. (1983). Systematically derived work dimensions: Factor analyses of the occupation analysis inventory. *Journal of Applied Psychology, 68*, 232–252.

Davis, B. L., Hellervik, L. W., Skube, C. J., Gebelein, S. H., & Sheared, J. L. (1996). *Successful managers handbook.* Minneapolis, MN: Personnel Decisions International.

Dierdorff, E. C., & Morgeson, F. P. (2008). Effects of descriptor specificity and observability on incumbent work analysis ratings. *Personnel Psychology, 62*, 601–628.

Dierdorff, E. C., & Wilson, M. A. (2003). A meta-analysis of job analysis reliability. *Journal of Applied Psychology, 88*, 635–646.

Dubois, D. D. (1993). *Competency-based performance improvement.* Amherst, MA: HRD Press.

Fine, S. A. (1955). A structure of worker functions. *Personnel and Guidance Journal, 34*, 66–73.

Flanagan, J. C. (1954). The critical incident technique. *Psychological Bulletin, 51*, 327–359.

Fleishman, E. A., & Quaintance, M. K. (1984). *Taxonomies of human performance.* Orlando, FL: Academic Press.

Gilbreth, F. B., & Gilbreth, L. M. (1917). *Applied motion study: A collection of papers on the efficient method to industrial preparedness.* New York: Macmillan.

Goleman, D. (1981, January). The new competency tests: Matching the right people to the right jobs. *Psychology Today*, 35–46.

Harvey, R. J. (1991). Job analysis. In M. D. Dunnette & L. M. Hough (Eds.), *Handbook of industrial and organizational psychology* (Vol. 2, pp. 71–163). Palo Alto, CA: Consulting Psychologists Press.

Hemphill, J. K. (1960). *Dimensions of executive positions* (Research Monograph No. 98). Columbus: Bureau of Business Research, Ohio State University.

Hinrichs, J. R. (1969). Comparison of "real life" assessments of management potential with situational exercises, paper-and-pencil ability tests, and personality inventories. *Journal of Applied Psychology, 53*, 425–433.

Hollincheck, J. (2007). *MarketScope for employee performance management software, 2007* (Gartner RAS Core Research Note G00147791). Stamford, CT: Gartner.

Kotter, J. P. (1996). *Leading change.* Boston: Harvard Business School Press.

Lawshe, C. H. (1975). A quantitative approach to content validity. *Personnel Psychology, 28*, 563–575.

Levine, E. L. (1983). *Everything you always wanted to know about job analysis.* Tampa, FL: Mariner.

Lievens, F., Sanchez, J. I., & De Corte, W. (2004). Easing the inferential leap in competency modeling: The effects of task-related information and subject matter expertise. *Personnel Psychology, 57*, 881–904.

Linkage. (1996, September 10–13). *Using competency-based tools and applications to drive organizational performance.* Chicago: Linkage.

Lombardo, M. M., & Eichinger, R. W. (1998). *For your improvement.* Minneapolis, MN: Lominger.

Lopez, F. M. (1986). *The threshold trait analysis technical manual.* Port Washington, NY: Lopez and Associates.

Lucia, A. D., & Lepsinger, R. (1999). *The art and science of competency models.* San Francisco: Jossey-Bass.

McClelland, D. C. (1973). Testing for competence rather than for "intelligence." *American Psychologist, 28*, 1–14.

McCormick, E. J. (1976). Job and task analysis. In M. D. Dunnette (Ed.), *Handbook for industrial and organizational psychology* (pp. 651–696). Skokie, IL: Rand McNally.

McCormick, E. J., Jeanneret, P. R., & Mecham, R. M. (1972). A study of job characteristics and job dimensions as based on the Position

Analysis Questionnaire (PAQ). *Journal of Applied Psychology, 56,* 347–368.

McLagan, P. A. (1990). Flexible job models: A productivity strategy for the information age. In J. P. Campbell & R. J. Campbell (Eds.), *Productivity in organizations* (pp. 369–387). San Francisco: Jossey-Bass.

Morgeson, F. P., & Campion, M. A. (1997). Social and cognitive sources of potential inaccuracy in job analysis. *Journal of Applied Psychology, 82,* 627–655.

Olesen, C., White, D., & Lemmer, I. (2007). Career models and culture change at Microsoft. *Organization Development Journal, 25,* 31–36.

Prahalad, C., & Hamel, G. (1990, May-June). The core competence of the corporation. *Harvard Business Review,* 79–91.

Prien, E. P. (1977). The function of job analysis in content validation. *Personnel Psychology, 30,* 167–174.

Prien, E. P., & Ronan, W. W. (1971). Job analysis: A review of research findings. *Personnel Psychology, 24,* 371–396.

Primoff, E. E. (1975). *How to prepare and conduct job element examinations* (Technical Study 75–1). Washington, DC: U.S. Civil Service Commission, Personnel Research and Development Center.

Primoff, E. E., & Eyde, L. D. (1988). The job element method of job analysis. In S. Gael (Ed.), *The job analysis handbook for business, industry, and government* (Vol. 2, pp. 807–823). Hoboken, NJ: Wiley.

Sanchez, J. I., & Levine, E. L. (1994). The impact of raters' cognition on judgment accuracy: An extension to the job analysis domain. *Journal of Business and Psychology, 9,* 47–57.

Schippmann, J. S. (1999). *Strategic job modeling: Working at the core of integrated human resources.* Mahwah, NJ: Erlbaum.

Schippmann, J. S. (2008). *In the words of our leaders: Work challenges and business strategies at Company X.* Unpublished proprietary report.

Schippmann, J. S., Ash, R. A., Battista, M., Carr, L., Eyde, L. D., Hesketh, B. et al. (2000). The practice of competency modeling. *Personnel Psychology, 53,* 703–740.

Schippmann, J. S., Hughes, G. L., & Prien, E. P. (1987). The use of structured multi-domain job analysis for the construction of assessment center methods and procedures. *Journal of Business and Psychology, 1,* 353–366.

Schippmann, J. S., & Newson, D. (2008). The role of the internal consultant: How internal consultants can promote successful change. In J. W. Hedge & W. C. Borman (Eds.), *The I/O consultant* (pp. 45–51). Washington, DC: American Psychological Association.

Schneider, B., & Konz, A. M. (1989). Strategic job analysis. *Human Resource Management, 28*, 51–63.

Schuler, R. S., & Jackson, S. E. (2005). A quarter-century review of human resource management in the U.S.: The growth in importance of the international perspective. *Management Review, 16*, 1–25.

Society for Industrial and Organizational Psychology. (2003). *Principles for the validation and use of personnel selection procedures* (3rd ed.). Bowling Green, OH: Author.

Spencer, L. M., McClelland, D. C., & Spencer, S. M. (1994). *Competency assessment methods: History and state of the art.* Boston: Hay-McBer Research Press.

Spencer, L. M., & Spencer, S. M. (1993). *Competence at work.* Hoboken, NJ: Wiley.

Taylor, F. W. (1911). *The principles of scientific management.* New York: HarperCollins.

Tett, R. P., Guterman, H. A., Bleier, A., Murphy, P. J. (2000). Development and content validation of a hyperdimensional taxonomy of managerial competence. *Human Performance, 13*, 205–251.

Thompson, H. A. (1970). Comparison of predictor and criterion judgment of managerial performance using the multi-trait multi-method approach. *Journal of Applied Psychology, 54*, 496–502.

Viteles, M. S. (1923). Job specifications and diagnostic tests of job competency designed for the auditing division of a street railway company. *Psychological Clinic, 14*, 83–105.

Williams, R. E. (1956). *A description of some executive abilities by means of the critical incident technique.* Unpublished doctoral dissertation, Columbia University.

Zemke, R. (1982). Job competencies: Can they help you design better training? *Training, 19*, 28–31.

Part Two

Assessment for Selection, Promotion, and Development

SO WHERE ARE THE PROMISED, PRACTICAL, AND PROVEN SELECTION TOOLS FOR MANAGERIAL SELECTION AND BEYOND?

A Call to Action

Judith L. Komaki

Looking back, maybe I should have known. But when my normally unflappable boss demanded a bulletproof way of selecting store managers, why . . . I couldn't resist. Nora didn't care what Judge Brack was going to decide. After weeks of preparing three senior-level managers for depositions, she had vowed "Never again." For the first time, Nora was actually eager to talk about managerial selection. I assured her that we could include valid tests with a criterion and predictor and evidence to boot. "Really . . .

Editors Note: The situation explored in this opening to this section is fictitious, but it represents a common problem for human resource (HR) managers and organizational psychologists working in companies today. Just as the character in this vignette finds, the practice of assessment in organizations can be complex. But researchers and practitioners who understand the issues can successfully navigate the landscape. The complexities involved with this endeavor provide the uphill climbs, but also the points of interest, in the landscape that accompanies this interesting journey. These complexities include the process of finding the right constructs, choosing or developing viable measures, conducting applied research in environments that do not allow for textbook research designs, and using new techniques and technologies to meet changing organizational demands. Different ways of handling these points of interest will be found in the chapters that follow.

evidence-based?" Just as I was about to launch into the assessment center literature, Nora started recounting all those lost weekends preparing for the case (*Gabler* v. *Oslo*, 2009).[1] She wondered out loud what would have happened if Oslo Drugs had used such a valid test.

The lawsuit . . . everyone here at Oslo had hoped we could dodge. But Hedda Gabler persisted. Must say I couldn't blame her for assuming that she would be a prime candidate for promotion. For fifteen years, Gabler had received exemplary reviews. Her district manager had already told her that she was ready to be promoted. So when Gabler received the news that George Tesman had gotten the job she sought, she was "upset . . . shocked," particularly when she found out about Tesman's performance appraisal ratings. In the preceding four years, three supervisors had given Tesman scores ranging from "an overall low of 2.85 and a high of 3.9" on a 5-point scale, whereas two supervisors, over nine years, had given Gabler overall scores ranging from 4+ to 4.5. Gabler was even more upset when she found out she didn't get the job because of her lack of experience in the household and food areas and "her poor interview performance." The senior staff was "impressed with Tesman's plans for developing the business," and all "found Tesman to be very confident in the interview." In contrast, the interviewers—the district manager of the Bergen, New Jersey, office, the then-area vice president, and the regional human resources manager—thought that Gabler "did not perform well." The VP characterized the interview as "pleasant, however, (Gabler) came across as having an edge, . . . (was) combative." The district manager blurted out that he "was disturbed by Gabler's remark that she would hold her people accountable"; he depicted her as "cocky." Although Nora thought the senior staff did a decent job of representing Oslo's extensive selection process, she was apoplectic that they let their biases slip out after weeks of coaching.

Whatever the outcome of the case, which was yet to be decided, Nora was convinced that Oslo had to do a better job of assessment. A week after the last deposition, Nora showed up in my office. "So you're absolutely sure that you've got a test appropriate for store managers? And it could be done by a neutral third party? Without knowing the gender, age, race, or whatever of the person? And it would be evidence-based?"

"Yes, yes, yes, and yes," I replied.

"Plus time's ripe. Just yesterday, the new area VP, a Dr. Rank, got the word: In one of his districts, volume's down in six branches. Injuries are up in eight. So Rank's up for a revamp. But the only way I can sell him on any new screening method . . . is better store managers and better performance.

"That's exactly what we'd look at: interpersonal and leadership skills needed to motivate others.

"Leadership . . . that's what it's all about. And it'll be proven, right? Rank's come up through pharmaceuticals. He's sold on evidence-based medicine. After the disaster with hormone replacement, he's not about to buy any more expert witness stuff. He's going to want to see hard data."

I assured her we would have the gold standard for selection devices, criterion-related validity with at least one criterion of supervisory effectiveness, a predictor of supervisory skills, and a significant but not perfect correlation between the two.

"I know Rank would respond to that. But you're sure you can get me the goods . . . the research articles? And we can use this test to select store managers one and two at a time for a reasonable price?"

Taking notes, she wrote:

- Supervisory/leadership
- Proven—with articles
- Practical

We talked at length about the practical. I argued for a battery of tests. But Nora immediately saw dollar signs and insisted on a single, reasonably priced test.

"I'll have it in six weeks," I told her. "By May 15."

"Make it May 1. Before Rank takes off for the corporate retreat."

Remembering all I had yet to do to prepare for our annual meeting, I stammered. "But May . . . "

"So on May 1, I'll go, articles in hand, to Rank."

A week later, I began what I naively assumed would be a fairly straightforward literature search.

Looking for supervisory prowess, I was not surprised to find calls from business leaders. The CEO of Delta Airlines, for example, searched for candidates who can "get along well with people . . . [and] be a part of a team and motivate people" ("He Wants," 2009, p. BU2). Hollenbeck (2009), a colleague, was even more direct: "We need not ask, 'Is leadership important?' but instead, 'Is leadership the ONLY thing that is important?'" (p. 133). Nor was I startled to find interpersonal skills and leadership prominent in taxonomies of managers. In their taxonomy, for example, Borman and Brush (1993) identified four mega-dimensions: interpersonal, leadership/supervision, technical, and other; together, the interpersonal (keeping others informed, maintaining good working relationships, and selling and influencing) and leadership (motivating and monitoring subordinates, coordinating to ensure the jobs get done) accounted for 47 percent of the variance.

In searching for tests of supervisory and interpersonal skills, I was not shocked to find guideline after guideline for the proper development of an instrument, starting with a job analysis and ending with the validation of the instrument. But as a member of an organization with limited staff and wide-ranging responsibilities, I knew I could not develop and then subject the test to the scrutiny it needed. I did find stand-alone tests in abundance with ample evidence of criterion-related validity. But they were in the realm of cognitive abilities and personality, not the interpersonal and social aspects of being a manager.

At first, I was buoyed by the number of calls for the noncognitive. Goldstein, Zedeck, and Goldstein (2002) characterized the current model of personnel selection as "incomplete" (p. 125) and recommended an "expanded conceptualization of the predictor domain" (p. 131). Other prominent researchers such as Hunter and Schmidt, Gottfredson, Hough and Oswald, Ployhart, and Outtz made a plea for the cognitive *and* noncognitive. But the noncognitive domain was typically left unspecified. When it was spelled out, the most often mentioned was personality (for example, traits such as conscientiousness, extraversion, agreeableness, neuroticism, openness to experience, integrity). Only occasionally was the interpersonal discussed. Sackett, Schmitt,

Ellingson, and Kabin (2001), in promoting a fuller spectrum of relevant characteristics of leaders, did suggest "personality and interpersonal skills" (p. 304). But they made no mention of a test appropriate for the interpersonal. Their call was just that—a call.

Reviews of the selection literature by Hough and Oswald (2000) and Sackett and Lievens (2008) confirmed the extensive use of cognitive abilities tests and, to a lesser extent, personality tests. Emotional intelligence was highlighted as a new predictor construct (Sackett & Lievens, 2008). But other than the assessment center (AC) literature, I kept looking in vain for a description of or even a reference to a test or scale for interpersonal, supervisory, or managerial skills that had been validated.

Bemoaning the promise I had made to my boss, I finally called my colleagues, some in the private sector, others in the public sector. Almost all were confident that such a test existed, pointing to the extensive AC research (for example, Arthur, Day, McNelly, & Edens, 2003; Gaugler, Rosenthal, Thornton, & Bentson, 1987). I too had been hopeful. But given the seemingly reasonable requirements my boss and I had agreed on, the problems were overwhelming. Affordability was an issue. A colleague who used to work at a Fortune 500 company admitted he could not have considered even a scaled-down traditional AC because of the prohibitive cost. The cost to conduct a half-day assessment with multiple tests was estimated at up to $7,000, and that was to fill a single executive position in 2005 (Holt, 2005). Another option was for the organization to take on the upfront costs and tailor an assessment, complete with design and validation. Depending on the size of the company and the breadth of the effort, estimates ranged from $65,000 to $250,000. Thereafter, the organization would pay from "$25 to $65 per test taker, depending on the number of candidates screened" (Holt, 2005, p. E1). "A rather expensive option for the average employer" is how Choragwicka and Janta (2008, p. 356) characterized it.[2] No way could I get Oslo to take on this option.

Just as critical, for interpersonal skills in particular, the evidence base was lacking. In virtually all AC studies, a composite score from a battery of exercises was the predictor, and the criterion was a global measure of performance. Hence, one could say that scores on the battery of tests were predictive of overall performance. Two studies using the AC strategy, however, did show the value of interpersonal skills. Pulakos and Schmitt (1996) and Goldstein, Yusko, and Nicolopoulos (2001) tapped human relations or the ability to relate to others using a battery of from five to eight tests. Although it was not possible to identify which test or section of a test would best predict these skills, they did show that assessing interpersonal skills, in addition to cognitive abilities, added incremental validity. But I still could not point to a stand-alone test predictive of candidates' managerial prowess.

So with my impending deadline, I redoubled my efforts. At a professional conference for industrial-organizational psychologists, I stalked the hallways and the cocktail hours, pressing my colleagues for viable predictors. With two notable exceptions, colleagues assured me that validated tests were indeed available. "Where?" I asked. "In-house," they said, but due to competitive and legal constraints ("shifting times," one noted), these tests were, alas, proprietary. So the research was being conducted, but neither the tests nor the data were available for scrutiny: a veritable catch-22.

Undaunted, several colleagues told me that validated tests could be obtained from consulting firms. When I looked further, I found a bewildering array of options. Among them was a company that promised in its voluminous promotional materials "the widest choice of tried and tested off-the-shelf . . . exercises in the world." But buried on one of the back pages titled "Validation of Exercises" was a disclaimer, "It is difficult to provide meaningful validation data," followed by four reasons explaining "the lack of hard validation data." For those of us who were "concerned about the question of validation," the company urged us to "undertake an internal validation study" and generously offered to lend a hand if necessary. Example two was a firm highly recommended to me by a colleague not connected to the firm. So convinced was he that the firm's assessments were indeed valid that he offered to e-mail me from the firm's Web site the references documenting the validation of their assessments. Eagerly I opened up the file—only to find articles about AT&T's AC research conducted decades ago. The third example included tailored-to-the-client AC exercises or core competencies developed and described to me by colleagues. I was duly impressed with the extensive development processes, lending themselves to face validity. When I probed further, however, I found gaps in the nature or existence of the criterion.[3] One colleague admitted that he had always wanted to do a criterion-related validity study for his exercise, but the criterion had proved tough to find and measure. My favorite was a firm that boldly asked: "How valid is your questionnaire?" And then I was directed to a Web site where I could read—yes!—a comparative study of eight questionnaires in predicting job performance. Alas, all the questionnaires dealt with personality.

In short, despite repeated searching and persistent questioning, nowhere could I find an article presenting hard validation data about a stand-alone test of supervisory or leadership skills.[4] Instead I came across numerous calls for leaders who can lead teams and motivate their staffs. Taxonomies of managers were replete with dimensions concerning interpersonal and leadership skills. Numerous guidelines existed for developing and validating instruments. Pleas were made to include both the cognitive and the noncognitive when selecting employees. But where were the tests? Where were the scales? Reviews of the selection literature in 2000 and 2008 indicated extensive use of tests of cognitive ability and, to a lesser extent, personality. But there was nary a mention of a selection tool for the interpersonal or supervisory aspects of a manager's job. A close examination of the AC research revealed potential problems with practicality and, most important, the evidence base. In-house research was supposedly being done, but the test and the results were proprietary and hence unavailable. Probing about vendors' tests revealed issues with affordability, especially for small- to medium-sized organizations and, most critical, the lack of criterion-related validity. This is not to say that all measures designed by consulting firms are high priced and poorly validated. But after combing the selection and assessment center literatures and buttonholing colleagues about their in-house efforts and consulting practices, I had to reluctantly conclude that even the most enterprising HR manager would have difficulty finding a practical and proven test for interpersonal and leadership skills.

When I got back from the conference, I had to break the news to my boss, who thankfully had not yet scheduled her meeting with the area VP. Nora did not exactly admit she thought it was too good to be true. But when she told me that the judge dismissed Hedda Gabler's claim in favor of Oslo,[5] I could only imagine her interest slumping. But much to my delight, she pressed even harder. "Rank's after me," she said. "More bad news. This time from the distribution centers. He's having to replace trucks right and left for lack of maintenance. So . . . he still wants help finding the best and brightest . . . whatever their gender or race. In two years, he's replacing thirty store managers in his area alone. I can probably hold him off for a year, but then we've got to have a test. With evidence. So we've got to come up with a new plan."

Remembering colleagues, several in leadership, on the outlook for their dissertation students, I said to her, "You'll have it."

Three suggestions I passed on. But my colleagues convinced me the gaps I had found were not unique to managerial selection. The same complaints occurred again and again when assessing hourly, skilled, administrative, professional, and sales personnel. Needless to say, these failures to find valid selection tools have huge legal and business implications. Hence, consider this call—edited for general distribution—for selection in general:

1. Invite researchers who have promising instruments to conduct criterion-related validity studies in your organization.[6] Offer a research sample in exchange for a trial use of the test *and* give permission to publish the results, keeping your organization confidential. If you find a significant relationship between the predictor and criterion, you will have data to support adding the instrument to your selection process in your organization. Consider as well going beyond concurrent validity to doing a predictive validity study.

2. Seek out vendors with evidence of valid instruments. For managerial skills in particular, do not be satisfied with face or even content validity. Insist on seeing the method and results of their criterion-related validity studies, ideally published.[7] Let them know that you expect that they will

be doing the heavy lifting of conducting validation studies with a broad range of managers in widely varying organizations. If vendors cannot immediately show you validity coefficients demonstrating the relationship between the test and criterion, keep asking. Consider giving preference to consulting firms based on published evidence about their instruments.

3. Set up or join a consortium with like-minded organizations to band together to develop or validate existing measures.[8] Police and fire departments could band together to come up with valid ways of promoting incumbents to supervisory positions.[9] If Oslo were to cooperate and form a consortium with other retail firms, it could do the same for store managers. Consortia make it possible to share the development costs and minimize deployment as the measure is shared across participating organizations.

4. Publish, publish, publish. Publish in a peer-reviewed journal to assure readers that the conclusions drawn are indeed warranted and to mitigate overblown claims. Publish so that the method and results will be readily available to readers such as you. Imagine where we would be today if AT&T had claimed that its assessment center results were proprietary. Because these landmark studies were published widely, they moved the field a giant step forward. Finally, publish so that you too can sit at the table in selecting the next director, VP, and CEO. Make sure that your expertise in predicting who would be exemplary at motivating teams to work productively and harmoniously together is well documented and recognized.

Notes

1. *Gabler* v. *Oslo* (2009), a fictitious case, was modeled after aspects of an actual case, *Johnson* v. *Penske* (1996). The employees portrayed (e.g., the corporate human resources VP, Nora Helmer, and the area VP, Dr. Ramp) as well as the organization, Oslo Drugs, are fictitious.
2. Six figures is the estimate Schmit and Strange (Chapter Twelve) made for developing and executing an assessment center including multiple job simulations.

3. The same frustration is reported by Howard and Thomas in Chapter Fourteen: "The most imposing problem is the difficulty of gathering appropriate criterion data." Moreover, McPhail and Stelly (Chapter Twenty-One) identify supervisor ratings as "often the best or only performance criteria available" but note that "supervisors are unable or unwilling to provide accurate evaluations of performance."

4. Evidently, neither could Howard nor Thomas (Chapter Fourteen). They simply state: "Evidence for the criterion-related validity of executive assessment procedures used for selection is seriously wanting."

5. In a similar case, *Johnson* v. *Penske* (1996), Judge Lechner ended up ruling against Johnson, who had filed an age and gender discrimination suit. He acknowledged the divergence in the ratings, stating: "On their face, a discrepancy between the Performance Appraisals and the Candidate Rating Forms. . . may exist." But he then proceeded to justify the discrepancy, concluding that "given the records," Johnson's appraisers were "more generous" than those of the chosen candidate. "What is considered by one supervisor to be average work and which earns a rating of 4," he tried to explain, "might be considered by another supervisor to be substandard work, earning a rating of 2." This generosity argument on the part of the court essentially discounted Johnson's exemplary ratings of her performance exhibited over an extended period of time by multiple raters. Furthermore, it attributes her exemplary appraisals to the "bias" of her raters and then condones that bias. The judge's decision bolsters the argument for a valid third-party assessment.

6. Drafting a criterion-related validity study that Michelle Minnich and I conducted (Minnich & Komaki, 2009), we were searching in vain for articles describing selection tools tapping managerial prowess that were both proven and practical. In fact, this chapter came about because of a series of conversations I had with one of the foresighted editors of this book, John Scott, during the course of the ultimately unsuccessful search.

7. At least one firm has conducted criterion-related validity studies on instruments tapping cognitive and managerial skills. They make this information available, but only to potential customers through a confidential request for proposal process. It is not available online or elsewhere.

8. Survey researchers in blue-chip companies have formed a consortium, the Mayflower Group, to administer and in some cases share the results of high-quality employee opinion surveys. Similarly,

members of life insurance companies originally formed the Life Insurance Marketing and Research Association (LIMRA); it assists with marketing and distribution, as well as "the identification and development of the next generation of leaders."

9. The Supreme Court decision in *Ricci* v. *DeStefano* (2009), which concerned the selection of supervisors in a fire department, provides an excellent illustration of the value of such a test.

References

Arthur, W., Jr., Day, D. A., McNelly, T. L., & Edens, P. S. (2003). A meta-analysis of the criterion-related validity of assessment center dimensions. *Personnel Psychology, 56*, 125–154.

Borman, W. C., & Brush, D. H. (1993). More progress toward a taxonomy of managerial performance requirements. *Human Performance, 6*(1), 1–21.

Choragwicka, B., & Janta, B. (2008). Why is it so hard to apply professional selection methods in business practice? *Industrial and Organizational Psychology, 1*, 355–358.

Gaugler, B. B., Rosenthal, D. B., Thornton, G. C. III, & Bentson, C. (1987). Meta-analysis of assessment center validity. *Journal of Applied Psychology, 72*, 493–511.

Goldstein, H. W., Yusko, K. P., & Nicolopoulos, V. (2001). Exploring black-white subgroup differences of managerial competencies. *Personnel Psychology, 54*, 783–788.

Goldstein, H. W., Zedeck, S., & Goldstein, I. L. (2002). g: Is this your final answer? *Human Performance, 15*, 123–142.

He wants subjects, verbs, and objects. (2009, April 26). *New York Times*, p. BU2.

Hollenbeck, G. P. (2009). Executive selection—what's right . . . and what's wrong. *Industrial and Organizational Psychology, 2*, 130–143.

Holt, S. (2005, February 2). Job hunters, simulate this. *Seattle Times*, p. E1.

Hough, L. M., & Oswald, F. L. (2000). Personnel selection: Looking toward the future—Remembering the past. *Annual Review of Psychology, 51*, 631–664.

Johnson v. *Penske Truck Leasing Co.* 949 F. Supp 1153 (1996).

Minnich, M.L.R., & Komaki, J. L. (2009). Focusing on the supervisory aspects of the job: A criterion-related validation of a theoretically-based in-basket simulation. Manuscript submitted for publication.

Pulakos, E. D., & Schmitt, N. (1996). An evaluation of two strategies for reducing adverse impact and their effects on criterion-related validity. *Human Performance, 9*, 241–258.

Ricci v. *DeStefano.* 129 S. Ct. 894 (2009).

Sackett, P. R., & Lievens, F. (2008). Personnel selection. *Annual Review of Psychology, 59,* 419–450.

Sackett, P. R., Schmitt, N., Ellingson, J. E., & Kabin, M. B. (2001). High-stakes testing in employment, credentialing, and higher education: Prospects in a post-affirmative-action world. *American Psychologist, 56,* 302–318.

CHAPTER 9

ASSESSMENT FOR TECHNICAL JOBS

Wanda J. Campbell

Technical jobs are prevalent in industries that produce durable goods as well as industries that produce services such as energy or telecommunications. Industries that rely heavily on skilled technical workers have made concerted efforts to develop valid employment tests to ensure that increasing levels of consumer needs are met. Because of my experience leading a nationwide testing consortium for the electric utility industry, many of the examples in this chapter come from that field, although the situations are transferable to other industries that benefit from the work of technical employees.

This chapter focuses on employment selection tests as a subset of a variety of selection procedures that have proven valuable in ensuring a qualified workforce and helping employees achieve their potential. It begins by describing technical jobs and the environment in which they occur. Labor organizations often play an important role in this environment, and their role is explored throughout the chapter. Technical and practical considerations for evaluating employment tests are identified, and commonly used employment tests are discussed with respect to these considerations. The rationale for cutoff scores is presented, along with three strategies for establishing them. Developing and implementing tests is dependent on the contributions of management and labor, and this requires attention to their concerns and issues, as well as making them aware of the benefits each will derive from the implementation of the employment test. Once established, employment tests are subject to both internal and external challenges. Ensuring adequate staffing levels through alternative recruitment strategies and providing developmental opportunities for employees and applicants can reduce internal challenges and mitigate damages of external challenges.

Background on Technical Jobs

Technical jobs are those where employees work with their hands to construct, operate, or maintain tangible objects. The jobs range from unskilled jobs (for example, laborer) that deal with a small aspect of a project or process to jobs that are responsible for the smooth operation of complex systems that involve multiple interrelated components (for example, nuclear control room operator). Examples of commonly recognized technical jobs are electrician, steelworker, mechanic, and carpenter. Characteristics that distinguish technical jobs from other types of jobs are the work environment, education and training, and the internal job progression.

Work Environment

The environment in which technical employees work varies depending on the nature of the work and the industry. Some jobs, such as in construction, require technical employees to work outside in all types of weather, while others occur in spotless plants (examples are nuclear power plants and some new automobile plants). Many of the jobs are physically demanding (maintenance is one of them), and some involve hazardous conditions, such as working with pressurized gas.

Education and Training

Many of the skilled technical jobs require completion of a multiyear apprenticeship program. Apprenticeship programs typically provide formalized classroom training as well as on-the-job training. Simulations may be used for training to avoid physical injury and protect expensive equipment until a certain level of proficiency is demonstrated. Progression in the apprenticeship program generally involves both classroom and job performance tests to ensure that the technical material is learned and can be applied in a work environment. Thus, organizations invest heavily in the education and training of individuals selected for the skilled positions. Therefore, it makes sense for them to invest in a high-quality employment test to ensure that individuals entering the apprenticeship programs have the ability to complete the training and perform the job.

Increasingly, community colleges and privately owned technical schools are expanding their offerings of technical programs, often forming partnerships with local businesses. Businesses have provided capital, industrial equipment for training, and the services of corporate technical trainers to teach some of the courses. Credential options for graduating students include certificates, two-year technical degrees, and associate degrees.

Internal Job Progression

Candidates for entry-level jobs are almost always external applicants. Apprenticeship positions for skilled jobs often have numerous internal applicants, many of whom are seeking advancement from entry-level jobs. The general procedure is to post apprenticeship and higher-level jobs internally before advertising them externally.

Labor Organizations

Labor organizations, whose role is to look after the welfare of the workers, are common in technical jobs. They intervene on behalf of their members on issues such as job security, wages and benefits, and employee safety. For labor organizations, seniority is a sacred cow. It is their preferred basis for employment decisions, both positive and negative, and this issue reoccurs throughout the process of developing and implementing an employment test.

Labor leaders are keenly aware of their status as elected officials. If the membership does not perceive the leaders to be sufficiently responsive to the needs of their constituents, they may be voted out of office. This sometimes accounts for aggressive behavior on the part of newly elected labor leaders or those who are concerned about retaining their office.

Relationships with and Among Stakeholders

The development of an employment test is a process that involves the contributions of at least two entities: management and the consultant (or internal resources). In the case of technical jobs, unions often constitute a third party of interest. In ideal circumstances, all three combine their best efforts to develop a valuable tool that will meet the needs of both management and labor. Some industries have created consortia where companies pool their resources to address shared staffing needs. In some formalized consortium programs, the consortium takes on the role of consultant to the industry.

Labor-Management Relationship

The success of the development of any selection procedure is predicated on a working relationship between management and labor. If the relationship is built on a history of honesty and trust, both parties can work together for an employment test that will benefit their joint and individual needs. By contrast, an acrimonious relationship is almost guaranteed to lead to confrontations that present multiple opportunities for delaying, if not terminating, the project. Typically the relationship lies somewhere between these two extremes. The relationship, however, is fluid, and over time, the actions of both parties may serve to strengthen or weaken the relationship. Achieving a positive working partnership is not easy and requires constant attention.

Consortium as Consultant

Section 1607.8A of the *Uniform Guidelines on Employee Selection Procedures* (1978) encourages the use of cooperative studies. The telecommunications, insurance, and electric utility industries have formed consortia to develop employment tests in the spirit of cooperative studies. Both the insurance and electric utility industries have established formal organizations that employ consultants as permanent resources for the consortium members.

Using this model, investor-owned electric utility companies initiated a number of testing projects that are currently used nationwide. As a result, these companies were able to develop higher-quality employment tests than would be economically acceptable to most individual companies. The cost savings were reflected not only in each company's cash contribution but also in labor costs, as fewer employees in each company were required to be taken off the job for test development and validation activities. A particular benefit of including companies from across the country was the ability to obtain higher representation of demographic subgroups that might have been in short supply in some geographical areas.

Because the consortium for the electric utility industry is owned and operated by the member companies, there is never a question regarding loyalties and special interests of the test provider. And since the consortium is a nonprofit entity, the products and services are provided at cost to its members.

Technical and Practical Considerations

The two major technical factors to consider when choosing an employment test are its validity and adverse impact. Other practical issues relate to cost and user acceptability. Three types of tests commonly used for technical jobs are described and compared relative to these factors. Issues related to combining tests and the use of cutoff scores are discussed as strategies to reduce adverse impact. Finally, different strategies for establishing cutoff scores are described.

Validity

The primary purpose for using an employment test is to predict performance on the job. Because of the high investment in training for technical jobs, the ability to predict performance in training also becomes an issue.

As a precursor to the development of a new employment test for technical jobs in the electric utility industry, an external consultant was hired to perform a meta-analysis of the validities of existing employment tests for these types of jobs. The 1988 meta-analysis contained 2,062 validity coefficients from 141 studies involving technical jobs. Table 9.1 presents combined excerpts from tables providing mean validities for job performance and training criteria. Validity coefficients, which represent the relationship between test scores and job-related performance, are uniformly higher for training than for job performance criteria. The best predictors for both training and job performance in technical jobs are a variety of cognitive abilities such as mechanical ability, spatial ability, perceptual speed, quantitative ability, and verbal ability. The least-effective predictors for technical jobs were noncognitive measures of personality, interest, and biographical data. While noncognitive tests traditionally are associated with lower validity coefficients than cognitive ability tests are, the results of this meta-analysis are more conservative than other research (Barrick, Mount, & Judge, 2001; Dudley, Orvis, Lebiecki, & Cortina, 2006). Perhaps one reason for this is that nonsignificant correlations were coded as zero in this meta-analysis. Another potential explanation is that technical jobs differ in some way from other jobs where noncognitive measures have been shown to be effective.

Table 9.1. Meta-Analysis Summary Correcting for Sampling Error, Criterion and Predictor Attenuation, and Range Restriction

	Mean Validities for Job Performance	Mean Validities for Training
Cognitive abilities		
Mechanical ability	.53	.76
Spatial ability	.49	.70
Perceptual speed	.41	.65
Quantitative ability	.45	.77
Verbal ability	.37	.68
Noncognitive measures		
Personality and interest	.04	.22
Biographical	−.02	.23

Source: Adapted from Jones & Gottschalk (1988).

Adverse Impact

A dilemma that many organizations face is the conflict between maximizing validity and reducing adverse impact. The *Uniform Guidelines on Employee Selection Procedures* (1978) require that employment tests that have adverse impact be shown to have evidence of validity. However, the *Guidelines* also require that organizations attempt to identify alternatives with less adverse impact.

Other Practical Considerations

Cost and user acceptability are inextricably tied from management's perspective. Acceptability to labor organizations also has cost considerations. Unions are most likely to challenge a test if they perceive it to be unrelated to performance on the job. And unsuccessful applicants seem to be more likely to allege that a test is discriminatory if it does not appear to be job related.

Types of Tests Commonly Used for Technical Jobs

There are a number of tests that have been proven effective for assessing the skills required for success in technical jobs. These tests range from cognitive ability measures to personality instruments and are briefly detailed following.

Cognitive Ability Tests

The validity of these types of tests for predicting performance both on the job and in training has been well established for decades. Unfortunately, cognitive abilities also are consistently associated with subgroup differences. Black-white differences of 1 standard deviation and Hispanic-white differences of approximately .60 standard deviation are commonly observed.

Cognitive ability tests have the advantage of being relatively inexpensive to administer and score. Large numbers of applicants, as is typical for technical jobs, can be tested simultaneously. User acceptability can be enhanced by incorporating technical language and job-oriented situations into the content whenever possible. Although labor organizations are not always fans of employment testing, they understand the importance of cognitive abilities and value the objectivity inherent in these types of tests.

Work Sample Test

These types of employment tests re-create a portion of the job and measure the applicant's ability to perform the work. Work samples typically have the highest validity coefficients of employment tests. In addition, they generally have less adverse impact than cognitive ability tests, but more than personality and biodata tests. The extent of the adverse impact is directly related to the cognitive demands of the task.

Work samples have the distinct benefit of having the potential to look like the job. The greater the similarity of the work sample to the actual work, the greater is the acceptance of management, labor organizations, and applicants. Work samples may at first glance appear to be a panacea, but they come with a price: the more the work sample mirrors the actual job, the more likely it is to be expensive to develop and to become outdated in environments with rapidly changing technology. Work samples for technical jobs may involve equipment such as that used on the job or computer simulations. Replicating complex work environments such as a nuclear control room generally is more expensive than sampling the ability to use hand tools unless the tools are being used on costly equipment such as an industrial generator.

A second consideration is the complexity of the job. The greater the number of distinct tasks performed, the more work samples may be required. Section 1607.14B(6) of the *Uniform Guidelines on Employee Selection Procedures* (1978) indicates that two factors contribute to a selection procedure being viewed as appropriate by the government: the validity evidence and the importance and number of aspects of job performance covered by the criteria. This section of the *Guidelines* goes on to caution, "Sole reliance upon a single selection instrument which is related to only one of many job duties or aspects of job performance will also be subject to close scrutiny." Whereas a number of work samples may be required to predict job performance for a moderately complex job, a cognitive ability test is able to predict a wide variety of job tasks economically. A related consideration is the number of job progressions that require the same abilities. In the electric utility industry, the same test battery can be used for employee selection for as many as six distinct job families. If work samples were used instead of cognitive ability tests, a minimum of six work samples would have been required, and even then, there is no assurance that all of the important abilities and characteristics required for technical jobs would have been measured.

Additional considerations are subjectivity and administration cost. If the work sample is not computer administered, a trained evaluator, typically a supervisor or trainer, may be required to observe and evaluate each applicant performing each work sample. Such evaluations are by their nature subjective and expensive. Observers need to be trained on what to look for and how to accurately rate the applicants' behavior on each aspect of the work sample. By contrast, cognitive ability tests and self-report measures can be administered to large numbers of applicants at the same time by a test administrator who is compensated at a lower rate than the technical evaluators.

Work samples make sense for jobs that are important, require extensive training, or are associated with high failure rates. As shown in the example, work samples may be combined with cognitive ability tests to capitalize on the benefits of each.

Combining Cognitive Ability Tests and a Work Sample: An Example

Line workers in the electric utility industry work with high-voltage electricity at the top of tall poles. The failure rate is often high because many recently hired employees are unable to climb poles or are afraid of heights. As a result, a number of electric companies have developed pole-climbing work samples. These work samples are expensive because companies must first teach the applicants the correct way to climb a pole. In addition, there are obvious safety concerns.

In an effort to increase the predictive ability of the selection procedures while minimizing costs, many companies first test the applicants on a battery of cognitive ability tests. Applicants who are successful on these tests, have received a release from a physician, and have signed a legal document absolving the company of responsibility in the event of injury are then sent to pole-climbing class. The more expensive work sample is thus reserved for applicants who have the cognitive ability to perform the work, and the legal exposure of the work sample is mitigated.

Personality and Biodata Tests

These types of tests measure a broad array of personal characteristics and experiences that are often related to job performance. One of the most appealing characteristics measured by personality tests for technical jobs is conscientiousness. This characteristic is particularly important when tasks must be performed in a particular fashion for the safety of the worker or to protect the equipment.

Although the validity evidence for self-report measures is relatively modest, these tests assess important characteristics that are not measured by cognitive ability tests. Thus, the inclusion of personality or biodata tests, or both, has the potential to increase the validity of the job performance predictions over that of cognitive abilities alone.

Personality and biodata tests have been shown to have little adverse impact (Hough, Oswald, & Ployhart, 2001). When they are used alone, the important issue is whether the adverse impact associated with these self-report measures is small enough to fall below the radar screens of government agencies responsible for investigating discrimination. The modest validity evidence often found for these measures could pose a problem in a legal challenge of discrimination.

A major concern associated with noncognitive measures is the ability and tendency of applicants to "fake good" on tests used for employee selection. This problem is largely undetected in validation studies of incumbents because their responses are used for research purposes only. Because there are no consequences, either positive or negative, related to their test scores, current employees have little motivation to fake. By contrast, applicants who portray themselves in a way they believe will be appealing to the potential employer can increase their test scores and their likelihood of being selected. Examinations of mean test scores invariably show higher scores for applicants than incumbents. These findings are not illogical: if applicants embellish their résumés and exaggerate their positive characteristics in interviews, why would we expect them to behave differently on a self-report measure used for selection?

The impact of faking on validity is still unclear. The initial research by Hough, Eaton, Dunnette, Kamp, and McCloy (1990) that was sponsored by the Army found that validity remained stable in the face of elevated socially desirable responses. White, Young, and Rumsey (2001) of the Army Research Institute subsequently found that high levels of response distortion (faking) dramatically reduced validity to low levels, often near zero. Even if the validity itself is unaffected, faking can affect the rank ordering of candidates as well as their standing relative to a cutoff score. Clearly more research is required to identify the characteristics and situations that will provide stable predictors of job performance.

Reducing the Adverse Impact of Employment Tests

Two compromise positions when work samples are not feasible are to combine cognitive ability tests with personality or biographical inventories and to use cutoff scores rather than rank ordering.

Combining Cognitive Ability Tests with Noncognitive Inventories

Combining personality or biodata instruments with cognitive ability tests may serve the joint goals of maximizing validity and reducing adverse impact. However, research has shown that the addition of noncognitive measures to a cognitive ability test does not necessarily result in a substantial reduction in the adverse impact unless the noncognitive battery receives an inordinately large weight (De Corte, Lievens, & Sackett, 2007; Sackett & Ellingson, 1997).

Surprisingly, research recently conducted on technical jobs in the electric utility industry has shown that the addition of personality and biographical measures to a battery of cognitive ability tests has had the greatest positive effect in terms of pass rates for whites. The positive effect on pass rates for blacks was minimal. By contrast, the addition of the personality and biographical information reduced the pass rates for Hispanics and Asian Americans by a much greater degree than it helped blacks.

Cutoff Scores Versus Rank Ordering

On the face of it, the decision between the use of rank ordering, or top-down selection, and the use of cutoff scores parallels the dilemma between enhancing validity and reducing adverse impact. The effectiveness or utility of an employment test is maximized by rank-ordering the applicants and selecting applicants who earned the highest scores. The use of cutoff scores does not take full advantage of the power of the employment test but does reduce adverse impact.

An important factor to consider is the level of validity evidence required to justify the use of rank ordering. Section 1607.5G of the *Uniform Guidelines on Employee Selection Procedures* (1978) states, "Evidence which may be sufficient to support the use of a selection procedure on a pass/fail (screening) basis may be insufficient to support the use of the same procedure on a ranking basis under these guidelines. Thus, if a user decides to use a selection procedure on a ranking basis, and that method of use has a greater adverse impact than use on an appropriate pass/ fail basis, the user should have sufficient evidence of validity and utility to support the use on a ranking basis."

As always, other considerations are important too. Employment tests do not measure everything that is important to an organization. This does not mean that employment tests are flawed for this reason, but rather that they should not be expected to meet all of the organization's selection needs. For instance, a cognitive ability test provides no information regarding the expected results of a drug screening, and vice versa. The use of rank ordering increases the weight given to employment test performance and may serve to virtually rule out a number of applicants who could perform well on the job. The use of cutoff scores provides a wider selection of successful applicants, who may then be evaluated based on other criteria of importance to the organization.

Practical issues should also be considered when choosing between rank ordering and the use of cutoff scores. Rank ordering is practical for large-scale testing conducted on a periodic basis such as that done for government agencies. In an environment of continuous testing, a condition that closely describes the hiring of technical workers in private industry, it is necessary to adjust the rank ordering with every test administration. A further complication arises with the issue of applicant feedback in a continuous testing situation in that each applicant's standing may potentially change with the next test administration. Finally, the use of a cutoff score constitutes a compromise between the predictive value of the employment test, adverse impact, and the role of seniority. In many unionized environments, jobs are awarded to the most senior employee who passes the employment test.

Establishing Cutoff Scores

There is a direct relationship between performance on the test and performance on the job: the higher the cutoff score, the higher the quality of the workforce as a whole. However, if cutoff scores are set too high, the organization will be unable to find a sufficient number of successful candidates to fill the technical jobs. By contrast, if the cutoff scores are set too low, job performance suffers. In the latter situation, technical employees may be unable to progress through the training program or earn necessary licenses, some required by law.

Cutoff scores for technical jobs are subject to legal scrutiny even when the employment test is shown to be valid and job related. Arguments have been introduced in court proceedings that the use of a lower cutoff score would constitute an alternative that has less adverse impact. The tests used by the electric utility industry have withstood this type of challenge, but the possibility of such exposure needs to be recognized. Therefore, it is essential that a psychologist with training and experience in employment testing be involved in establishing cutoff scores.

Section 1607.5H of the *Uniform Guidelines on Employee Selection Procedures* (1978) provides an evaluative standard with regard to the setting of cutoff scores. Specifically, this section states, "Where cutoff scores are used, they should normally be set so as to be reasonable and consistent with normal expectations of acceptable proficiency within the work force."

The importance of job requirements cannot be overstated in the establishment of cutoff scores. Labor market conditions and equal employment opportunity (EEO) goals are also important considerations when evaluating possible cutoff scores.

The approaches to setting cutoff scores differ somewhat by the relative ordering of the organization's goals. Two approaches that focus on job performance standards are judgmental standard setting and statistical standard setting. Both approaches involve testing current employees and evaluating their job performance. Thus, what constitutes acceptable job performance and the percentage of employees who meet this definition are important questions that need to be addressed with these approaches. A third approach that focuses on labor market conditions and EEO considerations is also described.

Judgmental Standard Setting

In this approach, the cutoff score is based on the test scores of current technical employees. Because employment tests are not perfect, some technical employees with low levels of job performance will earn higher scores than some employees whose job performance is viewed as satisfactory. Employees who perform poorly on the job despite passing the test are referred to as false positives, and employees who would perform adequately on the job but fail the test are referred to as false negatives.

Three approaches may be used when establishing cutoff scores judgmentally:

1. Set the cutoff score to exclude all employees whose performance is unsatisfactory.
2. Set the cutoff score to include all employees whose performance is satisfactory.
3. Set the cutoff at a level that maximizes correct decisions.

Establishing the cutoff score to exclude all poor performers will also exclude some technical employees whose job performance is satisfactory. Such a score often is viewed as being too high. The second alternative, setting the score so that all employees with acceptable job performance will be selected, results in a lower cutoff score but will enable some poor performers to pass the test. The third alternative is to examine the number of false positives and false negatives at different potential cutoff scores and work with management to set a reasonable compromise. Such a cutoff score would be one where the majority of the technical employees who passed the test are considered satisfactory and the majority of the employees who failed the test are poor performers. There is no way to eliminate both false positives and false negatives.

Statistical Standard Setting

When the test validation includes a determination of the statistical relationship between test scores and performance on a technical job, it is possible to use a regression equation to establish the cutoff score. This equation indicates the value of the cutoff score required to yield different levels of job performance. Once again, it is necessary to define the desired level of job performance.

Pass Rate Analysis for Standard Setting

This approach, based on projections of technical workforce needs, the number of applicants to be tested, and the pass rates at different score levels on the test, can be useful when labor market or EEO considerations are paramount. The pass rate is the number of applicants who pass the test divided by the number of applicants tested. If the pass rate at a certain score level is 50 percent, the organization needs a minimum of twice as many applicants as there are technical positions to be filled. Because applicants also must be successful on interviews and other selection procedures, such as drug screens and reference checks, the number of applicants tested will need to be higher. It goes without saying that the lower the cutoff score, the greater the number of people who pass the test. However, administering a test that everyone passes is a waste of time and money.

The same approach would be used if the goal was to increase the number of minority or female applicants hired into technical positions. The difference here is that the pass rate of the subgroup of interest would be substituted for the pass rate of the entire group of applicants. Generally the lower the cutoff score, the less adverse impact a test has. However, this presumes that the increase in pass rates is uniform across all subgroups. If the pass rate for white applicants increases at a faster rate than that of minority applicants at a lower cutoff score, the adverse impact will actually increase. Always look at the pass rate information by subgroup for each test score before making a decision.

Selling and Negotiating: Making Employment Tests a Reality

When an organization is implementing tests for selection into technical jobs, the first issue that needs to be addressed is the identification of the jobs to be included in the validation process. In addition to establishing the scope of the project, this process identifies the specific stakeholders within management and labor whose support is essential for test development and implementation.

Identifying Jobs to Be Covered by the Employment Test

Most employment tests for technical jobs are designed and developed for skilled positions. Typically these jobs entail a progression of increasingly difficult work with or without a formal apprenticeship program. Because many skills and abilities are required across a number of technical job progressions, organizations often are able to maximize the investment in the employment test by designing it to predict job performance for multiple job progressions, including all jobs within any given job progression. Candidates entering the technical job progression are thus tested only once regardless of their point of entry, and they can freely move across the job progressions covered by the test.

Benefits of a Valid Employment Test for Technical Jobs

The relationship between the effectiveness of an employment test and the increased effectiveness of the workforce is direct. This positive effect in technical jobs is most readily observable in training programs as evidenced by increases in the percentage of employees who successfully complete the training and potential reductions in the time required for training. As an example, the cost to train one nuclear plant operator is estimated at $250,000. One organization experiencing a high failure rate in training reported that the failure rate dropped to almost zero after the implementation of a valid selection procedure. Another organization found that candidates who scored at the highest levels on the same employment test were able to complete nuclear training a year ahead of candidates who scored just above the cutoff score.

Improvements in job performance echo the improvements identified in training. Often, however, the mechanisms for measuring the extent of improvement are more readily calculated in training than in job performance.

The ability of a valid employment test to reduce adverse employment decisions is often an overlooked benefit. Disciplinary actions in union environments require a great deal of time and energy on the part of line management, human resources, and labor organizations. During the period of time that performance issues are being addressed, the organization has a marginal or incompetent employee occupying a job that could be performed by a more effective employee. The use of an employment test, when appropriate to screen applicants for entry-level jobs, can substantially reduce grievances and arbitrations because applicants cannot file grievances. Furthermore, applicants are much less likely to file charges of discrimination than are employees who have experienced adverse employment decisions. Even if the organization is ultimately successful in such challenges, the cost of legal defense can be significant. In addition to the legal costs, substantial costs are associated with the recruitment, hiring, and training of replacement employees.

Employee safety may also be improved with employment testing. Although no one is immune to mistakes, those who are not qualified to perform their jobs are going to make more errors than most of their qualified counterparts. Depending on the nature of the job, the errors may be costly in terms of the health and well-being of the employees. Consider this example in which the labor organization saved an employment test.

One of the most dangerous jobs in the electric utility industry is that of line worker: individuals who work with high-voltage electricity at the top of electric poles. Mistakes can result in severe injury or even death. Therefore, it is essential that everyone working on the line crew knows exactly what he or she is supposed to do and performs the work properly.

A company that was facing a shortage of line workers proposed discontinuing the use of a valid selection test, believing that the test was eliminating too many job applicants. The union refused to go along with the discontinuation of the selection test and cited employee safety as the reason.

A more obscure basis for union support of an employment test is to minimize internal strife among the membership. Technical employees, like many other classifications of employees, do not tend to suffer in silence when they are required to shoulder additional responsibilities on behalf of less competent coworkers. This situation puts labor organizations in a difficult position since all of the parties involved are union members. In addition, labor leaders are not particularly pleased to be required to represent incompetent employees in labor disputes. Defending the indefensible is not pleasant, and the labor organizations would prefer to expend their resources on more meritorious issues.

Identifying Tests Acceptable to Management and Labor

In the absence of a union, organizations have considerable control over their employment policies. The major constraints are legislation (for example, Title VII of the Civil Rights Act), executive orders (Executive Order 11246, for example, which protects employees of covered federal contractors and subcontractors from discrimination in employment decisions such as hiring or promotion because of race, color, religion, sex, and national origin), and the *Uniform Guidelines on Employee Selection Procedures* (1978). Within these legal parameters, organizations are free to choose the types of tests that appeal to them and fit within their budget. This situation changes with the introduction of a labor organization.

Management prefers employment tests that are short and cost-effective. Often this means that the test will constitute a cognitive ability test battery, noncognitive measures, or some combination of the two. Management is often attracted to personality tests because of an interest in constructs such as conscientiousness and interpersonal skills. Work samples also are attractive to management because these employment tests look like the job. Elaborate work samples have much to offer if the job is important, training costs are high, or the failure rate (in training or on the job) is higher than management finds acceptable.

The presence of a union necessarily requires that the employment test be acceptable to the labor leaders. Labor organizations have substantial control over the participation of their members in test development and validation activities, and it is not unusual for represented employees to refuse to participate in the development of an employment test that has not been blessed by the union.

The clearer the relationship is between the test questions and the job requirements, the greater the acceptance is by union leaders and members. Labor organizations are attracted to work samples because they resemble the jobs, but they are cautious about any subjectivity inherent in the evaluation process. Labor organizations understand the value of cognitive ability tests because of their involvement with apprenticeship programs. Personality and biographical inventories are viewed as an invasion of the privacy of their members. The fact that the relationship between the questions asked (some of which are not scored) and job performance is not self-evident contributes to the negative perception of noncognitive measures. For example, one company received a grievance regarding an employment test for a technical job that included a cognitive ability test and a combination personality and biographical inventory. The grievance was taken to arbitration. It was not until well into the arbitration that it became clear that the basis for the grievance was the noncognitive components. A string of union members raised questions about the relevance of the questions included in the noncognitive measures. The arbitration was settled with two major concessions by management: the noncognitive component was removed from the company's employment test, and the company agreed to develop a tutorial to assist union members in developing the skills required to be successful on the cognitive ability test as well as the job.

The saliency of applicant reactions to the employment test seems to vary as a function of the relative supply of qualified candidates. In general, applicants tend to like work samples and understand the need for cognitive ability tests, particularly to the extent that the cognitive ability tests show an obvious relationship to the job requirements. Thus, many organizations make a concerted effort to design cognitive ability tests that not only predict job performance but also have the appearance of doing so.

Addressing Concerns of Management and Labor

In addition to the stakeholder preferences regarding the types of tests, there are also concerns that come into play regardless of the type of selection procedure adopted.

Line Management Concerns

Line managers are directly responsible for the productivity of the organization, which accounts for their power and influence with top management. Efforts to increase efficiency have led to reductions in the number of technical employees in many organizations. Taking employees off the job to participate in focus groups, complete job analysis questionnaires, or take experimental selection tests can pose real problems for line management in achieving short-term productivity goals. Furthermore, replacement workers may be difficult to find, and those who are available may need to be paid overtime, thus adding costs to the manager's budget. Potential resistance on the part of line management is certainly understandable.

Concerns of Labor Organizations

Labor organizations, like line management, exert substantial power and influence over the development of a selection process. While unions as a general rule are not overly concerned with selection procedures used to hire external applicants, they are very interested in the extent to which the employment tests will affect their members in areas such as promotion or transfer.

Successful implementation of an employment test frequently requires the following concessions:

- Current employees are grandparented within their line of progression.
- Current employees are given preferential consideration for jobs over external applicants.
- Seniority governs employment decisions among candidates who have passed the test.

Contributions of Line Management and Labor Organizations

Line managers often reach their positions by advancing through the technical job progression. Thus, many are useful resources for a thorough understanding of the job duties and the knowledge, skills, and abilities required to perform the jobs. Including an influential line manager who has the respect of his or her peers in the planning stages can facilitate the cooperation of other line managers during the development of the employment test. For example, the consultation of line management concerning the periods of time that would be least disruptive for data collection will facilitate development of the employment test.

As the recognized experts on the jobs and the ways in which they are performed, technical trainers are well versed in the knowledge, skills, and abilities required for successful job performance. Technical trainers are keenly aware of the deficiencies of current selection procedures and are tireless advocates and supporters of efforts to improve the process. Because of their role in the organization, they can be particularly helpful in the development of task lists and job requirements. as well as the identification of criterion measures.

The contributions of management are necessary but not sufficient for many testing situations. Incumbents are involved in focus groups and in the completion of job analysis questionnaires designed to identify important job tasks and determine the frequency with which the tasks are performed. While it is possible for supervisors or technical trainers to provide this information, the job incumbents are the best source because they are closest to the work that is performed. Identification of the knowledge, skills, and abilities required for successful job performance may be accomplished based on information provided by management alone, but the input of technical workers is desirable because of their familiarity with the work.

Thus, the efficient collection of high-quality data concerning the job components and requirements necessitates that the union be advised of and agree to the process. Information on the reasons for the development of the selection program, the proposed characteristics of the employment test, the benefits for the labor organization, and the role of their members in the test development should be shared as early as possible.

Implementing an Employment Test for Technical Jobs

The need to influence stakeholders continues with the implementation of an employment test. The implementation stage is also a time for formulating policy and procedures on the use of the test and training testing professionals accordingly.

Influencing Stakeholders

The employment test moves from abstraction to reality at the implementation phase. This recognition may bring with it a host of concerns and issues from both management and labor organizations. Management now must come face-to-face with the fact that the slate of candidates for technical positions will be limited. In addition, particular individuals they may have in mind for advancement may be culled out by the employment test. Labor organizations will experience a reduction in the power of seniority in selection decisions. Effective communication is the only way to address the reemergent concerns and issues. Specifically, the benefits discussed on selling the employment test must be resurrected in both meetings and written communication.

Formalizing a Selection Policy

Existing policies and procedures need to be reframed to include the new employment test. The selection policy should address the technical jobs covered by the employment test, grandparenting, test security, retest policies, and a delineation of information provided to the hiring manager and the applicant.

Some of these provisions will remain intact from the planning stage, whereas others may need to be adjusted to reflect the results of the validation study, recent negotiations with labor, and reconsiderations on the part of management. Validation studies may or may not support test use for all of the jobs initially considered for the test program. Negotiations with labor organizations may redefine the boundaries of the grandparenting provisions, and management must work with the psychologist to address practical issues such as the establishment of cutoff scores. Test security, retest periods, and the release of test results to the hiring manager and the applicant also need to be addressed.

Test Security

The employment test is an asset for the organization. Test security is most salient to management during the period of time that payments are being made, and this is the best time to formalize the precautions that will be taken to ensure the continued effectiveness of the test. Access to the test must be strictly limited, and the tests, answer keys, and test data must be stored securely when not in use.

Retest Periods

Test scores on cognitive ability tests are not likely to change very much from one administration to the next, although changes have been observed in personality and skills tests. Changes in test scores on cognitive ability tests may be due to extraneous conditions or real changes in applicant ability. For example, the test scores of an applicant who is tested immediately after working a double shift are unlikely to be a true measure of ability because of the detrimental effects of fatigue. And applicants who have engaged in sustained developmental activities during extended retest periods may actually have increased their ability levels. These situations, however, are the exception, and test scores remain very stable over time for cognitive tests.

Retest periods are established with consideration of test security, cost of test administration, and acceptability to the stakeholders. Repeated test administrations within a short time interval enable applicants to recall test content that poses a threat to the security of the test and reduces the predictive ability of the test scores. Retests involve labor costs as well as the cost of the test. When current employees are tested, the organization may be paying for the time of both the test administrator and the candidate. Unions often react negatively to ceilings on the number of retests permitted and long retest periods. Compromises normally take the form of retest periods between three and six months, with no upper limits. In many cases, disputes over the retest period cost more than the cost of test administration.

Providing Test Results

The information that will be provided to both the hiring manager and the applicant needs to be considered carefully. Providing the hiring manager with test scores may result in the operational use of a rank ordering among applicants who scored above the cutoff score. An alternative is to provide the hiring manager with a list of applicants who were successful on the test.

Organizations differ in the amount of information that they provide to candidates, particularly those who are unsuccessful on the employment test. Sometimes the feedback is limited to test results (for example, successful or not successful), and in other cases, test scores on both the composite score and individual test components are provided. Generally organizations are more likely to provide detailed feedback to current employees than to applicants. Percentile scores, accompanied by an explanation of how to interpret them, are more informative than test scores, which often have meaning only in relation to the cutoff score. Understandably most organizations are reluctant to divulge cutoff scores.

Formulating Testing Procedures and Training

Properly prepared tests come with administration manuals that provide detailed instructions for proper use. Additional procedures need to be established to determine applicant eligibility and authentication. Previously unsuccessful applicants are not eligible to retake a test until the passage of the retest period. Authentication can be accomplished by checking official photo identification such as a driver's license. Procedures must also be established to provide the selecting official and the applicant with test results in accordance with the testing policy.

Testing professionals need to be trained on the testing procedures and the importance of consistency. Deviations from the procedures may influence the test results and prompt grievances from internal applicants. An important component of the training is explicit instructions concerning the limits of access to test materials, scores, and results.

Defending Employment Tests in a Technical Environment

Once an employment test has been implemented, the primary emphasis is on protecting it from the inevitable challenges, both external and internal. For this chapter, internal challenges refer to concerns or attacks coming from management.

External Challenges

The validity of the test will almost always be included among external challenges even if the primary basis for the attack is differential treatment or a violation of the collective bargaining agreement. Handling these disputes often involves working closely with a management team that may include personnel representing labor relations, EEO or compliance, and legal. It is advantageous if people in each of these departments can be educated on employment testing in advance of a dispute. At the very least, it is important that they are aware of the need to contact the testing professionals whenever a testing issue arises. Defeating external challenges requires coordination and hard work for all members of the team.

Internal Challenges

The incumbents in line management positions change over time. Those managers who remain are preoccupied with current problems, and their memories of the contribution of the employment test fade with time. Most of the internal challenges are directly tied to difficulties line managers have in maintaining adequate staffing levels.

Challenges from line management often occur more frequently than external challenges. While external challenges may have more serious consequences for the organization as a whole, internal challenges have the power to put an end to the use of an employment test. In a number of examples in the electric utility industry, companies have eliminated valid employment tests to achieve goals such as reducing the time required for selection decisions, increasing the proportion of applicants hired for technical jobs, or reducing adverse impact. In almost all cases, the employment tests have been reinstituted. The performance losses and the cost of dealing with marginal and incompetent technical workers far outweighed the costs of the employment tests. These companies have since become the staunchest supporters of the effectiveness of the employment tests for technical jobs. It seems to be true that productivity losses are more easily recognizable and make a greater impression on decision makers than improvements do. This goes back to the frequent finding that individuals weigh negative information more heavily than positive information.

The only way to effectively combat these direct attacks by line management is to react swiftly, rounding up the support of patrons such as technical trainers and providing convincing evidence of the impact of the employment test. Unfortunately, the best time to collect the hard data is when you do not need it— shortly after test implementation when management is best able to recognize the positive effects. In the absence of concrete data, testimonials from line managers and technical trainers who witnessed the positive changes brought on by the employment tests and the experiences of those who have temporarily discontinued the use of tests are invaluable.

One company, for example, decided to discontinue a cognitive ability test designed to select individuals for meter reader positions because it viewed the test as a barrier in attaining its diversity goals. The meter reader job has high turnover, and the company realized after a year that it had serious problems: the error rate for meter readings had skyrocketed, customers were furious because their bills were inaccurate, and the company was expending tremendous amounts of money having meters read a second time. The selection test was reinstituted, and the error rate returned to levels achieved prior to discontinuance of the test.

Indirect Challenges

In addition to the direct challenges described, a number of indirect challenges are regularly encountered that inevitably are related to staffing levels. Two such indirect challenges include the use of contractors and temporary assignments.

Contractors

Contractors have long served as the solution to short-term staffing needs for technical jobs. Unfortunately, some contractors are still on the job years after they first stepped foot in the establishment. Using untested contractors to perform the same work as that performed by technical employees who were required to pass a test to obtain their positions can create a host of legal problems. First, the use of an employment test with adverse impact must satisfy two requirements to be legally defensible: the test must be job related, and the use of the test must constitute a business necessity. The longer the period of time that contractors are on the job, the greater the threat to the business necessity portion of the defense. Second, it is not unusual for contractors to become permanent employees. Hiring contractors as employees may be initiated by either the contractor or line management. The question facing the organization then becomes whether to test the contractor.

Contractors who have performed the technical work successfully and fail the employment test create direct challenges to the validity of the test. One source of challenges is that contractors may file charges of discrimination, and another source is the line manager who wants to hire the contractors. But if the organization does not test the contractors, it risks challenges by the labor organization and simultaneously weakens its position that the employment test is a business necessity.

Some solutions adopted by organizations to deal with this situation include testing technical contractors before they begin work, limiting the tenure of contractors, or limiting the types of work contractors are permitted to perform. In the situation where numerous contractors have been on the job for long periods of time, a solution that has been used occasionally is to establish a one-time policy of excluding contractors from the testing requirement if they have worked for a specified period of time and performed the technical work successfully. This is workable only if it is a one-time policy designed to correct the problem permanently.

Temporary Assignments

The main difference between temporary assignments and the use of contractors for technical positions is that in the former case, the work is performed by a current employee. A salient point related to this difference is that the employee in a represented environment can file a grievance if he or she is not selected for the position. Once again, the solutions described above may have applicability.

Thus, the chief cause of internal challenges to employment tests is the inability of line management to achieve or maintain adequate staffing. One of the best ways of preventing such challenges, or dealing with them before they become too serious, is to do everything possible to ensure an adequate supply of qualified applicants.

Recruitment and Employee Development

The electric utility industry has initiated a two-pronged approach to address the shortfall of qualified technical applicants and reduce adverse impact: aggressively recruit students at technical schools and provide developmental opportunities to entry-level employees and external job applicants.

Technical Education Partnership

A few years ago, the Edison Electric Institute (EEI) began a pilot program where a handful of technical schools, nominated by member companies as having rigorous technical programs, were targeted for participation in the Technical Education Partnership. Prior to their graduation, students at these technical schools were given the option to take the EEI employment tests on campus. The cost of the testing program has been borne by EEI, and the test scores and contact information of students who have passed the test are available to member companies on a secure Web site at no charge. Preliminary research indicates that the pass rates of upcoming graduates from these technical programs can exceed the pass rates from traditional sources by as many as six times.

Career Assessment and Diagnostic Instrument

The Career Assessment and Diagnostic Instrument (CADI) program was developed to test the current skills and abilities of employees and provide appropriate career counseling. The program includes batteries of diagnostic tests that have been correlated with a variety of cognitive ability test batteries used in the electric utility industry for selecting applicants for technical jobs. Personality and career interest assessments were also included for career planning purposes. These assessments are used for developmental purposes only; they may not be used for employee selection.

The CADI program has been used to provide career counseling for current employees in entry-level positions, some of which are being eliminated as a result of technological advancements. Based on the results of the diagnostic tests, employees are counseled on the job opportunities that most closely correspond with their current abilities, interests, and personal characteristics, as well as job opportunities that may be attainable with additional developmental efforts. In most cases, the CADI is administered one to two years in advance of job elimination to provide current employees with sufficient time to pursue developmental activities. Preliminary results are encouraging with respect to improved pass rates, and the program has done much to improve relations between management and labor organizations.

Skill Builders

In an effort to broaden developmental opportunities, EEI is working with consultants on a series of programs designed to provide focused skill-building exercises. The program will be computer based and accessible to job applicants as well as current employees at no charge through company career sites.

The initial program is identifying the mathematics required to perform a range of technical jobs successfully and matching up the math concepts to specific job tasks. In order to maintain interest, the skill builders will present the mathematical concepts within the framework of tasks performed by technical employees in a variety of jobs. In the interim, online practice tests have been developed and are accessible at no charge by company career Web sites.

Practice Tests

The purpose of practice tests is to provide applicants with a realistic preview of the components of the employment test and opportunities for elementary skill building. Each practice test has been designed to measure the same concepts as the selection tests and includes items of corresponding difficulty. At the end of each practice test, the correct answer is provided, along with an explanation regarding how to solve the problem. Resource lists also are provided for additional study.

In conclusion, information identifying the knowledge, skills, and abilities required for successful job performance can be used for development as well as employee selection. Enhanced recruitment and accessible developmental opportunities can address the staffing shortfalls. Given the experience of educational partnerships in urban areas, the developmental opportunities may provide the key to maintaining validity while reducing adverse impact. This is the basis for providing accessible diagnostic and skill-building programs to job applicants and employees nationwide at no charge through company Web sites.

Conclusion

Technical jobs range from unskilled jobs such as laborer to complex jobs such as electrician that may require a multiyear apprenticeship. Employees in technical jobs are frequently represented by labor organizations whose role is to look after the welfare of their members. Thus, unions often join management as important stakeholders in the development and implementation of employment tests.

Two major technical issues for employment tests are their validity and adverse impact. Practical considerations involve cost and stakeholder acceptability. Employment tests commonly used for technical jobs include cognitive ability tests, work samples, personality, and biodata tests. The validity of cognitive ability tests of constructs, such as mechanical ability, spatial ability, perceptual speed, quantitative ability, and verbal ability, as predictors of performance on the job and in technical training is well established, and so is the adverse impact associated with these tests. Work samples demonstrate high validity and typically have less adverse impact than cognitive ability tests, but the costs of development and use can be prohibitive unless the technical jobs of interest are very important, require extensive training, or are associated with high failure rates. Self-report measures such as personality and biodata tests typically demonstrate more modest validity and less adverse impact than either cognitive ability tests or work samples. Two major concerns faced by the electric utility industry for these types of self-report measures are the negative effects of faking on job performance and the negative reactions of labor organizations.

Efforts to reduce adverse impact for technical jobs often result in the combination of cognitive ability tests with self-report measures and the use of cutoff scores. The establishment of cutoff scores must take into account job requirements as well as labor market conditions and EEO goals. Judgmental and statistical standard-setting techniques focus on job performance standards. The pass-rate analysis approach to standard setting can take into account both labor market and EEO considerations.

Both management and labor derive benefits from the use of valid employment tests for technical jobs. For management, the primary benefits are improved productivity and reduced costs. Employee safety is important to both management and labor, although the connection between valid employment tests and worker safety seems more salient to unions. Finally, employment tests can reduce the internal strife faced by unions as well as reduce the need to defend incompetent members.

Management and labor provide unique contributions to the development and validation of an employment test. Their concerns, however, are somewhat different. An important management concern is minimizing the disruption to productivity when workers are taken off the job to participate in the test development and validation process. The concerns of labor organizations primarily deal with the terms of test implementation. Successful implementation of a test for technical jobs normally requires that current employees be grandparented within their line of progression, be given preferential consideration over external candidates, and be recognized for their job seniority. Other important issues for test implementation are provisions for test security, retest periods, and test results to management and job candidates.

Legal defense of employment tests is required in response to both external and internal challenges. The existence of a labor organization poses an additional threat over and above that posed by the Equal Employment Opportunity Commission and the Office of Federal Contract Compliance Programs. Internal challenges from management usually are made when there are shortages of technical workers.

The electric utility industry has addressed the shortfall of qualified applicants by developing partnerships with technical schools and providing developmental opportunities to employees and applicants. To the extent that the developmental efforts increase the supply of diverse job candidates, the potential benefits are twofold: reduction in challenges and adverse impact.

References

Barrick, M. R., Mount, M. K., & Judge, T. A. (2001). Personality and performance at the beginning of the new millennium: What do we know and where do we go next? *International Journal of Selection and Assessment, 9*, 9–30.

De Corte, W., Lievens, F., & Sackett, P. R. (2007). Combining predictors to achieve optimal trade-offs between selection quality and adverse impact. *Journal of Applied Psychology, 92*, 1380–1393.

Dudley, N. M., Orvis, K. A., Lebiecki, J. E., & Cortina, J. M. (2006). A meta-analytic investigation of Conscientiousness in the prediction of job performance: Examining the intercorrelations and incremental validity of narrow traits. *Journal of Applied Psychology, 91*, 40–57.

Hough, L. M., Eaton, N. L., Dunnette, M. D., Kamp, J. D., & McCloy, R. A. (1990). Criterion-related validities of personality constructs and the effect of response distortion on those validities. *Journal of Applied Psychology, 75*, 581–595.

Hough, L. M., Oswald, F. L., & Ployhart, R. R. (2001). Determinants, detection, and amelioration of adverse impact in personnel selection procedures: Issues, evidence, and lessons learned. *International Journal of Selection and Assessment, 9*, 1–43.

Jones, D. P., & Gottschalk, R. J. (1988). *Validation of selection procedures for electric utility construction and skilled trades occupations: Literature review and meta-analysis of related validation studies.* Washington, DC: Edison Electric Institute.

Sackett, P. R., & Ellingson, J. E. (1997). The effects of forming multi-predictor composites on group differences and adverse impact. *Personnel Psychology, 50*, 707–721.

Uniform Guidelines on Employee Selection Procedures. 29 C.F.R. §1607 et seq. (1978).

White, L. A., Young, M. C., & Rumsey, M. G. (2001). ABLE implementation issues and related research. In J. P. Campbell & D. J. Knapp (Eds.), *Exploring the limits in personnel selection and classification* (pp. 525–558). Mahwah, NJ: Erlbaum.

CHAPTER 10

ASSESSMENT FOR ADMINISTRATIVE AND PROFESSIONAL JOBS

Lia M. Reed, Rodney A. McCloy,
Deborah L. Whetzel

The majority of positions in an office environment are administrative or professional in nature. The types of assessments most useful for selecting individuals for these positions depend on the nature of the job, the volume and characteristics of the applicant pool, and the organization's assessment strategy.

This chapter discusses assessment for individuals in two broad classes of jobs:

- Administrative and clerical—jobs primarily involving administrative and clerical duties (including secretary, receptionist, and data entry clerk)
- Professional and technical—jobs requiring education or experience, or both, within a specific profession or technical area (including accountant, economist, attorney, psychologist, and foreign language interpreter)

We discuss these two job classes together because employees within these classes frequently work together in an office environment, and many of the skills required to do these jobs overlap.

Administrative and Clerical Jobs

Case Study 1: A Temporary Trap

It is a busy Monday afternoon, and the finance manager is frustrated. His secretary has just quit with only two weeks' notice. The timing of her departure could not be worse. The finance department has just begun to close out the books for the end-of-fiscal-year reporting. The company's human resource (HR) manager knows it will take a while to post the job and process the hundreds of applicants who will inevitably apply. Even if they could get candidates in the door quickly, the finance manager does not have time to conduct interviews. Therefore, the HR manager goes to a temporary agency and hires a secretary to fill in until they can staff the position permanently.

Two months later, the finance department has finished its year-end activities, and HR has lined up a number of apparently worthy candidates. All of them have passed the clerical test, the company's standard requirement for all secretary positions. They forward the candidate list to the finance manager. The next day, the finance manager calls the HR manager to ask why his current, temporary secretary is not on the list. The answer is straightforward: she did not pass the clerical test.

The finance manager, however, has been satisfied with the temporary secretary's performance and does not wish to train another secretary. So he asks about his options:

- *Can they just waive the test requirement?* No, because if they waive the test requirement for the temporary secretary, then they would need to waive that requirement for all of the other 178 applicants. The only screen after the clerical test is the interview, and the large number of applicants would make interviewing every applicant an onerous task.
- *Can the temporary secretary retake the test?* No, because then they would have to give everyone the option to take the test again—an expensive proposition. Furthermore, the test is reliable, such that most people who retake the test will likely get nearly the same score, meaning that the temporary secretary is likely to fail the test again.

When confronted with a situation such as this one, it is not uncommon for hiring managers (here, the finance manager) to jump to the conclusion that something is wrong with the assessment. Therefore, their first reaction is to ignore the test results. Even the most experienced HR professional will have difficulty persuading a manager to accept the test results in such a situation. It is important, therefore, to anticipate and prepare for such an eventuality.

This scenario is most typical in situations where the test has been in place for some time and the hiring manager is new to the process. One method for trying to prevent this dilemma would be to convene a meeting with the hiring manager before the test is administered. The goal of the meeting is to get the manager's buy-in by describing the types of items on the test and how they relate to the job. One should be prepared to answer questions about (and present evidence of) the test's ability to predict job performance. Thus, the hiring manager, although disappointed, will be less likely to ask that the test requirement be waived. Another way to avoid this dilemma is to require even temporary hires to pass any established job-related assessments.

The Value of Assessment

Numerous utility studies have empirically demonstrated the return on investment of a valid selection process. As HR professionals, we all can think of times when unqualified or underqualified employees made costly mistakes that a more qualified person most likely would not have. Nevertheless, when clerical and other staff must be hired quickly, people often resort to using unstructured interviews (with non-job-specific questions such as, "Tell me about yourself") because they can develop such interviews quickly and easily or believe that their judgment is sufficient to differentiate qualified from unqualified applicants. However, the easiest way is not always the most effective way when it comes to differentiating among applicants, and it rarely pays off in the long run. Unstructured interviews can be developed quickly but take a lot of time to administer and are not a realistic option for efficiently assessing large numbers of applicants.

In the case study, the finance manager might better appreciate the decision to abide by the test results if he considers both the long- and short-term implications of ignoring the test results. No manager can be allowed the luxury of turning the test on and off on a whim. If he ignores the test now, he must continue to ignore it in the future. Furthermore, most organizations have the same requirements for their secretarial jobs across all departments, which means ignoring the assessment results for all secretaries throughout the organization. Without a structured assessment such as a clerical test, the organization's ability to screen high volumes of applicants quickly and reliably is greatly reduced, in turn reducing its ability to efficiently differentiate among candidates in the future.

If the goal is to replace the test with another structured test, the organization needs to begin by determining its assessment strategy. The organization should consider both the nature of the applicant pool and the requirements of the job.

Applicant Pool

Due to the widespread availability of computers, many people today have basic clerical skills such as typing. This being the case, an organization seeking to fill an entry-level clerical job is likely to attract enough minimally qualified, interested applicants using local advertising without having to offer incentives, such as relocation or a signing bonus. Changing technology, however, is affecting the nature of these jobs. With the pervasiveness of personal computers and increasingly automated processes in the office environment, many professionals do their own typing and document creation and use automated data collection methods, thus reducing the need for secretaries, stenographers, and data-entry clerks to perform shorthand, dictation, and data entry. Rapid changes in technology are increasing the complexity of the tasks performed in clerical jobs, as well as the requisite knowledge and skills. Rather than straight typing, administrative employees are often asked to perform other clerical duties, such as editing documents that others typed, compiling spreadsheets, and creating presentations.

In addition, societal changes have influenced the applicant pool for these jobs. Historically women have dominated administrative and clerical jobs. Given greater educational and professional opportunities in industrialized nations, however, many women seek higher-level professional jobs and are less likely to be satisfied in clerical occupations. As qualified individuals take higher-level positions, lower-level jobs that offer lower pay may attract less-qualified applicants. With clerical jobs becoming more complex and higher-skilled workers being lured away to higher-paying jobs, a smaller proportion of applicants is likely to be qualified than has been the case in the past, even though an organization may see a high volume of applicants for clerical jobs. The challenge is to identify an effective and economical method for identifying qualified applicants.

When considering the case study, to the extent that clerical jobs are increasing in complexity with the advent of sophisticated technology, it might be that the temporary employee will be less able to assume more complex responsibilities than other candidates who obtained higher scores on the exam. The finance manager needs to consider the opportunity cost of not hiring someone with a higher level of skills. An effective assessment strategy must consider the requirements of the job now and in the future.

Requirements of the Job

The requirements of clerical and administrative jobs also drive the assessment strategy. These jobs traditionally have required skills such as shorthand, dictation, and typing. Thus, many organizations continue to require applicants for administrative and clerical jobs to type a certain number of words per minute—a measure of speed and accuracy. However, these jobs are trending away from some of the more routine typing and dictation tasks as more and more professionals have their own computers and type their own correspondence as they compose it. This reduces the volume of pure typing performed by clerical staff, thus making it less clear what level of typing speed should be required and altogether eliminating the value of skills such as dictation and shorthand. The International Association of Administrative Professionals (www.iaap-hq.org) explains on its Web site:

> Traditionally, a secretary was one who supported an executive by helping to manage their schedules, handle visitors and callers, and produce documents and communications. . . . However, for most

administrative professionals today, much more is expected. With more managers keying their own correspondence and more files being stored electronically, the nature of secretarial work is changing drastically. Managers are doing more clerical work; administrative assistants and secretaries are doing more professional work. . . . Job descriptions are expanding and new titles are being created, such as administrative coordinator, office administrator, administrative specialist and information manager, to name just a few.

With administrative staff spending less time typing, a job analysis is likely to find that administrative and clerical staff perform tasks that require complex computer and organizational skills. Although managers may increasingly draft their own correspondence, they still could rely on secretaries for proofreading and formatting correspondence, and possibly for creating other documents (such as presentations) or tracking information on spreadsheets. Thus, although typing tests with words-per-minute requirements were typical assessments in the twentieth century, organizations today are likely to find that assessments of individuals' abilities to use common computer software applications (for word processing, spreadsheets, e-mail, or presentations) are more relevant for today's administrative and clerical jobs.

Organizational skills are relevant for tasks such as creating and maintaining a filing system, maintaining a schedule, and coordinating meetings and travel—tasks that continue to be important for these jobs. Job analysis studies of administrative and clerical jobs are also likely to identify general cognitive ability and interpersonal skills as relevant and important. Indeed, as job complexity increases for these positions, general cognitive ability arguably becomes even more important than in years past. In addition, higher-level administrative jobs such as executive secretaries will likely need high levels of competence in all of these skills.

An important change in many clerical jobs is the increased use of service-relevant competencies such as customer service and interpersonal skills. For example, when coordinating business functions, clerical employees need to consider the needs of the participants and how to encourage staffs of other organizations (such as hotels and conference centers) to meet those needs. As a result, many employers screen employees using personality measures to determine the level of agreeableness of potential employees who must deal with the public.

The Occupational Information Network (O*NET; (Peterson, Mumford, Borman, Jeanneret, & Fleishman, 1999), the Department of Labor's comprehensive database of worker and job requirements, is a useful tool for identifying job requirements. It serves as the nation's leading source of occupational information, providing comprehensive information on many key attributes and characteristics of workers and occupations. The O*NET, originally designed to update the *Dictionary of Occupational Titles* (DOT; U.S. Department of Labor, 1991), provides a common frame of reference across nearly one thousand occupations in the U.S. economy. Each occupation possesses a numerical identifier from the Standard Occupational Classification. The content model specifies the data elements in the O*NET. It includes occupational tasks, knowledge, skills, abilities, generalized work activities, education and testing, work styles, work values, and the work context for each job. Since 2003, the abilities requirements portion of the O*NET has been updated in cycles, with each cycle consisting of updated information for approximately one hundred occupations. Data from the first nine cycles are available at the National O*NET Center's Web site (http://www.onetcenter.org).

The information in the O*NET is intended to provide a common language for the field of job analysis and for HR practitioners. One benefit of a common job analysis language is that different users of the O*NET—employers, job candidates, vocational counselors, occupational analysts, trainers, and policymakers, for example—can communicate with one another. This is an important consideration, because job analysts and the consumers of assessments can use the same language to discuss constructs needed and constructs assessed.

Exhibit 10.1 shows the O*NET knowledge, skills, and abilities (KSAs) for the job of Office Clerks, General (Code: 43–9061.00). Notice that the KSAs include not only clerical, but also economics and accounting as well as customer and personal service. A local job analysis is likely to yield similar patterns.

Exhibit 10.1. O*NET Knowledge, Skills, and Abilities for the Job of Office Clerk, General

Summary Report for: 43-9061.00—Office Clerks, General

Perform duties too varied and diverse to be classified in any specific office clerical occupation, requiring limited knowledge of office management systems and procedures. Clerical duties may be assigned in accordance with the office procedures of individual establishments and may include a combination of answering telephones, bookkeeping, typing or word processing, stenography, office machine operation, and filing.

Sample of reported job titles: Administrative Assistant, Office Manager, Receptionist, Clerk, Secretary, Office Assistant, Office Clerk, Customer Service Representative, Office Coordinator, Court Clerk

KNOWLEDGE

Customer and Personal Service—Knowledge of principles and processes for providing customer and personal services. This includes customer needs assessment, meeting quality standards for services, and evaluation of customer satisfaction.

Clerical—Knowledge of administrative and clerical procedures and systems such as word processing, managing files and records, stenography and transcription, designing forms, and other office procedures and terminology.

English Language—Knowledge of the structure and content of the English language including the meaning and spelling of words, rules of composition, and grammar.

Mathematics—Knowledge of arithmetic, algebra, geometry, calculus, statistics, and their applications.

Economics and Accounting—Knowledge of economic and accounting principles and practices, the financial markets, banking and the analysis and reporting of financial data.

SKILLS

Active Listening—Giving full attention to what other people are saying, taking time to understand the points being made, asking questions as appropriate, and not interrupting at inappropriate times.

Reading Comprehension—Understanding written sentences and paragraphs in work related documents.

Speaking—Talking to others to convey information effectively.

Writing—Communicating effectively in writing as appropriate for the needs of the audience.

Social Perceptiveness—Being aware of others' reactions and understanding why they react as they do.

ABILITIES

Oral Comprehension—The ability to listen to and understand information and ideas presented through spoken words and sentences.

Oral Expression—The ability to communicate information and ideas in speaking so others will understand.

Speech Clarity—The ability to speak clearly so others can understand you.

Speech Recognition—The ability to identify and understand the speech of another person.

Near Vision—The ability to see details at close range (within a few feet of the observer).

Written Comprehension—The ability to read and understand information and ideas presented in writing.

Information Ordering—The ability to arrange things or actions in a certain order or pattern according to a specific rule or set of rules (e.g., patterns of numbers, letters, words, pictures, mathematical operations).

Number Facility—The ability to add, subtract, multiply, or divide quickly and correctly.

(Continued)

Exhibit 10.1.   O*NET Knowledge, Skills, and Abilities for the Job of Office Clerk, General *(Continued)*

Mathematical Reasoning—The ability to choose the right mathematical methods or formulas to solve a problem.

Selective Attention—The ability to concentrate on a task over a period of time without being distracted.

Source: www.onetcenter.org.

Choosing Assessment Approaches

When considering the use of an assessment to screen applicants for jobs, a job analysis is needed to select appropriate assessments and document their job relatedness—that is, to identify which KSAs or competencies are needed for the job and thus should be measured by the test. In this section, we describe issues to consider when choosing among assessment approaches.

Case Study 2: Selecting a Clerical Assessment

An HR specialist has been charged with hiring an administrative assistant right away. The hiring manager says she needs someone who can proofread and edit correspondence, deal with customers, make travel arrangements, and work on presentations to clients.

On the basis of this information, the HR specialist realizes two things. First, this is not a typical clerical job that requires typing; rather, it requires someone who has interpersonal skills to deal with clients, and it requires someone who can edit and possibly draft presentations and correspondence. Second, she cannot develop a selection system right away that will cover everything the hiring manager needs.

The first thing that needs to be done is to conduct a job analysis to determine the job requirements. Based on what the hiring manager said, she may be looking for people with high levels of particular competencies, such as customer service, active listening, and written comprehension. Job analysts can use the O*NET definitions of active listening and written comprehension as a starting point for identifying the job requirements. Once the relevant KSAs have been identified, the next step is to identify the appropriate assessment methods for measuring the KSAs. Below, we describe issues to be considered when making assessment decisions.

Assessment Instruments for Clerical Jobs

Deciding which assessments to use entails a variety of logistic considerations, including the availability of qualified applicants and the resources available to develop or purchase assessments. For most administrative and clerical jobs, particularly entry- and midlevel positions, organizations are likely to find a large number of interested, minimally qualified applicants locally. When this is the case, highly structured assessments such as cognitive ability tests and work sample tests work well as an economical way to evaluate a large number of applicants for skills that are critical to the job. Time and money spent developing and administering structured assessments are worthwhile investments given the potential volume and frequency of testing. Furthermore, with so many applicants available locally, especially in and around metropolitan and suburban areas, requiring applicants to attend a proctored assessment should not be an unreasonable burden.

In contrast, organizations with fewer applicants may determine that the development or administrative cost of structured testing exceeds the risk of a bad hiring decision and thus may find that an interview, which might be slightly less predictive of job performance, is sufficient for their purposes. Interviews are generally cheaper to develop and easier to revise quickly to reflect changing organizational needs, although they are more time-consuming to administer per applicant. An interview by itself, however, will likely be a less precise measure of some key skills and abilities needed for clerical jobs, such as the ability to create data tables or other documents using computer software.

Once an organization has identified the specific KSAs relevant to its clerical jobs (using a locally conducted job analysis), the next step is to identify the appropriate assessment methods for measuring the KSAs. The organization may choose to use multiple assessment methods for one job. For example, it may use an off-the-shelf paper-and-pencil clerical test to assess clerical abilities, a computer-based assessment of skill with word-processing and spreadsheet software to assess computer skills, and a structured interview to assess interpersonal skills and attitudes toward work. The measurement methods that an organization chooses depend on the organization's assessment strategy, the resources available for developing and administering the assessments, and the consequence of error. In any event, the organization should select an assessment strategy that measures the majority of the critical KSAs for the job.

The assessment instrument can be purchased from a vendor or developed in-house. Chapter Two provides a description of considerations when deciding to build or buy an assessment. Table 10.1 provides a brief checklist of issues to consider when deciding whether to buy or build an assessment for clerical positions. For the position in case study 2, the HR specialist may choose an off-the-shelf measure of written comprehension (often measured using tests of reading comprehension) and personality (for example, some combination of the Big Five to cover active listening, such as agreeableness and conscientiousness).

Multiple assessments may be considered. One might supplement the assessments with a structured interview. Because interviews are fairly expensive to administer (interviewers must take the time to meet with each candidate individually), the decision might be to use a multiple-hurdle approach and interview only candidates who pass the written comprehension and personality assessments.

Once the decision is made to use an interview, which questions to ask and how to score the responses (assuming that a structured interview is used) must be determined. The interview

Table 10.1. Buy-Versus-Build Checklist for an Assessment Instrument

Issue	Buy	Build
Development costs: These include creating experimental items that measure constructs needed for clerical jobs, trying them out in a pilot test, and conducting analyses to determine which items to use in an operational test.	No development costs: vendors develop them.	Significant development costs: • Clerical subject matter expert knowledge of the job for content validity • Clerical employees to take test(s) • Clerical supervisors to rate performance (for criterion-related validity studies)
Maintenance costs: These include developing new test forms if a test is compromised and ensuring that the test continues to function similarly across administrations for clerical jobs.	No maintenance costs: vendors maintain them.	Significant maintenance costs if tests are compromised; also need to update norm data on clerical employees to ensure that the test performs consistently across administrations.
Access to data: Data include norm data for making comparisons across companies or across administrations of the test for clerical jobs.	Such data are often available through the test vendor and are useful for making comparisons across organizations to determine cutoff scores.	For small companies, fewer data are available for comparison; for larger companies, data can be used to compare across locations. May need data to be proprietary, in which case, a test and corresponding database need to be built.

(Continued)

Table 10.1. Buy-Versus-Build Checklist for an Assessment Instrument *(Continued)*

Issue	Buy	Build
Expertise: Whether expertise in industrial-organizational psychology and psychometrics is needed for test development and maintenance	Vendors typically have industrial-organizational psychologists or psychometricians available to analyze data and maintain their tests.	Companies may have expertise available. If not, consultants can be hired. The Society for Industrial and Organizational Psychology has a consultant locator on its Web site (www.siop.org) that can help identify consultants for various needs.
Validity study: Available and adequate	Vendors typically provide validity studies, but this needs to be considered carefully. Vendors may provide promotional material rather than an actual validity study, or they might not report nonsignificant results. Even if a validity study is available, a local validation should be conducted. Clerical KSAs need to be described in sufficient detail to permit transportability as needed.	Conduct an in-house validity study; this can be costly. It also requires subject matter expertise, along with legal expertise to defend if challenged.
Need for proprietary test	Not available	If a proprietary test (one owned by the company) is needed, a test for clerical jobs must be built.

Issue	Buy	Build
Need for alternate form	May be available through the vendor	If alternate forms are required, might need to develop them in-house. Need to ensure they are equivalent to existing tests of clerical skills.
Specialized or unique KSA identified in the job analysis	If a unique clerical KSA is identified in the job analysis, a corresponding test might not be available from vendors.	If the administrative or clerical job is expanded to include a unique skill, ability, or organization-specific competency, the company might need to develop a test in-house.
Number of anticipated examinees	Will likely have per-use charges. If anticipated volume is low, purchasing a test might be more cost-effective.	Given the likely high number of clerical applicants, a company might decide that it is cheaper to develop its own test than to be charged per applicant.

might contain situational questions, asking the candidate to project what he or she might do in situations similar to those likely to be encountered on the job. For the job in case study 2, the questions might focus on customer service ("What would you do if an irate customer called and asked about a service that was promised but not provided?"). Other questions might ask about behaviors performed in previous positions ("Tell me about a time when you dealt with a potential customer who was exploring the possibility of using the services of your company"). The interview should be scored using behaviorally based rating scales so that scoring is standard across interviewers. Behavioral anchors that could be used in a response scale to score the first question are provided in Table 10.2. Note that the anchors describe possible responses to the question that reflect low, medium, and high levels of responses. A challenge in creating low anchors for interview questions involves not making them so inadequate that no one would be so incompetent to say them in an interview.

Validity

In a landmark meta-analysis, Pearlman, Schmidt, and Hunter (1980) established the validity of various tests for predicting

Table 10.2. Behaviorally Based Rating Scale for Clerical Selection Interview

Low	Medium	High
• Informs the customer that service was provided and that you are not responsible • Describes the services that are provided in hopes that the customer will select something else • Transfers customer calls to others rather than handling issues; refers customer concerns to someone else • Encourages the customer to rethink his or her needs rather than adapting to meet the customer's needs	• Apologizes to the customer that service was not provided • Resolves customer's complaints in a timely manner • Provides accurate information to customers and appropriate referrals for additional information • Responds to complaints and follows up with employees and customers • Maintains a consistently positive attitude when dealing with customers	• Apologizes to the customer for service that was not provided and offers to reimburse any customer expenses • Proactively resolves customer complaints, providing solutions using a variety of options • Identifies novel and original solutions to customer issues • Conducts after-action review (for example, shares positive and negative customer experiences) to learn from previous successes and failures

performance in clerical jobs. Their study, however, is over thirty years old, and much has changed in the world of clerical testing and clerical occupations. With regard to tests, more measures are being administered by computer, and this includes measures frequently used for selecting administrative and clerical personnel. Although many tests are unaffected by the mode of administration, changing from paper-and-pencil testing to computerized testing can have a large effect on the performance of speeded tests (Mead & Drasgow, 1993). Many (though certainly not all) tests used for selecting clerical employees have a speed component, thus the question of their continued validity when moving from paper-and-pencil format to a computerized format is important to address. With regard to occupations, we raised the point previously that many elements of the traditional clerical position such as typing and dictation have been replaced by other elements that are arguably more cognitively complex. In short, both the testing process and the jobs have changed since the publication of Pearlman et al.'s meta-analysis.

To address these concerns, Whetzel, McCloy, Hooper, Russell, and Waters (2009) recently completed a meta-analysis of predictor constructs for clerical occupations. Two primary goals of the analysis were to determine whether changes in administrative and clerical occupations had resulted in changes to the criterion-related validity of various clerical tests and to examine (to the extent the literature permitted) the criterion-related validity of computerized clerical tests relative to those administered as paper-and-pencil tests.

The results of the meta-analysis can be summarized as follows (see Tables 10.3 and 10.4):

- The results continue to support the validity of clerical tests for predicting performance in clerical jobs.
- When corrected for range restriction and criterion unreliability (at the .60 level), mean meta-analytic validity estimates were positive. The cognitive predictor types examined were general cognitive ability ($\rho = .54$), verbal ability ($\rho = .49$), quantitative ability ($\rho = .43$), reasoning ability ($\rho = .48$), perceptual speed ($\rho = .50$), performance tests ($\rho = .56$), and

Table 10.3. Comparison of Corrected Validity Estimates for Cognitive Constructs to Pearlman et al. (1980)

	N	k	r	SD_r	ρ	SD_ρ	Corrected for Criterion Unreliability and Range Restriction 80% Credibility Interval Lower	Upper
General cognitive ability								
Whetzel et al. (2009)	1,260	9	.27	.11	.54	.17	.33	.75
Pearlman et al. (1980)	17,339	194	.26	.17	.52	.24	.21	—
Verbal ability								
Whetzel et al. (2009)	11,238	32	.24	.06	.49	.11	.35	.63
Pearlman et al. (1980)	39,187	450	.18	.16	.39	.23	.09	—
Quantitative ability								
Whetzel et al. (2009)	11,920	30	.21	.07	.43	.13	.26	.59
Pearlman et al. (1980)	39,584	453	.23	.14	.47	.14	.30	—
Reasoning ability								
Whetzel et al. (2009)	9,969	21	.24	.06	.48	.09	.36	.60
Pearlman et al. (1980)	11,586	116	.18	.13	.39	.15	.19	—
Perceptual speed								
Whetzel et al. (2009)	10,840	38	.25	.04	.50	.08	.40	.59
Pearlman et al. (1980)	70,935	882	.22	.16	.47	.22	.19	—

| | | | | | | Corrected for Criterion Unreliability and Range Restriction | |
| | | | | | | 80% Credibility Interval | |
	N	k	r	SD_r	ρ	SD_ρ	Lower	Upper
Performance tests								
Whetzel et al. (2009)	739	8	.29	.00	.56	.00	.56	.56
Pearlman et al. (1980)	6,265	67	.21	.24	.44	.43	−.11	—
Clerical aptitude								
Whetzel et al. (2009)	1,997	11	.24	.06	.49	.09	.38	.60
Pearlman et al. (1980)	11,927	142	.23	.17	.48	.24	.18	—

Note: A reliability estimate of .60 was used to correct the criteria for unreliability. N = number of participants across studies, k = number of studies included in the meta-analysis, r = uncorrected validity estimate, and ρ = corrected validity estimate. The standard deviation (SD) is provided for both r and ρ.

clerical aptitude ($\rho = .49$). As shown in the table, these are comparable to Pearlman's validity estimates of $\rho = .52$ for general cognitive ability, $\rho = .39$ for verbal ability, $\rho = .47$ for quantitative ability, $\rho = .39$ for reasoning ability, $\rho = .47$ for perceptual speed, $\rho = .44$ for performance test, and $\rho = .48$ for clerical aptitude.

- For the few studies available (k ranging from 2 to 6), computerized assessments have corrected validity coefficients that are for the most part similar to the corrected coefficients of paper-and-pencil assessments (see Table 10.4), although higher for general cognitive ability and verbal ability.

Table 10.4. Comparisons of Computerized and Paper-and-Pencil Measures of Predictor Constructs for Clerical Jobs

	N	k	r	SD_r	Corrected for Criterion Unreliability and Range Restriction		80% Credibility Interval	
					ρ	SD_ρ	Lower	Upper
General cognitive ability								
Paper-and-pencil	1,072	7	.25	.10	.51	.16	.31	.72
Computer administered	188	2	.37	.07	.69	.10	.56	.82
Verbal ability								
Paper-and-pencil	9,440	22	.25	.04	.50	.07	.41	.59
Computer administered	349	4	.35	.07	.65	.07	.56	.75
Reasoning ability								
Paper-and-pencil	9,706	19	.24	.06	.49	.11	.35	.62
Computer administered	263	2	.21	.00	.44	.00	.44	.44
Perceptual speed								
Paper-and-pencil	9,886	32	.25	.04	.50	.07	.41	.59
Computer administered	954	6	.24	.07	.48	.11	.33	.62

| | | | | | Corrected for Criterion Unreliability and Range Restriction | | | |
| | | | | | | | 80% Credibility Interval | |
	N	k	r	SD_r	ρ	SD_ρ	Lower	Upper
Quantitative ability								
Paper-and-pencil	11,053	23	.21	.07	.43	.13	.26	.60
Computer administered	746	5	.19	.00	.40	.00	.40	.40

Note: A reliability estimate of .60 was used to correct the criteria for unreliability. N = number of participants across studies, k = number of studies included in the meta-analysis, r = uncorrected validity estimate, and ρ = corrected validity estimate. The standard deviation (SD) is provided for both r and ρ.

- As shown in Table 10.5, when corrected for range restriction and criterion unreliability (at the .60 level), mean meta-analytic validity estimates for the Big Five personality constructs were positive across all but one predictor (Extraversion). The personality constructs examined were Extraversion (ρ = −.09), Agreeableness (ρ = .25), Conscientiousness (ρ = .39), Emotional Stability (ρ = .25), and Openness to Experience (ρ = .24). Conscientiousness was the most valid predictor of performance. Note that all the studies included in the meta-analysis were conducted using current employees.
- There were relatively few published studies available for analysis, a potential drawback of meta-analysis (Oswald & McCloy, 2000), and very few studies involving computerized assessments.

Clearly, more investigation into the criterion-related validity of computerized clerical tests should be conducted. The results obtained thus far, however, suggest that they function similarly to paper-and-pencil measures of the same constructs. In addition, the slight increase in the general cognitive ability coefficients is

Table 10.5. Corrected Validity Estimates for Noncognitive Constructs for Clerical Jobs

	N	k	r	SD_r	ρ	SD_ρ	Lower	Upper
							80% Credibility Interval	
Extraversion	3,637	9	−.04	.10	−.09	.21	−.36	.18
Agreeableness	2,583	12	.12	.01	.25	.02	.22	.27
Conscientiousness	5,411	15	.19	.05	.39	.09	.27	.50
Emotional Stability	5,264	15	.12	.05	.25	.11	.12	.39
Openness to Experience	2,318	8	.11	.08	.24	.17	.03	.46

Corrected for Criterion Unreliability and Range Restriction

Note: A reliability estimate of .60 was used to correct the criteria for unreliability. N = number of participants across studies, k = number of studies included in the meta-analysis, r = uncorrected validity estimate, and ρ = corrected validity estimate. The standard deviation (SD) is provided for both r and ρ.

consistent with the notion that administrative and clerical jobs have become more cognitively complex over the past decade or two.

Summary of Assessments for Administrative and Clerical Jobs

All organizations assess applicants to make hiring choices. Each organization should decide beforehand which assessments it will use and how it will use them—that is, its assessment strategy. Organizations with high applicant volume for administrative and clerical job postings often find highly structured assessments to be a cost-effective and relatively efficient method for differentiating among applicants. The organization's goals, the current requirements of the job, and the applicant pool are all factors to consider when determining the assessment strategy.

In selecting which assessments to use, organizations should begin with a job analysis to identify the job requirements. Increasing use of technology in the workplace has drastically changed the role of administrative and clerical jobs, so the job analysis is crucial for ensuring that assessments are relevant. Organizations will likely identify many administrative and clerical KSAs that lend themselves well to structured assessments, including tests of cognitive ability, personality, verbal ability, perceptual speed, software use, and clerical aptitude. All of these have demonstrated themselves to be valid predictors of performance in clerical jobs. Furthermore, there are a variety of ways to assess those KSAs, including multiple-choice tests, performance tests, online questionnaires, and structured interviews. The job analysis will help identify which KSAs to assess, and factors such as cost, anticipated volume, and availability of resources should be considered when deciding what types of assessments to use and whether to build or buy them.

When an organization is making these decisions for administrative and clerical jobs, its decisions will be more defensible if it also considers the unique issues affecting selection for these jobs. For example, they should avoid the "temporary trap" by using assessments in a consistent manner and working with hiring managers to facilitate buy-in to the assessment process. The use of current job information from the job analysis will help ensure that the assessments are appropriate for administrative and clerical jobs in today's high-tech world. Further, organizations should not take recruitment for granted; with more women entering the workforce at higher levels in the organization and with many administrative and clerical jobs requiring complex skills, it may be more difficult than expected to attract qualified applicants to clerical job opportunities.

Professional and Technical Jobs

Case Study 3: An Education and Years of Experience Mirage

A newly hired marketing manager is looking to fill two vacancies on his staff: one for a junior marketing specialist and another for a senior marketing specialist. The marketing manager has been charged with implementing a number of cutting-edge marketing initiatives in a short amount of time. He therefore decides that he needs to raise the bar for

(Continued)

Case Study 3: An Education and Years of Experience Mirage *(Continued)*

entrance into these jobs and is interested in revising the previous job requirements. In a meeting with the HR representative, the marketing manager says that the junior marketing specialist position requires a bachelor's degree in marketing and three to five years of experience, and the senior marketing specialist requires a bachelor's degree in marketing, with a master's degree preferred, and five to seven years of experience. That information is included on the job posting, and the posting is distributed to recruiting channels including the company's Web site, other commercial job search Web sites, and marketing professionals' networking organizations.

They post the job openings for one month. The senior-level job attracts a small number of applicants, one of whom was referred to the marketing manager by a colleague. After reviewing the applicants, the marketing manager selects the referred applicant as the best candidate. The candidate has ten years of experience as a marketing specialist, working for a competitor whose products and marketing strategy are similar to those of the hiring organization. However, the candidate does not have a degree in marketing.

The junior-level job attracts a much larger pool of applicants, but most of them are recent college graduates with little or no job experience. The marketing manager is under pressure to fill the jobs so he can begin implementing some of his new marketing initiatives. Therefore, he informs HR that because this is a junior position and others on staff can assist with training and guidance, he is willing to hire a candidate with a bachelor's degree and no experience.

In short, the marketing manager is asking HR to waive the education requirement for the senior position and waive the experience requirement for the junior position. Knowing that this cannot be defended legally and that this is contradictory to what were originally stated as the job requirements and therefore may lead to a bad hiring decision, HR instead closes the postings as unfilled, with no candidates meeting the minimum qualifications.

Assessment Challenges for Professional and Technical Jobs

Unfortunately, the situation in the case study is not atypical of the experience many HR professionals have faced when attempting to fill professional and technical jobs. The case study involves two personnel requirements that are frequently identified as "magic bullets": educational attainment (specifically, the bachelor's degree) and years of experience. Despite the hard-to-fill nature of professional and technical jobs, hiring managers frequently implement years of experience or education and certification hurdles because these are familiar and easy to assess. Their use, however, can be fraught with problems if not properly validated.

Problematic Magic Bullet 1: Bachelor's Degree

Professional and technical jobs are frequently the victim of the overused and undervalidated bachelor's degree requirement. On its face, a degree appears to be a valid requirement for these jobs. Hiring managers may perceive the degree as an easy way to quickly reduce the number of applicants they must consider. Often, however, they do not understand the difference between minimum qualifications (which are appropriately required at entry) and qualifications that reflect performance at satisfactory proficiency levels (which are not appropriate for screening applicants at entry). (Chapter Five discusses the importance of validating minimum qualifications appropriately.) Although a job might require a bachelor's degree, this is not always the case when the degree requirement is invoked. Therefore, job analysts must be especially vigilant when considering a bachelor's degree requirement for professional and technical jobs.

As an example, requiring an accounting degree for an accounting job or a marketing degree for a marketing job might seem appropriate at first glance. However, a brief conversation with the hiring manager might reveal that he or she would be interested in considering individuals who have gained the requisite knowledge and abilities through experience, even without the degree. Such managers often have staff members without the degree who are working effectively. When incumbents are performing the job satisfactorily without the degree, it can be difficult to support the degree requirement as job relevant and necessary at entry.

Requiring a bachelor's degree for professional and technical jobs is not a magic bullet to ease the hiring process. On the contrary, it is a standard that can make the organization vulnerable to litigation, which it might well lose if the degree requirement has not been appropriately validated. If subject matter experts or hiring managers make statements such as, "A bachelor's degree tells you that they can learn," or "A bachelor's degree tells you that they finish things that they start," this should be a red flag. These statements do not support the requirement of job relatedness. There are many ways to evaluate a person's ability to learn and propensity for completing what he or she starts. A bachelor's degree is a poor proxy for these competencies. Thus, even for professional and technical jobs, a thorough job analysis should be conducted to validate all requirements, including (indeed, especially) the education requirements.

Problematic Magic Bullet 2: Years of Experience

A "years of experience" requirement is another magic bullet that selecting officials think will make their jobs easier. When selecting officials state that the job requires a specified number of years of experience, they are usually talking about the amount of experience typical for individuals performing at satisfactory levels, not the amount of experience required at entry. They need to consider whether they would be interested in someone with slightly less experience, such as two years and ten months, or six and a half years. They frequently say they would want to be able to consider such an applicant as well. A more effective strategy is to describe the requirements qualitatively rather than quantitatively. For example, they should describe the specific KSAs that an applicant with that level of experience is expected to have. The years of experience requirement is frequently a shortcut for evaluating such KSAs—another poor proxy.

If an organization or selecting official insists on including an experience requirement, work with them to confirm the absolute minimum level. Remind them that although it is understood that more years of experience (or more education) are preferable to fewer, having a true minimum years requirement (rather than an inflated one) will allow them to filter the applicant pool without inappropriately deterring or rejecting applicants who are otherwise qualified. In addition, invoking a degree or education requirement might deter qualified applicants from applying. Thus, the screen begins to eliminate qualified applicants as soon as it is displayed on a job announcement. If, after setting the minimum years of experience requirement, the selecting official chooses to hire someone with less experience, that decision might be difficult to support in a legal challenge. An organization can avoid unfair application of this standard by working with the selecting official or subject matter experts to establish the absolute minimum.

Buster, Roth, and Bobko (2005) provided a process for content validation of education and experience-based minimum qualifications that has met with court approval and is consistent with the *Uniform Guidelines on Employee Selection Procedures* (EEOC, 1978). The process includes conducting a job analysis, developing and administering a Minimum Qualifications Questionnaire to SMEs, and identifying cutoffs for selecting questionnaire statements. A full description of this approach is beyond the scope of this chapter, but we recommend a process such as this to help alleviate the problems associated with both of these magic bullets.

We will return to the topic of considerations for identifying and validating requirements and assessments for professional and technical jobs. But first it would be helpful to step back and think about the applicant pool for this group and the related recruitment and assessment challenges.

Applicant Pool

An organization seeking to fill a high-level professional or technical job might need to invest in an active, geographically varied recruitment strategy and offer competitive salaries, bonuses, and other incentives, remunerative or otherwise, to attract qualified, interested applicants. For these jobs, recruitment often is conducted through the use of professional organizations and newsletters and by word of mouth. These jobs also can be difficult to fill if an organization is unable to pay competitive salaries. Consider the situation in which an organization in the public sector uses pay bands that are lower than salaries offered in private industry. These public sector organizations frequently have difficulty attracting qualified applicants into professional jobs in metropolitan areas where the cost of living is high and locality pay is not provided. Another challenge related to recruiting for these jobs is that once incumbents gain some level of experience, they often can find higher-paying positions elsewhere. Thus, turnover can be a challenge for organizations as they seek to be competitive and to retain talented employees.

The nature and level of the job drive the job requirements and, thus, which candidates will be minimally qualified. The proximity of the job to the organization's core mission, as well as the consequence of error, affects the extent to which the organization should tolerate imprecision in its assessment strategy. In high-level professional jobs, the consequences of error can be enormous (for example, the accountant who makes mistakes in the company's financial records, or the foreign language interpreter who incorrectly translates during an intense negotiation). Thus, organizations need to consider carefully the decision of whether or not to test. Issues to consider when making this decision are described below.

Professional and Technical Jobs: To Test or Not to Test?

Consider the challenges of filling a high-level, professional or technical job. Given a smaller pool of qualified potential applicants and the fact that experience, degree, or certification is easily identified and verified, many organizations find it useful to use training and experience questionnaires to evaluate candidates' education and experience, despite their relatively low validity (McDaniel, Schmidt, & Hunter, 1988). The organization then evaluates other skills (such as interpersonal skills and project management) in a structured interview, which is relatively inexpensive to develop and revise, provides a rich depth of information, and allows interviewers some degree of subjective judgment during evaluation. However, this combination of assessments might still miss some critical skills and abilities. If there is a high consequence of error, the organization should consider a more structured evaluation of critical knowledge or skills, even with a smaller applicant pool.

Organizations will benefit substantially from using structured assessment methods. They need to decide what type of assessment to use and whether it will be custom-made or purchased off-the-shelf. Before an assessment is chosen, however, a thorough job analysis should be conducted to identify the constructs (knowledge, skills, and abilities) to be measured.

Describing the Professional or Technical Job: Job Analysis

The process of identifying which assessment to use or develop typically begins with a job analysis. The job analysis is important not only for targeting appropriate knowledge, skills, and abilities, but also for documenting job relatedness to help establish legal defensibility, as described in the *Uniform Guidelines on Employee Selection Procedures* (EEOC, 1978). In-depth coverage of job analysis methods and content validation strategies for purposes of developing an assessment can be obtained from many sources, so we will not cover them here. However, we will discuss issues and challenges that might arise during job analysis studies for professional and technical jobs.

Organizations should conduct a job analysis before selecting assessments. We use information from O*NET to guide our illustration, a good starting point for any organization that is beginning a local job analysis.

Technical knowledge and ability requirements for professional and technical jobs are likely to be very job specific. Depending on the job, these include knowledge areas such as accounting, economics, law, and engineering, or abilities such as computer programming, technical report writing, and statistical analyses. Exhibit 10.2 shows a summary of the O*NET KSAs for the job of economist. Many of the nontechnical KSAs are similar across professional and technical jobs (such as reading comprehension, critical thinking, active learning, and complex problem solving). We chose the job of economist as an exemplar and a basis for comparison.

A comparison of Exhibits 10.1 and 10.2 for administrative and clerical occupations demonstrates how similar these occupations are in terms of their nontechnical KSAs (both require reading comprehension, writing, oral expression, and comprehension), as well as the contrast between the occupations. In general, and as shown here, professional and technical jobs require more

Exhibit 10.2. O*NET Knowledge, Skills, and Abilities for the Job of Economist

Summary Report for: 19-3011.00—Economist

Conduct research, prepare reports, or formulate plans to aid in solution of economic problems arising from production and distribution of goods and services. May collect and process economic and statistical data using econometric and sampling techniques.

Sample of reported job titles: Economist, Economic Analyst, Economic Consultant, Project Economist, Forensic Economist, Health Researcher, Research Analyst, Economic Analysis Director, Economic Development Specialist, Revenue Research Analyst

Knowledge

English Language—Knowledge of the structure and content of the English language including the meaning and spelling of words, rules of composition, and grammar.

Economics and Accounting—Knowledge of economic and accounting principles and practices, the financial markets, banking and the analysis and reporting of financial data.

Mathematics—Knowledge of arithmetic, algebra, geometry, calculus, statistics, and their applications.

Computers and Electronics—Knowledge of circuit boards, processors, chips, electronic equipment, and computer hardware and software, including applications and programming.

Law and Government—Knowledge of laws, legal codes, court procedures, precedents, government regulations, executive orders, agency rules, and the democratic political process.

Administration and Management—Knowledge of business and management principles involved in strategic planning, resource allocation, human resources modeling, leadership technique, production methods, and coordination of people and resources.

Skills

Reading Comprehension—Understanding written sentences and paragraphs in work related documents.

Critical Thinking—Using logic and reasoning to identify the strengths and weaknesses of alternative solutions, conclusions or approaches to problems.

Writing—Communicating effectively in writing as appropriate for the needs of the audience.

Mathematics—Using mathematics to solve problems.

Complex Problem Solving—Identifying complex problems and reviewing related information to develop and evaluate options and implement solutions.

Judgment and Decision Making—Considering the relative costs and benefits of potential actions to choose the most appropriate one.

Active Listening—Giving full attention to what other people are saying, taking time to understand the points being made, asking questions as appropriate, and not interrupting at inappropriate times.

Time Management—Managing one's own time and the time of others.

Coordination—Adjusting actions in relation to others' actions.

ABILITIES

Oral Expression—The ability to communicate information and ideas in speaking so others will understand.

Oral Comprehension—The ability to listen to and understand information and ideas presented through spoken words and sentences.

Written Comprehension—The ability to read and understand information and ideas presented in writing.

Written Expression—The ability to communicate information and ideas in writing so others will understand.

Deductive Reasoning—The ability to apply general rules to specific problems to produce answers that make sense.

Inductive Reasoning—The ability to combine pieces of information to form general rules or conclusions (includes finding a relationship among seemingly unrelated events).

Speech Clarity—The ability to speak clearly so others can understand you.

(Continued)

Exhibit 10.2. O*NET Knowledge, Skills, and Abilities for the Job of Economist *(Continued)*

Problem Sensitivity—The ability to tell when something is wrong or is likely to go wrong. It does not involve solving the problem, only recognizing there is a problem.

Mathematical Reasoning—The ability to choose the right mathematical methods or formulas to solve a problem.

Near Vision—The ability to see details at close range (within a few feet of the observer).

Source: www.onetcenter.org.

technical knowledge and complex problem-solving skills than do administrative and clerical jobs. This job-specific knowledge and abilities often lend themselves well to a structured multiple-choice or work sample test. For the same reason, many of these jobs have specific degrees or certifications that can be used to filter out applicants who are not minimally qualified. Remember that any education or certification requirement must be validated as a job-relevant minimum qualification. When the applicant pool is small and hiring for the job is infrequent, however, organizations often rely on a structured interview combined with a training and experience questionnaire.

Case Study 3, Continued: Job Analysis

How might the HR representative proceed now that she has not been able to fill the jobs? With hindsight, she realizes that she should not have accepted the marketing manager's assessment of the job requirements without conducting a job analysis. The marketing manager initially is resistant to waiting for a job analysis to be conducted. However, there are relatively few subject matter experts for these jobs (the marketing manager, one senior marketing specialist, three junior marketing specialists, and one trainer), so the job analysis will not take an excessive amount of time. In fact, the

HR representative estimated that the job analysis would take less time than the two months it would take to repost the current requirements, accept applications, and review the applications—a process that is likely to yield no suitable applicants. By explaining it this way, the HR representative helps the marketing manager understand that the time invested in conducting a job analysis is well spent: they will be able to refine the job requirements to more effectively attract and identify qualified applicants in less time than it would take to go through another potentially unsuccessful iteration of trying to fill the jobs without revising the requirements.

The job analysis yields the following information. Of the three junior marketing specialists currently on staff, only one has a bachelor's degree in marketing. The specialist with the bachelor's degree was hired directly out of school, and the other two were hired with between one and two years of experience. All three have been in their current job for at least two years, and the marketing manager believes they are performing at a satisfactory level. The one senior marketing specialist on staff has a bachelor's degree and seven years of experience as a marketing specialist. However, at the time that she was promoted into the senior position, she had only three years of experience as a marketing specialist. She too is currently performing at a satisfactory level.

The following KSAs were identified as needed at entry for the junior marketing specialist job:

- Knowledge of marketing techniques and strategies
- Ability to communicate orally and in writing
- Organizational skills
- Problem-solving ability
- Skill in using word processing and e-mail software

The job analysis for the senior marketing specialist job yielded the same KSAs as the junior job, plus:

- Ability to implement and manage a marketing program
- Project management skills
- Ability to advise others on marketing techniques and strategies

(Continued)

Case Study 3, Continued: Job Analysis
(Continued)

Discussions during the job analysis revealed that although obtaining a bachelor's degree in marketing is an acceptable way to acquire the knowledge of marketing techniques and strategies, this knowledge may also be acquired through other methods such as on-the-job training or related certification courses. For the junior position, the successful candidate could have as little as one year (or possibly less) of experience, but more years of job experience might be needed for individuals who are acquiring their knowledge of marketing through on-the-job experience rather than through formal education. Similarly, some individuals might quickly acquire the project management skills and program implementation ability necessary at the senior level, whereas others may take longer to acquire these skills and abilities if they are in a job with more routine, repetitive duties and little exposure to program implementation. Thus, setting a minimum number of years of experience for these jobs is difficult. The HR representative decides that directly assessing applicants' KSAs would be a more effective way to evaluate applicants' fit for the job rather than evaluating them indirectly by looking at their educational credentials and counting their years of work experience.

Developing an Assessment Strategy for Professional and Technical Jobs

Similar to administrative and clerical jobs, tests of general cognitive ability and competency-based assessments might be effective for screening applicants for professional and technical jobs, in addition to knowledge and ability assessments. As with the clerical occupations, an organization may choose multiple assessment methods for one job. For example, an organization that hires very few computer programmers for a minor technical support role may choose to evaluate applicants using a training and experience questionnaire to assess technical knowledge and related experience, followed by a structured interview to further assess technical knowledge, interpersonal skills, and work attitudes.

Demonstrating Assessment Validity

In addition to ensuring that assessments are job relevant, organizations should also ensure that the assessments predict job performance. Given the range of jobs described in this chapter, one can imagine the large numbers of assessments that have been researched and developed to predict performance. Such tests include measures of cognitive ability, accomplishment records, and personality measures, to name a few. The criterion-related validity of these tests has been discussed in previous chapters, as have other issues that should be considered such as subgroup differences and face validity. Here we highlight some of the research that has investigated criterion-related validity for tests that are frequently used for professional and technical jobs.

Because the value that individuals in professional and technical jobs provide to a company most often stems from their technical expertise, some of the most fitting tests for these jobs may be those of technical knowledge and skill, such as cognitive ability tests, knowledge tests, and work sample tests. Because these jobs typically attract a relatively small number of qualified candidates, many organizations find that the additional workload associated with conducting structured interviews is manageable and worth the time, given the depth and breadth of information they can elicit from applicants. Furthermore, because many professional and technical jobs require objective, verifiable qualifications such as degrees, certifications, or demonstrated experience performing specific tasks, training and experience inventories are also useful. In this section, we describe validity evidence for general cognitive ability, structured interviews, and training and experience measures.

General Cognitive Ability

Cognitive ability is a valid predictor of training and job performance for all jobs. Schmidt and Hunter (1998) reported on the validity of cognitive ability from a very large meta-analytic study conducted for the U.S. Department of Labor (Hunter, 1980). Data from more than thirty-two thousand employees in 515 widely diverse civilian jobs were included in the database. Schmidt and Hunter found that cognitive ability was a valid predictor of job performance for all jobs but was highest for more complex jobs. Validity estimates for predicting job performance were .58

for professional and managerial jobs, .56 for high-level complex technical jobs, .51 for medium-complexity jobs (which constitute 62 percent of all jobs in the U.S. economy), .40 for semiskilled jobs, and .23 for completely unskilled jobs.

Structured Interviews

Interviews are among the most widely used selection instruments. Structured interviews, in which the questions asked are the same across applicants and answers are rated against the same behaviorally based scale, have been shown to be valid predictors of performance. McDaniel, Whetzel, Schmidt, and Maurer (1994) analyzed 245 validity coefficients derived from 86,311 individuals. Results showed that interview validity depends on the content of the interview (situational, job related, or psychological), how the interview is conducted (structured versus unstructured, interview panel versus single interviewer), and the nature of the criterion (job performance, training performance, and tenure; research or administrative ratings).

Training and Experience Measures

McDaniel et al. (1988) studied the validity of training and experience (T&E) measures: those that attempt to predict future job performance through systematic, judgment-based evaluations of information provided by applicants on résumés, applications, or other documents. There are several methods for conducting T&E evaluations: point, task, behavioral consistency, grouping, and the KSA methods. Results showed that validity varied with the type of T&E evaluation procedure used. The Illinois job element and behavioral consistency methods each demonstrated useful levels of validity (.20 and .45, respectively) with small corrected standard deviations, thus supporting validity generalization. Both the point and task methods yielded low mean levels of validity (.11 and .15, respectively) with larger variability. The authors hypothesized that both the point and task methods were affected by a job experience moderator. Moderator analyses suggested that the point method was most valid when the applicant pool had low mean levels of job experience and was least valid with an experienced applicant pool.

Factors to consider when determining an assessment strategy include the KSAs that are being evaluated, the types of assessments that are appropriate for evaluating those KSAs, and any challenges, limitations, or constraints (such as the size of the expected applicant pool and the availability of organizational resources) that will affect the organization's ability to conduct the assessments effectively and in a timely manner. Table 10.6 sets out the assessment strategy that the organization in case study 3 chose for these jobs, and the case study picks up with the thought processes that brought them to this assessment strategy.

Case Study 3, Continued: Assessment Strategy

The HR representative has the results of the job analysis, including the KSAs that are needed at entry for each job. This list becomes the starting point for the next step: creating the organization's assessment strategy for these jobs. The screening process does not need to evaluate applicants on all KSAs needed at entry, but it should evaluate applicants on the important KSAs needed from the start. Furthermore, any decision not to evaluate one or more KSAs should be a conscious decision, not simply an oversight or the result of laziness on the part of the organization.

Table 10.6. Case Study 3 Assessment Strategy

KSA	Knowledge Test	Structured Interview
Knowledge of marketing techniques and strategies	Buy	
Organizational skills		Build
Ability to implement and manage a marketing program		Build
Project management skills		Build
Ability to advise others on marketing techniques and strategies		Build

(Continued)

Table 10.6. Case Study 3 Assessment Strategy *(Continued)*

Experience informs the HR representative that she can expect a large number of applicants for the junior position. The position requires knowledge of marketing techniques and strategies, making this an important KSA. Because that knowledge can be acquired in many ways, the organization decided to assess this KSA using a structured, multiple-choice assessment, which can be administered to a large number of applicants and scored objectively and quickly. Furthermore, the organization decided to administer the assessment online in a proctored environment to expedite the scoring process. Because the applicants are expected to be able to use computers on the job, the organization is not concerned about qualified applicants being put at a disadvantage by an online administration medium. (Chapter Nineteen discusses the factors to consider when selecting and implementing an online, proctored knowledge assessment.) Because the marketing knowledge that applicants are expected to demonstrate is general marketing and not knowledge specific to the organization, the organization has decided to look for an off-the-shelf measure. However, if it cannot find an off-the-shelf measure, it might need to commission a testing professional or company to build one for them. (Chapter Twenty-One provides guidance on searching for and appropriately validating an off-the-shelf measure.) KSAs such as written communication and computer skills can be effectively evaluated by a performance or work sample test. However, the organization determined that the level of written communication and computer skills required is relatively basic. Therefore, they decided not to spend resources on testing these skills. The organization decided to evaluate the remainder of the KSAs with a structured interview.

Although the volume of senior marketing specialist applicants is expected to be considerably smaller, the organization agreed that the applicants for the senior positions also should demonstrate their marketing knowledge. Accordingly, these applicants will take the marketing knowledge exam and will need to pass at the same score level as the junior job applicants.

Because the additional KSAs required for senior marketing specialist are more complex and best demonstrated through experience, the organization decided to evaluate them in the structured interview. This will afford a less restrictive venue where the interviewers can learn the depth and breadth of experience these individuals have in relation to these KSAs.

To make the structured interview process manageable, the organization decided to set up the two assessments as multiple hurdles: all applicants will take the marketing knowledge test; those who pass will be rank-ordered based on their test score, and only the top-scoring applicants will be invited to the interview.

Once the organization conducted the job analysis, identified the KSAs needed at entry, developed its assessment strategy, and selected and implemented the assessments, they revised the job announcement and reposted the jobs in the same recruiting channels used previously. When it came time to review the applications, the HR representative noticed that, as before, the junior job attracted a large number of applicants. However, in contrast to the first round of posting, the applicants had a range of marketing experience. Apparently the bachelor's degree requirement on the previous junior marketing specialist posting had had a chilling effect on the applicant pool: whereas the first applicant pool consisted primarily of individuals with a bachelor's degree in marketing and little to no experience, the current applicant pool was larger and included individuals with a range of marketing experience and some with no bachelor's degree.

A similar trend was seen with the senior marketing specialist job. Although the number of applicants was smaller than the number who applied for the junior position, this senior position applicant pool was larger than the first and included individuals with a greater range of experience. Furthermore, the person who was the marketing manager's preference in the first applicant pool applied again and was able to be considered now that the job announcement no longer specified an education requirement.

In sum, although there are legal reasons for conducting a job analysis and using a comprehensive approach to identify predictor measures, there also are positive selection outcomes that come from implementing such procedures.

Summary of Assessments for Professional and Technical Jobs

The technical expertise required for most professional and technical jobs often makes recruiting qualified applicants for these jobs somewhat difficult. Organizations might need to use a more geographically diverse recruitment strategy and rely on perks and competitive salaries to help attract qualified applicants. Hiring qualified candidates is critical for these jobs, which are often core to the mission of the organization or in a position where the consequence of error is high. Structured assessments will help organizations identify which applicants are qualified and differentiate among them.

As with administrative and clerical jobs, organizations should begin with a job analysis. It is likely that many professional and technical KSAs will lend themselves to assessments. Some qualifications, such as education or certifications, can be assessed easily and quickly, especially with the use of online questionnaires. Although job knowledge tests are often appropriate, other assessment methods have been shown to predict job performance effectively in professional and technical jobs, including cognitive ability tests, structured interviews, training and experience questionnaires, personality measures, and general competency assessments. An organization can use multiple assessments and should take care (as with all job types) that the assessments used measure most of the important job KSAs.

Although many professional and technical jobs require candidates to demonstrate acquisition of the appropriate technical skills through possession of a degree or certificate, the organization should conduct a careful job analysis to ensure that this requirement is necessary, and not just a hiring manager's magic bullet. The other perceived magic bullet of concern is years of experience. The job analysis might not support a requirement for a specific number of years of experience. Even if it does, SMEs should be queried to ensure that the number of years is truly a minimum and not an average. Remember from the marketing specialist case study that a qualitative description of the requisite KSAs often can help to facilitate a more effective recruitment and assessment strategy.

Conclusion

A variety of assessments have demonstrated validity for predicting performance in administrative, clerical, professional, and technical jobs. Therefore, the characteristics of the job under consideration and the availability of organizational resources should be considered when determining an assessment strategy.

It is important to begin with a job analysis to identify the KSAs necessary at entry for the job. Care should be taken to fully validate all requirements, including education and years of experience if used. Educational degree, certification, or years of experience should not be used as a proxy for knowledge and abilities that can be acquired through experience or other types of training. These proxy measures are difficult to defend if not properly validated, and even the managers who request them will be quick to ask for an exception when presented with otherwise qualified candidates.

Taken together, the assessments should measure the majority of the KSAs necessary at entry. Validating the assessments helps to ensure job relevance and the ability to predict job performance. For off-the-shelf instruments, reviewing the existing research is important but is no substitute for a local validation study. When implementing the assessments, proactively establishing guidance and protocols will help ensure that the assessments are used consistently. Reinforce the importance of assessment with those involved in the hiring decision, and consider requiring even temporary employees to pass established job assessments, to avoid the "temporary trap."

An interview will almost always be used to screen applicants for these jobs. If a high volume of applicants is expected, consider arranging the assessments as multiple hurdles, with the interview being the last hurdle. A structured evaluation process will help maximize the effectiveness of the interview.

Cognitive ability tests have been demonstrated to be effective predictors of performance in all of these jobs. For administrative or clerical jobs, consider including assessments of clerical aptitude, verbal ability, and computer software skills (as a performance test). The job analysis will likely reveal the importance of noncognitive competencies such as customer service and organizational skills. And depending on the job, a measure of mathematical or numerical skills may also be appropriate.

An assessment strategy for professional or technical jobs is likely to focus more on technical knowledge, skills, and abilities. Although basic computer proficiency is generally required, limited time and resources may necessitate that the assessment strategy focus on the most critical and differentiating job requirements. Thus, the assessments are likely to focus more on technical competencies and high-level nontechnical competencies such as project management, critical thinking, and complex problem solving.

References

Buster, M. A., Roth, P. L., & Bobko, P. (2005). A process for content validation of education and experienced-based minimum qualifications: An approach resulting in federal court approval. *Personnel Psychology, 58*, 771–799.

Equal Employment Opportunity Commission, Civil Service Commission, Department of Labor, & Department of Justice. (1978). Uniform guidelines on employee selection. *Federal Register, 43*(166), 38290–38315.

International Association of Administrative Professionals, The 21st Century Administrative Professional. (n.d.). *Career paths for administrative support staff* (p. 5). Retrieved February 15, 2010, from http://www.iaap-hq.org/researchtrends/21centuryadmin.htm.

Hunter, J. E. (1980). *Validity generalization for 12,000 jobs: An application of synthetic validity and validity generalization to the General Aptitude Test Battery (GATB)*. Washington, DC: U.S. Department of Labor, Employment Service.

McDaniel, M. A., Schmidt, F. L., & Hunter, J. E. (1988). A meta-analysis of the validity of methods for rating training and experience in personnel selection. *Personnel Psychology, 41*, 283–314.

McDaniel, M. A., Whetzel, D. L., Schmidt, F. L., & Maurer, S. D. (1994). The validity of employment interviews: A comprehensive review and meta-analysis. *Journal of Applied Psychology, 79*, 599–616.

Mead, A. D., & Drasgow, F. (1993). Equivalence of computerized and paper cognitive ability tests: A meta-analysis. *Psychological Bulletin, 114*(3), 449–458.

Oswald, F. L., & McCloy, R. A. (2003). Meta-analysis and the art of the average. In K. R. Murphy (Ed.), *Validity generalization: A critical review* (pp. 311–338). Mahwah, NJ: Erlbaum.

Pearlman, K., Schmidt, F. L., & Hunter, J. E. (1980). Validity generalization results for tests used to predict job proficiency and training success in clerical occupations. *Journal of Applied Psychology, 65,* 373–406.

Peterson, N. G., Mumford, M. D., Borman, W. C., Jeanneret, P. R., & Fleishman, E. A. (Eds.). (1999). *An occupational information system for the 21st century: Development of the O*NET.* Washington, DC: American Psychological Association.

Schmidt, F. L., & Hunter, J. E. (1998). The validity and utility of selection methods in personnel psychology: Practical and theoretical implications of 85 years of research findings. *Psychological Bulletin, 124,* 262–274.

Whetzel, D. L., McCloy, R. A., Hooper, A. C., Russell, T. L., & Waters, S. D. (2009). *Meta-analysis of clerical predictors of job performance.* Alexandria, VA: Human Resources Research Organization.

CHAPTER 11

ASSESSMENT FOR SALES POSITIONS

Steven H. Brown

From the broadest perspective, a business cannot be successful unless it finds a way to sell its products or services. Although there are many ways to accomplish this task, most often an individual is responsible for making the sale. Sales positions bring in customers and revenue; the success of a company's sales efforts is often critical to total organization success. Having an effective sales effort is a key objective in most businesses, but as you might expect, there are many ways to reach success.

A Wide World of Sales Positions

When people think of sales positions, they rarely imagine the wide range of position types that exist. The Bureau of Labor Statistics (U.S. Department of Labor, 2008) lists over twenty occupational codes under "Sales and Related Occupations." It estimates that nearly 16 million people in the United States—nearly 11 percent of all employees—are employed in sales occupations. The median annual income for these positions is about $23,700, ranging from $17,200 for the 3.5 million cashiers, to $80,300 for the 76,000 sales engineers. Projections over the 10 years between 2006 and 2016 suggest that sales employment will grow by over 1 million jobs (Dohm & Shniper, 2007). With turnover, the Bureau of Labor Statistics estimates that 6.2 million sales positions will need to be filled through 2016, nearly 12 percent of all job openings in the United States. Clearly, effective assessment can play a significant role in selecting sales employees.

What is common across these positions is that all have a desired outcome of selling a product or service to a prospective customer. Other similarities emerge when we look at O*NET content models for a group of sales positions. Table 11.1 shows knowledge, skills, abilities, work activities, work context, and work styles for ten representative sales positions. To be included in Table 11.1, a characteristic had to be rated as important or above for eight of the ten sales positions. The characteristics are listed in descending order, from most important on average across the positions. Note that there are relatively few knowledge, skills, or abilities (KSAs) that are consistently important across these sales positions. Those that emerge tend to be various types of communications skills and abilities. The most important work activities and work context characteristics continue the communication theme. Finally, the most important work styles tend to focus on characteristics that are related to building and maintaining trust and being conscientious.

In general, these are knowledge, skills, abilities, and other characteristics (KSAOs) that will be the focus in most sales selection or assessment programs. They are more or less universal across sales positions. Rarely, however, will the possession of these generic sales position KSAOs be sufficient for sales success. Positions vary in other ways that can be important when considering who will be successful in a specific position. For example, some sales positions sell tangible products; others sell services. Some sell to the public and some to businesses. There are retail sales positions and wholesale sales positions. Some sell over the telephone; some sell person-to-person in a store. Still others sell person-to-person at a customer's location.

Some sales positions do not require specific prior education, and others require substantial levels of education. For some, the position represents a career, and for others, it is a short-term job. Some salespeople make many sales each day, while other salespeople make only one or a few sales per year. Some positions are geared toward finding and qualifying prospective customers, and other salespeople are brought in to provide technical sales support in understanding complex customer needs and crafting

Table 11.1. O*NET Content Characteristics with High Importance Ratings Across Ten Sales Positions

Knowledge	Skills	Abilities
• Sales and marketing	• Active listening	• Oral expression
• Customer and personal service	• Speaking	• Oral comprehension
• English language	• Reading comprehension	• Speech clarity
	• Social perceptiveness	• Speech recognition
	• Service orientation	• Information ordering
	• Instructing	

Work Activity	Work Context	Work Styles
• Performing for or working directly with the public	• Telephone	• Integrity
• Getting information	• Contact with others	• Dependability
• Selling or influencing others	• Face-to-face discussions	• Cooperation
• Establishing and maintaining interpersonal relationships	• Freedom to make decisions	• Self-control
• Identifying objects, actions, and events	• Structured versus unstructured work	• Attention to detail
• Communicating with supervisors, peers, or subordinates	• Indoors, environmentally controlled	• Persistence
• Updating and using relevant knowledge	• Deal with external customers	• Stress tolerance
	• Work with work group or team	• Adaptability, flexibility
	• Importance of being exact or accurate	• Independence

(Continued)

Table 11.1. O*NET Content Characteristics with High Importance Ratings Across Ten Sales Positions (*Continued*)

Work Activity	*Work Context*	*Work Styles*
	• Level of competition	• Initiative
	• Frequency of decision making	• Achievement, effort
	• Impact of decisions on coworkers or company results	• Concern for others
	• Physical proximity	• Leadership
		• Social orientation

solutions for sale. Furthermore, salespeople are compensated in a variety of ways: hourly wages, salary, salary plus commission, salary plus bonus potential, and commission only with no salary.

All of this matters because although sales occupations are often grouped together as being very similar, important differences are seen when assessing KSAOs that differentiate strong from weak performance. It is important to understand the particular target sales position as completely as possible. Just as the skills needed to be a cashier differ from those needed to be a sales engineer, the skills needed for success in sales at one product distributor can be quite different from those needed at a second distributor.

Assessments for Selecting for Sales Positions

Earlier chapters in this book discuss many types of assessments. For the most part, there are situations where each is appropriate when selecting for sales positions. Here we address the most popular and more valid assessments used in selecting salespeople with a focus on any particular nuances in their use. Specifically, we look at cognitive and sales ability assessment, personality assessment, and biodata assessment. In a meta-analysis of predictors of sales performance, Vinchur, Schippmann, Switzer, and Roth

(1998) found that general cognitive ability, sales ability, biodata, and two personality dimensions (conscientiousness and extraversion) were strong predictors of sales success.

Clearly the most popular assessment step used in all sales selection processes is the interview—usually an unstructured interview. And while research has consistently shown that unstructured interviews have limited validity, they continue to be heavily relied on in sales selection, as well as in most other selection decisions. Those conducting the interviews firmly believe that interviews are more effective than other assessment techniques (Highhouse, 2008) and that, as interviewers, they are more effective than other interviewers.

Beyond the dismal predictive performance of unstructured interviews, Vinchur et al. (1998) point to a few other assessment types that have not shown great success in sales selection. For example, neither quantitative nor verbal ability shows much predictive power for sales positions, nor do the Big Five personality factors of Emotional Stability, Agreeableness, and Openness to Experience or the subdimensions of Affiliation or Dependability.

The following sections discuss sales-specific issues that should be considered when choosing assessments for selecting sales personnel. Note that these three categories of predictors (cognitive and sales ability assessment, personality assessment, and biodata assessment) tend not to be highly intercorrelated and therefore offer potential for real incremental prediction when used together.

Cognitive and Sales Ability Assessment

Impressive evidence exists that cognitive abilities are important in almost any job (Schmidt & Hunter, 1998), and this applies to sales positions as well. Empirical evidence suggests that telemarketers, insurance agents, and financial services salespeople with higher cognitive ability scores generate more sales and stay on the job longer than do those with lower scores. However, earlier research suggested that cognitive ability tests may not be consistently predictive across all sales jobs or all sales criteria (Hunter & Hunter, 1984). The Vinchur et al. (1998) meta-analysis suggests that this could be a function of the criterion being predicted in the study. They found that general cognitive ability was highly predictive of performance ratings but generally failed to predict objective sales criteria. My experience with telemarketers and financial services salespeople suggests that cognitive ability does predict quantitative sales results, especially for sales of complex products.

Bertua, Anderson, and Salgado (2005) found that cognitive ability tests are strong predictors of training success. As cognitive complexity requirements for sales positions increase, we find that the importance of cognitive skills also increases. For example, cognitive ability tests are useful in identifying whether a particular job candidate will have difficulty learning the material necessary to pass a certification or licensing exam, a frequent requirement for selling many financially oriented products and services.

Sales ability tests are generally designed to measure knowledge of selling techniques. These tests can be generic and off-the-shelf, or they can be developed for a specific type of job or a specific job within a given company. Like general cognitive abilities tests, most sales abilities tests have correct answers; therefore, test security is of prime importance. Vinchur et al. (1998) found strong validities for these tests in predicting both ratings (.45) and objective sales results (.37) criteria. Although validities are high, these tests may be less appropriate for entry-level sales positions where sales techniques are learned on the job and are not required at hiring. A number of general sales ability tests are available from test publishers, but experience suggests that the more customized the test is to the particular company and the particular sales position, the greater is its actual effectiveness. Customized sales ability tests may be feasible only for large companies with the resources to develop these sorts of assessments. Another concern with published sales ability tests is that the sales approach (relationship selling, consultative selling, or single-need selling) modeled by the test may be somewhat different from that desired by the employer. Those selecting an off-the-shelf sales ability test should be certain not only to review the test's psychometric properties and any available validation studies (see Chapter Two), but also to study the test's questions and scoring for consistency with the desired on-the-job sales behavior.

Personality Assessments

Perhaps more than for any other position, personality is thought to be a significant factor in the success of a salesperson. Many sales managers strongly believe in the predictability of personality assessments, and many personality test vendors are heavily targeting this market. Nevertheless, many personality tests have not been professionally developed, they are aggressively marketed, and they are often worthless, or even detrimental, to the effective selection of new salespeople. One particularly misleading approach is to offer to test a small number of the most successful salespeople and build a personality profile for the company. These sales tactics, as well as others listed in Exhibit 11.1, too often convince sales leaders, unsophisticated in selection testing,

Exhibit 11.1. Sales Assessment Warning Signs

Be skeptical about a sales assessment if the publisher or developer:

- Claims near-perfect results
- Touts years of sales and sales management experience rather than psychometric expertise
- Puts down traditional approaches to the assessment of sales talent
- Pushes you to prove it works on a few of your best salespeople
- Discourages conducting a validation study regardless of the number of salespeople in the company
- Bases the test's validity support primarily on testimonials
- Claims to have found the secret to identifying great salespeople
- Offers to build a company-specific profile based on a few of your top salespeople
- Claims to have the approval of the Equal Employment Opportunity Commission
- Does not share empirical studies conducted during the test's development
- Bases all or nearly all validity studies on differentiating among existing salespeople rather than predicting future successes
- Gives you, or more likely your sales executives, the hard sell
- Promises much improved productivity and improved retention

that a certain personality test predicts for their situation. Not only do a number of personality test vendors approach potential clients with these offers, many clients actually want this kind of specious evidence as "proof" that the test actually works.

Still, there is evidence that certain personality factors, particularly conscientiousness and, to a lesser extent, extraversion (Barrick & Mount, 1991) are related to sales success. Vinchur et al. (1998) found that Achievement, a subdimension of the Big Five factor Conscientiousness, and Potency, a subdimension of the Big Five factor Extraversion, predicted both sales performance ratings and objective sales results.

Perhaps the greatest challenge in using a personality test in sales selection is ensuring that a test that differentiates between current stronger or weaker salespeople can actually predict who will be successful in the future. All too often, personality test validation studies are based on current employees rather than on prospective candidates. Although this may be a good starting point for validating a personality test, as we shall see, results from such studies can be misleading.

Biodata: Background and Experience Measures

Biodata (biographical inventories or weighted application forms) have long been used in the selection of both entry-level and experienced salespeople. This form of assessment is based on the premise that past success is the best predictor of future success. Success can be defined broadly, as in being successful in a wide range of prior life experiences, or more narrowly, such as being successful at past experiences directly related to well-defined aspects of the position, such as prospecting, making sales, generating long-term clients, or effectively meeting customer needs.

Meta-analyses that have included biodata assessments for sales positions have found that biodata are typically strong predictors of both sales performance ratings and objective sales results (Vinchur et al., 1998). Similarly Ford, Walker, Churchill, and Hartley (1987) reported that personal history predictors were the most promising predictors of sales performance. Like sales ability measures, biodata measures generally perform better the more customized the questionnaire and scoring is to the target position as well as to the target applicant.

Issues in Using Assessments for Sales Selection

Finding the right assessments for sales selection is only part of the challenge. Ensuring that the assessments are implemented and used appropriately and knowing that they are meeting the needs of the company are also important goals that pose some challenges unique to sales selection. The sections that follow examine the challenges associated with the realities of selecting salespeople in widely dispersed locations with little or no human resource (HR) involvement, where the person doing the assessing and selecting is also incented to meet personnel growth goals, where testing is often unproctored, and where experienced candidates are viewed de facto as successful.

Dispersed Locations

The use of assessments in preemployment screening for sales positions presents unique challenges. In many companies, the sales organization is segregated from the rest of the organization, particularly when the product is marketed directly to consumers who are geographically dispersed. For example, many large organizations have sales offices located throughout the country or throughout the world. These offices are typically small and may consist of a sales manager, an administrative assistant or office manager, and several sales representatives. A single company may have hundreds of these offices reporting through a home office sales organization. It is not unusual for a corporate HR department to have little or no direct influence over practices and procedures used in these dispersed offices. Moreover, the salespeople are often independent contractors, not employees of the organization. In this case, the sales manager is typically responsible for recruiting, selecting, training, and supervising his or her sales personnel. The sales manager is often a recently promoted salesperson, has received only introductory training in management practices, and has received very little training in effective selection practices. Retail stores, especially smaller ones, often fit this pattern as well. The company may have a prescribed selection process, and testing may well be an important step in the process. However, the execution of the process takes on nearly as many forms as there are sales offices in the company.

The assessment is typically administered by computer in the local office. When completed, the assessment is scored online, although some scoring is still done with a template or scoring key in the local office or by sending a completed answer sheet to a scoring bureau. The results may be a pass-fail score, a single total score that needs some interpretation, multiple subscores, or a full interpretive report. Depending on the prescribed process, the results may dictate exactly what the manager is to do next in the selection process, or they may simply provide information to the manager. In the latter situations, sales managers may not be prepared to make effective use of testing in the selection of sales managers, and they often do not understand or appreciate the need for controlled test administration practices. They rarely see enough candidates or make enough hiring decisions to experience the value of testing firsthand. This creates a situation where the quality of implementation of an assessment is as important as, or even more important than, its ability to predict.

Roles at Odds

Compounding the challenge of many small, widely dispersed sales offices or outlets is that in certain industries, growth is a function of adding sales personnel in an office. To this end, the sales manager often has a personnel growth objective that must be met. For example, a manager may be compensated not only for office productivity but also for meeting salesperson recruiting goals and net manpower growth goals, and he or she may receive higher commission percentages on sales made by a new salesperson compared to those made by an established salesperson. This situation results in significant pressure to hire new sales staff, and it becomes a matter of quantity over quality all too often. Hiring managers become motivated to get candidates through the selection process and on board, not to potentially eliminate them through the results on tests or other assessments. Furthermore, recruiting is a difficult and time-consuming part of the sales or office manager's job. Any step in the selection process that potentially prevents hiring a candidate is viewed with suspicion, potentially ignored, and occasionally even manipulated.

Unproctored Testing

Another issue in assessing candidates for sales positions is the appeal of unproctored Internet testing, especially when recruiting and hiring are dispersed over a broad geographical area. When salespeople are being recruited to cover an area located some hours from even the closest sales office, the use of proctored screening assessments is often not cost-effective. Whether it is the HR department, the sales organization, or the local sales manager, today there is intense pressure for "better, faster, and cheaper." Screening candidates through the Internet is nearly always faster and cheaper. Appropriate unproctored Internet testing can be "better" too. The question becomes, "How can we make assessment effective using the Internet?" not, "Can we do effective assessment using the Internet?" If unproctored testing is necessary, then assessments with no correct answers, that are not timed, that do not require high-speed connections or special software, where information or results can be verified later, and where a less-than-ideal testing environment is acceptable are likely to be more effective. Biodata and personality measures can fit these criteria; cognitive and sales ability tests typically do not.

The Experienced Candidate

Where turnover is high, the sales recruiter invariably talks with many candidates who have sales experience. The candidate's experience may be similar to or different from that being recruited for, but to the harried recruiter, sales experience is all too often the equivalent of a green light for hiring. The important difference between sales experience and sales success is lost, especially when the pressure to fill positions is significant and the perceived cost of a poor hiring decision is small. In designing and implementing assessments and selection processes for sales personnel, we must be careful to consider the potential for differing procedures for experienced and inexperienced candidates.

Special Validation Issues in Sales Selection

Validating assessments used for selection is always a challenging task. Validating assessments for sales positions is no less challenging, but the process can be a bit different. One key difference is the potential for the use of objective sales results as criteria in the validation process. Here, the goal is to show that scores on the assessment are systematically related to an objective sales measure important to the organization. I discuss the advantages and disadvantages that objective sales criteria can bring, as well as the special challenges of using performance ratings with sales personnel. It is very important to communicate the effectiveness of a test or assessment in words and metrics that mean something to the end users, as well as to the corporate decision makers. This section ends with a discussion of special issues in validating both personality and biodata assessments for salesperson selection and the role of consortium studies.

Defining Success as a Salesperson

Key to any validation study is finding a way to measure success among employees—in our case, salespeople. What are the important aspects of performance for the sales position we are interested in, and how can we best measure them? Are we interested in the quantity sold, the quality of the sales, or both? Do we care about how something is sold, or only that it is sold? Do we want to predict how many sales are made, how much revenue is generated, or how satisfied the customer is? Do we want to predict short-term or long-term performance? Do we want people who are satisfied with their performance? Do we want to reward team performance or individual performance? Do we want to foster good corporate citizenship or just foster strong sales performance? Do we want to predict tenure or job survival or job productivity? Do we need people who can readily and effectively adapt to changing environments, products, and regulations? The list can go on and on.

Chances are that we will not be able to focus our work on all of these, but we do need to have a good discussion with the sales leaders to understand their priorities. In most sales jobs, the top priority will be some measure of sales. Everything else becomes secondary. Nevertheless, there are still judgment calls to make.

If we think of overall performance as comprising task-oriented, contextual, and adaptive performance, we can begin to see the challenge. To some sales leaders, the primary concerns are sales made and job survival over a certain period of time. These outcomes could be considered measures of task performance, or they may result from a combination of all three performance domains. We could argue that sales results are little more than the result of effective task performance. Or we might effectively argue that certain objective performance measures are the result of far more than simple task performance. MacKenzie, Podsakoff, and Fetter (1991) showed that managerial ratings of overall performance are roughly equally determined by contextual performance, primarily organizational citizenship ratings, and by measures of sales, commission, and quotas met. To these sales managers, overall performance is more than just sales production. In my experience, the primary objective sales measure varies from company to company and often is deeply embedded in the corporate culture.

Of course, not all assessments are developed to measure overall performance, and there are certainly cases where predicting only sales results is appropriate. But we and other company decision makers need to be aware that by concentrating on objective sales results, we may be overlooking other aspects of performance that, if addressed, could also yield overall productivity improvements. In addition, there is a certain degree of chance in making sales; therefore, quantitative measures are not a perfect reflection of individual task performance.

Risks and Rewards of Objective, Quantitative Sales Results Criteria

Perhaps more than any other occupation, salespeople are measured on results: number of sales, total revenue generated, commissions earned, prospects generated, number of prospects called or seen, close ratios, number of referrals obtained, net gain in revenue, and combinations of these measures. Some sales jobs require a number of sales per day. For others, a sale a week is more the norm, and for still others, one or two sales a year meet the sales goal. In organizations where turnover is high, number of months of tenure or simply remaining on the job for a certain period of time is a significant measure of success.

There are some real advantages to the use of quantitative results in the validation of selection procedures. For one, they have inherent, important meaning to the senior management of the company. Second, it is very persuasive to provide the sales leadership with validity information, not in correlation coefficient terms, but in terms of impact on revenues per employee or the increased percentage of newly hired employees who will survive. Finally, because individual sales results are routinely collected, periodic validation studies can be relatively easy and inexpensive to conduct, allowing a company to assess the effectiveness of its selection processes on an ongoing basis.

Understanding the Numbers

Not all sales measures are what they seem to be. The unsuspecting researcher or HR consultant may be seduced into validating a test against a sales criterion that depends less on the salesperson's actual performance and more on environmental or other factors beyond the control of the salesperson. Generally four types of objective sales criteria are commonly available and used in validation studies: sales revenues, number of sales, commissions, and tenure or survival. Each class of objective criteria comes with its own set of strengths and drawbacks; no one type of measure is inherently better than the others. Most quantitative sales measures are more than they appear to be on the surface. It is incumbent on the test specialist, the HR consultant, and the sales leaders to understand the sales effectiveness measures being used as criteria in assessing test validity. By way of example, Exhibit 11.2 depicts some of the questions to ask when using commissions as the sales criteria. Similar questions are necessary for the other forms of objective sales criteria.

In validating a selection assessment tool, the goal is to show that scores on the tool are related to employee performance on the job. To this end, any quantitative sales criteria used should be the result of the individual's sales performance and not be driven by circumstances that are not within his or her control.

Exhibit 11.2. Potential Issues When Using Objective Sales Criteria

- Do the commissions cover all major products used to define salesperson success?
- Is there a base level of compensation? A base salary? If so, what is the target level of total compensation that the base salary represents?
- How representative are the sales commissions of actual sales performance?
- What are the key factors that determine compensation? Examples might include actual sales, mix of products sold, returns, customer satisfaction, sales of targeted products or special promotions, job tenure, and job level.
- What is the effect of experience on sales commission rates?
- What is the typical growth curve for commission growth by experience?
- Is ongoing client service required, and, if so, how is it compensated?
- Do new salespeople get any special salaries or accelerated commissions? If so, how are they represented in the criteria?
- Do experienced salespeople get the best markets or territories? Do they get their choice of markets or territories?
- What is the turnover rate among new salespeople, and to what extent do the terminations lead to a restricted sample for our study?
- Has there been any change in the commission plan over the time period that commission earnings are available?
- Has there been an appreciable change in products, product mix, or product competitiveness? If so, have all salespeople been equally subjected to the changes?
- What impact might local factors, such as cost of living and union contract, play in the compensation?

For example, a salesperson opening up a new territory in an area where company products are not well known is likely to sell less than an equally talented and qualified salesperson in a well-established territory. For validation purposes, any sales criterion should roughly equate their two levels of performance.

Similarly, many sales compensation plans award bonuses for reaching certain increasing sales targets. If a criterion includes bonuses, we may exaggerate the differences between average and strong performers (depending on when bonuses are awarded) and contaminate the results of the study. Although there are times where this may be appropriate, more often it is not.

As a final example consider the past year's gross sales as a criterion. Potential contaminants include the effect of experience on results, the possibility that not all salespeople were employed by the company for all twelve months, territory or store differences, product availability, local economic factors, and the effects of local sales contests. We probably cannot adjust or correct for all of these factors, but we may be able to address the factors that contribute most to contaminating individual performance differences among salespeople.

Controlling for contaminating factors can take several forms. First, by understanding the factors that are contributing to a particular sales measure, both those that are under the control of the salesperson and those that are not, we might discover that more appropriate measures can be made available. For example, we might find that an average monthly sales measure exists to replace a total sales results criterion, thereby minimizing (at least to some extent) the effect of individuals not being employed for the full year. Second, we might consider standardizing, or otherwise adjusting, the criterion within a territory to eliminate the unwanted effects of territory. Still, there are times when territory differences are not arbitrary and are primarily the result of true sales performance differences. In these cases, an adjustment that equalizes the average performance across territories would not be desirable. Only by fully understanding the available sales measures and the overall situation can we truly understand what a test is actually predicting.

Predicting Focal Product Sales or All Product Sales

On occasion, a company wants salespeople who are good at selling one specific product within a line of products that they will be expected to sell. In this situation, how do we define a strong salesperson? Do we simply look at this one focal product line and validate against it? If we do, we may find that the lowest producers in this product line are just as likely to be overall strong producers as not. We would find there are excellent salespeople who sell a lot of this product and other excellent salespeople who sell very little of it. An alternative approach might be to define the validation sample as including only those who focus on this line of business. We might define an individual as focused on this line wherever the product line represents at least 50 percent, or some other appropriate percentage, of his or her total sales. This might be appropriate if we are seeking people to generate strong sales by concentrating on this particular line of business.

Again, neither approach is right or wrong, so long as it aligns with the company's goals. In either case, traditional assessments of sales potential may be of little use if we are trying to differentiate not only strong sales potential from weak but also between two approaches to sales success (differing product lines). Other factors may play into success within the product line; some of these may be individual difference factors such as past experience or some preexisting relationship with the market, or the differences could be primarily situational, a function of training or prospecting techniques used. If we try to understand all that we can about selling the focal product line compared to the others, we may be led to consider additional or different KSAOs as targets for the assessment process.

There is no best approach to dealing with objective sales criteria. The goal of this discussion is to stress the need to thoroughly understand the available data in order to design the data collection, preparation, and analysis to address the many potential issues. Undoubtedly there will be a need to rely on professional judgment to determine if the study will lead to results that will make the project worth conducting.

Sales Results and Meeting the Assumptions of Statistics

In many cases, the best salespeople far outperform the average as well as the mediocre salesperson. The 80–20 rule is alive and well when considering sales productivity, and this creates challenges in using objective performance measures as criteria. Often a distribution is highly skewed to the right; the mean is often roughly equal to the standard deviation, and there are invariably a few outliers with extremely high production who make the nonnormality even more extreme. Given that statistics typically used to summarize relationships between predictors and criteria make assumptions of normal bell-shaped distributions and the equality of variance, we must be careful in how we evaluate and report validation results. For example, the correlation coefficient can be an inaccurate estimate of the actual relationship between an assessment score and sales production. Modern, robust statistical techniques are now readily available that help alleviate the problems inherent in traditional methods when assumptions do not hold (Erceg-Hurn & Mirosevich, 2008).

Performance Ratings of Sales Success

At this point, we might be tempted to forgo using quantitative productivity results and decide that a better choice is to collect performance ratings specific to this project. Some evidence shows that managerial ratings of sales performance are easier to predict than are objective measures. Barrick, Mount, and Strauss (1993) looked at two personality factors (conscientiousness and extraversion), cognitive ability, and the prediction of both sales volume and supervisory ratings of job performance. They found that conscientiousness and cognitive ability directly predicted performance ratings; only cognitive ability directly predicted sales volume. Vinchur et al.'s (1998) meta-analysis of predictors of sales performance showed that across all predictors, relationships with ratings criteria were somewhat higher than those with sales criteria. Only extraversion, conscientiousness, and achievement had higher corrected correlations with objective sales criteria.

Although the use of performance ratings may overcome some of the challenges with objective sales criteria and tend to be more easily predicted than actual sales results, we could be going from the frying pan into the fire without appropriate caution. First, many salespeople work one-on-one with their prospects and clients, often outside the company office. Given that many sales managers rarely, if ever, actually observe the salesperson interacting with the prospect, any rating of the quality of task performance is likely to be based on what the sales manager actually observes, such as sales results and customer comments or complaints. Ratings of how the salesperson interacts with the customer or of behavior in the actual sales process are not likely to be based on actual observation. In this case, we simply get a rating of task performance that is highly correlated with sales results.

In addition, if most sales managers rate only a few individual salespeople, we need to be able to account for rater differences, just as we need to account for store or territory differences in quantitative studies. Rarely are multiple raters available, so reliability estimates are a challenge. Experience suggests that significant differences occur in the mean ratings across raters and often across companies. Local (store or manager) adjustments may still be needed.

If, rather than task performance, we are interested in contextual or adaptive performance, the issue of lack of managerial observation or familiarity generally goes away. Sales managers are able to assess dimensions such as following organizational rules, volunteering to carry out activities beyond the scope of the formal job, handling stress, and demonstrating interpersonal adaptability.

Communicating Value to the Sales Leaders

As selection professionals, our challenge is not only to develop sales assessments that work, but also to show the end user, often the sales manager, that use of these assessments is beneficial to them and their company. Effectively communicating validity is paramount. Several approaches to this include showing the benefit in metrics other than traditional statistics, using data combination approaches that allow end-user input, and using stories that emphasize others' experiences with the test (Kuncel, 2008). In addition, gaining reluctant end-user buy-in usually means paying attention to face validity and logistics such as simplicity and ease of use and to easily understood score reports. A test with great validity is of little value if the sales manager or other end user does not believe in it and refuses to use it.

For this reason, whenever possible, communicate the validity of a selection procedure through the use of expectancy tables, using metrics that incorporate costs saved, revenues generated, and the return on investment. Not only does this approach avoid the correlation coefficient, but it communicates the assessment's impact using numbers with which the sales leaders are comfortable.

In some recent work for LIMRA Services, a financial services industry research association with member companies located throughout the world, I completed an analysis for a relatively new user of a biodata assessment, the Career Profile+ (CP+), for selecting sales representatives. In a recent validation study, commissions were collected for the sales advisors for their first twelve months after hiring or until they terminated if they left the company in less than a year. The company also provided the salesperson's assessment score, hiring date, and termination date if he or she was no longer with the company. A strict cutoff score is not used, but the company encourages geographically dispersed hiring sales managers to pay attention to test scores in their hiring decisions. Descriptive statistics for the sample show that the mean test score for those hired is higher than for the tested population and that the standard deviation is restricted. Commissions for survivors are substantially higher than for terminators. For earned commissions, the standard deviation is roughly equal to the mean.

The correlation between twelve-month survival and the test score is .17 when corrected for dichotomization and range restriction. For sales commissions, the correlation, corrected for range restriction, is .25. Sample sizes are large, and both correlations are statistically significant. Still, the correlations are not high; in fact, some might argue that this test is of little benefit to the user and probably should be dropped. More important, most sales leaders would not know how to interpret these results. Through many years of working with sales leaders in the financial services industry, I have found that the approach that I outline next effectively communicates a test's real value to sales leaders.

First, an expectancy table is created using actual experience to date and based on the regression equations for the correlations noted. In this case, we found that for each increase in test score, the company can expect a 1.0 to 1.3 percent increase in the odds of surviving for one year and a twelve hundred dollar increase in commissions earned over the first year. It is clear that hiring candidates with higher CP+ scores is in the company's best interests.

Table 11.2 takes this approach a step further by grouping the scores into score ranges, or classes, and relating the predicted results to the historical actual results for the company. Scores are grouped for two reasons: to reduce the impact of variation due to small sample sizes for individual scores and to facilitate a discussion of the impact of test use. Table 11.2 shows that the percentage of applicants hired from Classes A1 and A2 (high CP+ scores) is greater than the percentage of applicants from these two classes (49.5 versus 27.7 percent): the sales managers are paying at least some attention to test scores when making hiring decisions. The table also shows that nearly 10 percent of hired applicants are coming from the lowest class (Class C) of test scores and their results, while slightly better than predicted, are below average.

Next we turn to the impact of making changes in how the test is implemented. As seen in Table 11.3, to estimate the impact of CP+ use, we adjust the percentages hired by each score class (reflecting increasing selectivity) and use the expected survival and commission numbers to calculate a return on the investment in testing. The calculations can be based on actual results or predicted results generated through the regression equation that summarizes the relationship between the CP+ and survival or commissions. Table 11.3 shows the results for several scenarios using the regression-based expectancies and assumes five hundred new salespersons hired each year and a fixed test price of $120,000 per year.

The first row in this table shows the impact of discontinuing use of the CP+, and the second row shows the results as the CP+ is currently used. If the company chooses to drop the test, first-year survival rate would be expected to decrease from 67.6 to 64.8 percent, a 4.0 percent drop. Total commissions for the five hundred new salespersons over the first year would be down over $1.5 million to $12,628,000. The $120,000 test cost yields fourteen more surviving salespeople and nearly $3,000 greater commissions per person. Rows 3, 4, and 5 show what the company might expect if it increased the average CP+ score of its

Table 11.2. CP+ Validity Grouped into Score Classes

Rating Class	CP+ Range of Ratings	Percentage of Tested	Percentage of Hired Applicants	Expected Twelve-Month Survival Rate	Actual Twelve-Month Survival Rate	Expected Average Commissions per Hire	Actual Average Commissions per Hire
A1	17–19	11.3%	25.4%	73%	77%	$34,000	$37,700
A2	14–16	16.4	24.1	70	68	30,500	27,000
B1	11–13	21.0	22.6	67	62	27,000	24,800
B2	7–10	28.3	19.1	63	61	23,100	22,400
C	1–6	23.1	8.8	57	66	18,200	24,800

Table 11.3. Estimates for CP+ Use at Various Cutoff Assumptions Using Regression-Based Expectancies

Summary for 500 New Employees	First-Year Survival Rate	Total First-Year Commissions	Average Commissions per Hire	CP Cost	Return in Increased Commission in Year 1	Survival Rate Improvement
Without CP+	64.8%	$12,628,000	$25,260	—		
Current use of CP	67.6	$14,051,000	28,100	$120,000	1,088%	4.2%
Assume no C Class agents hired	68.5	$14,423,000	28,800	120,000	1,396	5.2
Assume no C or B2 Class agents hired	70.0	$15,233,000	30,500	120,000	2,071	7.4
Assume mostly A Class agents hired, with a small percentage of B Class agents	71.1	$15,862,000	31,700	120,000	2,596	8.8

new salespeople by implementing increasingly selective cutoff scores. As expected, the return increases as the hiring standards become tougher. Communicating validity in this way conveys the test's value in terms that have meaning to sales leaders and allows them to visualize the bottom-line impact of test use scenarios.

Challenges of Using Personality Testing in Hiring for Sales Positions

Personality tests are popular in sales selection processes. According to the lore, the sales personality is outgoing, aggressive, and persuasive. This stereotype is especially strong for salespeople who earn commissions. It is common in movies, television, and books; almost anywhere we see salespeople, we see them with a variant of this personality. It is a short jump, then, to suggest that personality testing be an important component of any process for assessing sales candidates. Personality testing fell out of favor with personnel psychologists several decades ago, but recent renewed interest in it has been reinforced by some promising validity evidence. As a result, personality testing is in the mainstream today more than ever before.

A second reason for the popularity of personality testing for sales selection is that its use is less likely to lead to adverse impact. Recent research suggests that although adverse impact does exist for some personality factors and some racial groups, most effects are small or negligible (Foldes, Duehr, & Ones, 2008). Finally, evidence is building that even if personality factors may not be consistently strong predictors of task performance, they are effective predictors of contextual performance (Borman & Motowidlo, 1997).

What the Personality Test Really Measures

To assess the potential effectiveness of a personality assessment, we need to look first at the research conducted during the development of the test and other validation studies to understand if the test is psychometrically sound and what it actually measures. Personality tests in particular result in more than one score, corresponding to each of the personality characteristics being measured. In assessing the test, we need to know that each of these personality measurements is reasonably distinct from the others and that each score is reliable.

Second, we need to understand what the test actually measures. Anyone can write a few items and claim that by adding the responses together, they have a measure of assertiveness or of some other personality characteristic. As a potential user of a test, we need to ask how we know that the test actually measures assertiveness. The developer should be able to provide additional information about people with high assertiveness scores. For example, do people with high scores on this assertiveness scale also tend to get high scores on other tests of assertiveness? If we know that assertiveness and conscientiousness are unrelated in the population, are the assertiveness scores from this test also unrelated to conscientiousness scores from this or other tests? Reputable test developers will have these and other test development research results readily available in either the test manual or in technical reports outlining the efforts taken in developing the test.

For some reason, people with no formal psychometric background and no understanding of appropriate strategies for test development, validation, or use seem to think that they can develop a good sales personality test. It is not unusual for these tests to have been developed by successful salespeople or sales managers who believe they know how to measure sales potential. They try it out on successful salespeople they know, and more often than not, these people get high scores. As successful salespeople, they are effective at selling their tests: they approach top sales executives in a company and convince them, and perhaps a few of their top salespeople, to take the test. Again, high scores are seen. A simple Internet search for sales personality tests finds a number of such offers:

■ ■ ■

• Vendor A: "One of the most powerful tools is to test a sampling of your currently successful salespeople. We analyze their test results for any common success factors and, along with the other pieces of information, establish your target profiles."

• Vendor B: "What makes these sales assessment tests so effective is the customized benchmark we develop for your company's sales positions. Here's how it works. First, we assess several top-performing salespeople. Sophisticated software assigns a score of between 1 and 10 to each talent that is measured by the sales assessment tests. The sales assessment test scores are merged together for the top performers. This produces a desirable score range (usually three to four numbers wide) for each talent. Finally, the combination of desirable score ranges for all of the talents measured by the sales assessment tests makes up the benchmark. Once a benchmark has been developed, other individuals can be assessed and their scores compared against the benchmark. If an individual's scores are a close match to the benchmark, their talents are similar to those of the top sales performers whose scores were used to create the benchmark. If these talents are developed through training and experience, these individuals are much more likely to become top sales performers than people whose sales assessment test scores are not a close match to the benchmark."

• Vendor C: "With our benchmarking process, you have the ability to assess the exact requirements of your sales position and your unique company culture first. Then you can measure your candidates against the same criteria."

• Vendor D: "We invite you to take the challenge. For qualified situations, we will allow you to sample our powerful system with six team members—three high performers and three low performers. We will tell you which ones are which."

■ ■ ■

Presented with this sort of so-called profile analysis, sales leaders frequently become convinced that the test is predictive and use their influence to implement the test. The problem, though, is that the test has not been validated. We do not know that average or poor salespeople perform any differently from the top performers on the assessment. While it tells us a little about top performers, it reveals nothing about predicting success. In cases where an attempt to differentiate between top and poor or average performers is made, too often the samples are so small as to yield meaningless results. A sample of six tells us nothing. Assuming an estimated population correlation of .25 (typical for a personality test), the percentage chance of obtaining statistically significant correlations for a sample of 25, 50, 100, and 150 is 22 percent, 42 percent, 71 percent, and 87 percent, respectively. Small samples are simply not effective for assessing a test's validity for selecting salespeople or any other employees.

Even when we have an adequate sample size and the results confirm our hypotheses, a concurrent study of a personality test tells us only that the test can differentiate among successful and unsuccessful salespeople who are already working for the company. It does not tell us that it can predict, from among job candidates, who will be more successful and who will be less successful. Why? First, candidates and current employees differ in their motivations when taking a test. Candidates who are trying to get a position are motivated to describe themselves in the best light possible. Candidates for sales positions tend to generate more extreme personality factor scores than do incumbents. Couple the motivation to exaggerate with a job that has a distinct, well-known personality stereotype, and the differentiating ability of the test can easily be diminished or eliminated in a predictive situation. Many personality tests do attempt to deal with this with various types of lie detection scales, often a social desirability scale. While meta-analytic research suggests that controlling for social desirability in personality test scores leaves the operational validities for many occupations intact (Ones & Viswesvaran, 1998), my experience with sales selection suggests that controlling for faking is often ineffective.

A second reason that a concurrently validated personality test may not predict success is self-learning. For example, consider the question, "I know how to convince others." An individual with no experience cold-calling households may answer "strongly agree," but after a few months of rejection in making cold calls, the same individual may answer in the midrange of the scale. Self-knowledge grows from job experience, and the responses to personality test items are better reflections of the personality relative to the work requirements of the incumbent's job. As a result, improved differentiation is likely in a concurrent evaluation, but we may also see an overestimate of the test's effectiveness in actually selecting new salespeople. Similar to the experience of others who have implemented personality testing based on validation designs using current employees, concurrent validation (White & Moss, 1995), we typically find that concurrent validities are substantially higher than are those actually seen when the test is used predictively.

Biodata: Background and Experience Questionnaires

Another effective type of assessment for the selection of salespeople is the use of background and experience measures, or biodata. Biodata have a long history of successful use predicting sales among insurance salespeople. The first documented use was in the 1920s by the Phoenix Mutual Life Insurance Company and grew out of the recognition by the manager of the sales research division that biographical data collected at the time of employment as life insurance agents from 1919 to 1921 were related to future success and survival ("History of the AIB," 1980). This work was brought to the Life Insurance Sales Research Bureau, now LIMRA Services.

In the 1930s, the leaders of the association contracted with two leading psychologists to take the basic process used by the company and apply it across a number of companies—perhaps the first selection test consortium project. The questionnaire included a number of biodata items, including questions about number of dependents, current occupation, employment status, time with most recent employer, membership and offices held in organizations, net worth, minimum living expenses, amount of life insurance owned, and length of interest in selling life insurance. The validation process was a classic predictive design whereby insurance agents were tested at the time of hire, but no scores were generated or provided to the hiring managers. Twelve months later, the companies provided productivity information (survival for twelve months and commissions earned) on each tested agent. The individual responses to each of the biodata items were compared to the first-year sales results of the agents who endorsed the response.

Using scoring for key development procedures similar to those used by insurance industry actuaries to predict risk of loss, scores were developed specifically to predict sales production. Scoring keys were developed on a validation sample of agents and cross-validated on a smaller holdout sample. The resulting key not only predicted agent success in the mid-1930s, but was still able to predict agent success in the early 1970s (Brown, 1978). In reviewing the items, it is immediately clear that these are the kinds of items that appear on many employment application forms. Of course, times have changed and several items no longer can be asked, but the basic approach works well today and is still employed in the selection of financial services sales representatives around the world. The process works because it is both logical and empirical in nature. Very large sample sizes are used, and care is taken to ensure that any item response–productivity relationships are stable and explainable.

The approach is not without controversy. Early use of biodata was often undertaken from a "dust bowl" empiricism philosophy. The goal was to find and implement test items that predict employee success, not necessarily to understand why. As the approach has evolved, it has become less driven purely by prediction and more by understanding. New test questions are written and selected as potential indicators of a candidate possessing a KSAO that a job analysis has suggested is important for strong job performance. If a relationship is discovered that does not support the hypotheses about how an item should predict, the item is not immediately put into a scoring key. Rather, the item is tracked over time to see if the relationship holds in other samples. The hypotheses are reviewed and, if appropriate, revised, and additional items are explored to test the revised hypothesis through additional background or experience perspectives.

Another common challenge in using biodata is that there may be no obvious face validity. Since sales assessment users are often geographically dispersed sales managers with little or no training in testing, judging a candidate's success potential based on a number of biographical questions makes little intuitive sense. However, when these decision makers understand what the test predicts for their situation, how it predicts, and, just as important, what it does not predict, their acceptance of the process increases. Face validity can also be addressed by adding questions to the test that may not be predictive but might, to the lay observer, be related to sales success. These questions are not scored, but they can improve the acceptability of the test to sales managers.

Face validity is rarely a concern when biodata tests are developed for selecting the best from among candidates who have held similar positions previously. In many industries, often for very good reasons, salespeople change positions frequently. Using a series of questions directly related to experiences in previous sales positions, empirical biodata questionnaires can be developed explicitly for this situation. Unlike those for the new salesperson, these questionnaires for experienced candidates can be extremely face valid and are readily accepted by the sales manager. Although sales managers have access to most of the information collected in a biodata questionnaire for experienced salespeople, they often do not critically assess it. More often, they equate "experience" with "successful experience," which often is not the case. Many experienced salespeople are seeking employment because they have not been particularly successful in their past positions. Biodata questions help identify which experienced candidates have had successful experience and which have just had experience.

Consortium Studies

Only the largest companies hire a thousand or more salespeople over, say, a few years. On their own, most companies are not able to use the empirically validated biodata approach unless they are able participate in industry or cross-industry consortium test development and validation studies. A consortium study is an effective means for developing and validating selection assessments. It accumulates data from a number of companies and can effectively reduce the costs for the individual company. Smaller companies are able to gain access to assessments validated for their particular position, and larger companies are able to save substantially on the cost of custom test development. Still, consortium studies have some pitfalls. To take advantage of having multiple companies in a study requires measuring salesperson productivity on a common scale. This can be challenging because companies define sales success in many different ways and often collect only the data needed to measure their specific definition of success. To this end, the criteria, especially quantitative sales criteria, need to be combined in a way that accounts for both intracompany and intercompany differences.

Once a test is developed and we want to look at the validity of the test in use, the company differences present themselves in different ways. Assuming we can deal with nonnormality and heteroskedasticity issues, we may be able to evaluate the validity of the assessment across companies through meta-analytic techniques. Validity generalization methods allow us to correct for artifacts such as range restriction, unreliability, and sampling error, but company differences can still play a role. A study of eleven companies using a biodata assessment for new salespeople found that company differences in average productivity, recruiting sources, and quality of new employees moderated the validity of the test. In each group of companies, the biodata test was valid, but in companies with more effective management practices, the use of the test resulted in a net gain in productivity that was 50 percent higher than experienced in the other company group (Brown, 1981). These company differences are at play not only in assessing the in-use validity of a test, but also in the earlier steps of test development and initial validation.

Summary of Assessments for Sales Positions: The Selection Process

Thus far, we have been looking at potential steps in a selection process, one at a time. Table 11.4 reviews a number of assessment approaches and notes strengths, weaknesses, and other characteristics associated with each type. To be effective, however, a selection process will put together a number of assessment steps, in a logical order, leading to the development of assessment results

Table 11.4. Pros and Cons of Assessment Tools for Sales Selection

Assessment Method	Effective Measurement Uses	Strengths	Weaknesses	Useful for Small or Midsized Sales Force?
• Cognitive ability test	• Valid predictor of training success and licensing	• Easy to score and to administer • Very predictive • Short testing time	• Needs proctoring • Needs strong test security • Higher adverse impact against minority groups	• Effective off-the-shelf, general-purpose, and licensing prediction tests are available.
• Sales ability test	• Sales performance and knowledge of selling and marketing	• Easy to score and administer • Evidence of generally good validity • Short testing time • Strong face validity	• Needs proctoring • Needs strong test security • Selling model tested may not fit desired selling model	• Off-the-shelf tests are available, but customized test are likely to be better predictors.
• Biodata questionnaire	• Predicts objective sales outcomes, as well as retention of salespeople	• Low to moderate adverse impact • Nonproctored testing is feasible • Good validity	• Limited face validity • Large numbers needed to create and validate empirical scoring keys	• Simple weighted application, blank questionnaires, or rationally developed scoring keys may be feasible for midsized sales forces. • Expect some loss in predictive power.

354

Method	Description	Advantages	Disadvantages	Comments
• Structured interview	• A strong measure of communication skills and interpersonal skills	• Easy to administer and score • With multiple interviewers, can get multiple perspectives • Low adverse impact • Moderate evidence of validity • Inexpensive to develop	• Interviewers may be uncomfortable with structure and often stray toward nonvalid unstructured format • Requires strong interviewer training and follow-up	• Good method for customized assessment for small-to-medium sales forces.
• Unstructured interview	• Interviewer "liking" of applicant	• Inexpensive • Face valid	• Not valid	• Should not be used as part of selection process regardless of company size.
• Assessment center, job simulation	• Most useful for complex or high-level sales positions • A several-hour process simulating one or more aspects of job	• Strong validity • Face validity	• Expensive to build and operate • Need to keep assessors well trained • Requires significant applicant and assessor time	• Assessment centers or simulations built and operated by I-O consulting firms may fit the needs of small organizations with complex sales positions. • Interactive, online versions may reduce costs.

(*Continued*)

Table 11.4. Pros and Cons of Assessment Tools for Sales Selection *(Continued)*

Assessment Method	Effective Measurement Uses	Strengths	Weaknesses	Useful for Small or Midsized Sales Force?
• Personality testing	• A well-developed personality test can provide good measures of con-scientiousness and extraversion, both valid predic-tors of sales per-formance ratings	• Low adverse impact • Some traits shown to predict performance	• Significant potential for faking • Testing time can be significant • Many traits are typically measured, but few are predictive • Limited face validity • Many poorly developed sales personality tests are marketed	• If chosen and implemented with professional guidance, a good off-the-shelf person-ality test can be effective in sales selection for smaller sales organizations.
• Realistic job preview	• Assesses an applicant's understanding of the sales position applied for • Particularly use-ful for positions that are not well understood by the public • A good approach to reducing early turnover	• Highly face valid • Generally inexpen-sive to develop	• Can require significant applicant and organiza-tion time • Not appropriate for all sales positions	• Can be effective in any sales organization.

356

covering each applicant's standing on the position's most important KSAOs.

A process tends to be most efficient when the least expensive assessments are used as early as possible. Efficiency is also increased when clearly unqualified candidates are eliminated as soon as possible. For this reason, we might use basic unproctored, online screening questionnaires, automated application forms, or work availability questionnaires as early steps in the process. For sales positions, a short, structured initial interview can be an effective early step. More in-depth testing typically occurs after the initial screening has reduced the applicant pool significantly. Generally there will be a trade-off between the amount of information generated about candidates and the testing and interviewing time and money available.

One approach to mitigating this dilemma, at least to some extent, is to use a test that has been validated against an important quantitative sales metric. The premise is that the quantitative results already take into account the key KSAOs, so if an assessment predicts sales results, the need to predict an applicant's standing on each KSAO is lessened.

Finally, much early turnover in sales positions is the result of inadequate understanding of the position's demands by new salespeople at the time of hire. Some form of realistic job preview can effectively reduce this type of voluntary turnover.

A sample selection process is depicted in Table 11.5. To be sure, locally developed or validated assessments are expensive and usually require large numbers of employees in the focal positions. However, companies with small or medium-size sales forces can still take advantage of improved selection through the use of customized structured interviews and realistic job preview activities. Occasionally other methods of validating an assessment, such as content validation (see Chapter Twenty-One), are also appropriate. Testing may also be within reach through the use of industry-validated assessments or through off-the-shelf tests. I-O psychologists at a local university or specialists identified through the Society for Industrial and Organizational Psychology Web site can be a valuable resource in helping identify and build a rationale for the use of testing for improving sales force productivity.

Table 11.5. An Effective Selection Process for Sales Personnel

Proposed Step	Why?	Examples
1. Short screening assessment (online if feasible)	• To reduce a large applicant pool to a more manageable number • To eliminate applicants with little chance of meeting minimum standards for the position	• Short background and experience questionnaire • Cognitive ability test validated to obtaining needed licenses (proctored) • Availability for work questionnaire to ensure legal status, availability for hours required, and bona fide occupational qualification (BOQ) eligibility
2. Short initial interview	• To assess very basic communication skills and abilities • To provide candidate with a basic understanding of position requirements (for self-deselection)	• Fifteen- to twenty-minute structured interview guide • Standard description of the position, prerequisites, and performance expectations • After-interview rating of status on measured communication skills and abilities
3. Second validated assessment	• To generate an objective sales success prediction • To measure standing on key important KSAOs	• Biodata, especially to predict quantitative sales results and tenure • Sales ability to assess understanding of sales and marketing concepts • Personality test to assess conscientiousness and extroversion

4. In-depth structured interview	• To assess key KSAOs required for sales success, especially KSAOs that are not measured through testing • To allow multiple interviewers to observe and assess the applicant	• A sixty- to ninety-minute highly structured interview organized around KSAOs • Behavioral interview formats have proven successful at generating examples of past behaviors related to the KSAO being assessed • Breaking the interview into two shorter sessions can alleviate fatigue issues and facilitate the use of multiple interviewers

5. Realistic job preview	• To allow the applicant to better understand the position
	• Especially useful for positions not well understood (or often misunderstood) by the general public
	• To effectively reduce early voluntary turnover
		• Activities might include:
		  • A detailed brochure explaining a day in the life of a salesperson with the company
		  • A Q&A session with current salespeople
		  • Spending a few hours with a current (often a recently hired) salesperson
		  • Participating in a sales training session
		  • Actually performing some aspects of the position

Implementation Issues

In cases where sales personnel are housed and supervised at major company offices or plants and HR professionals recruit and screen new sales personnel, selection test implementation issues are the same as those for any other position. However, this is often not the case in sales selection. Here, we consider the unique challenges of implementing a selection or assessment process in geographically dispersed environments. Key among these challenges are training test administrators and test users and ensuring test security.

Training Dispersed Administrators

Effective testing programs rely on a reasonable degree of consistency in the use of the test. Whether testing occurs in a home office, a regional office, a local sales office, a specialized testing facility, or some other location, test administration should follow prescribed procedures that standardize key elements of the testing experience for the candidate. When testing takes place in a sales office, the sales manager or the office administrator or manager is responsible for following the protocol. Neither is a specialist in testing or test administration, and both have far more pressing tasks to do than to proctor a testing session. A key need for all testing programs is to train test administrators and test users in how to appropriately administer the tests and interpret the results.

Technology has provided some help in this area with the advent of Internet-based teleconferencing capabilities as well as Internet-based training platforms. An ongoing challenge for keeping test administrators trained is the frequent turnover of sales managers and office administrators. With each change in personnel comes a need for training in virtually all of the office's standardized procedures, including testing. Just-in-time online learning platforms can be a cost-effective and timely means of training or retraining test administrators. While most companies offer some form of training in appropriate testing procedures, candidates still experience a wide variety of test-taking situations. For example, testing in the office waiting room, at a job fair, or in a coffee shop are relatively common practices among sales managers. Certainly these are not the majority of cases, but the challenge of providing a quiet, secure, private location to test a job candidate in a busy sales office environment is very real. Working closely with the end users at the time of implementation of a testing program is an important step in minimizing these sorts of challenges. Alternatives might include defining a dedicated testing room within the sales office, training all within the office to respect the need for quiet when testing is going on, testing only on a computer dedicated to testing, or contracting with a local commercial test administration site to provide testing services.

As technology continues to advance, new testing options are beginning to offer a form of proctored online testing. For example, the testing system might continuously monitor testing sessions and send messages to the test taker as necessary. If necessary, the system could also take actions such as pausing, suspending, or stopping the test based on test taker behaviors or actions (*Kryterion's Webassessor Test Delivery Options*, 2008). Although this approach does not guarantee standardized testing environments, the approach can identify problems in real time and allow HR professionals to take steps to minimize them, office by office.

Test Security

Test security includes steps taken to ensure that a test or test scoring keys are available only to those who are authorized to use them and identify if and when test administration has been compromised. Today much selection testing is conducted over the Internet. In some ways, this is an improvement over test security because paper test materials are often no longer needed in offices, and scoring keys almost never need to be divulged to test administrators. However, the Internet offers a variety of new test security challenges, especially if the test administration is not proctored. Despite programming efforts to minimize misuse, savvy individuals can often find a way to print test questions, use the Internet during testing to seek correct answers to questions, or defeat test timing mechanisms to allow a break or extra time for testing. For true high stakes-testing, proctored administration is imperative. In contrast, in many cases, unproctored testing for sales positions is acceptable. Not all personnel psychologists would agree, and the issue remains controversial (Tippins, 2009).

Making Sales Assessment Work

The basic steps for designing and implementing an improved sales selection process are simple:

1. Understand the job. O*NET is a good starting point, to be supplemented with a job analysis study.
2. Understand what you are trying to predict. The criteria may be quantitative sales results or performance rating provided by sales managers, or both. You need to determine which are most appropriate for your situation and fully understand the criteria you decide to use.
3. Determine the minimum qualifications that are required to be a successful salesperson in your company.
4. Identify the assessment steps that will effectively measure the key KSAOs and will most likely predict the various criteria of interest to you.
5. Build or find the validity evidence needed to support the use of the assessments you would like to use. Occasionally this is a matter of documenting a content validity argument. Other times you will want to develop empirical validation support for your specific company, and still other times, you will be able to make a case based on a large number of previous studies completed on positions very similar to your sales positions.
6. Put the individual assessment steps into a well-thought-out, organized sales selection process.

During the process, spend time building and communicating realistic expectations about the impact of a new selection process. Rarely do selection tests alone turn a faltering organization around. Productivity is unlikely to double, and turnover rates are unlikely to be cut in half. Do set realistic expectations—perhaps 5, 10, or even 15 percent improvements in the metrics of importance to the company. Also recognize that productivity improvements through improved selection occur over many years.

As an increasing proportion of the sales force is selected using the new valid process, overall productivity and retention grow.

References

Barrick, M. R., & Mount, M. K. (1991). The Big Five personality dimensions and job performance. *Personnel Psychology, 44*, 1–26.

Barrick, M. R., Mount, M. K., & Strauss, J. P. (1993). Conscientiousness and performance of sales representatives: Test of the mediating effects of goal setting. *Journal of Applied Psychology, 78*, 715–722.

Bertua, C., Anderson, N., & Salgado, J. F. (2005). The predictive validity of cognitive ability tests: A UK meta-analysis. *Journal of Occupational and Organizational Psychology, 78*, 387–409.

Borman, W. C., & Motowidlo, S. J. (1997). Task performance and contextual performance: The meaning for personnel selection research. *Human Performance, 10*, 99–109.

Brown, S. H. (1978). Long-term validity of a personal history item scoring procedure. *Journal of Applied Psychology, 63*, 673–676.

Brown, S. H. (1981). Validity generalization and situation moderation in the life insurance industry. *Journal of Applied Psychology, 66*, 664–670.

Dohm, A., & Shniper, L. (2007, November). Occupational employment projections to 2016. *Monthly Labor Review Online*. Retrieved from http://www.bls.gov/opub/mlr/2007/11/contents.htm.

Erceg-Hurn, D. M., & Mirosevich, V. M. (2008). Modern robust statistical methods. *American Psychologist, 63*, 591–601.

Foldes, H. J., Duehr, E. E., & Ones, D. S. (2008). Group differences in personality: Meta-analyses comparing five U.S. racial groups. *Personnel Psychology, 61*, 579–616.

Ford, N. M., Walker, O. C., Churchill, G. A., & Hartley, S. W. (1987). Selecting successful salespeople: A meta-analysis of biographical and psychological selection criteria. In M. J. Houston (Ed.), *Review of marketing* (pp. 90–131). Chicago: American Marketing Association.

Highhouse, S. (2008). Stubborn reliance on intuition and subjectivity in employee selection. *Industrial and Organizational Psychology: Perspectives on Science and Practice, 1*, 333–342.

History of the AIB. (1980, March 1). *Managers Magazine*, pp. 30–33.

Hunter J. E., & Hunter, R. F. (1984). Validity and utility of alternative predictors of job performance. *Psychological Bulletin, 96*, 72–98.

Kryterion's Webassessor Test Delivery Options. (2008). Retrieved from http://www.kryteriononline.com/test_delivery.htm.

Kuncel, N. R. (2008). Some new (and old) suggestions for improving personnel selection. *Industrial and Organizational Psychology: Perspectives on Science and Practice, 1,* 343–346.

MacKenzie, S. B., Podsakoff, P. M., & Fetter, R., (1991). Organizational citizenship behavior and objective productivity as determinants of managerial evaluations of salespersons' performance. *Organizational Behavior and Human Decision Processes, 50,* 123–150.

Ones, D. S., & Viswesvaran, C. (1998). The effects of social desirability and faking on personality and integrity assessment for personnel selection. *Human Performance, 11,* 245–269.

O*NET Online. (2003). *Find occupations.* Retrieved from http://online.onetcenter.org/find.

Schmidt, F. L., & Hunter, J. E. (1998). The validity and utility of selection methods in personnel psychology: Practical and theoretical implications of 85 years of research findings. *Psychological Bulletin, 124,* 262–274.

Tippins, N. T. (2009). Internet alternatives to traditional proctored testing: Where are we now? *Industrial and Organizational Psychology: Perspectives on Science and Practice. 2,* 2–10.

U.S. Department of Labor, Bureau of Labor Statistics (2008, September). *May 2007 national occupational employment and wage estimates.* Retrieved from http://www.bls.gov/oes/current/oes_nat.htm/.

Vinchur, A. J., Schippmann, J. S., Switzer, F. S. III, & Roth, P. L. (1998). A meta-analytic review of predictors of job performance for salespeople. *Journal of Applied Psychology, 83,* 586–597.

White, L. A., & Moss, M. C. (1995, April). Factors influencing the concurrent versus predictive validities of personality constructs. In F. Schmidt (Chair), *Response distortion and social desirability in personality testing for personnel selection.* Symposium presented at the 10th Annual Conference of the Society of Industrial and Organizational Psychology, Orlando, FL.

CHAPTER 12

ASSESSMENT FOR SUPERVISORY AND EARLY LEADERSHIP ROLES

Mark J. Schmit, Jill M. Strange

Chris, a dedicated, hard-working customer service agent for the Sam Hill Agency, consistently received outstanding performance ratings from his boss, peers, and customers. He quickly moved up through the customer service ranks to his current position of senior customer service agent. Having reached this level, Chris was also at the top of his pay grade. He loved his job, but times were financially challenging, and he believed that a supervisor job would be his best chance at financial stability. He had never had any supervisor responsibilities before this time, but he had seen others do the job and thought, "How difficult can it be?" So Chris applied for the job of customer service supervisor.

Chris's supervisor, Cindy, was delighted that Chris wanted to become a supervisor and strongly recommended him, explaining what an asset Chris had been in providing exceptional customer service to the agency's clients in a professional and consistent manner. She went on to say that she thought Chris would be an excellent supervisor.

(Continued)

The next week, Chris interviewed with Janice for the supervisor job. She asked Chris about his career aspirations and why he thought he would be a good supervisor. The interview was short and pleasant—at best an informal discussion about the position and why Chris thought he was qualified for it. Although Janice had some initial concerns about Chris's lack of supervisory experience, his performance record was better than that of any other applicant. The agency had a superior metric system for evaluating the performance of customer service agents that was developed and validated by the leading consulting firm in the industry. Not wanting to second-guess such a good system, Janice promoted Chris to customer service supervisor.

Chris was initially excited about the new opportunity and the higher pay that came with the position. However, after three months in the position, he was completely frustrated. All of the customer service agents who loved him before he was supervisor now seemed to hate him. He was not accustomed to feeling like a failure, but he could not help feeling that way now. Every day he had to handle issues with the angriest customers, and he had to try to motivate agents who had far less passion for the job than he ever had. The peer who was assigned to help him learn his job kept telling him, "Hang in there; it gets easier eventually." However, she was frequently fighting her own fires and had little time to help Chris handle his problems. Chris felt he was in over his head and wanted to go back to the job he loved. Just five months into his tenure as a supervisor, he left the Sam Hill Agency and took a job as senior customer service agent at a competing firm.

When Chris left, Janice was concerned. It seemed to her she just could not find stable supervisors for the call center. She believed in promoting from within, but she now doubted the effectiveness of this policy. She had over 80 percent turnover in the supervisor ranks and wondered what was going wrong. What could she do to stop the bleeding?

A *Washington Post* columnist wrote: "If I could make a bar graph to chart the subjects on which I get e-mail every week, one subject would tower over the others: manager. You have bad managers, you could do a better job than your own manager. You are a new manager and don't know what you are doing. You are a new manager and just want a little respect. You are a new manager and you miss your old non-managerial job. You wish your company offered your managers some training. You wonder whether training would actually help. You want to go home and hide under the covers" (Joyce, 2003, p. H5).

The Business Need

In many organizations, more than half of first-line supervisors fail, costing the organization thousands of dollars in lost productivity for each failed supervisor. The case study that began this chapter poses a difficult question: Why do so many supervisors fail? The first answer is that they were likely set up for failure by the organization. The natural tendency is to promote good workers to management. Most organizations do this without any pretraining for those promoted to supervisors. In addition, the training on the job after promotion often comes in doses of too little or too late. The specific knowledge and skills needed to perform the job of an individual contributor generally comprise the majority of the job requirements. However, for the supervisor job described in the case study, the individual contributor tasks requiring these skills and knowledge will comprise only a minor part of the job; the majority of the activities are specific to the application of supervisory knowledge and skills. The overlapping requirements are important but not substantial, leaving many new supervisors ill prepared for the new job and ultimately resulting in their failed performance.

Job candidates for supervisory positions, like Chris in the case study, often want the job because it comes with a higher earning potential than the wage range typically associated with an individual contributor position. However, many candidates are blinded by the money and do not consider whether a supervisory job will be a good fit for them. The opportunity for a higher salary and a new career path in management often attracts many applicants, feeding the frenzy of those competing for the job. The result is that candidates often self-select into the applicant pool for a supervisor job not on what the job entails but on what outcomes the job might offer. This shortsighted approach can set candidates up for nearly immediate job dissatisfaction and ultimate failure in the position. In the case study, Chris participated in setting up his own failure by not examining what would be truly required of him in his new, and very different, position.

With both organizations and candidates creating unrealistic expectations for new supervisors, the failure rates of supervisors seen in published statistics are not surprising. So what can be done to quell this perfect storm of events? Assessment is one of the answers. However, it is often the case that the pool of supervisory candidates is filled with many individuals who do not have previous supervisory experience. This begs the age-old question: Are leaders born or made? If people are born with the natural competency to lead, then assessment can be the simple answer: assess the traits required of a leader, and be done with it. However, years of research have shown that leadership is not an innate ability. Rather, some individual characteristics may help to facilitate the learning and use of leadership skill, but motivated adults can learn the skills to be a leader. Consequently, assessment may be part of the answer to selecting supervisors, but it is not the full answer. Reducing the failure rate of supervisors can begin with assessment, but it must also entail other organizational interventions.

Assessment can be used in several ways as a beginning point to selecting and developing supervisors. Initial assessments might be used as a baseline for establishing an individual's readiness to move into a supervisory job and determine if he or she has traits or characteristics that facilitate the ability to lead. In addition, assessments can help determine if candidates know how to motivate employees, solve problems, manage conflict, and lead the execution of work. A baseline assessment can answer these questions. In later sections of this chapter, we describe the types of assessment that can be used to accomplish this goal.

Once a baseline assessment is conducted, organizational interventions can be implemented to develop individuals in supervisory and other early career leadership roles. For example, team lead roles are often implemented to give aspiring supervisors a realistic job sample of what it might be like to be a supervisor. These positions are often set up to provide the incumbent with limited decision-making authority, but with restricted responsibility for ensuring that the motivation and execution of the team is at peak levels. The team lead is closely monitored and mentored by a supervisor with greater authority. In this type of intervention, people who were previously individual contributors can learn to become supervisors in a protected or safe environment. Internships, manager-in-training programs, mentorships, and new manager training opportunities are other effective means of closing the gap between assessed and expected levels of supervisory competence in a way that keeps the incumbent from being thrown into a position that is over his or her head, as was the case for Chris in the case study.

The failure to correctly assess, select, and develop employees in supervisory and early leadership roles is endemic to organizations. For assessment and selection, many organizations rely on the old adage that past performance is the best predictor of future performance. Although assessment and selection methods based on this premise have strong validity in many instances, this approach can backfire when an employee is moving from an individual contributor to a leadership role. Many organizations miss the fact that the past performance must be similar in nature to the future expected performance if it is to be a good predictor. In addition, assessing and selecting on personality traits and cognitive ability can provide a solid foundation for supervisor and early career leadership roles, but these facilitating characteristics are not enough. First-time supervisors and leaders need additional interventions to learn to lead and ultimately ensure successful performance in these roles. Consequently, success in assessing, selecting, and developing leaders can be achieved only through a systematic program of interrelated human resource (HR) interventions. We focus the remainder of the chapter on the assessment component of this system, but we reinforce the concept that assessment is but one component of the larger systematic intervention.

The U.S. Office of Personnel Management (2001) described findings of research to assess the status of efforts in federal agencies to identify, select, develop, and evaluate first-level supervisors. Here is what they found:

- Most agencies still do not identify employees with supervisory potential and develop them for future leadership positions.
- Supervisory selections primarily emphasize technical expertise without adequate attention to leadership competencies.
- Supervisors believe that leadership development is given a low priority.
- Poorly performing supervisors are ignored and receive little feedback on how to improve, and effective supervisors are not adequately recognized and rewarded.
- Agencies need to do a better job of selecting and developing first-line supervisors.

Our experience as consultants leads us to conclude that the state of supervisors in the private sector mirrors these findings from the government sector.

Assessment Instruments

There are two primary ways to approach assessment for leaders: those based on a theoretical perspective about leadership and those based on a direct study of the job or role at hand (that is, through job analysis). A typical practitioner approaches the development of an assessment for supervisors using a combination of the approaches. That is, the practitioner studies the job requirements, understands what is needed from the role both now and in the future, and then draws from theory and assessment research to construct an assessment program that fits the needs of the organization.

Leadership Theories and Supervisor Selection

First-line supervisors are usually the future high-level leaders of the organization and are leaders in their own right the day they step into the supervisor job. Many organizations, however, ignore this fact and instead focus solely on the day-to-day managerial aspects of the job. When selecting supervisors, organizations would be well served to assess leadership potential in addition to the more day-to-day characteristics of the job. Several theories outlined in the leadership literature offer helpful guidelines for determining potential leader success and can be tied to assessments to help identify this potential (see Table 12.1).

Assessment can provide the guideposts along the way to ensure that the early-career leader is ready to start down the path toward success and stay on it. Each leadership theory in the professional literature contains implications for assessment techniques. Specifically the theories generally dictate the type of assessment method that is most appropriate and the psychological constructs that are most likely to influence success as a leader. Table 12.1 outlines the implications of each leadership theory for assessment.

Leadership theories over the years have ranged from those describing a "great man" born to lead to those depicting leaders as those who simply exchange rewards for work performed by followers. These two examples are extreme, but they still play into perceptions of leaders today. Many do agree that leadership can be learned, but much of leadership cannot be taught in formal classroom settings. Leadership is an apprentice trade, as leaders often learn a majority of their craft on the job. Early-career leaders learn from watching other leaders and emulating their behavior. They choose role models and seek out mentors. They ask other leaders about how to handle situations. Leaders become leaders through others.

The Ohio State Leadership Studies identified two qualities of leaders that make them successful to varying degrees: consideration and structure initiation (Bass, 2008). These two dimensions represent two major aspects of supervisory work (people orientation and task orientation), and good leaders know when to use more of each characteristic at a given time. If an organization is faced with a short deadline and has a great amount to accomplish quickly, an effective leader initiates structure in order to get a grasp on the situation and becomes very task oriented and possibly directive. In times of crisis, such as organizational downsizing, a good leader uses more of his or her consideration skills

Table 12.1. Comparison of Key Leadership Theories and Implications for Selection

Theory Type	Examples	Key Assumptions	Implications for Selection Instruments
Trait based	• Four primary traits (McCall & Lombardo, 1983) • Servant leadership (Greenleaf, 2002)	• Born leaders will arise to greatness in times of need. People are born with certain inherited traits enabling them to be good leaders.	• Potential leaders can be identified through the assessment of certain personality traits.
Behavior based	• Role theory (Merton, 1957) • Managerial grid (Blake & Mouton, 1961)	• Leaders can be made through learned behaviors.	• Potential leaders can be trained and assessed through high- or low-fidelity simulations.
Participative leadership	• Leadership styles (Lewin, Lippit, & White, 1939; Likert, 1967)	• Good leaders involve others in making decisions; followers therefore are more invested in the results and more committed to the leader.	• Potential leaders can be assessed through high-fidelity simulations such as leaderless group discussions.
Situational leadership	• Situational leadership (Hersey & Blanchard, 1969) • Normative model (Vroom & Yetton, 1973) • Path goal theory of leadership (House, 1971)	• Good leaders adapt their style to match the situation rather than always responding the same way.	• Potential leaders can be assessed through high- or low-fidelity simulations.

Contingency theories	• Least-preferred-coworker theory (Fiedler, 1964) • Cognitive resource theory (Fiedler & Garcia, 1987) • Strategic contingencies theory (Hickson, Hinings, Lee, Schneck, & Pennings, 1971)	• Leadership style is based on several factors including the leader's preferred style, followers, and situation.	• Potential leaders can be identified through the assessment of certain personality traits, biodata, and low- or high-fidelity assessment methods.
Transactional leadership	• Leader-member exchange theory (Dansereau, Graen, & Haga, 1975)	• Effective leaders motivate their followers through reward and punishment.	• Biodata and performance evaluations can help identify potential leaders.
Transformational leadership	• Transformational leadership theory (Bass, 1985) • Transformational leadership theory (Burns, 1978) • Leadership participation inventory (Kouzes & Posner, 2003)	• Leaders inspire and motivate followers through a well-articulated vision for the future.	• High- and low-fidelity simulation assessments can help identify potential leaders.
Authentic leadership	• Authentic leadership theory (Avolio, Gardner, Walumba, Luthans, & May, 2004)	• Good leaders are self-aware and transparent, and they act in accordance with accepted ethical guidelines.	• Trait- and emotional intelligence-based personality measures, structured interviews, and high- and low-fidelity assessments can help identify potential leaders.

Note: For additional information about leadership theories, see Bass (2008).

in order to calm the workforce and help them get through the trying time. Being able to evaluate not only a person's potential for having consideration toward people and task orientation but also the ability to switch back and forth between these two styles is quite valuable to organizations searching for supervisors and future leaders of the organization.

Two other leadership theories of use to selecting potential supervisors are those of transactional and transformational leadership. Transactional leaders rely on traditional reward and punishment strategies to gain follower compliance, whereas transformational leaders engage followers in such a way as to motivate them and satisfy their intrinsic needs through articulating an inspiring vision for the future. Although these two concepts have generally been applied in the realm of political leadership, they have definite utility in the selection of supervisors. Hiring managers must take care to ensure that potential supervisors can exhibit both types of leadership styles as they progress through the organization. While in a first-line supervisor job, employees may have to rely on more transactional strategies to motivate direct reports to reach their goals (for example, if they show up for work, they get paid). However, as the supervisor progresses through the organization, leadership needs change, and the supervisor may be called on to motivate direct reports by laying out strategies for the organization's future and provide motivation of a more intrinsic nature. Being able to assess both transactional and transformational qualities in an applicant can be quite useful from a long-term planning standpoint.

A final leadership theory that is important to examine when selecting supervisors with leadership potential is that of authentic leadership. An authentic leader is one who is ethical, transparent, self-aware, and balanced in his or her thinking. These leaders have a high degree of unwavering integrity, focus on developing positive psychological states in their followers, and are transparent in their goals for the organization, which can be highly motivating for followers. Assessing these qualities in a potential leader is particularly relevant for organizations now, when integrity throughout the organization, and especially in the leadership ranks, is of utmost importance.

These theories all show characteristics and behaviors that could cause a supervisor to become an outstanding leader. In addition, several of these theories allow room to train supervisors to take on leadership roles later. By assessing for and selecting applicants based on the traits established to contribute to leadership, allowing applicants to exhibit leadership qualities through low- or high-fidelity assessments, and later training them in effective leadership techniques, hiring managers could find the best supervisor for the organization's current needs and also the best potential leader for the future.

Understanding the Requirements of the Supervisor Job

Although it is easy to discuss the need for assessment of supervisors and the benefit of assessment to the organization, it is first necessary to understand the requirements of supervisory jobs. O*NET (online.onetcenter.org), the Department of Labor's comprehensive database of work and worker requirements for jobs in the U.S. workforce, describes the knowledge, skills, abilities, and other requirements (KSAOs) for twenty types of first-line supervisors (for example, retail, production, administrative). To collect this information, the Department of Labor performed job analyses on hundreds of supervisor jobs using a common taxonomy of work and worker characteristics. What the O*NET data show is that while specific knowledge and work context characteristics differ based on the type of job being supervised, there are many common elements across supervisor jobs (see Table 12.2). These include administrative, managerial, and communication-related job components.

As in the case study, organizations typically make the mistake of evaluating and basing the hiring decisions of a supervisory applicant on the KSAOs specific to the applicant's current individual contributor job rather than his or her supervisory KSAOs. As a result, those hired might not be suited for the supervisor job. Second, the common work styles (similar to personality characteristics) differ from individual contributor jobs in that supervisors need work styles enabling them to focus more on the leadership of people and management of overarching workplace issues. Although these characteristics would undoubtedly be helpful to a person in a nonsupervisory position, organizations may overlook

Table 12.2.   Common O*NET Elements Across Various Supervisor Jobs

Knowledge	Abilities	
• Administration and management • Customer and personal services • Education and training	• Deductive reasoning • Inductive reasoning • Information ordering • Near vision • Oral comprehension • Oral expression	• Problem sensitivity • Speech clarity • Speech recognition • Category flexibility • Written comprehension • Written expression

Skills		Other Personal Characteristics	
• Active learning • Active listening • Complex problem solving • Coordination • Critical thinking • Instructing • Judgment and decision making • Learning strategies • Management of personnel resources	• Mathematics • Monitoring • Negotiation • Persuasion • Reading comprehension • Service orientation • Social perceptiveness • Speaking • Time management • Writing	• Achievement, effort • Adaptability, flexibility • Analytical thinking • Attention to detail • Concern for others • Cooperation • Dependability	• Independence • Initiative • Innovation • Integrity • Leadership • Persistence • Self-control • Social orientation • Stress tolerance

Note: The dimensions listed apply to at least 75 percent (fifteen of the twenty) of supervisor jobs listed in O*NET.

the fact that in most cases, the personality characteristics that it takes to be an exceptional supervisor may need to be very different from those of an exceptional individual contributor. Finally, the work context or environment itself may contribute to issues when selecting and retaining supervisors. A former individual contributor, like Chris in the case study, may become disenchanted with the supervisor job when he realizes that his favorite aspects of the previous job (interacting with the customer and being out in the field) are not part of the new supervisory position.

The most important aspect of the information gathered in O*NET, though, is that it provides evidence that supervisory jobs are inherently different from individual contributor jobs and that supervisory jobs have common KSAOs across industries. The supervisor jobs in O*NET cover diverse job families in the U.S. economy (for example, correctional officers, retail, office administration, aquaculture) and exhibit a surprising degree of commonality. Although the knowledge requirements might be very different according to career field, supervisors across industries need many of the same characteristics in order to succeed.

Competencies Versus KSAOs

In the previous section, we focused primarily on KSAOs. In recent years, however, much emphasis has been placed on the measurement of competencies: observable performance dimensions influenced by KSAs that can be linked to high performance and provide the organization with a competitive advantage. Rather than evaluating one small aspect of performance, competencies encompass a set of related work behaviors and provide a more organization-specific slant. In the case of Chris, one competency for the supervisory job might be "call center staffing and scheduling," which might entail knowledge and skill in identifying staffing options, calculating staffing requirements, calculating telephone resources, and creating workforce schedules.

Traditional KSAOs can be defined in a very discrete way. Often they are not connected to anything and leave little room for promotional pathways or performance levels. KSAs or other personal characteristics identified for an individual contributor may also be identified for an executive with little to no differentiation between the level at which the employees must use the KSA in their day-to-day jobs. Competency frameworks, however, have clearly defined performance levels marked by specific behaviors so that all employees understand their performance expectations. This can establish a more clearly defined work environment, eliminate role ambiguity, and create promotional pathways. In the case of the first-line supervisor, knowledge of call centers might be critical to both the individual contributor and the supervisor job. However, the supervisor may need to know how to conduct day-to-day operations and handle conflict, whereas the individual contributor may need to know only how to answer and handle calls. Competencies allow the company to move beyond that discrete knowledge requirement and incorporate concrete behavioral performance indicators as well.

Since competencies call on several aspects of the job, they are often better measured through more complex means, such as high-fidelity simulations and structured interviews, as opposed to assessment types measuring only one type of construct (ability or knowledge tests). Aside from this, competencies can be implemented into the test development process with relative ease through the same process KSAOs typically are: job analysis, analysis to determine optimal testing methods, and test validation to ensure job relatedness and the ability to predict performance.

Choosing the Right Assessment Tool

Once the job analysis has been completed and a set of KSAOs or competencies established for the position, the next step is to choose assessment tools that measure these important elements of success. However, finding the best way to determine who is a qualified applicant can prove challenging. With the many different types of assessments available, how can an organization know that the KSAOs necessary to be an effective supervisor are measured and also find candidates who will stay in the job? The answer is straightforward: by evaluating pros and cons of various types of selection instruments in light of the job requirements necessary to be a first-line supervisor.

Table 12.3 describes the types of dimensions measured by several selection or promotion methods that may be useful when

Table 12.3. Selection and Promotion Methods for Supervisors

| | Dimensions Measured | | | | | | | |
	Knowledge	Skills	Abilities	Work Style	Preferred Work Context	Past Performance	Strengths	Weaknesses
Cognitive ability testing			X				• Valid predictor of performance • Inexpensive • Not time-consuming • Easy to score and administer	• Higher adverse impact against minority groups
Assessment centers	X	X	X	X			• Low adverse impact • Valid predictor of performance • High face validity	• Costly • Complicated to score and administer • Time-consuming to develop and administer • May not validate across departments
Biodata				X	X	X	• Low adverse impact • Valid predictor of performance • High face validity	• Potential for faking

(Continued)

Table 12.3. Selection and Promotion Methods for Supervisors *(Continued)*

	Dimensions Measured							
	Knowledge	Skills	Abilities	Work Style	Preferred Work Context	Past Performance	Strengths	Weaknesses
Situational judgment tests	X	X	X	X			• Low adverse impact • High face validity • Valid predictor of performance • Off-the-shelf tests available	• Costly and time-consuming to develop • May not validate across departments
Structured interviews	X	X		X	X	X	• Low adverse impact • Valid predictor of performance • Easy to score and administer	• Interviewers tend to ignore scripts and training over time, fading into unstructured format
Unstructured interviews	?	?		?	?	?	• Inexpensive	• Inconsistent • Not a valid predictor of performance
Personality testing: Trait measures				X	X		• Low adverse impact • Valid predictor of performance	• Potential for faking • Low face validity • Lack sufficient predictive validity as a sole measure of potential

				Benefits	Drawbacks
Personality testing: Emotional intelligence		X		• Low adverse impact	• Potential for faking • Low face validity • Limit predictive validity • Limited in scope
Knowledge testing	X			• Valid predictor of job performance • High face validity • Easy to score and administer	• Requires frequent updating • Potential for adverse impact
Performance evaluations			X	• Evaluates actual performance on the job	• Constructs evaluated may be unrelated to supervisor job • May be perceived as subjective
Probationary periods			X	• Evaluates actual performance on the job	• Cost of training lost if supervisor does not succeed • Can lead to failure if not properly executed

evaluating potential supervisors. In addition, strengths and weaknesses of these selection methods are presented in the table. This table is a starting point for evaluating different types of assessment methods. Assessment methods are complex and should be chosen or developed in conjunction with trained professionals such as industrial and organizational psychologists. Given the complexity of assessment methods, entire chapters in this book are also dedicated to describing them more fully along with the pros and cons of each.

Templates for Supervisor Assessment

Practitioners often ask for guidance on specific combinations of assessments that have proven useful across organizations faced with similar needs. We provide some recommendations in Table 12.4, which focuses on the most common situations facing employers developing supervisor assessment systems:

- A large applicant pool for a smaller number of supervisor openings or a single opening
- A small applicant pool for a single supervisor job
- A pool of only internal candidates for a supervisor job
- An opening in a high-impact job
- A company decision to minimize potential adverse impact
- A development context

Each of these situations creates circumstances that may call for a different set of assessment tools. Table 12.4 provides examples of different combinations of assessments that we have found useful in meeting the needs of organizations in each of these situations.

Supervisor Selection Assessment Versus Training and Development Assessment

Up to now, we have focused on assessments used for the selection and promotion of supervisors. Assessments linked to training and development, however, can have just as much impact on an organization's ability to identify and retain good supervisors.

Table 12.4. Example Supervisory Assessments for Specific Situations

Situation	Assessments	Rationale
Large applicant pool (option: organizational decision to minimize adverse impact)	Cognitive ability, situational judgment, biodata, structured interview	• Cognitive ability is the best single predictor of supervisor success, but will also have adverse impact against African Americans and Hispanics. Decision to include depends on risk tolerance of organization. If the test is validated, it is not illegal to have adverse impact. If organization decides to minimize adverse impact as part of a diversity initiative, any assessment including cognitive ability components should be carefully considered or appropriately weighted. • Situational judgment and biodata have less or no adverse impact. Off-the-shelf tests are available from test publishers for supervisory jobs. These are efficient and valid assessments for screening large numbers of candidates. • Structured interviews would be used following the screen and would focus on job-specific knowledge, if relevant, and questions regarding the most important competencies identified through job analysis.
Small applicant pool	Structured interview	• Structured interviews can include both situational and behavioral interview questions. • The situational questions may focus on leadership scenarios, and the behavioral interview questions may focus on the applicant's experience in other important competencies identified through job analysis.

(Continued)

Table 12.4. Example Supervisory Assessments for Specific Situations *(Continued)*

Situation	*Assessments*	*Rationale*
Internal candidates only for promotion to supervisor	Performance evaluations, training data, structured interview	• Performance evaluations are useful only for competencies that are important at the supervisor level. This is typically a subset of the evaluation ratings at the lower level. • Supervisor training, mentoring, or on-the-job training assignments can be conducted prior to making promotion decisions. Outcome data from these experiences are useful in making promotion decisions. However, all candidates should be given equal opportunities to the experiences to ensure fairness. • Structured interviews can be used in the same way as for small applicant pools.
High-impact supervisor job	Assessment center	• For jobs where the success or failure of the supervisor will have a significant impact on the organization or unit, in-depth assessment centers are appropriate. This type of assessment might include job simulation exercises, tests, interviews, and an integration of all assessment data by a trained assessor.
Development	Assessment center performance evaluations, training data, 360-degree feedback	• A development assessment center might include job simulation exercises, tests, interviews, and a 360-degree feedback assessment. • Integration of all assessment data and training data by a trained assessor who can provide feedback to the person being assessed.

384

Assessments that are used in training and development of supervisors focus on how well knowledge and skills are learned and then applied on the job. However, the more important assessment of successful training and development is whether the knowledge and skills learned are used on the job. This type of assessment is known as a transfer-of-training assessment. Without an assessment, there is no systematic way to know the impact of the training on the job performance of supervisors.

Assessments used in selecting and promoting supervisors assess the potential an individual has for performing well on the job. The premise of these assessments is that they lead to better inferences about which candidates will perform better on the job. Similar to training assessments, without knowledge of the impacts of the interventions it is impossible to systematically know if good selection or promotion decisions are being made regarding supervisors. Consequently, it is important to show that the scores obtained on the assessments, whether used in training and development or in selection and promotion, are related to performance on the job of supervisor.

Aside from the obvious difference in premise between supervisory assessments for selection versus training, the stakes resting on them are another major difference between these purposes of testing. Selection assessments are typically more high-stakes situations for both the candidate and the organization for several reasons. First, the possibility of adverse impact (the manifestation of unintentional minority versus majority group score differences that result in differential hiring ratios between the groups) and resulting litigation can be increased. Second, there is a higher need to ensure that the tests are related to performance and that the right people are hired. Training and development situations have considerably lower stakes because they are often voluntary, and continued employment is usually not based on test results.

Special Considerations for Implementation

A number of assessment options are available to employers, all of which, if employed properly, can help select the best candidate for the supervisory job and save organizations from making costly mistakes. There is no one best selection method to use, and the implementation of any of the selection tools already identified should be based on a careful analysis of the job, the potential validity of the tool or combination of tools, and the potential for adverse impact against protected groups. A combination of selection methods should always be considered to enhance overall validity, ensure competency coverage, and minimize potential adverse impact. Whichever methods are ultimately chosen, there are other implementation issues to consider in optimizing the usefulness of the program.

An important consideration is whether to promote supervisors from within or to hire externally. The external applicant pool is often more diverse in KSAOs, experiences, cultural and ethnic background, and other less important factors. The internal applicant pool is more knowledgeable about company-specific operations, policies, and procedures. In addition, internal candidates have already learned the culture and values of the organization, giving them an inside advantage in that respect. Internal candidates are likely to be resentful toward those hired externally, perceiving them as taking their potential promotion opportunities away. Accordingly, the decision is a difficult one that must balance the needs of the organization and the workforce. A combination of internal and external hiring is likely to be most effective.

The validity of the tools discussed earlier is likely to be solid if the methods are chosen or developed by trained professionals. However, a valid predictor of performance potential may still not fulfill important company goals. Adverse impact against minority group members, women, or older workers may still exist, given that the most valid predictors of supervisor performance may demonstrate the highest adverse impact against segments of these protected populations. That is, the most valid supervisor assessments may result in the largest group differences in scores and passing rates between majority and minority group members. The supervisor job is the largest entry point to management. Accordingly, it can serve as an iron gate to the protected population, which will affect the diversity of the applicant pools to management jobs above the entry level, particularly in organizations with strong internal promotion values. Thus, it is exceedingly important to develop assessment and selection systems for the supervisory job that minimize adverse impact and optimize opportunities for protected group members.

Judiciously setting entry requirements and providing diverse training opportunities can help in inclusiveness efforts. If an organization always demands supervisory experience as a minimum requirement, it will tend to perpetuate limited opportunities for diverse populations. Organizations that assess and select for supervisory potential based on a wide host of factors, including both cognitive and noncognitive elements, will open more doors for diverse populations. However, opening the door is not enough. Potential cannot be realized without a price. As a result, training and development efforts will be needed to help optimize potential. Training and development are maximized for diverse adult populations by providing multiple avenues for learning that are tailored to specific groups and individuals. One size does not necessarily fit all. Of course, assessment is a necessary part of training and development, in that measures of pre- and post-intervention are needed to determine progress. Hiring for potential and developing for performance is a good path to inclusiveness.

Other steps can be taken to reduce adverse impact against protected groups in the assessment and selection of supervisors. Initial steps include:

- Adding noncognitive test components, such as biodata, to the selection battery
- Employing alternative weighting of the cognitive test elements
- Using compensatory selection models versus multiple hurdle methods where cognitively loaded elements may have a greater impact
- Using selection bands rather than absolute passing scores
- Identifying alternative tests that result in less adverse impact

Another approach to reducing the adverse impact of cognitive ability test elements is to remove a portion of the written language component of the test. For example, a situational judgment test measuring judgment and decision-making ability could be delivered in a video format, thereby removing much of the written content that would be found in an equivalent paper-and-pencil format. Research and experience have shown that this type of method change may result in reduced adverse impact.

It is always wise to offer candidates a test orientation. These orientations can take many forms, including live practice sessions, interactive Web site programs, or orientation brochures or videos. While test orientation or coaching sessions may have some effect on group differences, these differences tend to be small but can help to level the playing field. The real benefit of test orientation sessions is that they are typically viewed as positive by applicants, who report favorable impressions of organizations that offer these types of programs; accordingly, complaints about the test, as well as potential litigation, are likely to be reduced.

Implementation of supervisory assessment and selection systems is a complex decision-making process with many issues and technical solutions to consider. It is always best to consult with multiple trained professionals, including those trained in industrial and organizational psychology and employment law, before finalizing implementation plans.

Managing the Assessment Program

The ongoing management of the supervisor assessment process is as important as the original design. Currently numerous employment court cases target the selection and promotion systems used for hiring management employees, including first-line supervisors. Several of these cases focus on alleged use of subjective decision-making processes in the hiring or promotion process. Specifically, it is frequently asserted that subjective decision-making processes allow hiring managers so much discretion that they may consciously or unconsciously harbor and use stereotypes. These stereotypes are alleged to be the root of discriminatory decisions against a protected group member. The ongoing management of the supervisor assessment process must be managed correctly to ensure that a defense is built against these possible threats.

Two primary mechanisms defend against the possibility of discrimination cases involving what plaintiffs refer to as subjective decision making. First, decision making should be fully job related. If a decision is fully job related, then it is a business judgment decision, not a subjective or arbitrary decision. Second, a system of checks and balances should be developed that holds managers accountable for the business judgments that they make regarding hiring and promotion decisions. Together these two mechanisms can mitigate the possibility of discrimination law suits.

The job relatedness of a supervisor assessment is established through job analysis techniques and validation studies. The content of the assessments should closely resemble the content of the job. Alternatively the content of the assessments should be shown to predict performance on the job. The ongoing job relatedness of a supervisor assessment is affected by changes in the job, and if the job changes, the assessments may need to change as well.

Accountability for managerial decisions made through a supervisory assessment process can be established by a system of checks and balances put in place to ensure the fair and equitable treatment of all candidates for a job. The selection and promotion of candidates to supervisor positions is usually a high-stakes process that typically includes many applicants vying for substantially higher pay and greater responsibility. The higher the stakes, the more potential there is that the process will be challenged. A system of checks and balances can help ensure a fair and defensible process:

- Validate and document all supervisory assessment practices and systems.
- Provide a training and certification process for designers, implementers, and users of supervisory assessment practices that focus on job-related decision making.
- Audit assessment process implementation and execution using clear behavioral standards, and provide immediate, specific feedback to designers, implementers, and users.
- Ensure the consistent application of all supervisory assessments.
- Use multiple interviewers or raters with multiple perspectives.
- Implement higher-level management and HR reviews of supervisory hiring and promotion decisions.
- Develop multiple avenues of appeal for supervisory candidates affected by manager decisions in the assessment process.

- Challenge managers to justify assessment decisions with behavioral examples and job-related outcomes.
- Provide developmental feedback to internal supervisor candidates that will enable them to develop skills and knowledge for possible future promotion opportunities.

Evaluation and Return on Investment

The usefulness of assessment in hiring, promotion, and development of supervisors is often challenged by management. The typical response is, "Why would we want to spend so much on assessment? Let's just get these supervisors working!" Assessments can be quite costly. For example, an assessment center with multiple job simulations can run into the six figures to develop and execute in a large organization. Consequently it is important to show the business impacts of the assessments, that is, the expected return on investment (ROI). Demonstrating the ROI of assessments can provide a business case for the investment, in addition to yielding important metrics showing the ongoing improvements made in the organization following program implementation. The potential for a high ROI can certainly help convince management of the usefulness of assessments.

For supervisors, there are three primary categories of performance indicators that are typically analyzed to determine ROI: job performance and productivity, employee attitudes and turnover, and third-party interventions. Here are some measures that fall into these three categories (see Cascio, 2000, for methods of calculating ROI for these performance indicators):

Job Performance and Productivity

- Supervisor ratings of competence
- Supervisor ratings of performance
- Business unit productivity
- Direct report productivity
- Customer satisfaction
- Number of accidents
- Number of safety violations
- Lost work time

Employee Attitudes and Turnover

- Percentage of annual direct report turnover
- Percentage of direct report turnover in first ninety days
- Percentage of annual absenteeism of direct reports
- Direct report attitudes toward supervisor
- Direct report job engagement

Third-Party Interventions

- Number of grievances or complaints filed
- Number of times HR involvement is required in disputes
- Number of times lawyer involvement is required in disputes

The assumption is that if accurate decisions about candidates are made in selection and promotion or transfer of training is taking place, then performance and productivity should be maximized, employee attitudes should be positive, turnover should be low, and the number of instances where third-party interventions are required should be minimized. These metrics of performance can then be used as indicators of ROI.

ROI is determined by looking at changes in these metrics before and after the implementation of assessments and related interventions such as training or development programs. Accordingly, dollar values must be placed on the metrics. For example, how much does the turnover of a supervisor's direct report or a supervisor cost the organization in replacement costs for recruiting and hiring, training costs, or production loss, for example? Or what does it cost to resolve the typical grievance filed with the union? Once dollar values are associated with performance indicators, the changes in performance are monetized, and a true ROI of an assessment and related interventions can be determined.

ROI becomes the lifeblood of the assessment programs. Whenever the cost or impact of an assessment program is challenged, these data can be referenced. Without ROI data, it is very difficult to sustain an assessment program. Furthermore, it is in the best interest of the organization to know how well programs are working so that they can be modified or eliminated if there is not sufficient ROI. Without some form of ROI, supervisory assessment may be a futile exercise, and management, employees, and applicants will let you know it.

The Way Forward

Effective selection, promotion, and development of first-line supervisors are essential to an organization's talent pool. It is the largest pool of talent from which higher-level managers can be drawn. Yet organizations are often reluctant to spend the time and money on employees at this level. Assessment is a key element of these HR processes. Some of the common arguments are, "We are just training them to go elsewhere, so why spend the money?" and, "We don't need expensive processes to select leaders. We know them when we see them." If organizations do not assess potential supervisors correctly or adequately train them, they will also go elsewhere, probably even faster, as we saw with Chris in the opening case. Assessment and training are investments. As with any other investment, there are upsides and downsides. The price to assess and train first-line supervisors is quite low compared to the upside gained from a first-line supervisor who progresses through and is successful in two or three more levels of management. All organizations will lose a few people to other companies, but their odds of keeping and having more successful supervisors and future managers are much more likely with investment. Like any other business decision, you should go with investments where the data tell you the odds are stacked in your favor.

The academic research literature provides a good source of information regarding the assessment of first-line supervisors, though it is rapidly aging. Specific sectors of employers have struck out on their own, using existing academic literature as a base, but building on it with practical collective experience. Two such sectors are the federal government and call centers. Both have recognized the harsh realities of not paying enough attention to first-line leaders, and both have extensively pooled resources to improve their situations. A scan of information available on the Internet from these employment sectors can be informative to approaches to assess, select, develop, and retain first-line supervisors.

Moving forward, there are workforce changes and unique supervisory positions to consider. The enlargement of the remote workforce population offers special challenges to the assessment, selection, and development of supervisors of these workers. The aging and diversification, even globalization, of incumbents to supervise also pose new challenges. These challenges need to be met with new types of assessments and developmental experiences. In most cases, the topics addressed in this chapter will remain the core issues to consider, but emerging challenges will incrementally add to the issues to consider and develop new solutions for the successful assessment, selection, promotion, and development of first-line supervisors.

References

Avolio, B. J., Gardner, W. J., Walumba, F. O., Luthans, F., & May, D. R. (2004). Unlocking the mask: A look at the process by which authentic leaders impact follower attitudes and behaviors. *Leadership Quarterly, 15*, 801–823.

Bass, B. M. (1985). *Leadership and performance beyond expectation.* New York: Free Press.

Bass, B. M. (2008). *Bass and Stogdill's handbook of leadership: Theory, research, and managerial applications.* New York: Simon and Schuster.

Blake, R. R., & Mouton, J. S. (1961). *Group dynamics: Key to decision making.* Houston: Gulf Publishing.

Burns, J. M. (1978). *Leadership.* New York: HarperCollins.

Cascio, W. F. (2000). *Costing human resources: The financial impact of behavior in organizations* (4th ed.). Cincinnati, OH: South-Western College Publishing

Dansereau, F. Jr., Graen, G., & Haga, W. J. (1975). A vertical dyad linkage approach to leadership within formal organizations: A longitudinal investigation of the role making process. *Organizational Behavior and Human Performance, 13*, 46–78.

Fiedler, F. E. (1964). A contingency model of leadership effectiveness. In L. Berkowitz (Ed.), *Advances in experimental social psychology* (Vol. 1, pp. 149–190). Orlando, FL: Academic Press.

Fiedler, F. E., & Garcia, J. E. (1987). *New approaches to leadership, cognitive resources and organizational performance.* Hoboken, NJ: Wiley.

Greenleaf, R. K. (2002). *Servant leadership: A journey into the nature of legitimate power and greatness* (25th anniversary ed.). New York: Paulist Press.

Hersey, P., & Blanchard, K. H. (1969). *Management of organizational behavior: Utilizing human resources.* Upper Saddle River, NJ: Prentice Hall.

Hickson, D. J., Hinigs, C. R., Lee, C. A., Schneck, R. S., & Pennings, J. M. (1971). A strategic contingencies theory of intra-organizational power. *Administrative Science Quarterly, 16,* 216–229.

House, R. J. (1971). A path-goal theory of leader effectiveness. *Administrative Science Quarterly, 16,* 321–339.

Joyce, A. (2003, January 5). Lessons for a command performance: Training programs help new managers avoid the pitfalls of taking charge. *Washington Post,* p. H5.

Kouzes, J. M., & Posner, B. Z. (2003). *The leadership challenge* (3rd ed.). San Francisco: Jossey-Bass.

Lewin, K., Lippit, R., & White, R. K. (1939). Patterns of aggressive behavior in experimentally created social climates. *Journal of Social Psychology, 10,* 271–301.

Likert, R. (1967). *The human organization: Its management and value.* New York: McGraw-Hill.

McCall, M. W. Jr., & Lombardo, M. M. (1983). *Off the track: Why and how successful executives get derailed.* Greensboro, NC: Center for Creative Leadership.

Merton, R. K. (1957). *Social theory and social structure.* New York: Free Press.

National Center for O*NET Development. (2008). *O*NET Online.* Retrieved from http://online.onetcenter.org.

U.S. Office of Personnel Management. (2001). *Supervisors in the federal government: A wake-up call.* Washington, DC: Author.

Vroom, V. H., & Yetton, P. W. (1973). *Leadership and decision-making.* Pittsburgh, PA: University of Pittsburgh Press.

CHAPTER 13

EXECUTIVE AND MANAGERIAL ASSESSMENT

Ann Howard, James N. Thomas

Given the complexity of today's global markets, the need has never before been greater for organizations to have the right executives and managers leading the way. Every high-level selection or placement has become a high-stakes decision for organizations, their shareholders, and their associates.

These decisions are made in the pressure cooker of competition for resources from a rapidly shrinking talent pool. Executives of the baby boom era are approaching retirement, and the traditional replacement pool of those thirty-five to forty-four years old is not nearly large enough to fill the empty chairs. Moreover, many in the right age group are not up to the challenges of increasingly demanding executive roles. In a recent large selection study in North America, 65 percent of staffing directors reported strong competition for executives, and 43 percent indicated that there were fewer qualified candidates for such positions (Howard, Erker, & Bruce, 2007).

Finding available candidates is only a prelude to filling the leadership gap; executive failure rates are astounding. In 2008, 35 percent of the CEO successions in the world's twenty-five hundred largest public companies were the result of the incumbent being forced out by the board (Karlsson & Neilson, 2009). Published estimates of managerial failure range from 30 to 67 percent, with an average of about 50 percent (Hogan, Hogan, & Kaiser, in press). The financial penalty for these failures is equally astounding: costs that include search firm fees, severance packages, hiring bonuses, relocation expenses, base compensation, stock options, and training average about $1.5 million per executive hire (Governance Focus, 2006).

Industrial-organizational (I-O) psychologists can hardly be blamed for these failures, as they are infrequently at the table where selection decisions are made. The decision makers are essentially untrained amateurs (boards of directors and other executives). Moreover, executive recruiters, the primary professionals involved in helping the selection process, overrely on unstructured interviews and reference checks—tools that inhabit the low end of the validity continuum (Howard, 2001).

Organizational programs to develop executives, though less publicized, are no more successful than those used to select them. A recent worldwide study of more than 12,200 leaders found that only two in five (41 percent) were satisfied with their organization's development offerings, and only 29 percent of human resource (HR) professionals rated their leadership development programs as high quality. These data denote a dismal return for programs estimated to cost more than $45 billion annually in the United States alone. Perhaps as a consequence of both selection and development failures, only 42 percent of leaders had high confidence in their senior leaders' ability to ensure the long-term success of the organization (Howard & Wellins, 2008).

Clearly there is a pressing need for better ways to select and develop executives and managers. Today many organizations are turning to professionally developed assessment methods to help them make executive selection decisions and guide managerial development and succession planning. The purposes of the assessment and the organization's particular situation dictate the choice of methods to combine into an assessment system. This principle guides this chapter's discussion of the design, implementation, and evaluation of assessment systems for executives and managers.

Objectives of Executive and Managerial Assessment

Assessment answers the fundamental question, "Does the participant possess the attributes necessary to succeed in a given managerial or executive role?" The specific design and implementation of the assessment are driven by its underlying purpose. For selection, a future role is anticipated; for development, the purpose might be to shore up performance in a current role or prepare a leader to take on a future role. Assessment used for selection focuses on prediction, whereas assessment to guide development focuses on diagnosis.

Various business purposes determine the extent to which an assessment is predictive or diagnostic. For example, an organization or business unit that is changing its strategy (as from transactional to consultative selling) might want to select new managers (predictive assessment), strengthen its current managers in areas requiring a different focus (diagnostic assessment), or some combination of the two. Mergers and acquisitions often require predictive assessments to determine the appropriate placement of current employees into a new structure. An organization anticipating multiple retirements in the near future might want to focus on prediction, whereas a firm with a longer-term replacement horizon might want to focus on diagnosis to carry out an orderly development and succession plan.

In this chapter, we treat selection and development as separate initiatives to illustrate how purpose and situation affect program choices as well as measurement of their effectiveness. Yet even if selection is the primary business purpose for executive assessment, typically there is also some element of development, at least for internal candidates. As Day (2009) pointed out, executive selection should be considered not as a stand-alone decision but as part of comprehensive succession planning. At the same time that assessment helps determine who is ready for a new position, it also evaluates others' potential for future opportunities and the development they need to make them ready for such opportunities. Thus, succession planning at its best is an ongoing process that incorporates aspects of selection, leadership development, and performance management.

When the purpose for an intervention is specific, as is often the case, the attributes targeted by the assessment will diverge, and the processes used will vary as a consequence. For example, an assessment center conducted to diagnose development needs should focus on competencies that are clearly developable. In contrast, an assessment center designed to support selection is more likely to include cognitive ability tests, personality inventories, or other measures of constructs that are difficult to develop yet important prerequisites for success.

Other factors beyond purpose also influence the design and implementation of assessment processes for this employee group. These factors include the unique nature of the executive and managerial population and the type of work that they perform.

The Executive and Managerial Population

Managers and executives generally have the latitude to act, or not to act, on initiatives of concern to them and thus are seldom compelled to participate in an assessment effort against their will. Assessment processes targeted at this group must therefore be carefully designed and deployed to obtain buy-in and commitment. Senior leaders who have not been involved in the design of assessment processes, or have not had information about the purpose, process, and intended outcomes of assessment programs often find ways to derail, delay, or redirect such initiatives.

Executive temperament poses some unique challenges for assessment practitioners. All executives are not alike, of course, but as a group, they tend to stand out in several respects. Data from two personality questionnaires, collected from more than thirty-six hundred participants in DDI executive assessment centers (Howard & Watt, 2008), showed that executives on average scored high (in the seventy-sixth percentile of working adults primarily in leadership roles) on ambition, meaning they tended to be competitive, self-assured, and assertive. On the negative side, they were moderately at risk of being easily bored or distracted, self-promoting and attention seeking, and having a strong sense of entitlement.

Managers and executives have generally worked their way up the organizational hierarchy and proved their mettle. The idea of assessment might be off-putting to those who believe they are beyond such evaluations and that their experience should speak for itself. However, having years in a position is not the same as becoming better in a position or being qualified for the next hierarchical level. Thus, the professional's need to assess executive candidates to fully understand their capabilities and capacities runs up against executives' egos and their natural human resistance to a potentially high-stakes assessment experience over which they have little control.

Executives' sense of importance and entitlement also affects their expectations. They typically expect first-class treatment that shows respect for them and their time. Whereas lower-level managers are often relegated to an online guide, executives' experiences are usually designed to be high touch. They also expect to get as well as give. For example, executives who demonstrate what they would do in a business simulation might inquire about how you interpret their behavior, how they stack up against others in similar situations, and how they can hone their performance.

Executives' and managers' time is limited. Even if an effective case is made to spend the time on assessment, it can be difficult to schedule executives and to have their undivided attention when they do attend. Processes need to take this into consideration, for instance, by allowing ample lead time when scheduling, designing experiences that can fit within busy calendars, and avoiding meetings that must be synchronized with other hard-to-schedule leaders.

Executive and Managerial Work

The nature of executive and managerial work requires that practitioners carefully consider the management levels targeted for assessment, the nature of the tools and processes to be used, and how processes are deployed. The higher a position is in the managerial hierarchy, the greater are its scope (number of units managed) and scale (complexity, diversity, and ambiguity). For this reason, success at one level of management is no guarantee of success at the next level, and each transition to the next level can be a struggle initially. The transition from operational to strategic leader is considered particularly difficult; it is not just a step up in scope and scale but a step beyond, into a different kind of responsibility. In the worldwide leader study, more than half (52 percent) of leaders rated the transition to strategic leader difficult or very difficult compared to only 39 percent who rated the transition to operational leader this way (Howard & Wellins, 2008).

Thus, assessment designs need to represent the appropriate level in the managerial hierarchy; a one-size-fits-all management assessment process will be inadequate.

Executive positions entail not just more accountability than those lower in the hierarchy but more visibility, which increases stress. In fact, a common assessment simulation for executives is a media interview, where leaders are challenged to explain and defend the foibles of their organizations. Practitioners must consider how to integrate the more stressful nature of executive work into assessment design and implementation.

A variety of contextual influences make each executive role unique. The organization's circumstances (for example, a crisis, start-up, turnaround, or focus on growth) at the time when selection decisions are made define the particular accountabilities the executive will have. Assessments should be tailored to the organization's culture and business situation, or their outcome will not fully satisfy organizational requirements. Moreover, executives must fit with the executive team. This carries inherent tensions, for executives must represent their divisions or functions as well as participate in organizationwide strategy and decision making.

Assessing Executives Compared to Other Leaders

Because of the nature of the candidate population and their roles, executive assessment differs from that for lower-level managers. Table 13.1 summarizes some key factors that affect the assessment process at each level.

The priorities for executive assessment should be driven by business strategy. Although strategy development might be the role of only the top tier of executives, managers at various levels are responsible for its execution, which is often a make-or-break factor in their success. Making the right things happen requires an ability to communicate and collaborate with key players across the organizational spectrum. This is why the notion of fit for an executive goes beyond suitability to the job and compatibility with the organization culture. Executives must have the experience and skills to carry out the organization's strategy (for example, to turn around a flailing organization) and be able to collaborate effectively with other members of the executive team as well as the board of directors while doing so.

Table 13.1. Factors Distinguishing Assessment
of Managers by Level

	Lower Level	*Midlevel*	*Executives*
Focus of role	Functional	Operational	Strategic
Assessment priorities	Job driven	Mixed	Business-strategy driven
Fit	Job, organization culture	Job or role, organization culture	Role, organization culture, executive team, board
Candidate sources: external	College campus, Web	Web, executive search	Executive search
Candidate sources: internal	Frontline workers, individual contributors	Lower-level leaders, succession pools	Succession pools
Selection decision makers	Line management with HR leadership	Line management with HR partnership	Board of directors, CEO, executive teams
Assessment approach	High-tech, structured, fast	Mixed	High touch, flexible, slow
Importance of stakeholder input in assessment design	Low	Moderate	High
Importance of pre- and post-assessment communication	Moderate	High	Very high

Whereas selection of candidates at lower levels might lend itself to a multiple-hurdle paradigm, dropping candidates with each sequential step, executive selection is more of a holistic, dynamic process where synthesis is more important than cutoffs.

Because executive selection is a high-stakes decision, it needs to be informed not just by accurate information but by nuanced insight to interpret the data within the context of executive challenges (Smith & Howard, 2009).

Lower-level managers are often selected using structured, technology-driven methods that have the needed efficiency to address large numbers of candidates. However, executives make up a smaller, more elite candidate pool. Practitioners need to use flexible methods that can accommodate their schedules and sense of importance.

Individual Assessment Tools

Executive assessment can take advantage of many classic evaluation techniques, such as tests, biographical data, and assessment centers. However, the applications of those techniques must fit with the variety of circumstances illustrated in Table 13.1. This section describes tools or methods that might be considered and gives their advantages and disadvantages for assessing executives.

Types of Assessment Tools

Assessment tools can be arrayed across a continuum that ranges from signs of behavior (predispositions to act in a certain way, as from a personality test scale of extraversion) to samples of behavior (demonstrations of complex behaviors, like coaching a direct report) (Wernimont & Campbell, 1968). Table 13.2 provides examples of executive and managerial assessment methods that take three positions along that continuum from signs (inferences about behavior) to samples (demonstrations of behavior).

Inferences are made about how people will behave in leadership situations from their answers to tests (which have correct and incorrect answers), inventories of their personal qualities or beliefs, or other techniques. These methods are typically closed-ended (multiple choice). They answer the question, "Who am I?" and by inference suggest, "What I might do." For example, a test might identify a leader as "conscientious" or "smart" and then be used to infer that this person can make challenging managerial or executive decisions.

Table 13.2. Executive and Managerial Assessment Methods

Inferences about Behavior	Descriptions of Behavior	Demonstrations of Behavior
• Cognitive tests • Situational judgment tests • Personality inventories • Integrity tests • Leadership questionnaires • Motivational fit questionnaires • Projective techniques	• Biographical data • Career achievement records • Reference checks • Interviews • Multisource ratings	• Administrative simulations (in-basket, planning, fact finding, analysis) • Interactive simulations (interaction role play, media interview, group discussion, business game)

Source: Adapted from Howard (2006).

Descriptions of knowledge or experience are expressed in written or oral form. These include factual information about the candidates' backgrounds as well as perspectives on their past behavior. These methods answer the questions, "What have I done?" and "What do I know?" For example, a biographical data form might describe a candidate as experienced in hospital administration.

Demonstrations of leader behaviors are elicited from work samples and simulations. These methods answer the question, "What can I do?" For example, a candidate to head a hospital might demonstrate in a simulated interaction with a physician (a role player) that he or she can gain the physician's cooperation to cut hospital costs. Demonstrations of behavior are always open-ended (free response).

Criteria for Selection of Assessment Tools

Organizations should consider several criteria when evaluating assessment methods. Some of these criteria are more important for selection and others for development.

Relevance

The most important question is whether a proposed method measures what is needed to be successful in the executive role. The assessment method must produce evidence that will help decision makers understand how the candidate will perform in the major aspects of an assignment. This is important not only for selecting the best-qualified candidate for a given position, but also for identifying the most important competencies or skills that need to be developed to enhance success in a current or future position.

Traditional concurrent or predictive validation requires measuring executives' job performance. This is fraught with difficulties, as discussed later in this chapter. Thus, there is very little evidence of criterion-related validity for any tools used to select executives. More typical is the use of a content validation strategy, whereby the competencies required for success in the executive role are mapped to competencies measured by the selection tools.

Informing Individual Development

Whether an assessment method produces information on changeable qualities or skills is a critical criterion for an assessment conducted to guide development. But even when assessments are aimed at selection, executives expect, and may even demand, feedback that they can use for their personal development.

Demonstrations of behavior provide the most useful information for individual development. Simulations usually elicit skills that can be improved, and feedback based on their actual behavior helps managers see and accept where their performance was effective or fell short. Tests and inventories that measure relatively hardwired characteristics, such as intelligence and personality traits, provide the least useful information for development, although executives can benefit from instruction on how to leverage their strengths and compensate for their potential derailing characteristics.

Acceptance

Practitioners who deploy assessments for managerial and executive populations need to be concerned with how participants and users of assessment data perceive the process. Without face validity, assessment processes are not sustainable in most organizations.

Whether the assessment is used for selection or development, candidates want to feel that their true skills, abilities, and potential are being evaluated and that going through the process will be worth their time and effort. With qualified executives scarce, organizations are particularly sensitive to negative reactions to the evaluation process for fear that good candidates might withdraw from the competition. Candidate acceptance is generally highest with descriptions of behavior, such as interviews, and biographical data, and lowest with inference-making tools that are less well understood.

Legal Defensibility

Civil rights legislation and subsequent court cases have emphasized the importance of equal opportunity and the need for selection methods to be unbiased. Although formal charges of bias have been infrequent at the executive level, it is essential for candidates at any level to feel that evaluations of their capabilities are fair and unbiased. Given the need for buy-in at the executive level, this requirement takes on additional import.

Efficiency

Assessment methods that cost less and can be administered quickly and easily are naturally favored by organizations. Closed-ended tools lend themselves to computer scoring and are more efficient. Thus, they are often favored for selection at lower levels of management, where candidate pools are large.

Organizations are much more tolerant of thorough, more expensive procedures for senior managers, where the payoff is clearly worth the investment. Even here, volume raises the demand for efficiency. For example, assessment for development in current positions might be open to all managers and executives as much to motivate their commitment to the organization as to develop their capabilities. In these cases, multisource feedback questionnaires might substitute for more expensive simulations, which are reserved for high-potential candidates who are being developed to move up the hierarchy.

Efficiency cannot be ignored when assessments are deployed for high-level talent because organizations compare prices among competitive vendors. Thus, assessment centers, even at the executive level, are becoming increasingly dependent on computer technology for administration and other purposes. Electronic in-baskets, for example, not only save time and costs but better represent what leaders do today (Howard, 2006).

Using Assessment Tools with Executives and Managers

The individual tools listed in Table 13.2 have unique advantages and disadvantages for the assessment of executives and managers. This section highlights particular strengths and shortcomings, which are summarized in Table 13.3.

Table 13.3. Pros and Cons of Assessment Methods for Executives and Managers

	Pros	*Cons*
Inferences about behavior		
• Cognitive tests	• Help determine high potential in early career	• High adverse impact; low acceptance by executives
• Situational judgment tests	• More face validity than cognitive tests	• Executive situations too complex for useful items
• Personality measures	• Important to consider enablers and derailers given the stress and visibility of top jobs	• Might be misleading if executives cover deficiencies with well-developed skills
• Integrity tests	• Might reassure organizations with ethical concerns	• Measures not well established for senior managers
• Leadership questionnaires	• Focus specifically on leader characteristics and potential	• Some tests not validated; some useful for development
• Motivational fit questionnaires	• Can help determine fit of external candidates	• Usually too general to capture the nuances of executive roles
• Projective techniques	• Identify underlying motivations, such as the motivation to manage	• Require a trained scorer, challenging efficiency

	Pros	*Cons*
Descriptions of behavior		
• Biographical data	• A screen for needed experience and knowledge	• Scored forms too general for higher-level executives; data need elaboration
• Reference checks	• Small but significant correlations with job performance	• Many organizations reluctant to provide very meaningful data
• Career achievement records	• Give candidates a voice in restructuring situations; seen as fairer than many performance evaluations	• Time-consuming and costly to create and score; difficult to verify behaviors
• Interviews	• Descriptions of past behavior can capture nuances of executive jobs; can be tied to important competencies	• Time-consuming; ratings can be influenced by executives' social and communication skills
• Multisource ratings	• Useful sources of information about executives' reputations to guide development in current role	• Raters lack training and skills of assessors; different points of view can be confusing. Poor for selection or mixed use: ratings might not be relevant to future jobs, and raters might have goals other than accuracy
Demonstrations of behavior		
• Simulations	• Successfully predict later managerial performance. Live behavior requires no speculation or opportunities to fake and candidates accept it well. Can be directed at future jobs or challenges and provide good fodder for feedback.	• Labor intensive and expensive; need to check regularly for interrater reliability

Cognitive Tests

Cognitive measures are especially useful for culling out high-potential leaders early in their careers. Ability to learn is essential for mastering the increasing complexity encountered with each step up the management ladder; research has shown that cognitive tests are more predictive for complex jobs than simple ones. However, legal defensibility is always a challenge with cognitive tests because they have greater adverse impact than other measures. As managers rise in the hierarchy, average cognitive test scores also rise, although there is only a modest restriction of range that can reduce the predictive value of these tests (Ones & Dilchert, 2009). Cognitive tests are highly efficient but less acceptable to candidates, particularly since what they measure is not amenable to short-term development.

Situational Judgment Tests

Tests that require making judgments about how to handle specific management situations appear more job relevant to candidates than general cognitive tests. However, it is difficult to depict executive situations in a simple way because a host of issues and contexts must usually be considered. Thus, these tests are more suitable for lower levels of management where situations are less complex.

Personality Inventories

Because the stress and visibility of high-level positions are likely to draw out a person's underlying nature, it is important to identify the characteristics that could enable and derail executive performance. However, the dark side of personality can coexist with well-developed social skills and might never emerge. Thus, practitioners should be careful not to overrely on personality measures that make inferences about what might mar an executive's performance.

Personality inventories show a serious reduction in score variability for executives compared to the general population, which can reduce their predictive value (Ones & Dilchert, 2009). Moreover, self-report inventories are subject to faking, although the extent to which this happens remains controversial. However, the inventories are easily administered and can engage executives' interest and acceptance if they are interpreted in a business context. If these tools are used for development purposes, candidates should be coached around understanding and coping with their fundamental nature, not trying to change it.

Integrity Tests

When constructed as offshoots of personality questionnaires, integrity tests might appeal to organizations with ethical concerns. There is evidence for the validity of integrity testing for lower-level employees, where it has been related to counterproductive behaviors such as theft, illegal activities, violence, and absenteeism. However, it is questionable whether these results generalize to senior leadership levels. Moreover, the content of the overt type of integrity test could easily insult savvy executives. The importance of leader integrity and ethical leadership has surfaced with recent scandals, but these constructs have not yet become well established in psychometric measures.

Leadership Questionnaires

These measures focus specifically on leader characteristics and potential, which help establish their relevance. Older tests, such as the Leader Behavior Description Questionnaire, did not report criterion-related validity. Better-established instruments, such as the Bass Multifactor Leadership Questionnaire, are most often applied to help executives understand their leadership styles and encourage their development.

Motivational Fit Questionnaires

By querying candidates about their likes and dislikes and comparing them to opportunities in the position (such as amount of autonomy or need to tend to details), these tools identify whether a candidate will be personally satisfied with the role and organization. These measures can be useful for judging how external candidates will fit in, particularly if followed up in an interview. However, they are unlikely to be specific enough for understanding how an executive will fit with an organization's culture or the nuances of a particular role within an existing leadership team.

Projective Techniques

These tools provide ambiguous stimuli to which candidates' responses supposedly reveal their underlying motivations. These techniques rest on the assumption that personality structure influences the way individuals interpret their environment. Although longitudinal research has shown limited usefulness for projective exercises in predicting long-term managerial success (Howard & Bray, 1988), multiple studies have validated the Miner Sentence Completion Scale, which measures motivation to manage (Miner, 1993).

Projective tests have difficulty meeting the efficiency criterion because the level of inference is so great that they require a trained scorer. Moreover, executives are likely to object to these tests' obscure nature and lack of usefulness for development.

Biographical Data

Biographical experiences, such as academic achievements and early leadership roles, relate to later performance as a leader, although executives might struggle to see the relevance of such historical information. Quantified descriptions of past activities and accomplishments can be efficient screening tools for those hired externally, but these are likely to be too general and impersonal for higher-level executives. Résumés can also provide basic information about experiences, although résumé inflation is a frequent problem. In general, biographical information needs to be explained and explored by other means (an interview, for example) to be useful for executive selection and development.

Reference Checks

Research has shown small but significant correlations between reference check data and job performance, but references often have limited value. Bosses and colleagues, whose loyalty is to the candidate and not the hiring organization, usually praise generously and criticize sparingly (Howard, 2001). On top of that, problems with lawsuits in the United States have made many organizations reluctant to provide very meaningful data. This undercuts the efficiency of reference checks, as many calls might have to be made to collect useful data.

Career Achievement Records

Also known as the behavioral consistency method, these records capture key experiences that demonstrate effective performance of competencies. They are typically completed by candidates and reviewed by managers. These methods can be especially useful in mergers and acquisitions or realignments, where selecting and placing leaders in a new organizational structure are important. They have the advantages of giving candidates a voice in decisions and being seen as fairer than most regular performance evaluations. It is also easy to establish the relevance of these tools because they are built around competencies identified as important to success.

Career achievement records are not very efficient; they are time-consuming and costly to create and score. Another problem is that verifying documented behaviors can be difficult, which casts suspicion on their accuracy.

Interviews

Interviews structured around key competencies can readily demonstrate their relevance to executive positions. Those that ask for descriptions of past behavior have been shown as more valid for jobs with high complexity, such as executive positions, than interviews that pose hypothetical questions about what a candidate would do. This difference likely occurs because it is difficult to represent the necessary details of a complex job using a few specific and standardized hypothetical questions (Huthcutt, Conway, Roth, & Klehe, 2004).

Interviews are not a very efficient selection method because they require time from other executives for both interviewing and pooling their judgments about candidates. One threat to interview validity is that executive candidates' social and communication skills tend to be high and can unduly influence interviewers. Interviewers should receive training and skill practice in effective interviewing and data evaluation techniques in order to avoid common rater errors and make sound judgments. It might be tempting to shortcut interviewer training in order to improve efficiency, but this jeopardizes the quality and long-term value of the assessment process.

Multisource Ratings

Ratings by those able to observe executives' behavior can provide useful information about their reputations. Multisource ratings are most relevant for development within the current position; properly chosen raters have observed on-the-job behavior, and their motivation to fill in ratings accurately should not be compromised. With the appropriate software, electronic multisource ratings can be relatively efficient.

We do not recommend multisource ratings for selection or promotion, however, because observers might have other motivations that would compromise their providing accurate information. Multisource ratings that can influence selection decisions can strain interpersonal relationships among raters and targets, causing damage that far outweighs their usefulness. In addition, they might be vulnerable to legal challenges because evaluating or controlling for rater bias among minimally trained or unknown raters is very difficult.

Organizations might be tempted to leverage the same multirater process for both selection and promotion and for development as a means of driving efficiency. These mixed-use applications of multirater assessment should be avoided because of the different response biases that underpin each use. For selection, raters understand the high-stakes nature of the data and generally operate with a positive bias. Developmental uses of multirater tools generally work best when raters have a neutral or negative bias; raters must be comfortable providing low ratings. Mixed-use applications almost always contain a positive bias, which is all but useless for developmental diagnosis.

A problem with multisource ratings, even if used solely for development, is that the varying points of view from different sources can confuse candidates and make them wonder about the method's accuracy. In addition, raters lack the training and practice of experienced assessors and often struggle to differentiate among competencies. One solution is to use a "live 360," where observers offer examples of the candidate's behavior that can be weighed and evaluated.

Simulations

Assessment centers, which rely on simulations, have a long track record of successfully predicting managerial performance.

Simulations are based on competencies central to success in a managerial or executive role; they are readily accepted by candidates and have had few legal challenges. At the executive level, simulations might include strategic planning and analysis exercises, decision challenges, visioning exercises, and role plays with various characters in an executive's internal or external network, including members of the media. An executive assessment center is typically organized around one role in a fictional organization (a "day in the life" design), which gives participants the opportunity to experience many of the conflicts and complexities of executive life.

Simulations have many advantages for executive assessment. They elicit live behavior, so there is no need to speculate about what a candidate might do, and the opportunities to fake are limited. Exercises can be directed at current challenges or future roles. Usually aimed at competencies that can be developed, simulations provide good fodder for feedback.

The major drawback to simulations is that they can be labor intensive and thus expensive. Logistics can also be difficult with busy executive schedules, as when the organization wants to hold a group discussion with several candidates at once. It is also necessary to regularly check for interrater reliability among assessors.

Designing and Implementing Assessment Systems

Given that each type of tool brings different advantages and disadvantages, most selection and development systems use more than one technique to get a well-rounded view of each participant. Therefore, creating and implementing an assessment system should follow a careful strategy.

Designing Assessment Systems

Executive selection and development should be viewed as a core business decision central to strategy execution (Smith & Howard, 2009). To support business strategy, assessments must begin and conclude with the bottom-line business challenges that are top-of-mind for executive decision makers. Boards and senior executives want to know if candidates are ready for specific business challenges, such as entering a new market, enhancing process efficiency, or implementing a new global segmentation strategy. Because business challenges are too abstract to be primary measurement targets, they need to be linked to specific human capabilities that will help executives meet those challenges.

The assessment design process thus requires an understanding of the talent implications of the organization's strategic and cultural priorities. This allows development of a comprehensive profile of the characteristics that will be most important to executives' success. This profile allows the practitioner to select or develop assessment tools and processes that provide relevant information that will resonate with stakeholders.

The success profile for an executive should include information about what the candidate has done (experience), knows (knowledge), and can do (competencies) and who the person is (personal attributes, including intelligence, personality, and other qualities). The three types of assessment methods along the continuum of signs to samples contribute to different segments of this success profile. Moreover, each type has distinct advantages and disadvantages for executive selection and development. Table 13.4 summarizes how the three types of assessment tools compare when stacked against the primary criteria for executive selection and development.

Each type of tool has a particular strength for assessing managers and executives. Tests that make inferences about behavior

Table 13.4. Strengths and Weaknesses of Categories of Assessment Methods

Tool Category	Relevance	Inform Development	Acceptance	Low Adverse Impact	Efficiency
Inferences about behavior	Strong	Mixed	Very weak	Mixed	Very strong
Descriptions of behavior	Strong	Strong	Very strong	Strong	Weak
Demonstrations of behavior	Strong	Very strong	Strong	Strong	Weak

are the most efficient, descriptions of behavior are the most widely accepted, and demonstrations of behavior provide the best information to guide competency development. On the negative side, tests have the least user acceptance (including considerable adverse impact among cognitive tests) and limited value for development because they typically measure fundamental characteristics that are unlikely to change significantly or easily. Descriptions of behavior are tied to past or current positions and are not very useful for predicting success in new or different roles. Demonstrations of behavior can be more costly than most other methods.

Creating an assessment system is thus a balancing act, bringing together elements from each type of measurement method to provide optimal coverage of the success profile. Practitioners must be able to envision how results from the different methods can be interpreted through the lens of the business strategy. That is, bits of information about an individual executive must be assembled like pieces of a jigsaw puzzle and presented to higher management as a picture of how he or she will carry out key business priorities.

Stakeholder Analysis

Involvement of stakeholders in both the design and implementation of managerial or executive assessment is central to its short-term success and long-term sustainability. Stakeholders are people with a direct connection to the design, implementation, or use of the assessment. Their positions and job titles will depend on the organization's particular structure.

Where the assessment is used for selection, the hiring manager is an obvious stakeholder, as are candidates, particularly if they are internal. A local HR person is also intimately involved, and there might be a corporate center of excellence with a stake in designing and defending the assessment method. Although there is a primary decision maker, he or she usually gets advice or consensus from a larger group. For top positions, that might be the board of directors or the chair of the board. For other executives or managers, people who will be dependent on the applicant if hired can be consulted and might even get to interview candidates. For example, applicants for a top hospital administrator position might be interviewed by the heads of the various departments.

Stakeholders for an assessment used to diagnose development needs are usually different from those involved in selection. Participants and their leaders or coaches are key stakeholders. Development sponsors are less likely to be local HR generalists and more likely to be specialists in a training and development function or center of excellence. There also might be corporate sponsors or a talent management advisory committee.

Practitioners should complete a stakeholder analysis in the project planning stage and then involve key stakeholders or their representatives in the assessment process to the maximum extent practical. Any person or group that will have a significant role in the design, deployment, or use of the assessments in question should be identified. An effective analysis should consider the following questions:

- Whose participation is required to ensure the effective design of the assessment process?
- Who must be involved to deploy the assessment process successfully?
- Who has the authority to approve or provide the resources needed to design and deploy the assessment?
- Who will receive or use the data resulting from the assessment?
- Who will determine whether the assessment process is successful? And what criteria will they use to determine success?

The stakeholder analysis should also lead to an appreciation for stakeholders' needs and how they will evaluate whether their needs have been met by the assessment program. These concerns guide effective implementation and measurement tactics.

Implementing Assessment Programs

The implementation and management of assessment programs for managers and executives must address the special circumstances of the senior leader population noted earlier.

Communications

Significant attention needs to be paid to communication with participants and stakeholders throughout all phases of program design and implementation. A summary of communication best practices is provided in Table 13.5.

Table 13.5. Stakeholder Communications for Managerial and Executive Assessment

Stakeholder Communication Practices

Design

Define assessment targets	• Involve participant representatives and important stakeholders in definition of characteristics to be assessed (for example, a success profile).
Develop and select assessment tools	• Involve participant representatives and other stakeholders in design or selection of specific assessment tools and processes.

Implementation

Develop implementation time lines and schedules	• Consider time constraints and scheduling challenges associated with executives when designing assessment processes or scheduling participants. Provide adequate lead times and completion times that consider other leadership or executive job requirements such as travel or quarter-end closing; appreciate difficulties associated with synchronizing calendars (as may be required for group activities).
Preassessment communications	• Provide business-focused rationale for choice or configuration of assessment tools to all participants and stakeholders.
	• Provide clear and accurate instructions to enable participants to prepare for and complete all assessment processes.
	• Provide information on time schedules, travel, and other logistics.

(Continued)

Table 13.5. Stakeholder Communications for Managerial and Executive Assessment *(Continued)*

	Stakeholder Communication Practices
Preassessment communications *(Continued)*	• Provide accurate information about how assessment data will be used, who has access to data, and data storage and life span expectations. Keep these commitments without fail.
Post-assessment communications	• Provide all participants with feedback on assessment performance and implications for their performance in current and future roles. (Note: Different processes may provide varying degrees of information, but all executive participants will want some level of feedback.)
	• Provide participants and stakeholders with information related to individual and organizational outcomes resulting from assessment, such as the value of the program. Effective assessment program evaluations enable existing processes to be sustained and build support for future assessment applications.
	• Share success stories with potential participants and stakeholders.

Communications must focus at a minimum on the overall objectives of the program and the mechanics important to participants. They should also clearly delineate who will receive results and the form in which they will be shared, such as detailed results or summaries. To ensure trust, there must be strict adherence to these stated policies once the assessment program begins.

Staffing Assessment Programs

Another important implementation consideration, often overlooked, is development of the staff needed to support the assessment process. The *Standards for Educational and Psychological Testing* (American Educational Research Association, American Psychological Association, & National Council on Measurement in Education, 1999) provides specific guidelines for organizations using assessment processes. It is impossible to comply with these guidelines without training and equipping staff members involved in all phases of the assessment program design and implementation. Important staffing issues implied by the *Standards* include the following:

- Do those charged with administering assessment processes have the proper training and skills?
- Are assessors, interviewers, or other evaluators trained and managed to perform to a certain standard of reliability?
- Are the end users (assessment program managers, participants, and other stakeholders) equipped to interpret the information provided and use it effectively for selection and development decision making?

Depending on the nature of the assessment processes, staff training can be substantial. For example, assessors in assessment centers typically receive several days of training and complete an apprenticeship before being certified. Formal training and certification may also be required to interpret standardized assessment tools such as personality inventories.

Assessment process managers must have the skills to ensure that stakeholders receive information in ways that help them use it effectively. For selection, this often means that an assessment expert formally presents the data to decision makers. This meeting includes a review of all of the individual assessment results as well as a holistic interpretation and discussion of what the individual data points suggest about a manager's or executive's potential to address business challenges successfully.

For initiatives geared toward development, assessment process managers must ensure that there are trained coaches or feedback providers who can review assessment results with participants and other stakeholders such as participants' managers and help them extract meaning from the data. Effective coaches also help participants prepare an actionable development plan that relates to business, role, and personal development needs. Thus, coaches need training on the assessment processes as well as on conducting effective feedback discussions.

A key determinant of the usefulness of assessment for development is whether participants are motivated to follow through on their development plans. A best practice is to have a coach or another accountable person, such as an HR representative or the participant's manager, follow up with assessment participants on a regular basis regarding their progress on their development plans.

Case Studies

The following cases studies typify sound managerial and executive assessment practices in use within organizations. Although they embody many of the recommendations discussed in this chapter, they do not necessarily represent best practices in all respects. Unfortunately, the practical realities of organizations do not always permit implementation of all the elements of a best practice selection or development system. Nevertheless, it is still possible to extract meaningful data in both circumstances.

Assessment for Executive Development

In order to build greater senior leadership bench strength, a global media/publishing company deployed an executive-level diagnostic assessment to support development action planning among the company's executive corps. The large population subject to the program necessitated that simple, low-cost processes be employed, as opposed to more comprehensive assessment techniques—an example of organizational realities that can sometimes constrain optimal choices among the possible elements of talent management systems. Thus, the program included multisource ratings and several personality inventories.

The multisource ratings were built around an executive competency model that had been in use for several years and was well accepted by leaders throughout the organization. The competencies assessed were important for success in a broad range of senior leadership positions. The personality inventories provided insights into the ease or difficulty that might be associated with the development of competencies viewed as gaps. These inventories, proprietary to a third-party consulting organization, were built around well-established executive enabler and derailer constructs.

During the design process, program managers engaged with stakeholders to validate the relevance of the existing competency profile and define current business challenges. This enabled designers and coaches to interpret results from the individual assessment tools in a holistic way that related to the role requirements of the executives instead of simply providing competency scores and personality dimension scores.

Great care was taken during the design of the program to make clear to all concerned the success factors that would be evaluated and the tools that would be used. The director of the global executive development function championed these efforts, which involved focused communications to the executives subject to the program, as well as to the HR leaders who supported the various business segments or units where the executive participants worked. The communications provided detailed information about the assessment tools, the mechanics for their completion, access to results, and intended uses for the results.

Significantly, ownership of assessment data resided with the participants; other stakeholders, such as HR professionals and leaders of participants, received summaries of multirater data only. Participants were obligated to provide HR and their leader with a development action plan, but they had wide latitude regarding how the actual assessment data were shared. In addition, participants were provided with a coach (a representative from a third-party consulting firm) to review the detailed assessment results and support preparation of a draft development plan. Coaches also facilitated a meeting with the assessment participants, their leader, and an HR representative to review the draft development plan and secure commitments

(Continued)

Assessment for Executive Development *(Continued)*

from each stakeholder group to ensure that the plan would be activated successfully.

The assessment program management staff prepared development planning guides to simplify and make more consistent the efforts of the individual coaches. These electronic guides enabled coaches and participants to easily identify possible action steps in response to the assessment data. They recommended training courses, readings, and on-the-job work activities that could be used to support the development of each competency covered by the program. Although the guides were not intended as a comprehensive listing of all possible development actions, they provided an important discussion starter and point of reference for corporate-supported training activities.

This process has been operating continuously within the organization for several years with good success. Participants report considerable satisfaction with the process, and compliance with development planning and plan execution requirements is high. As the program grew in popularity, HR representatives were trained to act as coaches to supplement those from the third party and enable the program to be expanded. All prospective internal coaches must complete a two-day feedback and coaching workshop that involves concept training and extensive skill practice—a requirement that underscores the importance of the coach role and appreciation for the skills involved.

Assessment for Executive Selection

A global hospitality company recently reorganized its national sales and marketing functions. Prior to the reorganization, sales and marketing events were highly regionalized and decentralized: sales channels only focused on a subset of the firm's brands, although many of the properties were located in close proximity to one another. The reorganization centralized many sales and marketing functions, consolidated sales call centers, and increased the coordination of sales assets focused on specific brands. As a result, leadership roles were changed dramatically, with leaders assuming greater responsibility for coordination of sales and marketing efforts across a wide brand portfolio within their respective geographical areas.

The leadership role changes were viewed as so significant that the organization decided to use an open posting process to fill all of the restructured leader jobs within the revised sales organization. Posting was open to all employees. After evaluating and making decisions about the suitability of the internal candidates, the organization sought additional candidates from outside the organization to fill the remaining vacancies. However, internal candidates filled the vast majority of the vacancies.

HR team members supporting this change effort readily understood that assessment could be used to predict a candidate's success in the new sales organization. They collaborated with the senior executives who were designing the new structure to define a success profile for each new leadership role. The success profile identified business challenges and leadership imperatives that leaders would face in their new roles. It also defined the related work experience, technical knowledge, behavioral competencies, and personal attributes associated with success in these roles. Current leaders were also engaged in the success profiling effort using interviews and focus groups to establish the accuracy of the success profiles and ensure that the profiles would be readily accepted by all stakeholders once developed.

Assessment processes were selected or designed to align with the success profile. The specific assessment tools used for any one position were tailored to the appropriate job level, but all senior leader assessments followed this set of processes:

- *Career achievement profile*, an online form that allowed candidates to provide career history and information about experiences that indicated the presence of critical behavioral competencies.

(Continued)

Assessment for Executive Selection *(Continued)*

- *Behavior-based interview*, which allowed candidates to describe examples from their previous work experience that related to competencies and motivations associated with success in the redesigned jobs. Senior manager teams conducted the interviews.
- *Behavioral simulations*, designed to mirror the business analysis, leadership, and collaborative challenges associated with senior leader roles within the new structure. A consulting firm conducted the behavioral simulations, which were in a "day in the life" assessment center format.
- *Personality inventories*, completed online and used to assess executive enabler and derailer attributes.

Once the processes were developed, the assessment team communicated with senior stakeholders and current sales leaders, who would be subject to the assessments if they applied for the posted jobs, through a series of e-mails, Webinars, and manager-led communication events. Communications stressed the origins of the assessment tools, the purpose of the tools, preparation for participation, data sharing, and feedback. Following a pilot assessment, senior leaders within the organization created a video covering many of these same topics along with the pilot's success story. A significant part of this video communication was the senior executives' personal commitment to the effective deployment of the process and use of the resulting data.

Following completion of all assessment activities, the consulting firm consolidated the data and prepared a presentation covering each assessment participant. The presentation was delivered in a collaborative meeting with senior leaders of the sales function, including the national head of sales and key staff members involved in the decision. The review outlined each participant's performance across all factors assessed, summarized trends, and rated the likelihood that each participant would be able to successfully perform against the business challenges and leadership imperatives that framed the success

---

profile. Selection decisions were based on all of the assessment data, with heavy emphasis placed on results from the interviews and simulations.

Once selection decisions were made and announced, assessment participants received their full assessment results and had access to a third-party executive coach to review the results and help them prepare a development plan. For participants selected for a new role within the redefined organization, these development plans took on the character of transition plans. If participants were not selected, their development plans focused on helping them build skills that would enable them to compete successfully for future opportunities within the parent organization.

The success of the assessment process was evidenced by the pilot restructuring project, which encompassed one geographical region. Senior leaders reported a high degree of confidence that selectees were equipped for success (the reorganization is in progress so more objective measures are not yet available). They also expressed satisfaction with the perceived fairness of the process and the accuracy and comprehensiveness of the development and transition information. These perceptions were captured and shared throughout the organization by the video. Participants also indicated that they perceived the process as highly relevant and fair, particularly in comparison to previous restructuring and internal selection efforts.

Evaluation of Assessment Programs

Evidence for the criterion-related validity of executive assessment procedures used for selection is seriously wanting. Book chapter authors consistently lament the lack of evidence, and the latest *Annual Review of Psychology* chapter on personnel selection (Sackett & Lievens, 2008) did not even include the topic because no empirical research was found (Hollenbeck, 2009).

In the executive arena, several practical problems are associated with the classic validity paradigm in which assessment scores from selection are correlated with performance on the job. One problem is sample size; no more than a handful of executives might be evaluated at one time. A synthetic validity paradigm is a possible workaround for this problem, although variations across organizational settings can pose serious complications.

Perhaps the most imposing problem is the difficulty of gathering appropriate criterion data. We have personally been frustrated time and again trying to get organizations to agree to have higher-level executives rate the performance of direct reports who were assessed a year or two earlier. Executive clients who are satisfied with the assessment experience do not feel they need further proof of its value. "Don't you know that it works?" they often ask. Even if we were successful in gathering performance data, it might be argued that standardized performance evaluations will not capture the uniqueness of managerial positions (Hollenbeck, 2009).

Evaluations of assessment programs for development encounter similar measurement challenges. Here the issues are less related to the validity of the tools than to the value of the assessment-guided development undertaken—a slippery proposition for measurement. Many development programs have been introduced with much fanfare, only to die a slow death as other priorities compete for resources.

We believe that some of these problems can be overcome by introducing measurement as essential to the managerial and executive assessment process from the very beginning of the initiative. Assessment program managers must have a strong measurement plan in place—and yielding relevant metrics—to sustain the momentum of any significant assessment initiative.

A lack of convincing proof that assessment at the executive and manager level leads to desired organizational outcomes is an obstacle to getting I-O psychologists to the table where decisions about executive careers are made. We do not believe that this is because we have our selection priorities backward—that the order of emphasis should be character, competence, and then competencies rather than vice versa, as Hollenbeck (2009) argued. Rather, we support the position that the determination of assessment priorities, as well as the evaluation of the assessment's effectiveness, must be guided by the organization's business challenges (Smith & Howard, 2009). Practitioners need to emphasize that the achievement of the business challenges that are driving the assessment is what the evaluation is meant to determine, not just whether the assessment "works." This requires a much broader approach to evaluation than the classic validity model (see Chapter Twenty-Three).

Although leadership is a collective phenomenon, meta-analytic studies show that researchers have focused more on perceptions of individual leader effectiveness ("approval" ratings) than on how they influence the teams they are responsible for. But attributes that help managers gain approval and advance their careers do not necessarily help the organization prosper (Kaiser, Hogan, & Craig, 2008).

Our preferred evaluation model, described in the following sections, makes a distinction between leaders' individual performance and their influence on others. It also differentiates outcomes that reflect the behavior, attitudes, and performance of leaders and their teams (the organization's talent) from results that indicate an impact on the organization itself (the organization's business).

Evaluation Stages

Evaluations of the value of executive assessment should target four areas: the program's focus, the process of executing the program, the workforce outcomes, and the program's eventual impact on organizational performance. These areas are dependent on one another and occur in a time sequence in the order presented above. Although these areas can be meaningfully addressed for any major talent management initiative at any organizational level, they are particularly relevant to managerial and executive assessment, given its proximity to organization-level challenges and solutions.

The key evaluation challenges in each measurement stage and the types of metrics to evaluate them are shown in Figure 13.1. The graduated shading signifies that the influence of a program diminishes with each step along the continuum as other factors come into play.

Figure 13.1. Measurement Stages and Types of Metrics

INITIATIVE		RESULTS	
FOCUS	PROCESS	OUTCOMES	IMPACT
Did the solution:			
Target critical business needs?	Get delivered in a sustainable way and meet user needs?	Enhance available talent and their contributions?	Advance the business, its customers, and other external stakeholders?
Types of metrics:			
• Needs • Relevance	• Implementation • Execution • Stakeholder reactions	• Behavior/capacity • Attitudes/motivation • Work performance	• Customers/outsiders • Business results • Financial results

Focus

The important evaluation question in the focus stage is whether the program targets critical business needs. A direct link should be made from business challenges to the knowledge, experience, competencies, and personal characteristics critical to executive success, and these in turn form the substance of the selection or development program.

Another key theme in the measurement of focus is relevance. This has been the concern of regulatory bodies—selection procedures must be job relevant—and is typically established for tests by a concurrent validation study with employees already on the job. Because of their expense, assessment centers do not lend themselves to this type of validation. Instead, through a process of content validation, knowledgeable executives confirm that the assessment content fairly and adequately represents the managerial role and that it is aligned with the current business challenges.

Process

The process refers to the implementation of the talent management initiative. The important evaluation question in this stage is whether the program was installed in a sustainable way that met users' immediate needs. Relevant metrics might evaluate whether the assessment adequately differentiated candidates, if higher-level managers supported the process, or if candidates reacted positively to the assessment or feedback experience. For development-focused initiatives, measures could track whether feedback meetings were conducted, useful development plans were prepared, and developmental actions took place.

Outcomes

Outcomes refer to how the process affected the workforce. The key evaluation question is whether the process enhanced the organization's talent and their contributions; it pertains to the executives assessed or developed, as well as the people whom they influence. This stage can include predictive validation, relating individual assessment performance to later job performance. However, it also includes other factors, such as whether an executive's enhanced job performance, due to either selection or development, resulted in different performance or attitudes among his or her direct reports or other colleagues.

Impact

The impact of the assessment on the organization derives from its success in the earlier outcomes. The key evaluation questions focus on how changes in the organization's talent affect the business and its external stakeholders, particularly customers. If business objectives were included in the design—for example, reduced operating costs, new and innovative products, or new strategic external partnerships—the impact measures can evaluate the extent to which organizations or business units achieved these objectives. Broader examples of impact measures might include customer retention or financial indexes.

The Logical Path Method of Measurement

The key to creating a comprehensive measurement plan is to diagram across the four evaluation stages a logical path that traces how the selected or developed executives can be expected to affect organizational performance. Figure 13.2 provides two simple examples of a logical path.

Figure 13.2. Logical Path Examples for Executive Selection and Development

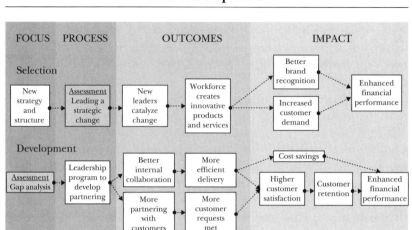

Each box in Figure 13.2 represents an opportunity for measuring the effectiveness of the initiative. An assessment plays differing roles, depending on whether its purpose is selection or diagnosis for development. For selection, the assessment itself is the intervention that should lead to desired outcomes; it is therefore located in the process box. For development, the assessment is a tool for giving focus to the development initiative; it is therefore placed in the focus box. Although the accuracy of the assessment is essential for making the development successful, the realization of the development effort is what brings the desired outcomes.

A traditional predictive validation model for selection (the first example in Figure 13.2) requires a statistically significant correlation between the assessment process (ability to lead a strategic change) and the first outcome box (rating of how well leaders catalyze change on the job). However, the logical path model points the way toward accumulation of a broader array of evidence that leads to business impact. That is, it is not just the performance of the leader that is important, but the leader's influence on others (the workforce under the leader) and how their changed behavior in turn brings positive results for the executive's business unit or the organization at large. This does not, of course, eliminate the need to measure the executive's behavior and actions; however, it takes the onus off the executive's "performance evaluation" by making what the executive does a catalyst in a larger process.

The development model (the second example in Figure 13.2) requires no less attention than the selection model to content validation of the assessment process and ensuring its connection to business priorities. However, in this measurement paradigm, the assessment's role is a gap analysis to make sure that the resulting development program has the appropriate focus. The immediate outcome of the development program should be a change in leader behavior; different leader behavior is achieved by bringing in new leaders in the selection paradigm and through changing current leaders in the development paradigm. Similar to the logical path for selection, behavior change is just the first step in a chain of events that result in a business payoff.

The logical path model still leaves significant challenges for evaluating executive assessment, particularly since so many other factors (for example, acceptance by other executives, relationship with the board, internal and external constraints) can become executives' undoing. These other factors diminish the impact of an executive's behavior, illustrated by the fading background as measurement moves from the focus to the impact areas in the model. However, a careful look at what happens at each step in the logical path between the assessment and business performance can help diagnose many of the barriers to individual executive success and shine important light on the organization's culture. Gathering metrics at each stage of the logical path also avoids leaving an unidentified black box between a selection or development initiative and evidence of business impact, helping to track the causal arrow from executive or managerial assessment to business-level improvements.

Earning—and Keeping—a Seat at the Executive Table

Opportunities for I-O psychologists to support organizations abound in managerial and executive assessment, especially given the high number of executive failures and disappointments. But there are significant risks. Practitioners courageous enough to champion these programs must appreciate the unique characteristics and challenges associated with working at this level and build the skills to accommodate this complex reality.

As we noted at the beginning of this chapter, I-O psychologists have traditionally not had a seat at the executive table where important selection decisions are made. This chapter has provided many guidelines and examples to illustrate how to conduct executive and managerial assessments that will win management acceptance. In conclusion, we want to reinforce what we have presented here by highlighting four important steps that I-O psychologists must take in order to earn and keep a seat at the executive table.

Build a Relationship with Senior Managers

The implementation of managerial and executive assessment programs must take into account the considerable sophistication and position power that both participants and stakeholders possess. Executives must be enlisted as willing partners in the process instead of passive participants, as may be the case with lower-level programs. To facilitate this partnership, the I-O psychologist must build a relationship with senior managers and other key stakeholders.

Executives want advisors who can listen to them and understand how they function in their unique environment. Psychologists can draw on their basic training to meet executives' needs to be heard and understood on a personal level, but psychological training is not enough to meet senior leaders' practical needs. I-O psychologists who can speak executives' language pay them the ultimate sign of respect. For most of us this means becoming bilingual, combining English (or your primary language) with the language of business (Smith & Howard, 2009). Mastery of this second language can be a high goal, but research into the challenges of the organization's industry or reading business publications such as the *Wall Street Journal* can help.

Focus on Business Challenges

Executive and manager assessment should start and end with the business challenges that have created the need for the assessment.

Executive selection and development are not ordered in a vacuum; there is a purpose behind these initiatives that the I-O psychologist must recognize and build on in designing the assessment program and making sense of its results.

The focus on business challenges is an important reason to interpret the findings from various assessment methods holistically. Practitioners need to pull the results together like a jigsaw puzzle, creating a picture of how a participant will tackle the business challenges he or she will face in one or more target positions. Psychologically tuned senior managers might have some interest in how a candidate scored on conscientiousness on a personality inventory or how he or she was rated on decision making in an assessment center. But what most senior managers really want to know is how the candidate would likely approach "opening the new office in Beijing" or "cutting manufacturing costs in Clarksville by 20 percent" and how successful that approach is likely to be under different sets of circumstances.

Connect Assessment Results to Organizational Outcomes

The assessment program, whether created for selection, development, or both, will have the most meaning if it connects what senior leaders do to organizational outcomes (Kaiser et al., 2008). This means going beyond establishing whether the assessment worked to finding out how it contributes to organizational functioning in the long run.

This conceptualization of evaluation research, such as diagrammed in our logical path method, establishes the link between what senior leaders do, how that affects their team, how team performance affects business results, and how business results affect the bottom line. The logical path can also be worked backward; that is, the immediate cause of a key business result (say, customer satisfaction) can be tracked to specific team actions (say, customer-facing work teams), those team actions traced to the behavior of frontline leaders, and frontline leader behavior traced to the actions taken by middle and higher managers. The point is to hypothesize a causal chain of events and then attempt to verify each link in the chain with solid research.

Assessment practitioners must increase their attention to the collection, analysis, and reporting of a chain of metrics that ultimately demonstrates the value of managerial and executive assessment programs. Although measurement challenges persist, there are practical solutions that should engage executive interest. These measurement initiatives need to be made an integral part of program design instead of tacked on as an afterthought, as is so often the case.

Capitalize on Other Opportunities to Add Value

Senior executives will not suffer advisors, coaches, consultants, or program managers who do not possess credible expertise in assessment processes and do not provide immediate value to help them make critical selection and development decisions. Besides being mindful of their own need for preparedness, practitioners must ensure that organizational staff are trained and supported so that they can successfully deploy and sustain the assessment programs.

For I-O psychologists, an initial challenge is to provide a nuanced and insightful interpretation of what the assessment data reveal while avoiding jargon and technical terms. That is, you must find a way to translate your message into language that resonates with senior managers without dumbing it down.

Part of the beauty of a measurement model like the logical path is that it provides many avenues for adding value to the organization. The various links in the model are opportunities to bring in a wide array of I-O research. You can help organizations not just with selecting and developing executives and managers—the front end of the path—but with the various links that follow. These links can be explored using insights from I-O research on leadership, teams, empowerment, organizational climate, social learning processes, and much more. Once you master the steps that get you to the executive table, the depth and breadth of I-O psychology can anchor your seat deep within the organization's foundation.

References

American Educational Research Association, American Psychological Association, & National Council on Measurement in Education

(1999). *Standards for Educational and Psychological Testing.* Retrieved from http://www.apa.org/science/standards.html.

Day, D. V. (2009). Executive selection is a process not a decision. *Industrial and Organizational Psychology: Perspectives on Science and Practice, 2*(2), 159–162.

Governance Focus (2006, April 19). *The high price of executive turnover.* Retrieved from http://governancefocus.blogspot.com/2006/04/high-price-of-executive-turnover.html.

Hogan, J., Hogan, R., & Kaiser, R. B. (in press). Management derailment: Personality assessment and mitigation. In S. Zedeck (Ed.), *American Psychological Association handbook of industrial and organizational psychology.* Washington, DC: American Psychological Association.

Hollenbeck, G. P. (2009). Executive selection—What's right...and what's wrong. *Industrial and Organizational Psychology: Perspectives on Science and Practice, 2*(2), 130–143.

Howard, A. (2001). Identifying, assessing, and selecting senior leaders. In S. J. Zaccaro & R. Klimoski (Eds.), *The nature and context of organizational leadership* (pp. 305–346). San Francisco: Jossey-Bass.

Howard, A. (2006). Best practices in leader selection. In J. A. Conger & R. E. Riggio (Eds.), *The practice of leadership: Developing the next generation of leaders* (pp. 11–40). San Francisco: Jossey-Bass.

Howard, A., & Bray, D. W. (1988). *Managerial lives in transition: Advancing age and changing times.* New York: Guilford Press.

Howard, A., Erker, S., & Bruce, N. (2007). *Selection forecast 2006–2007: Slugging through the war for talent.* Pittsburgh, PA: Development Dimensions International.

Howard, A., & Watt, B. (2008). *Leaders without sea legs: Threats to staying afloat in uncertain times.* Pittsburgh, PA: Development Dimensions International.

Howard, A., & Wellins, R. W. (2008). *Global leadership forecast 2008–2009: Overcoming the shortfalls in developing leaders.* Pittsburgh, PA: Development Dimensions International.

Huthcutt, A. I., Conway, J. M., Roth, P. L., & Klehe, U. (2004). The impact of job complexity and study design on situational and behavior description interview validity. *International Journal of Selection and Assessment, 12*(2), 262–273.

Kaiser, R. B., Hogan, R., & Craig, S. B. (2008). Leadership and the fate of organizations. *American Psychologist, 63*(2), 96–110.

Karlsson, P., & Neilson, G. L. (2009, June 10). CEO succession 2008: Stability in the storm. *strategy+business*, pp. 1–12.

Miner, J. (1993). *Role motivation theories.* London: Routledge.

Ones, D. S., & Dilchert, S. (2009). How special are executives? How special should executive selection be? Observations and recommendations. *Industrial and Organizational Psychology: Perspectives on Science and Practice, 2*(2), 163–170.

Sackett, P. R., & Lievens, F. (2008). Personnel selection. *Annual Review of Psychology, 59,* 16.1–16.32.

Smith, A. B., & Howard, A. (2009). Executive selection as a strategic business decision. *Industrial and Organizational Psychology: Perspectives on Science and Practice, 2*(2), 144–150.

Wernimont, P. F., & Campbell, J. P. (1968). Signs, samples, and criteria. *Journal of Applied Psychology, 52,* 372–376.

CHAPTER 14

THE SPECIAL CASE OF PUBLIC SECTOR POLICE AND FIRE SELECTION

Gerald V. Barrett, Dennis Doverspike, Candice M. Young

Selection for public safety jobs can be characterized as high stakes and extremely litigious. Creating test batteries for public safety jobs requires that a practitioner deal with political pressures, unions, lawyers, escalating costs, and reduced budgets. There is also the high cost of a mistake: selecting the wrong police officer or firefighter can potentially have a disastrous impact on public safety and welfare. This makes public safety selection an exciting area, because assessment professionals are called on to apply their full knowledge of the testing enterprise within significant practical constraints. In this chapter, we discuss the area of public safety testing—specifically, assessment for police and fire positions.

The testing process can be thought of as occurring at two distinct points in a career. The first is for entry level or initial entry into the organization. The second is promotional testing, which for police includes, among others, detective, sergeant, lieutenant, and chief. For fire, the promotional ladder is from engineer, to lieutenant, to captain, to chief.

We can then think of public safety testing as being a 2×2 matrix consisting of type (police or fire) by level (entry or promotional). There are enough differences in these four types of testing that they can be considered independently, although for this chapter, we have collapsed our discussion of typical tests into entry-level and promotional assessment.

In writing this chapter, we have taken primarily the perspective of the assessment professional involved in developing and validating safety force test batteries. Admittedly we have taken an unabashedly scientist-practitioner focus; viewing the issue from a different perspective—for example, that of a plaintiff's attorney or expert—could lead to very different areas of emphasis and conclusions. In addition, given this chapter is in a book on assessment, we have discussed only those aspects of tests that we consider to be somewhat unique within the public safety domain. We begin with an illustrative case involving a testing professional's first encounter with the labyrinth of public safety testing.

A Typical Public Safety Project

John Adams is an industrial-organizational (I-O) consultant who has always worked in the private sector. One of his colleagues suggested that he put in a bid in response to a Request for Proposal (RFP) for a city that wanted to contract with a testing firm to develop and administer an entry-level test for firefighters and a promotional test for fire lieutenant. He reviewed the RFP, which was over fifty pages in length and contained various requirements for minimum compensation for associates in the firm, declarations regarding minority subcontracts, and a unique indemnification clause. There was also a requirement that he obtain various types of insurance, including a $2 million professional liability insurance policy. Adams's firm put together a successful proposal and obtained the contract to do both the entry-level and promotional-level tests for the city.

Meeting with Stakeholders

During the initial meeting with the city, a number of issues were discussed with the various parties involved in the testing process. The mayor's chief of staff noted many problems in the past with other consultants, including allegations of tests being improperly scored or lost and information given to applicants before the test administration, and he warned Adams that the city did not want more bad publicity. The nonminority union representative stated that his members were still mad about a previous court order giving additional points to minority candidates for promotions, and the minority union representative stated emphatically that his members wanted tests to be administered that had no adverse impact. The head of the law department stated that there had been continued litigation with every fire test given since 1973, when Title VII of the Civil Rights Act of 1964 was applied to public organizations, and he was confident that there would be a lawsuit. The civil service director stated that the city had strict rules that the consulting firm had to follow on rank ordering, a 70 percent cutoff for all tests, and extra points for various factors including residency and being an ethnic minority. The human resource (HR) director explained that there were established scoring and appeals processes for all examinations that had to be followed.

Job Analysis and Test Development

Over the next several months, Adams spent quite a bit of time in job analysis, test development, and preparing for the test administration. Some members of the fire department who were still involved in litigation from the most recent test did not want to cooperate with the job analysis. The media alleged that supervisors involved as subject matter experts (SMEs) were leaking details of the potential items and tests to applicants. Adams worked through these problems, completed the job analysis, and developed a weighted battery of tests for both the entry-level and promotional positions.

Test Administration Challenges

Test administration day arrived, and the HR department had stipulated that the entry-level test was to be given in the morning and promotional examination in the afternoon, which

(Continued)

A Typical Public Safety Project *(Continued)*

put a strain on the consultant's resources. As a further complication, the HR department informed Adams that Saturday was a religious holiday for some candidates. This meant that he would have to give exams on Monday that were equivalent to those given on Saturday.

The morning of the test administration, Adams noticed a man who appeared to be in his fifties taking the entry-level exam. The HR director explained that the man in question was a fire captain who had had a lucrative test training program for the past thirty years. Furthermore, the captain had instructed some of the test takers to memorize, in sequence, every item on the test, so it could be used in subsequent training programs. By the end of the day, the captain would have reproduced all of the items on the entry-level test.

Adams was aghast! He told the HR director that this meant that the people taking the test on Monday could in theory have all of the test items and answers. The HR director agreed: "Yes, that's true, and it's your problem." He explained that cheating was prevalent during test administrations and suggested that Adams confiscate all electronic devices because test takers had been known to download information while in the restroom.

The overall entry-level process appeared to work well except for some problems with scoring and, of course, the additional hassles of the Monday retest. According to the contract between the union and the city, the tests had to be scanned and scored on the spot, and some of the machines malfunctioned. Finally, all answer sheets were scanned, and preliminary scores were given to all applicants. The answer sheets were then copied and given to HR.

The promotional exam in the afternoon began on an uneasy note when one of the outside raters for the assessment center failed to show up; fortunately there was an extra assessor. Although there were a few small problems, such as malfunctioning video cameras and sticky computer keys, each problem was addressed in turn, and the assessment center scores were generated and reported to the city and the candidate.

As part of the promotional appeals process, Adams sent a keyed copy of the written job knowledge test to the HR department, so the candidates could protest any of the items they believed to be incorrectly scored or not job relevant. At the end of the appeals process, all one hundred promotional items were challenged. The HR director informed Adams that this was common: candidates appealed any item they felt they might have missed. In the end, the appeals process resulted in five items being eliminated and the keys changed to reflect the final scoring for the fire lieutenant position.

Litigation and Charges of Discrimination

The Civil Service Commission posted the results of the exams and certified the lists to the fire chief as eligible for hire and promotion. Six months later, the law department informed Adams that the U.S. Department of Justice (DOJ) had found that adverse impact existed in both assessment procedures, the tests were not valid, and alternative selection procedures existed that were equally valid and not used by the city.

One week after the DOJ decision, the minority union filed a lawsuit charging discrimination in both the entry-level and promotional tests. A broad discovery request was submitted to both the city and Adams Consulting. The request included all of the notes, e-mails, and written reports (including drafts) concerning both tests.

As a result of the court filing, the lists stood in limbo, and no one was hired or promoted. Finally, about two years after the signing of the initial contract, Adams learned that the plaintiffs had chosen experts to attack his test: a statistician, sociologist, social psychologist, linguist, and I-O psychologist from a local college.

At that point the plaintiffs added to the list of defendants John Adams personally, as well as his consulting firm. The next day Adams received a call from the city's law department informing him that he should immediately contact his professional liability insurance carrier because the law department

(Continued)

A Typical Public Safety Project *(Continued)*

was invoking the clause he signed indemnifying the city for any legal fees incurred. Adams protested that he had done nothing wrong and did not understand why he was being sued. The law director said, "It doesn't matter. You signed the agreement and are responsible for all legal costs." Adams was worried, and as he read over his policy, he found that he and his firm could be held personally liable for all legal fees, costs, and awards; the insurance company would not cover him if the jury found that he intentionally discriminated.

Two weeks later, all five plaintiffs' experts alleged numerous shortcomings in the validation process, including substantial adverse impact. The statistician's report included an unusual structural equation modeling approach. He testified that this model showed discrimination as well as adverse impact for six items. The sociologist, social psychologist, and I-O psychologist had analyzed all the items on the entry level and promotional tests and claimed to have discovered many biased or poorly written items. The I-O psychologist, linguist, and sociologist all opined that the job analysis was inadequate and stated that there was not enough detail in the job description, although it extended over twenty pages. The social psychologist claimed that the assessment center allowed assessors to be influenced by ethnic and sex stereotypes and had not eliminated stereotype threat by taking into account racial identity theory. The city's law department informed Adams that under federal rules, he had only thirty days to respond to the experts' reports. The court would not give him an extension of time.

Adams responded in the thirty days and diligently attempted to answer the critiques from the five experts. This took an enormous amount of time, and Adams, having been naive about work in the public sector, had signed a fixed-price contract. The contract included a clause that obligated his firm to defend allegations of discrimination without increased compensation.

During the deposition phase of litigation, the opinions of the plaintiffs' experts were fleshed out. The I-O expert testified that there were techniques that could be used to weight different tests to optimize validity and minimize adverse impact. Although the tests administered were not valid, valid alternative procedures that were valid with no adverse impact did exist. Adams testified that in order to use the mathematical model suggested would require obtaining a statistical correlation between all the tests and a criterion, none of which was available before or after the tests were given since content-valid tests were administered for both entrance and promotional tests.

The I-O psychologist also testified that personality tests should have been used to reduce adverse impact, in particular a measure of emotional intelligence. She also questioned the cutoff score, saying the 70 percent value was arbitrary and had not been validated. She insisted that a variation of the procedure known as banding, where scores are collapsed into three score ranges and all scores within a category are treated as equal, should have been used instead of rank ordering.

The social psychologist criticized the job analysis, stating that only one-third of the incumbents involved were minorities. She testified that it was a well-known fact that minority incumbents use different procedures to fight fires than nonminority incumbents and stated that the job analysis may have missed critical pieces of information due to the small number of minorities involved. Therefore, the job knowledge test may have asked the wrong questions.

The social psychologist further testified that the cut score should have been adjusted for ethnic group status to account for the mean differences. However, in cross-examination, she was unable to cite any empirical research suggesting racial differences in firefighting techniques.

The linguist, in her expert report, stated that any competent consultant would have included linguistic analysis because of the large number of Hispanic candidates. She stated that the evidence for the Flesch-Kincaid reading level of the tests was of no value, and a qualitative reading analysis should have been conducted by a professional linguist.

(Continued)

A Typical Public Safety Project *(Continued)*

During the depositions, all five experts admitted that they had never validated or developed a test other than classroom tests. The statistician, linguist, and sociologist had never had a graduate course in testing, psychometrics, or personnel selection. Despite these gaps in their experience, the court allowed their testimony.

The Decision

In the end, John Adams's tests were found to be valid and non-discriminatory. Adams was found not to be personally liable. However, the city still lost the case because of actions the HR department had taken that were found to involve disparate treatment and retaliation. Therefore, the original list was thrown out and replaced with a new list generated through an agreement with the DOJ. The plaintiffs' attorneys were awarded significant legal fees because they had prevailed on some of their claims, although the test had been found to be valid.

Adams tried to bill the city for all the time he spent in preparing for the trial, responding to expert reports, and his own legal fees. The city refused to pay based on the initial contract. Adams's insurance company did end up paying a portion of his legal fees, but soon after, the company cancelled the firm's professional liability insurance. Although Adams's firm was not responsible for all of the legal fees, the firm took a major loss on the contract.

Adams and the firm decided to concentrate their business in the private sector henceforth. They never submitted another proposal in response to a public sector RFP.

Entry-Level Hiring for Police and Fire

The tests used for entry-level hiring are similar enough for both firefighters and police that we can consider them together. In this section we examine traditional instruments, a few newer or nontraditional instruments, and supplemental screening methods such as physical ability tests, reference checks, and clinical screenings.

In designing the selection system, the agency and the consultant, like their private sector counterpart, must pay attention to the *Uniform Guidelines on Employee Selection Procedures*, professional testing guidelines, and federal laws. This includes, at a minimum:

- *Uniform Guidelines on Employee Selection Procedures* (Equal Employment Opportunity Commission, Civil Service Commission, Department of Labor, & Department of Justice, 1978)
- *Standards for Educational and Psychological Testing* (American Educational Research Association, American Psychological Association, & National Council on Measurement in Education, 1999)
- *Principles for the Validation and Use of Personnel Selection Procedures* (Society for Industrial and Organizational Psychology, 2003)

In addition, and complicating the process, the test must be designed to comply with any collective bargaining agreement, state laws, local laws, and state or local civil service regulations.

Minimum Qualifications and Prescreens

In larger cities, the usual minimum qualifications are a high school diploma and a driver's license. Generally there is no requirement of previous experience. In smaller cities, some type of previous academy training may be required.

There have been initiatives to try to raise the educational requirement to two or four years of college, but these are usually met with resistance due to the potential for adverse impact. For firefighter positions, it has been more common to add the requirement of prior completion of an emergency medical services or paramedic program. Another controversial issue is residency requirements, which may be current residency or the willingness to establish residency within some specified time period.

Written Cognitive Ability and Related Tests

This technique typically involves paper-and-pencil or computerized measures of an individual's general mental ability. The cognitive ability literature has demonstrated the validity of cognitive ability tests to predict academy training (often the first three months of the job) and performance across all job categories, including police and fire (Barrett, Polomsky, & McDaniel, 1999; Hunter & Schmidt, 1996). It is also evident that whites typically score one standard deviation higher than blacks on cognitive ability tests, which results in adverse impact against the latter group, although differences in education between ethnic groups explain portions of the test performance difference. The problem with off-the-shelf cognitive ability tests is that they are not compatible with a content validity strategy. Thus, their validity must be established through a criterion-related validation study or through validity generalization, which usually has not been accepted by the courts in police and fire litigation.

Reading Ability

Reading tests require the candidate to read a section of the test and then respond to questions, usually in a multiple-choice fashion, based on only the material provided. Such tests may be off-the-shelf instruments or locally developed and validated. Locally developed tests are designed to include safety force content relevant to the specific jurisdiction. Written tests typically are designed to require a reading level at or below the level required on the job. This can be accomplished by comparing the reading level of the test to reading materials and source documents provided by the agency. A Flesch-Kincaid or similar quantitative readability analysis is usually used for safety force documents and the test.

Mathematical Ability

Mathematical tests require the applicant to apply simple arithmetic operations to solve applied problems. For firefighters, a question might ask, "How many total feet of hose have to be combined if three different hoses of known length have to be used?" Again, these can be off-the-shelf or locally developed.

Mechanical Comprehension

Tests involving mechanical comprehension are often found on entry-level firefighter examinations. Barrett, Carobine, and Doverspike (1999) found that mechanical comprehension was a valid predictor of performance among firefighters. In fact, mechanical comprehension was found to be a better predictor of performance in comparison to other cognitive measures; "however, the superiority of mechanical tests is consistent with substantial mechanical demands inherent in the successful performance of firefighter duties" (p. 511). This was an intriguing finding since general cognitive ability tests have had a reputation of yielding greater validity coefficients than any other predictor.

Short-Term Memory Tests

In short-term memory tests, the candidate is given several minutes to memorize some content, for example, the face of a criminal or the layout of a building that is on fire. He or she is then asked questions about the information memorized. Such tests are found on both police and fire exams (Barrett et al., 1999).

Situational Judgment Tests

Situational judgment tests present the candidate with a brief scenario and then ask him or her to select the best choice or indicate what he or she would do (in some cases, candidates might be asked both what they would do and what they should not do). Scoring of situational judgment tests can become quite complicated. However, these tests have garnered popularity because they can be given in paper-and-pencil format, by computer administration, using video, or even in an interview. Because of the costs of developing situational judgment tests, they are often purchased off-the-shelf. Although local development is possible, a criterion-related strategy is required.

Personality Tests

Controversy surrounds the use of nonclinical personality testing as a selection device for fire and police. It is clear that personality is important for both police and firefighter jobs. Police have substantial amounts of interaction with the public, and firefighters have to live together; both jobs involve working within a highly structured, paramilitary-style organization. However, the issue is one of developing reliable and valid measures of personality that cannot be faked, not whether the constructs themselves are job related.

In terms of validity, there are surprisingly few empirical data relating personality tests to police or fire performance. Meta-analysis results from the studies we could locate do not indicate that personality measures consistently predict police or fire job performance (Barrett, Miguel, Hurd, Lueke, & Tan, 2003). It is extremely difficult to support the use of a personality test based on a content-validity argument; thus, transfer, criterion-related, or construct-validity approaches must be relied on. However, the positive results found using concurrent validation designs for personality tests disappeared under actual test conditions using a predictive validation design (Henderson, 1979). In high-stakes situations, the temptation to "fake good" can reduce validity and lead to a variety of problems with implementation, including faking, no right answers, test takers' negative reactions, and public relations issues (Barrett, 2008). In addition, coaching can drastically raise personality test scores (Miller & Barrett, 2008). The Department of Justice rigorously advocated personality tests until this position was not supported in the legal arena (*United States* v. *City of Garland, Texas*, 2000).

Biodata

Biodata are similar to the personality test in that they are also noncognitive measures that attempt to assess life history data. The purpose of the biodata is to reveal and assess the individual's past behavior as a predictor of future behavior. As a scientific generalization, this has some merit if one carefully examines how one defines past and future behavior. For example, high school grades from a transcript predict college grades.

Some research supports the use of biodata in police entry-level processes. For example, in a sample of officers from the New York City Police Department, it was found that background ratings predicted performance problems (Cohen & Chaiken, 1973). Although the research shows some positive results for the use of background and biodata information for hiring, biodata instruments require careful development and validation, using a criterion-related validation strategy.

Nontraditional Tests

During trainability testing, a person is assessed as to how well he or she can learn the knowledge and behaviors required to perform a job; this can be accomplished using a minicourse or a job-related test preparation manual. During testing, the test taker answers questions from memory about information contained in the manual or completes a work sample based on the minicourse. A recent study (Kuthy, 2008) found that a trainability test resulted in less adverse impact for entry-level firefighter applicants than a cognitive ability test and was a valid predictor of job performance.

Supplemental Tests

We have referred to a number of selection devices as supplemental tests, for lack of a better term. Many of the selection hurdles listed below are given after an offer has been made, although some may be given before the offer. They usually do not enter into the ranking of individuals, although an exception could be physical ability screenings.

Physical Ability

Physical ability assessments include tests of aerobic capacity, physical fitness, and physical agility. For both entry-level fire and police, we believe that locally developed, job-related physical ability tests represent the most defensible option. Such tests simulate the physical requirements of the job. For example, a physical ability test for police officers might include a trigger pull, a weight carry, and a run over a short distance simulating chasing a perpetrator. A physical ability test for firefighters might include an aerial ladder climb, a body drag, and a stair climb.

Physical ability tests require the setup of apparatus and can be costly to administer. For that reason, they are usually given later in the selection process, after the number of candidates has been reduced. Physical ability tests are likely to have adverse impact as a function of sex and age.

Minnesota Multiphasic Personality Inventory

The Minnesota Multiphasic Personality Inventory is a clinical personality psychological test that can be given as part of an overall psychological evaluation. Approximately 72 percent of police departments report using it (Cochrane, 1999). They are used to screen out applicants who may be problematic due to a personality or clinical disorder, though there are legal issues surrounding the use of clinical personality tests. The Americans with Disabilities Act (ADA, 1990) prohibits the use of clinical personality tests until after an offer of employment has been made because these tests are considered medical tests.

References and Background Checks
This selection technique entails using judgments and information of persons familiar with the applicant. Research indicates this technique lacks reliability and typically has low validity as a predictor of performance. For the safety forces, it tends to be used to screen individuals out due to problems such as a criminal record and includes fingerprint and criminal record checks.

Promotional Testing for Police and Fire

This section looks at the various types of tests used in the selection of applicants for promotion within a police or fire department. In promotional testing, the assessment center method may be used to organize the administration of tests; therefore, we discuss it here as a type of test, since it is a method that may contain a variety of tests.

Minimum Requirements

The typical minimum requirement is a certain number of years of acceptable performance in a lower-level job. For example, promotion to sergeant may require three years of previous experience as an entry-level police officer.

Job Knowledge Tests

Promotional examinations are tests for which candidates can study and develop their skills. Job knowledge tests that are incorporated into promotional examinations provide an incentive for test takers to learn important procedures that may be overlooked but are still required on the job. In most cases, candidates are given a list of source materials to study for the job knowledge test; this differs from the trainability test for entry-level safety forces in that the source material to be studied is not necessarily viewed as new material.

Assessment Centers

With the assessment center method, applicants complete multiple tests, simulations, and role plays in a structured, standardized environment. They may complete some of the role plays or simulations with other candidates. Raters observe the various exercises and make evaluations that may be combined through statistical methods or human judgment. Usually for safety forces, the content is based on local materials and specific issues concerning that particular jurisdiction such as sexual harassment.

It is possible to package any set or types of tests into an assessment center. Assessment centers take a great deal of management and administrative time and can be quite costly. In order to reduce costs, organizations have moved to shorter exercises that can be administered and scored by computer. Assessment centers are more commonly used with promotional testing. Personnel testing research supports the validity of the assessment center as a personnel selection method or means of delivery of tests. In the following sections, we discuss some of the more common assessment center exercises: in-baskets, interviews, leaderless group discussion, and role plays.

In-Basket Test

An in-basket test simulates an in-box on the desk of a particular position (say, a fire lieutenant) in which memos, messages, reports, and other pieces of information accumulate as they are received on the job. The purpose of the test is to assess the ability to handle the administrative aspects of the position. For example, a candidate may be asked to attend to the materials he or she finds on the desk and address them in order of importance.

Interviews or Oral Boards

This technique entails the job candidate's giving oral responses to job-related questions asked by an interviewer or panel of interviewers. The interviewee is then rated on such dimensions as work history, motivation, creative thinking, and presentation. The scoring procedure for oral interview boards has typically been subjective, and there are a number of concerns, including security of questions, training of raters, cost, and time required. In response, many jurisdictions have moved to the video or voice recording of the interview or oral board. This allows an independent panel of trained raters to provide ratings in a more structured and objective setting.

Unless all of the interviews can be completed on the same day and the candidates sequestered, security problems can arise due to the sharing of questions. The subjective nature of this procedure may allow bias such as favoritism and politics to enter into the process.

Leaderless Group Discussion

The leaderless group discussion is an exercise often found in an assessment center where applicants meet as a group to discuss an actual job-related problem. As the meeting proceeds, the candidates are observed to see how they interact and what leadership and communications skills each person displays.

Role Plays

Another exercise traditionally used in assessment centers is the role play, in which the candidate assumes the role of the incumbent of the position and must deal with another person in a job-related situation. A trained role player is used and responds in character to the actions of the candidate. Performance is assessed by raters observing the interaction.

Performance Appraisal Ratings

Performance appraisal measures fall into the general categories of objective and subjective. Ratings of police and fire personnel generally involve subjective assessments completed by higher-level supervisors; the ratings may be made solely for the purpose of the assessment, or operational ratings may be used. Operational ratings are characterized by extreme restriction in range.

Individual Assessments

In individual assessment, a psychologist makes an evaluation of an individual for personnel decision-making purposes. Individual assessments are used most often by either very small departments for entry-level testing or by departments of any size for higher-level selection.

Adverse Impact

Most tests used in safety force selection have significant group mean differences for ethnicity or sex. Cognitive ability tests usually result in a one standard deviation difference between whites and blacks. Mechanical comprehension and physical ability tests often result in sex differences. The existence of such differences, combined with the large number of applicants and small number of new employees or promotions, almost guarantees that adverse impact will be an issue. It should be noted that adverse impact is not a property of the test but exists only within the context of specific decisions concerning applicant pools and hiring rates.

For test developers, it is often frustrating to repeatedly be confronted with the many myths and misinterpretations of adverse impact. However, it is understandable that individuals who are not experts in the field of testing make erroneous allegations. In the public sector, test developers are constantly told that their clients do not want their selection systems to have any adverse impact. There are certain myths about adverse impact. One suggests that adverse impact is a property of tests in general. Another suggests that the existence of adverse impact automatically indicates discrimination.

A number of statistical methods have been, and could be, applied to determine the adverse impact of tests used in safety force hiring. The most basic methods are the 80 percent rule and the Fisher exact test. The 80 percent rules states that the ratio of the hiring rate (hires divided by applicants) for the protected class has to be at least 80 percent of the hiring rate for the majority group. The Fisher exact test is a statistical test that can be applied to a contingency table where the rows indicate whether the applicants were members of the protected class or not and the columns indicate whether the applicant was hired or not hired. The Fisher exact test tests the hypothesis that any differences or relationship is due to chance. Different methods can lead to different results. Furthermore, slight modifications to the numbers can change the results dramatically. In many cases, especially for promotional tests, the sample sizes may be too small to be of probative value.

Cutoff Scores

An issue related to that of adverse impact is the establishment of cut scores on tests, often a highly contentious and litigious area. The issue of cutoff scores, always important, has received increased scrutiny by judges in recent years.

Multiple Predictors and Weighting

Adding a personality test to an ability test for employee selection has been suggested as a means of improving validity while reducing adverse impact of the system. Ryan, Ployhart, and Friedel (1998) concluded that the use of personality testing did not compensate for the adverse impact related to cognitive ability testing and that the applicant pool characteristics and nature of the personality measure were important considerations. Other studies have looked at the effects of forming multipredictor composites on group differences and adverse impact, and the results suggest caution in presuming a reduction in adverse impact by the addition of personality measures. Practically speaking, there are no easy methods of reducing adverse impact while maintaining optimal prediction of performance. Beyond that, complicated weighting schemes are difficult to explain to stakeholders, and unit weighting tends to lead to results close to optimal.

Techniques for Reducing Adverse Impact

The scientific literature indicates that most of the procedures developed to reduce adverse impact have only a small, if any, impact on adverse impact. Nevertheless, in Table 14.1, we have listed some possible approaches to reducing adverse impact.

Table 14.1. Methods for Reducing Adverse Impact

Methods	Critiques
Conduct a literature review to identify tests with less adverse impact.	The literature suggests a trade-off between validity and adverse impact; there is a mixing of constructs and methods in the literature.
Perform item bias analyses including pretesting items and expert review.	Tends to have minimal, if any, impact on adverse impact.
Follow good test writing practices.	Tends to have minimal, if any, impact on adverse impact.
Avoid items that tap beliefs or values with known group differences.	Tends to have minimal, if any, impact on adverse impact.
Reduce the reading demand.	Will tend to reduce adverse impact; however, reading may be a job-related KSA.
Increase the time limits.	Overcomes some of the problems due to reading load; however, the pass rates of all groups will go up as time limits increase.
Include memory tests.	Will reduce adverse impact and can be both face and content valid; however, increases the complexity of administration.
Use tests that are unrelated to cognitive ability.	Tests that are not correlated with cognitive ability tend to have lower validity.
Use job sample tests.	Job or work sample tests are not appropriate for entry-level safety force tests; job sample tests introduce subjectivity into scoring.
Use personality tests.	If given sufficient weight, will lower adverse impact; lower validity, can be faked, hard to explain scoring and results.

(Continued)

Table 14.1. Methods for Reducing Adverse Impact *(Continued)*

Methods	Critiques
Use a trainability test.	If given sufficient weight, will lower adverse impact; more applicable to entry-level test; may tap past knowledge, giving advantage to those with experience.
Use assessment centers.	There is no one standard assessment center. Adverse impact tends to be similar to the amount found in job knowledge tests.
Offer training in how to take the test.	Impact on adverse impact unclear, but at best minimal.
Apply greater weight to low adverse impact tests.	In order to have an impact, the weights given to low-impact tests must be much larger, approaching 100 percent.
Lower the cut score.	Lowering the cut score solely to reduce adverse impact will result in reduced utility and a greater number of incorrect decisions.
Instead of rank ordering, collapse the full score range into a smaller number of groups or categories, where scores within a category are treated as equal; this technique is referred to as "banding."	If random selection within categories or bands is used, the reduction in adverse impact may be minimal.

Alternative Selection Devices

Employers have a genuine interest in finding alternatives that will reduce or eliminate adverse impact while maintaining or increasing predictive validity. Since the sure techniques of race and sex norming are not viable options due to the Civil Rights Act of 1991, interest has turned to examining the efficacy of including personality tests in selection batteries and alternative means of test administration.

The most common allegation by plaintiffs is that an alternative selection procedure (ASP) is equally valid and has less adverse impact than the procedure a jurisdiction is using. For example, over the past ten years, the U.S. Department of Justice has alleged (*United States* v. *City of Garland*, 2000) that personality tests should be used for the selection of safety forces (that is, as part of the preoffer selection battery and for the ranking of candidates). Plaintiffs' experts routinely testify in court that if the consultant had used an emotional intelligence test, a personality test, or an oral exam, there would have been no adverse impact. In many cases, the plaintiffs' experts are not I-O psychologists but come from fields such as sociology, English, linguistics, human resources, education, industrial relations, and various disciplines in psychology, including cognitive and clinical. Their assessment experience is often limited to giving exams to undergraduates, and they have never validated a police or fire test. No matter what tests or procedures are used, experts can propose, from their armchair, a better test or procedure in court with no empirical evidence.

Reflections

Within the area of police and fire selection, few changes in test content have occurred in the past fifty years. Yes, we have new technologies for the delivery of assessments, such as computer-administered and video tests. There are new validation technologies, including meta-analysis and the use of regression equations to determine weights. Of course, there has been a great deal of discussion of adverse impact, but with not much to show in terms of results. Consequently, the basic structure and content of the tests used today look very much like the instruments used fifty years ago. There have been no new grand theories or approaches to explaining individual differences in performance as a police officer or firefighter. We do not know much more about the constructs that predict performance than we knew fifty years ago. Basically the field knew eighty years ago that cognitive ability tests predict success in police and fire academies, with lower levels of success for predicting job performance in the safety forces. Unfortunately, no systematic peer-reviewed research has led to improved professional practice in the area of selection for the safety forces. Why so little progress? There could be many reasons.

Professional Practice Has Been Driven by the Attempt to Reduce Adverse Impact

As a field, we have spent an incredible amount of time and effort trying to solve the problem of adverse impact. The research and practice of developing selection and promotion tests have been dominated since the early 1970s by the specter of adverse impact. Most major cities, and their consultants, have sought to eliminate or reduce adverse impact, but with limited success. Most cities remain mired in constant litigation; a jurisdiction administers a test and is sure to face a lawsuit. The U.S. Department of Justice has spent millions on expert and attorneys' fees advocating received doctrine, such as that personality tests are the holy grail. This has led to a number of undesirable consequences. All of them negate the merit principle; more important, none of this litigation has led to major advances in research knowledge, professional practices, validity, or reduced adverse impact. We can predict continued alleged adverse impact and litigation, with courts making personnel decisions on flimsy evidence from single studies.

The I-O psychologist's obligation of developing the most valid procedures and then selecting among those procedures with the least adverse impact has been changed by political pressures to one of selecting the procedure with the least adverse impact and marginal validity. Procedures are hailed that reduce adverse impact, while resulting in only minimal reductions in validity. This is best illustrated by the pressure applied by the U.S. Department of Justice to use personality tests to select safety forces, based on the reasoning that personality tests are not only allegedly valid for the safety forces but have no adverse impact. However, we know that the use of personality testing does not compensate for the adverse impact related to cognitive ability testing and that the applicant pool characteristics and the nature of the personality measure are important considerations (Ryan et al., 1998). Overall, results suggest caution in presuming a reduction in adverse impact by the addition of personality measures or through any of the techniques developed over the past thirty years. Strategies that reduce adverse impact for one minority group may actually increase it for another group.

Professional Practice Has Been Limited by Security Issues Inherent in High-Stakes Testing

Due to security issues and problems, jurisdictions in medium to large cities have moved to the use of locally developed tests. But to guard against test leakage, those tests must be rewritten and recreated each time they are administered, a costly and time-consuming process. Also, from a scientific standpoint, it means that the wheel is constantly being reinvented, and thus little progress has been made.

Most of the research has been conducted by consultants and therefore is considered proprietary. Even if the consultant did want to publish the result, many cities do not want the results published for financial or legal reasons.

Impact of Recent Litigation

Starting in the mid-1970s and continuing to the present, litigation has been a common theme in safety force selection. Safety force jobs account for as much as 75 percent of all litigation involving service jobs. One reason for such a hefty percentage is due to the fact that these jobs are routinely targeted by the Department of Justice (Ugelow, 2005). This is largely because of the high stakes, the number of interested parties, and the ease with which adverse impact is alleged for this type of testing. Selection batteries typically include cognitive ability tests or job knowledge tests, which tend to result in adverse impact as a function of ethnicity. For fire selection, physical ability and mechanical comprehension tests often lead to adverse impact based on sex.

It is beyond the scope of this chapter to discuss the many court cases involving assessments in police and fire departments. But because of its importance and primacy we will briefly discuss *Ricci* v. *DeStefano*, which was decided in 2009 by the U.S. Supreme Court. The City of New Haven had a consulting firm administer promotional exams (a job knowledge and oral assessment) for fire lieutenant and captain. The results presented to the Civil Service Board (CSB) indicated adverse impact. For the captain's exam, the probable promotion rate for Hispanics and whites was nearly identical. There was no statistically significant difference between blacks and whites or Hispanics and whites. The CSB should have been advised to certify the captain's promotional exam. The adverse impact found in the lieutenant promotional process was more complex. The *Uniform Guidelines* state, "If only one more black had been hired instead of a white the selection rate for blacks . . . would be higher than that for whites." If one white candidate had been replaced with a black or Hispanic candidate, no adverse impact would have been found. For both the lieutenant and captain exams, the sample sizes were very small—probably too small for any conclusion of adverse impact to be warranted.

The CSB decided against certifying the lists, whereupon the white and Hispanic candidates with a high probability of being promoted sued the City of New Haven. The city relied in part on the testimony of an I-O psychologist who opined that there was adverse impact that would have been avoided if alternative selection procedures, such as an assessment center, were used. However, he presented no analyses or citations to support this idea. One ironic aspect of this case is that the same I-O psychologist who recommended an assessment center as a technique to avoid adverse impact and litigation had been sued by a client city for indemnification when the city was sued by a candidate in the assessment center he administered.

Of even more importance for *Ricci*, there seems to be a received doctrine that assessment centers have little or no adverse impact. In fact, 2008 was the first year a meta-analysis of subgroup differences in assessment centers was even published. Dean, Roth, and Bobko (2008) found moderate subgroup differences ($d = 0.52$), but this is probably an underestimate because assessment centers in the public sector are usually used after the applicants have been prescreened using other assessment devices. In the end, the Supreme Court stated that there must be a "strong basis in evidence" to fail to certify an exam. The CSB did not have this evidence, and summary judgment was given to the white and Hispanic plaintiffs.

It is well beyond the scope of this chapter to even partially review all of the issues in *Ricci*, but it does closely track, and return us to, the case study that opened this chapter with allegations that the fire promotional tests were not valid and numerous alternative selection procedures were available to the I-O consultants who developed the tests. *Ricci* departed from our case study in that the CSB refused to certify a list before reviewing a validation study and assumed a new selection procedure would not have any adverse impact. (For those wondering, the case study at the beginning of this chapter was written completely independent of the knowledge of the facts in *Ricci;* any similarities are a coincidence.)

Conclusion

The traditional scientific model was one that involved hypothesizing that certain constructs would predict job performance, developing operational measures, validating, and then reporting the results in peer-reviewed publications. However, the science of merit and validity has been replaced by the science of social consequence testing. Whether this is good or bad depends on your viewpoint, but from the perspective of building a science of selection for the safety forces, it has redirected focus and hampered attempts to build on replicable results and produce a cohesive body of knowledge.

References

American Educational Research Association, American Psychological Association, & National Council on Measurement in Education. (1999). *Standards for educational and psychological testing.* Washington, DC: Author.

Americans with Disabilities Act of 1990, Public Law No. 101–336, 104 Stat. 328 (1990). Codified at 42 U.S.C., Section 12101 et seq.

Barrett, G. V. (2008). Practitioner's view of personality testing and industrial-organizational psychology: Practical and legal issues. *Industrial and Organizational Psychology: Perspectives on Science and Practice, 1,* 299–302.

Barrett, G. V., Carobine, R. G., & Doverspike, D. (1999). The reduction of adverse impact in an employment setting using a short-term memory test. *Journal of Business and Psychology, 14*(2), 373–377.

Barrett, G. V., Miguel, R. F., Hurd, J. M., Lueke, S. B., & Tan, J. A. (2003). Practical issues in the use of personality tests in police selection. *Public Personnel Management, 32*(4), 497–517.

Barrett, G. V., Polomsky, M. D., & McDaniel, M. A. (1999). Selection tests for firefighters: A comprehensive review and meta-analysis. *Journal of Business and Psychology, 13*(4), 507–513.

Civil Rights Act of 1991, Public Law No. 102–166, 105 Stat. 1071 (1991). Codified as amended at 42 U.S.C., Section 1981, 2000e et seq.

Cochrane, R. E. (1999). *Psychological testing and the selection of police officers: A national survey.* Unpublished doctoral dissertation, Wright State University.

Cohen, B., & Chaiken, J. M. (1973). *Police background characteristics and performance.* Lanham, MD: Lexington Books.

Dean, M. A., Roth, P. L., & Bobko, P. (2008). Ethnic and gender subgroup differences in assessment center ratings: A meta-analysis. *Journal of Applied Psychology, 93*(3), 685–691.

Equal Employment Opportunity Commission, Civil Service Commission, Department of Labor, & Department of Justice. (1978). Adoption by four agencies of uniform guidelines on employee selection procedures. *Federal Register, 43*, 38290–38315.

Henderson, N. D. (1979). Criterion-related validity of personality and aptitude scales: A comparison of validation results under voluntary and actual test conditions. In C. D. Spielberger (Ed.), *Police selection and evaluation: Issues and techniques* (pp. 179–195). Westport, CT: Praeger.

Hunter, J. E., & Schmidt, F. L. (1996). Intelligence and job performance: Economic and social implications. *Psychology, Public Policy, and Law, 2*(3–4), 447–472.

Kuthy, J. (2008). *Examination of relationship of general mental ability and study time to scores on a study-guide style reading test used for pre-employment testing.* Unpublished doctoral dissertation, University of Akron.

Miller, C. E., & Barrett, G. V. (2008). The coachability and fakability of personality based selection tests used for police selection. *Public Personnel Management, 37*(2), 1–13.

Ricci v. Destefano, 557 U. S. 071428 2009.

Ryan, A. M., Ployhart, R. E., & Friedel, L. A. (1998). Using personality testing to reduce adverse impact: A cautionary note. *Journal of Applied Psychology, 83*(2), 298–307.

Society for Industrial and Organizational Psychology. (2003). *Principles for the validation and use of personnel selection procedures* (4th ed.). Bowling Green, OH: Author.

Ugelow, R. S. (2005). A lawyer's view: I-O psychology and the Department of Justice. In F. J. Landy (Ed.), *Employment discrimination litigation: Behavioral, quantitative, and legal perspectives* (pp. 463–490). San Francisco: Jossey-Bass.

United States v. City of Garland, No. 3–98-CV-0307-L (N.D. Tex. 2000).

Part Three

Strategic Assessment Programs

CHAPTER 15

THE ROLE OF ASSESSMENT IN SUCCESSION MANAGEMENT

Matthew J. Paese

The challenge of succession management has become significantly more complex in recent years and, at the same time, more central to business vitality, which makes it troubling that so many organizations struggle to execute effectively in this arena. Who will replace senior executives when they retire? Who steps in when a new leadership position is created to address a pressing business challenge? Who replaces a senior leader who leaves unexpectedly to join a competitor? As our business changes, how will we prepare lower-level leaders to step up and take on the increasingly complex leadership challenges that emerge? These questions among others have been at the heart of succession management efforts for many decades. More recently, the response needed from top leaders and human resource (HR) leaders has shifted dramatically away from traditional approaches toward methods more appropriate in today's dynamic environment, and many are struggling to make the transition (Howard & Wellins, 2008).

At the heart of this challenge is understanding and then developing leadership capabilities. This begins with the requirement that organizations craft and execute assessment processes that uncover hidden leadership potential from within the organization, accurately gauge current skills against future requirements so that the right developmental investments can be made to close the gap as quickly as possible, and fully assess the success profile of potential successors to ensure effective decision making as leaders are promoted. But assessment pays dividends in succession management only when the subsequent development (after assessment) makes a difference that benefits both the individual and the organization. This chapter focuses on both assessment in the context of succession management and how to ensure that the investment in assessment pays dividends in overall leadership capability.

The Contemporary Succession Management Challenge

Competitive organizations have long worked to be ready for the moments when key leaders depart, seeking to maintain leadership continuity by taking stock of critical leadership positions, and identifying the individual who would step in should incumbents in these critical slots vacate their positions unexpectedly. The traditional approach, often termed replacement planning, has been to assemble senior management (usually annually in a private session, open to no one outside the senior team except the top HR leadership) to scan the organization chart and, for each critical position, agree on the few internal successors—the individuals who could step in to replace the incumbent should she or he depart suddenly. Then, when vacancies occurred, the list was used to identify the immediate replacement. This all worked quite well for a while.

This process of replacement planning has proven to be insufficient or impossible for more than a few of the top C-suite positions. Today's leaner organizations with fewer levels of management and fewer apprentice-type roles face rapidly shifting business demands and fierce competition. As a result, lists of ready replacements are reduced to near zero. Meanwhile, the roles requiring backups are becoming ever more dynamic and complex. The result is a widening gap between leadership supply and demand, and for an increasing proportion of organizations around the world, succession management has become synonymous with survival (Martin, 2007).

And so the contemporary challenge for organizations is not simply to identify or name successors, but to search for those with leadership potential within the organization and to accelerate their growth so that the organization's overall leadership readiness is enhanced. This means moving away from simply surveying talent (watching and noting when they will be ready) toward actively developing talent by intervening directly in leaders' careers to increase the rate of growth toward future leadership assignments. This is a fundamental shift in both the HR role and the management role in ensuring that organizations have a supply of leadership capability to respond to current and emerging business demands.

Unfortunately the lessons of traditional replacement planning have done little to prepare organizations for this shift. Replacement systems operated on a set of realities that seldom exist in today's environment. With more layers of management, leaders in waiting were often plentiful, and their responsibilities were more comparable to those of the target position for which they were being considered. This made the challenge of assessing readiness for promotion quite straightforward. Current performance was enough. Now organizations lament that only a very small proportion of key positions have ready replacements, and aggressive measures must be taken to heighten the readiness of those with less experience (Martin, 2007). The annual meetings to review the organization chart and tag replacements as ready or not was far simpler to execute and worked well enough for its time, but it is far from sufficient for the contemporary challenge.

Current conditions require more aggressive action, and as we will see, assessment is the most fundamental element in becoming more aggressive. Organizations have fewer potential successors who have wider gaps in their leadership capability, and closing those gaps means more than identifying replacements; it means developing them. To do so, organizations must develop excellence in assessment, identify individuals with leadership potential, assess their most crucial developmental gaps, and assess their readiness for promotion into more business-critical roles. A mistake in any of these arenas means sacrificing precious developmental resources or, worse, putting the wrong leaders into critical roles. This means engaging high-potential leaders, their managers, and senior executives in an effort to alter the experiences of high-performing leaders so that they are more immediately exposed to and involved in the challenges their superiors face. Yet many organizations remain rooted in traditional practices, failing to make the transition to more growth-oriented methods of succession.

The actions required for organizations to shift from a traditional replacement-focused system to a more contemporary growth-focused system are not always intuitively obvious, but they are also not complex. Six fundamentals represent the building blocks for making this critical shift:

1. *Align succession management with business strategy.* This is perhaps the most frequently recognized need, and at the same time the most seldom accomplished in reality.

2. *Define success holistically for all levels of leadership.* Narrow definitions and the absence of clear points of transition make this an area where many organizations can improve.

3. *Identify leadership potential with a focus on the ability to grow.* This is the most commonly applied element of succession management, as well as being the subject of considerable confusion and failure.

4. *Accurately assess readiness for leadership at higher levels.* Developing human capability requires a deep understanding of people, making in-depth assessment well worth the effort.

5. *Adopt a creative, risk-oriented approach to development.* Over and over, organizations execute effectively until after assessment has taken place, and then development becomes lackluster and ineffectual. More ingenuity is needed to engage emerging leaders in development experiences that build their readiness for more pressing business challenges.

6. *Establish management accountabilities with teeth.* HR cannot execute succession management to achieve its necessary outcomes. Management must own the growth and accelerated readiness of high-potential leaders, with HR as a critical partner.

This chapter delves into each of these fundamentals, examining the role that assessment plays in ensuring that succession management outcomes are achieved. As will become clear, the ability to effectively assess both leadership potential and readiness for future roles is at the heart of what makes world-class succession management systems cultivate leadership growth beyond traditional replacement.

Fundamental 1: Align Succession Management with Business Strategy

When asked how he became so successful, the great hockey champion Wayne Gretzky quipped that his approach was to skate not to where the puck is but to where it will soon be. In the same way, anticipating movement and change in a business is at the heart of developing leadership capability for the future. This means something that only the very best have been able to implement.

Imagine that the CEO and senior team of a consumer products organization declare a long-term business strategy focused on developing unique products to capture untapped market potential. Innovation and speed to market are pivotal. Senior leaders will need to generate effective strategies for product development and launch, and drive focused execution of these plans.

Now imagine the subsequent (and distinctly different) conversation about succession management and which leaders can step in to senior roles at a moment's notice. It is likely that senior executives' minds remain rooted in the language of the business: *We need people who can develop new products and penetrate new markets.* HR, however, appropriately recognizing the need to translate these business demands into something behavioral and measurable, is likely to drive discussion toward variables such as strategic thinking, driving execution, leading change, and likely a long list of others. Senior executives are now asked to shift their thinking and focus to a more microlevel set of variables in order to consider the capabilities of key leaders.

And here lies the first and most fundamental point at which succession management systems break down. In the pursuit of measurement precision and accurate characterization of human capability, we in HR often (despite our best intentions) steer our senior leaders away from the fundamental business purpose of succession management: to create more leaders who are ready to take on pressing business challenges.

This is not to say that measurement precision and lists of well-defined behavioral competencies are not essential. They are, as we will see when discussing the assessment of readiness. However, if succession management efforts are to be truly aligned to the business strategy, the system must be continually anchored to the business outcomes desired, particularly when discussing individuals, and their readiness to step up. This means defining the high-level leadership needs that emerge from a particular business strategy and declaring these as the targets (that is, the metrics) for the succession management system: *Because our business strategy is to . . . , we need leaders who can . . .* The answer to the second part of this statement cannot be a long list of variables. In order to create focus on the most critical outcomes, these high-level needs must targeted and few in number—say, three to five.

The core of a business-focused succession management system is the measurement of progress toward having more leaders ready to step up to the most pressing leadership demands—for example, create and launch new products, penetrate new markets, engage employees, or drive greater efficiency. These are examples of the kinds of high-level leadership growth targets that business leaders articulate when they declare what is needed from a succession system, and our job in HR is to ensure that we communicate and measure progress in a way that maintains focus on them.

The ownership and accountability for these growth targets, however, cannot reside in HR alone; senior leaders must own talent growth. HR may be well equipped to provide development experiences to individuals and to build and facilitate the succession management process, but true growth toward business leadership targets will not occur without the direct involvement and energy of line leaders.

This means that aligning succession management to the business strategy includes aligning the accountabilities of senior leaders to the metrics of system success. Senior executives must own talent growth in the way that sales leaders must own sales growth. We almost always know who owns "the number" for sales growth. A territory, region, or unit is summarized neatly with a revenue number, and we can look at its growth or decline over time. We also know precisely who is responsible for the number. Why should talent growth be any different? If a consumer products company needs more leaders who can develop new products and penetrate new markets, who owns the growth of talent to make that happen? The answer is not HR—at least not alone. Certainly these accountabilities must be shared to some extent, but without a clear answer to the ownership question, achievement of meaningful business outcomes is unlikely.

Moreover, a succession strategy that is truly aligned to the business strategy is a plan to ensure a stable supply of leaders ready to fulfill critical business challenges when they emerge, and the primary measure of the success of such a strategy is the availability of ready leaders at the times when needs emerge (and, of course, the subsequent success of these leaders when challenged). Two fundamental principles are needed to make this plan work:

- Leadership growth targets must be direct extensions of the business strategy (and must not be long lists of competencies or other highly specific variables).
- Senior leaders must be directly accountable for the growth of leaders toward these targets.

Fundamental 2: Define Success Holistically for All Levels of Leadership

Accurately identifying those with leadership potential is a strong step forward, but it is not particularly useful if the target toward which they will be developed has not been clarified. For this section, two critical success factors in defining leadership effectiveness will be stressed:

- Leadership success profiles should be holistic, such that any assessment of an individual is able to describe the whole person, and avoids fragmented evaluations of leadership capability.
- Leadership success profiles should cascade from one level of leadership to the next, illustrating clearly where new and different skills must be applied to succeed at the next level.

A great deal of research and practice has been devoted to the development and construction of behavioral leadership competencies, and those discussions will not be extended here. Instead, the focus here is on how these variables should be organized, and what additional information should be coupled with competencies to ensure that measures are appropriately designed or selected, and that development and promotion decisions are made with the most accurate and comprehensive information.

Aside from any academic definitions or theoretical principles, it is undeniable that if we are to be truly successful in accelerating the growth of leadership capability, we must be prepared to have full and complete conversations about that capability, and we must be precise. Telling the complete truth about talent first requires will, followed closely by discipline. Differently stated, if the definition of success is fragmented or incomplete, then we can reasonably expect that when evaluations are conducted against that definition, the subsequent discussion of the individuals being evaluated will be similarly fragmented. Instead we must have definitions of success that cover the entire range of attributes that interact to create an individual's tendencies and behavior patterns. At any level of leadership (or nonleadership) four elements of success are critical to define:

- *Organizational knowledge*—Requisite knowledge and awareness of how the organization operates, including systems, processes, functions, products, services, and other stable elements of the organization (What I know)
- *Experience*—Job challenges and situations that one must encounter in order to be successful in a given role or job family (What I have done)
- *Competencies*—Clusters of behaviors that are related to job success and under which data can be reliably classified (What I am capable of)
- *Personal attributes*—Stable individual dispositions or abilities, including personality, cognitive ability, and motivation that are related to job success (Who I am)

These factors, and the assessment tools often associated with each, are shown in Table 15.1.

Table 15.1. Success Profile Elements and Associated Assessment Tools

Success Profile Elements	Definition	Associated Assessment Measures
Knowledge	What one knows, particularly about the organization (systems, products, processes)	Résumés Experience inventories Interviews
Experience	What one has done (manage multiple teams, manage profit and loss, work in multiple cultures)	Résumés Experience inventories Interviews
Competencies	What one is capable of—behavioral skill sets (coaching, strategic planning, leading teams)	Interviews 360-degree feedback Assessment centers (simulations)
Personal attributes	Who one is—stable personal characteristics, including personality, cognitive ability, and motivation or work values	Personality inventories Cognitive ability tests Work values inventories Motivational fit inventories

From the standpoint of succession management and the acceleration of readiness, it is crucial to identify the different levels of "developability" of these four components. Knowledge and experience have traditionally received the greatest amount of management attention when evaluating leadership capability. The academic degrees an executive has, the jobs he or she has held, certifications, accomplishments, results achieved: all of these tend to be quite well known among management and HR (or easily obtained) and have traditionally played the biggest role in driving management decisions about both potential and readiness. The irony is that they are the easiest to develop and, as most would recognize, the least associated with success, particularly at higher levels of leadership where knowledge and experience play a lesser role in success. (Ironically, the overemphasis on knowledge and experience is most prevalent in the riskiest succession situation: CEO succession. For a more complete discussion of CEO succession management, see Paese, 2008.)

More critical to discern as one climbs to higher levels of leadership are competencies and personal attributes, the variables that more starkly differentiate success from failure. From the standpoint of competencies, that is, observable behavioral skill sets, a critical design premise is that competency sets must be aligned to the primary levels of leadership in an organization, such that the skill "transitions" between leadership levels is clear.

Table 15.2 illustrates the point. In this example, only one category of competencies has been selected and arrayed across three levels of leadership: how the competencies and job families are defined. (The remaining competencies that should populate each job family are ignored for this discussion. Interested readers may refer to Byham, Smith, & Paese, 2002, for a more detailed discussion.) A quick scan reveals that at the middle manager level, a new competency, business acumen, is introduced. Similarly, entrepreneurship becomes critical at the executive level.

When arrayed across all competencies, and any additional levels of leadership that might be required to define a given organization's leadership hierarchy, the overall picture illustrates the points at which transitional competencies are introduced. These are the competencies that were not required for success in the prior role level but emerge as critical at the next. Creating success profiles that clearly illustrate these transition points serves two key purposes. First, individuals seeking to understand or

Table 15.2. Cascading Competencies

Frontline Supervisors	Middle Managers	Executives
Planning and organizing	Mobilizing resources	Driving execution
Decision making	Operational decision making	Operational decision making
	Business acumen	Business acumen
		Entrepreneurship

develop their skills for higher levels of leadership are shown a clear picture of what is necessary, which helps to clarify the skill components of career progression. Second, this framework provides a blueprint for the design of an organization's assessment system. This is particularly useful for succession management, since we can see clearly where our measures must focus to ensure that we capture the ability to make the jump to the next level. Those identified as high-potential leaders will typically not have prior experience in the transitional competencies because their roles have not likely required it, which renders some measures less useful for succession management—for example, interviews and 360-degree feedback, which rely on current and past performance.

Because the goal is to rapidly accelerate the development of high-potential leaders, the first step is to define all the elements of the success profile. This enables comprehensive development strategies to be employed and avoids the common mistake of summarizing individual capabilities in terms that are too narrow. The second critical step is to illustrate clearly where profile transitions occur throughout the leadership pipeline, enabling effective career discussions and assessment system design.

Fundamental 3: Identify Leadership Potential with a Focus on the Ability to Grow

A midwestern mining corporation found itself in a vulnerable succession situation not long ago. With the CEO soon to retire and several longtime C-suite members to follow soon after, more than half of the senior team was expected to be gone in less than three years, and the question of who would fill their seats became a sudden business crisis. In a discussion with the CEO, the HR vice president summarized the choices well. Option 1 was to promote from within—clearly the most desirable option, except that no internal candidates were seen as ready for any of the positions. Scratch that option. Option 2 was to hire from the outside—a highly undesirable option because it risked eroding the strong culture on which this organization had relied for decades. Scratch that too. Option 3, as the HR vice president put it plainly, was to close the doors and go out of business. Another scratch.

Quickly the conversation turned to the only real option remaining: reach down into the organization and identify the few leaders with the greatest potential for growth toward these roles and dramatically accelerate their development in the hope that they could be ready to fill the soon-to-be-vacated slots.

The need to accelerate the growth of select leaders introduces the first and most fundamental assessment need in succession management: identifying leadership potential. Because resources are scarce and time is short, executives must make crucial investment decisions about talent growth, and these investments cannot be spread evenly and democratically across the organization. In order to prepare the organization for emerging leadership vacancies and business challenges, less-experienced leaders must be developed to quickly take on more senior-level roles. For that reason, the investment in growth must be disproportional in the direction of those who can and will respond to growth opportunities. (This does not imply no investment for all other employees, only that those who can grow into positions of greater responsibility will receive the added support needed to get them there sooner.)

Acknowledging these realities openly is crucial to growth-oriented succession management, and not acknowledging them can be crippling. Before engaging in the business of identifying high-potential leaders, it is critical to confirm that acceleration of a select group of leaders is a business necessity; everyone is eligible, and those receiving special developmental experiences will likely rotate periodically; everyone in the organization still receives development; and not being offered special development does not lessen one's value to the organization. Clearly there are nuances to these types of communications that must be crafted to fit the unique organizational culture and circumstances, but in general, it is difficult to imagine the successful acceleration of development under conditions of secrecy.

When the decision to differentiate among people in terms of their leadership potential has been made, the next obvious question is, How should this be done?

First, a common tripwire is in the definition of terms. Many organizations equate potential with performance and readiness for a position. It is common for organizations to host an annual talent review meeting to identify high-potential leaders in which performance, potential, and readiness for promotion are discussed all at once. This triple-purpose approach can be a barrier to success, as we will see, but first some definitions. Table 15.3 illustrates important distinctions among these three variables.

For the purposes of growth-oriented succession management, the definition of *potential* must be anchored to the intent to rapidly develop these individuals. Toward that end, *leadership potential* is the likelihood that one will respond to development opportunities and grow quickly, ideally to the point of being ready for the next level. This is distinct from the evaluation of current performance and from the determination of readiness for a job or position. Yet many organizations equate the three, and confusion mounts.

This implies several distinct process steps.

1. Identify those with leadership potential.
2. Assess strengths and development needs.
3. Develop toward future roles.

Because so many equate potential with readiness for promotion, a common mistake is to combine steps 1 and 2 into a talent review meeting, relying on subjective manager judgment to arrive

Table 15.3. Definitions of Performance, Potential, and Readiness

	Definition	*How It Is Measured*
Performance	How one is performing now in current role	Performance management
Potential	One's likelihood of leadership growth	Inventory of potential plus management integration
Readiness	One's fit with a specific future role, job, or job family	Role-specific assessment methods such as interviews, simulations, and tests

at both evaluations. Not surprisingly, this can result in poor decision making in both development and promotion.

Although senior leaders and line managers can be relied on to examine current and past performance and make judgments about who has potential, more accurate, in-depth assessment is required to evaluate the fit between an individual and a more advanced role. Best practices in assessment of readiness are discussed later, but first we should examine how organizations can efficiently and accurately identify those with leadership potential.

Presuming that we have agreed to isolate the evaluation of potential from the assessment of readiness for promotion, the challenge is to move as efficiently as possible in step 1 so that we can proceed with step 2. This requires a talent review discussion with a focus on the right factors—those that signal the person's likelihood to respond and grow if provided with stretch assignments and learning opportunities.

At this point, many organizations are tempted to introduce competencies, with the logic that examining the skills required at the next level up is the best way to examine one's potential. This approach has at least two inherent problems. First, lists of competencies are commonly quite long and require a great deal of time to discuss—too much time in this instance. Second, most, if not all, people being evaluated have not yet performed at the level of the competencies in question, so evaluators have to make an inferential leap and project how current performance will predict performance in competencies not yet performed. Of course, tremendous error exists in these judgments if they are not aided with appropriate measurement tools (hence, the presence of a huge field of research and practice in leadership assessment, and the section below on assessing readiness; see also Chapter Thirteen, this volume).

Since it is far too inefficient (and expensive) to conduct in-depth assessments of all employees for the purpose of identifying potential, what is needed is a smaller set of variables that focus the judgments of evaluators on a more appropriate prediction: In which leaders should we invest extra time and money to accelerate their growth? A recent review of potential by Silzer and Church (2009) offers a comprehensive treatment of the construct, segmenting it into a series of factors: cognitive, personality, learning, leadership, motivation, and performance. In practice, the following simpler structure (which is inclusive of the Silzer and Church factors) has been found to facilitate this judgment accurately and efficiently:

- *Leadership promise.* Describes individuals who readily step up to take on leadership roles (either formally or informally) when challenges emerge and bring out the best in others when doing so. They operate with authenticity and an unselfish interest in achieving outcomes that help the organization and others.
- *Developmental orientation.* Describes individuals who grow from their experiences by leveraging feedback and new learning. They show positive responses to others' suggestions for improvement and actively search for ways to gather personal feedback. Having received feedback, they quickly adjust their approaches based on what they have learned.
- *Mastery of complexity.* Describes individuals who navigate effectively through complex challenges by focusing on the few right things and adapting to change. They demonstrate the ability to think conceptually and navigate the ambiguity associated with difficult assignments, as well as adapting their own personal approaches as situations around them change.
- *Balance of values and results.* Describes individuals who achieve positive results in a way that fits with the organization's culture. They are strong pillars of the organization's cultural environment and demonstrate a passion for seeing assignments through to completion and achieving tangible outcomes.

These factors have been applied in many organizations with strong outcomes in both efficiency and prediction (Bernthal, 2007). In practice, arriving at final judgments of individuals against these four factors proceeds in the following primary steps:

1. *Orientation.* Nominators (typically senior leaders or executives) are brought together to be briefed on the purpose of identifying potential and intended outcomes of the process, the definition of potential and how it is different from performance

and readiness, the factors to be evaluated, and the upcoming steps in the process and their expected roles in each.

2. *Ratings of potential.* Managers select and evaluate individuals within their respective organizations whom they view as having leadership potential. Ratings of both current performance and leadership potential are gathered so that the distinction between the two can be explicitly discussed. The four factors of potential are represented in a series of subfactors and behavioral statements, against which each nominee is rated. Each nominee is evaluated by at least two raters (if only one person is knowledgeable enough to rate the individual, more exposure is recommended before the individual is considered for special development). All ratings are then compiled into individual and aggregate summaries for use in the next step.

3. *Integration discussion.* Raters come together in an integration discussion to review each nominee and arrive at final determinations of who shows the greatest amount of leadership potential and will subsequently be eligible for specialized development experiences. This discussion is facilitated by an expert who ensures that conversations about individuals maintain a behavioral focus (avoiding unreliable inferential leaps or personal biases) and drives consensus around both performance and potential evaluations by using the nine-box performance potential grid shown in Figure 15.1.

To arrive at this array, the integration discussion is conducted in two parts: confirmation of the overall performance ratings on the vertical axis and discussion of potential on the horizontal axis. Note once more that these two judgments, performance and potential, are isolated to avoid the common mistake of equating the two.

Of particular note is that this nine-box discussion is the product of survey prework and subsequent discussion among managers who are familiar with the performance of the nominees. Although the survey and four potential factors bring structure, objectivity, and reliability to the process, under no circumstances should the evaluation of leadership potential be left solely to the outcome of a test or inventory. In the interest of driving greater efficiency and lower cost, it may be tempting to rely solely on a test, but the most accurate judgments are drawn from rich discussion of individuals:

Figure 15.1. Nine-Box Performance-Potential Grid

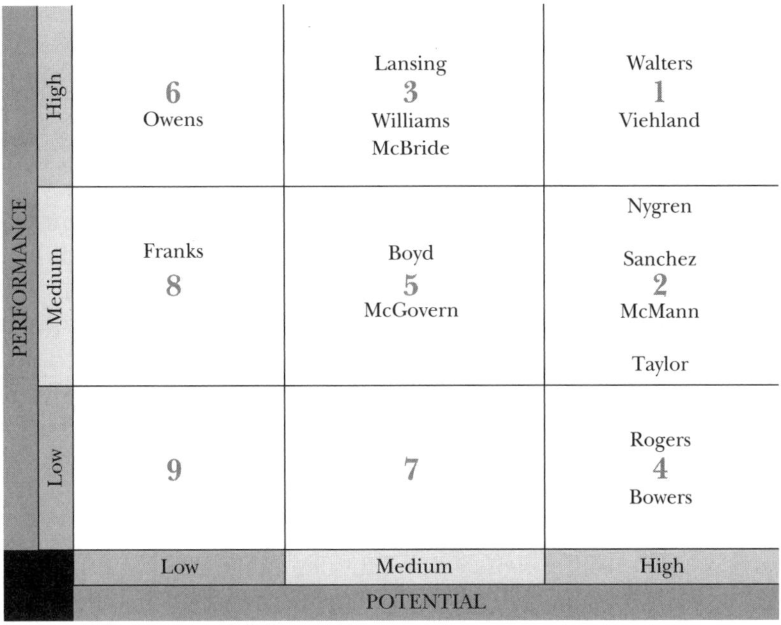

PERFORMANCE		Low	Medium	High
	High	**6** Owens	Lansing **3** Williams McBride	Walters **1** Viehland
	Medium	Franks **8**	Boyd **5** McGovern	Nygren Sanchez **2** McMann Taylor
	Low	**9**	**7**	Rogers **4** Bowers
		Low	Medium	High
			POTENTIAL	

their work histories, behavioral tendencies, and overall performance patterns as they relate to an objective definition and framework for leadership potential. If conducted thoroughly, these conversations result in a deeper understanding of each individual and also a greater felt need to look more closely through the application of objective assessment methodologies. Before discussing assessment of readiness, however, it is critical to ensure that success at the various levels of leadership in an organization has been defined and articulated in a way that enables growth-oriented succession management to thrive.

Fundamental 4: Accurately Assess Readiness for Leadership at Higher Levels

In 2007, Lenny was chief operating officer of a large global home product manufacturer, and the organization he and the CEO had built was struggling. For twelve years, they had grown at breakneck pace from a small outfit to a multibillion-dollar organization, but structure and discipline were not their strengths. Performance reached a plateau, and then it started to decline. Soon they were purchased by a well-known private equity firm that sought to turn the floundering ship around and turn a profit at the same time.

As is customary in these situations, Lenny's boss (the CEO) was fired and replaced by a deputy of the private equity firm. The new CEO, Kurt, was on a mission to get in, make positive change, and get out—all as quickly as possible. However, to get out, he would need a successor. Word came to him that Lenny was the clear and obvious choice: a gifted salesman (the best in the company), knowledgeable of every aspect of the organization, infinitely energetic, with high integrity, and loved by the entire fifteen-thousand-person organization. Interviews conducted by the private equity firm corroborated this assessment. Lenny was the clear choice.

Kurt needed to be sure. A professional assessment was conducted, using interviews, simulations, personality inventories, and cognitive testing. After reviewing the results, Kurt elected to hire a CEO from the outside because Lenny was not ready. But the most compelling (and relevant) part of the story was Lenny's reaction to the assessment feedback. Disappointed to learn that he would not be put into the CEO role and with an understanding of why, Lenny responded by saying, "This assessment is absolutely correct, but I still want to be CEO, and now I know how to get there."

This true story (names changed) illustrates two fundamental axioms of assessment within the context of succession management. First, assessments based on examination of current and past performance (for example, interviews, 360-degree feedback) often fall short, providing only a portion of the information needed by hiring managers, and often leading them toward the wrong conclusions about readiness for promotion. Second, a comprehensive assessment of the entire success profile, using professionally validated tools and methods, yields far greater perceived validity, acceptance of feedback, and developmental insight than assessments conducted in more cursory fashion.

High-quality assessment serves three essential functions in a succession management system:

- *It confirms potential.* Whereas the identification process illuminates who has potential, the assessment process clarifies the specific nature of that potential.
- *It targets developmental actions.* More granularity in the diagnostic enables more specific development actions that result in more impact, more quickly.
- *It guides promotion decisions.* Armed with more detailed assessment information, management can make more effective placement decisions, ensuring that the fit between individuals and roles is optimal.

Table 15.1 showed several of the most common methods for assessing the various elements of the success profile. Clearly many different combinations of tools and methods can be applied to different leadership levels, and at different levels of depth and precision. And since roles at all levels of leadership have requirements in all four of the success profile areas, measuring all components of the success profile is essential.

But how much assessment is the right amount? A truism of leadership assessment is that as the role becomes more complex, the methods of assessment must meet the complexity of the role to ensure accurate prediction (Frisch, 1998; Jeanneret & Silzer, 1998; Thornton & Byham, 1982). In practice, this means that for the more complex leadership roles of managers and executives, multiple methods of assessment must be used to fully assess the entire success profile.

Yet the default for most is to focus on knowledge and experience. These are variables that industry insiders understand and that are easily detected and verified through a résumé, interview, or internal HR records. But rendering judgment after assessing only knowledge and experience leaves critical profile elements unaddressed. The assessment of competencies such as strategic planning, influence, leading change, and driving execution requires deeper and more focused assessment. Certainly competencies can be measured with interviews and 360-degree feedback, but these methods often inadequately measure transitional skills, which are pivotal in the succession process. To gather more reliable competency information, some organizations turn to leadership simulations in which many of these skill sets can be observed in live situations.

A much-neglected area in assessment for succession is the measurement of personal attributes. These are stable, unchanging characteristics such as personality and cognitive ability that cannot be measured accurately in interviews or 360-degree feedback, but play a pivotal role in the success and failure of senior leaders (Hogan & Holland, 2003; Hogan, Hogan, & Warrenfeltz, 2007).

Factors such as emotional adjustment, ambition, and learning orientation (to name a few) sit on the bright side and show the positive and more noticeable aspects of a leader's profile. Arrogance, perfectionism, volatility, imperceptiveness, and others sit on the dark side and show the less obvious aspects of one's profile that can (and do) emerge when leaders feel stress, and derail leadership success if they are not mitigated (Hogan et al., 2007; Dotlich & Cairo, 2003). These well-researched aspects of human personality are the stable, relatively unchanging attributes of individuals and are instrumental in understanding what underlies the behavior that we observe in others. All leaders have elements of both sides of the equation in their profiles, and differences have been shown through considerable research to be predictive of leader behavior patterns (Hogan & Holland, 2003; Hogan et al., 2007).

Another frequently missed opportunity in assessment as it pertains to succession management is the application of assessment centers. As Howard and Thomas point out in Chapter Thirteen (this volume), failure rates among leaders are staggeringly high, particularly at higher levels of leadership where roles are more complex. In these high-stakes promotion situations, simulation-based assessment plays a more crucial role in supplying decision makers with the insight needed to make effective judgments around both development and placement. The value of multimethod approaches that include behavioral observations derived from realistic simulations and reliable evaluation by trained and certified assessors can add substantial value to the insight gained by interviews and tests alone (a common application).

Consider a regularly observed situation in which a high-potential leader is referred to as highly "strategic" by his manager and colleagues. His reputation in the organization is one of a strong thinker and influencer on critical long-range plans and proposals. He can relate stories of his direct involvement in the construction of strategy. In addition, personality test results indicate that he is creative and inquisitive, naturally inclined toward wading into complex associations to search for ideal solutions. To corroborate the pattern, cognitive ability testing reveals a bright and vibrant mind capable of sound judgment and critical thinking.

Stopping here, we would likely conclude that we have a strong strategist on our hands. However, when placed into a leadership simulation (aimed at a level or more above his current standing) in which he was required to analyze complex information and data, extract key trends from a dynamic business scenario, and organize his observations into a coherent plan, he missed critical issues, skimmed over important information, failed to identify the core problems and challenges, and ultimately crafted a strategy that would not have addressed the issues inherent in the scenario. Of what significance is this finding? What does it mean when experience and personal attributes point in one direction, and job-relevant simulations showing actual behavior in future-focused settings point in another?

The reality is that these incongruous patterns emerge regularly. For this high-potential leader, we may find that his personality also includes tendencies toward arrogance and argumentativeness, which might account for his reputation for being influential, bright, and inquisitive, while also signaling warning signs for larger leadership responsibility. A second possibility is that his pattern of strategic thinking capability is valid, but he has not yet had the opportunity to work with the complexity that the next level of leadership presents, and so the simulation caught him flat-footed. Would a complex role at the next level of leadership also catch him flat-footed? What would be the effect of a developmental assignment aimed at this gap? In either instance, the presence of simulation-based behavioral patterns against which to reflect prior experiences and personal attributes such as personality and cognitive ability represents a critical point of insight in making judgments relevant to succession management. How might we have elected to develop this person had we not included the simulation observations? For which roles would we have deemed him a good or bad fit? Clearly judgments are sharper with the inclusion of assessment center insights.

An ongoing challenge in this field is the continued demonstration of empirical evidence for the incremental validity of these multiple methods of assessment. As most will readily recognize, this type of research is uniquely challenging to conduct due to organizational realities of time, availability, and resources, but more so due to the presence of complex intervening variables that make traditional validation difficult and, in many cases, impractical at senior levels. For example, if we make an accurate assessment of the strategic capability of this person but his business unit fails when he is promoted, have our assessment conclusions been rendered invalid? Despite the absence of traditional incremental validation evidence, the tremendous utility in the integration of personal attribute data with assessment center data in drawing meaningful conclusions about leadership performance trends is clear. Having valid personality data at hand when interpreting behavior patterns from a representative set of simulations (and vice versa) leads to a level of understanding that explains why certain patterns have emerged and, more important, how those patterns might be leveraged, developed, or mitigated in actual work situations.

Equal to the importance of powerful assessment tools and methods is the discussion and integration of the results with the key stakeholders in the organization. Routine are the requests by well-intentioned customers of professional assessment to have the assessment administrator "just send the report." But the absence of thoughtful discussion and professional integration of multisource assessment data neutralizes the potentially powerful insight gained by comparing and contrasting perspectives between people who know the behavior of the individual and professionals who have interpreted many different individual profiles. Together these perspectives bring insight to the developable and nondevelopable elements of one's capabilities and can thereby elicit far better judgments about both development and readiness.

At this point, a reference back to fundamental 1 (align succession management with business strategy) is in order. Recall the strong recommendation that organizations should focus on the small number of leadership growth targets (driving efficiency, penetrating new markets, and developing new products, for example) that will propel the business forward. Assessments of readiness must similarly be anchored against these targets. For example, if an organization needs leaders who can drive the development of new products, then it must identify which specific elements of the success profile (knowledge, experience, competencies, personal attributes) will be needed to execute against that target and then provide outputs illustrating readiness against that target. This requires that success profiles and their detailed elements be wired to the broader growth targets, such that assessment outputs can report at both levels of detail. In the example, we would share overall readiness against the ability to drive the development of new products, as well as evaluations against the details within the success profile such as competency scores and personality scale scores. In this manner, senior leaders responsible for the growth of those with high potential have access to business-level information about leadership readiness, as well as individual-level information about the person. Traditional assessment has reported only on the latter, leaving both development and placement decision making with an important and difficult interpretive leap to be made.

A final word about the assessment of readiness has to do with how much assessment to apply at different levels of leadership. By and large, more assessment for more complex roles is a rule of thumb, but the transition from middle manager to executive is one that many organizations view as worthy of special attention. It is at this point that decisions have greater consequences, and therefore organizations tend to invest more heavily in ensuring that they are made effectively. Acceleration pools (Byham et al., 2002) or groups of high-potential leaders who receive special developmental attention are typically formed at this level and above, and sometimes at a level below, but seldom at frontline leadership levels where more general (and therefore less individualized) approaches to succession management are more prevalent. At these lower levels of leadership, more streamlined assessment alternatives that rely on less management discussion are more useful in driving the broad understanding of capability that leaders seek, and they provide the information needed to prescribe more generalized leadership development.

Fundamental 5: Adopt a Creative, Risk-Oriented Approach to Development

The most efficient organizations often have few layers of leadership, providing fewer formal job assignments as stepping-stones for leaders in development. For that reason, development assignments must be created by means beyond job rotation. The result is that highly meaty development assignments are a form of organizational capital. There is only so much to go around, and organizations must spend it wisely if they are to exact a meaningful return on the investment in accelerated growth. Effective assessment provides the insight needed to construct development assignments that will challenge leaders' capabilities and appropriately stretch them into new leadership territory without putting the organization's investment at risk.

A situation at a midwestern insurance organization helps to illustrate the point. A group of approximately twenty high-potential leaders had participated in an assessment process not unlike the multimethod design described in this chapter, including future-oriented assessment simulations. A review of both group and individual results was conducted with the senior team, and for each high-potential leader, development suggestions were made, and accountability was assigned to work with the individual to craft a specific development plan and to report back quarterly on progress. After approximately half the group had been reviewed, a senior team member asked what would be done when there were no more naturally occurring developmental assignments to be handed out. To that point in the meeting, development assignments had been either key jobs or roles on well-established committees, teams, or task forces. The group was at a loss for a response.

In traditional replacement planning scenarios, job rotation (or perhaps simply staying in one's current job until the time came) was the principal development intervention. Because most senior leaders today came up through systems of this nature, few have experience with alternative ways of developing others, and therefore they struggle to imagine what accelerated development can look like in the absence of jobs in which to place people. But it is in these moments of uncertainty that opportunity is born. Growth requires tension. Seldom does a leader (or anyone else for that matter) recount the comfortable, care-free experience that resulted in powerful new learning. To the contrary, accelerated learning is routinely coupled with excitement and, perhaps more common, fear. And to say that this fear, or better, *learning tension*, should be felt by only the high-potential individual is to forget the goal.

Learning tension should be felt and shared by the learner as well as the sponsor, mentor, or manager who is helping to facilitate that learning. This means that in moments when the developmental path forward is unclear, a unique opportunity exists to leverage uncertainty and work to generate a new opportunity to apply new skills or test untested capabilities. This requires creativity, and risk in most cases, particularly if the development is to benefit the business as well as the individual, which it clearly must. Action learning teams may be generated, new task forces created, new roles assigned, or jobs restructured. Many of the most powerful learning experiences come from assignments that do not require a job change. With practice and regularity, organizations can become expert at generating these assignments and thereby establish a means of increasing their developmental capital.

Make no mistake: job rotations and assignments are some of the most powerful experiences available and should be leveraged as much as is practical in succession management. Of course, determining what *practical* means is at the heart of establishing a growth culture. Marginal performers who occupy roles with high learning value should perhaps be moved to make room for high potentials who might perform better and move on more quickly, making room for another high potential. Furthermore, establishing movement between businesses and functions is essential to ensure that untapped skill sets are exercised, unleash talent that may live dormant within a single unit, and prepare leaders for the multidisciplinary challenges that lie ahead.

Few would argue that the greatest learning is achieved when development is dominated by new and challenging experiences that tap into different skill sets and require leaders to take novel approaches. Job rotations, new assignments, short-term assignments on task forces and committees, and in-role development can be powerful in this regard. In addition, formal training and individual coaching play pivotal roles. Training focused on building awareness or skill in a particular element of the success profile may be essential to enable leaders to make the jump to the next level. University programs, event-based action learning, skill practices, courses, and other focused learning offerings are essential to have available for high-potential leaders. Naturally as roles become more complex, these offerings will need to be applied more individually as opposed to systematically.

This is true as well for executive coaching, a vast and ever-growing field that many organizations and individual leaders value. With respect to succession management, executive coaching has often been used as a fallback when no natural job or assignment is available and no alternative development strategy has been crafted. This can be valuable if the high-potential leader is uniquely self-motivated and developmentally oriented, but it can be disappointing to business leaders who hope for visible changes in leadership capability after coaching takes place. If the purpose, intended outcomes, and metrics of success for executive coaching are crystallized and adhered to, then the engagement can be successful. If, however, the engagement is the product of uncertainty about how to develop a leader, the likelihood of meaningful growth is small. Byham et al. (2002) offer a thorough discussion of assignments, short-term experiences, training, executive education, and professional coaching.

Fundamental 6: Establish Management Accountabilities with Teeth

The value of high-quality assessment and creative development planning cannot be realized if management accountabilities are not aligned to ensure follow-through on plans and learning objectives. Organizations frequently struggle with this component of succession management, and a few basic points should be emphasized.

One of the best ways to understand the needed accountabilities in succession management is to consider the perspective of a high-potential leader. In most organizations, the prospect of accelerated development is presented to high-potential leaders as a unique and special opportunity to learn and grow. Certainly this is not inaccurate, but by itself, it does not fully represent the depth of commitment that is often required or present acceleration as something that requires the involvement and commitment of senior management in conjunction with emerging leaders. All too often organizations take the position that individuals drive their own development, but in reality, they seldom can.

Senior management must not only share accountability for growth; they must take it on themselves to create a collective effort focused on the acceleration of readiness. If, as so many lament, the business is short of talent ready to move up, then emerging leaders must be brought closer to the organization's leading edge by senior leaders who are on that edge. This requires not only the creative, risk-oriented development planning discussed but also a shared ownership of growth. Senior leaders must work hand-in-hand with emerging leaders to familiarize them with the immediate and potential future leadership dilemmas being faced.

This is not intended to supplant the accountabilities of the high-potential individual, his or her manager, and HR, all critical to this collective endeavor. It does, however, elevate the ownership of growth to the top. Unless this elevation takes place, the system is likely to languish and achieve far more modest outcomes.

Conclusion

Growth-oriented succession management requires that organizations execute a series of interlocking processes. The business requires more leadership of a certain ilk, which means that leaders with potential must be identified so that their growth can be accelerated toward higher levels. This requires that leadership potential be defined as the likelihood of growth. To accelerate leadership growth, accurate assessment of capability against the future standard must be conducted to determine the true gap between current and required capability. Once the gap is understood, powerful development strategies with appropriate learning tension must be enacted. This learning tension must be shared by the high-potential individual, his or her sponsor, and the appropriate support players, for example, HR or this person's direct manager. The primary means of ensuring that learning tension is felt is to track development progress and hold the development sponsor accountable for growth (along with the individual and other stakeholders) such that the individual's overall readiness for promotion is clear.

This approach to succession management departs dramatically from traditional replacement planning, from which so many contemporary leaders have emerged. As a result, few senior leaders are instinctively inclined to support and drive growth-oriented succession in the way it needs to occur. Shifting the orientation of senior leaders requires painting a simple picture of how the business depends on a collective approach to leadership growth, in which senior leaders engage directly with emerging leaders to create experiences that prepare the latter for tomorrow's leadership challenges.

References

Bernthal, P. (2007). *Assessing the leadership potential factors.* Pittsburgh, PA: Development Dimensions International.

Byham, W. C., Smith, A. B., & Paese, M. J. (2002). *Grow your own leaders.* Upper Saddle River, NJ: Financial Times–Prentice Hall.

Dotlich, D. L., & Cairo, P. C. (2003). *Why CEO's fail: The 11 behaviors that can derail your climb to the top, and how to manage them.* San Francisco: Jossey-Bass.

Frisch, M. H. (1998). Designing the individual assessment process. In R. Jeanneret & R. Silzer (Eds.), *Individual psychological assessment: Predicting behavior in organizational settings* (pp. 135–177). San Francisco: Jossey-Bass.

Hogan, R., Hogan, J., & Warrenfeltz, R. (2007). *The Hogan guide: Interpretation and use of Hogan Inventories.* Tulsa, OK: Hogan Assessment Systems.

Hogan, R., & Holland, B. (2003). Using theory to evaluate personality and job-performance relations: A socio-analytic perspective. *Journal of Applied Psychology, 88*, 100–112.

Howard, A., & Wellins, R. W. (2008). *Global leadership forecast 2008–2009: Overcoming the shortfalls in developing leaders.* Pittsburgh, PA: Development Dimensions International.

Jeanneret, R., & Silzer, R. (1998). Individual psychological assessment: Predicting behavior in organizational settings. San Francisco: Jossey-Bass.

Martin, K. (2007). *The looming leadership void: Identifying, developing, and retaining your top talent.* Boston: Aberdeen Group.

Paese, M. (2008, November–December). Your next CEO: Why succession management is more important than ever. *Conference Board Review*, pp. 18–23.

Paese, M., & Wellins, R. (2007). *Leaders in transition: Stepping up not off.* Pittsburgh, PA: Development Dimensions International.

Silzer, R., & Church, A. H. (2009). The pearls and perils of identifying potential. *Industrial and Organizational Psychology: Perspectives on Science and Practice, 2*(4), 377–412.

Thornton, G. C., & Byham, W. C. (1982). *Assessment centers and managerial performance.* Orlando, FL: Academic Press.

CHAPTER 16

ASSESSING THE POTENTIAL OF INDIVIDUALS

The Prediction of Future Behavior

Rob Silzer, Sandra L. Davis

Sonia, the vice president of human resources at a major retailer, brought her ideas about the inherent talent implications of the company's strategy to the CEO's executive team. She pointed out that doubling the size of the company's revenues over the next ten years would require a larger number of senior product merchandisers than the company currently had. By extrapolating the demand and noting that the company was committed to growing talent from within, she showed how big the gap would be between today's hiring levels and tomorrow's talent demands. Knowing that hiring recent college graduates and bringing in some experienced merchandisers was still feasible, she stated: "Our next hires on college campuses have to be capable of moving into senior buyer roles within five to seven years of hire. We need to be able to accurately assess the potential of new college hires as well as the potential of employees who have been in the system for three or four years. We know senior buyers need both merchandising skills and leadership talent; I need your help to put in the processes and systems now to be ready for the future."

If you face similar issues, you may need to find ways to define and measure the potential of individuals. This chapter directly addresses this complicated challenge by focusing on the assessment potential in individuals. It is an extension of recent work by Silzer and Church (2009, 2010).

The Talent Challenge in Organizations

Business organizations now more than ever are competing in a global marketplace. Their success is linked to having both the financial resources and human resources needed to achieve their strategic objectives. Organizations know that it is now critical to have the right talent to achieve business strategies. Increasingly, leading-edge companies view their critical talent as a strategic, competitive advantage. Their high-value, hard-to-replace talent pool (Dowell, 2010) allows the organization to accomplish unique and differentiating business objectives and gain a significant competitive advantage. As organizations realize the strategic value of critical talent, there has been greater competition for that talent (Michaels, Handfield-Jones, & Axelrod, 2001). This talent is in greater demand now than in the past, and there is a perceived shortage of individuals who can fill these roles.

Progressive senior executives and CEOs now see talent resources as important as financial resources to sustaining organizational success. Over the past decade, organizations have given significantly greater strategic attention to identifying, developing, deploying, and retaining critical talent in order to achieve business strategies (Silzer & Dowell, 2010a). Cumulatively this effort is often referred to as "talent management," which has been defined as "an integrated set of processes, programs and cultural norms in an organization designed and implemented to attract, develop, deploy and retain talent to achieve strategic objectives and meet future business needs" (Silzer & Dowell, 2010b, p. 18.).

In some companies, talent management reviews get equal attention as a core business process to organizational strategic reviews and annual operating plans (Dowell, 2010). As part of talent management efforts, organizations are devoting significant resources to identifying and developing the existing talent in the organization. However, there is also growing interest in identifying individuals who have the "potential" to be effective in other future roles that have broader responsibilities and are at higher levels in the organization. This expands leadership development efforts to the development of individuals for long-term future performance to meet future business needs. To effectively accomplish this, organizations are focusing on identifying and building the talent internally that will be needed in the future.

Identifying and developing talent for future organizational needs is more complex than typical employee selection and development programs for several reasons:

- The future business needs and objectives may be difficult to specify.
- The skills and abilities needed in the future to achieve those objectives are hard to identify and define.
- The individuals who have the most potential to develop those skills and abilities in the future are hard to identify accurately.

The challenge for organizations is that both the future business objectives and the skills and abilities needed to achieve those objectives are difficult to specify with any detail. Consequently the future we are trying to predict is somewhat ambiguous.

Predicting long-term future individual performance is very different from the usual short-term selection issue. Identifying future potential involves making a long-term prediction, often over a period of five to ten years. It requires predicting how much potential an individual has, given additional growth and development, to perform successfully in future organizational roles. That includes consideration of the individual's potential to learn and grow over the years. The future positions themselves, as well as the individual, will change and evolve over the years before a promotion into a specific target role actually occurs.

Defining Talent and Potential

Many organizations are creating processes and systems to identify, assess, and develop high-potential talent (Church, 2006; Silzer & Church, 2010). Over the years, the percentage of organizations that in various surveys report having a high-potential program has increased, from 42 percent of twenty-one companies surveyed in 1994 (Silzer, Slider, & Knight, 1994) to 55 percent of one hundred companies surveyed in 2003 (Hewitt Associates, 2003; Wells, 2003). In 2003, all one hundred companies identified in the top quartile for total shareholder return in 2003 (Hewitt Associates, 2003; Wells, 2003) had high-potential programs, as did 100 percent of twenty major corporations surveyed in 2008 (Silzer & Church, 2010).

Talent and *potential* are conceptual terms that have been used in different ways and for different purposes. Different definitions have been used for both terms (Silzer & Dowell, 2010b; Silzer & Church 2009, 2010).

Defining Talent

The term *talent* has a long history, in various time periods meaning a measure of weight, a unit of money, and later a person's value or "natural abilities" (Michaels et al., 2001). A distinction can be made between having natural abilities in an area (these individuals might be called *gifted*), and learned skills and knowledge. Of course individuals have a mix of both natural abilities and learned skills. A person's natural abilities typically can be further developed by what the person learns and through her experiences.

The term *talent* is used in three different ways in organizations (Silzer & Dowell, 2010b), referring to:

- *An individual's knowledge, skills, and abilities.* "He has talents," for example, referring to what the person has done and is capable of doing or contributing to the organization in the future.
- *A specific person.* "She is a talent," for example, implying she has exceptional knowledge, skills, and abilities in one or more areas.
- *A group in an organization.* "The talent in the marketing function," for example, referring to a specific pool of individuals.

Frequently companies have multiple talent pools (Dowell, 2010), which are sometimes called acceleration pools or pivotal talent pools. *Talent* is distinguished from *high-potential* talent or *high potentials,* in that the term *talent* usually refers to current and demonstrated knowledge, skills, and abilities, while *potential* is the possibility of developing knowledge, skills, and abilities in the future.

Defining Potential

Many organizations use the terms *potential* or *high potential* to refer to individuals who might be able to develop additional skills and abilities in order to perform and contribute effectively in broader or different organizational roles in the future. Potential is associated with performance possibilities for the future rather than with current performance. Organizations want to find the talent with the greatest potential to help maximize future organizational success. Typically high-potential talent programs in organizations (Silzer & Church, 2009) seek to identify individuals with the potential to be effective in broader roles at least several career steps into the future, beyond the next promotion, or to identify individuals earlier in their career (sometimes labeled "diamonds in the rough") who might have long-term potential.

The term *potential* can be either a noun (*he has potential*) or an adjective (*he is a potential general manager*). As a noun it is defined as "something that can develop or become actual"; as an adjective it is defined as "existing in possibility, capable of development in actuality" (Merriam-Webster, 2002). Both uses suggest that the person with potential should be capable of future development and growth. If someone is identified as having *potential,* we should be able to conclude that the person has characteristics that suggest the individual is likely to develop and grow in the future. The definition of *potential* inherently includes the possibility of further development.

This raises a separate question of whether an individual's *potential* is an inherent and unchanging capability—either one has or does not have potential—or is something that can be changed or developed in an individual. Some consulting firms have asserted that potential factors "are extremely difficult to develop" (Rogers & Smith, 2007, p. 8). Our experience indicates that some key components of potential can be developed and more fully realized through specific development opportunities. That is, a person's potential capability may change over time, such as developing more with additional experiences.

Another relevant question is whether potential is a single construct that can be identified and measured independent of the context or expected future role and that is constant across situations, much like general intelligence. Alternatively, does a person's potential depend on the situation or the future role or position and require answering the question, "Potential for what?" Is there one definition and standard for potential, or do they vary depending on the career path?

Some companies have multiple categories of potential or talent pools (Dowell, 2010) depending on the nature of the future roles, such as leadership potential or finance management potential. They suggest that you need to first answer, "Potential for what?" before you can identify the individuals who have potential or are the high-potential talent. This raises the question of whether the purpose (that is the answer to "potential for what?") drives the definition of potential. Is the definition of *potential* specific to the context or career path or is it a general trait?

Recently Silzer and Church (2010) surveyed twenty major corporations and identified several different definitions that are used for *high potential*:

- *By role*—the potential to effectively perform in top or senior management roles (35 percent of companies)
- *By level*—the potential to effectively perform two positions or levels above current role (25 percent of companies)
- *By breadth*—the capability to take on broader scope and leadership roles and to develop long-term leadership potential (25 percent of companies)
- *By record*—a consistent track record of exceptional performance (10 percent of companies)

Other organizational definitions include:

- *By strategic position*—the potential to effectively perform in key positions that may be at the core of the organization's success (perhaps a subset of *by level* definitions but targeting specific positions)

- *By strategic area*—the potential to perform effectively in key functions, business units, or geographical areas that are central to the organization's strategic objectives

Most of these definitions have specific target roles or job levels in mind, and 65 percent of the companies in this sample have more than one category or group of high-potential talent. This suggests that the definition of *potential* in many of these companies depends on answering the question—Potential for what?

Several issues regarding potential have been raised by Silzer and Church (2009):

- How can potential be identified, measured, or predicted if it exists in possibility and is not yet actual?
- Is potential a singular, immutable characteristic that is independent of the situation, or is it more specific to the context or the target role (potential for what)?
- Is potential something that a person just has naturally, or can it be developed?
- Is potential a measure of an existing skill and ability trajectory moving along a predictable path to the future, or can an individual's potential be significantly changed and altered in the future?

These issues will be discussed later in this chapter.

High-Potential Candidates

Typically candidates considered for designation as a *high potential* are internal employees who have a demonstrated performance track record with the company. Although only 10 percent of the companies mentioned above actually use performance track record as the primary and sole definition of *high potential,* all of the companies (100 percent) consider an individual's performance record as one identification factor among others that is considered when selecting high potentials (Silzer & Church, 2010). Newly hired employees usually need to establish an internal performance track record for several years before they can be nominated as having high potential.

Many companies, however, work hard to separate current performance from future potential (Dowell, 2010), having learned that performance in current roles (such as sales positions) is often not a good predictor of performance in future roles (such as sales management positions). So having a strong performance track record is usually seen as necessary but not sufficient to be designated as a *high potential* in most organizations.

Several steps that are frequently included when organizations identify high potentials (Silzer & Church, 2010) are:

1. Agreement on categories and definitions of potential
2. Solicitation of nominations
3. Nominations by managers
4. Assessment of candidates
5. Review by senior management and identification of final candidates
6. Development activities for high-potential individuals

Managers who nominate candidates usually are asked to evaluate them against company criteria or definitions for identifying high potentials. Although the identification process varies across companies, companies often use similar identification factors.

Key Factors for Identifying Potential

Because of the increased interest in identifying high potentials in organizations, a number of models of potential have been developed, usually by external consulting firms. Silzer and Church (2009) reviewed eleven models and corporate surveys of factors of potential and found common categories across the models (see Table 16.1):

- Cognitive skills; some version is included in all eleven models and surveys
- Personality variables, included in eight models or surveys
- Learning variables, reported in eight models or surveys
- Leadership skills, included in nine models or surveys
- Motivation variables, included in ten models or surveys
- Performance, included in three models or surveys
- Other factors, included in seven models or surveys

Table 16.1. Summary of Current Models of Potential

Cognitive abilities	• Conceptual or strategic thinking, breadth of thinking • Intellect, cognitive ability • Dealing with complexity and ambiguity
Personality variables	• Interpersonal skills, sociability • Dominance • Maturity, stability, resilience
Learning variables	• Adaptability, flexibility • Learning orientation, interest in learning • Openness to feedback
Leadership skills	• Leadership capabilities, manage and empower people (general) • Developing others • Influencing, inspiring, challenging the status quo, change management
Motivation variables	• Drive, energy, engagement, tenacity • Aspiration, drive for advancement, ambition, career drive, organizational commitment • Results orientation, risk taking
Performance record	• Performance track record • Leadership experiences
Other variables	• Technical and functional skills, business knowledge • Qualifiers: mobility, diversity • Cultural fit

Source: Silzer and Church (2009).

Cognitive Skills

These variables are likely to be highly correlated with each other. There is growing interest in strategic thinking skills and ability to deal with ambiguity and complexity, which are needed to address the business challenges faced by senior executives. Earlier in careers, cognitive skills may be useful as entry variables to being named a high potential since they can be used to screen in individuals who have the intellectual abilities to learn, grow, and develop during their careers.

Personality Variables

Many organizations are now selecting for and developing interpersonal skills in organizational leaders. A number of these variables, including interpersonal dominance, emotional stability, and sociability, have been found to predict designation as a *high potential* and also later career progress.

Learning Variables

Ability and motivation to learn have been gaining in popularity and acceptance by industrial-organizational psychologists and human resource professionals. Silzer and Church (2010) found that 65 percent of the twenty corporations surveyed use some version of learning skills as an indicator of high potential, although it may be called *learning ability, learning motivation,* or *learning agility.* Also an individual's adaptability and flexibility is widely viewed as an important factor in a person's ability to be effective in a range of new situations and unfamiliar challenges.

Leadership Skills

Leadership skills, or at least early indictors of leadership ability, are widely used in identifying high potential. Two other related factors, developing others and influencing others, are gaining in importance. However, leadership skills may be relevant primarily for individuals who are being considered for long-term leadership careers in the future rather than for careers in research or for other high-potential pools.

Motivation Variables

Although these factors have often been considered in identifying potential, they are gaining in importance as the needs, ambitions, and interests of the individual are given greater consideration in promotion and advancement decisions. It seems clear that personal ambition, drive, and results orientation are more highly valued by organizations now than in the past. In the Silzer and Church corporate survey (2010), 90 percent of the twenty companies consider a person's career drive and ambition in determining whether the person is identified as a high potential.

Performance Record

Clearly a past performance track record may not adequately predict potential to handle future roles. However, when past performance is in experiences that are similar to likely future roles, then the past performance record in those experiences is useful in identifying an individual's potential. For example, success in leading a cross-functional strategic task force may be a useful indicator of how the person might later handle broad strategic initiatives across the organization as a senior executive.

Other Variables

The importance of technical and functional skills and business knowledge varies depending on the particular career path. Mobility has been a key screening factor in the past, but organizations are becoming more open to considering individuals as high potentials even if they are not fully mobile at certain points in their career (Silzer & Church, 2010). Additionally, cultural fit has become a more important consideration as organizations focus on identifying and selecting individuals who match the company's values and cultural norms.

An Integrated Model of Potential

A new "integrated model of potential" has been proposed by Silzer and Church (2009). They considered which components of potential are relatively stable and hard to change and which components are more easily learned and developed. Most human resource professionals understand this dichotomy and often separate them into selection and development variables. Silzer and Church refer to them as *foundational dimensions* (those that are hard to change and develop) and *career dimensions* (those that are more easily developed). They also identify a third group of components, *growth dimensions,* which "impact learning and act as intervening variables that facilitate or inhibit a person's learning and development. They can influence whether a person actually develops in other areas" (p. 399). Examples include an individual's adaptability and openness to feedback. The growth dimensions also can be developed over time through development experiences and opportunities. Silzer and Church propose three types of potential dimensions: foundational, growth, and career (see Table 16.2).

Foundational Dimensions

Silzer and Church (2009) view these dimensions "as consistent and hard to change; in adulthood they are relatively stable across situations, experiences and time" (p. 399). The emphasis here is on cognitive skills and personality variables that are unlikely to develop or change much "without extraordinary intervention and support from others" and probably could be measured "at the same level or near the same level throughout a person's adult career"(p. 399).

Growth Dimensions

These dimensions are seen as "facilitating or hindering a person's growth and development." They are intervening variables to learning, and can be used to indicate whether a person will develop further and learn additional skills. They may vary somewhat across situations and are more likely to be demonstrated when the "person has strong personal interests in an area, has an opportunity to learn more in those areas of interest and has a supportive encouraging environment" (p. 399). Given the right experiences, individuals can change on these dimensions over time.

Career Dimensions

These dimensions are usually career specific and can serve as early indicators of later success in specific careers. A useful example is that effective supervisory skills are likely to be a good indicator of potential for more advanced leadership roles. Which of these are important depends on the particular career path and the answer to the question, potential for what?

Table 16.2. Integrated Model of Potential

- Foundational dimensions, which are consistent and stable and therefore unlikely to develop or change
  - Cognitive
    Conceptual or strategic thinking
    Cognitive abilities
    Dealing with complexity
  - Personality
    Interpersonal skills, sociability
    Dominance
    Emotional stability, resilience
- Growth dimensions, which facilitate or hinder growth and development in other areas
  - Learning
    Adaptability
    Learning orientation
    Open to feedback
  - Motivation
    Drive, energy, achievement orientation
    Career ambition
    Risk taking, results orientation
- Career dimensions, or early indicators of later career skills
  - Leadership
    Leadership capabilities, manage people (general)
    Developing others
    Influencing, challenging status quo, change management
  - Performance
    Career-relevant performance record
    Career experiences
- Knowledge, values
  Technical and functional skills and knowledge
  Cultural fit—career-relevant values and norms

Source: From Silzer and Church (2009).

Common and Specific Dimensions of Potential

The integrated model of potential (Silzer and Church, 2009) addresses the question of whether potential is a single general characteristic or is specific to different careers. Their model has both "common general components that apply in most situations and specific components for specific career paths" (p. 401). Common components of the foundational dimensions are cognitive and personality and of the growth dimensions are learning and motivation. Career-specific components of the career dimensions are leadership, performance, and technical/functional skills.

Silzer and Church (2009) suggest that both the foundational dimensions and the growth dimensions may predict potential for a wide range of careers and talent pools, irrespective of the career path. Of course the level of the foundational dimensions (cognitive skills and personality variables) that is needed will vary depending on the target career roles.

The growth dimensions also are relevant to future learning and development in any career path. Clearly a person with potential is unlikely to currently have the end-state skills needed in future roles and needs to develop them over time. These growth dimensions are indicators of a person's potential to learn and develop those end-state skills.

The career dimensions, such as leadership skills and functional skills, vary in importance depending on the specific career path or talent pool. Leadership skills may be an indicator of potential for an executive leadership position, but they may not be relevant for individuals pursing a research or technical career track.

So potential has both common and career-specific dimensions. The common dimensions (foundational and growth dimensions) may be important for individuals in all potential groups, while career dimensions are relevant to answer the question, Potential for what?

In our view, the integrated model of potential captures the critical underlying factors of potential (Silzer & Church, 2009). This model is used as the basis for our discussion on assessing potential.

Useful Assessment Techniques

This section outlines our combined best practices for assessing the potential of an individual. First, it is important to have a definition and a working model of potential; then reliable assessment methods need to be chosen for measuring each of the key elements of potential. Measuring foundational, growth, and career dimensions usually requires using multiple techniques because no single test inventory, interview, rating scale, evaluator, or crystal ball can provide a simple, numerical, accurate prediction of long-term potential. Evaluating potential from multiple approaches provides a richer, more accurate, and more comprehensive picture of an individual's potential than relying on a single measure. In addition, measuring potential should not be just a one-time judgment (people do change and learn and grow); potential needs to be periodically reevaluated in order to gauge the individual's current potential as it evolves. This approach rejects those who think that potential is an immutable, unchangeable, and undevelopable characteristic.

Assessing potential begins with an answer to the question, Potential for what? In the case of the retail organization at the beginning of this chapter, the answer was, "potential to be successful in a senior merchandising role," which requires both leadership capability and role-specific knowledge or judgment. The second question the organization has to answer is, "Whose potential should be measured, and at what point in their careers?" The choice of assessment approach will be much different when evaluating entry-level job candidates, versus external associate buyer candidates, versus internal experienced associate buyers who may be only several career steps away from a senior-level merchandising leadership role.

The assessment approach that is used needs to measure the level of potential that can be expected for individuals at that particular career stage. For example, the expected level of merchandising knowledge or leadership skills would be different for each of these three different candidate groups (entry level, external, internal experienced). External assessment psychologists assess for, and routinely comment on, an individual's ability to be successful in a specific immediate role and on his potential to be effective in higher-level roles. If you oversee internal or external assessment psychologists, it is usually reasonable, for both selection and development assessments, to ask for conclusions about the candidate's potential to be effective in higher-level roles and potential for further development and growth. Rather than giving absolute predictions, since assessors are being asked about future success far beyond a judgment about success today or tomorrow, an individual can be placed in one of four categories related to her potential for effectively performing higher-level roles in the future: too soon to tell, unlikely, possible, or highly probable. This is based on assessing the individual on foundational and career dimensions and using the growth assessment to gauge the person's likelihood of further growth and development.

If none of the candidates (for either immediate selection or for high-potential identification) has potential for higher-level roles, then you may need to find additional candidates and new sources for candidates, particularly if the objective is to identify high-potential talent.

As an example of looking at an entire candidate pool, one high-technology company that needs both technical talent and technical leadership set an arbitrary rule that at least 30 percent of its new technical hires need to have long-term leadership potential. The company does not need every newly hired employee to have long-term leadership potential, but if they pay no attention to the need for future technical leadership as they hire new employees, they will be relying on chance to meet their future technical leadership needs.

Table 16.3 outlines the assessment techniques that can be used to assess the foundational, growth, and career dimensions related to potential. It is clear to us that there is no single "right" measure for any of these dimensions. Usually the more relevant the data that can be collected across several different assessment approaches to reach conclusions about an individual on a particular dimension of potential, the more accurate the assessment will be. Typically it is best to look at the pattern of data across several measures to reach an accurate assessment on a dimension. Then, based on the assessment of the various dimensions of potential, a more reliable and valid judgment can be reached about an individual's overall potential.

Tests and Inventories

The foundational dimensions (cognitive abilities and personality) are generally consistent, stable and unlikely to develop or change. Cognitive abilities and personality traits lend themselves especially

Table 16.3. Useful Techniques for Assessing Potential

	Tests and Inventories	Interviews	Multirater Feedback Surveys	Immediate Manager Evaluations	Special Rating Scales	Behavior Samples	Performance Measures
Foundational							
Cognitive	X	(x)		(x)	X	X	
Personality	X	X		(x)	X	X	(x)
Growth							
Learning	X	X	(x)	X	X	X	(x)
Motivation	X	X	X	X	X	(x)	(x)
Career							
Leadership		X	X	X	X	X	X
Performance		X		X	X		X
Knowledge	X	X	(x)	X	X	X	X

Note: X—most useful assessment techniques; (x)—secondary assessment techniques.

well to measurement through psychometrically reliable and valid tests and inventories; such tests are widely used as screening devices. The more data an organization has about the current successful performers in particular target roles or levels, the more definitive the assessor can be about whether an individual has the foundational qualities to be that future star performer.

Tests of conceptual thinking skills can be used quite effectively as an early-career screening tool for long-term potential. As a profession, industrial-organizational psychology has extensive data that show a positive relationship between cognitive skills and eventual senior leadership success. However, selecting only those who score the highest on cognitive measures would rule out many individuals with midlevel results, who could also become successful senior leaders because of their other skills, abilities, or traits. Rather than identify only the highest-scoring individuals at early-career stages as having long-term potential, an organization should screen out those who fall in the lower levels on cognitive skills (perhaps the bottom quartile in comparison to others based on organizational test norms).

Personality measures are valuable for the foundational dimensions of personality (dominance, emotional stability) and also for the growth dimensions of learning (adaptability and openness to feedback). Providing a list of the most commonly used measures would be an exhaustive task and outside the review of this chapter. There are several valid and reliable measures of dominance—emotional stability, adaptability, and openness to feedback, for example. In assessing the foundational variables of sociability, dominance, and emotional stability, it is helpful to look for a threshold capacity. If traits and foundational variables are thought of as providing a threshold for future capability and development, then the judgment made early on is whether an individual is at enough of a threshold level that she can become even stronger in the future.

As an example, dominance as a trait tends not to change dramatically over time, so an individual who scores low on dominance today is unlikely to have the influence, drive, or skills to be effective in higher-level roles in the future. Again, the objective is not to look for the most dominant individuals (which may in some situations be a negative indicator of potential), but rather to be sure that there is "enough" dominance for the individual to have the propensity to influence others and take charge in the future (for future leadership positions).

Psychologists have multiple personality measures to choose from when measuring the growth dimensions of learning (adaptability and openness to feedback). These variables can change significantly over time based on situational changes, so assessing them only at one point as a predictor of potential with early-career talent could result in the assessment being less accurate over time as the individual changes. However, scores on these variables tell us how likely an individual is to seek out new experiences, learn from experience, and be open to coaching, feedback, and suggestions. They are especially useful predictors in early- to midcareer situations when an individual scores low on these variables. For example, the associate merchandise buyer who is rigid and closed to feedback would likely be a poor candidate for future senior buyer or merchandising manager roles.

Interviews

A quick review of Table 16.3 shows that interviews emerge as a useful assessment methodology for all dimensions of potential—foundational, growth, and career. Interviews can be conducted by anyone trained in the art and science of structured behavioral interviewing, and specific questions can be crafted that relate to each of the variables under the dimensions.

Measuring true cognitive capability through an interview can cause numerous problems and be influenced by interviewer bias, but strategic thinking, strategic experiences, and long-term perspective can certainly be assessed. In our view, interviews are most appropriate for assessing the growth dimensions, especially motivation. One significant issue in identifying high-potential individuals in an organization is that some strong performers are actually not interested in moving up into higher-level roles. Bosses tend to assume that the high performer wants to move up, but that is certainly not always the case. The identification of high-potential talent must include discovering the individual's aspirations, motivations, and drive.

Sometimes talented individuals need information to see that moving up is a real possibility for them. Recently a banking organization asked a young assistant branch manager whether she was interested in advancement. Her first answer was "no." Probing a little deeper, the human resource manager discovered that the young woman never thought the branch manager job was a reality for her. Once she understood that it was possible and how it might lead to other roles in the future, she agreed to participate in an initiative for high potentials. Organizations that are concerned about diversity in their talent pool may need to use broadly inclusive criteria and not just include individuals who are overtly ambitious for upward career progress.

Multirater Feedback Surveys

Leadership is much more than the innate traits, capabilities, or initiating behaviors of an individual. Leadership is an interaction between a leader and her followers. Therefore, identifying future leaders is not just identifying who has dominance, but discovering how the individual interacts with followers. Methods for identifying leadership potential should include collecting data about leadership impact on others: Are others inspired and motivated by the individual? At lower levels in an organization, one can identify positive, informal leaders in a group by making on-site observations rather than by using a written survey. Who in the group do others seek out for advice? Who can influence others to accept a new company policy?

Some 360-degree mulitrater feedback surveys ask directly about potential, but that can be problematic because there is little understanding of the frame of reference that the respondent is using for defining potential. The most value from multirater surveys stems from the observations others have about the growth dimensions and the career dimensions. By definition, multirater surveys are embedded in the work setting, and respondents have had the opportunity to directly observe how an individual adapts and accepts feedback. They can be especially useful in assessing career dimensions (such as leadership skills and cultural fit) related to real on-the-job behavior, especially leadership.

Immediate Manager Evaluations

The task of identifying and nominating individuals as high-potential candidates should be separated from the task of evaluating their current skills and abilities. For the identification and nomination process, organizations should use a specific definition and targeted criteria for deciding whether an individual is a high-potential candidate. These criteria might involve asking the immediate manager and others for input on select dimensions of potential. For example, as part of the nomination process, the immediate manager and others familiar with the individual's skills and abilities might rate the individual on the growth dimensions (learning orientation and motivation) and on a few of the most relevant career dimensions (such as leadership and cultural fit for leadership potential). The immediate manager might rate the individual using special anchored rating scales or might respond to open-ended questions asking for behavioral examples for each dimension. The nomination process is usually designed to advance an individual's candidacy as a high potential in the organization's decision process. It is not designed to identify the individual's development needs.

Later in the decision process, many organizations complete a more thorough assessment of the individual. This assessment often includes tests, inventories, 360-degree feedback surveys, and other assessment tools. The immediate manager and others may also be asked for their input on the individual's skills, development needs, or experience gaps. Some organizations conduct this more comprehensive assessment of potential before the final high-potential candidate selection decisions are made so they have that data available as final decisions are made. This often results in more accurate identification decisions. Other organizations reverse the process: they identify the final high-potential individuals first and then have all the selected individuals participate in a more comprehensive assessment to identify development needs and gaps in experience. This more thorough assessment process drives development and career planning, while the nomination process generally does not.

Designating individuals as high potential requires clear criteria based on answering, Potential for what? Creating and using anchored rating scales around the specific criteria greatly improves the reliability and validity of the identification process. Managers need to understand that they must use the organization's definition and criteria for potential and not their own personal definitions or biases. They need solid, observable criteria that they can use to determine how well an individual stacks up on the key dimensions of potential. Immediate managers should be one of the best sources of information on the career dimensions. They have seen how an individual leads, manages assignments, achieves results, and demonstrates technical depth and knowledge. These managers can be an excellent source of data about growth dimensions (particularly motivation) if they have behavior criteria to guide them and if they understand an individual's career aspirations, drive, and results orientation. For example, managers can be coached on how to have a career aspiration discussion with their direct reports so the individual's actual motivations are known, and not taken for granted. In our view, immediate managers are a less reliable and less valid source of data on the foundational dimensions (cognitive and personality).

The level of the immediate manager needs to be considered in the nomination process. That is, a director generally has less experience in seeing individuals progress to higher levels in the organization and has a more limited understanding of the target roles or levels. A vice president, by virtue of his role, has a different vantage point and might be in a better position to accurately identify high-potential talent. Relying on the judgment and nomination of a single manager only one level above the high-potential candidates, particularly for early-career candidates, can be problematic. That is why nominations from directors or below are usually reviewed and screened by higher-level managers for their insights and perspectives to ensure that the nominations have merit before they are submitted to the organizational talent review process for a final decision.

Whether an organization nominates first and assesses in-depth later or whether in-depth assessment is used to help identify candidates, data about individuals exist in the organization and can be captured if the right questions are asked to draw out relevant observations. Therefore, reference interviews (targeted interviews with immediate and former managers, direct reports, peers, and others) can be a valuable source of rich and relevant data when assessing an individual's potential.

Special Rating Scales

All of the dimensions of potential lend themselves to behaviorally anchored rating scales for rating individuals and comparing individuals to each other. Asking managers and others to rate the potential of a person can introduce many problems, since each manager brings his own personal and conceptual understanding of what constitutes potential. By asking managers about behaviors they have observed and how they evaluate an individual in comparison to others on specific dimensions, an organization can build useful and reliable anchored ratings scales for assessing potential.

Here is an example. Senior leadership in a construction products organization had identified the general manager role as central and strategic to the company's long-term success. Because the senior leaders intended to significantly grow the organization, they knew they would need a pool of individuals ready to move into general manager positions. Central to their criteria for identifying someone as high potential was evidence of strong leadership skills and business analysis skills. In addition to considering past job performance, they asked managers to rate individuals on two behaviorally anchored rating scales that provided a common evaluation approach for leadership and business analysis skills across candidates. The scales were also used in calibration meetings that required higher-level managers to use the common scales to rate and compare all the candidates. Those ratings were combined with an external assessment and past performance track record to identify their high-potential general manager talent pool and provide them with special development opportunities.

Table 16.4 presents a sample behaviorally anchored rating scale for career motivation. Behavioral scales can be developed for all of the dimensions of potential, including learning orientation, cultural fit, resiliency and adaptability. Managers find them very helpful in guiding their own evaluations and decisions regarding potential.

Behavior Samples

Assessment centers and behavioral exercises have been shown to predict future behavior and advancement. By having an individual

Table 16.4. Sample Career Motivation Anchored Scale

Career Motivation: The level of interest and effort by an individual to advance one's career

Needs Development 1	2	Moderate 3	4	High 5
• Shows little understanding of own career goals and issues • Gives little thought to best career matches for own interests, skills, and abilities • Takes little action to develop self for future career • Reacts to career opportunities as they occur, but takes no proactive steps to plan career • Fails to see benefits of assuming new responsibilities		• Outlines career goals that are unrealistic or unrelated to own skills and abilities • Tries new responsibilities only at the encouragement of others • Is motivated more by financial rewards than by the work or career advancement • Plans career one step at a time; has no longer-term career plan • Pursues development objectives and action steps once identified by others		• Keeps an updated long-term career plan • Outlines specific career steps for achieving long-term career goals • Proactively seeks new responsibilities and roles • Is motivated by the work and personal accomplishments • Identifies own personal development goals and action steps needed to move career forward

complete behavioral tasks and exercises that are realistic samples of higher-level roles, it is possible to observe the individual's behavior and evaluate the person's potential to perform effectively in higher-level roles. Assessment centers are used in some organizations to help evaluate the long-term potential of employees. One common practice that is a poor measure of future potential is having individuals present to the board of directors or senior leadership on a given topic. The thought is that through the process of presenting to senior leaders, there will be an opportunity to evaluate the person's leadership potential. However, the relationship between a single presentation and long-term potential is weak. Whether an individual can make an effective presentation and field questions from senior leaders does not measure foundational, growth, or career dimensions.

Performance Measures

The career dimensions can possibly be measured by performance ratings that focus on career-related skills and past achievements. However, the use of past performance appraisal scores should not solely determine potential in the talent review process. Past performance and future potential are very different from each other (see Silzer & Church, 2009, 2010, for a more complete discussion). Specifically, past performance needs to be carefully reviewed for relevant indicators of the career dimensions. However, past performance ratings also frequently reflect specific situational variables and may not portray the individual's actual skills and abilities (such as an individual getting high performance ratings because he had few real job challenges, an immediate manager who makes all the decisions, or a supportive and highly seasoned peer team that carries most of the workload). In addition, the skills and abilities required to perform past jobs may not be relevant to the skills and abilities required for the career dimensions (such as doing administrative work). The work challenges of past positions may not require the skills and abilities that will be required in higher-level positions and may not be good indicators of future potential.

All of that said, skills and abilities relevant to the specific career dimensions might be observed by performance raters. However, the career-relevant skills and abilities need to be specifically identified and evaluated. General performance ratings can be affected by a wide range of variables, many of them irrelevant to indicators of potential.

Individual Psychological Assessment

Many organizations use individual psychological assessments to evaluate the long-term potential of individuals. Jeanneret and Silzer (1998) define this approach as "a process of measuring a person's knowledge, skills, abilities and personal style to evaluate characteristics and behavior that is relevant to (predictive of) successful job performance" (p. 3). It is not listed separately in Table 16.3 because individual psychological assessment usually includes several of the other assessment techniques, such as tests and inventories, interviews, and behavioral exercises. In addition, for assessments of potential (with development implications), reference interviews with others, such as behavioral interviews with a immediate manager, peers, and direct reports, can be a valuable addition to the assessment process.

Of course, individual psychological assessments are also commonly used for assessing an individual's likelihood of being successful in a particular next job. This approach usually focuses on matching the individual to specific job requirements. Assessors are often asked to evaluate the individual's future potential beyond the immediate job in consideration. In such circumstances, assessors need to broaden the assessment to consider both the immediate job requirements and the dimensions of potential discussed above.

Some organizations include individual psychological assessments as part of the identification process and later review the assessment results and other data to make the final identification decisions. In these cases, the individual assessment results are integrated with other internally collected data to provide an in-depth picture of the individual. Candidates might be appropriately concerned if they thought their fate rested solely on an external assessment. However, an external assessment is usually more objective than internal data and can more easily overcome internal biases and corporate politics.

Other companies wait until after the high-potential individuals have been identified and then have them go through an individual psychological assessment for development and career planning purposes. This removes the individual assessment from the decision process but gives it significant influence in determining later career and development plans.

Assessing the Potential of Individuals

The integrated model of potential and the assessment methods discussed can be used to structure an assessment process to evaluate high-potential candidates. First, the critical components need to be identified that are relevant to the organization's strategic needs and the particular high-potential talent pool that is being considered. Exhibit 16.1 provides an example of an evaluation of a candidate for the merchandising leadership high-potential talent pool in a large consumer products company. This example illustrates a common profile found in early-career talent. This candidate demonstrates solid cognitive, learning, and job performance skills but perhaps needs more experience to gain additional leadership and technical skills and to clarify her career ambitions. She would be a solid candidate for designation as a high potential providing she gains these skills and knowledge in additional work assignments.

The decision on an individual's potential should be based on the entire profile of relevant dimensions. In particular, the foundational and growth dimensions provide insight into basic components, while the career dimensions give some insight into the individual's career direction and the appropriate talent pool for the person.

Special Assessment Issues

Setting up organization processes to create a robust high-potential identification and assessment process brings a number of challenges. No matter how the organization answers the question, Potential for what?, there are predictable and important issues to address.

Exhibit 16.1. Assessment of Potential: Results for Sally Sample

Date: October 30, 20xx

Division/Business Unit: Women's Apparel

Current Position: Business Analyst

Future Consideration: General Merchandising Manager (GMM)

This analysis includes elements related to this candidate's potential. The data from several sources were used to determine overall potential at this point in time. These data are to be used for discussion about the candidate's development and action plans for capitalizing on and increasing the candidate's potential.

	Psychological Assessment	Structured Interviews	Manager Ratings	Business Case Sample	Performance Record
Foundational Dimensions					
Cognitive: • Compared to GMMs	←				
Personality: • Resilience	↕	↕	↕		
Personality: • Dominance	↕	↕	←	↕	
Growth Dimensions					
Learning: • Openness to Feedback	←	←	←	←	
Motivation: • Career Ambition	↕	↕	←		

Motivation: • Risk Taking	←			←	
Career Dimensions					
Leadership: • Managing People		→	←	→	↕
Performance: • Job Record		←	←		←
Knowledge: • Technical		→	←		→

Recommendation: This profile reflects an individual at an early stage in her career. Some elements of potential are unknown due to her limited experience, but she shows enough indicators to be considered as having solid potential for the future, providing she gains experience in managing people, learns whether leading others is truly her career ambition, and gains more technical merchandising knowledge. These actions should help to increase her potential for future leadership roles in merchandising.

← Data suggest high potential	↕ Data suggest moderate potential
→ Data suggest limited potential	Blank No data

Transparency or Secrecy

Invariably as an organization implements the process of identifying high-potential talent, someone will ask, "Should we tell the individuals who are high potential?" and, "What do we tell individuals who are not identified as high potential?" There are several fears lurking behind these questions: a fear of fostering elitism among those identified, a fear of demotivating strong performers who are not the highest-potential talent, and a fear of creating a sense of entitlement for selected individuals. In addition, some organizations have simply said that they do not believe their managers are sophisticated enough or do not have the right skill sets to be able to have the delicate conversations with individuals about their future potential that transparency requires.

Silzer and Church (2010) found that most of the companies in their survey of twenty companies do not release this information to individuals. They have concerns about "misinformation, shifts in performance, labeling biases, retention and creating culture of entitlement" (p. 239). This is often compounded by the fact that it is often the leaders just a few levels above the candidate who ultimately make the decision about potential. This can make it difficult for the candidate's immediate manager to explain to the individual why she is not in a particular high-potential program.

As a general rule of thumb, transparency is a better practice than secrecy, and interest is growing in having open, honest, and transparent conversations with individuals. Highly talented individuals need to know they are well thought of and that career opportunities exist for them. Organizations that believe they can retain "A" players under a mantle of secrecy are misguided. At the same time, if an organization only pays attention to developing high-potential talent and has no development offerings for other individuals to learn and grow in their careers, they may risk demotivating those who are not in a high-potential pool. Investing in talent development broadly, with programs for high potentials being only a part of the mix, is one way to keep all employees engaged and feeling valued.

Status often can be communicated indirectly through new assignments and development opportunities. Because of complicating factors, many organizations rely on human resources to communicate with individuals about their status, either quietly or indirectly.

There is also a question about what to tell an individual about where he stands, especially if an organization uses a typical nine-block performance and potential matrix to rate individuals. Placement on a performance–potential matrix should be dynamic and open to change as individuals move up the organization, refine their motivations, learn new skills, or move to new assignments. The more that potential and development are seen as dynamic, the less concern there will be about telling an individual where he stands at this particular moment in time.

Involvement of Candidates

It makes sense that formal assessment requires the candidate's agreement to participate. Individuals should understand the purpose and implications of participating. Informed consent is necessary; individuals need to know who might see their assessment data, how the information will be used, and what kind of feedback they will receive. Unless the assessment is being conducted for external selection purposes, most organizations expect an assessment to fulfill more than one purpose—judgment about potential and information for development, for example. In several organizations, assessments have become so much a routine part of development planning that individuals are actually pleased, rather than apprehensive, to be asked to participate. They see it as a clear indication that the organization is actively managing their careers and giving them special development opportunities. Often it is a sign that the individual has achieved a certain level of visibility and attention in the organization.

In some organizations, all individuals who move to certain organizational levels participate in an assessment, and the assessors are asked to provide ratings on competencies and potential. Those ratings are then reviewed in the formal talent review process. The more that assessment in an organization is common and "business as usual," the easier it is to gain cooperation—even enthusiastic engagement.

Performance Versus Potential

Personality inventories and intellectual measures are powerful indicators of foundation and growth dimensions. Their use, along with the role of external individual assessments, in the high-potential identification process is a widely discussed issue in organizations. Some managers and high-potential candidates are unenthusiastic about the use of tests and inventories in the high-potential decision process. They believe that their performance track record should be the primary indicator of their potential rather than some tests or inventories over which they have little control or influence.

Although their concerns may be understandable, they are based on a lack of distinction between performance and potential. Past performance is not necessarily a good predictor of long-term potential. Organizations introduced the performance-potential matrix to help distinguish these constructs and evaluate them separately. Unfortunately, many organizations have been slow to move away from past performance as their key indicator of potential. Silzer and Church (2010) found that 100 percent of the twenty companies in their survey use past performance as one factor in the identification of potential, although only 50 percent indicate that it is a critical factor.

Future potential is typically better measured by tests, inventories, and individual assessment than by past performance. Some candidates who have strong performance track records want to rely on the performance they have demonstrated already rather than put their candidacy at risk by taking cognitive tests, personality inventories, and an individual assessment. They are trying to ensure their candidacy and avoid getting rejected based on factors they believe they cannot control. Organizations and senior managers often fail to see the difference between performance and potential, or they do not want to have to defend the use of tests and assessments as identification tools.

It is possible that both a performance track record and an evaluation of potential can be relevant to future potential. Past performance may reflect strong indicators of learning and motivation. Our point is that past performance should not be accepted blindly as a valid measure of potential. An individual's performance record needs to be carefully evaluated and parsed for specific indicators of the dimensions of potential. If this is done carefully, past performance may indeed provide relevant data for assessing potential. But equating the two, as some organizations do, is misleading at best and often a wrong conclusion. Ultimately in the future, organizations, senior managers, and even high-potential candidates will better understand the difference between performance and potential and will come to accept these more valid and reliable approaches to assessing potential. Once they become comfortable using the tools, they will see that they provide more relevant and accurate data. At the same time, better ways of analyzing the relevance and predictive power of past performance will be developed so that the focus is on the behavior from past performances that are clearly relevant to having future potential for a particular career path. Both of these efforts are now starting to occur and will likely evolve substantially over the next five years.

Regarding confidentiality of the candidate profiles, actual test and inventory scores and the assessment results should be restricted to key decision makers in the company. Often human resources has responsibility for ensuring this confidentiality.

Internal Versus External Assessment of Potential

When an organization chooses to use a formal leadership assessment process to assess potential (which often includes standardized tests and inventories, behavioral exercises and simulations, an interview, and 360-degree survey components), it may have the option of using an internal or an external assessment psychologist. Some larger global entities may have that assessment resource internally, while midsize and smaller companies typically do not. In either case, the psychologist needs to know how the company defines potential, what dimensions need to be assessed, and what judgments they expect the psychologist to make.

An internal psychologist typically will know the organizational culture better and through their work experience and knowledge of candidate data also know many current high-potential individuals as an assessment benchmark. However, it can be challenging to conduct an internal assessment for potential.

Internal assessors often have biases that are inherent in knowing the candidate's business unit or function and the internal political dynamics. For these and other reasons, many organizations turn to external assessors for objective, unbiased judgments. In addition, external assessors bring a comparative perspective and normative data from having worked with multiple organizations. The question often asked is, How do our high-potential performers stack up against those from other companies?

Ultimately, the assessment of potential is likely to be best served and accomplished by using a combination of internal and external assessment. Internal assessors are better positioned to evaluate specific past performance and experiences to identify how skills and abilities demonstrated in the past are relevant to future career paths, roles, organizational culture, and business strategy. External assessors can often provide a more objective and norm-based assessment of an individual's potential on the critical dimensions of potential.

Evaluating Progress and Success

Organizations have begun measuring the effectiveness of their high-potential programs. Silzer and Church (2010) found that 75 percent of the companies in their survey track the ongoing performance and career moves of high-potential individuals, but most do so only informally or are just starting more formal tracking efforts. They found that the typical tracking measures are:

- Promotion rates for high potentials
- Movement of high potentials to new assignments
- Performance of high potentials
- Time spent by high potentials in positions
- High-potential attrition and churn rates

These measures on high-potential groups are often compared to similar measures collected for a comparative group of internal managers—perhaps high performers. However, these measures are often contaminated since the individuals making related decisions (such as promotions and performance ratings) are usually aware that the individual is a high potential. (For further discussion of talent management measures see Scott, Rogelberg, & Mattson, 2010.)

Better measures need to be developed of the impact of high-potential decisions on business outcomes. Once accurate measures are identified, HR will gain much greater influence in leading organizations.

A Few Lessons Learned from Experience

Over the years we have done thousands of assessments with executives and managers and have regularly evaluated the long-term potential of these individuals. Along the way, we have identified a few valuable lessons on assessing potential:

■ ■ ■

1. *Use a clear definition of potential.* It is central to the reliability and validity of the assessment process that there is agreement on the definition and key components of *potential.* It is usually helpful to ask, Potential for what? A clear and objective definition (including key components) provides internal agreement among managers and executives on what they are looking for and minimizes the impact that their personal biases can have on who is identified as a high-potential talent. Clarity of definition also leads to appropriate choices for a process.
2. *Include rich data.* The assessment should tap into the strongest and richest sources of data available on the individual to make an accurate judgment about potential. It is important to have relevant and multiperspective data for making the decision calls about potential and for understanding skill and experience gaps. Assessments can not only be ineffective but also damaging to individuals and organizations if they are based on the wrong criteria and or personally biased data. Industrial-organizational psychologists know how to do this well, and it is important that these assessments are conducted professionally and effectively.
3. *Conduct a professional assessment.* Whether you are using individual psychological assessments conducted by an industrial-organizational psychologist or behaviorally anchored rating

scales completed by the immediate manager, it is critical that the integrity and professionalism of the assessment process be maintained. This means maintaining the objectivity and integrity of the data, minimizing personal biases, focusing on the best data available, and honestly reporting the assessment results. Keep in mind that the assessment results can have significant impact on the candidates and their careers as well as on the long-term success of the organizations.

4. *Match the individual to the definition and criteria of potential.* Carefully compare the individual's results on various potential components with the stated criteria for potential. We support a compensatory approach to evaluating potential, considering how a strong score on one component might help compensate for a moderate score on another component. However this approach has limits. For example a strong score on cognitive skills might not necessarily compensate for weak scores on learning or interpersonal skills. It depends on the specific criteria for a particular potential assessment. Keep in mind that the definition and criteria might be different for different answers to the question, Potential for what?

5. *Identify development needs and experience gaps.* Every assessment provides data that can be leveraged in several ways. Most immediately, the results can be used to make informed and valid decisions for identifying high-potential talent. However, almost all assessment data can and should be used to identify an individual's development needs and experience gaps. Unfortunately this step is often skipped over; it should become a routine.

6. *Assess potential over time.* Assessing potential is not just a one-time judgment; people learn and grow, and even the definition of *potential* can change dramatically over time in a company's evolution. For example, as organizations become flatter and more global in nature, it will be more apparent that assessing potential is not solely about upward mobility, but about an individual's potential contribution broadly to the organization's success and strategic direction. In addition, while a person may not change much over time on the foundational dimensions, there is great opportunity for an individual

to change and develop on the growth and career dimensions over time. Some organizations fully understand this and reconsider a person's potential status on a regular basis.

■ ■ ■

Both organizations and individuals have a great deal to gain by using reliable and valid assessments of potential. This chapter provides some guidelines that should help to develop and implement those assessments. Organizations and human resources professionals should be encouraged to focus efforts and resources on building this critical strategic initiative to more successfully achieve organizational objectives. Preparing for the future starts now.

References

Church, A. H. (2006, May 6). Bring on the high potentials—Talent assessment at PepsiCo. In *Talent management: Will the high potentials stand up?* Symposium at the Annual Conference of the Society of Industrial/Organizational Psychology, Houston.

Dowell, B. E. (2010). Managing leadership talent pools. In R. F. Silzer & B. E. Dowell (Eds.), *Strategy-driven talent management: A leadership imperative* (pp. 399–438). San Francisco: Jossey-Bass.

Hewitt Associates. (2003). *Managing high potentials.* Lincolnshire, IL: Hewitt Associates.

Jeanneret, R., & Silzer, R. (Eds.). (1998). *Individual psychological assessment: Predicting behavior in organizational settings.* San Francisco: Jossey-Bass.

Merriam-Webster. (2002). *Merriam-Webster's collegiate dictionary* (10th ed.). Springfield, MA: Merriam-Webster.

Michaels, E., Handfield-Jones, H., & Axelrod, B. (2001). *The war for talent.* Boston: Harvard Business School Press.

Rogers, R. W., & Smith, A. B. (2007). *Finding future perfect senior leaders: Spotting executive potential.* Bridgeville, PA: Development Dimensions International.

Scott, J. C., Rogelberg, S. G., & Mattson, B. W. (2010). Managing and measuring the talent management function. In R. F. Silzer & B. E. Dowell (Eds.), *Strategy–driven talent management: A leadership imperative* (pp. 503–548). San Francisco: Jossey-Bass.

Silzer, R. F., & Church, A. H. (2009). The pearls and perils of identifying potential. *Industrial and Organizational Psychology: Perspectives on Science and Practice, 2*(4), 377–412.

Silzer, R. F., & Church, A. (2010). Identifying and assessing high potential talent: Current organizational practices. In R. F. Silzer & B. E. Dowell (Eds.), *Strategy–driven talent management: A leadership imperative* (pp. 213–279). San Francisco: Jossey-Bass.

Silzer, R. F., & Dowell, B. E. (Eds.). (2010a). *Strategy–driven talent management: A leadership imperative.* San Francisco: Jossey-Bass.

Silzer, R. F., & Dowell, B. E. (2010b). Strategic talent management matters. In R. F. Silzer & B. E. Dowell (Eds.), *Strategy–driven talent management: A leadership imperative* (pp. 3–72). San Francisco: Jossey-Bass.

Silzer, R. F., Slider, R. L., & Knight, M. (1994). *Human resource development: A benchmark study of corporate practices.* St. Louis, MO, and Atlanta, GA: Anheuser-Busch Corporation and Bell South Corporation.

Wells, S. J. (2003). Who's next: Creating a formal program for developing new leaders can pay huge dividends, but many firms aren't reaping those rewards. *HR Magazine, 48*(11), 44–64.

CHAPTER 17

ASSESSMENT FOR ORGANIZATIONAL CHANGE

Mergers, Restructuring, and Downsizing

John C. Scott, Kenneth Pearlman

Staffing needs that arise from organizational change present a unique set of challenges not typically faced in standard staffing situations. Whether as a result of a corporate merger, restructuring, or reduction in force (RIF), staffing for organizational change generally occurs under conditions of high stress, unrealistic deadlines, and uncertainty. Because of the tremendous pressure to staff the new organization as quickly as possible, expediency often takes precedence over sound selection decisions. Unfortunately, organizations frequently risk making staffing decisions in this context without the benefit of a clear vision as to what is required for the long-term success of the new organization. Without a structured and well-communicated staffing model to guide them, employees and managers alike often perceive the resulting selection decisions as arbitrary and unfair. Research and experience over the past twenty years have shown that companies using such unstructured approaches experience decreased productivity, eroding morale, and, with alarming frequency, employment litigation.

An examination of 115 federal district court opinions involving age discrimination litigation and organizational downsizing revealed the importance of sound personnel practices in influencing litigation outcomes (Wingate, Thornton, McIntyre, & Frame, 2003). This study highlighted how closely the courts scrutinize personnel practices associated with an RIF and detailed specific practices that are most meaningfully linked to judicial verdicts. For example, a defendant organization is more likely to prevail if it has a written layoff policy, has conducted assessments of the plaintiff's capabilities prior to termination, has documentation of substandard plaintiff performance, has executed an independent review of the termination decisions, and does not replace the laid-off employees. This review serves to identify some key components that should be incorporated into any staffing model involving organizational change and RIF decisions.

Another important legal development that bears directly on RIF staffing practices is a recent U.S. Supreme Court ruling (*Meacham et al.* v. *Knolls Atomic Power Laboratory,* 2008) that extends the burden on employers when defending RIF decisions and avoiding liability under the Age Discrimination in Employment Act (ADEA). This ruling requires extra vigilance on the part of the employer to ensure that RIF decisions are based on reasonable factors other than age (RFOA). Employers who are defending a disparate-impact claim under ADEA must not only demonstrate that their layoff decisions were based on RFOA, they must also be able to persuade a judge or jury of the reasonableness of that factor. While the court's decision increases the difficulty and cost for defending a disparate impact claim, an appropriately designed staffing plan will lay the foundation for legal defensibility by establishing reasonable job-related factors on which staffing decisions can be made.

Fortunately, the defining characteristics of a staffing model that retains the best and the brightest are the same characteristics that render it legally defensible. It is not necessary to make a trade-off between these two goals. Whether companies confront the staffing process internally or enlist the help of experts, it is crucial to understand the key principles that should guide a strategic staffing model when dealing with an organizational change.

This chapter outlines the principles and practices that are necessary to build an effective staffing model that will withstand legal scrutiny and place the right employees, with the right competencies, into the right roles. The chapter begins by highlighting the different routes that should be considered when confronting various types of corporate change initiatives (for example, mergers and acquisitions, organizational restructuring, and across-the-board RIF) and outlining a five-step process for ensuring that the infrastructure is in place for successful execution of the staffing model. It then offers practical guidelines for conducting sound assessments and making proper selection decisions. The processes and guidelines we present should be regarded as suggestions rather than prescriptions, since tactical and procedural details of planning and implementation must always be adapted for the prevailing circumstances under which an organizational change is initiated. Nonetheless, we have found these strategies to be applicable and appropriate in a wide range of settings. Interspersed through the chapter is a case study that highlights the staffing principles discussed and selection decisions reached by a hypothetical organization involved in an organizational change initiative. Despite the considerable challenges facing an organization undergoing significant transformation, this is an opportunity to build the most capable workforce possible and position the organization for future success.

Building the Staffing Model Road Map

The obvious goal of any staffing model used during a period of organizational change is to ensure that a superior workforce is placed (or retained) in the new organization. The key to building a legally defensible, best-in-practice staffing model in this context is to ensure that the components of the process are structured, fair, and job related. The particulars of the staffing model road map obviously vary depending on the nature of the organizational change and many other factors specific to each organizational setting, but should generally follow five key steps, regardless of the type of initiative or special circumstances: (1) establish guiding principles, policies, and tools; (2) develop and implement a comprehensive communication plan; (3) identify the positions requiring staffing decisions; (4) create job requirements for the targeted positions; and (5) develop and validate assessment tools.

Step 1: Establish Guiding Principles, Policies, and Tools

The first step in the process is to establish the guiding principles and ground rules for staffing the organization. A good idea at this stage is to assemble a review board comprising the organization's business leaders and high-ranking members of the legal, human resources (HR), and corporate communications departments. The major responsibility of the board is to establish and agree on the set of guiding principles that will drive the staffing process, determine how displaced employees will be dealt with, agree on communication and rollout strategies, and commit the resources needed to effectively carry out the staffing process. The review board will also evaluate all selection decisions across the organization before they are finalized and announced. While this auditing role appears at first to be a daunting task, it is managed by the fact that the staffing decisions are generally made in successive waves, typically beginning at the top layers of the organization and cascading down through the organizational levels. In addition, some organizations choose to train smaller review committees that operate within each business unit and report their findings and any issues to the review board.

Although there are a number of ways to proceed and each organization faces its own unique challenges, the review board should discuss and agree on a set of guiding principles that will direct decision making throughout the staffing process. The following set of recommended principles should be considered when establishing the staffing plan.

Guiding Principle 1: Adapt the Staffing Model to Organizational Initiatives

The objectives of the staffing process vary based on the nature of the organizational initiative, and this will bear on the tools used in the assessment and selection phases. The three primary organizational initiatives that lead to head count reductions are mergers and acquisitions (M&As), restructuring, and targeted or across-the-board RIFs.

The principal objective of a staffing process in an M&A is to select the most qualified incumbents from the different legacy companies for positions in the new organization. The challenge is to execute a fair staffing process that affords equal opportunity to employees from each company who are vying for the same positions in the new organization. The hiring managers in the new organization will be familiar only with candidates from their own company. As a result, the staffing process used must close this knowledge gap and provide an objective and fair assessment that places all candidates on a level playing field.

In a restructuring, the principal objective becomes one of properly placing the most qualified incumbents into new positions in the restructured organization. The challenge is determining which employees have the skills needed to succeed in the newly designed roles and which employees no longer meet the requirements of the organization and hence must be displaced—and potentially replaced. The hiring managers will likely be familiar with all of the candidates' performances but will need to be able to assess them against a new set of criteria required for the newly designed roles.

In a conventional downsizing or RIF initiative, the principal objective is to select out the least qualified incumbents in the targeted positions. The primary challenge here is to differentiate among current incumbents to determine who should be displaced and who should be retained. Faced with tight deadlines and inexperience, organizations frequently rely on archival performance measures, such as recent performance appraisals, to make these assessments. Since the organization's existing performance appraisals were not designed (or validated) for this purpose and typically produce inflated ratings, they tend to be ineffective, and hence minimally defensible, for differentiating among incumbents for the purpose of making termination decisions.

The common feature among these three initiatives is that they all target incumbents who have a history of performance (that is, work-related behavior) with the organization. Since it is virtually axiomatic in our field that past behavior is the best predictor of future behavior, a well-designed staffing model that capitalizes on this rich behavioral history is not only the most logical approach but also the most defensible. However, this is true only to the extent that such prior performance-related and behavioral information is appropriately organized and evaluated, as in the competency-based assessment approach we describe later in the chapter, which should serve as the core feature of a staffing model across all three initiatives.

The specific tools that comprise this core assessment may differ in order to address the different organizational objectives appropriately. For example, in the case of a merger or acquisition, the use of self-assessments, interviews, business cases, and other objective measures can help place candidates from the different legacy companies on a common scale and bridge the knowledge gap between the selecting leaders and employees from the different companies. (Note that we use the term *selecting leader* in this chapter to denote the individual who is responsible for making decisions on placement and displacement.) In the case of a restructuring, an assessment of core and functional competencies tied to the newly designed job requirements can help differentiate top candidates within the incumbent group. In a downsizing, differentiating criteria such as a special license, seniority, or a unique job-related skill can help break ties in the assessment process. Moreover, in some cases, such as certain types of M&As and restructurings or disaggregations, staffing decisions are made by the sending organization (the organization from which employees will be drawn) rather than the receiving organizations (the organizations to which employees will be assigned and may not yet exist), making it important to balance the prospective needs of the new organizations with one another or with the sending organization. The point is to adapt the specific assessment tools, methods, and processes to the unique demands of the organizational initiative while using the assessment of appropriately organized performance-related and behavioral information as the core feature.

Guiding Principle 2: Ensure Job Relatedness

A fundamental requirement for a viable staffing model is that it be job related. That is, the criteria used for selecting or displacing a candidate must be tied directly to the requirements of the target job. Although this seems intuitively obvious, many approaches to staffing for organizational change do not take the steps necessary to ensure this linkage. This can lead to a skills gap between the demands of the job (whether new or existing) and the skill level of the person selected or displaced. Ensuring job relatedness requires the specific identification of success factors that are critical for effective execution of job responsibilities. Therefore, before any assessment and selection decisions can occur, a job analysis or competency modeling study must be conducted on the jobs in the new, restructured, or targeted-for-RIF organization. (There are many definitions and interpretations of *competency modeling;* we regard it as a particular form of job analysis; see Chapter Eight.) To the degree that the organizational change initiative also involves changes in organizational strategy or in the context or culture in which a job is performed, it will also be important to incorporate relevant organization-level variables—those that might imply the need for worker competencies driven by strategic or contextual factors, such as the need for multiskilled workers—into the job analysis process. Once the job requirements have been determined, it is necessary to validate the assessment tools against these critical requirements.

A validation study should be conducted to support the use of the assessments used in this context. Both the *Uniform Guidelines on Employee Selection Procedures* (1978) and the *Principles for the Validation and Use of Personnel Selection Procedures* (Society for Industrial and Organizational Psychology, 2003) describe alternative strategies and standards for demonstrating the validity of selection procedures.

Guiding Principle 3: Ensure Procedural Justice

A common mistake made by organizations undergoing any kind of RIF is to be secretive about the staffing process and share information only on a need-to-know basis. This is generally motivated by both a lack of confidence that the staffing process is fair, valid, and legally defensible and a related concern that too much information shared with affected employees can be risky. The decision to share only the basics, such as time frame and percentage of head count reduction, is a shortsighted strategy that often results in the very challenges the organization is seeking to avoid. Employees who feel that they have been treated unfairly or presented with minimal information will make assumptions about the process that may or may not be true, often resulting in negative reactions.

Regardless of the particular staffing model and circumstances surrounding an RIF, employees need to know what to expect, by what means they will be evaluated, and from what source decisions will be made. A great deal of recent research suggests that fair and transparent procedures can often compensate for the undesirable outcomes that employees experience, such as termination or displacement into a pool. There is no need to conceal any aspect of an appropriately designed staffing model. In fact, sharing the particulars of the model will tend to enhance employee and manager perceptions of fairness and thereby engender their support of the process.

When organizations commit themselves to investing in a thorough and fair evaluation of their employees' capabilities, everyone reaps the benefits. After observing an impartial staffing process in action, employees are less likely to suffer from the declining morale so often observed after an RIF occurs. Organizations armed with a process that is demonstrably job related face considerably less risk of a legal challenge resulting from employee terminations and should feel comfortable communicating such decisions to their workforce.

Guiding Principle 4: Execute Quickly and Effectively

Once the new organization has been designed or the desired head count determined, the staffing process should move rapidly and efficiently so as to minimize disruption to the organization and its employees. That said, the process should not be unnecessarily rushed because important decisions are in the balance, and key steps must be executed. Rather, the process should proceed in an orderly, reasoned fashion. For M&As and restructurings, the staffing process should proceed in a cascading manner, beginning with the top layers of the organization and focusing first on mission-critical jobs, with candidates for key positions at the top level of the organization selected first. This phased approach allows individuals selected at each level to participate in the staffing of their own organizations. New managers are afforded the opportunity to take ownership of their areas and participate in determining who will be supporting them in the new organization. In addition, a cascading approach to the staffing allows individuals not selected during a prior phase to be considered in pools for a subsequent phase.

Guiding Principle 5: Identify and Involve Key Stakeholder Groups
Several distinct activities need to be performed when staffing for organizational change, and each requires the involvement of different sets of key stakeholders who will take the lead at different phases of the process. We have previously discussed one of the most critical stakeholder groups, the review board, which comprises key business leaders, legal, HR, and corporate communications. This group plays an essential role in the success of the staffing initiative by establishing the guiding principles, committing the resources necessary to carry out the work, auditing the staffing decisions, and serving as champions of the process. While every organization will have a unique set of circumstances and the nature and size of the initiative will also be a determining factor on team configuration, the review board and following teams will play an integral role in ensuring that the staffing process proceeds smoothly and that sound selection decisions are made. Three teams will likely overlap in their membership:

- *Design team.* This team comprises individuals who were involved in defining the new organizational structure. During the staffing process, they will be responsible for identifying the status of each job in the organization (existing, redesigned, new, to be eliminated), creating competency models for each job requiring a staffing decision, and helping to define the criteria for candidate pools. Typically design team members are organized into group- or unit-specific subteams to facilitate this process.
- *Assessment team.* This team provides evaluations of candidates' competencies based on the requirements of the job. These evaluations, which ideally are made during consensus rating sessions, serve as the basis for selection decisions. Assessment teams consist of supervisors of the candidates in the pool (typically first-level supervision) and, ideally, a core group that participates across the assessment sessions (typically second-level supervision).

- *Selection team.* This team is responsible for decisions related to the selection of candidates. These responsibilities fall into two categories: population of candidate pools and selection of candidates based on assessment results. The team comprises key design team members, the selecting leaders within the organization, HR staff, and external consultants if they are involved with the process. The selection team identifies members of the assessment team based on the composition of candidate pools.

Guiding Principle 6: Build a Rigorous and Fair Assessment and Selection Process

The key elements of the staffing process are identifying the important requirements of the organization's targeted jobs, reliably assessing candidates against those requirements, and making selection decisions based on fair and accurate assessments.

The staffing model recommended here relies on a competency-based assessment, using multiple perspectives, to determine candidate suitability for the target positions. During the assessment stage of the process, multiple sources of input and group consensus ratings are advisable, so that evaluations are consistent and properly calibrated across candidates. This contributes to both the fairness and the validity of the rating process.

Guiding Principle 7: Review and Audit All Decisions

To ensure that both the assessment of candidates and subsequent selection decisions are fair and accurate, it is necessary to audit the results of these two processes. This audit should bring to light any rating inconsistencies, evidence of rater bias, rater errors, and adverse impact against protected groups. These reviews may result in follow-up discussions with supervisors or the gathering of additional documentation necessary to justify the selection decisions, for example, a critical skill set or an essential business-specific knowledge that precipitated a particular selection decision. The review board should generally assume the role of conducting this audit.

Step 1 in the staffing road map serves to establish the principles, ground rules, roles, and responsibilities that will guide the staffing process from beginning to end. The particulars of the seven guiding principles will vary based on the unique circumstances of the organization and initiative. However, the establishment of a governing body that agrees on such a set of principles and roll-out strategies will immeasurably help the organization navigate through the various phases of the staffing process.

Table 17.1 shows how these guiding principles would be tailored to a hypothetical M&A situation. This situation will serve as our case study, the other facets of which are illustrated in the tables throughout this chapter.

Step 2: Develop and Implement a Comprehensive Communication Plan

Without an aggressive, proactive, and comprehensive communication plan, resistance to any organizational change process can rise to almost unmanageable levels. In conjunction with a staffing process where employees could stand to lose their jobs, the anxiety level within the organization can stall productivity and accelerate turnover of key talent. Although it is not a complete antidote to the anxiety brought about by change, the most effective way to combat its negative effects is to get out in front of the change process with a well-thought-out, multifaceted communication plan. Employees need to understand the full nature of the changes and how they are likely to be affected. This means providing more than an overview of the process. Employees must be presented with a detailed explanation of how the process will work, how decisions will be made, who will be making the decisions, what will be expected of employees, what (if any) recourse they will have, as well as a solid estimate of the time frame involved.

Corporate communications should play a key role throughout the process and make use of all forms of media to get the message out: video, newsletters, town hall meetings, intranet, Q&As, and facilitated focus group meetings, for example. This will help ensure that employee questions are answered quickly and that the key information is being properly disseminated in a timely fashion. The organization's management needs to buy in early regarding the importance of communication and support these initiatives. This is often more easily said than done; management is sometimes reluctant to share much information due

Table 17.1. Application of Guiding Principles to a Merger and Acquisition Initiative: Staffing Model Road Map Step 1

Key Tasks	*Decisions Reached*
1. Agree on guiding principles 2. Establish scope and time line 3. Define process and its application 4. Clarify roles and responsibilities	A. Principal objective of the staffing process is to select the most qualified incumbents for positions in new organization. B. Staffing process will cover all jobs identified on new company (NewCo) organization charts and be competency driven, relying on a consensus approach for assessment and selection. C. Job relatedness will be accomplished by conducting a competency modeling study to determine the core and functional competencies required for success in the affected jobs. Assessment procedures will be developed to accurately assess these competencies. D. Procedural justice will be established by fully outlining all aspects of the assessment and selection process through a variety of media (town hall meetings, intranet, newsletters, CEO communication video). Managers will be trained to discuss the process with employees, and an appeals process will be implemented. E. Timing: Organization charts for the new organization will be available after January 1 and the following time line proposed and communicated for decisions at each organizational level: Tier 1: CEO direct reports (end of December) Tier 2: Vice presidents (January) Tier 3: Directors (February) Tier 4: Managers and professionals (March-April) Tier 5: Sales (May)

(Continued)

Key Tasks	Decisions Reached
	F. Key stakeholder groups will be a review board, design team, and assessment and selection team. Legal counsel will participate on the review board.
	G. Assessment will comprise a consensus-based rating process that taps the core and functional competencies and a structured interview; all of these will be validated against job requirements.
	H. Selection decisions will be made in a consensus format following an analysis of the assessment data for potential bias, adverse impact, rating errors, and heritage company rating differences.
	I. Selection recommendations will be reviewed and audited by the review board, which will take all appropriate action to ensure integrity of process and fairness of decisions.

to the sensitive nature of the decisions being made, general inexperience in dealing with these situations, and reservations about committing to the final process and firm time lines.

The importance of early and frequent communication in this process cannot be overemphasized. It is an essential ingredient for making a smooth transition to the new organization and ensuring key talent retention as well as sustained productivity and morale. If employees are provided with full disclosure regarding the process, they will be less likely to distrust the organization's motives and stand in the way of its success. The goal is to provide a transparent outline of what is going to happen and when—and to make it clear if decisions have yet to be made. The sample newsletter in Exhibit 17.1 can be an effective way to share information on a timely basis.

Exhibit 17.1. Sample Newsletter for NewCo Merger

January 30, 2011 Staffing Process Communications Series Edition 2

Staffing Update

The organizational structure for the new company has been finalized, and we are now in the process of matching the heritage company job titles to those in the new organization. Once the job-matching process is finished, we can identify candidate pools and begin the staffing process for Tier 2 (VPs/SVPs).

The specifics of the staffing process are presented in the chart shown here. You will note that there are several steps in this sequence that must be completed prior to conducting the assessment and selection processes. Step 1 (job matching and candidate pool identification) is currently being finalized for the Tier 2 positions and should be finished by March 10. Step 2 (determining which jobs will require selection) can only be made once employees have indicated their decisions concerning relocation. The process by which these decisions will need to be communicated is also being finalized. This process will also be in place by March 13. In step 3, hiring managers will conduct informational interviews with all of the candidates for the jobs that require selection decisions.

These informational interviews will be designed to allow an active interchange between the hiring manager and candidates from both companies. The hiring manager will discuss the position with the candidates, gain an understanding of each candidate's background and interests, and provide expectations for the job in the new organization. Candidates will also have a chance to ask questions and discuss any issues around the process.

In step 4, managers will evaluate their direct reports

(Continued)

1	NewCo hiring manager confirms job structure and corresponding candidate pool.	Feb 28–Mar 10
2	Candidates affirm relocation decision. NewCo jobs needing assessments are identified.	Mar 10–13
3	Hiring manager conducts informational interviews. *Proceed to step 9 for noncompetitive positions.*	Mar 10–17f
4	Supervising managers independently make candidate assessment ratings.	Mar 15–20
5	Consensus rating session conducted with legacy company supervising managers and NewCo hiring manager.	Mar 16–24
6	Structured interviews are conducted as needed.	Mar 20–24
7	NewCo hiring manager makes selection decisions.	Mar 20–24
8	Review board reviews decisions and identifies any issues to be resolved.	Mar 27–31
9	Develop compensation packages and prepare communications: Offer letters delivered: April 10 All offers finalized: April 14 All staff communication: April 17	Apr 3–17

on a set of competencies that have been determined to be required for success in the new organization. These competencies are currently being finalized for the Tier 2 positions and will be communicated in the next *Update*. In step 5, managers from both companies will come together in a facilitated meeting to present and justify their ratings on each of the competencies. This facilitated meeting will ensure that raters from both companies are calibrated and interpreting the competencies similarly.

Step 6 allows for the contingency where two candidates are considered equally qualified for a position based on manager ratings and background information. When these situations occur, a

(Continued)

structured interview will be conducted to gather additional information on the required competencies to help "break the tie."

In step 7, hiring managers will review the assessment information and make their selection decisions. Before these decisions are actually communicated, a review board (step 8) will review all decisions to ensure fairness and process integrity.

All offers will be finalized by April 17.

For more information on this process, please call our merger hot line at 1-800-555-1212.

Another critical goal of proactive communication (in addition to sustaining productivity and morale) is to prevent turnover of key players before offers can be made. Beyond the steps recommended above, it is usually wise to identify and counsel key talent who may be turnover risks during this time of transition. Although no promises can or should be made since staffing decisions will not have occurred, it is important to meet with these employees, acknowledge the stress around the change, ask for their input, and reiterate the vision of the organization. The employee should be engaged, as appropriate, in a collaborative discussion about his or her career goals, with the manager providing information and guidance to the extent possible. The employee's value should be reiterated and an environment created in which he or she feels comfortable sharing concerns and is able to engage in conversation about the future of the organization. Table 17.2 shows an example of how a communication plan was designed and executed for our M&A case study.

Step 3: Identify the Positions Requiring Staffing Decisions

In this step, the organizational chart is created and the jobs requiring staffing decisions are identified. The design team is

Table 17.2. Design of Communication Plan for the Merger and Acquisition Initiative: Staffing Model Road Map Step 2

Key Tasks	Decisions Reached
1. Design and execute communication plan.	*Primary focus:* Build transparency into the process by disclosing full details of the plan: how the process will work, how decisions will be made, estimated time lines, and the recourse available:
	• Fill the information vacuum.
	• Establish perceived fairness and sense of procedural justice.
2. Detail the staffing process and its objectives, as well as scope and time line.	• Gain the support of the middle managers who fill a crucial role in the process.
	Preparation: Plan communication to businesses and employees:
	• Work with legal, benefits, employment, and EEO to determine what prenotification is required and will be provided.
	• Coordinate with corporate communications and public affairs (for example, on the need for press releases).
3. Use full multimedia resources.	• Develop a reengagement strategy for retained employees.
	• Train management on communication message and approach.
4. Build turnover management process.	*Delivery:* Broad, multimedia communication rollout throughout legacy organizations as soon as the staffing process and relocation and severance packages have been finalized:
	• Town hall meetings.
	• Newsletters.
	• Web sites and videos.
	• Group and one-on-one meetings.
	• Conduct meetings prior to and after notifications.
	Interactive dialogue:
	• Employees asked to affirm their intentions (desire to work for new organization).
	• Informational interviews conducted to provide an opportunity for the candidate to become familiar with hiring manager and position.
	• Managers trained to conduct turnover management coaching sessions.

responsible for establishing the criteria for matching existing jobs to the new organization chart, identifying which jobs require staffing, and working with the selecting leaders to identify the candidate pools.

The identification of candidate pools—in effect, determining which employees are eligible for which jobs—is a highly consequential issue requiring careful thought and planning. Some of the more common policy issues to resolve include such questions as whether an employee will be permitted to be in more than one pool (that is, to be a candidate for multiple jobs where they involve separate selection decisions); whether an employee will be given the option to be in a pool that is not mapped to his or her current job; and whether the assessment or selection teams will be given the option to import employees into a pool from which they would otherwise have been absent. Because such policies constitute one of the few mechanisms in an organizational change initiative that can provide employees some degree of control or input over their fate, they can have an important effect on attitudes toward, and ultimate acceptance of, the new or restructured organization.

The goal of this step is to specify the job titles that will be covered and what layer in the organization will be reached. For M&As and restructurings, it is necessary to develop a process for qualifying candidates for new and redesigned jobs and to decide whether candidates can be allowed to compete for multiple jobs at the same level, or for higher or lower levels, in the organization. For RIFs that do not involve a restructuring, a business plan should be developed that includes a proposed organizational chart with the targeted jobs identified. The rationale should be provided for which jobs and employees are being targeted, what layer in the organization will be reached, and how this aligns with the business need.

The design team identifies whether each targeted job is (1) an existing job for which the head count will not change, (2) an existing job that requires a reduction or expansion in head count, (3) a redesigned job (for example, one where there has been more than a 50 percent change in responsibilities), or (4) a newly created job. Organizations engaged in an M&A or restructuring may decide that certain subsets of the positions for which there is a one-to-one match of current incumbents to future positions (condition 1 above) are exempt from the selection process. Although this discussion focuses on circumstances where new staffing strategies and processes are needed, it is important to note that such needs can be minimized by first identifying groups of employees and functions where people will simply follow their work into the new or restructured organization. This greatly simplifies the overall position-filling process, while also permitting more targeted communications only to employees who are subject to new staffing processes, thereby limiting the overall disruption and anxiety associated with the change initiative.

Incumbents in conditions 2 through 4 above—as well as those in condition 1 who are allowed to apply for additional positions—require an assessment and selection process. In terms of the candidate pools for these positions, it is generally desirable to consider internal candidates first, with external candidates being considered for open positions at the end of the process.

Table 17.3 provides an example of the criteria used for identifying positions requiring staffing for our M&A case study.

Step 4: Create Job Requirements for the Targeted Positions

Job requirements will be identified by the design team or its designees. These team members will be job experts who clearly understand the role and expectations of the jobs in the new or downsized organization. As part of their task, they will be asked to create a position profile, which includes the key responsibilities, competency requirements, and minimum qualifications. They will also define the criteria for candidate pools.

Competency models should consist of both organizational and job-specific success factors. All competencies should have a clear, concise, and unambiguous definition and a set of clearly differentiated performance levels defined in terms of observable work behaviors. It is important that the competency model developers meet with leaders of the function in order to fully understand

Table 17.3. Identifying Positions Requiring Staffing Decisions for a Merger and Acquisition Initiative: Staffing Model Road Map Step 3

Key Tasks	Decisions Reached
1. Identify specific job titles that will be covered and what layer in the organization will be reached.	• Organizational chart • Legacy company job titles will be matched to same and redesigned jobs in new organization. • Job titles may be matched to more than one job in the new organization
2. Establish criteria for matching existing jobs to organization chart.	• New or redesigned jobs will be matched with existing job titles with similar functions and skills to the extent possible. • All jobs requiring selection will be identified.
3. Identify which jobs require selection.	• Candidate pool • Legacy company incumbents will be considered only for jobs to which their current job titles are matched.
4. Determine criteria for candidate pool.	• Positions for which there is a one-to-one match of current incumbents to future positions are exempt from the selection process (the follow-your-work principle).
5. Develop process for qualifying candidates for new or redesigned jobs.	• Legacy company incumbents may be included in a candidate pool if their skills fit with that job family even if they are currently not incumbents in a matched job.
6. Decide whether employees will be allowed to compete for multiple jobs (same level, higher level, or lower level).	• Displaced employees • For thirty days after the end of the initial selection process, displaced employees will be considered for any jobs in their tier that remain unfilled and for which they meet minimum qualifications. • Jobs that are not filled by displaced employees will be posted publicly for any candidate to apply.

the skills required to drive organizational performance in the context of the business strategy and any expected changes in organizational context.

Once the competency model has been developed, it is necessary to evaluate the criticality of the competencies against the jobs for which they have been developed. A group of job experts, ideally independent of the experts who developed the competencies, should be convened to make a series of importance ratings for each competency. This serves to validate the importance of each competency for a particular job and ensures that the selection criteria, which will be driven by these competencies, are based on the essential requirements of the job. A typical importance rating scale is shown in Table 17.4.

The job experts are asked to individually rate each competency and then as a group reach consensus on their ratings. Only competencies receiving consensus ratings of 2 or 3 will be retained for further analysis. The behavioral anchors are evaluated through a similar process to ensure that they adequately distinguish performance levels. The result of this step is a list of critical competencies for each job under review. Table 17.5 shows several sample behavioral anchors associated with a *Leads Strategically* competency, which is defined as follows:

Table 17.4. Importance Rating Scale

3	Critical	This job could not be performed at even a minimally acceptable level without this competency.
2	Important	It would be difficult to perform this job effectively without this competency.
1	Of minor importance	This job could be performed somewhat effectively without this competency.
0	Not applicable	This competency is not required for this job.

Table 17.5. Sample Competency for Leads Strategically: Staffing Model Road Map Step 4

Level	Rating	Behavioral Evaluation Standards
Exceptional Performer: Describes performance that sets the standard of excellence and exceeds the requirements of the job	5	• Creates and conveys a clear, overarching vision for the future that capitalizes on the corporate purpose and mission • Builds commitment to strategic plan, and anticipates and resolves barriers (for example, interpersonal, financial, informational) to successful execution • Leads the development of focused, well-articulated, strategic business plans that are aligned with the corporate mission and vision and meet organizational goals • Develops and promotes innovative strategies designed to create a significant competitive advantage • Ensures that strategic plans are translated into specific, measurable, attainable, and timely objectives and tactics
Above Expectations: Describes performance that exceeds some of the requirements of the job but does not fully meet the standards of excellence	4	• Candidate described experience, performance or knowledge that exceeded the standards listed under Valued Performer, but did not fully meet the standards listed under Exceptional Performer.
Valued Performer: Describes performance that fully meets the requirements of the job	3	• Develops strategic business plans that meet organizational goals and align with the corporate vision • Works to create breakthrough opportunities for growth and success • Incorporates business strategies that provide a competitive advantage to the company

Level	Rating	Behavioral Evaluation Standards
		• Builds alliances and networks that facilitate cross-functional collaboration on strategic plans • Translates strategic plans into actionable objectives and tactics • Communicates the strategic vision to employees so that they can deliver on goals and objectives
Improvement Opportunity: Describes performance that requires improvement or does not fully meet the requirements of the job	2	• Candidate described experience, performance, or knowledge that exceeded the standards listed under Below Expectations, but did not fully meet the standards listed under Valued Performer.
Below Expectations: Describes performance that is clearly below the requirements of the job	1	• Develops superficial or poorly defined business plans that are unlikely to meet or are not aligned with organizational goals • Employs a silo mentality, emphasizing own efforts with little attention to cross-functional collaboration • Reactively responds to obstacles or misidentifies threats to implementation of strategic plan • Communicates the strategic vision in a limited or impersonal manner • Criticizes employees for failure to achieve goals without providing support and guidance

Creates a clear and compelling vision for the future that is aligned with the purpose and mission of the organization. Develops and leads breakthrough business strategies for transforming own organization and achieving a competitive advantage. Translates company strategic imperatives into specific business plans. Communicates the strategic vision to employees, motivating them to work toward common plans and objectives.

To ensure the optimal focus of the selection process, it can often be helpful to determine the relative importance to success in the target job of the competencies that were identified through the job analysis. By, in effect, prioritizing among competencies already determined to be important, this step allows the assessment tools to be honed to the most critical aspects of the job and to ensure high predictability of job success. It also provides guidance should practical constraints make it difficult to fully incorporate all important competencies into the assessment tools. One relatively straightforward way to accomplish this is to have job experts weight the competency model by distributing one hundred points across the competencies, based on the relative importance of each competency to the target job. In Table 17.6, functional expertise was fixed at 25 percent.

Step 5: Develop and Validate Assessment Tools

In this final and critical step of the staffing model road map, the assessment tools by which candidates will be evaluated for target jobs in the new or downsized organization are developed and validated. The next two subsections detail the process for building the assessment tools and gathering the necessary evidence to support the high-stakes staffing decisions that are required during a merger, restructuring, or downsizing.

Develop the Assessment Tools

The competencies identified as most important (those receiving the greatest weight in the competency weighting process) serve as the primary dimensions against which assessments of candidate suitability for the target job are made. Candidates can be evaluated on these competencies through a number of alternative approaches, including self-assessments, manager assessments, structured interviews, business cases or simulations, and minimum

Table 17.6. Competency Weighting

	1	2
	Sales Director	*Sales Vice President*
Leadership		
1. Leads strategically		
2. Builds ethical culture		
3. Leads change		
Drives the business		
4. Drives for excellence and quality		
5. Achieves market growth and competitive advantage		
6. Manages finances		
Talent management		
7. Assesses and develops talent		
8. Embraces and fosters a diverse environment		
Builds relationships		
9. Builds strategic alliances and relationships		
10. Champions the customer		
Functional expertise		
11. Functional expertise	25%	25%
Total weightings	100%	100%

and preferred qualifications. (Archival performance measures, such as prior years' performance appraisals, are another potential option, but they should be used advisedly, since they were not designed for this purpose and are likely to be neither optimal nor defensible in this context.) Sometimes organizations will seek, for expediency, to evaluate incumbents with a standardized cognitive ability or personality test with the goal of selecting out those with the weakest test scores. We strongly advise against this course of action for several reasons:

- In all cases, we are dealing with incumbents with rich performance histories that, when accurately assessed, provide the best predictor of future success.

- Test scores do not correlate perfectly with performance, and an incumbent who is terminated due to low test scores need only point to his or her years of stellar performance ratings to support a challenge.
- These sorts of tests require significant research within the organization (for example, a criterion-related validation study) that, for a variety of reasons, including time and resources required and significant test security issues, is typically infeasible in this context.

Standardized testing in this context is fraught with logistical and legal concerns and therefore is not an efficient option.

The following assessments have been successfully implemented across a wide range of situations involving reductions in force:

■ ■ ■

- *Self-assessments.* Self-assessments provide the candidate with an opportunity to more actively participate in the process, which leads to a greater sense of control over the selection decision and a belief in the overall fairness of the system. In addition, self-assessments frequently provide a valuable source of information that supervisors may have otherwise overlooked, though this must be tempered by awareness of the potential for job candidates to inflate such assessments, particularly for relatively abstract and complex competencies, as opposed to more concrete (and hence more verifiable) technical and functional skills or knowledge. In general, candidates should make self-assessment ratings on the same instrument that managers will use in making their assessments, to facilitate managers' use of this information. (Because of the potential for rating inflation, we do not encourage direct use of self-assessment ratings by selecting leaders. They should be used as input only.) The obvious drawback of this sort of assessment is the additional amount of administrative activity involved in collecting, reviewing, and incorporating these data. However, a number of organizations have found the added value to be well worth the extra effort.

- *Manager assessments.* In this process, candidates are rated by their supervisors on the key competencies required for success. In making their ratings, supervisors consider a candidate's self-assessment (if such data have been collected), past performance documentation (covering the past several years, if available), and other relevant sources of input. The point here is to ensure that the new set of ratings is not significantly misaligned with the candidate's performance history, which can sometimes occur in this high-stakes context. The accurate and most reliable means for conducting managerial assessments is through a facilitated consensus rating process involving first- and second-level supervision. Direct and one-over managers participate in these facilitated assessment sessions to rate the competencies of their direct reports who are candidates for the target position. Although this is the recommended means for collecting such ratings, some organizations, particularly those undergoing large-scale layoffs, may opt to collect supervisory ratings without consensus because of time or resource limitations. However, these ratings should always be reviewed by the second-level manager to ensure accuracy and proper calibration across his or her direct reports.
- *Structured interviews.* Three primary categories of interviews can be used as part of this staffing process: an informational interview, a targeted interview, and a full interview. The purpose of the informational interview is to get to know the candidate—his or her background, experiences, and expertise. This type of interview is particularly useful in an M&A where the selecting leaders will not be familiar with candidates from the other company. It is also an opportunity for the candidate to become familiar with the selecting leader. Although this interview is conducted prior to any formal assessment and is designed to allow a mutual sharing of information in a relaxed atmosphere, it is still considered part of the overall assessment and, as such, it needs to be validated and administered under specific guidelines.

The targeted interview occurs during the assessment phase and is conducted by trained interviewers representing the line organization, HR, or the selecting leaders. These interviews are geared only toward competencies that could not be adequately evaluated through the competency rating process (that is, the person received a "cannot rate" rating). After processing the ratings from the supervisory assessment, the assessment facilitator identifies individuals for whom insufficient data were provided (those who received one or more "cannot rate" ratings). These interviews will be shorter than the typical full interview since they will be targeting only performance areas that could not be rated. The ratings from these assessment interviews will be made on the same scale used for the supervisory ratings. The interview ratings can then be substituted for the missing supervisory ratings, thereby allowing a composite assessment score to be generated (based on a combination of supervisory and interview ratings).

A full interview taps all performance areas and relevant experience required for the job. These interviews should be conducted in a panel format with at least two, but no more than four, interviewers (supervisors, selecting leaders, or HR) participating. An overall consensus rating is determined based on the interview results. Some organizations rely on these full interviews only during the selection phase, when two or more finalists for a job have indistinguishable composite assessment rating scores and no other job-related information is available to further differentiate these candidates.

- *Business cases or simulations.* Business cases or other types of simulations are also sometimes used to assess candidate capabilities for managerial jobs and higher. These cases are designed to tap a subset of the required competencies using scenarios that bear a strong resemblance to those that the candidate would encounter on the job. Candidates are asked to analyze the case, outline priorities and recommendations, and make a presentation to demonstrate their command of the situation. Assessor ratings of the business cases are placed on the same scale as the interview and competency assessments, and subsequently they are combined to form a composite score for the candidate.

- *Minimum and preferred qualifications.* Minimum qualifications (MQs) are designed to serve as a basic applicant screening tool by determining whether candidates will be minimally able to perform the target job. This is accomplished through the establishment of minimally required levels of education and experience or specific licensure or certification requirements that have been shown through a job analysis and content validity study to be required for success in the target job. The MQs allow a determination of whether candidates meet the basic requirements to be considered further for the target job. The preferred qualifications (PQs) offer a method for selecting among qualified candidates when they are otherwise equally matched on the minimum qualifications and competency assessments. PQs can be employed in cases where additional information beyond the competency assessment and interview is needed to make a selection decision. In some instances, a particular PQ might be regarded as unique, critical, or irreplaceable (for example, a particular knowledge base relevant to a key customer's technical requirements) so instead of functioning exclusively as a tiebreaker, it will be permitted to override certain MQs or the results of other assessments. It is essential, however, that such applications be supported by an appropriate job analysis, as discussed below.

Validate the Assessment Tools

The procedures included in a staffing model need to be validated in accordance with professional standards and legal guidelines to ensure technical rigor and legal defensibility. A content validation strategy is typically used to demonstrate the job relatedness of the selection procedures used in this context. This type of validation study is not only the most logical, as the types of assessments we are using readily lend themselves to this approach, but incumbents are not needed to conduct the study as they would be with a criterion-related study. Therefore, the assessments can be validated without requiring incumbent input and unnecessarily jeopardizing the security of the assessment measures. According to SIOP's *Principles* (2003), evidence of content validity typically consists of a demonstration of a strong linkage between the content of the selection procedure and important work behaviors and worker requirements. The job analysis results serve as the foundation for the development and validation of the assessment tools.

Chapter Twenty-One in this handbook provides an in-depth review of validation techniques relevant to these procedures; an overview of the process is provided in Table 17.7.

Table 17.7. Overview of Major Project Steps Undertaken to Demonstrate Content Validity

Job analysis

- A thorough job analysis is conducted for the target jobs, resulting in competencies that are operationally defined in terms of observable work behaviors.
- The job analysis identifies important and requisite competencies necessary for effective job performance.

Assessment procedure development

- Assessment tools are developed to measure requisite competencies as determined by the job analysis.
- Minimum qualifications are developed based on entry requirements identified in the job analysis.
- Preferred qualifications are developed based on job-related requirements that served to distinguish among equally qualified top candidates

Content validation evidence development

1. Competency assessments (self- and manager assessments)
   - Competency assessments are drawn directly from the job analysis and are based on the competencies determined to be important.

- Evaluation standards are developed to ensure reliability and accuracy of the rating scales. Subject matter experts evaluate these standards to ensure that they are relevant to the competency (a relevance rating) and accurately describe the corresponding performance level (a performance effectiveness rating).

2. Additional assessments (interview and business case)

   - The structured interview questions and business case scenarios are validated by subject matter experts to ensure that they adequately measure the targeted competencies.
   - The realism of the business case scenarios is judged by subject matter experts (business case scenario realism rating) to ensure they faithfully represent what one would or could encounter on the job.
   - Evaluation standards for the interview and business case assessments are judged by subject matter experts to ensure that they are relevant to the competency (a relevance rating) and accurately describe the corresponding performance level (a performance effectiveness rating).

3. Minimum qualifications

   - The job relatedness of the minimum qualifications is judged by subject matter experts (job-relatedness rating and linkage to job requirements) to ensure that each is important and related to effective job performance.
   - The level of each minimum qualification is judged by subject matter experts (a minimum level rating) to ensure that the qualification is required at the appropriate level (that is, of a minimally acceptable candidate).

4. Preferred qualifications

   - The job relatedness of the preferred qualifications is judged by subject matter experts (job-relatedness rating and linkage to job requirements) to ensure that each is important and related to effective job performance.
   - The level of each preferred qualification is judged by subject matter experts (importance and entry requirement ratings) to ensure that the qualification is important for the job.

Table 17.8 shows an example of some decisions reached regarding the development and validation of an assessment process for our M&A case study.

Table 17.8. Development and Validation of Assessment Tools for a Merger and Acquisition Initiative: Staffing Model Road Map Step 5

Key Tasks	Decisions Reached
Develop assessment tools • Develop assessment specifications based on required competencies. • Build assessment tools that map onto critical competencies. • Consider whether MQs are required and PQs desired. **Validate assessment tools** • Ensure all tools are content-validated. • Ensure operational validity.	*Competency-based assessment* will be built around competencies and evaluation standards: • A five-point behavioral evaluation rating scale will be developed for each competency. • Multiple perspectives for ratings (consensus) will be used. *Minimum qualifications* will be developed as required for each target job for use with candidates applying forpromotion. *Preferred qualifications* will be developed as appropriate to help differentiate among similarly qualified candidates. *Structured interviews* will be created only as need may arise to help differentiate similarly qualified candidates. *Self-assessments* will not be used. • Informational interviews will be conducted. *Other assessment information* will be identified for use as appropriate (for example, list of experiences, training courses). • Competency validation forms the basis for competency-based assessment; MQs, PQs, and interviews will be content-validated. • Operational validity will be established by training assessors, having professionally facilitated consensus rating meetings, and monitoring results.

Conducting Assessments and Making Selection Decisions

By following the five steps outlined in the staffing model road map, we have ensured that the assessment process is job related and competency based, and it will enable the accurate evaluation of candidate capabilities. The competencies identified as important for the target jobs will serve as the primary dimensions against which assessments of candidate suitability will be made. This section describes the steps that need to be taken to conduct the assessments, score and interpret the results, and make final selection decisions.

Conducting Competency-Based Assessments

We have argued that a competency-based assessment process is the most logical and defensible means for staffing an organization undergoing organizational change. Since the evaluation of employee behavior is often fraught with such challenges as rating inflation and conscious and unconscious biases that are magnified under the stressful conditions of organizational change, it is necessary to take steps to ensure the reliability and accuracy of these assessments. Assessor training plays an important role in sensitizing raters to avoid common errors; however, additional measures need to be taken to ensure that candidates are assessed fairly. Beyond assessor training, two key activities should be built into the assessment process to ensure accuracy: rater calibration and consensus ratings.

Rater Calibration

The use of behaviorally anchored rating scales (BARS) helps increase the objectivity and standardization of competency ratings by providing examples of performance at varying levels on the competency rating scale (see Table 17.4). The use of these evaluation standards helps reduce rater reliance on non-job-related factors and generates a common understanding among raters as to what each point on the rating scale translates into in terms of observed behaviors. To further ensure rater calibration, it is necessary for one-over managers to review and compare their direct reports' ratings to one another. This review will highlight rater trends and patterns, discrepancies with past performance results, and potential errors that may require follow-up and adjustments. The most direct and effective way to calibrate raters is to follow up the individual rating activity with a consensus rating session. Consensus sessions force raters to develop a common interpretation of the evaluation standards and create a culture where raters assist their peers in making the proper judgments.

Consensus Ratings

The consensus-based rating process is designed to minimize individual rater biases and inconsistencies and ensure an accurate evaluation of candidates. In each session, first- and second-level managers are instructed to review the independent ratings of the candidates against each competency. First-level supervisors are informed that they will be required to justify their ratings by referencing the defined behavioral examples of the competency, as well as describing specific projects, roles, and responsibilities. Ratings are then adjusted up or down based on the consensus and input from the larger group of raters. All participants are instructed and encouraged to raise questions and constructively challenge ratings that seem out of place (too low or too high) given their knowledge of the candidate's performance record. Any argument for adjustment must be substantiated with behavioral examples that show the participant is higher or lower on the scale than the initial rating would suggest.

Final consensus scores for each candidate are rolled up into a database in which an overall competency rating is calculated for each candidate. This overall rating is determined by multiplying the consensus rating for each competency by the competency's weight (if weights were established) and summing the weighted scores. This number is then divided by 5 to place it back on the 100-point scale. An example of the output from the consensus-based assessment process is shown in Figure 17.1.

Group Differences Analyses

It is a good idea to conduct analyses of potential mean group differences in ratings at least once, and potentially twice, during this process. This first point would be after the independent ratings have been collected and entered into the database. Group

Figure 17.1. Example of Assessment-Process Data

- Name of position and organization

- Set of critical competencies and professional skills for position

CANDIDATE COMPETENCY ASSESSMENT (Sample)
Production Services Organzation
Position: Manager IMC Operations

Rating Scale: 5=Extremely Competent/4=Very Competent/3=Competent/2=Somewhat Competent/1=Not Sufficiently Competent

Competencies and Professional Skills

- Set of candidates for position

- Candidate ratings on competencies and professional skills

- Overall candidate assessment scores

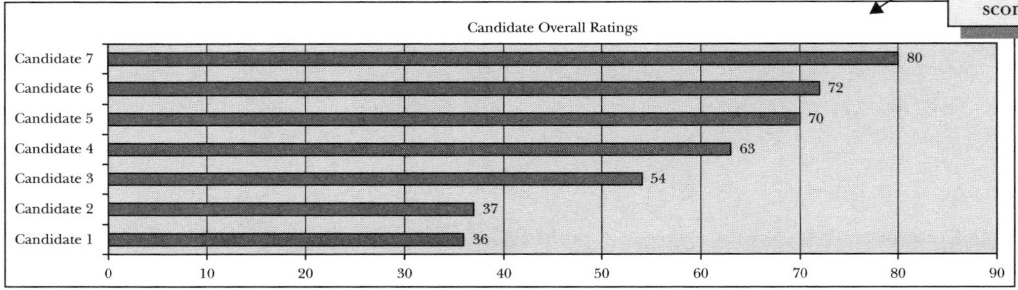

Candidate Competency Ratings

Competencies and Professional Skills	Weight	Candidate 1	Candidate 2	Candidate 3	Candidate 4	Candidate 5	Candidate 6	Candidate 7
Team Commitment	10	2	3	4	4	4	4	4
Self-Confident Integrity	10	1	2	3	3	3	4	4
Developing Others	5	3	1	2	3	5	3	5
Learning from Experience	15	1	2	2	3	5	3	3
Budget Preparation and Financial Management	10	2	3	3	3	3	2	3
Operations and Services Management	30	2	1	3	2	3	4	4
Technical Knowledge of Networking, Client Server	20	2	2	2	4	3	4	5
Weighted Score:		36	37	54	63	70	72	80

Candidate Overall Ratings

Candidate 7	80
Candidate 6	72
Candidate 5	70
Candidate 4	63
Candidate 3	54
Candidate 2	37
Candidate 1	36

567

differences and rater bias analyses should be conducted on these ratings to detect any potential issues regarding protected groups that can be ironed out in the consensus meetings or as part of the one-over manager's review if no consensus rating sessions are to be conducted. If desired, such analyses may be conducted a second time on the consensus data (or on ratings that were adjusted based on one-over manager review). Where the analysis identifies any problems in this regard, the assessment team is informed and asked to reexamine all affected candidates.

Administering Additional Assessments

Some organizations decide to supplement the competency-based assessment with additional tools, particularly in situations like M&As, where candidates may not be personally known to the selecting leader, or restructurings, where promotions may be involved and candidates have not necessarily demonstrated all of the competencies required for the newly designed positions.

In most circumstances, the supplemental assessment tools will consist of an interview and possibly some sort of simulation, such as a business case. It is a good idea to conduct these assessments using a panel of assessors who have attended a training program outlining the purpose and process components of a competency-based interview and simulation.

Combining Assessment Scores

A composite score is calculated for each candidate by averaging the overall competency rating with the scores from any additional assessment measures. The overall competency assessment and supplementary assessment scores can be equally or differentially weighted, a decision that should be made by the review board in advance of the assessment process. Candidates are placed into an assessment band (for example, one of five bands), based on their composite score. Assessment bands are simply score ranges within which scores are considered equivalent, which helps ensure that small differences between scores do not have an undue effect on process outcomes. These bands are used to determine the most qualified candidates for the target job.

Making Selection Decisions

Following candidate rating sessions, overall assessment scores are calculated for each candidate, producing a preliminary ranking of candidates for each job. The selecting leaders, the HR representative, and any other key decision makers meet to review the assessment results and determine whether any additional information is required to make final selection decisions. These individuals will collaboratively discuss the best decision to meet the business needs. These meetings will be professionally facilitated to ensure that all perspectives and business goals have been taken into account. In cases of rating ties between candidates, tenure, diversity requirements, or other job-related factors should be considered.

Table 17.9 shows a typical worksheet completed by the selecting leaders when making decisions on a job-by-job basis. This worksheet is used to facilitate decision making and document the staffing decisions. Information such as incumbents' willingness to relocate and assessment results is summarized in these worksheets for each job. In the example, Mike Johnson was placed in the highest assessment band, but because he was unwilling to relocate, he was not selected for this job.

Table 17.10 lists a set of disposition codes, which provide a means for documenting the reasons selection decisions are made on a job-by-job basis. By the end of the staffing process, every candidate should have been assigned a disposition code, and this should be stored in the staffing database. These disposition codes become very useful when conducting audits of the staffing process.

Selecting leaders who are making decisions in an M&A context should focus on resolving overlapping selections (the same person selected for multiple positions), evaluating the degree of heritage company representation in the postmerger organization, anticipating impact on the business during the transition, and assessing legal vulnerability. Managing this process effectively will also require active consideration of each nonselected candidate for possible selection for other vacant positions. A plan for communication of selection decisions and separation from the organization should also be thoroughly communicated and strictly followed. A summary of the tasks and decisions made for our M&A case study is presented in Table 17.11.

Table 17.9. Selecting Leader Worksheet

Director, Deal Management			Willing to Relocate	Disposition Code	Selected	Weighted Average	
Candidate	Current Job	Company					Assessment Bands
Mike Johnson	Business analyst	Olson, Inc.	N	10	N	4.0	Exceptional performer
William Jennings	Senior manager, contract negotiation and execution	Olson, Inc.	Y	1	Y	3.4	Valued performer
Joseph Cummings	Senior program manager, financial analysis	Riggs	Y	5	N	3.2	Valued performer
Dianna York	Program manager, business analysis	Riggs	Y	5	N	3.2	Valued performer
Michelle Henry	Senior program manager, business analysis	Olson, Inc.	Y	5	N	3.0	Valued performer

In a restructuring, the selection team will make tentative selections for every job based on the assessment data, the needs of the business, and other considerations as appropriate. Once the tentative decisions have been made, an adverse impact analysis is conducted to determine whether there are any issues related to protected group members. If none are identified, the tentative selections become final. Where issues arise, all appropriate

Table 17.10. Candidate Disposition Codes

Candidate Disposition	Code
Placed into matched job (Competitive)[a]	1
Placed into matched job (noncompetitive) (follow-your-work principle)	2
Promoted (competitive)	3
Promoted (noncompetitive)	4
Not selected for matched job (competitive)	5
Not selected for matched job (noncompetitive)	6
Not selected for promotion (competitive)	7
Turned down offer (relocation)	8
Turned down offer (other)	9
Unwilling to relocate	10

[a]Assessment was conducted.

action is taken to ensure the integrity of the process and the fairness of the decisions. One immediate action might be to have a discussion with the selecting leader to ensure that decisions were based on assessment data and not extraneous (non-job-related) factors. All final decisions should be documented, talking points prepared for hiring managers to communicate decisions, and candidates informed.

In an RIF, assessments are compiled and delivered to the review board or legal counsel, or both. Employees of targeted jobs are rank-ordered within competency band by seniority, and adverse impact data are presented for all demographic groups. All issues and concerns are reviewed and all appropriate actions taken to ensure the integrity of the process and fairness of decisions. All final selection decisions should be documented.

Audit the Results

All selection decisions, regardless of the type of initiative, should be presented to the review board to ensure these decisions have

Table 17.11. Selection Process for Merger and Acquisition Initiative

Key Tasks	Decisions Reached

Conduct candidate assessments and selections.
 	
• Consensus-driven rating process whereby candidates are assessed against the competencies developed for the target positions.
 	
• A composite rating will be determined for each candidate. Candidates will then be placed into one of five bands, based on their composite score.
 	
• The selection team meets collaboratively to review assessment results, determine whether any additional information may be required, and make staffing decisions aligned with business needs.
	A. Conduct facilitated consensus rating sessions with assessment and selection teams to evaluate candidates' proficiency on the designated competencies.
	B. Assessment and selection teams will each have five or six members:
	  • Two direct and second-level managers of all candidates for position(s)
	  • One hiring manager
	  • One or two legacy company HR (recommend representatives from both companies)
	  • One outside facilitator
	C. Self-assessments will not be collected.
	D. Assessment data will include:
	  • Banded ratings from competency-based assessment
	  • Banded scores from panel interviews (if conducted)
	  • Other relevant data such as experience or other special skills
	E. Where candidates' scores are roughly equal, other considerations such as the following may be taken into account:
	  • Unique skills or qualifications
	  • Experience
	  • Diversity
	F. After assessment, selection teams will proceed to make tentative selections for every job, based on the assessment data, the needs of the business, and other considerations as appropriate, subject only to the analysis described below.

- Create database of selection decisions indicating hire/no-hire and reason codes for nonselections.

Review board addresses outstanding issues and concerns; selection decisions are communicated.

- Report and document all final selection decisions.
- Communicate decisions to organization.

G. All tentative selection decisions will need to be kept highly confidential, as they may change.
H. Since incumbents may be matched to multiple jobs, selection meetings will need to be coordinated to take that into account.
I. Will conduct analysis of assessment and selection data to identify any of the following issues:
   • Rater error patterns
   • Adverse impact (using combined populations of both companies as basis)
   • Heritage company rating differences
J. Where no issues are identified, the tentative selection becomes final.
K. Where the analysis identifies any issues, the assessment and selection team is informed and reexamines all affected candidates to make a new selection decision (possibly same as prior decision).
L. The review board will address any significant issues raised by the analyses and reexamination.

been made based on appropriate consideration of rating data and business needs. The review board will audit the results of the staffing process, ensuring that the assessments of candidates and the subsequent selection decisions are fair, accurate, and legally defensible. Specifically, this audit will surface any rating inconsistencies, evidence of rater bias, rater errors, and potential adverse impact against protected groups. At this point, follow-up discussions with the HR and legal departments and with hiring managers will ensure that appropriate selection decisions have been made, reducing the risk of litigation related to terminations and reassignments that are perceived as unfair or illegal.

Conclusion

The strength of this process lies in its ability to be both a predictor of success and a legally defensible means of managing organizational change. The process is driven by several key factors:

- *Collaboration.* All phases of this process are collaborative in nature, which ensures open communication and no surprises for the key stakeholders involved.
- *Consensus.* Decisions that are based on a consensus among the key stakeholders are more reliable and accurate and are subject to greater support and less potential undermining, which is critical for moving forward.
- *Calibration.* All ratings are calibrated across raters and competencies to ensure that candidates are fairly assessed and treated. This is accomplished through the development of behaviorally anchored rating scales, rater training, and continual push-back throughout the assessment and selection phases.

We further suggest that as staffing is routinely conducted in the context of change for an increasing number of organizations, many elements of this process are likely to be useful as components of the normal, ongoing, staffing model in such organizations.

Although business leaders and hiring managers may resist any process that seems to threaten their ultimate control over the selection decision, these concerns can be substantially allayed by educating them on their essential role in an objective assessment process. In our experience, previously skeptical hiring managers frequently become vocal supporters of this approach to staffing because it provides them with a great deal of rich information on which to make their selection decisions, and it allows them to feel comfortable in justifying to unsuccessful candidates why they were not selected.

A well-designed staffing model will rely on the input of the hiring manager throughout the process, from identifying critical competencies and assessing those competencies to making the final selection decisions. The hiring managers who participate in this process are therefore much more likely to support the final decisions and be heavily invested in the success of the organization they helped to create.

References

Equal Employment Opportunity Commission, Civil Service Commission, Department of Labor, & Department of Justice. (1978). Uniform guidelines on employee selection procedures. *Federal Register, 35*(149), 12333–12336.

Meacham et al. v. *Knolls Atomic Power Laboratory*, 128 S.Ct. 2395 (2008).

Society for Industrial and Organizational Psychology. (2003). *Principles for the validation and use of personnel selection procedures* (4th ed.). Bowling Green, OH: Author.

Wingate, P. H., Thornton, G. C., McIntyre, K. S., & Frame, J. H. (2003). Organizational downsizing and age discrimination litigation: The influence of personnel practices and statistical evidence on litigation outcomes. *Law and Human Behavior, 7*(1), 87–108.

CHAPTER 18

GLOBAL APPLICATIONS OF ASSESSMENT

Ann Marie Ryan, Nancy T. Tippins

Much has been made of the increasing connectivity across nations, the globalization of business markets, and the dispersion of talent around the world. These trends stimulate the creation of multinational organizations and affect all aspects of business, but they also pose particular challenges and opportunities for human resource (HR) practices. These multinational organizations, as well as many domestic organizations that need to source employees globally, have turned the attention of assessment specialists toward practices that result in effective global assessments, the focus of this chapter.

By "global assessments," we mean any attempts by an organization to bring some standardization to how assessment is conducted for the same job, the same group of jobs, or the same program or purpose (leader development or training needs, for example) across countries. Assessments may be used for hiring, promotion decision making, evaluation of training program success, certification, performance management, employee and leader development, executive coaching, and many other contexts. Thus, our discussion here is relevant to the organization using the same assessment tools for a given purpose on a worldwide basis, as well as to the organization requiring some standard elements of the assessment tools and practices but allowing some variation by country depending on local needs.

Numerous benefits can accrue to organizations with a globally standardized assessment process:

- Ensuring consistency in the quality of those hired and those chosen for advancement, training, or a specific program
- Identifying employees capable of working in many different locations in the organization
- Providing a consistent staffing brand image to applicants and employees worldwide
- Reducing assessment development costs through standardization
- Increasing efficiencies in administration
- Collecting data that are more useful for strategic talent management on a global basis

Despite these benefits, organizations may be reluctant to pursue standardization of assessment practices globally because of the many challenges in doing so. In this chapter, we focus on the challenges most likely to be the purview of organizational psychologists, recognizing that other important business decisions impinge on the success of a global assessment program—for example, determining the organization's strategic focus in terms of use of expatriates versus host country nationals or determining whether there are economic advantages of local hiring given availability of talent pools. We organize our discussion into two major areas: challenges in design and challenges in implementation.

Throughout this chapter, we highlight specific points through a series of vignettes. Although the company described is fictitious, the issues presented represent examples of concerns real organizations have in designing and implementing global assessment systems.

A large U.S.-based multinational company manufactures and repairs electronic equipment. Because of the unavailability of appropriately trained labor in the United States and fractious union relationships, the company carefully researched options abroad and discovered that the cost of shipping parts is off-set by the savings from cheaper, foreign labor. Consequently the organization establishes foreign manufacturing and repair shops around the world.

The electronic equipment is complex and vital to many technological systems, ranging from security systems to commercial aircraft. The technicians must assemble a number of different pieces of equipment. The company needs to maintain a highly qualified workforce like it once had in the United States and has decided to develop a global assessment process to select qualified manufacturing technicians. The company hopes to develop an assessment that will be challenging and support its image of high standards and manufacturing excellence.

Key Challenges in Designing Global Assessments

Whether designing a global system or considering the use of a single assessment tool in new locations, organizational psychologists must assess the viability of tools used across countries and cultures. A number of frequently encountered challenges stymie efforts to develop global assessments:

- Jobs with the same or similar titles are different in terms of the work actually performed across locations.
- The economic and legal contexts in different locations necessitate differences in approaches to assessment.
- Assessment traditions or familiarity with particular kinds of tools differ across locations.
- The infrastructure and human resources required for assessment differ across locations.

To meet these challenges, the organizational psychologist must understand the context in which the assessment program will be designed and later implemented. In this section, we highlight the key questions that need to be answered to design a successful global assessment system.

What Are the Objectives of the Assessment?

The organizational psychologist must understand why there is a desire for a global assessment and the ultimate goals of the assessment program. For example, some organizations embark on a global assessment project to increase efficiencies in hiring, while others are seeking consistency in the quality of employees worldwide. Although the organizational psychologist may design the global assessments, the management of the organization often sets the objectives for the system in conjunction with current overall business plans as well as intended future plans. Thus, to increase initial acceptance of the program and avoid quick obsolescence of the assessment or the inability to use it in a new location, the objectives of the assessment program need to be considered in light of the future strategic thrust of the organization and take into account factors such as which regions of the business will grow or contract, what job categories will expand, how the work is performed today and how it will be performed in the future, and how rich the applicant pools are in various locations.

The company is clear on the objectives of the assessment process for selection of manufacturing technicians: it wants to identify qualified technicians as efficiently as possible wherever the jobs may be located. The first step of the organizational psychologist who leads the project is to interview the leaders of the manufacturing and repair business to gain an understanding of the job, its challenges, and the changes that will likely be made in the coming years. The psychologist also speaks with HR staffing leaders around the world to learn about typical education and experiences that applicants can be expected to have, customary ways of sourcing candidates, local labor organizations, and employment laws as well as the resources available for an assessment program.

The psychologist learns a number of things about the job and the staffing environment:

- The manufacturing technician jobs vary slightly from location to location. Importantly, the psychologist learns that some countries use two job titles (manufacturing technician and repair technician) but others use only one (equipment technician).

- The manufacturing job will become somewhat easier in the future because of plans to use robotic machines to do more of the assembly.
- In some countries, applicants have had little experience with multiple-choice tests because examinations in their country are generally essay or oral evaluations.
- Although all the locations have a good supply of well-qualified applicants, the credentials each brings vary substantially, making prescreens based on education and experience difficult.
- Some repair shops are small and have no HR personnel colocated.
- One country in Africa does not have computers in the HR office.
- Data privacy laws in many countries restrict the conditions under which assessment data can be transported. Some countries require informed consent prior to the assessment.
- The employment laws in some Eastern European countries require that the labor organizations be fully informed of hiring practices.

What Will Be the Nature of the Project Team?

When a design team for a successful domestic assessment effort is being put together, attention is paid to the key stakeholders and how their needs and objectives can be identified and met. Moving to a global project requires even greater forethought regarding the composition of the team that will define the parameters of the assessment and guide the development process. Identifying the stakeholders in each country can be challenging, and gaining access to incumbents, managers, local HR representatives, legal counsel, training and development specialists, career counselors, labor leaders, and others on such a scale can require considerable effort. Efforts in the planning stage to identify global needs

To ensure the success of this project, the organizational psychologist creates an internal review board to advise the assessment design team throughout the project and review assessment components once they are developed. The board is composed of three subgroups: the technical group, which advises the assessment design team primarily on job requirements; the staffing group, which advises the design team on the staffing context; and the legal and labor group, which advises the design team on employment laws and labor requirements in all locations. The entire review board meets periodically throughout the project to receive information about the assessment design, plans for collecting job analysis and validation data, and so forth and to discuss common issues. The subgroups also meet independently to discuss issues that are relevant to their subgroup. These decisions are communicated to the entire board at the regular meetings.

and understand the cultural context in which the system will be used will help ensure that the requirements for the assessment are clearly defined and can be met. In addition, global input at the design stage can forestall potential resistance and other challenges to the selection system during implementation. The literature on managing global teams effectively (Uday-Riley, 2006) can be helpful in creating the team that will design, develop, and implement the assessment and in establishing ways of working within the team.

How Comparable Are Jobs Across Locations?

Job title or job description similarity is often the beginning point for considering using the same assessment in locations across the world. However, mistaken assumptions regarding job comparability across locations lead to major problems in assessment utility. The work performed under the same job title may not be standard across cultures. Similarly, unique job titles may mask similarities across locations, and opportunities for standardization of processes can be missed. The systematic collection of information on job requirements, work performed, and job context is essential. Although the thought of job analysis in each location in which an assessment tool may be implemented is daunting, a clear understanding of the jobs is necessary, and similarity should be demonstrated rather than assumed.

Despite obvious cultural differences, the psychological literature demonstrates that many jobs are similar across national boundaries. Taylor, Li, Shih, and Borman (2008) studied over one thousand workers from 369 organizations in first-line supervisor, office clerk, and computer programmer jobs in four locations and found similarity in rank ordering of importance, ratings of work activities, and job requirements ratings. Kaminski and Hemingway (2008) found considerable overlap in tasks and competencies for sales manager jobs in hotels in one company across four regions. Review of job analysis information can focus design on areas of overlap rather than points of divergence.

The organizational psychology literature contains considerable guidance on how to determine if different jobs are sufficiently similar to warrant common assessment selection processes (Society for Industrial and Organizational Psychology, 2003). The process for conducting job analysis in multiple countries is not unlike a job analysis in multiple domestic locations when the intent is to confirm the similarity of jobs in diverse locations. The process should define the tasks and the knowledge, skills, abilities, and other characteristics (KSAOs) that are necessary to perform the tasks in each location and assess the degree of overlap across locations.

A number of methods are available for determining job similarity. Gibson and Caplinger (2007) summarize three common approaches: the Pearson product moment correlation, critical overlap statistics, and the squared Euclidean distance. Care must be taken to recognize what is considered in making comparisons (for example, two jobs may differ only on tasks that are not particularly important to the job). Actual data collection in the job analysis may not be quite so simple for a number of reasons. For example, each approach to establishing consistency across jobs requires a common job analysis questionnaire containing the same set of tasks and KSAOs. Unless there is a good reason to believe the jobs are identical across locations, the job analysis must include steps such as observations and interviews to confirm that all tasks and KSAOs are captured in the job analysis questionnaire. Another concern is the different languages of incumbents and their supervisors and the necessity of translations, which require a careful evaluation of the equivalence of statements and rating scales. (We discuss issues in translation and equivalence further below.) In addition, there are few accepted standards answering the question, "How similar is similar enough?"

The organizational psychologist conducts a traditional job analysis that includes interviews with employees who work in the manufacturing and the repair divisions and their supervisors across all the countries, as well as focus groups to develop comprehensive task and KSAO lists, which are then placed into a job analysis questionnaire. Using information collected in the common questionnaire and the critical overlap statistic, the psychologist confirms that there are two distinct jobs: manufacturing technician and repair technician.

The design team reviews the results of the job analysis with the internal review board, which agrees that the best approach to selection for them will be two distinct assessment programs. The HR staffing group is concerned that two separate assessment programs will be very difficult for them to manage efficiently. As a compromise, the technical group and the staffing group agree that there will be an initial screen that measures core KSAOs common to both jobs, such as basic math skills and knowledge of electronics, and this will be followed by specialized screening for each job—vigilance for the manufacturing technicians and troubleshooting for the repair technicians, for example.

How Might the Various Labor Markets Affect the Assessment Process?

Often organizations expand their hiring to new locations because of labor market conditions: available cheap labor, available labor with appropriate skills, and other labor market conditions. For example, many technology companies have increased outsourcing to China, where talent has been cheaper than in India or the United States (Preston, 2007). How these specific labor market conditions affect the usefulness of an imported assessment needs to be given careful consideration to determine, for example, how much recruiting must be enacted and how many applicants will need to be processed. An assessment that is labor intensive may not work efficiently in a labor market that is rich in qualified applicants. An assessment that has many steps spread over time risks the loss of capable applicants in labor markets that are highly competitive. We recommend examining how local labor conditions affect applicant quantity and quality and also how the organization's presence might change the local labor market over time. Effective methods of attracting candidates can vary by location, as can recruitment timing or cycles. Cultural adaptation of Web sites has received considerable attention in the marketing literature, and such adaptation may be needed in recruitment as well (Baack & Singh, 2007).

When the company moved work offshore, it chose places that had plentiful supplies of well-qualified applicants. Initially applicants were willing to do whatever it took to get a well-paying job; however, as time elapsed, some of the countries have seen rapid expansion and increased competition for well-trained applicants. The HR subgroup recommends that the assessment program be as brief as possible so that they can attract the best applicants regardless of the location. In contrast, the technical group and the legal group are vitally aware of the ramifications of manufacturing and repair errors. Consequently they want a highly rigorous assessment program that minimizes errors.

After a great deal of discussion in the review board meetings, everyone agrees that the design team should create an assessment program for each job that takes about four hours if the person is successful. In addition, the international

(Continued)

> staffing organization will develop a recruiting campaign that describes the benefits of working for this company, which include comprehensive training and high levels of responsibility, and emphasizes that only the best are chosen for the privilege.
>
> The psychologists on the design team suggest that the assessment begin with a prescreen that can be administered by computer or paper and pencil. This prescreen measures the basic skills common to both jobs. Those who qualify on the prescreen complete a detailed work sample and a series of interviews with a staffing representative and the local management team.

Because education varies so much across countries, the design team, in conjunction with the staffing group, decides to allow each country's staffing organization to define whom they will invite to test in each country. One challenge many assessment specialists face is the interpretation of educational credentials. Applicants with identical educational achievement may have very different skill levels associated with them from location to location. Thus, screening on educational credentials may need careful attention. A related problem is the variability in literacy and education around the world.

What Legal Issues Should Be Considered?

Many countries have laws that govern employee selection and hiring processes, and these laws must be taken into consideration when designing assessments for these purposes. In addition, U.S. laws are sometimes applicable to global selection practices. For example, U.S. citizens who are hired by U.S. companies to work internationally are protected by many federal laws. Posthuma, Roehling, and Campion (2006) noted that organizational psychologists trained in the United States often have false assumptions regarding the applicability of U.S. laws to multinational corporations. They note that U.S. law is not applicable in these situations:

- Employees located outside the United States when the employer is not a U.S. entity regardless of the citizenship of the employee

- Non-U.S. citizens working for a U.S. organization outside the United States
- When compliance with U.S. laws would violate local laws such as a local quota or within-group norming requirements that violate U.S. civil rights laws

Three legal areas are of particular concern when designing selection systems for global use: discrimination law, regulations on hiring foreign workers, and privacy laws. Myors et al. (2008) provide an excellent review of the specific discrimination laws of various countries, so we will not repeat that here except to note a key conclusion: "disadvantaged groups" are different from country to country (some countries cover demographic characteristics, sexual orientation, or political opinion), and the permissible ways of treating these groups differ (some countries mandate quotas while some disallow them, and some allow within-group norming while some bar the practice). Hence, any undertaking in different locations requires investigating local laws and ensuring that the assessments comply with them

Second, countries' regulations regarding the hiring of non-citizens vary. Many require that new employees have appropriate work visas and other documents. Consequently such regulations can affect sourcing. For example, difficulty in getting work visas for software developers has led some U.S. companies to move work outside the United States (Hansen, 2008). Posthuma et al. (2006) suggest matching attractive candidates with locations where they can get visas and timing recruitment efforts with the granting of visas by countries.

A third area where the organizational psychologist needs to take notice is privacy laws that limit the transfer of personal information across borders or impose requirements for disclosing the purposes for which the data collected will be used (for example, European Commission's Directive on Data Protection). Such laws can pose challenges for electronic data collection and centralized databases for tracking recruits and internal talent. The U.S. Department of Commerce and the European Commission developed the safe harbor framework to allow U.S. companies to be certified as providing adequate privacy protections under the European Directive definitions. In addition to requiring that organizations meet strict security provisions for the protection of data, the safe harbor principles (www.export.gov/safeharbor/eg_main_018236.asp) require providing notice to individuals regarding uses of their data, the opportunity for an individual to opt out of uses other than those originally intended, and access to correct any errors in the data collected.

In addition to varying laws regarding employment processes, there are other constraints on how assessments can be administered and the assessment data can be stored. Many countries have labor organizations with varying amounts of influence that can affect selection systems. Collective bargaining coverage differs from location to location, and the developer of a selection system must have an understanding of what role such units might have to play in approval of selection systems in various locations.

Many countries, particularly in Europe, also have laws, rules, or expectations about various aspects of the assessment process. For example, some require informed consent prior to administration, and others require face-to-face feedback by a qualified professional. Many such practices are likely to be included in the ISO 9000 work to set standards for assessment (PC230) currently underway (although not yet approved). Thus, companies that want to be compliant with ISO 9000 standards or are required to be compliant must adopt these practices.

Laws and regulations in every country change. Organizational psychologists designing assessment programs should confer with their legal advisors in the countries in which they will work to confirm their understanding of current laws and the implications for assessment design.

The design team, the legal group, and the staffing group create a comprehensive list of laws and regulations that apply in each country. To achieve economies of scale, the design team has planned one database that will reside in the United States. In order that only one database be used, the design team takes the most restrictive security requirements and designs the database and data transfer systems to meet them. To meet the requirements of various privacy laws, the team again takes

the most restrictive stance and builds in the appropriate protections. In addition, features such as the ability to change certain pieces of information are built into the system, although
such features are not required by all countries.

In contrast to the single strategy to meet privacy and data
protection laws, the groups agree that the antidiscrimination
laws vary too much across countries and must be handled on
an individual basis. Therefore, each country's staffing organization develops its own set of guidelines regarding who may
apply, what kinds of outreach to protected groups must be
undertaken, what records must be retained, and so forth. The
centralized database is designed so that ad hoc reports can
easily be constructed for local reporting purposes.

Similarly, the rules for interacting with labor organizations
differ significantly. Thus, each country must include guidance
for those interactions in their local procedures.

How Should Cultural Differences Be Considered in Assessment?

An important question for the assessment designer to address is
when and how cultural differences should affect choices of assessment content and methods. Usually the job or program requirements determine what the assessment should measure. However,
cultural considerations make some approaches to assessment
more acceptable to the people taking the assessment and stakeholders in the organization than others and may make some
approaches more useful than others. For example, the definitions of cheating and plagiarism vary across cultures, as does the
acceptability of such behaviors (see Cizek, 1999, for a review).
Behaviors that are considered duplicitous in one culture are seen
as merely appropriate collaboration in another. Cultures also
vary in the familiarity assessment candidates have with certain
forms of assessments. For example, multiple-choice tests may be
uncommon in places where the education system uses only essay
and oral examinations. Knowing cultural perspectives on such
behaviors may influence how a tool is designed, what instructions

are provided, and how it is administered (for example, in levels of proctoring and security procedures). To heighten the probability that the assessment will be accepted, the professional must take cultural differences into account.

Considerable research has been undertaken on how individuals differ across cultures (House, Hanges, Javidan, Dorfman, & Gupta, 2004), and to describe the findings of that body of work would be a book in itself. Instead we note a few key conclusions.

Everyone involved with the development of the assessment is adamant that the assessment tools measure skills required by the job. Although representatives from several countries are concerned that many people in their culture are not likely to challenge authority, the job analysis makes clear that at times, an employee is required to speak up. Although a lingering concern is that applicants in some countries will not do as well as those in other countries, the assessment process includes a measure of an individual's willingness to point out problems.

The job analysis indicated that several noncognitive skills such as teamwork and conscientiousness were critically important for successful job performance. Although personality measures based on self-report worked well in the United States, the design team decides that the cultural differences in response sets will limit this kind of instrument's effectiveness. Instead, the team develops a situational judgment inventory and develops a scoring key that works in all cultures.

Members of the HR group report that cheating is a significant concern in several countries, so the company decides to use work sample tests that require applicants to display their knowledge and skills. Representatives from countries whose education systems do not regularly use multiple-choice test formats are particularly pleased because the work sample option does not penalize applicants from their countries. However, they also understand that the work sample approach will require assessor training and monitoring and realize they must find and commit the resources.

Groups can be described in terms of such shared values and beliefs as acceptable status differences and desire for personal achievement, and there are differences in national averages in these. However, a great deal of variability is found within countries in values as well (Oyserman, Coon, & Kemmelmeier, 2002). That is, some nations, including India and Belgium, have strong subgroup cultures, and some individuals do not have a strong cultural fit with the dominant values of their nation. Individual values vary according to nationality as well as ethnicity, geographic region, religion, and socioeconomic class. Hence, we urge organizational psychologists to step away from broad stereotypical pronouncements such as, "Asians are more collectivist," and instead focus more directly on how a cultural value might affect assessment acceptability and the performance of those assessed.

Considerations of culture should occur throughout the assessment process. A review of tools can be made with common cultural distinctions such as individualism and collectivism in mind to assess potential concerns. For example, those high in individualism or achievement may favor processes that allow them to showcase past achievements (Steiner & Gilliland, 2001), and those low in power distance may expect a more participative approach to assessment (Groeschl, 2003). Detailed orientation and preparation materials may be necessary to combat unfamiliarity with certain types of assessments in certain countries. Interviewers and administrators must be trained to recognize how their own cultural values and those with whom they interact may affect decision making.

One last caveat is that when an assessment tool meets resistance in a certain location, it may be due to cultural unacceptability, but often it is due to unfamiliarity or infeasibility given the context of assessment. Before dismissing the viability of a method due to culture, the professional should investigate the reasons for resistance and determine if modifications are possible. While cultural differences and their potential impact on acceptability are often discussed in the literature, the empirical research that exists does not support a strong influence of culture on reactions to assessment (see Ryan et al., 2009, for a recent example of such research).

As a prelude to the next section, we note that one area with concrete evidence of the influence of cultural differences is in response styles on self-report measures such as personality tests. Culture does relate to acquiescence tendencies (Smith, 2004), use of scale extremes (Hui & Triandis, 1989), and self-enhancement and modesty biases (Church et al., 2006). Recent advances in assessment formats to counter response bias effects, including improved forced-choice item development, may help in addressing these limitations. Cultural norms may also affect responding to assessments that require realistic responses. For example, situational judgment inventories that require a candidate to select an appropriate response or simulations and role plays in which the candidate generates an appropriate response require careful attention to scoring to avoid penalizing certain responses that are accepted ways of behaving in some cultures. Furthermore, differences in score comparability and system effectiveness can and do occur by country, although these are due more to human capital differences such as educational systems than to culture. Thus, country differences need to be considered in score interpretation and in evaluations of the validity and usefulness of assessments.

How Does One Ensure Assessment Tools Are Equivalent Across Countries?

Measurement equivalence exists when items and response scales measuring a construct are interpreted the same way across cultures and languages. Hambleton (2005) noted three major issues in adapting tools for use in one location from another: translation quality, measurement equivalence, and appropriate support materials.

Many discussions of this topic point out amusing translation errors; however, even when the translation error is not egregious, it can have a significant impact on an applicant's understanding of the meaning of a question, a rating scale, or instruction, leading to changes in that individual's score. In other words, translation quality can greatly affect measurement error, so the translation process is not a place for cutting corners or skimping on costs. (Brislin, 1986, and McKay, 2007, provide practical tips for reducing translation costs and increasing translation accuracy.) Although back-translation is often discussed as an accepted best practice, many have noted that this process is no guarantee of an error-free translation, particularly if the translators are unfamiliar with the company, job terminology, the construct being measured, or testing in general. We advocate careful translations as a starting point, with the inclusion of multiple reviews of the translated version by independent translators and in-country company experts, and detailed instructions for translators and reviewers on maintaining equivalence of concepts and difficulty of text.

Before the organizational psychologist ever gets to the issue of translations, there are ways of writing assessment items and exercises that boost the likelihood that the item can be used effectively cross-culturally. Some example guidelines on what to avoid in assessment tool development include the following:

- Culturally offensive or confusing content
- Specific measurements (for example, metric versus English system for weights and measures, monetary units)
- Colloquialisms
- Country-specific topics such as political, historical, or sporting events
- Nuanced word meanings
- Behaviors that are differentially appropriate according to culture—for example, how one interacts with strangers

In sum, the best way to approach ensuring equivalence is to invest in the development and translation process and involve cultural and job experts.

Two analytical frameworks are commonly used for evaluating measurement equivalence statistically: confirmatory factor analytical approaches and item-response theory approaches. The mechanics of establishing equivalence is beyond the scope of this chapter, and we refer readers to Vandenberg and Lance (2000), Raju, Laffitte, and Byrne (2002), and Meade and Lautenschlager (2004) for a review of confirmatory factor analytical and item-response theory methods for establishing equivalence. Meade and Lautenschlager note that because the two methods have different assumptions, provide different types of information, and have different limitations, one would use both methods whenever feasible in the ideal world. These techniques require considerable sample sizes for each culture or language group to be compared. Thus, more traditional item statistics, such as item-total correlations, standard deviations, and difficulty and discrimination indicators, often are used to identify points of concern. In the practical world, partial equivalence is often considered acceptable, and judgments to make changes or retain specific items that are not equivalent are made (see Robert, Lee, & Chan, 2006, for a discussion of this issue).

Robert et al. (2006) note threats to measurement equivalence, some of them particularly relevant when designing a global assessment or adapting a tool for international use:

- Item content can differ in construct relevance across countries.
- Extreme response sets may be used.
- Acquiescence response sets may be used.
- Differences in frame of reference can occur when individuals are comparing themselves to local cultures that differ on average in a trait; for example, labeling oneself as above average in extraversion means different things when "average" is based on different local cultures.
- Colloquialisms, idioms, and metaphors can be misinterpreted.
- Translations overshoot or undershoot intended meaning for words expressing quantity (for example, *few*), probabilities (*often*), times (*rarely*), and evaluation (*excellent*), and when individuals are answering questions in a language in which they have low ability, such as interview questions in English when English is a second language and applicants vary in proficiency.

Thus, one approach to developing measurement equivalence is avoidance of assessment tools that are more difficult to use cross-culturally. Finally, the quality of support materials should be carefully studied.

What Types of Evidence Are Needed to Support Effectiveness on a Global Basis?

The *International Test Commission Guidelines for Test Adaptation* (International Test Commission, 2001) is an important guidebook for those seeking to adapt or create tools for use across cultural and linguistic groups. The checklist emerging from these guidelines suggests that the user verify the following aspects of the assessment process:

- Appropriateness of language for all populations where used
- Familiarity of techniques and formats for all populations where used
- Measurement equivalence across versions
- Validity in each of the populations for which the assessment is used
- Consistency in the assessment administration environments across locations

This information may need to be sifted to determine where specific changes might improve the system in one or more locations. For example, comparable validities across countries do not rule out the need to determine if some individual items have been poorly translated or are in other ways nonequivalent and therefore require adjustment. Validity may be better with culturally tailored scoring algorithms than with a global scoring key. Hence, a professional review of all the information supporting the appropriateness of the assessment across cultures is needed.

Despite the importance of establishing evidence of validity for a particular use of an assessment, international validity studies present several problems that are not usually found in studies of validity within a single country. The first is the problem of identifying an appropriate criterion that is universally understood and consistently used. Performance dimensions and rating scales may not have common meanings despite the quality of the translations, and attitudes toward the assessment of individual performance may vary across cultures. Second, psychologists may find themselves in a challenging position with respect to establishing validity in each location while simultaneously ensuring that cultural differences do not systematically affect test scores. Few organizations have enough assessment information and criterion data on the same set of people to compute statistics related to validity or cultural equivalence despite the importance of such studies. Many companies use the transportability approach to establishing validity and transport the validity found in one culture to other cultures; however, this approach relies on the use of common job analysis tools with equivalent meanings and assumes measurement equivalence of the assessment tools across all cultures.

Key Issues in Implementation

All of the tools used in the assessment project (including the job analysis questionnaire, situational judgment inventory, work sample instructions, rating materials, and criterion measures) are translated into the local languages. The initial translations are reviewed by another professional translator and then sent to the HR organization in each country for an in-country review. Concerns are sent back to the professional translators for resolution.

The organizational psychologist designs a complex validation study that allows the company to establish the effectiveness of the assessment battery. In each location where there are more than three hundred employees, a concurrent criterion-related design is used. In locations where there are fewer than three hundred employees, a transportability approach based on the common job analysis questionnaire to establishing validity is used. The test is also administered to one hundred or more people so that appropriate norms can be determined.

In addition to the validity analyses, the organizational psychologist takes two approaches to establishing equivalence. First, conceptual equivalence is established by having three to five bilingual assessors compare situational judgment inventory items and work sample instructions and rating materials in English, the language in which they were written, and the local language to ensure they appear to be equal in difficulty. The psychologist also uses confirmatory factor analysis to confirm the measurement equivalence of the items.

Just as there are challenges in designing a global selection system, there are also many challenges in implementing one. The assumption that a well-designed and well-developed assessment that meets the organization's objectives can be easily deployed is often false. The careful professional must investigate the assessment contexts, ensure the assessment can be used appropriately in the intended locations, and adapt the assessment procedures when necessary.

How Does One Balance the Goal of Efficiencies in Cost, Time, and Technology with Local Needs?

Although one of the central benefits of standardization across countries is cost savings and efficiencies, these benefits can be lost if implementation is ineffective. To ensure an effective implementation that balances standardization and local effectiveness, several important variations in test design and administration procedures should be considered, and the professional must determine which are warranted.

First, some variations in the assessment tools themselves or their administration may be deemed necessary for legal, cultural, or other reasons. In most assessment programs that span international boundaries, some variations in the assessment tools themselves or their administration may be deemed necessary for legal, cultural, or other reasons. For example, situational judgment test videos may need to be created for each location to reflect the race and gender of workers, the type of equipment used, or geography, or alternate biodata items may need to be created to include the educational alternatives in a particular country. Such variations add to development time and costs, as well as administration costs, and their development and maintenance must be budgeted. Eliminating unwarranted variations in the assessment can reduce costs, yet eliminating all variations may render the global process useless in some parts of the world.

Second, costs of system administration likely vary by location (for example, cost of assessor time and cost of computer setups), and budgets for ongoing use must reflect those variations. The amount of time required for administration of the entire assessment process might also differ by location due to local markets and local staffing contexts at the same time the cultures vary in expectations regarding the acceptable amount of time that should be spent in assessment. In some countries, it may be necessary to alter the order of assessment components because of traditional sourcing strategies. For example, interviews may precede tests in countries where job applicants must travel long distances and the interview can be conducted over the telephone. Some organizations may alter the mechanics of the administration process itself depending on the availability of assessors and equipment. For example, tests might be administered in a paper-and-pencil mode in some areas and by computer in others. Scoring keys might be entrusted to trained administrators in some areas, but the same organization might require an untrained administrator to fax answer sheets to a centralized location for scoring. A careful review of administration requirements early in the design phase will provide the opportunity to explore less costly alternatives such as scoring by hand versus scanner versus faxed in versus computer based.

Third, despite the rapid spread of technology, Internet use and computer availability are not uniform globally, particularly among applicants and others external to the organization. Assessing the true state of technology availability is vital to success. Considering what, if any, variations might be required to accommodate technological differences globally is important.

Fourth, centralization decisions can certainly enhance efficiencies, but care must be taken to ensure that such decisions are made with thoughtful consideration of the needs of local management to participate in the design process. By involving the remote users, central designers can ensure that the assessment tools and administration processes work in multiple cultures and boost the likelihood that assessments can be reliably executed. Moreover, local participation may reduce resistance to the new system and even firm up commitment to it.

Finally, factors such as application rates and selection ratios are drivers of costs (and time requirements), so a locally efficient system may not translate into a globally efficient system. For example, automated multiple-choice tests may be useful in screening large numbers of applicants in one location, but in another location with fewer applicants, it might be better to choose a different method to assess the same competencies.

What Characteristics of the Local Assessment Environment Are Important in Global Implementation?

Consideration of the local context can ensure a successful implementation. What often makes global assessment difficult are the variations across locations. Even within the same corporations, HR staffs in various locations can have personnel who differ in terms of number, education, and experience in testing and attitudes toward testing as well as facilities that are more or less conducive to good practices. Some contextual challenges can be amplified in global system implementation—for example:

- Qualified administrators may not be available at each location for various system components.
- Training of system administrators may vary by location.
- Appropriate facilities for administering the assessment may not be available in all locations.
- Administration policies on such matters as retesting, exemptions, confidentiality, and test security policies need to be understood and accepted everywhere.

Without a consideration of these context issues, a well-designed tool or system may not deliver what was expected. Although these are all issues with a single country system, the variation in context found globally is often great in technology, physical environments for assessment, and qualifications of administrators.

How Much Flexibility Should Be Allowed?

Case studies of successful global selection systems (Ryan, Wiechmann, & Hemingway, 2003) suggest that some flexibility is needed if an assessment tool is going to work equally well in a variety of cultural, linguistic, economic, and legal environments.

Some variation to meet local cultural practices, legal requirements, and other requirements does not mean a system is not global; the global nature comes from the commonality of aims, objectives, and general structures rather than the comparability of specific elements. In our view, the challenge is not in what variations should be designed into the system to accommodate differences, but in avoiding unjustified regional variations and drift from a global standard.

What Should Be the Basis for Score Interpretations?

One of the more challenging questions assessment developers face with global systems is whether comparisons are to be made on a local or global basis. Recently test developers (Bartram, 2008; Ramesh, Hazucha, & Bank, 2008) have investigated the appropriateness of different norms (multinational norms, regional norms, within-nation norms, and language-based norms, for example), and there is no short and simple answer. The most appropriate normative group depends on the goals of the system, the source of candidates, the evidence for measurement equivalence across groups, and test content. For example, ample evidence suggests that differences in personality test scores across countries necessitate local norm groups (Schmitt, Allik, McCrae, & Benet-Martinez, 2007). In contrast, a selection program that qualifies individuals for placement anywhere in the world may require a single global norm.

Some tips for successful implementation of a consistent system are:

- Use well-developed administration training and printed guidance.
- Use scripts for assessment administrators to follow and read aloud.
- Have FAQs and scripted responses.
- Role play assessment problems with administrators to ensure consistency.
- Set up a hotline for unexpected issues that occur so that administrators can get answers in unanticipated situations.

What Is Needed to Market the System to Stakeholders Globally?

Stakeholders from different countries may have many justifiable concerns regarding new assessment methods based on their own economic, legal, and cultural environment. Having a good internal marketing strategy is important, but this effort will be successful only if there has been involvement from the start of individuals from different countries in the decisions that led to the system. Without initial input, unseen obstacles may emerge at later points in the process where modifications will be costly; for example, a need may arise for an additional translation for a variation in dialect or a paper-and-pencil version for remote sites with poor Internet accessibility. In addition, communications will need to describe how cultural and other differences were taken into account in the design of the process, opportunities were available for input, and how that input was incorporated. As with any new selection process, the rationale for change needs to be made evident.

What Types of Monitoring Should Be Put in Place?

Many small local changes can lead to a system with little consistency globally. Thus, those responsible for assessments must be vigilant for drift from the standard and attempt to determine which changes are necessary and which are merely preferred. Although monitoring activities depend on the nature of the assessment process, some examples of how tracking can occur include the following:

- Assessment scores (by country and by legally protected groups in each country)
- Adherence to administration procedures and policies such as time limits, retesting, training of administrators, security practices, and confidentiality
- Assessee reactions to processes
- Recruiting metrics such as time-to-hire and yield ratios
- Appropriate selection and training of administrators and scorers for assessment tools

Monitoring for drift in a variety of areas can inform decisions about when global standardization is useful and when it should be relaxed.

Prior to implementation, the organizational psychologist takes an inventory of the facilities and personnel available for administration of the assessment process. Although the African location does not have computers, the international HR organization believes that consistency of administration and data recording is so important that it funds the computers needed out of its own budget.

The inventory also included testing policies and procedures and revealed that there were few outside the United States and Europe. The HR team developed a list of policies that covered retesting, exemptions, training requirements for assessors, data reporting requirements, and others that the technical group reviewed. Later it became clear that a standard set of policies and procedures could not be implemented in all locations, so a model set of assessment policies and procedures was developed that clearly delineated which sections could not be amended. For example, security procedures and data recording policies and procedures generally cannot be changed. Ultimately the model assessment policies and procedures are distributed, and each country must accept or amend the model policy and have it approved by the review board.

The HR organization, regardless of location, is staffed by highly educated people; however, many have little experience in formal assessment processes. The organizational psychologist develops user guides for administration of all the components of the assessment process and a training program that can be delivered through Web meetings. In addition, hourlong monthly assessment meetings are held at rotating times (to share the pain of unreasonable times across time zones) to discuss problems that arise. In addition, the psychologist's team conducts monthly audits of each location's assessment records and has conference calls monthly to discuss anomalies. The psychologist develops a protocol for reviewing assessment procedures that can be used to check on administration of the assessment procedures throughout the world

Success metrics are developed by each country and applicant reactions are monitored. After the assessment program is implemented, the review board meets every three months to review the feedback and reactions to the program.

Final Thoughts

Global assessments can be difficult to develop and implement; however, successful projects share several important characteristics. First, those responsible for the assessment make a considerable effort to identify all of the important stakeholders and engage them in a participatory process to define the requirements of the system. Second, developers undertake careful research to help them understand all of the cultural contexts in which the assessment will be used. Third, they balance the need for consistency with the need for local adaptations to the process. Fourth, successful developers carefully and often communicate information about the development, ranging from the objectives of the assessment and plans for development and implementation to the expectations of participants in the related research studies and requirements of administrators. Fifth, monitoring systems help ensure that the selection system is fulfilling its intended goals.

As more organizations become multinational, the importance of global assessment will grow. The same forces that encourage international expansion also emphasize the need for efficient and cost-effective hiring practices. Thus, organizations that are moving manufacturing operations overseas for cost savings or hiring engineers from developing nations to meet the demand for skilled labor will also be looking for assessments that can be deployed around the world. As the demand for international assessment increases, organizational psychologists must refine the methods used for single-country assessment development to consider multiple cultural, linguistic, economic, and educational contexts from the start. Through these efforts, they will build a repository of knowledge regarding assessment methods that work best in various contexts.

References

Baack, D. W., & Singh, N. (2007). Culture and web communications. *Journal of Business Research, 60,* 181–188.

Bartram, D. (2008). Global norms: Toward some guidelines for aggregating personality norms across countries. *International Journal of Testing, 8,* 315–333.

Brislin, R. W. (1986). The wording and translation of research instruments. In W. J. Lonner & J. W. Berry (Eds.), *Field methods in cross-cultural research* (pp. 137–164). Thousand Oaks, CA: Sage.

Church, A. T., Katigbak, M. S., del Prado, A. M., Valdez-Medina, J. L., Miramontes, L. G., & Ortiz, F. A. (2006). A cross-cultural study of trait self-enhancement, explanatory variables and adjustment. *Journal of Research in Personality, 40,* 1169–1201.

Cizek, G. J. (1999). *Cheating on tests: How to do it, detect it, and prevent it.* Mahwah, NJ: Erlbaum.

Gibson, W. M., & Caplinger, J. A. (2007). Transportation of validation results. In S. M. McPhail (Ed.), *Alternative validation strategies: Developing new and leveraging existing validity evidence* (pp. 29–81). San Francisco: Jossey-Bass.

Groeschl, S. (2003). Cultural implications for the appraisal process. *Cross Cultural Management, 10,* 67–79.

Hambleton, R. K. (2005). Issues, designs, and technical guidelines for adapting tests into multiple languages and cultures. In R. K. Hambleton, P. F. Merenda, & C. D. Spielberger (Eds.), *Adapting educational and psychological tests for cross-cultural assessment* (pp. 3–38). Mahwah, NJ: Erlbaum.

Hansen, F. (2008). Microsoft's Canadian move a swipe at stiff U.S. visa policies. *Workforce Management.* Retrieved from http://www.workforce.com/section/06/feature/25/33/66.

House, R., Hanges, P., Javidan, M., Dorfman, P., & Gupta, V. (Eds.). (2004). *Culture, leadership, and organizations: The GLOBE study of 62 societies.* Thousand Oaks, CA: Sage.

Hui, C. H., & Triandis, H. C. (1989). Effects of culture and response format on extreme response style. *Journal of Cross-Cultural Psychology, 20,* 296–309.

International Test Commission. (2001). *International Test Commission guidelines for test adaptation.* London: Author.

Kaminski, K. A., & Hemingway, M. A. (2008, April). *Assessment around the world: A case study from Starwood Hotels.* Paper presented at the Annual Conference of the Society for Industrial and Organizational Psychology, San Francisco.

McKay, C. (2007). *Nine tips for increasing translation quality while decreasing translation cost.* Retrieved from www.translationdirectory.com/article413.htm.

Meade, A. W., & Lautenschlager, G. J. (2004). A comparison of item response theory and confirmatory factor analytic methodologies for establishing measurement equivalence/invariance. *Organizational Research Methods, 7,* 361–388.

Myors, B., Lievens, F., Schollaert, E., Van Hoye, G., Cronshaw, S. F., Mlandic, A. et al. (2008). International perspectives on the legal environment for selection. *Industrial and Organizational Psychology: Perspectives on Science and Practice, 1,* 206–246.

Oyserman, D., Coon, H. M., & Kemmelmeier, M. (2002). Rethinking individualism and collectivism: Evaluation of theoretical assumptions and meta-analyses. *Psychological Bulletin, 128,* 3–72.

Posthuma, R. A., Roehling, M. V., & Campion, M. A. (2006). Applying U.S. employment discrimination laws to international employers: Advice for scientists and practitioners. *Personnel Psychology, 59,* 705–740.

Preston, R. (2007, August 13). Global outsourcing not a one-way street from U.S. *Information Week,* p. 72.

Raju, N. S., Laffitte, L. J., & Byrne, B. M. (2002). Measurement equivalence: A comparison of methods based on confirmatory factor analysis and item response theory. *Journal of Applied Psychology, 87,* 517–529.

Ramesh, A., Hazucha, J. F., & Bank, J. (2008). Using personality data to make decisions about global managers. *International Journal of Testing, 8,* 346–366.

Robert, C., Lee, W. C., & Chan, K. (2006). An empirical analysis of measurement equivalence with the Indcol measure of individualism and collectivism: Implications for valid cross-cultural inference. *Personnel Psychology, 59,* 65–100.

Ryan, A. M., Boyce, A. S., Ghumman, S., Jundt, D., Schmidt, G., & Gibby, R. (in press). Going global: Cultural values and perceptions of selection procedures. *Applied Psychology: An International Review, 58,* 520–556.

Ryan, A. M., Wiechmann, D., & Hemingway, M. (2003). Designing and implementing global staffing systems: Part II—best practices. *Human Resource Management, 42,* 85–94.

Schmitt, D. P., Allik, J., McCrae, R. R., & Benet-Martinez, V. (2007). The geographic distribution of Big Five personality traits: Patterns and profiles of human self-description across 56 nations. *Journal of Cross-Cultural Psychology, 38*(2), 173–212.

Smith, P. B. (2004). Acquiescent response bias as an aspect of cultural communication style. *Journal of Cross-Cultural Psychology, 35*, 50–61.

Society for Industrial and Organizational Psychology. (2003). *Principles for the validation and use of personnel selection procedures.* San Francisco: Jossey-Bass.

Steiner, D. D., & Gilliland, S. W. (2001). Procedural justice in personnel selection: International and cross-cultural perspectives. *International Journal of Selection and Assessment, 9*, 124–137.

Taylor, P. J., Li, W., Shih, K., & Borman, W. C. (2008). The transportability of job information across countries. *Personnel Psychology, 61*(1), 69–111.

Uday-Riley, M. (2006). Eight critical steps to improve workplace performance with cross-cultural teams. *Performance Improvement, 45*, 28–32.

Vandenberg, R. J., & Lance, C. E. (2000). A review and synthesis of the measurement invariance literature: Suggestions, practices, and recommendations for organizational research. *Organizational Research Methods, 3*, 4–70.

Part Four

Advances, Trends, and Issues

CHAPTER 19

ADVANCES IN TECHNOLOGY- FACILITATED ASSESSMENT

Douglas H. Reynolds, Deborah E. Rupp

The expanding influence of Internet technologies on human resource (HR) practices in organizations is undeniable. New technologies have been introduced to facilitate personnel processes ranging from initial job search to executive development and succession management. Yet despite the increasing expectation for HR processes to be technology enabled, research on these new technologies has lagged behind their design and application.

Both researchers and practitioners have discussed a wide range of applications of technology that may be deployed within the HR function (Guental & Stone, 2005; Reynolds & Dickter, 2010; Rupp, 2008; Rupp, Gibbons, & Snyder, 2008). Many of

We acknowledge and thank Assesta, Development Dimensions International, Iscopia Software, Job Performance Systems, and Procter & Gamble for their partnership and permission to use their work as examples in this chapter. We are also grateful to Jon Bricker, Alyssa Gibbons, Robert Gibby, Mark Johnson, Myungjoon Kim, Doug Rosenthal, and our chapter reviewers for their helpful assistance with and support of this project.

these technology applications include assessments in the services they provide. This chapter summarizes the key issues associated with the use of technology to facilitate assessment in organizations and provides examples of how technology has extended the value provided by assessment. We use the term *assessment* broadly in this context, referring to all measures of human capability ranging from standardized tests of abilities, skills, and knowledge to large-scale behavioral simulations and assessment centers.

We begin by examining the conditions that have enabled the growth of technology-facilitated assessment, as well as the applicable professional standards, guidelines, and legal considerations that are specific to technology-based assessments. Next, we turn to a summary of the primary applications of technology to assessment and provide some examples of technology-based assessments that are currently available. We end with a review of some of the new issues that are being raised and concerns that are heightened when technology is used to deliver assessments. We also share some thoughts on the trends that will influence technology-based assessment into the future.

We are neither advocates nor critics of the pervasive trend toward the automation of assessment. Rather, our aim here is to discuss what technology has made possible, consider both the full potential and boundary conditions of high-tech assessment, and point out the regulatory, legal, and structural challenges that the implementation of technology into assessment programs creates. We see great opportunity for technology to improve assessment programs. At the same time, we strive to be realistic, providing recommendations to assist assessment practitioners in making informed decisions regarding their use of technology. The objective of this chapter is to help users of technology-based assessments approach the issues they face with an understanding of both the benefits and challenges associated with these new tools.

Drivers for Technology-Based Assessment

The use of technology, and the Internet in particular, to facilitate the delivery of assessment has exploded since the late 1990s. Beyond faddish application of technology for its own sake, the trend has reshaped how assessments are designed and delivered.

What accounts for this rapid shift? What guidance can be offered to those who are working with these new technologies? Where are the boundaries of reasonable practice when technology has changed many aspects of the assessment landscape? The answers to these questions provide a foundation for understanding the value (and risks) associated with these new practices.

Technology Availability

One potent driver for technology-based assessment is the availability of technology, its ease of use, and its applicability to global assessment practices. Even ten years ago, industrial-organizational psychologists, psychometricians, and HR practitioners may have felt overwhelmed, underskilled, and lacking the resources to leverage technology into their assessment programs. With increases in the availability, affordability, and usability of technology, this landscape has changed considerably.

The Internet as we know it began to be used by large groups of people in 1995. In the intervening years, its use has become widespread and commonplace. As of 2007, about 39 percent of Internet users are in Asia, with 26 percent of users in Europe and 18 percent in North America. Regions with the least amount of Internet penetration are currently experiencing the fastest growth in use. From 2000 to 2009, Internet use grew by 380 percent worldwide (internetworldstats.com). This growth means that more people than ever before are becoming familiar and comfortable with Web-based environments, a critical factor for those developing assessments in organizations.

This growth can largely be attributed to two simultaneous trends: an increase in the speed of the Internet and a decrease in the cost of an Internet connection. The issue of channel data capacity (or bandwidth) and speed is of critical importance for the practice of technology-enabled assessments. Without a stable and consistent broadband connection, much of the technology reviewed in this chapter is impossible. Real-time interaction, streaming video, and complex algorithms such as those used for computer adaptive testing all require the rapid transmission of very large quantities of data. The cost of broadband access is to some degree driven by economic policy and infrastructure.

At present, the United States lags behind many other industrialized nations in broadband speed (Asia by far is the market leader, with Europe and the United States behind), which has made implementation of assessment technology challenging. However, Web speed is getting both faster and cheaper at an exponential rate. For example, in recent years we have seen an increase in broadband availability from 50 percent to 80 percent of U.S. homes, and from 81 percent to 94 percent in U.S. workplaces.

A number of emerging technologies also show promise for increasing the feasibility and accessibility of sophisticated assessment technologies. Among these are new standards (802.11n) for wireless local area networks (LANs) that would allow much faster connection speeds—ten times or more than current average speeds. These types of speeds also allow more graphically sophisticated and interactive forms of assessment. Another key transition is that from current 32-bit computer systems to 64-bit systems. These newer systems use more RAM (or working memory) and can process more data at faster rates.

Similarly the development of WiMAX—high-speed wireless that does not run using wired or cellular networks—allows high-speed access anywhere in the world, even in very remote locations where traditional cable-based broadband is not available. Finally, it has been projected that there will soon be a dramatic jump in the number of Internet protocol (IP) addresses available worldwide facilitated by the transition from IP version 4 to version 6, such that assessment may be conducted using a wider range of electronic devices, and assessees and assessors can be networked through a number of different channels. Indeed, the demand for the delivery of assessments on mobile platforms may become the most significant opportunity and challenge to assessment over the next decade.

Perhaps the largest perceived barrier to implementing complex technology-based assessment is that of software design and development. Yet even this task is becoming simpler. Some vendors now offer authoring tools for designing traditional multiple-choice tests, situational judgment tests, and even avatar-based simulations and other technically advanced assessments. Thus, assessment developers need not become programmers (or hire them) to take advantage of these technologies.

Technology trends and innovations will continue to influence assessment deployment options. Look for the growing impact of cloud computing, for example, where all aspects of computing power can be shared across organizations, allowing access to extensive computing power for those who may not otherwise have the hardware, software, and infrastructure capacity to support complex automated assessments. Also, consider the growing trend for handheld devices to be a primary access point to the Internet in many countries. These trends exemplify the growing levels of access to the sophisticated technologies required to support many of the innovations we describe in this chapter. Future innovations and trends will continue to push in the direction of greater access levels, higher computing power, and more flexibility for both users and providers of technology-based assessments.

Business Efficiency

The most common reason that technology is deployed to enable an HR activity is to improve the efficiency with which the task is performed. Consider the introduction of technology to the job application process: by having job applicants complete the process on the Internet, organizations have been able to reduce the labor associated with collecting, reviewing, and maintaining job applications—a time-consuming, paper-laden activity. Given the fact that most assessment processes involve routine and repetitive tasks, the introduction of technology allows many opportunities for efficiency gains.

Several characteristics of modern software allow such gains. First, well-designed software systems are built on a database that houses individual data records that may be used for multiple purposes. The database serves as a virtual warehouse that replaces paper storage and supports the reuse of information, eliminating redundant data collection. For example, applicant information can be reused to populate an employee's record when the applicant is hired, thereby eliminating the need to enter the information twice. Second, most business software is built to contain business logic that automates decisions and actions. Continuing the recruitment example, software may be written to select from among all applicants only those who indicate they have a college degree (for jobs where a degree requirement has been validated). By constructing software rules in this manner, organizations can eliminate the need to have people review information and make simple and routine decisions. Third, by using a browser or Internet-based interface for broad access to the system, organizations are provided with a low-cost distribution method whereby a large number of people can access the system with a minimal increase in associated cost. Compared to business processes deployed by paper or telephone, once the initial technology investment is made, the cost to replicate, distribute, and store information is nearly invariant as user volume increases.

Better Insight About People

Beyond efficiency benefits, technology also promises to improve how assessment is conducted and, in turn, provide deeper insights into those who complete technology-based assessments. This promise has yet to be realized for most assessment applications, but the foundations exist for improvements over traditional assessment delivery methods. Technology could be expected to yield benefits to assessment in a number of areas:

- By increasing efficiency in the assessment delivery process, technology can reduce the amount of time required to administer a given assessment, thereby allowing the administration of more assessment material within a given time period. The addition of content can yield an assessment that is more reliable and has the potential to become more valid.
- By including audio, video, or replicas of computer-based work processes, technology-based assessments may enable assessment experiences that are more true-to-life than non-computerized alternatives.
- By enabling advanced administration techniques such as adaptive testing, technology can enhance measurement precision.
- Techniques such as question randomization and parallel form administration can improve the security, and consequently the accuracy, of an assessment.
- Technology can assist in streamlining and standardizing the process by which interviewers, assessors, and other raters in

behavioral assessment processes carry out their tasks. For example, technology can be used to more easily classify observed behaviors into predetermined performance dimensions.

- Technology allows tracking and recording of behaviors that are difficult to capture through other means. By monitoring such variables as where test takers click within a set of information and how much time they spend on computer-based tasks, it may be possible to uncover new metrics for use in assessment.

For many of these potential benefits, it is too early to draw conclusions about their effectiveness. However, a variety of assessments are available that incorporate these concepts so the potential benefits should become clear as research is conducted with these new tools.

Strategic Perspective and Impact

Technology tools can also yield benefits for strategic decision making in organizations, especially as data are aggregated across individuals, time, and assessment events. For example, by examining trends in recruiting quality, an organization may be able to better prepare new employees for entry into the organization by adding training events aimed at filling common deficiencies. Organizations can also optimize job selection procedures based on changing job conditions, predict job vacancy rates, and tie cultural and business outcomes to earlier interventions. Technology tools facilitate these goals by capturing and storing information across assessment events such as entry-level hiring systems, culture surveys, developmental assessments, and customer satisfaction measures. Although these connections are possible to make without technology, having integrated technology systems enables faster and more flexible analyses. Organizations are using integrated technology tools and data warehousing as one method for informing strategic decisions, fueling a marketplace trend toward the management of people in organizations as one integrated system, compared to separate systems for the major talent functions of recruitment, selection, development, performance management, and succession.

Applicable Standards, Guidelines, Regulations, and Best Practices

With the rise of technology-enabled assessment, new issues arise for evaluating the psychometric quality of assessments and ensuring their ethical use. Unfortunately, many of these issues have not been addressed by the professional testing guidelines we currently have available, among them the Society for Industrial and Organizational Psychology (SIOP) Principles for the Validation and Use of Personnel Selection Procedures, the Guidelines and Ethical Considerations for Assessment Center Operations, and the APA Standards for Educational and Psychological Testing. To address this need, a number of reports, guidelines, and programs have been created to assist practitioners in using technology in their assessment programs.

APA Taskforce Report on Internet-Based Testing

The American Psychological Association's Committee on Psychological Tests and Assessment formed the Taskforce on Psychological Testing on the Internet (Naglieri et al., 2004) to analyze the state of technology-enabled assessment and its implications for test validation. After studying the issues in depth, the committee concluded that although current psychometric standards should be applied when developing high-tech assessments, the technological advancements being made in the field push the boundaries of existing psychometric theory.

In their report, the committee encouraged practitioners to see beyond the "flash and sparkle" that technology offers and remember that regardless of the increases in availability, efficiency, and convenience that technology can provide, no utility will be gained if the assessment scores lack reliability and validity. The committee also highlighted a number of new issues that must be addressed when conducting Web-based assessment: the security of data transferred over the Internet, identity protection, item and measurement equivalence (when all test takers do not receive the same items or test forms), and equality of access to the Internet and technology used across populations of test takers, for example. These issues are heightened when data are housed on third-party servers and assessments are delivered in nonproctored environments or over nonsecured networks such as handheld devices.

The APA taskforce made several recommendations to practitioners using the Internet to deliver assessments:

- Using assessments that require identity confirmation through the use of secure test sites or short on-site verification tests for those who pass an open administration.
- Using a multiserver configuration where the Internet, test applications, data, scoring and reporting applications, and backups are each contained on a separate server, with the data residing safely behind a firewall.
- Implementing systems that will discourage the copying and printing of test content from within the application. This can be done by disabling hot keys and the right mouse context menu, as well as by installing a test security agent that prohibits leaving the test application when it is operable.

International Test Commission Guidelines for Internet-Based Testing

Another effort to provide guidance to developers, publishers, and users of computer-based tests and assessments is represented by the International Test Commission (ITC) *Guidelines on Computer-Based and Internet-Delivered Testing* (2006). These guidelines provide recommendations for technology design, test security, administration policies, and other tools and processes that affect assessment quality. The ITC guidelines also introduce important distinctions between different modes of test administration when tests are delivered over the Internet. These categories vary based on the level of oversight and control asserted over the assessment process, including:

- *Open access.* The test can be accessed by the Internet from any location with no authentication of the test taker (proof that the test taker is who he or she claims to be) and no direct supervision of the assessment session.

- *Controlled delivery.* The test is made available only to known test takers, yet no direct authentication or supervision of the assessment session is involved.
- *Supervised delivery.* Test taker identity can be authenticated, and there is a degree of direct supervision over test taking. For example, an administrator may log in a candidate and confirm that the test has been properly administered and completed.
- *Managed delivery.* This is the highest level of supervision and control over the test-taking environment, often achieved by the use of dedicated testing centers where there is control over authentication, access, security, qualification of test administration staff, and quality and technical specifications of the test equipment.

These categories provide useful distinctions for the design of assessment programs and for organizing future research.

European Union Data Protection and U.S. Safe Harbor Program

The European Union (EU) has developed the most extensive set of rules and guidelines for protecting personal and sensitive data, such as data collected in assessment programs used in organizations. The United States created a program to mirror the requirements of the EU guidelines to help U.S. organizations comply with the EU standards. The U.S. approach, known as the Safe Harbor program, emphasizes seven elements that should be present when handling personal data:

- *Notice.* Individuals must be clearly informed, as early as possible, about the reasons for collecting and using their personal information.
- *Choice.* Individuals must be allowed to decide if and how their information is to be disclosed to third parties and used beyond the purpose originally specified.
- *Onward transfer.* Personal information may be transferred to a third party only when the data provider has been given both notice and choice about the data transfer.

- *Access.* Within reason, individuals must have access to and be able to correct, add to, or delete their personal information where it is inaccurate.
- *Security.* Data must be reasonably protected from loss, misuse, unauthorized access, and disclosure.
- *Data integrity.* Personal information must be relevant, reliable, accurate, current, and complete and used only for the purpose that was originally specified.
- *Enforcement.* Mechanisms should be provided for complaints and recourse, as well as for verifying adherence to the Safe Harbor principles.

More information about the Safe Harbor program can be found at the U.S. Department of Commerce Web site (www. export.gov/safeharbor).

Internet Applicant Rule and Record-Keeping Regulations

The United States has employment regulations regarding Internet-based personnel selection processes. In 2005, the U.S. Department of Labor's Office of Federal Contracts Compliance Programs published a rule that connected the established federal *Uniform Guidelines on Employee Section Procedures* (Equal Employment Opportunity Commission, Civil Service Commission, Department of Labor, & Department of Justice, 1978) to Internet-based employment processes. This new rule applies to the multitude of organizations that contract with the U.S. government and thus fall under the purview of this office. The rule has implications for organizations that use assessments as part of an online recruiting and selection procedure because it requires records to be maintained on all applicants and for anybody who takes a test (defined broadly as nearly any form of assessment) during the process of applying for a job. The rule defines exactly which job seekers are to be considered job applicants when Internet-based selection processes are used. The regulations specify that applicants must meet carefully defined basic qualifications as well as other criteria related to their interest in the job and adherence to the requirements of the selection procedure.

Because Internet-based procedures can generate large pools of interested job seekers, the identification of qualified job applicants should be done according to the requirements of the regulations before tests and assessments are provided. More information about these regulations is available from the U.S. Department of Labor (2005).

Tips for Ensuring Professionally, Legally, and Psychometrically Compliant Technology-Enabled Assessment

- Be knowledgeable about applicable standards, regulations, guidelines, and legal requirements when designing and implementing technology-based assessments.
- Consider how the features of your technology options support the planned administration method (open, controlled, supervised, or managed).
- Determine whether your technology providers comply with the Safe Harbor principles for data protection, and specify how each principle will be met for your assessment process. Consider having your legal department review the process, especially if your assessments are to be used in multiple countries.
- If your assessment is used for employee selection, map your process against the Internet applicant definition. Ensure that proper records are maintained for participants in the process.

Applications of Technology to Assessment

The list of ways in which technology is being used to increase the efficiency and effectiveness of assessment is increasing each year. Examples of such uses include Internet-administered prescreens, applications, and selection tests; the use of computer-adaptive testing algorithms; neural network scoring methodologies; and media-rich assessments by broadband delivery (virtual reality assessments, video-based situational judgment tests, and avatar-based simulations are examples). Technology-mediated assessments have been used to assess cognitive ability and integrity, collect biodata, and assist with interviewing. We briefly describe some of the most prevalent of these applications.

Internet Applications and Screening

One HR management tool that has gained tremendous popularity is the online job application. Such systems allow individuals to explore job openings, submit online résumés, complete screening questionnaires and job applications, and, when paired with an applicant tracking system (ATS), allow recruiters to easily access applicant data to efficiently prescreen candidates and schedule further assessment. Properly developed online screening tools provide an effective and efficient method to reduce a pool of job seekers down to those with the highest potential to succeed on subsequent portions of the assessment process and ultimately on the job. This outcome is achieved by weighting and scoring responses to the online questionnaires to allow sorting and ranking of candidates against defined qualifications.

Online applications and screening tools are often bundled within ATS systems. When this is the case, the assessment tools may be configured by users based on predefined libraries of questions, or custom content must be populated by a knowledgeable user. These features provide a wide range of flexibilities, but they also increase risk when users are not careful when constructing requirements. Poorly specified requirements can lead to the incorrect rejection of qualified job seekers and discrimination against protected classes based on factors that are not related to the job. Thus, it is essential that all applicant-screening content be appropriately validated with the same rigor as other aspects of the selection process.

Computer-Based Testing

One of the most researched topics within the realm of technology and assessment is in the area of computerized and Web-based testing. The term *testing* in this context refers to standardized measures of knowledge, abilities, or traits. Examples include licensure exams, college entrance exams, and employment selection tests. Because of the large numbers of individuals who take such exams, practical demands are placed on test developers and administrators to manage the logistics of large-scale test administration while protecting the security of the tests. Advances in technology, coupled with advances in contemporary psychometric theory, have not only created opportunities for vastly improving the efficiency of test administration but have also allowed more sophisticated tests.

The combination of technology, psychometrics, and cognitive science has made possible an integrated series of systems where technology enables item generation, item pretesting, examinee registration, test administration, scoring, reporting, and data management. The use of computer adaptive testing, where items are chosen by the system depending on the test taker's responses to previous items, shortens the test administration, reduces the threat of security breaches, and allows controlled test administration at times of convenience for the test taker. In addition, with increases in speed and bandwidth, more sophisticated test content, such as audio, graphic, and video-based stimuli, can be incorporated into test questions. Also, with more computational power, more advanced scoring algorithms can be used, allowing the inclusion of questions that allow more complex constructed responses, for example, essay questions that are scored automatically by searching for key words and themes. Finally, the availability of advanced technology and greater bandwidth now allows smaller testing operations to conduct advanced forms of testing.

Despite these advancements and efficiencies, computer-based testing programs can still be quite costly. For example, large pools of pretested items are required for computer adaptive testing, and given the newness of these technologies, local validation is typically a requirement. Furthermore, although new technologies and procedures have been developed to address the security concerns that arise when testing is conducted without a proctor, many high-stakes programs cannot accept the risks inherent with this approach and dedicated testing centers are thus required. New advances in biometric verification such as fingerprints and typing patterns offer promise for improving online test security as well.

Assessment Centers and Simulations

Behavioral forms of assessment such as assessment centers require participants to take part in simulation exercises and have their behavior observed, recorded, classified, and rated by trained assessors. Because the method traditionally requires assessees, assessors, role players, and administrators to come together in the same place at the same time and because of the time required to integrate assessment data about candidates and generate feedback reports, the demand for the application of technology to aid assessment center efficiency has been strong. By providing assessors video access to assessee performance using the Web (either live or streamed from a stored file on a server), assessment centers can be conducted remotely, reducing the need for travel, physical space, and other costly resources. If technology can be used to bring assessors together in a virtual environment, the integration of data and report generation can be further streamlined.

Recent work has explored the feasibility of such video- and Internet-enabled remote assessment centers (Rupp, 2006, 2008). Although the video recording of simulation exercises is not new, the use of small, portable, and affordable video equipment and the streaming of video over a reliable connection (eliminating the need to ship videos or contend with long download times) have broadened the options for deploying these technologies. Software has also been developed to assist assessors in completing their duties. These applications use an Internet-based platform for taking behavioral observation notes, rating candidates in the exercises, having consensus discussions, developing feedback reports, administering feedback, presenting development plans, and carrying out follow-up activities. Preliminary results have indicated that both the hardware and software for long-distance assessment centers are well within reach technologically and are quite affordable.

High-Fidelity Technology-Based Assessments

Beyond the possibilities for automating testing and simulation processes, technology also allows advancements in the content of assessments. These advancements include the use of embedded audio, video, and animated images to increase the realism of the assessment experience. For example, a typical automated test of situational judgment may present written scenarios of common events in the workplace, such as a conflict between two coworkers. Through the use of embedded video files, the test material could include a vignette of an argument between the coworkers, thereby enabling the test taker to be influenced by factors such as the appearance, emotion, mannerisms, and setting of the hypothetical situation. These elements add realism that could lead to improvements in the accuracy and depth of measurement.

In addition to improvements in the display of assessment materials, advancements in technology have also broadened the options for how participants respond to assessments. By using animated controls such as hot spots (areas of the screen that can be clicked to indicate an action), drag-and-drop images (where users click an on-screen object and move it to another location), as well as simulated documents, spreadsheets, and Web forms, assessment designers are able to simulate a far greater range of activities than is possible with traditional multiple-choice responses. For example, an assessment for bank processors may require job applicants to inspect images of checks and enter information into a form that replicates software that the bank uses. This assessment could be scored based on the number of errors made and the number of checks processed during a fixed time period.

Due to improvements in programming technology and Internet bandwidth, creating and deploying assessments that use high-fidelity features have become relatively easy. However, these tools also have drawbacks that limit their use in some circumstances. Highly graphical assessment material can place greater demands on the bandwidth of the Internet connection at the assessment site and may require compatible software on the local computer to support the assessment. In turn, these requirements can increase installation and maintenance costs. In addition, if participants are unfamiliar with the technologies used, prior experience with graphical content can interfere with the abilities being targeted by the assessment. For this reason, adequate practice time should be provided to all assessment participants.

Tracking and Administrative Tools

For assessments during the hiring process, ATSs play a critical facilitating role. These systems are designed to collect, track, and report information about open positions and job seekers. They can also orchestrate the progression of job seekers through the application and selection process, as well as manage the integration of various subsystems that may be included in a hiring process, such as background check procedures and registration for health screening (Electronic Recruiter Exchange, 2007). Although many ATSs do not contain much in the way of assessment, they typically serve as integrators. Some systems offer the capability to integrate a range of preselected assessments that may be chosen by the user and deployed to construct a seamless assessment experience for the participant in the process.

Research on Technology-Based Assessments

Some research has been conducted on the effectiveness of technology-based assessments and the appropriate conditions for their deployment. For example, it has been shown that job applicant perceptions of the speed and ease of use of Internet-based screening and selection tools have an impact on how they view an organization as a potential employer (Sinar, Reynolds, & Paquet, 2003). Other research has demonstrated that using automated assessments, such as interactive voice response screening, can be just as effective as more cumbersome face-to-face or telephone screening interviews in presenting a positive organizational image (Bauer, Truxillo, Paronto, Weekly, & Campion, 2004). Older research has shown that using video rather than face-to-face assessment techniques does not appear to affect the accuracy of scores (Ryan, Daum, Bauman, & Grisez, 1995).

Although these findings show promise, it is important to interpret the results in the proper context because the availability and flexibility of technology today is far greater than it was when these studies were published. As the technological potential of assessments grows, we will increasingly find ourselves in uncharted territory. As these advancements are made, it is crucial that, as with any new assessment technique, evaluation studies be carried out to ensure that the assessments in fact show validity for the purposes they serve, that validity is maintained once the tool is implemented, and that the rights of test takers are protected. Evaluation after implementation is especially important if the deployment conditions (such as open access testing) are different from the validation conditions (such as proctored testing). (Chapter Twenty-Three in this book provides an overview of various approaches for conducting applied evaluation research of this nature.)

Case Studies

In this section we profile several technology-based assessment solutions that have been described in the professional literature or presented at assessment conferences. In each of these cases, technology was used not only to gain efficiency but also to add value to the assessment process.

Unproctored Adaptive Testing

As the use of online testing increases, traditional examination models are evolving, and boundaries of practice are being pressed by practical demands. For example, unproctored administration of online tests has become a frequent practice. Some risks associated with this practice are clear: test security is threatened because unproctored Internet delivery exposes test questions to large groups of test takers, and candidate identity is unverified. Although no complete solution to these issues is available, the use of adaptive testing in this context can assist with the first concern.

Gibby, Biga, Pratt, and Irwin (2008) described a program of research being conducted at Procter & Gamble where an Internet-delivered computer adaptive test (iCAT) was deployed for the purpose of selecting employees around the globe. Adaptive testing is well suited to this application because the technique exposes each candidate to only a small subset of the operational test questions. In adaptive testing, questions are chosen for administration to a given candidate based on his or her estimated ability level on the construct being assessed. P&G's iCAT uses very large banks of test questions, strict time limits, and algorithms to control and restrict exposure of the test questions to ensure the security of the test content. Frequent monitoring of the system allows for the replacement of questions when their exposure rate (that is, the number of times they are administered to candidates) begins to climb. The P&G process also includes a second (proctored) test in the hiring process to verify the initial unproctored score. This process discourages candidates from having a stand-in take the first exam, because the job candidates need to perform at comparable or better levels once they are on-site for the proctored test. Aside from the security benefits, adaptive tests such as P&G's iCAT also provide a more accurate assessment of candidate ability compared to traditional tests because candidates are asked questions that are closer to their true ability levels.

P&G's preliminary research on the iCAT has been extensive, with over 200,000 job candidates participating in the required calibration research and many more in various validation samples. Research has also been conducted to determine whether job candidates would have a negative impression of the iCAT—a possibility due to the perceived difficulty of adaptive tests; however, the findings from this work show that candidate perceptions of fairness and appropriateness did not vary substantially compared to traditional forms of testing.

High-Fidelity Testing of Job Candidates

Kauffman (2008) presented on a technology platform that was used to construct simulated manufacturing tasks that could be performed as part of an Internet-administered assessment. The assessment requires candidates to assemble components of a product by dragging images across the computer screen and dropping them into place according to a set of predefined rules that each candidate is required to learn at the outset of the assessment. For example, "parts" must be assembled in a prescribed order for the final product to be correctly assembled. By replicating key aspects of the manufacturing process including repetition, attention to detail, and vigilance, the assessment is able to provide a higher-fidelity replication of actual work activities than standard online tests such as multiple-choice job knowledge tests.

Validation research using this assessment has been conducted at several manufacturing facilities. High-fidelity test scores correlated with composites of supervisor ratings of technical performance (.26 to .45, uncorrected) and with on-the-job measures of work pace and quality (.32 to .34, uncorrected). These findings tend to be comparable with other studies of the predictive capability of simulation-based assessments.

The Console Operator Basic Requirements Assessment (COBRA) described in Chapter Six is another technology-enabled high-fidelity test. The COBRA was developed to simulate the tasks required of petroleum and chemical processing plant operators. During a four-hour assessment, job candidates with no prior knowledge of processing plant operations are instructed on the parts and operations of a simulated refinery; they are also instructed on how to operate the plant in a safe and environmentally sound manner. By manipulating on-screen controls, candidates run the refinery and respond to common events in the refining process. The computer records the extent to which applicants are successful in running the simulation according to the rules provided to candidates at the outset of the simulation. The computer also scores applicants on how closely they achieve their production goals, create high-quality products, and are able to minimize energy use within the simulated environment.

COBRA has been validated in several petroleum and chemical processing environments (Rosenthal, 2008). Results from these studies show that the computer-based simulation is predictive of real-world operator performance (validities range from .20 to .44, uncorrected), again indicating that work activities simulated on a computer screen can be predictive of real-world performance.

Technology-based measures of this variety show promise for simulating on-the-job work activities in a realistic manner while providing the benefits of automated delivery. Of course, one of the main benefits of simulation-based assessment is the ability to replicate key aspects of the work, and technology-based simulations may still fall short on realism for some jobs. In these situations, technology-based simulations can be paired with more true-to-life simulations that include, for example, activities that require physical activities that closely mirror the job and can be conducted in a realistic work environment. This combination can contribute to both measurement fidelity and face validity. Nonetheless, computer-based task simulation has great potential for advancing standardization, efficiency, and measurement precision.

Portable, Long-Distance Assessment Centers

Rupp, Kim, and Gibbons (2006) presented results of a feasibility study for a video and Internet-based assessment center program that enabled assessees and assessors to be in different locations. Prior to the technology upgrade, the program required assessors to travel to the locations where the assessment centers were being administered (Illinois and South Korea). This original low-tech version of the assessment center program was completely paper based: assessors took behavioral observation notes by hand while observing participants took part in behavioral simulation exercises; they made ratings using paper forms and had face-to-face integration discussions. The process required additional staff to enter data, calibrate ratings, generate reports, and file documents.

Consequently this program implemented a series of technology-based improvements to increase its efficiency and portability. High-quality, low-cost, and small-sized video cameras, microphones, and Web servers were obtained that could be transported and quickly set up in any location where the behavioral assessments would be carried out. A Web-based interface was created that allowed the camera and sound equipment to be controlled locally or remotely (for example, a remote assessor observing a candidate can change the volume, camera angle, or zoom settings from anywhere in the world). The Web server was set up such that assessors could access a live video feed of candidates going through exercises, or stream stored video at a later time (see Figure 19.1).

Another Web interface was created that assisted in the facilitation of all of the major assessor tasks. Using a single screen, assessors view candidates working through simulation exercises, take observation notes, classify behaviors into performance dimensions, and make ratings. Data are instantly recorded and available to assessors to support integration discussions (using Web videoconferencing and instant messaging technologies; see

**Figure 19.1. Technology-Facilitated Assessment
Center Delivery System**

Source: Courtesy Assesta.

Figure 19.2) and the preparation of feedback reports. The same tools are used to facilitate interactive feedback sessions, and assessors can show assessees actual clips of their behaviors during the exercises for developmental purposes. Although this program was experimental, using available hardware and software to push the boundaries of assessment center technology, it is illustrative of what is possible within this domain.

User-Constructed Assessment Platforms

As the role of technology in assessment has expanded, so too has the cost of assessment design and development. The financial benefits of technology-based assessment begin to accrue

Figure 19.2. Assessor Integration Tools

Dimension	Definition	ASS-A	ASS-B	ASS-C	AVG
• Problem Solving	• Problem Understanding	5	6	5	5
	• Thinking Solutions Through	6	7	5	5
	• Decisiveness	5	5	5	5
• Conflict Management /Resolution	• Effective Strategies	2	5	3	3
	• Handling Conflict	1	2	2	2
	• Constructive Solutions	3	3	4	3
• Leadership	• Guidance of Others	5	5	5	5
	• Balance of Needs	6	6	6	6
	• Personal Effectiveness	5	5	5	5
• Oral Communication	• Verbal/Nonverbal Expression	6	6	6	6
	• Message Clarity	5	5	5	5
	• Appropriate Communication Style	6	6	6	6
• Fairness	• Interpersonal Sensitivity	5	5	5	5
	• Appropriate Outcomes	6	6	6	6
	• Executing Processes	5	5	5	5
• Cultural Adaptability	• Understanding Cultural Differences	6	6	6	6
	• Culturally Sensitive Judgments	5	5	5	5
	• Culturally Appropriate Communication	6	6	6	6

	ASS-A	ASS-B	ASS-C

ASS-A says : the person is discouraging the group by downplaying the importance of conflict

ASS-C says : I think other members are discouraged by the unappropriate communication style

ASS-B says : The tone and gesture was definitely negative

ASS-A says : the person did not listen to other member's opinion

ASS-C says : I agree with that

ASS-B says : at least he/she understands what the conflict is

Effective Strategies

	Assessor-A	Assessor-B	Assessor-C
• First	downplays the importance of conflict, discourage other group members	seeks areas of agreement in order to make decision, suggests alternatives to other group members	Accurately identifies the conflict, but does not show respect to other group members
	[2]	[5]	[3]
• Second	3	5	3
• Final			

SEND

Source: Courtesy Assesta.

as the tools are deployed; often substantial development costs are required to build the initial software platform. Therefore, some software providers have sought ways to reduce the cost of development of customized technology-based assessment. Iscopia Software developed a set of assessment authoring tools for conducting technology-based assessment that allows assessment designers to create assessments without requiring a software engineer.

Designers using the Iscopia system can choose among several existing assessments, such as popular cognitive and personality tests, to construct a multitest process with consistent branding, integrated results and reporting, and tools to track participant progress through the system. Users may also enter their own tests into the platform. Various assessment system formats can be designed (multiple cutoff and multiple hurdle, for example), and reports can be generated for multiple purposes: hiring, applicant tracking, development coaching, and so on.

Iscopia's platform also allows users to construct animated images, tools, and sequences to support their assessments. For example, avatars (a computer-animated representation of a person) can be configured to create in-basket simulations and situational judgment tests (see Figure 19.3). Participants may see an animated work space, such as e-mail, calendar, phone, documents, and an office space where avatars might visit "in person." The assessment designer may configure these tools such that participants are faced with multiple stimuli (phone ringing, e-mail pinging, disgruntled employee barging in) and must choose their actions by clicking on the stimuli they view as the highest priority. The system then tracks a variety of behaviors, such as question

Figure 19.3. Assessment Design Using an Avatar

Source: Courtesy Iscopia Software.

responses, priorities, response times, and task completion, that can be used to compute scores on the assessment.

This flexible approach to technology-based assessment distributes control to the assessment designer and, with it, the responsibility to conduct and document appropriate evaluation research. Highly animated assessments have appeal to assessment sponsors and participants; however, these intriguing elements should add value to the experience without detracting from the fundamental requirements of reliable and valid assessment.

Common Issues Raised by Technology-Based Assessment

As new technology has become increasingly intertwined with the practice of assessment, some new issues have emerged, and some old ones have increased in importance. We discuss the most prominent of these concerns briefly.

Assessment Equivalence

Many assessments available today were originally designed and researched in paper-and-pencil formats. As new technologies became available to improve the efficiency of assessment administration, these assessments were converted to electronic formats. In this conversion, it is possible for aspects of the technology, such as screen resolution, navigation controls, and transmission speed, to interfere with the effectiveness of the assessment. Although research has shown that most assessments can be automated without serious consequence to their measurement properties, some assessments, especially when speed of completion is a strong factor in the scoring, have been shown to be affected by computerization.

Users of assessments should be cautious when comparing tools that are administered in different formats, and evaluation should be carried out to demonstrate that format differences produce equivalent assessments. This type of research will carefully compare computerized and noncomputerized measures that have been administered to the same people or large groups of similar people to determine whether the computer format has an effect on the scores. When conducted appropriately, this type of research can be complex, and guidance from a measurement expert is recommended.

Appropriate Deployment Conditions

The use of the Internet to deploy assessments provides the potential for participants to access assessments at a time and place of their choosing. While heralded as a huge advantage for reaching wide audiences with limited cost, Internet-based assessments raise fundamental concerns that the security of the process cannot be assured, the identity of the participant remains uncertain, and the testing conditions can be highly variable across participants. These concerns are elaborated in Tippins (2009) and a series of responding articles.

Users of technology-based assessments should carefully consider the implications of their assessment deployment approach and choose tools, techniques, and strategies to reduce the risks that can arise with Internet delivery. Techniques such as adaptive administration used by Gibby et al. (2008) represent one of several available approaches to mitigating some of these risks. Other technology-based solutions are emerging to help with the security of unproctored assessments such as typing cadence measures (where test takers are asked to type a phrase repeatedly throughout an assessment and the typing patterns are compared across the phrases to ensure that the same person is responding each time) and online proctoring where test takers are monitored by Webcam.

Cultural Adaptation

Internet deployment also allows assessment processes to cross national and cultural borders with relative ease. Here again, this can be an advantage for organizations that seek to operate globally consistent assessment practices. Ease does not imply effectiveness, however. Assessments can be highly sensitive to nuances of culture and language, and they should not be assumed to be effective in cultures other than the one in which they are developed unless research is undertaken to demonstrate appropriateness in the second culture. Here again, the tools and procedures for evaluating appropriateness across cultures can be complex, and assessment users are encouraged to seek advice from a measurement specialist before attempting to apply assessments across cultures. (Chapter Eighteen in this book provides additional guidance.)

Data Security and Privacy

Privacy and security go hand-in-hand. Without security, privacy cannot be assured. Several tools and techniques are available for maintaining the security of information transmitted over the Internet, and these technologies are evolving rapidly. For assessment software used in workplace applications, a variety of security features are commonplace:

- Use of passwords or even various forms of biometric identification such as fingerprints and palm prints can help to verify the identity of the test taker.
- Role-based access is often used to ensure that administrators, recruiters, and other system users have access to only the information they need to conduct their jobs.
- Use of history or log files can track changes made to records held within the system.
- Encryption of information that flows between systems can prevent the interception of data as it travels over the Internet.
- Secure network configurations and carefully secured facilities help to prevent accidental damage or theft of system hardware.

Software technology specialists are frequently consulted to conduct an audit of system security features when an assessment system holds sensitive data that are to be used for critical decisions. Audits of this nature can help ensure that assessment software systems use current technologies for maintaining data and system security.

Software Maintenance

When an assessment tool is supported by software, the ongoing cost of maintaining the software comes into play. Typically software maintenance is funded by fees that are either bundled within the assessment use fees or as a separate yearly charge to maintain the system. These maintenance fees help to fund system upgrades and enhancements. The model for software delivery can have a big impact on the costs, benefits, and flexibility of maintenance upgrades.

Although many software delivery models exist, most fit in two broad classes. First, software can be implemented such that only one client organization uses a particular copy of the software. This can allow customizations to be made to the program so that it fits the unique needs of the organization. Maintenance costs are often higher (and upgrades less frequent) because each client is paying for the upkeep of their system individually. The second model is often more desirable for users and vendors of software. Under this model, several clients use the same instance of the software, but their data are kept separate so that users never see information from other organizations. This model (now commonly known as software as a service, or SaaS) is supported by maintenance fees from all clients of the software and allows vendors to maintain only one version of the software. The disadvantage of the model is that it limits the degree to which the software can be modified for any one client. Typically modifications must stay within a range of allowable configurations predesigned within the software. When purchasing assessment software, organizations should consider the trade-off between the need for software customization and the cost of long-term maintenance.

Regardless of the software delivery model, users of technology-based assessments should ensure that there is a documented service-level agreement in place with the software provider. This agreement is a contractual element that defines the support to be provided by the vendor for various types of errors and issues that may be encountered by users. It also defines the levels of support that the licensee must provide; for example, it is common for the users' organization to provide the first line of help when issues arise.

Integration

Organizations typically use assessments as part of larger processes. Short screening assessments are used for applicant prescreening, tests are used in the hiring and promotion processes, and behavioral simulations and assessment centers are used for hiring, promotion, and leadership development programs. Each of these organizational processes may have multiple automated components as well as associated tracking and administrative tools such as an ATS or a performance management system. Because organizations are motivated to automate each of these processes to gain efficiencies, there is pressure to integrate related systems under a common umbrella. Therefore, providers of tests and assessments that are used in combination with other technology systems often must integrate their technology with others. This process can be complex and costly, but new approaches to software design such as services-oriented architecture and programming methods such as extensible markup language have emerged to facilitate easier integration among software systems.

The trend toward talent management systems is perhaps the most extensive example of software integration to support the HR function in larger organizations. The idea behind talent management as a software-driven process is that each major people management process—recruitment, selection, development, performance management, and succession—can be automated and tied together under a common system that allows the outputs from one stage to be easily input into others. Automated forms of assessment that are not easily integrated into these larger frameworks are at a disadvantage as organizations seek to consolidate the number of technology systems they operate.

Future Opportunities and Challenges

Advances in computer technology have moved faster than advances in assessment, and this pattern will likely continue into the future, suggesting that many of the innovations in technology-based assessment will probably be borrowed from applications of technology in other areas. A few examples of technologies that are likely to bridge into assessment applications are provided here.

Applications of Social Networking Technology

Advances to techniques in training and development can be forerunners of assessment applications. Recent developments in the training domain have called for what has been referred to as *third-generation instruction* (Kraiger, 2008). This perspective advocates for learning using social networks. In such a program, learning is maximized through instructor-learner, learner-content, and learner-learner interactions. Training programs over the Internet, known as Web-based instruction, can foster learning through social networks. In such environments, the role of the instructor is diminished, which motivates trainees to seek information using multiple channels, such as file sharing, chat rooms, threaded discussions, video or audio conferencing, e-mail, course postings, or instant messages. Because these same tools are becoming increasing popular in the workplace, it is possible to envision simulated organizational social networks being used to support behavioral assessment. Participants in such an assessment could be provided with access to a network of information and role players contributing to electronic interactions through a variety of communication tools. In fact, some assessment platforms are already incorporating interactive simulations that are facilitated through Web tools such as Second Life. As these social networking technologies become commonplace in organizations and in education, the transfer into use for assessment becomes more viable because participants are familiar with the medium.

Assessments Incorporating Virtual Reality

Another rapidly advancing area that might hold promise for assessment applications is that of virtual reality. Virtual reality (VR) requires the participant to wear special VR glasses and other sensory equipment that simulate a three-dimensional, animated environment within which the participant interacts. This technology is similar to the avatar technology described earlier in this chapter, but instead of viewing an avatar on a computer screen, the participant is immersed in the environment. To date, HR applications of VR technology have mostly been within training and development. VR is used to train surgeons, fighter pilots, and even dancers and martial artists (rather than learning tai chi by watching and mimicking a teacher, for example, you can actually "step into" a holograph of the teacher and move as he or she moves).

Using VR in assessment contexts is not difficult to envision because the VR simulations created for training contexts could be modified for assessment purposes. As the cost of VR technology declines, it is likely that VR simulations of complex skills will be used for assessment purposes; however, the needs for precision, standardization, and control of these technologies are stronger in an assessment context, so the direct use of training tools for assessment can be problematic.

Future Challenges

The advances described are just a sample of what technology might offer assessment practice. Knowledge of these trends allows us to envision the future of assessment. Perhaps there will be a point when many assessments are conducted using virtual environments. Perhaps mobile devices will become a common tool for accessing Web-based assessments. Perhaps traditional proctoring will be replaced with biometric identifications such as fingerprints or monitoring of typing pattern. Perhaps the assessment industry will shift to an open source environment, where assessment content and format are shared and customized for client use. Our goal in this chapter has not been to make precise forecasts about what the future of assessment will look like; however, these advances could very well change assessment practice as it is known today.

The incorporation of new technology into assessment often begins because the technology is available and its incorporation into the assessment process appears to add value that resides in added novelty or user attraction: there is an undeniable fact that new technology can engage the user if it is executed effectively. However, if the benefits of a new technology do not extend beyond stylistic flair, the usefulness of the advancement will decline as fads and trends change.

The challenge for technology innovations applied to assessment is in the demonstration of added measurement value. Technology-based assessments should be studied for their effect on variables such as measurement reliability, validity, and precision, as well as on outcomes such as test security, user acceptance, and efficiency gains. In addition, technology applications can have benefits for measurement outcomes. For example, technology-based assessments might serve to help level the playing field among underrepresented groups as a broader range of measures can be more easily deployed with the assistance of technology. The sustainability of advancements in technology-based assessments will be dependent on these demonstrated benefits to measurement, not simply by user engagement. In fact, technology that is too novel may interfere with the quality of the assessment, because familiarity with the technology could moderate assessment scores. If deployed effectively, technology should fade to the background of the assessment experience, allowing the participant to focus on the experience itself.

References

Bauer, T. N., Truxillo, D. M., Paronto, M. E., Weekley, J. A., & Campion, M. A. (2004). Applicant reactions to different selection technology: Face-to-face, interactive voice response, and computer-assisted telephone screening interviews. *International Journal of Selection and Assessment, 12*(1/2), 135.

Electronic Recruiter Exchange. (2007, September). *Applicant tracking systems: Industry analysis and buyer's guide.* New York: Author.

Equal Employment Opportunity Commission, Civil Service Commission, Department of Labor, & Department of Justice. (1978). Uniform guidelines on employee selection procedures. *Federal Register, 35* (149), 12333–12336.

Gibby, R. E., Biga, A., Pratt, A., & Irwin, J. (2008, April). *Online and unsupervised adaptive cognitive ability testing: lessons learned.* Paper presented at the conference of the Society for Industrial and Organizational Psychology, San Francisco.

Guental, H. G., & Stone, D. L. (Eds.). (2005). *The brave new world of eHR: Human resources in the digital age.* San Francisco: Jossey-Bass.

International Test Commission. (2006). International guidelines on computer-based and internet delivered testing. *International Journal of Testing, 6,* 143–172.

Kauffman, J. (2008). *Mechanically-scored behavioral simulations for high volume selection.* Paper presented at the 34th International Congress on Assessment Center Methods. Washington, DC.

Kraiger, K. (2008). Transforming our models of learning and development: Web-based instruction as enabler of third generation instruction. *Industrial and Organizational Psychology, 1,* 454–467.

Naglieri, J. A., Drasgow, F., Schmit, M., Handler, L., Prifitera, A., Margolis, A. et al. (2004). Psychological testing on the Internet: New problems, old issues. *American Psychologist, 59*(3), 150–162.

Reynolds, D. H. & Dickter, D. N. (2010). Technology and employee selection. In J. L Farr & N. Tippins (Eds.), *Handbook of employee selection* (pp. 171–193). New York: Psychology Press.

Rosenthal, D. (2008). *Summary of validation studies completed on the COBRA hiring test.* Alexandria, VA: Job Performance Systems.

Rupp, D. E. (2006). *The future is here: Recent advances in assessment center methodology.* Invited talk presented at the Society for Industrial and Organizational Psychology Fall Consortium, Charlotte, NC.

Rupp, D. E. (2008). *Using technology to enhance assessment and development programs.* Workshop presented at the 23rd Annual Conference of the Society for Industrial and Organizational Psychology, San Francisco.

Rupp, D. E., Gibbons, A. G., & Snyder, L. A. (2008). The role of technology in enabling third-generation training and development. *Industrial-Organizational Psychology, 1*, 495–499.

Rupp, D. E., Kim, M.-J., & Gibbons, A. M. (2006). *Remote assessment: better, faster, cheaper?* Paper presented at the 33rd International Congress on Assessment Center Methods. London, England.

Ryan, A. M., Daum, D., Bauman, T., & Grisez, M. (1995). Direct, indirect, and controlled observation and rating accuracy. *Journal of Applied Psychology, 80*(6), 664–670.

Sinar, E. F., Reynolds, D. H., & Paquet, S. L. (2003). Nothing but 'Net? Corporate image and Web-based testing. *International Journal of Selection and Assessment, 11*(2), 150–157.

Tippins, N. T. (2009). Internet alternatives to traditional proctored testing: Where are we now? *Industrial and Organizational Psychology, 2*, 2–10.

U.S. Department of Labor (2005). Obligation to solicit race and gender data for agency enforcement purposes; final rule. *Federal Register, 70*(194), 58947–58961.

CHAPTER 20

THE LEGAL ENVIRONMENT FOR ASSESSMENT

R. Lawrence Ashe Jr.,
Kathleen K. Lundquist

Almost thirty years ago, the Second Circuit Court of Appeals commented on the intersection of law and science at the heart of employment testing:

> The study of employment testing, although it has necessarily been adopted by the law as a result of Title VII and related statutes, is not primarily a legal subject. It is part of the general field of educational and industrial psychology, and possesses its own methodology, its own body of research, its own experts, and its own terminology. The translation of a technical study such as this into a set of legal principles requires a clear awareness of the limits of both testing and law. It would be entirely inappropriate for the law to ignore what has been learned about employment testing in assessing the validity of these tests. At the same time, the science of testing is not as precise as physics or chemistry, nor its conclusions as provable. While courts should draw upon the findings of experts in the field of testing, they should not hesitate to subject these findings to both the scrutiny of reason and the guidance of Congressional intent.[1]

The courts have taken the opportunity to interpret and evaluate the findings presented by industrial-organizational psychologists, and as a result have both influenced and been influenced by the evolution of scientific thought and measurement practice in the intervening time period.

The use of assessment in the workplace has also evolved, with both public and private employers increasingly using assessment procedures. According to a 2001 survey by the American Management Association, 41 percent of large employers test job applicants in basic literacy or math skills (or both), 68 percent measure job-specific skills, 20 percent use cognitive ability tests, 14 percent use some form of managerial assessment, 13 percent administer personality tests, and 10 percent of employers use physical simulations of job tasks.[2]

It is important to note that the term *selection procedure* as used in the legal context is quite broad. The federal *Uniform Guidelines on Employee Selection Procedures* (1978) defines a selection procedure as

> any measure, combination of measures, or procedure used as a basis for any employment decision. Selection procedures include the full range of assessment techniques from traditional paper and pencil tests, performance tests, training programs, or probationary periods and physical, educational, and work experience requirements through informal or casual interviews and unscored application forms [29 CFR sec. 1607.16(Q)].

The increasing use of tests and other selection procedures by employers has resulted in greater scrutiny by the courts and enforcement agencies. This chapter outlines the legal environment for employee assessment and describes how the dual evolution of legal standards and scientific advancements raises new questions and issues for those using assessment information to make decisions about employees.

The Legal Framework

Discrimination cases are brought under two main theories of discrimination: disparate treatment and disparate impact. Under the disparate treatment theory, an individual alleges that he or she was intentionally treated less favorably as a result of his or her protected status: race, gender, age, religion, national origin, and so forth. Proof of a discriminatory motive is critical to a disparate treatment case. As part of the U.S. Supreme Court's seminal decision in *Griggs* v. *Duke Power Co.*, a second theory of discrimination emerged: disparate impact.[3] Under the disparate impact theory, individuals allege that a facially neutral policy or practice resulted in a significant adverse impact against their protected group, even in the absence of a discriminatory intent. In actual practice, the distinction between the two theories has been blurred, particularly in challenges to subjective employment practices, and cases are frequently brought invoking both theories (see Table 20.1).

Tests are typically challenged under the disparate impact theory of discrimination, although it is possible to challenge a test under disparate treatment where administration is inconsistent or the examinees are selectively administered the test (for example, women must take the test but men are not required to test).

Selection procedures have been subjected to challenge under federal, state, and local employment discrimination laws. The requirements of these statutes have been interpreted by the courts, enforced by regulatory agencies, and often informed by professional standards.

The Statutes

Several statutes set the boundaries of what is an acceptable personnel selection procedure. Beyond prohibiting intentional discrimination, these statutes, as interpreted in the *Griggs* v. *Duke Power* decision and its progeny, identify even facially neutral actions as illegal if they have a disparate impact on protected groups, are not demonstrably job related, or, even if validated, there are known less adverse, equally, or more useful alternatives available.[4] The sections that follow address the key federal statutes.

Title VII of the Civil Rights Act of 1964

Title VII of the Civil Rights Act addresses the use of tests and employee selection procedures: "It shall not be an unlawful employment practice for an employer to give and to act upon the results of any professionally developed ability test provided that such test, its administration or action upon the results is not

Table 20.1. Theories of Discrimination

Theory of Discrimination	Basis	Illustrative Case	Usual Claim	Example	Comment
Disparate treatment	Discriminatory intent	*Teamsters v. United States,* 431 U.S. 324, 14 FEP 1514 (1977)	Individual	Individual not selected for promotion because of her gender	Pattern and practice class action may also be brought alleging the discriminatory practice is the employer's regular and standard operating procedure.
Disparate impact	Discriminatory result	*Griggs v. Duke Power Co.,* 401 U.S. 424 (1971)	Class action	Women denied promotions because they failed a physical ability test	Individual cases and cases alleging both disparate treatment and disparate impact occur in practice.

designed, intended or used to discriminate because of race, color, religion, sex or national origin."[5] An employer may use professionally developed tests as long as it does not do so with the purpose to discriminate and the test either does not have a significant adverse impact on protected groups or is shown to be job related.

Americans with Disabilities Act

The ADA, recently amended, governs the impermissible use of tests that screen out those with disabilities:

> (6) using qualification standards, employment tests or other selection criteria that screen out or tend to screen out an individual with a disability or a class of individuals with disabilities unless the standard, test or other selection criteria, as used by the covered entity, is shown to be job-related for the position in question and is consistent with business necessity; and

> (7) failing to select and administer tests concerning employment in the most effective manner to ensure that, when such test is administered to a job applicant or employee who has a disability that impairs sensory, manual, or speaking skills, such test results accurately reflect the skills, aptitude, or whatever other factor of such applicant or employee that such test purports to measure, rather than reflecting the impaired sensory, manual, or speaking skills of such employee or applicant (except where such skills are the factors that the test purports to measure).[6]

To bring a claim under the ADA, a candidate must demonstrate that she or he is qualified to perform the essential functions of the job, with or without appropriate accommodations. The courts, however, are split on whether the employee challenging an assessment procedure must show that she is qualified to perform the job in general or that she is able to perform the assessment.[7]

Age Discrimination in Employment Act of 1967

The ADEA, as amended, may be relevant to evaluating the use of employment selection procedures if the tests are implemented to inappropriately screen applicants or have an unintended adverse impact on employees over the age of forty.[8] The Supreme Court has recently held that challenges to assessment procedures under the ADEA include challenging the disparate impact of tests on those over the age of forty.[9]

Legal and Professional Standards

Legal and professional standards establish the basis against which the adequacy of assessments is judged. Tests must be developed in accordance with the recognized legal and professional standards for establishing job relatedness described below, including the federal *Uniform Guidelines on Employee Selection Procedures* (1978), the *Principles for the Validation and Use of Personnel Selection Procedures* (2003) developed by the Society for Industrial and Organizational Psychology (SIOP), and the *Standards for Educational and Psychological Testing* (1999) developed by the American Educational Research Association, the American Psychological Association, and the National Council on Measurement in Education.

Uniform Guidelines on Employee Selection Procedures

The *Uniform Guidelines*[10] were adopted by the Equal Employment Opportunity Commission (EEOC), the Civil Service Commission, the Department of Labor, and the Department of Justice in 1978 with the purpose of incorporating "a single set of principles which are designed to assist employers, labor organizations, employment agencies, and licensing and certification boards to comply with the requirements of Federal law prohibiting employment practices which discriminate on grounds of race, color, religion, sex, and national origin."[11] The *Uniform Guidelines* apply to Title VII but not to the ADA or the ADEA.[12]

Under the *Uniform Guidelines*, tests are not required to be validated unless there is evidence of adverse impact. In fact, there is an inference of discrimination according to the *Guidelines* if adverse impact is shown. Plaintiffs and defendants alike frequently use the four-fifths rule of thumb articulated in the *Guidelines* to measure impact.[13] However, the *Uniform Guidelines* contemplate the possibility that smaller differences in selection rates can still constitute adverse impact. Smaller differences may constitute an adverse impact "where they are significant in both statistical and practical terms or where a user's actions have discouraged applicants disproportionately on grounds of race, sex, or ethnic group."[14]

The *Uniform Guidelines* require employers to maintain validity data for any selection criteria found to have an adverse impact. Employers are required to maintain documentation to make adverse impact determinations of their personnel selection procedures, which will dictate whether job-relatedness documentation evidence is necessary.[15]

The courts have given the *Uniform Guidelines* weight and deference, but they are beginning to move beyond them in analyzing validity and disparate impact.[16] The General Accounting Office (GAO) in 1982 criticized the *Uniform Guidelines* as outdated even then and called for review and revision. No action was taken, and in 1993, an announcement was made that there would be no changes. Since the publication of the *Uniform Guidelines*, both the relevant professional standards have each been revised twice to reflect the evolution in professional thought and practice. Arguably the *Uniform Guidelines* (at least implicitly, if not expressly) incorporate the revisions of these professional standards when they state: "The provisions of these guidelines relating to validation of selection procedures are intended to be consistent with generally accepted professional standards for evaluating standardized tests and other selection procedures . . . and standard textbooks and journals in the field of personnel selection."[17]

One example of the contrast between the *Uniform Guidelines* and current professional thought is in the area of validation methodology. While the *Uniform Guidelines* discuss the three methods of validation—criterion-related validity studies, content validity studies, and construct validity studies—as discrete validation methods appropriate to particular types of test content, current professional standards reject the rigid categorization of validation studies and view proper validation as incorporating evidence from multiple strands of validity evidence.

Professional Standards

The SIOP *Principles* and the APA *Standards* articulate professional standards for development and validation of assessment procedures. As professional standards, they reflect the ongoing evolution of thought and science over time. The APA *Standards* were revised in 1966, 1974, 1985, and 1999, and the next revision is under development at the time of this writing, while editions of the SIOP *Principles* were published in 1975, 1980, 1987, and 2003. The SIOP *Principles* are the more directly relevant for evaluating employment tests. According to SIOP, the purpose of the *Principles* is to outline established scientific and professional procedures in the field of personnel selection psychology focusing "on the accuracy of the inferences that underlie employment decisions."[18]

Both the *Standards* and *Principles* articulate a movement away from the *Uniform Guidelines'* rigid segregation of validation categories into content, criterion-related, and construct validity. The *Standards* and the *Principles* view validation as a unitary concept with different types of evidence and theory that can support the predictive nature of a test score on job performance. But just as some courts have moved away from exclusive reliance on the *Uniform Guidelines'* 80 percent rule toward a greater appreciation of the value of statistical analysis, the courts may embrace the continued development of construct validation research, particularly related to the use of personality and noncognitive measures to predict employment outcomes such as turnover and absenteeism.

Regulatory Agencies

Regulatory agencies such as the EEOC and the U.S. Department of Labor's Office of Federal Contract Compliance Programs (OFCCP) play an important role in review and litigation of personnel selection procedures. In response to complaints of discrimination by individuals, the EEOC can investigate and ultimately file a lawsuit against an employer's assessment practices. In March 2006, an EEOC task force released a report recommending the EEOC take an even more active role in identifying and combating systemic discrimination by initiating class action lawsuits on behalf of groups of employees.[19] With a large emphasis on acquiring and analyzing new data, the EEOC seems poised to turn a spotlight on personnel selection procedures and the validation studies supporting those procedures. Further information about the EEOC's approach to evaluating assessment procedures is published in a fact sheet on its Web site.[20]

The OFCCP, which also plays a large role, is charged with administering and enforcing Executive Order 11246, which applies to any federal contractor doing more than ten thousand dollars in business with the federal government in a year. Contractors are required to comply with certain provisions that prohibit discrimination in employment and require the development of written affirmative action programs. Since 2005, the OFCCP has increased its focus on the defensibility of assessment procedures, increasing the emphasis on testing in audits of contractor compliance and initiating legal action on that basis. In addition to back pay and other forms of relief to victims of discrimination, the OFCCP can impose the penalty of debarment (a company that loses may become ineligible for federal contracts), which can easily dwarf the size of an adverse court verdict for a major government contractor.

Of particular interest to employers is the increasing emphasis by regulatory agencies on the age of a validation study. Although neither the *Uniform Guidelines* nor professional standards articulate an "expiration date" for validation studies, the ongoing use of a validated assessment can be challenged when the test user fails to demonstrate that the jobs have not significantly changed over time and that the original validation evidence is still applicable.

Private Plaintiffs

Employees may also challenge assessment procedures by bringing legal action through private attorneys in the form of an individual complaint or a class action. Such litigation has recently challenged a wide range of assessments within a given organization, including measures associated with hiring, promotion, compensation, performance management, development, and succession planning.[21] These large-scale class actions are frequently settled, resulting in injunctive relief requiring the employer to institute new or revised practices that comply with professional standards and often with best practices. As a result, the bar has been raised for the types of procedures plaintiffs and their attorneys expect employers to implement.

Order of Proof

There is a substantially similar series of steps involved in litigating under Title VII, the ADA, and the ADEA. A plaintiff begins by identifying a personnel selection device and establishing that it has an adverse impact on a relevant protected group. This shifts the burden to the defendant to show that the procedure is job related and consistent with business necessity. If the defendant is successful, the plaintiff can prevail only if she can then show that less adverse alternatives are reasonably available that are at least comparably job related to satisfy an employer's needs (see Figure 20.1). The plaintiff bears the burden of proving the existence (or nonexistence) of less adverse, equally acceptable alternatives:[22]

■ ■ ■

• *Step 1: Plaintiff establishes adverse impact.* A plaintiff must prove, generally through quantitative comparisons, that the challenged practice or selection device has a substantial adverse impact

Figure 20.1. Order of Proof in Testing Cases

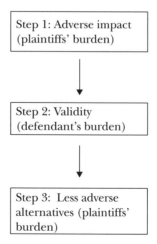

Step 1: Adverse impact (plaintiffs' burden)

Step 2: Validity (defendant's burden)

Step 3: Less adverse alternatives (plaintiffs' burden)

on a protected group.[23] There are a variety of approaches, and statistical significance is one method of showing that the adverse impact is unlikely to be the result of chance. In response, the employer can then criticize the plaintiff's statistical analysis or offer different statistics to show a lack of disparity.

There is a distinction, however, between Title VII and the ADEA relevant to establishing the adverse impact of a selection procedure. Since a plaintiff must identify the specific selection device responsible for the adverse impact, this can be difficult when multiple test components and procedures are combined in the hiring and promotion process. Title VII was amended by the Civil Rights Act of 1991 to excuse plaintiffs from this requirement when the processes are not easily capable of separation. But the ADEA was not amended by this act, so plaintiffs alleging age discrimination claims are likely to continue to be required to identify the component responsible for the disparate impact to establish a prima facie case.

- *Step 2: Employer establishes test is job related and consistent with business necessity (validity).* A defendant may rebut the prima facie case by demonstrating that the scored test is job related and consistent with business necessity; this is accomplished by showing that the test is valid, although a formal validation study is not necessarily required.[24] The goal of the validation process is to show that the test is an adequate predictor of future job performance. The employer may alternatively show that the test does not cause adverse impact. When multiple tests or selection procedures are used to make selection decisions, each decision point must be separately justified as valid or failing to cause adverse impact.
- *Step 3: Existence of equally acceptable, less adverse alternatives.* Even if the employer proves that a test is job related and consistent with business necessity, the plaintiff may still prevail by showing that the employer has refused to adopt a known alternative employment practice that would satisfy the employer's legitimate interests without having the same disparate impact on a protected class.[25] This framework is not applicable to ADEA cases, however, which allow employers to escape liability if they can

show that the adverse decision was based on a "reasonable factor other than age."[26] There, a plaintiff must show that the articulated nonage factor was unreasonable. The Supreme Court specifically held that Title VII's business necessity test, which looks at alternative ways to achieve business goals with less adverse impact, is not part of the ADEA inquiry.[27]

The Current Legal Landscape: Implications for Practice

Litigation continues to influence and be influenced by the evolution of assessment practices. Recently, the courts have grappled with types and quality of evidence needed to establish adverse impact, the appropriateness of subjective evaluations and scoring methods, and the suitability of less adverse alternatives.

Adverse Impact

Not surprisingly, courts appear to employ an informal continuum when a test has an adverse impact. The greater the adverse impact, the higher the correlation and the better the validity evidence must be to defend the assessment. Similarly, the more critical the impact of successful job performance (for example, the job performance of a surgeon or a pilot), the more lenient the validity standard becomes.

There are a variety of approaches to measure adverse impact, including the 80 percent rule and use of statistical significance testing.[28] One circuit has held that satisfaction of the four-fifths rule is "highly persuasive proof that there was not a significant disparity."[29] Another has held that a passage ratio in excess of 90 percent defeated a plaintiff's prima facie case.[30] Still another has held that a 7.1 percent differential among test takers does not, as a matter of law, state a prima facie case of disparate impact.[31] But the vast majority of cases refer to the four-fifths rule as only a rule of thumb used as enforcement guidance for the relevant federal agencies. The 80 percent rule has been criticized as an arbitrary standard that fails to take into account differences in sample sizes and test results in the applicant population.[32]

While the EEOC may feel somewhat constrained by the *Uniform Guidelines*, a private plaintiff can challenge any procedure with statistically significant adverse impact. Language in the *Uniform Guidelines* allows a departure from the four-fifths rule in certain circumstances (when there is both statistical and practical significance), and recent cases, involving both private plaintiffs and the EEOC,[33] support the notion that a plaintiff may be able to establish a prima facie case of adverse impact despite the employer's satisfaction of the four-fifths rule. In *Bew* v. *City of Chicago*,[34] the Seventh Circuit found: "Even though 98.24% of the African American test-takers passed compared with 99.96% of the whites so the four-fifths rule was not violated, the challenged test had a disparate impact because there was evidence that there was a statistically significant correlation between race and test failure. The fact that the difference in magnitude between the pass rates was so small was not relevant because the difference was statistically significant."[35] In *Bew*, the difference was a little more than five standard deviations.[36] This decision on impact is atypical and extreme. Further, a test with such high pass rates has little or no apparent utility for selection.

Sometimes the decision on a plaintiff's prima facie case may hinge on the court's interpretation of "practical significance." According to the *Uniform Guidelines*, even differences that satisfy the 80 percent rule can constitute an adverse impact if they are statistically and practically significant.[37] Conversely, greater differences might not constitute adverse impact where the sample size is too small or the applicant pool is atypical of a normal applicant population.

Unlike statistical significance, practical significance is difficult to define, and therefore courts have considerable discretion in making a determination on the prima facie case. Courts have used several types of analysis to assess practical significance: the four-fifths rule, shortfall analysis, and case-by-case analysis. All three illustrate the key relationship between practical significance and sample size.

In several decisions, courts have cited the four-fifths rule itself is a gauge of practical significance.[38] When the sample size is extremely large, even trivial disparities can be statistically significant. The use of the 80 percent rule is then a valuable tool to examine practical significance. In August 2009, in *Stagi v. National Railroad Passenger Corp.*, the Eastern District of Pennsylvania held that a plaintiff failed to establish a prima facie case of disparate impact, despite a showing of statistical significance, because the differences were not practically significant. In its decision, the court noted the importance of this additional test, particularly in cases with large populations where statistical significance is routinely established:

> "Statistical significance" is a term of art within the science of statistics which means simply that the disparity was unlikely to have been produced by chance. Statistical significance is routinely established in cases where observations are made among a reasonably large population. For this reason, courts look for practical significance as an important signifier of impact in addition to statistical significance. [39]

At least one court has recently held that the EEOC established a prima facie case, despite the employer's satisfaction of the four-fifths rule, because the large number of affected individuals established practical significance. In *United States v. City of New York*,[40] the government brought an action challenging the fire department's reliance on written examinations in the selection process. In its analysis of practical significance, the court focused on the aggregate number of minority applicants denied an opportunity to join the fire department as compared to whites— known as the "shortfall."

A third approach to practical significance is case-by-case analysis. It is not at all uncommon for a court, in conclusory fashion, simply to cite the 80 percent rule and statistical significance test results and then assert that, considering all the evidence, there is more likely than not practical significance.[41] More often, though, courts try to determine if either side's set of numbers would be considered borderline. Courts seem to follow a sort of de facto continuum and allow cases to proceed if the test barely satisfies the four-fifths rule while the statistical significance is high.[42] In contrast, courts are more willing to block actions based on borderline or even higher statistical significance when the test passes the four-fifths rule by a wider margin.[43]

Subjectivity in Assessments

Challenging subjectivity in the assessment process is a logical attack for plaintiffs, as discretion to use subjective criteria can more easily be viewed as a pretext for intentional, or even subconscious, discrimination.[44] For this reason, subjective criteria are more commonly challenged on the basis of disparate treatment rather than disparate impact, although the Supreme Court has affirmed that the disparate impact model is appropriate to challenge the use of subjective hiring and promotion criteria.[45]

Employers can safeguard against claims that their assessment procedures are overly subjective by providing proper training and direction to evaluate candidates on core and functional competencies. In *Anderson* v. *Westinghouse Savannah River Co.*, the Fourth Circuit rejected an administrative assistant's challenge to the hiring and promotion process.[46] The process contained nineteen steps, three of which related to interviews and were challenged due to alleged subjectivity. During the interviews, the interview panel considered six core competencies: teamwork, leadership, communications, business results, self-management, and employee development. The panel also considered functional competencies, which were selected to be specific to the position sought, such as being proficient in heating and air-conditioning design. The court held that the reliance on core and functional competencies in evaluating the candidates sufficiently addressed concerns of subjectivity.

Courts look to a variety of factors when evaluating the appropriateness of subjective criteria in personnel selection, including whether a proper job analysis has been completed, adequate instructions are given to the evaluators, objective criteria are available, interactions between the rater and ratee are significant, and the rater or decision maker is a member of the same protected group.[47] Recent decisions show that courts are more willing to uphold subjective criteria as valid when raters or decision makers are well trained and focus on certain core competencies and functions. There is also substantial recognition that higher-level jobs require more subjectivity in selections.

Cutoff Scores

The use and setting of cutoff scores are often the subject of litigation for several reasons. First, courts have increasingly found that the cutoff score itself must be valid, requiring the employer to show that the score adequately differentiates those who can perform the job satisfactorily (or better) from those who cannot.[48] Second, the selection and justification of a cutoff score open the door for arguments that there are one or more less discriminatory alternatives known to the employer. A plaintiff can argue that a lower cutoff or the use of test score bands would be less adverse alternatives.

Cutoff scores and rank ordering are frequently challenged—often successfully—since it is generally difficult to justify fine gradations among candidates. The *Uniform Guidelines* state that cutoff scores "should normally be set so as to be reasonable and consistent with normal expectations of acceptable proficiency within the work force."[49] Courts have begun to frame the issue as setting a threshold of minimum qualifications for the job. A thorough job analysis will help an employer establish that a certain level of proficiency on the assessment correlates with the minimum ability to do the job. The use of Angoff and other professionally accepted techniques for setting cutoff scores has received favorable commentary by the courts.[50]

While professional standards recognize the expected linear relationship between cognitively based assessments and job performance (SIOP *Principles*), courts generally reject a per se "more is better approach" to justifying cutoff scores. The Sixth Circuit had an opportunity to weigh in on the appropriate validation standard for cutoff scores in 2005 in *Isabel* v. *City of Memphis*.[51] African American police officers alleged that a facially neutral written test administered by the City of Memphis had a disparate impact on minority promotions within the police department. The promotional process consisted of four parts: a written test, a practical exercise test, performance evaluations, and seniority points. However, only those who passed the written test, which had a cutoff score of 70, would be allowed to continue in the promotion process. Finding that the cutoff score violated the four-fifths rule, the City of Memphis reduced the cutoff score to 66. The test developer had advised the city against the use of a cutoff score and admitted at trial that the score was not able to distinguish between candidates who could and could not perform the job. The Sixth Circuit held that any cutoff score must be a measure of minimum qualification. Citing evidence that a nonminority applicant who had a score of 66 was the second-highest-rated candidate overall in the entire promotional procedure, the court ruled against the employer's use of the 70 cutoff score.

Similarly, in *United States* v. *Delaware*,[52] the court held that the test cutoff score was set too high. The federal government challenged Delaware's use of the Alert test to hire state troopers. The 160-item multiple-choice test consisted of 60 items designed to measure reading comprehension and 100 items designed to measure four aspects of writing skills: spelling, clarity, grammar, and detail. It was undisputed that the reading and writing skills were relevant to the job responsibilities of a state trooper. The criterion-related validity studies found small but statistically significant correlations with job performance. On these facts, the court rejected the "more is better rationale" of the cutoff score and held that a lower passing score was appropriate.

In addition to lowering the cutoff score, banding may be an acceptable less adverse alternative. In *Biondo* v. *Chicago*, the Seventh Circuit endorsed banding as an alternative when a valid test has a disparate impact.[53] The case involved tests for promotion within the fire department. Not confident that the use of strict rank ordering was appropriate in light of likely adverse impact, the department created racially segregated lists and made 29 percent of all promotions from the minorities-only list. In a scathing opinion, the Seventh Circuit held that compliance with a governmental regulation (the 80 percent rule under the *Uniform Guidelines*) was not automatically a compelling interest to justify such a race-based decision-making process. The court also held that the city could have used bands reflecting the standard error of measurement to respect the limits of the exam's accuracy without resorting to race or ethnicity as the basis for selection.

Less Adverse Alternatives

Recent cases have supported the notion that it is not sufficient merely to articulate a less adverse alternative; there must be some showing that the alternative provides substantially the same validity as the assessment it seeks to replace. In 2003, the Seventh Circuit, in *Allen* v. *Chicago*, rejected a challenge to a promotional test because the plaintiffs lacked sufficient data to support their proposed less adverse alternative (promotions based on merit).[54] Validation studies rest on empirical data, and the plaintiff's assertions about the ability of supervisors to make promotions lacked this evidentiary base. As the court noted, plaintiffs must prove a correlation between their proposed alternative procedure and job performance in the same manner that employers must validate their test. This can be an expensive and problematic proposition for a plaintiff, as employers typically have the benefit of extensive data and validation studies to support the challenged personnel selection procedure.[55] Increasingly plaintiffs rely on generalizing validation data from a similar job or skill rather than gathering local validation evidence for the less adverse alternative.

The Supreme Court in *Albermarle Paper Co.* v. *Moody* placed this burden on the plaintiff.[56] In *EEOC* v. *Dial Corp.*, however, the Court held it was the defendant's burden to show that there was no acceptable less adverse alternative to the use of a strength test.[57] While this decision seems inconsistent with *Albermarle*, there was evidence that accidents were decreasing after other safety measures were taken, as well as evidence that women had lower injury rates than men. In effect, the employer's validity evidence was held to be badly flawed.

Even when evidence is available to validate an alternative, the viability of implementation can also be an issue. In 2006, in *Adams* v. *Chicago*, the Seventh Circuit heard a case brought by minority members of the Chicago police force challenging an exam used in the promotion process.[58] The challenged exam consisted of three parts: multiple-choice questions covering the law, department procedures, and other regulations sergeants needed to know; multiple-choice questions testing the administrative functions performed by sergeants; and an oral exam based on a written briefing. The only issue for the court was the viability of the alternative, because the city conceded that the test had a disparate impact and the plaintiffs conceded that the test was validly job related. The plaintiffs argued that merit promotions (based on supervisory evaluations of officers' on-the-job performance) were a less adverse alternative to the examination. This alternative was recommended by a task force reviewing the exam one month prior to its administration (a recommendation that the city did not implement). The plaintiffs pointed out that the city used merit promotions to fill 20 percent of certain police positions. At the time the promotions were made, no procedure was in place for evaluating the job performance of potential sergeants, and the history of litigation over promotion procedures in the city made it difficult to obtain objective, reliable performance evaluations to serve as the basis for any merit procedure. The task force, in its recommendation, had instructed the superintendent to develop and distribute appropriate criteria for making merit promotion decisions. As a result, an expert spent months doing an appropriate job analysis to develop criteria to select candidates. The court rejected the alternative for two reasons. First, the merit promotions already in place were for nonsupervisory positions, so the process could not be presumed to be an equally valid method for promoting officers into the supervisory position of sergeant. Second, because there was insufficient time to implement the recommendations (the city's later implementation of a merit system took nineteen months), it was not an available alternative at the time of the 1997 promotions.

A recent case in Tennessee, *Johnson* v. *City of Memphis*, illustrates that employers must be thorough in checking the prior testimony and experience of their experts, which can support the viability of an alternative.[59] In *Johnson*, the court accepted plaintiffs' arguments that a merit promotion process was a viable alternative in large part because the city's expert had successfully used a merit process in a different city.

Case law continues to evolve on the subject of less adverse alternatives and the criteria used by the courts to evaluate them. Demonstration that the alternative is indeed equally valid, less adverse, available, and feasible (both logistically and financially) to implement are all factors considered in the evaluation.

The *Ricci* Decision

A recent Supreme Court decision, *Ricci et al.* v. *DeStefano et al.*, makes addressing adverse impact post hoc problematic for an employer, creating a dangerous catch-22 situation.[60] If an employer receives information that a test has a disparate impact, it might nonetheless be limited in its ability to stop using that test. When an employer aims to eliminate a statistical disparity against a minority or other protected group of employees and takes retroactive action that may give rise to a claim of disparate treatment by nonminority employees (reverse discrimination), then the employer must have a strong basis in evidence of disparate impact liability to justify not using the test results.

In *Ricci*, the City of New Haven, Connecticut, hired an outside company to design and develop examinations that would form the baseline for promotion decisions in its fire department. The examination results showed a marked adverse impact on minority candidates, and the ensuing political controversy led the city to disregard the examination results.

Several white firefighters and one Hispanic firefighter brought suit against the city and several individual decision makers under Title VII and Section 1983,[61] alleging intentional race discrimination. The district court granted summary judgment for defendants, finding that "Defendants' motivation to avoid making promotions based on a test with a racially disparate impact, even in a political context, does not, as a matter of law, constitute discriminatory intent."[62] The Second Circuit affirmed without opinion, then subsequently vacated and reaffirmed in a one-paragraph anonymous opinion. Adopting the district court's reasoning, the Second Circuit stated, "Because the Board, in refusing to validate the exams, was simply trying to fulfill its obligations under Title VII when confronted with test results that had a disproportionate racial impact, its actions were protected."[63]

In a sharply divided five-to-four decision, the Supreme Court reversed. The Court "beg[a]n with [the] premise" that the city's actions constituted intentional discrimination, "absent some valid defense."[64] It continued: "All the evidence demonstrates that the City chose not to certify the examination results because of the statistical disparity based on race—*i.e.*, how minority candidates had performed when compared to white candidates."[65]

The Court then determined that an employer's aim to eliminate such a statistical disparity is not a valid defense absent "a strong basis in evidence of disparate-impact liability."[66] Applying this standard, the Court held that the city lacked a "strong basis in evidence" that, if it certified the test results, it would violate Title VII's disparate impact provisions.[67]

Two concurrences and a dissent were filed in addition to the majority opinion. Justice Scalia's concurrence warned of the possible future demise of Title VII's disparate impact provisions. Justice Alito's concurrence noted that in addition to the majority's reasoning, a reasonable jury could have found that the city's purported justification (compliance with Title VII's disparate impact provisions) was pretext for political appeasement of minority groups. Justice Ginsburg wrote a dissent that expounded on the city's justification for its decision and emphasized the employer's impossible predicament in the wake of the majority's holding.

Implications of *Ricci*

The first major implication of *Ricci* is a heightened standard for taking any race-conscious action once a procedure has been developed and validated: the employer must have a strong basis in evidence for believing it would be liable to a disparate impact claim.[68] The dissent makes the point that the *Ricci* majority has not only transplanted this evidentiary burden, it has toughened it: "It is hard to see how [the majority's] requirements differ from demanding that an employer establish 'a provable, actual violation' against itself."[69]

This heightened standard may not apply to assessments on initial hiring, because initial employment does not carry the same sort of expectations as seniority systems and methods for promotion relied upon by incumbent employees:

> Nor do we question an employer's affirmative efforts to ensure that all groups have a fair opportunity to apply for promotions and to participate in the process by which promotions will be made. *But once that process has been established and employers have made clear their selection criteria, they may not then invalidate the test results, thus upsetting an employee's legitimate expectation not to be judged on the basis of race.* Doing so, absent a strong basis in evidence of an impermissible

disparate impact, amounts to the sort of racial preference that Congress has disclaimed, § 2000e-2(j), and is antithetical to the notion of a workplace where individuals are guaranteed equal opportunity regardless of race.[70]

Another implication of *Ricci* is that it provides a new defense for employers. The employer can certify the test results, regardless of the disparate impact, because failing to do so would constitute a strong basis in evidence that subjects it to liability. The Supreme Court acknowledged as much near the end of the opinion that the "strong basis" standard is a two-way street, both directions seemingly favorable to nonminorities:

> Our holding today clarifies how Title VII applies to resolve competing expectations under the disparate-treatment and disparate-impact provisions. If, after it certifies the test results, the City faces a disparate-impact suit, then in light of our holding today it should be clear that the City would avoid disparate-impact liability based on the strong basis in evidence that, had it not certified the results, it would have been subject to disparate-treatment liability.[71]

This statement suggests that an employer may avoid disparate impact liability by proving a strong basis in evidence that it would have faced and lost a disparate treatment claim. The conclusion is that the "strong basis in evidence" standard is not only a hurdle discouraging well-meaning employers from attempting to remedy disparate impact discrimination in less than obvious cases; it is a defense to any disparate impact claim, increasing the disparate impact plaintiff's burden.[72] Before making a racially motivated change to employment practices, an employer should now consider whether *Ricci* will apply to the decision; it should then evaluate the possible sources of evidence.

Even when the employer does its best to ensure a strong basis in evidence, some elements of the new doctrine are left uncertain. For example, it is unclear whether a court will view evidence as a strong basis in the aggregate if none of the component parts individually constitutes a strong basis. What if there are substantial questions on both the "job-related/business necessity" prong of disparate impact liability and the "equally valid alternative" prong, but the quantum of evidence falls short of a "strong basis" for either individually? Further, what are the effects of an employer's need to introduce such sensitive and self-critical evidence to defend itself?

Second, it is not entirely clear whether the court or the jury will decide whether a strong basis in evidence exists in a particular case. While traditional disparate impact testing cases have been tried to the bench, the reverse race cases are disparate treatment claims, and therefore the plaintiffs are entitled to a jury trial. Hence, it appears that the employer presenting a strong basis in evidence of disparate impact liability to defend a treatment claim may well be presenting disparate impact statistics and validity evidence to a jury.

Conclusion

The increased use of assessment procedures in the workplace has led to greater scrutiny by courts and enforcement agencies. Even the neutral use of selection procedures can be illegal if they have a disparate impact on protected groups, are not demonstrably job related, or, even if they are validated, an alternative method is available that would serve the employer's legitimate expectations in a less adverse way.

In addition to monitoring the impact of selection procedures on certain protected groups and relying on sufficient validity evidence when choosing a procedure, employers can minimize their litigation exposure in a variety of ways. Proper training and direction to evaluate candidates on core and functional competencies reduce subjectivity in assessments and enhance the validity of selection procedures. The use of bands instead of more rigid cutoff scores respects the limits of an exam's accuracy. And a periodic reassessment of selection procedures keeps the employer abreast of both the procedures' continuing validity and the potential existence of alternatives.

Notes

1. *Guardians Association of New York City Police Department, Inc.* v. *Civil Service Commission of City of New York*, 630 F.2d 79, 89 (2d Cir. 1980).

2. http://www.amanet.org/research/pdfs/bjp_2001.pdf.
3. 401 U.S. 424 (1971).
4. This chapter is not intended to explore these provisions in detail. For more comprehensive coverage on federal employment discrimination laws, see this well-known treatise: Lindemann, B., & Grossman, P. (2007). *Employment discrimination law* (4th ed.). Washington, DC: Bureau of National Affairs.
5. 42 U.S.C. § 2000e-2(h).
6. 42 U.S.C. § 12112(a), (b)(6)–(7).
7. Compare *Monette* v. *Electronic Data Systems Corp.*, 90 F.3d 1173, 1184 (6th Cir. 1996) (plaintiff bears the burden of showing he is qualified to perform the essential functions of the job, absent the challenged job requirement), and *Bates* v. *UPS*, 465 F.3d 1069, 1081 (9th Cir. 2006), rehearing en banc granted, (same), with *Davidson* v. *AOL, Inc.*, 337 F.3d 1179, 1188–1189 (if job requirement is job related and consistent with business necessity, employee must show she is qualified to perform the requirement).
8. 29 U.S.C. § 623.
9. *Smith* v. *City of Jackson*, 544 U.S. 228 (2005). Also see n. 12, *infra.*
10. 29 C.F.R. § 1607 et seq. (1978).
11. 29 C.F.R. § 1607.1B.
12. 29 C.F.R. § 1607.2D.
13. The four-fifths rule of thumb identifies adverse impact as occurring when members of a protected class are selected at a rate less than four-fifths (80 percent) that of the highest-performing group. For example, if 50 percent of white applicants receive a passing score on a test but only 30 percent of African Americans pass, the relevant ratio would be 30/50, or 60 percent, which would violate the 80 percent rule.
14. 29 CFR § 1607.4D (1981).
15. 29 C.F.R. § 1607.15A.
16. See, e.g., *Isabel* v. *City of Memphis*, 404 F.3d 404, 412–413 (6th Cir. 2005).
17. 29 C.F.R. § 1607.5C.
18. Society for Industrial and Organizational Psychology. (2003). *Principles for the validation and use of personnel selection procedures* (4th ed., p. 1). Bowling Green, OH: Author.
19. Equal Employment Opportunity Commission. (2006, March). *Systemic task force report.* Washington, DC: U.S. Government Printing Office. Retrieved from http://www.eeoc.gov/abouteeoc/task_reports/systemic.pdf.
20. http://www.eeoc.gov/policy/docs/factemployment_procedures.html.

21. See, for example, the record settlements by Texaco ($176.1 million) and Coca Cola ($192.5 million) that led to sharp changes in company practices. Wiscombe, J. (2003, April). Corporate America's scariest opponent. *Workforce Management*, pp. 34–41. Retrieved from http://www.workforce.com/archive/feature/23/42/44/index.php.

22. *Albermarle Paper Co. v. Moody*, 422 U.S. 405, 425 (1975).

23. See 42 U.S.C. § 2000e-2(k)(1)(A)(i).

24. 29 *CFR § 1607.5(B); see also Watson* v. *Fort Worth Bank & Trust Co.*, 487 U.S. 977, 998 (1988); *Albermarle Paper Co. v. Moody*, 422 U.S. 405, 431 (1975).

25. 42 U.S.C. § 2000e-2(k)(1)(A)(ii).

26. 29 U.S.C. § 623(f)(1) (2000).

27. *Smith* v. *City of Jackson*, 544 U.S. 228 (2005).

28. *Brown* v. *Nucor Corp.*, 576 F.3d 149 (4th Cir. 2009).

29. *Waisome* v. *Port Authority of New York and New Jersey*, 948 F.2d 1370 (2d Cir. 1991).

30. *Moore* v. *Southwest Bell Telephone Co.*, 593 F.2d 607, 608 (5th Cir. 1979) (affirming holding that pass ratio of 93 percent defeated prima facie showing of disparate impact).

31. *Frazier* v. *Garrison Independent School District*, 980 F.2d 1514, 1524 (5th Cir. 1993).

32. *Eubanks* v. *Pickens-Bond Construction Co.*, 635 F.2d 1341 (8th Cir. 1980); *Reynolds* v. *Sheet Metal Workers Local 102*, 498 F. Supp. 952 (D.D.C. 1980).

33. See *United States* v. *City of New York*, 2009 WL 2180836 (E.D.N.Y. July 22, 2009) (granting summary judgment for plaintiffs on written examination that satisfied 80 percent rule due to practical and statistical significance). See also *United States* v. *New York City Board of Education*, 487 F. Supp. 2d 220, 224 (E.D.N.Y. 2007) (as an alternative to the 80 percent rule of thumb, a prima facie case can be established by showing a statistically significant disparity of two standard deviations).

34. *Bew* v. *City of Chicago*, 252 F.3d 891, 893 (7th Cir. 2001).

35. Zimmer, M., Sullivan, C., & White, R. (2003). *Cases and materials on employment discrimination* (6th ed). New York: Aspen Publishers.

36. 252 F.3d 891 (7th Cir. 2001).

37. 29 C.F.R. § 1607.4D.

38. See *Groves* v. *Alabama State Board of Education*, 776 F. Supp. 1518, 1528 (M.D. Ala. 1991): "It may well be true that a measure of difference between black and white selection rates, such as the four-fifths rule, incorporates an important test of practical significance not captured by the Hazelwood and Shoben formulas' focus on

statistical significance." See also *Delgado* v. *Ashcroft*, 2003 WL 24051558 *8 (D.D.C. May 29, 2003) (admitting that the 80 percent rule is often the measure of practical significance but rejecting under the circumstances).

39. *Stagi* v. *National Railroad Passenger Corp.*, 2009 WL 2461892, 12 (E.D. Pa. Aug. 12, 2009) (citations omitted).

40. 2009 WL 2180836 (E.D.N.Y. July 22, 2009).

41. 776 F. Supp. 1518, 1528 (M.D. Ala. 1991).

42. See *United States* v. *City of New York*, 2009 WL 2180836, *15 (E.D.N.Y. 2009) (distinguishing *Waisome* because the 2.68 standard deviation was a "borderline" case); *Groves* v. *Alabama State Board of Education*, 776 F. Supp. 1518, 1526–1527 (M.D. Ala. 1991) (82.3 percent passage ratio versus 9.5 and 10.7 standard deviations).

43. *Waisome* v. *Port Authority of New York and New Jersey*, 948 F.2d 1370 (2d Cir. 1991) (87.23 percent versus only 2.68 standard deviations); *Moore* v. *Southwestern Bell Telephone Co.* (93 percent passage ratio versus 3.93 standard deviations); *Stagi* v. *National Railroad Passenger Corp.*, 2009 WL 2461892 (E.D. Pa. Aug. 12, 2009) (98.63 percent versus 8.42 standard deviations). But see *Bew* v. *City of Chicago*.

44. See *Thornton* v. *Coffey*, 618 F.2d 686 (10th Cir. 1980).

45. *Watson* v. *Forth Worth Bank & Trust*, 487 U.S. 977 (1988).

46. 406 F.3d 248 (4th Cir. 2005), cert. denied, 126 S. Ct. 1431 (2006).

47. See Lindemann & Grossman (2007).

48. See *Albermarle Paper Co.* v. *Moody*, 422 U.S. 405, 434 (1975); *Isabel* v. *City of Memphis*, 404 F.3d 404, 413 (6th Cir. 2005); *Lanning* v. *Southeast Pennsylvania Transportation Authority*, 308 F.3d 286, 294, n.1 (3d Cir. 2002).

49. Section 5H.

50. See *U.S.* v. *City of Garland*, 2004 WL 741295, *12 (N.D. Tex. Mar. 31, 2004); *Gulino* v. *Board of Education of City School District of the City of New York*, 2003 WL 25764041, *16 (S.D.N.Y. Sept. 4, 2003).

51. 404 F.3d 404 (6th Cir. 2005).

52. 2004 WL 609331 (D. Del. March 22, 2004).

53. 382 F.3d 680 (7th Cir. 2004), cert. denied, 543 U.S. 1152 (2005).

54. *Allen* v. *Chicago*, 351 F.3d 306 (7th Cir. 2003).

55. See *Association of Mexican-American Educators* v. *California*, 231 F.3d 572, 587 (9th Cir. 2000) ("Validation studies 'are by their nature difficult, expensive, time consuming and rarely, if ever, free of error'").

56. *Albermarle Paper Co.* v. *Moody*, 422 U.S. 405, 425 (1975).

57. 469 F.3d 735 (8th Cir. 2006).

58. *Adams* v. *Chicago*, 469 F.3d 609 (7th Cir. 2006).

59. *Johnson* v. *City of Memphis*, 2006 WL 3827481 (W.D. Tenn. 2006).

60. —U.S.—, 129 S. Ct. 2658 (June 29, 2009).
61. 42 U.S.C. § 1983 provides a federal remedy against those who, under color of state law, violate federally protected rights. Section 1983 provides a private cause of action for the violation of federal statutory rights, in addition to constitutional rights violations. See Lindemann & Grossman (2007).
62. *Ricci v. DeStefano*, 554 F. Supp. 2d 142, 160 (D. Conn. 2006) (footnote omitted).
63. *Ricci v. DeStefano*, 530 F.3d 87 (2d Cir. 2008).
64. 129 S. Ct. 2658, 2673 (2009).
65. Id.
66. Id. at 2676.
67. The Court declined to reach the equal protection issues because it held that the city's decision violated Title VII.
68. See, e.g., Cotter, 323 F.3d at 169. *Concrete Works of Colorado*, 321 F.3d at 971; *O'Donnell Construction Co.*, 963 F.2d at 424.
69. Id. at 2701 (Ginsburg, J., dissenting).
70. *Ricci v. DeStefano*, 129 S. Ct. 2658, 2677 (June 29, 2009) (emphasis added).
71. Id. at 2681.
72. It is no wonder Justice Scalia's concurrence in *Ricci* speaks ominously of the future of disparate impact.

CHAPTER 21

VALIDATION STRATEGIES
S. Morton McPhail, Damian J. Stelly

With any form of workplace assessment we are dealing with the topic of measurement. In this sense, measurement generally involves describing something about a person that can be difficult to observe (such as a personality characteristic) or predicting an individual's (or groups of individuals') future behavior or success. Thus, we are making inferences that go beyond simply responses to assessment procedures; we draw conclusions about people. For example, we might conclude that:

- Their typical behavior patterns are consistent with competencies important to some valued outcome—perhaps success in performing certain tasks or growth and development in preparation for other positions.
- They possess some underlying personal characteristics, interests, or motivations required for performance in existing or future roles.
- They have (or do not have) the minimum qualifications to perform the work.
- They have (or do not have) the requisite knowledge and skills to perform the work competently.
- They are more (or less) likely to perform the job better than other candidates.

When we make such inferences, the extent to which we can have confidence in them is a function of the extent to which they are "valid." We define validity, then, as the strength of the evidence we have to support the conclusions we reach based on the assessment (*Principles*, 2003).

In this chapter, we discuss the scientific, legal, and business imperatives that affect the quest for evidence regarding our inferences. We examine a range of strategies for obtaining validity evidence under various circumstances.

We begin with the two most commonly used research approaches: criterion-related and content-oriented strategies. Turning to alternatives, we have organized our discussion into two broad categories: those that leverage existing evidence for additional purposes and those designed to develop new evidence. We conclude with a discussion of the issues involved in selecting a strategy in practice.

The Rationale for Validity

The effort necessary to conduct validation research can sometimes be complex, time consuming, and costly. The question must arise for managers of why it should be undertaken at all. The answer to this question has a number of facets, each of which provides a compelling justification for the effort.

Scientific Importance of Validity

The definition of *validity* we offered has a number of important implications. First, it says that validity resides not in the instruments, procedures, or processes of assessment, but in the evidence supporting the particular inferences we are planning to make based on them. Simply put, tests are neither valid nor invalid. Rather, we must judge the strength of the evidence supporting the inferences that we draw from test scores. Indeed, some conclusions from a particular assessment may be well supported, while others may not. Whenever we make inferences based on test scores, we are asserting a hypothesis that may be falsified or supported empirically. It is the business of science to test such propositions using methods designed to reduce the chance that we will be deluded by our intellectual investment in or expectations about the outcome.

Suppose we were to administer a very good measure of mental ability to a group of candidates being considered for a position as chief financial officer. If we draw inferences from that measure that include the likelihood that those candidates will be able to grasp new ideas quickly, identify logical flaws, interpret complex verbal information accurately, and analyze data effectively, the evidence available from a great deal of research on cognitive ability would give us confidence that our conclusions would be quite accurate.

If, however, we go further and reach conclusions about how well these managers will present complex information to the board, manage a team of highly skilled and independent professionals, deal with overseas partners, and carefully and diligently follow rules, regulations, and legal requirements, our confidence in these conclusions would be at best limited and perhaps nonexistent. The assessment process in this example is not flawed; rather we simply have little evidence to support the latter inferences. It might be that the assessment is capable of predicting some of these aspects of job performance, but we are going to need evidence of that before we are willing to rely on it for such purposes. In effect, we need to test the hypothesis that the measure will be useful for these more extended purposes (Landy, 1986; Messick, 1988).

Legal Requirements for Validity

In addition to the scientific imperative to seek evidence supporting the inferences we draw from assessments, there are legal requirements to do so as well. Virtually every aspect of the employment relationship is governed by statutes, regulations, or case law. In the United States (and in some similar ways in other countries as well), assessments may not discriminate on the basis of race/ethnicity, color, gender, national origin, religion, age, or disability in any aspect of employment. The primary statement of the regulations governing the use of assessments in employment is found in the *Uniform Guidelines on Employee Selection Procedures* (Equal Employment Opportunity Commission, Civil Service Commission, Department of Labor, & Department of Justice, 1978). The extent of coverage goes beyond selection to include such components as promotion, compensation, performance evaluation, work assignments, termination, admission to training programs, and availability of developmental opportunities. The *Guidelines* apply to all selection procedures, including tests, interviews, and other methods.

Two broad approaches to discrimination have been identified by the courts. The first approach, disparate treatment, has to do with how people are treated. Discrimination occurs when a member of a subgroup is treated differently from members of another (usually more favored) subgroup. For example, if women were required to take a mechanical aptitude test to qualify for a job but men were not, a clear case of disparate treatment, the most obvious kind of discrimination, would arise.

The second approach, disparate (or adverse) impact, refers to cases where an employer imposes a requirement that is on its face neutral but in fact results in fewer members of one subgroup being successful than members of another. Disparate impact means that the proportion of successful candidates from one subgroup is substantially less than the proportion that is successful from another subgroup. "Substantially" is defined as being so different that the resulting disparity has a low probability of occurring by chance alone. As a rule of thumb, this definition became operationalized as the four-fifths, or 80 percent, rule: adverse impact occurs when the pass rate of one group is less than 80 percent of the pass rate for the most successful group (see Figure 21.1). Disparate impact may also be evaluated using more sophisticated statistical tests.

Disparate or adverse impact does not necessarily indicate discrimination. Instead, it raises questions about the assessment process and triggers the requirement that the employer produce evidence supporting its validity.

Organizations must be able to show evidence supporting the validity of any procedure that has disparate impact with respect to protected groups. We must have evidence to back up the job-related inferences we wish to draw and be able to show that our use of the assessment procedure is consistent with business necessity. Thus, to the extent we wish to predicate employment decisions (whether to hire, admit to training, promote, or terminate) on an assessment outcome, we have to be able to demonstrate

Figure 21.1. Illustration of the 80 Percent Rule

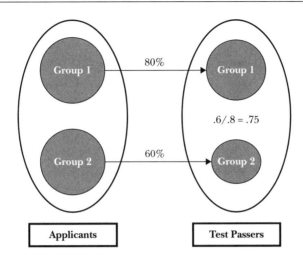

the job-related reason for that decision and that it promotes the legitimate interests of the organization.

Business Case for Validity

There is also a business case to be made for the development of validity evidence in addition to the scientific and legal arguments for validation research. For employers using assessment instruments to inform human resource (HR) decisions, there is risk in the form of costs and potential returns. For example, costs might include the expense of the hiring process (recruitment, assessment, and onboarding, for example) and the expense of an unsuccessful hiring decision (an employee who performs ineffectively). In addition, there is the opportunity cost of failing to hire a more successful employee. Conversely, potential returns come in the form of identifying and hiring a highly successful employee and avoiding hiring a less successful one. Indeed, research has shown that even modest gains in the productivity of higher-performing employees can produce substantial cost savings and productivity improvements.

Employers who make employment decisions on the basis of assessment processes are trying to reduce the risk and increase the return by improving the chances those decisions will result in positive outcomes. Evidence for validity provides information about the extent to which the assessments are likely to be effective in producing those outcomes. A test for which there is no validity evidence may fail to contribute to improving the chances of making good decisions, while incurring costs for its use and risk of challenge by equal employment opportunity enforcement agencies or potentially disadvantaged individuals. Assessments for which good evidence exists to support the inferences provide organizations with competitive advantage in identifying what one senior manager called their "unfair share of the best employees."

Obtaining Validity Evidence

Although we will review various approaches for obtaining validity evidence, it is important to note that all of these specific methods are focused on a single unitary concept: validity. Thus, it is appropriate to think about the specific methods described here as different approaches or lines of evidence for validity and not different types of validity. Most of the options discussed in this chapter are treated in much greater detail in a recent volume of the Society for Industrial and Organizational Psychology (SIOP) Professional Practice Series (McPhail, 2007); specific citations to that volume are made only where particularly relevant or when quoted. Some methods are based on conducting applied research to create new evidence to support the inferences we seek to draw from an assessment process. Other methods involve leveraging existing evidence to show that the process under consideration provides meaningful and accurate inferences in different situations or under different conditions, or even that the conditions for making those inferences are not very different from those where evidence was developed previously. Note that stating that the process "looks as if it ought to work" or formulating a rationale in the absence of professional validation research is not an appropriate option.

Traditional Strategies: Tried-and-True Approaches

Reflecting professional thought about validity dating back to 1954, the *Guidelines* specifically identified three strategies for validation research: criterion related, content oriented, and construct. They then effectively dismissed construct as imposing heavy burdens on employers. Thus, the two approaches that have been used most often, researched most extensively, and subjected to judicial review most stringently are criterion and content. The following section introduces these now traditional strategies for developing validity evidence.

Criterion-Related Evidence

The most direct and straightforward evidence for validity is obtained empirically by relating individuals' scores on the assessment measure to performance on a relevant criterion measure. If we are evaluating an assessment for selecting salespeople, we hypothesize that candidates scoring higher on our assessment will be more successful in selling. Relevant outcomes might include sales volume, order increases, customer retention, up-sales, and lag time to sale. For many jobs, however, the only performance information available is a supervisor's judgment of how well incumbents are performing, so supervisory ratings are common criteria. Regardless of the types of criteria, the correlation coefficient is a typical method for evaluating the relationship between the assessment and performance. The correlation answers the question: "To what extent do people who perform well on the assessment also perform well on the job and vice versa?"

Developing criterion-related evidence depends on having information about individuals' performance on appropriate assessment procedures (given the job in question) and relevant information about their job performance. To ensure we have appropriate and relevant information, we start with job analysis to better understand the job and the knowledge, skills, abilities, and other characteristics (KSAOs) required for its performance. Job analysis is fundamental to any validation strategy we choose, and the quality of the validity evidence we develop often hinges on the thoroughness and adequacy of the job analysis. Without job analysis, we may choose inappropriate assessment procedures to include in our validation research or define and measure performance inappropriately.

There are two substrategies for obtaining information needed to conduct a criterion-related study. In the concurrent approach, we solicit the participation of current employees to respond to the assessment measure, while simultaneously (that is, concurrently) obtaining information about their job performance. An alternative strategy, the predictive approach, requires assessing applicants, setting the data aside, using other hiring methods in the interim, and then waiting an adequate amount of time for information about the performance of new employees to develop before correlating test and assessment results.

There are a number of requirements for using criterion-related strategies. Most important, enough incumbents must be available to allow an adequate sample for statistical analyses. Some researchers argue that sample sizes under one hundred result in too much sampling error to have confidence in the results. For samples of fewer than fifty, not only must we deal with sampling error, but the statistics themselves become unstable. One way to think about sampling error is in terms of the probability that subsequent samples from the same population will differ from each other just because of the luck of the draw. By *instability*, we mean the extent to which changes in a single or very small number of cases can result in substantial changes in the statistics we compute.

A second requirement for this strategy is that there must exist meaningful and reliable ways to assess performance of individuals. Sometimes known as the criterion problem, being able to measure performance accurately has long been a concern for validation research. There are several aspects to the criterion problem. First, the performance measure must be relevant to work performance, that is, it must be job related, meaning that a person's standing on the measure is associated with overall job performance. Second, the measures of performance need to capture all or most of the important aspects of performance (*criterion sufficiency*).

Key Requirements for Criterion-Based Research

- Job analysis
- Sufficient sample size
- Identification of alternative possible predictors
- Willing participation of employees and supervisors
- Meaningful and reliable performance measures

Unfortunately, performance is often rather poorly assessed by objective measures, especially as the United States has transitioned from a manufacturing to a service economy. In addition, the increasing importance of team-based environments complicates the process of measuring job performance. One result of the insufficiency of objective measures and complicated and interactive work structures is that supervisor evaluations are often the best or only performance criteria available. It is clear that supervisors can generally identify the best employees, and usually they can identify the worst too. However, with increasing spans of control, less immediately observable work outcomes, and greater time constraints, it often is difficult for supervisors to differentiate among the majority of employees whose performance is about average. Despite these challenges, being able to obtain accurate, reliable, and unbiased supervisory evaluations is a central requirement for most criterion-related validation research.

One of the most important advantages of empirical research is the ability to show how well an assessment predicts job performance. Having such data available can also inform decisions about appropriate passing scores, allow evaluation of test fairness, and provide estimates of the utility or value of the assessment measure or process.

The efficacy of validity data may be limited by a number of conditions. In the case of a concurrent study, assuming the current incumbent pool has been selected using tools or procedures somewhat similar to those being investigated in the current study, the workforce likely will not include the full range of test scores or performance (most incumbents generally meet or exceed the performance standards). The result of this restriction in range is to attenuate (reduce) the size of the correlations we will obtain; this situation in turn requires even greater sample sizes to allow meaningful research. In addition, a concurrent validation strategy requires current incumbents to participate willingly and put forth effort on the assessment being validated as if they were applicants. Several factors may lessen their willingness to do so, including distrust about how data will be used, fatigue, disaffection with the employer, or unwillingness of bargaining unit leaders to sanction the research.

On the criterion side, supervisors may be unable or unwilling to provide accurate evaluations of performance for several reasons. Large spans of control may prevent supervisors from having sufficient knowledge of individual performance, supervisors may be concerned about how their evaluations will be used, team-based environments may make individual performances indistinguishable except to team members, and criterion measures may be difficult or time-consuming to use.

Criterion-related validation potentially can provide strong and convincing support for our assessment measures. Such evidence is often considered by EEO enforcement agencies to be of great value (some have even called it the gold standard, which may be only partly hyperbolic) in supporting the use of selection procedures. On the other hand, done properly, such research may be expensive and time-consuming in terms of both elapsed time and employee commitment.

For managers, perhaps the greatest risk in this strategy is that as in all other research, the outcome cannot be known in advance. The results of testing a hypothesis may not provide the evidence we are seeking. We may invest time and resources in research, only to discover the data do not support the use of the tests. Nevertheless, investing adequate time and resources is important because a poorly conducted study may produce erroneous results or results that will not survive scrutiny. Although the goal may be to perform the research to the highest possible standards, there are many ways, both technical and practical, in which criterion-related research may be flawed, and perfect studies are rare, if not absent altogether.

Content-Related Evidence

A second common approach taken by practitioners to support test development and use involves showing that the assessment is composed of a representative sample of a specific content domain—say, a job or a KSAO. As a scientific process, content-oriented test development has its roots in domain sampling theory. However, it is worth noting that despite its benefits (including legal defensibility), there has been compelling criticism of content-oriented validation research as a method for evaluating validity (for example, Murphy, 2009).

The process of content validation is typically based on the systematic collection and analysis of judgments by subject matter experts (SMEs). Job analysis is used to define the relevant domain for the job of interest, including work behaviors, KSAOs, and work products. The relationship between work behaviors and KSAOs also must be documented. Although there is no single preferred job analysis approach, more rigorous methods that are deliberate in design and aligned with professional standards will likely produce a better and more legally defensible result. Practitioners should focus on developing a research plan that identifies appropriate SMEs (in terms of expertise, representation of key variables, and so forth), acquiring job information from multiple sources, designing research processes and tools to facilitate objective data gathering, and documenting research in accordance with the *Guidelines*. The job analysis should identify the KSAOs truly necessary at job entry and not learned on the job during a brief orientation period; only these KSAOs are appropriate targets for the selection process.

Based on the *Guidelines*, content-oriented development of selection procedures is appropriate in the case of direct work samples and measures intended to assess certain categories of KSAOs. Work samples should be developed to be representative of behavior required on the job or to result in a representative sample of work produced on the job. When selection procedures are intended as measures of KSAOs, it is important that KSAOs be operationally defined. For measures of skills or abilities in particular, the skill or ability being measured should be defined in terms of observable aspects of work behavior; the selection procedures must not rely on inferences about unobservable components of work or mental processes. Knowledge measures must be shown to assess knowledge that is used on the job and necessary to perform important work behaviors; the actual test questions do not necessarily have to be operationalized in terms of work behavior.

The SIOP (2003) *Principles for the Validation and Use of Employee Selection Procedures* support the use of content-oriented test development regardless of the type of KSAOs in question—an important distinction from the *Guidelines*, which explicitly state that measures of KSAOs involving inferences concerning mental processes such as traits or constructs are inappropriate targets for content validation. The linkage of the assessment to work behaviors may be established in several ways, including how the KSAO is defined, whether data such as SME judgments indicate a dependency between the KSAO and job tasks, or if the KSAO is represented by the display of key work behaviors (for example, the scoring key for a structured interview).

Subsequent to a job analysis, it is necessary to identify selection approaches such as work samples, structured interviews, and job knowledge tests to assess critical work behaviors or KSAOs. Assessment development should involve staff with specialized expertise (in addition to other SMEs who may be involved). There also must be a process for evaluating assessment components and scoring procedures that includes how they are formally judged, discarded, or revised. Selection procedures are more supportable when they minimize the assessment of extraneous factors, such as reading level, and approximate the level and complexity of the job. Formal documentation of the links between assessment components and the KSAOs or work behaviors they are intended to measure should be developed. Once assessments are developed, it should be clear how the assessment content representatively samples important aspects of the observable job domain or the body of knowledge that is a prerequisite for observable work behavior.

When properly applied, content validation research has benefits beyond the obvious fact that it is a legally defensible strategy for providing evidence to support implementation of a selection process. It also can improve other types of studies, such as criterion-related validation, and provide additional support and defensibility. In the context of test development, content-oriented research supports the construction of high-quality instruments through the systematic evaluation of test content relative to job requirements.

Content studies are often possible when criterion studies are not feasible, such as when sample sizes are too small or the organization is unwilling to collect test and criterion data. However, greater feasibility should not be equated with ease of use; in fact, conducting high-quality content-oriented research and test development can be challenging. Even in well-developed research, some elements will be vulnerable to criticism based on scientific principles or legal guidelines.

To some extent, vulnerabilities arise due to the many decisions made during study design and development, along with the organizational realities of time and resource limitations. In addition, content validation does not produce a single source of evidence as intuitively (or statistically) appealing to outside observers as a validity coefficient. Although this does not make criterion-related research better as a validation strategy, it makes content-oriented studies vulnerable to challenge in that the strength of the evidence is dependent on the soundness of the evidentiary framework built in the course of the research. When a compelling challenge is made to any component of the framework, the entire structure can be weakened.

There is additional vulnerability when assessment development involves sampling from broader constructs (KSAOs) compared to more conventional applications of content-oriented procedures such as work samples and knowledge tests. In such applications, particular attention must be paid to KSAO-work behavior linkages and operationalization of selection measures in terms of work behaviors. It is common to see content validation research that relies on indirect KSAO linkages (for example, work behavior, KSAOs, and assessment components). Based on the *Guidelines*, this approach is more vulnerable as compared to approaches in which assessments and scoring procedures directly reflect work behaviors.

To ensure the quality of evidence needed to support test use based on content validation, the research process must be carefully designed and executed. Limited consideration of factors related to study design will undermine the quality of the approach. We have seen research challenged based on a variety of factors such as which SMEs should participate, weighting of assessment components, which facilities should be involved in the research, what types of ratings should be collected, and what types of quantitative analyses should be conducted. Documenting the representativeness of assessment instruments can be challenging, given that there is no single straightforward standard for doing so. Because of the technical issues, assessment developers must have appropriate expertise. Although it is unlikely all potential threats can be addressed, skilled developers can make reasoned judgments that balance science, legal defensibility, and practical constraints.

Alternative Strategies—On and Off the Beaten Path

Evidence for the validity of a selection procedure may already exist. The challenge for users then becomes how to properly leverage that existing evidence to support implementation of the procedure in a new or different context. In other cases, neither criterion nor content evidence for validity of an assessment may be available. For these situations, we consider alternative means for developing suitable evidence anew. In this section, we differentiate these circumstances and offer nontraditional alternatives.

Leveraging Existing Evidence

Assessment experts have been studying the relationships between tests and other assessment methods for many years and have developed a substantial knowledge base in doing so. In some cases, this existing knowledge can provide the validity evidence needed to support the use of assessments in particular situations. Several strategies for doing so are described below.

Transporting Validation Evidence

When the *Uniform Guidelines* were being framed, the idea that validation evidence was specific to a particular job and perhaps even a particular place (the "situational-specificity hypothesis") was still widely accepted, but reservations about it were growing. The idea arose that it might be possible to transfer the validity evidence developed about an assessment measure for a job in one location to apply that measure for the same job in another location. Certainly there would be significant efficiencies and savings for employers if such transportation of validity were acceptable. With this goal in mind, the *Guidelines* included a specific provision for doing so:

> A. *Validity studies not conducted by the user.* Users may, under certain circumstances, support the use of selection procedures by validity studies conducted by other users or conducted by test publishers or distributors and described in test manuals. While publishers of selection procedures have a professional

obligation to provide evidence of validity which meets generally accepted professional standards (see section 5C of this part), users are cautioned that they are responsible for compliance with these guidelines. Accordingly, users seeking to obtain selection procedures from publishers and distributors should be careful to determine that, in the event the user becomes subject to the validity requirements of these guidelines, the necessary information to support validity has been determined and will be made available to the user [*Uniform Guidelines*, sec. 7.A.].

Thus, users can borrow evidence from an empirical, criterion-related validation study conducted in one setting; transport it; and apply it to a similar jobs in another setting without repeating the empirical validation research. The *Guidelines* contain four requirements for demonstrating transportability:

1. Criterion-related validation evidence
2. Fairness analyses
3. Job similarity
4. Absence of extraneous factors that might undermine the inferences, such as differences in applicant pools

First, there must be an empirical study of the validity of the assessment that satisfies the technical requirements of the *Guidelines*. Although the *Guidelines* contain statements about using evidence based on content and construct studies for most practical purposes, they require criterion-related validation studies when transporting validity evidence. The language of the *Guidelines* also requires that the original validity evidence "clearly demonstrate[s] that the selection procedure is valid" (*Uniform Guidelines*, 1978, sec. 7B). Gibson and Caplinger (2007) conclude from this "that the evidence must be persuasive; that there should be no doubt that validity has been demonstrated" (p. 31). A corollary to this requirement is that the original study must be available to the borrowing user. Because the borrowing user will be predicating all of the validity evidence, and therefore any subsequent defense of the assessment, on research conducted elsewhere, it is prudent for the employer to have the report of that research in hand and that the borrowing organization make an evaluation of the extent to which it complies with the reporting requirements in the *Guidelines*. In addition, the organization that sponsored the original research must grant permission to the borrowing employer to use that research and report. Legal issues may arise here. For example, questions of data ownership and availability may arise, and the organization where the original research was conducted may object to provision of the validation evidence to enforcement agencies.

Second, users must show by an appropriate job analysis that the job to which they wish to apply the test and borrowed validation evidence performs "substantially the same major work behaviors" (*Uniform Guidelines*, 1978) as the job on which the validity evidence was originally developed. Job similarity is perhaps the central issue in transportability analyses, and the *Guidelines* provide no clear guidance about how similar jobs must be to support transporting validity. Two broad categories of issues arise in assessing job similarity:

1. How to measure similarity
   - Overlap of critical elements
   - Distance measures
   - Correlation of frequency, importance, or other ratings
2. What should be similar
   - Tasks
   - Duties
   - Generalized work activities
   - Underlying KSAOs

One common problem researchers must cope with is that to evaluate job similarity, useable job analysis data from the original study must be available. There must also be sufficiently detailed and documented job analysis information to allow a comparison of the original and target jobs. It is not uncommon to find that such data are unavailable either because they do not exist or because someone refuses to provide them—the organization, the researcher, or the test publisher, for example.

A third requirement for using this strategy is that to the extent it is technically feasible to do so, an analysis of test fairness should have been included in the original study. If such an analysis was not included, the borrowing employer must undertake to accumulate sufficient data to do so. This constraint implicitly requires that the employer conduct a local criterion study at some future time when it becomes technically feasible.

The final requirement is that there not be other variables that might undermine the evidential inferences when the assessments are used in the borrowing organization. The *Guidelines* specifically mention that applicant pools should be similar, but in the questions and answers to the *Guidelines*, this admonition is broadened to include any other factors that might serve to make the inferences inappropriate. Guion (1998) noted, however, that "it is less certain that broader similarity is truly necessary, and very nearly certain (from research done in the 1970s) that demographic similarity is not necessary" (p. 86).

This strategy was not originally a theoretically based approach; it reflected a pragmatic acknowledgment that validation research is expensive and complicated and that smaller employers would have difficulty conducting it. However, subsequent research has broadened our understanding of the relationships between assessment measures and job performance and largely found that concerns about situational specificity were unfounded. Accordingly, the *Principles* (2003) include the transportation of validation evidence as part of the larger context of validity generalization and define it as "a strategy for generalizing evidence of validity in which demonstration of important similarities between different work settings is used to infer that validation evidence for a selection procedure accumulated in one work setting generalizes to another work setting" (p. 71).

In part because of the increased knowledge base and in part because of the litigation history of transporting validity, this strategy has been more broadly applied since the publication of the *Guidelines*. One significant expansion has been to use it to extend the definition of job similarity. In some cases, researchers have argued that jobs may be treated as similar for the purposes of assessment if the skills, abilities, and personal characteristics required to perform the job are similar. On this basis, a number of researchers have transported validation evidence across job titles on the basis of similar requirements.

When all of the basic requirements are met, the process of conducting the necessary research is largely composed of collecting job analytic information to allow comparison of the similarity of the original and target jobs. If no job analysis has been conducted for the target job, it may be appropriate (and even recommended) to use the same instrument as the originating study did to collect data. The advantage is direct comparison of the jobs at the same level of detail as used in the validation research. However, conducting an independent analysis of the target job seems to have merit in that it is objective and unbiased by knowledge of the previous job. The problem, of course, is then meshing two approaches that may differ on the basis of level of specificity, task organization, rating scales, or other issues. These issues are sometimes addressed effectively by analyzing both jobs on a well-developed standardized job analytic tool like the Position Analysis Questionnaire (PAQ) (McCormick, Jeanneret, & Mecham, 1969) or the Occupational Information Network (O*Net) (Peterson, Mumford, Borman, Jeanneret, & Fleishman, 1999).

When transportability is feasible, organizations can gain efficiencies in both time and resources by leveraging existing information and avoiding replicating costly research or contributing to the problem of small samples in the research. Based on previous litigation, the courts seem open to carefully constructed and documented arguments for the validity of selection instruments derived from previous research.

The disadvantages for this approach lie in the availability of both technically adequate validation research and job analysis data. Many organizations are reluctant to subject their assessment procedures to scrutiny arising from another employer's use of them. In addition, test publishers sometimes do not provide adequate details of validation research and may not have or be willing to provide job analysis data for comparative purposes. Finally, organizations adopting a transportability strategy must rely on research conducted outside their control.

These conditions present some risk. Organizations using this strategy must show that adequate job analysis data are available to allow comparison of the original and target jobs. Moreover, even if the borrowing user is successful in demonstrating the similarity of the target job with the original, if the underlying validation research is flawed, it provides little support for using the assessment. The *Guidelines* and good sense indicate that users should obtain copies of the original technical reports and maintain them along with the report of the transport analyses.

Synthetic Validation Evidence
Synthetic validation refers to a family of techniques for building up, or synthesizing, validity evidence from existing empirical information. The term *synthetic validation* derives from the ultimate outcome or synthesis of component validities into overall validity estimates for specific jobs or job families based on their job components. Although it relies on previously conducted research, it is distinguishable from transportation of validity evidence because it does not rely on the previous study of one particular job. In this way, it shares some conceptual elements with validity generalization, which is discussed in the next section.

Synthetic validation is a methodological approach rather than a single technique for developing validity evidence. Several synthetic validation techniques have been developed since the concept's original inception by Lawshe (1952). The underlying common element of these techniques is that although jobs may differ regarding the tasks performed, if those tasks have components imposing the same or similar requirements on workers, common selection methods will predict performance. Thus, if we have information about the relationships between assessments of specific skills, abilities, and personal characteristics and job components across jobs, we can combine those relationships for any particular job's set of components to build up validation evidence for a battery of assessments.

Some early approaches to synthetic validation used expert judgments of the relationships (for example, Primoff, 1959), and both empirical and judgmental methods are still used to estimate the validity of a test relative to a specific job component. In fact, both methods may be used in any one application of synthetic validation research depending on the available sample sizes and commonality of job components among jobs.

With the advent of a large database of standardized job analysis data, McCormick and his colleagues (see McCormick et al., 1972, and McCormick, Denisi, & Shaw, 1979) operationalized what came to be called job component validity using the PAQ. These studies used job-level information from the U.S. Employment Service's validation research on the General Aptitude Test Battery (GATB). Job components in the form of PAQ dimension scores for jobs included in GATB validity studies were used to predict a variety of parameters, including validity. The resulting regression equations can be used to predict these parameters for other jobs analyzed with the PAQ to develop test batteries that could then be linked to commercially available tests (see Hoffman, Rashkovsky, & D'Egidio, 2007, for additional details). Subsequent research using O*NET parameters has extended these findings to the O*NET job analytic model and included personality constructs in the predictions.

Alternative but related conceptualizations of synthetic validity have used psychometric equations to accomplish the buildup process. There often is a need to implement selection processes for multiple related jobs for which there are too few incumbents in each job to conduct criterion-related validity studies. Synthetic validation focuses on common work behaviors (job components) across jobs in a single study rather than the requirements of each job separately in multiple studies. This method is particularly useful when a group of jobs under consideration has many job components in common and assumes that validity with respect to job components is job invariant.

An important advantage of synthetic validation is its potential application to future jobs having components similar to those included in existing validity research. Based on data collected in the original validation study, it is possible to estimate the validity of a new test battery for a job that does not yet exist. The success of this strategy hinges on the job analysis. The new job must be analyzed using a methodology consistent with and relevant to the job components identified in the original study. For this reason, careful consideration should be given to designing a synthetic validity study of the job components expected to be part of future jobs and the need to ensure coverage of these components in the initial research.

Although synthetic validation is not mentioned in the *Guidelines*, it is recognized by the *Principles* as an acceptable methodological strategy for generalizing validity. Interestingly, Johnson (2007) points out that the synthetic validity approach is described in the operational definition of construct validity provided in the *Guidelines*. To this extent, the methodological approach is circuitously addressed. However, some caution is warranted in situations where there is a need to rely on judgment rather than empirical data as a basis for validity estimates. The *Guidelines* are clear that judgmental evidence is inadequate for supporting the use of measures of psychological constructs. Although the risks may be small if the job in question includes a small number of incumbents or if little hiring is expected, it may be prudent to conduct follow-up criterion research if it becomes feasible to do so.

The legal precedent for the defensibility of synthetic validation approaches is limited. Although job component validity and validity generalization have been successfully defended in some court cases, other applications of synthetic validity have not been challenged. Despite the fact that the approach is largely untested with respect to defensibility, it is helpful that the approach is grounded in sound job analysis and consistent with standards of professional practice.

Notable deficiencies exist in our current understanding of synthetic validation. For example, studies have tended to find that synthetic validity equations developed for one job lead to similar results when applied to another even when the job components might be expected to differ. This lack of discriminant validity may (along with other criticisms inevitable in many validation studies) undermine the credibility of a particular application of synthetic validation. However, as one reviewer of this chapter noted, the lack of discriminant validity is consistent with findings from validity generalization research that tests (especially cognitive ability measures) predict performance quite robustly across specific job tasks; as such, it may provide evidence supporting synthetic validation. That most synthetic validity research has focused on cognitive, perceptual, and psychomotor measures is noteworthy. Although more recent research has incorporated other measures such as personality constructs, the literature is not extensive concerning the application of synthetic validation techniques. However, despite its limitations, synthetic validation remains an important alternative validation approach that should be given serious consideration when selection processes must be developed for a variety of related jobs with limited numbers of incumbents.

Meta-Analytic Validation Evidence

Meta-analysis refers to mathematical techniques for combining the results of individual research studies to allow scientists to draw more general conclusions. These techniques are widely used across many scientific disciplines and offer great power in increasing our understanding and knowledge base. In the assessment arena, one of the primary uses of meta-analysis has been to combine validation studies to estimate with greater precision the actual relationships of assessment processes to subsequent performance. Based on meta-analytic findings, industrial-organizational psychologists have been able to draw conclusions about the effectiveness of assessments across situations and jobs. We now have a better understanding of the sampling error introduced by small-sample local studies and the limitations in interpreting them. These techniques and the resulting conclusions have come to be known as *validity generalization,* and they have wide-ranging implications for the validation and use of assessments of all kinds, particularly as they may apply to selection.

It is widely accepted in the scientific community that meta-analytic research provides more accurate conclusions concerning the validity of test use than local validation studies do. Relying on meta-analytic research to support test implementation is consistent with applicable professional standards (the *Principles* and the *Standards*) provided that evidence for generalizing to the local situation can be assembled. Although it always makes sense to consider existing meta-analytic evidence when initiating validation research, such evidence is particularly useful in situations in which local validation is not feasible. For example, a common need is to develop a selection program for complex jobs that require strong problem-solving and decision-making skills. However, there are often far too few incumbents to conduct a criterion-related validity study. In these situations it is appropriate to consider supporting test use based on existing research. In the example just noted, the extensive meta-analytic research supporting the use of cognitive testing is particularly relevant.

Those who are deciding whether to rely on meta-analytic research as a validation approach must consider the implications relative to research requirements and professional practice, the difficulty of developing evidence for test use, and the business

Questions to Ask when Considering Meta-Analytic Evidence as a Validation Approach

- How relevant or applicable are previous meta-analyses to the situation at hand?
- What evidence can be assembled to show that existing meta-analytic evidence is applicable to the job in question?
- Are the potential legal risks associated with the approach manageable?

case for balancing quality of evidence with legal risk. Sometimes there is no easy answer.

As a defense in adverse impact cases, meta-analysis has met with mixed success in the courts. Legal risks associated with adopting a meta-analytic strategy for supporting test use are due in part to the fact that the *Guidelines* preceded the widespread use and acceptance of meta-analytic methodology and thus do not explicitly include validity generalization as an appropriate validation strategy. Although the scientific community has embraced validity generalization since the *Guidelines* were published, the *Guidelines* have not been updated to keep pace with the evolution of the research and professional practice. The *Guidelines* do condone reliance on validity studies not conducted by the test user and use of criterion-related validity evidence from other sources. Employers, however, have the burden of providing evidence that the underlying validation studies were conducted in a manner consistent with the technical standards of the *Guidelines* and that the jobs examined in the studies are substantially similar to the target jobs (see the previous discussion of transporting validity evidence).

In supporting test use based on meta-analytic findings, some may choose to make their case entirely on the availability and quality of existing meta-analyses rather than organization-specific research. Such arguments might well be made for cognitive ability measures given that such tests have been found to predict performance across virtually all types of jobs studied in the empirical literature and that choosing tests that clearly measure the constructs is a relatively simple matter. With this sort of argument, job content becomes irrelevant. This approach clearly carries greater risk if it is the sole justification for test use. A more conservative (and prudent) approach, and one that better conforms to the *Guidelines,* is to develop evidence to link the target job to those included in meta-analytic research based on similarity of work behaviors.

When possible, a systematic approach for demonstrating the relationship between a target job and jobs included in a meta-analysis is needed to document that the jobs are substantially similar. The basis of this strategy is an analysis of the jobs in sufficient detail to compare the target job to those included in existing meta-analyses. Reliance on existing standardized methods for comparing jobs may provide an organizing framework around which a generalizability argument may be developed. This sort of systematic approach is not necessarily straightforward. Although a meta-analysis may describe the types of jobs included (often placing them in categories), the information included may be too general to allow a clear demonstration of job similarity at a level of detail sufficient to address requirements of the *Guidelines.* To deal with this problem, it may be beneficial to acquire original studies used in a meta-analysis or contact meta-analytic researchers to gain a better understanding of how studies were classified—for example, what categories of jobs (say, clerical, managerial, or sales) were referenced in the meta-analysis.

Some Key Questions in Managing Legal Risk

- Is the level of exposure too great to warrant sole reliance on meta-analysis as a basis for test use?
- Does the quality of evidence available present a compelling case for test use?
- Can the various components of the selection process be combined in a manner that will minimize the potential for adverse impact?
- Is it possible to set cut scores (or use score bands) to minimize adverse impact?

Characteristics of the meta-analysis itself also may have important implications. At a basic level, the quality and scope of a meta-analysis are relevant considerations. Practitioners should seek to determine whether the meta-analysis was conducted based on a broad and representative sample of the job or job family in question and whether procedures were consistent with current accepted practice (for example, accounting for nonpublication bias). It may also be useful to consider whether the tests and criteria in the meta-analyses are comparable to available tests and existing criteria in the current situation. Finally, meta-analysis applied to assessments that measure identifiable constructs, such as cognitive ability or personality assessments, would appear to lend themselves more directly to validity generalization arguments than those targeted to methods and techniques (assessment centers, structured interviews, and work samples, for example) that do not measure the same things each time they are implemented.

The types of jobs being considered may affect the risks associated with the use of meta-analyses. For example, meta-analytic research suggests that job complexity moderates the relationship between cognitive ability and performance, with larger relationships observed for more complex jobs. Thus, there may be less risk associated with implementing cognitive tests for jobs of a complex nature (for example, managers, technical specialists, and other professionals).

Just as the type of job may have implications for legal risk, so may the type of assessment instrument. Measures that have consistently demonstrated adverse impact in previous use are likely to carry greater risk potential. Use of cut scores that screen out large numbers of applicants will exacerbate risks further. In the current legal environment, it may be prudent to augment meta-analytic evidence with other validity generalization methods, such as transportability or job component validity, or to conduct local validation research in the event it becomes feasible.

Developing New Evidence

Of course, the traditional strategies described previously provide new or additional evidence for the validity of assessments, but other approaches for developing new evidence also exist.

In the next section we first discuss an alternative approach for carrying out traditional validation research and then turn our attention to the somewhat difficult and troubling concept of construct validation.

Conducting Consortium Studies: Sharing the Trouble and the Costs

Empirical validation research can be expensive and time-consuming, and it is subject to technical constraints in terms of sample sizes, prior selection, and criterion development and collection. When an organization faces substantial issues of technical capability and resource availability, one approach may be to pool the resources of multiple organizations. A consortium may allow conducting empirical validation with larger populations of employees or applicants and may provide greater variation within the samples on the constructs measured. The basic and ancillary costs (both monetary and organizational) for data collection activities may be shared, reducing the burden on any particular employer. The *Guidelines* actually encourage such "cooperative studies" (sec. 8.A), and the *Principles* acknowledge consortia as viable venues for empirical validation research.

For this discussion, consortium or cooperative studies are those in which independent organizations join together without having other mutual obligations beyond the research. Thus, we are not including circumstances in which multiple units of an organization cooperate in conducting validation research. Perhaps the most common situations in which consortia studies have been conducted are professional groups developing credentialing examinations, organizations in a common industry with highly similar jobs or groups of jobs, and test publishers that provide various inducements to solicit cooperation from organizations during test development research efforts. Tippins and Macey (2007) note: "A validation study conducted in a consortium need not require exactly identical positions, although 'common interests' almost always involve similar positions across organizations. Theoretically, at least, different positions containing similar components (such as knowledge, skills, abilities, or personal characteristics or similar job dimensions like communications requirements) might also be the foundation for a consortium-based synthetic validation study" (p. 233).

Once a consortium group has been identified, the organizations must reach agreement on a variety of issues, some allocation and some legal. Allocation decisions consider relative sizes of organizations, alternative contributions in terms of HR staff time and in-house expertise, and particular organizational circumstances. Among the potential legal issues are the obligations of members of the consortium after completion of the study (for example, response in the event of challenge, record keeping, test security), ownership of data collected, and ownership of assessment tools developed in the research.

As an example, eight member companies of a national industry organization participated in a consortium project to develop and validate physical ability tests for construction jobs. At the completion of the study, other members of the organization sought to use the tests. A formal process to allow transport of the validation research was developed, and the participants had to reach agreement on the costs to new users, whether those costs should be allocated back to the original participants, and what contractual obligations new users would have to the participants in terms of how the tests would be implemented.

One of the reasons cooperative studies fail is that they require sustained effort over relatively long periods of time. Much time and effort are needed to collect job analysis data, search for alternatives, identify or develop appropriate assessment instruments, design common criteria for use in the research, collect test and criterion data, conduct data analyses, develop implementation options, and prepare reports documenting the validation evidence. If one or more of the consortium members have professional expertise in validation research, members must agree regarding their time commitments to the research. Using external organizations such as industry trade groups, professional organizations, or consulting firms to manage the detailed planning and execution of consortia is a common solution.

Consortia studies have a number of advantages:

- Availability of larger sample sizes to make criterion-related research feasible
- Ability to share resources such as technical expertise, job analysis information, and existing assessment tools

- Sharing direct project costs, such as consulting fees, test purchase, and project management
- Reducing indirect costs for each participating organization such as employee and supervisor time and operational disruptions
- Explicit recognition in the *Uniform Guidelines*
- Improved defensibility due to sufficient resources to perform research with particular thoroughness

The challenges of this strategy tend to be practical in nature, having to do with both technical issues such as job similarity and procedural concerns such as project management and equitable cost sharing:

- Defining job similarity across participants to allow inclusion in or require exclusion from the research
- Obtaining common and comparable performance criteria across participants
- Planning, coordinating, and managing research complexities
- Resolving technical and practical issues among professionals from different organizations
- Resolving cost allocation issues
- Addressing concerns regarding protection of intellectual property, appearances of improper restraint of trade, or loss of competitive advantage in hiring
- Dealing with implementation issues such as test security, allowing new users, and applying the test differently across organizations
- Resolving legal issues and obligations to provide information

Although the *Guidelines* support the use of cooperative studies, they also impose limitations and requirements. In particular, they indicate there should not be "variables in the user's situation which are likely to affect validity significantly" (*Uniform Guidelines*, sec. 8.B). It is not clear what those variables might be; however, such things as job similarity, differences in organizational structures, and variations in the demographics are likely candidates for scrutiny. The *Guidelines* also include additional requirements for documentation of cooperative studies beyond those already

specified for criterion-related research. In choosing to participate in a cooperative study, organizations must of course weigh
the costs and benefits. Such evaluations should include input
from professionals in HR management, testing, legal, and operations management.

*Validation Evidence Based on Knowledge of What Is Being
Measured (Construct Evidence)*
Practitioners rarely view employee selection research as an
opportunity for construct validation. The organizational reality is often one of limited time and limited resources and one
in which demonstrating broad theoretical support for selection
processes is less important than finding a practical and legally
defensible research strategy. In many organizations, the breadth
of the concept of construct evidence and its lack of a straightforward path or formula for completion quickly eliminate this
strategy from consideration. This lack of popularity is unsurpris-
ing given the warnings in the *Guidelines* that construct validity
research requires "an extensive and arduous effort" (sec. 14.D.1.).

The traditional notion of construct validation has involved
accumulating evidence that a predictor is a representative sampling of a construct domain, an essential component of the job
performance domain. Part of this process may also involve accumulating evidence that a criterion measure adequately samples
the performance domain, the predictor is related to the criterion
measure, and, by inference, the predictor is related to job performance. Thus, construct validity evidence includes traditional
content-based research and criterion-related research, in addition
to broader research strategies typically discussed as construct validation, such as multitrait/multimethod (MTMM) analyses, review
of previous research concerning constructs, and experimental
research. Construct validation can indeed be viewed as the primary validation strategy to be pursued (which may include traditional criterion and content-oriented research). In fact, extensive
construct validity research, in addition to typical criterion- or
content-oriented studies, may be justifiable even from a practical perspective when the cost of bad hiring decisions is particularly high. These situations notwithstanding, time and resource
limitations are often such that practitioners will consider more

conventional approaches as primary. Realistically, it more often makes sense to consider construct-based research as a supplementary approach to enhance the overall quality of validity evidence produced by a more conventional validation study. As such, for any validation effort, we should look for opportunities to pursue relevant construct-related validity evidence and avoid limiting our focus exclusively on a single type of validity. In the most practical sense, the application of construct-based research is really about considering opportunities to build evidence for key linkages between the job, the performance domain, key constructs, and predictor and criterion measures—for example:

- Identifying constructs underlying performance based on job analysis and relevant literature
- Developing measures using procedures to sample representatively from constructs of interest
- Identifying or creating an assessment to sample from the performance domain (content validation)
- Defining criterion measures by sampling behaviors from the performance domain and identifying groups of related behaviors using statistical procedures such as factor analysis or cluster analysis to provide evidence that items are linked to specific construct domains
- Obtaining estimates of criterion-related validities from testing experts as an additional source of data when a criterion study is not feasible or to supplement weak criterion studies
- Using expert judgment to link predictors and performance domains to constructs
- Developing and confirming measurement and structural models to provide evidence for the relationship between predictor and criterion constructs
- Generalizing validity evidence from other research using methods discussed in this chapter, such as meta-analyses, transportability research, and synthetic validity
- Examining relationships between predictor and criterion measures within a nomological network to demonstrate that predictor or criterion measures reflect constructs of interest

Because there is no simple, by-the-book approach for applied, construct-oriented research, procedures in any given situation depend on the selection process under consideration, the purpose of the research, and, most important, the degree to which the goal is to rely on construct-oriented evidence as the sole strategy for supporting test use. There also are legal implications regarding the choice of research methods. Not only do the *Guidelines* require the presence of extensive research and documentation in construct validation, they also require criterion-related validity research to support inferences concerning constructs or mental processes such as intelligence or personality. These requirements mean that in some cases, construct-oriented evidence may be deemed unacceptable by the courts as the sole justification for test use, despite the theoretical position that it is constructs for which validity evidence is being sought in every situation.

In some situations, construct-oriented research may be extensive enough to provide strong support for test use, particularly when it includes, among other things, strong statistical evidence, such as transportability research or meta-analytic evidence, to support validity generalization. Clearly legal exposure in terms of adverse impact or large-scale testing programs may affect decisions regarding the sufficiency of construct evidence. An additional consideration may be the difficulty of explaining or summarizing this type of evidence in a way that is easily understood by the courts. The fact that the *Guidelines* provide less of a formula for this approach emphasizes this point.

Selecting a Strategy

Given the number of options for conducting validation research, the choice of a specific strategy for a given situation can be complex. Understanding the return on investment for the validation approach can help guide the choice; however, strong validation strategies are likely to result when a variety of factors are considered within the context of the assessment application.

Return on Investment for Validation Research

One of the first questions managers often ask at the outset of validation projects is, "Do we really have to go through all of this effort and expense?" In part they are asking if there will be a return on their investment. Traditionally HR practitioners have answered this question in two ways: they have relied on the legal argument ("The law says we have to do this or we'll be in trouble" or "The legal department says we have to do this or we can't use a test"), or they have tried to provide some dollar value to show the benefits of using tests (though the real question is often not about whether to test, but why they have to go through what they sometimes refer to as "all this trouble about validation").

Both responses are in some sense reasonable. Indeed, it is clear that if assessment tools have adverse impact relative to some protected group, we are obligated to provide evidence of job relatedness and business necessity. The legal and regulatory environment surrounding assessment in the employment context has its share of the big sticks associated with assessment, but other sticks also include the business imperatives of hiring or promoting the best candidates. Failure to accomplish this task efficiently and effectively can be as negative as a bad investment decision or failure to source parts or equipment properly.

The payoffs from identifying and selecting qualified employees can be substantial in terms of improved productivity, reduced errors, lower turnover, and competitive advantage. The problem is that for payoffs to occur, the assessment tools must predict outcomes of interest. A rational decision maker would not undertake to purchase new equipment, institute a quality assurance process, or invest in a new line of business without evidence that valued outcomes have a reasonable probability of occurrence. Similarly, a company should not rely on a selection procedure without evidence that it is likely to increase the probability of improving selection outcomes over what would be obtained otherwise. Thus, it is important to define successful outcomes of a new selection procedure and then evaluate the evidence showing it produces those outcomes.

We have sophisticated methods for estimating the utility of selection tools in terms of financial benefits. Although in some cases, these methods produce estimates that (no matter how mathematically correct) do not seem credible to managers, using conservative assumptions when calculating utility may improve the credibility of estimates. Moreover, if technical methods of utility analysis are considered too difficult to explain to stakeholders, it is fairly straightforward to make a case for the cost of poor hiring decisions through a basic demonstration of the cumulative costs of different stages of the hiring process: sourcing, selecting, onboarding, and training.

A Balancing Act

Although the arguments that succeed in getting the research approved and funded are clearly important, they do not represent the range of relevant considerations for choosing a validation strategy and evaluating validity evidence. A more sophisticated rationale must acknowledge that validation research is an applied and practical endeavor in its own right and speaks directly to a business need. From an applied perspective, the type and amount of validation research undertaken in a given application may in part be a function of the value of such research based on relative costs and benefits. In addition to the question of basic feasibility, practitioners need to consider potential costs beyond obvious budget constraints when deciding among the different validation approaches described here, including time to complete the research project, urgency of implementation, difficulty or time to design complicated research strategies, and challenges in explaining sophisticated research methods to stakeholders. Nevertheless, these costs must be balanced against the benefits of finding an effective approach to address the needs of the situation, performance and productivity gains associated with effective selection decisions, the availability of sound research to win stakeholder support, legal defensibility, and even professional integrity in ensuring that new assessment programs serve their intended purposes.

In Table 21.1 we have summarized some of the key issues with which researchers must deal in selecting a strategy or strategies for developing validation evidence.

Even such a brief overview highlights the fact that there are no perfect solutions; every option presents trade-offs. In many cases evaluation of these trade-offs can lead users to the best strategy for their particular situation and organization; in others, it may be necessary to use multiple strategies to accumulate adequate evidence to support the inferences users wish to draw from their assessments.

Table 21.1. Summary of Research Strategies

Strategy	Overview	Advantages	Disadvantages	Comments
Criterion-related validity	Relies on empirically correlating assessment (predictors) with job performance (criteria)	• Provides a concrete and appealing statistical metric (correlation) • Covered in *Guidelines* • Most acceptable to enforcement agencies	• Difficult to obtain sufficiently large sample sizes • Difficult to obtain adequate criterion measures • Small sample sizes and other statistical issues may limit use	• Enforcement agencies may view this strategy as the gold standard of research models. • May be necessary when evaluating constructs or mental processes.
Content-related validity	Relies on showing that predictor is an adequate sample of the job content (tasks or KSAs)	• Covered in *Guidelines* • Acceptable to enforcement agencies • Does not have the sample size problems associated with criterion-related strategy	• *Guidelines* caution against use with tests measuring latent constructs or mental processes • No single metric to estimate level of validity	• Requires detailed job analysis and, done right, may require level of effort similar to criterion studies.
Transport of validity	Relies on showing that a job to which validity is to be transported is substantially similar to a job for which a criterion-related study has already been conducted	• Covered in *Guidelines* • Acceptable to enforcement agencies • Much less expensive than conducting a new criterion-related study • Useful alternative for smaller organizations or when sample sizes are inadequate	• May be difficult to obtain permission to use another organization's study • May expose original study to scrutiny • Definition of "substantially similar" is not clear • Lack of availability or inadequacy of job analysis or other data from original study	• Courts seem open to arguments for validity based on previous research provided it is carefully constructed and documented.

Synthetic validity	Relies on methodological approaches for building up overall validity estimates for specific jobs or job families based on their job components	• Useful technique when selection processes must be developed for multiple related jobs • Allows empirical research with limited numbers of incumbents in any one job • Can provide a method for estimating validity for future jobs	• Not covered in *Guidelines* • Caution is warranted if using judgment data as a basis for validity estimates • Credibility of the common finding of similar validity estimates across different jobs • Limited past research or application to personality constructs (compared to abilities)	• Strategy is grounded in sound job analysis and consistent with professional practice; however, there is limited legal precedent, particularly considering the variations possible in different applications of the methodology.
Meta-analytic validation evidence	Relies on methods to mathematically combine results from individual studies to draw conclusions regarding validity for a particular job, class of jobs or occupations, or test constructs	• Useful when local validation is not feasible • Overcomes the issue of sampling error in small-sample local studies • Widely accepted in the scientific community as providing more accurate conclusions concerning validity than local studies • Availability of considerable meta-analytic evidence in the research literature	• Not covered in *Guidelines* • Has met with mixed success in courts • Can be difficult to show that a specific job is substantially similar to those in the meta-analysis • Requires evaluation of the methodology and characteristics of the meta-analysis (and whether the underlying studies were consistent with the *Guidelines*)	• Users should seek to develop a sound evidentiary link between the target job and those included in the meta-analysis. It is not prudent to rely casually on previous research only—particularly when there is substantial legal risk due to adverse impact or high-volume testing.

(Continued)

Table 21.1. Summary of Research Strategies (*Continued*)

Strategy	Overview	Advantages	Disadvantages	Comments
Consortium studies	Relies on multiple organizations pooling resources, technical capabilities, and employees and applicants to conduct empirical validation research	• *Guidelines* appear to encourage research of this type • Pooling resources saves time and reduces expenses • Enables the sharing of limited technical skills or resources to conduct research • Enables empirical research with only small numbers of employees in an organization	• Issues arise concerning responsibilities and obligations of consortium members (for example, in response to challenge, test record keeping, test security) and ownership of data and assessment tools • Project management and planning for a sustained cooperative effort over time may create some challenges • Job dissimilarity and incomparability of performance criteria across organizations may complicate research	• A common solution for dealing with project management challenges and clarifying member responsibilities is to use external organizations such as industry trade groups, professional organizations, or consulting firms to manage the detailed planning and execution of consortia.

| Construct validity research | Relies on accumulating evidence that a predictor is a representative sampling of a construct domain, which is an essential component of the job performance domain | • Can enhance the quality of more common approaches such as content- and criterion-related validity studies
• Improves legal defensibility when used to augment other approaches
• In some circumstances, may be sufficient to be the sole support for test use, particularly when strong statistical evidence exists (for example, transportability studies, meta-analyses) | • Not a simple by-the-book approach
• Time and resource limitations often preclude adoption as the primary validation strategy
• May require criterion-related research when applied to measures of latent constructs or mental processes | • Although construct validity probably is not widely viewed as a primary validation strategy, there are great benefits to thinking about validity more broadly than in terms of specific types of validity. Considering opportunities for construct-based research helps keep practitioners focused on the ultimate purpose of validation: to accumulate evidence supporting the inferences to be drawn from assessments. |

At some point in the decision-making process the balancing act can be summarized by two key questions:

- What validity evidence do we have and need?
- How should we leverage what we have or get what we need, given our situational constraints?

The first question involves an evaluation of the quality of job analysis and validity evidence we have (or plan to obtain), as well as a determination of key vulnerabilities or weaknesses in our research. Although the strength of the evidence will be the primary consideration, the degree of legal risk associated with the implementation of the assessment process also must be considered. The validation strategy also may affect the answer. For example, we may decide that an alternative validation method such as synthetic validity or transportability is inadequate as the sole support for test use. The second question involves a practical evaluation of the best way to use or obtain needed evidence given resources such as available staff, SMEs, time, and costs. The answer affects the methods pursued and where we choose to focus resources in terms of building an evidentiary case for validity. Of course, we may judge that what needs to be done cannot be achieved with existing resources, indicating that it may be appropriate to attempt to acquire additional resources, cooperation, or assistance.

Answers to these questions will not always be straightforward. It often will be a matter of professional judgment as to whether our validity evidence should be considered adequate in a given situation. Judgment comes into play not only in relation to the decision that available evidence supports the inferences we wish to make, but also in situations where there is an obvious divergence of professional standards and legal guidelines. In the end, our goal is to choose one or more validation strategies that best meet the organization's needs in consideration of the full range of costs and benefits. In some cases, it will be difficult to find the right balance of all of these factors. Regardless of the chosen validation strategy, there should be significant focus on research design and execution based on professional standards with appropriate consideration of how legal vulnerabilities might be mitigated.

References

Equal Employment Opportunity Commission, Civil Service Commission, Department of Labor, & Department of Justice. (1978). Uniform guidelines on employee selection procedures. *Federal Register, 43*(166), 38295–38309.

Gibson, W. M., & Caplinger, J. A. (2007). Transportation of validation results. In S. M. McPhail (Ed.), *Alternative validation strategies: Developing new and leveraging existing validation evidence* (pp. 29–81). San Francisco: Jossey-Bass.

Guion, R. M. (1998). *Assessment, measurement, and prediction for personnel decisions.* Mahwah, NJ: Erlbaum.

Hoffman, C. C., Rashkovsky, B., & D'Egidio, E. L. (2007). Job component validity: Background, current research, and applications. In S. M. McPhail (Ed.), *Alternative validation strategies: Developing new and leveraging existing validation evidence* (pp. 82–121). San Francisco: Jossey-Bass.

Johnson, J. W. (2007). Synthetic validity: A technique of use (finally). In S. M. McPhail (Ed.), *Alternative validation strategies: Developing new and leveraging existing validation evidence* (pp. 122–158). San Francisco: Jossey-Bass.

Landy, F. J. (1986). Stamp collecting versus science. *American Psychologist, 41*(11), 1183–1192.

Lawshe, C. H. (1952). Employee selection. *Personnel Psychology, 6,* 31–34.

McCormick, E. J., DeNisi, A. S., & Shaw, J. B. (1979). Use of the Position Analysis Questionnaire for establishing the job component validity of tests. *Journal of Applied Psychology, 64,* 51–56.

McCormick, E. J., Jeanneret, P. R., & Mecham, R. C. (1972). A study of job characteristics and job dimensions based on the Position Analysis Questionnaire (PAQ). *Journal of Applied Psychology, 56,* 347–368.

McPhail, S. M. (Ed.) (2007). *Alternative validation strategies: Developing new and leveraging existing validation evidence.* San Francisco: Jossey-Bass.

Messick, S. (1988). The once and future issues of validity: Assessing the meaning and consequences of measurement. In H. Wainer & H. I. Braun (Eds.), *Test validity* (pp. 33–45). Mahwah, NJ: Erlbaum.

Murphy, K. R. (2009). Content validation is useful for many things, but validity isn't one of them. *Industrial and Organizational Psychology: Perspectives on Science and Practice, 2(4),* 453–464.

Peterson, N. G., Mumford, M. D., Borman, W. C., Jeanneret, P. R., & Fleishman, E. A. (Eds.). (1999). *An occupational information system for the 21st century: The development of the O*NET.* Washington, DC: American Psychological Association.

Primoff, E. S. (1959). Empirical validation of the J-coefficient. *Personnel Psychology, 12*, 413–418.

Society for Industrial and Organizational Psychology. (2003). *Principles for the validation and use of personnel selection procedures.* Bowling Green, OH: Author.

Tippins, N. T., & Macey, W. H. (2007). Consortium studies. In S. M. McPhail (Ed.), *Alternative validation strategies: Developing new and leveraging existing validation evidence* (pp. 233–251). San Francisco: Jossey-Bass.

CHAPTER 22

ADDRESSING THE FLAWS IN OUR ASSESSMENT DECISIONS

James L. Outtz

This chapter reviews some common problems with the implementation of selection procedures and the resulting selection decisions. The issues raised here stem from two basic premises. The first is that the classical model does not accurately represent the work environment that exists in most organizations. The second is that the assessment tools often used in organizations may lack sufficient validity evidence to support the inferences typically drawn from them. If these premises are correct, they create moral and ethical dilemmas for users of assessment that they are often ill prepared to handle. This chapter discusses each premise and then describes the ethical and moral consequences, along with suggestions for resolving them.

The focus of this chapter is on those who implement assessment in organizations: practitioners who apply the science of industrial-organizational (I-O) psychology and managers and human resource (HR) professionals in organizations who design and implement decision-making systems that incorporate assessments. Professionals who work in this arena face selection situations that affect the lives of thousands of individuals each day. In today's world, these professionals must consider the consequences of their work from multiple perspectives: organizational goals, legal requirements, social values (such as diversity in the workforce), and social consequences (such as the perpetuation of class differences and disproportionate distribution of poverty by race and ethnicity). The wide-ranging impact of selection decisions based on assessment instruments can exacerbate the moral and ethical conundrums that frequently arise when selection systems operate.

The Flawed Classical Selection Model

According to the classical selection model, criterion-related validity supports the accuracy of inferences drawn from a selection tool. This model is typically represented by a bivariate distribution with test scores along the x-axis and performance arrayed along the y-axis. "Test" in this case is defined broadly to mean any instrument designed to predict job performance. The basic model is illustrated in Figure 22.1.

When each person's test score is plotted against job performance, evidence of validity is said to exist if job performance increases as test scores increase. This classical model appears straightforward. Obviously the applicability and utility of the model depend on what constitutes the test and the manner in which job performance is defined. This in turn determines the applicability of the model to a given selection situation.

Figure 22.1. Classical Selection Model

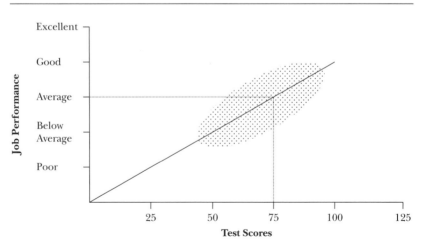

Job performance, for example, is multidimensional with any number of facets, each of which may be more or less important depending on the values of the organization. The content of a given test or test battery may or may not reflect all or even many of the various facets of job performance. Practical considerations typically limit the number of relevant attributes measured by any given test or selection procedure. Therefore, not all or even most of the facets of performance are typically measured by a test depicted in the model. This creates a disconnect between the model and the actual selection situation. In reality, several or even many tests would probably be needed to cover all of the performance or criterion space. In addition, if all of these tests were part of a selection process, each applicant would no doubt perform differently on each test. Thus, each applicant would vary with regard to predicted performance based on all of the predictor-performance relationships. In the classical selection model, however, each applicant is depicted as having a single score based on one test or composite test battery. This will result in each candidate being placed in one of four quadrants. The quadrants can be shown by building on Figure 22.1. If the employer sets as the goal hiring individuals who will perform at average level or higher, the passing score on the test could be set at 75—the point where performance is predicted to be average or higher. Four categories of applicants result:

- *True positives*—applicants who score at or above the cutoff and perform at or above average on the job
- *True negatives*—applicants who score below the cutoff and who perform below average on the job
- *False positives*—applicants who score above the cutoff but below average on the job
- *False negatives*—applicants who score below the cutoff but above average on the job

These quadrants are shown in Figure 22.2.

The problem with the model in Figure 22.2 is that each candidate will not simply fit in one of four quadrants. If the full set of relevant predictors were used, there would in fact be many sets of four quadrants for each applicant. That is, an applicant may

Figure 22.2. Four Categories of Applicant Results

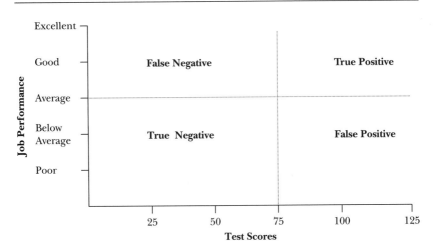

be a true positive based on one predictor and its relationship to a specific facet of job performance and a true negative based on another predictor, and so on.

A more realistic model is shown in Figure 22.3, where quadrant patterns for four applicants are based on four predictors. Obviously this illustration could be expanded based on the actual number of applicants and relevant predictors.

Figure 22.3 shows why the classical selection model may result in flawed assessment decisions. This occurs because assuming assessment decisions are valid even though they are based on an incomplete representation of the selection situation will usually result in erroneous conclusions. Unfortunately much of the best practices literature used by those who develop and implement selection procedures is based on this flawed model. For example, the model has been used to support the practice of establishing cognitive ability tests as the centerpiece of any selection system. Studies showing that cognitive ability tests alone are significantly correlated with measures of job performance have been used to support the conclusion that cognitive ability is the "best" or most important predictor of performance for almost all jobs. But these conclusions are unwarranted if they do not simultaneously consider facets of job performance that exist, the relative importance

Figure 22.3. Quadrant Patterns for Four Applicants Based on Four Predictors

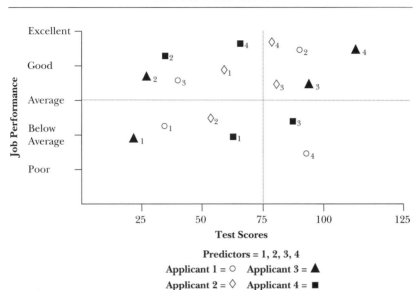

Predictors = 1, 2, 3, 4
Applicant 1 = ○   Applicant 3 = ▲
Applicant 2 = ◇   Applicant 4 = ■

of each facet to job success, the number of facets accounted for in the selection process, and the accuracy of each predictor with regard to each facet.

Even if, for example, we were to take the four tests shown in Figure 22.3, put them in a composite battery, and use a statistical approach such as multiple regression to weight the various components, this would still not solve the problem of determining which individual has the ideal combination of predictor scores. If we consider further that each of the tests in Figure 22.3 probably measures more constructs than intended and the unintended constructs may correlate with demographic variables such as race, ethnicity, or gender (see, for example, Newman, Hanges, & Outtz, 2007), it becomes apparent that the classical selection model may do little more than scratch the surface with regard to the types of issues practitioners face daily.

The disconnect between what classical selection theory purports to demonstrate and what it actually demonstrates has led to a number of serious misconceptions about the benefits, appropriateness, and legal defensibility of many selection procedures.

As an example, some managers believe that a statistically significant relationship between a predictor and a measure (any measure) of job performance is sufficient validity evidence for the following conclusions:

- The predictor measures a construct that is important to job performance.
- The higher a person scores on the predictor, the better he or she will perform on the job as a whole.
- The person with a higher score on the predictor is more qualified than anyone with a lower score.

The misconceptions result in flawed assessment decisions that include setting a high cut score (without consideration of predictor underrepresentation) to "get the very best performers" or making selections in strict rank order as a means of ensuring "merit-based selection." Such decisions have very little probability of producing the desired outcomes. Selecting individuals with high scores on a given predictor will yield higher job performance only to the extent that the aspect of performance predicted is necessary and sufficient to materially affect individual performance overall and linearly related to organizational effectiveness. Thus, typical selection decisions may simply give the illusion of merit. More important, the flawed decisions and the incorrect premises on which they are based create serious ethical problems for practitioners.

Ethical Problems Created by a Flawed Model

Many practitioners may be aware of the flaws in the classical selection model. Yet they must constantly consider the degree to which the misconceptions created by the flawed model should influence the way they develop selection systems and implement them. As an example, in deciding on the components of a selection procedure under development, practitioners are (or should be) aware of the types and combinations of predictors that produce similar validity but may differ substantially in the level of adverse impact they produce against different demographic groups. The practitioner must decide whether to inform his or her employer or client of such matters. The practitioner could simply take the position, for example, that the selection procedure has some validity based on the classical model and nothing else really matters. Or the practitioner may determine that a composite battery has validity based on a regression-weighted paradigm. The weighted paradigm, however, may have severe adverse impact. Is it ethical for the practitioner to reject use of an alternative weighting procedure that may have similar validity and portray the regression-weighted model as the only appropriate approach based on "merit"? This may be a particularly thorny issue in public sector selection. Many jurisdictions are constrained by state law, civil service rules, or labor agreements with regard to the content of their selection procedures and the weighting of selection system components. Such constraints may not be problematic if the resulting selection process is free of adverse impact. If, however, the results of the selection procedure have adverse impact, meaning that certain demographic groups are disproportionately rejected, the fact that the structure and implementation of the process are based on civil service rules or labor agreements will not suffice as a defense against Title VII discrimination claims.

Suppose the practitioner determines prior to implementation of a test battery with weights set by labor agreement that the weighting structure is not consistent with the proper weighting based on a job analysis. Assume further that the labor agreement weights will almost certainly result in adverse impact. Should the practitioner agree to go ahead and implement the process using the labor agreement weights? If the process ends up having adverse impact, should the practitioner recommend that the weights be changed to those supported by the job analysis? These are not only legal issues; they are also moral issues given that adverse impact could mean the unwarranted rejection of applicants from underrepresented groups. Moreover, these individuals will be led to believe they are less qualified as a racial group and may be perceived by others in a similar light.

Users of assessments have a responsibility to keep abreast of research literature on the types of assessments that are less likely to produce subgroup differences. Practitioners in this area have a clear legal obligation to search for alternatives under the *Uniform*

Guidelines on Employee Section Procedures (Equal Employment Opportunity Commission, Civil Service Commission, Department of Labor, & Department of Justice, 1978). There is also an ethical obligation for practitioners to keep abreast of the research literature to facilitate such a search. If employers, applicants, and other stakeholders believe that any difference between scores on a selection device is sufficient grounds to consider the higher-scoring applicant more qualified, then assessment professionals also have an obligation to explain why such inferences may be inappropriate. Some suggestions are offered below as to how these issues might be resolved.

Resolving the Moral and Ethical Issues

Two critical activities must be carried out in order to minimize or directly address the moral and ethical issues described above. First, job analysis methodology must be employed that goes beyond what is typically described in texts and published research on selection. Second, practitioners must become more adept at converting job analysis results into selection procedures that best mirror the requirements of the job.

An analysis of work or job analysis should serve as the foundation for a selection procedure. The question is what should be included as part of the job analysis. The recommendations for job analysis that follow can help address issues regarding selection procedure content, component weighting, and fidelity with the job.

First, learn as much as possible about the context in which the job is performed before analyzing the job. It is often thought that selection system development begins with a job analysis. In actuality, a number of actions should be taken before the job analysis begins in order to maximize the likelihood that all applicants will have a fair opportunity:

- Determine the best sources of information about the job (incumbents, supervisors, peers, subordinates, or others).
- Determine if there are factors that might serve as a hindrance to getting accurate information about the job—for example:
  - Labor-management conflict

- Recent negative activity such as downsizing
- A slow or atypical work cycle such as a seasonal slowdown in production
- Determine which individuals are most knowledgeable about the job and request that they be part of the subject matter expert sample from whom job analysis information is gathered.
- Ensure that initial information (for example, information that subsequently will be included in a job analysis questionnaire) is obtained from a diverse sample in terms of demographics such as race, ethnicity, gender, and tenure. During focus groups, be sure to solicit information from all participants, particularly members of diverse groups. They may be able to provide a different perspective.
- If possible, interview employees individually and in small focus groups. Focus groups allow employees to bounce information off each other, allowing the practitioner to assess the consistency of the information.
- Play devil's advocate with interviewees and challenge the information being given to ensure that employees are not simply telling you what they think you want to hear.

A second approach is to ensure that a range of job information is provided. For example, information regarding the relative importance of major job components (task groups), tasks, work behaviors, knowledge, skills, abilities, and other personal characteristics may be quite helpful. Major job components (task group categories) might be rated to determine their relative importance. Table 22.1 provides an example of how this might be done.

The job tasks for the position in Table 22.1 have been organized into clusters or task groups. You are being asked to distribute two sets of one hundred points each among only these task groups. The first set of one hundred points is allocated according to the relative importance of each task group to the position and the second set of one hundred points is allocated among the task groups according to the relative amount of time spent performing them.

Job tasks might be evaluated as to importance, frequency of performance, and whether they must be performed on the first

Table 22.1. Determining the Relative Importance of Major Job Components for a Settlement Specialist

Average "Importance" Points Assigned to Task Groups		Average "Time Spent" Points Assigned to Task Groups	
Relative Importance Points	Task Group	Relative Time Spent Points	Task Group
32.5	Reviewing and analyzing the purchase and assumption agreement	31.87	Analyzing, documenting, preparing, and processing the settlement
18.5	Preparing for and conducting initial settlement meeting with an assuming institution	28.12	Reviewing and analyzing the purchase and assumption agreement
18.5	Analyzing, documenting, preparing, and processing settlement	12.5	Entering all relevant data, generating reports and relevant documents, producing schedules, and collecting documentation
18.37	Entering all relevant data-generating reports and relevant documents, producing schedules, collecting documentation	11.87	Preparing for and conducting initial settlement meeting with an assuming institution
12.12	Preparing, processing, and funding interim and final settlements	8.12	Preparing, processing, and funding interim and final settlements

day in the position. Rating scales for doing this are exemplified by the following questions that might be put to persons who are knowledgeable about the position:

- How often does an incumbent perform this task?
- How important is this task to effective performance on the job as a whole?
- Is this a task that someone newly hired or appointed to the position would be expected to perform during the first six months on the job? A typical rating scale for assessing task importance might be:

  1 = Not important. Improper task performance results in virtually no error or consequences.

  2 = Minor importance. Improper task performance may result in minor consequences.

  3 = Moderately important. Improper task performance may result in moderate consequences.

  4 = Very important. Improper task performance may result in serious consequences.

  5 = Crucial. Improper task performance may result in very serious consequences.

- Knowledge statements should be evaluated on: importance, whether more of the knowledge leads to better performance, and whether the knowledge must be brought to the job or acquired while in the job and the level of recall, for example. The level of recall becomes important when considering whether an assessment procedure for the position should require participants to respond to test questions from memory. Job analysis questions designed to address such issues might include:

  - How important is this information or knowledge to effective performance in the position?
  - Would more of this information or knowledge result in better overall performance of the job?
  - Is it important that a person have this information or knowledge at the time of hiring or appointment to the position?
  - What level of recall is needed from memory of the specific aspects of this knowledge?

- Abilities can also be rated on factors such as importance and whether they must be brought to the job from the outset.
- Areas of knowledge, skills, abilities, and other personal characteristics (KSAOs) should be linked if possible to the major job components—for example:

Please indicate whether a knowledge, skill, ability, or personal characteristic is needed for each task group using the following rating scale:

2 = Essential. This knowledge, skill, ability, or personal characteristic is essential to the performance of this task group. Without this knowledge, skill, ability, or personal characteristic, an incumbent would not be able to perform these tasks effectively.

1 = Useful. This knowledge, skill, ability, or personal characteristic is useful in performing tasks in this task group but not essential. These tasks could be performed without this knowledge, skill, ability, or personal characteristic, although it would be more difficult or time-consuming.

0 = Not relevant. This knowledge, skill, ability, or personal characteristic is not needed to perform tasks in this task group. Having this knowledge, skill, ability, or personal characteristic would make no difference in the performance of tasks in this task group.

These recommendations are designed to illustrate the level of detail that may be required to address validity and fairness issues regarding a given selection procedure.

The job analysis results should identify the following information:

- The most critical job duties or major job components and the KSAOs needed to perform the position
- The job tasks that must be performed immediately on entering the position and the relative importance of each
- The KSAOs required immediately on entering the position and their relative importance

A proper job analysis is a necessary rather than sufficient basis for establishing that the assessment process is absent of critical flaws. Moreover, the scales described are intended as examples of how job analysis information might be collected. The job analysis information must be properly converted into a selection tool or process that accurately reflects the attributes required on the job.

Converting the Job Analysis into a Selection Process

The practitioner must make a number of important decisions in determining how to convert the job analysis information into a valid selection tool. In making these decisions, the practitioner should keep in mind that the ultimate objective is to predict job performance. Therefore, the definition of *performance* is important. Unfortunately the classical selection model is typically not applied based on the wealth of knowledge in the I-O literature on the multidimensionality of job performance (see for example, Murphy, 2010). In realistic selection situations, the practitioner must consider the relationship between individual performance and organizational effectiveness. Job performance must be considered from multiple perspectives:

- The organization's mission, vision, and values
- The degree to which individual performance translates to organizational effectiveness
- The organization's emphasis on team performance versus individual performance
- The organization's emphasis on contextual performance versus task performance

One decision that must be made is whether to use a commercially available selection device or develop a customized selection tool. Many off-the-shelf tools measure some facet of cognitive ability, and they are most often structured in a multiple-choice format. The primary advantages of using them are that they are relatively inexpensive compared with other devices, they are readily available, and a considerable research literature on their validity exists. There are also disadvantages however. These tests:

- May rely too heavily on research that tends to overestimate the significance of cognitive ability relative to other constructs that underlie individual job performance (Outtz & Newman, 2010; Goldstein, Scherbaum, & Yusko, 2010)

- May too often be supported on the basis of validation research that focuses on individual productivity at the expense of the larger perspective of organizational effectiveness (Murphy, 2010)
- Produce greater adverse impact than other selection devices with similar validity (Sackett & Shen, 2010)
- May produce greater adverse impact than combinations of predictors that have higher validity
- Can produce racial subgroup differences that can be much larger than differences on measures of actual job performance

Even when a paper-and-pencil test is appropriate, it may not be necessary to use only a multiple-choice format. This format is based on a cognitive process known as convergent thinking (Guilford, 1956). In this form of thinking there is usually one conclusion or answer that is considered correct.

Assessment tools formatted on the basis of convergent thinking may produce flawed selection decisions because they are incongruent with the kinds of problem solving used in actual work situations. That is, for many jobs, successful performance depends on divergent thinking: generating multiple answers to a set problem. Assessment decisions based on devices that require convergent thinking, even though successful job performance is a function of both divergent and convergent thinking, may screen out many applicants who in fact would make excellent employees.

There is a way to use the paper-and-pencil medium that incorporates an element of divergent thinking. It requires formatting test questions in what can be called a multiple-list format. In this format, the stem of the question is presented in the usual manner. However, a list of many responses is presented rather than the four or five typically used with multiple-choice items. Rather than selecting the one best answer, the test taker is instructed to choose the set of responses that together best solve the problem. What follows is an example of an item presented in a multiple-choice and a multiple-list format.

The multiple-list format allows the test taker to formulate a strategy rather than choose one answer. Formulating a strategy is probably more in line with what actually happens on the job. The multiple-list format also acknowledges that there may be several

---

Multiple-Choice Format

Choose the single best response: When two coworkers are arguing over financial projections for the upcoming quarter, as their manager, you should:

   a. Ask each coworker to clearly state his or her position.
   b. Instruct the coworkers to stop overreacting.
   c. Figure out the projections yourself.
   d. Tell the coworkers that teamwork is important.

Multiple-List Format

Choose the three responses that together best represent what you as the manager should do: When two coworkers are arguing over financial projections for the upcoming quarter, as their manager you should:

   a. Ask each coworker to clearly state his or her position.
   b. Counsel the coworkers independently.
   c. Instruct the coworkers to stop overreacting.
   d. Figure out the projections yourself.
   e. Document the incident (make a written record of it).
   f. Tell the coworkers that teamwork is important.
   g. Take disciplinary action against both coworkers.
   h. Attempt to clarify what the disagreement is based on.

---

equally effective strategies for solving the problem. This format may be most effective when used as part of a situational judgment test designed to measure attributes such as decision making, interpersonal skills, and flexibility and adaptability.

Beyond the use of off-the-shelf multiple-choice tests, the practitioner must decide what, if any, other assessment tools may be appropriate—for example:

- Personality measures
- Assessment centers
- Biodata inventories
- Accomplishment records

- Interviews
- Work samples
- Situational judgment tests
- Measures of job perception
- Trainability tests

Determining the appropriateness of each category requires consideration of a number of technical questions based on the job analysis. These considerations focus on test characteristics for each component of the process—for example:

- What will be the best medium for presenting test content?
- What will be the best medium through which the test taker is allowed to respond: spoken response, written response, overt action, or something else?
- Will test items be homogeneous (the same kind of response is required for each item) or heterogeneous (an assessment center, for example)?
- Will items have immediate meaning or referent meaning, that is, will they refer to situations or information outside the test itself?
- Will there be many discrete items or one global situation?
- Will the test require cognitive judgment, affective response, or both?

Questions about test characteristics are important because they can affect both validity and adverse impact. Answers to the questions above cannot be pulled directly from the job analysis. They require professional judgment using the job analysis as input. It is in making these judgments that practitioners must confront important ethical and moral issues. For example, is it appropriate to ignore the possible adverse impact of certain test characteristics and focus only on a traditional approach? If a practitioner is unfamiliar with the possible ramifications of using various test characteristics, is he or she obligated to become acquainted with these issues before developing or recommending a selection process? The manner in which the practitioner resolves these dilemmas can have a significant impact on the appropriateness of the selection process and the results.

Conclusion

Practitioners rely on the classical selection model to guide them in developing and implementing selection procedures. Unfortunately, the model is an oversimplification of selection situations as they actually exist. Gaps in the fit between the model and the context in which selection decisions take place are too large for practitioners to rely on professional judgment alone. Users of assessments should be familiar with the common ethical dilemmas that arise when assessment tools are used for decision making. Comprehensive knowledge of alternative assessment methods and an accurate yet broad understanding of the job will help resolve these dilemmas.

References

Equal Employment Opportunity Commission, Civil Service Commission, Department of Labor, & Department of Justice. (1978). Uniform guidelines on employee selection procedures. *Federal Register, 35*(149), 12333–12336.

Goldstein, H., Scherbaum, C., & Yusko, K. (2010). Revisiting *g*: Intelligence, adverse impact, and personnel selection. In J. Outtz (Ed.), *Adverse impact: Implications for organizational staffing and high stakes selection* (pp. 99–138). New York: Routledge

Guilford, J. P. (1956). The structure of intellect. *Psychological Bulletin, 53*, 267–293.

Murphy, K. (2010). How a broader definition of the criterion domain changes our thinking about adverse impact. In J. Outtz (Ed.), *Adverse impact: Implications for organizational staffing and high stakes selection* (pp. 141–164). New York: Routledge.

Newman, D. A., Hanges, P. J., & Outtz, J. L. (2007). Racial groups and test fairness: Considering history and construct validity. *American Psychologist, 62*, 1082–1083.

Outtz, J. L., & Newman, D. (2010). A theory of adverse impact. In J. Outtz (Ed.), *Adverse impact: Implications for organizational staffing and high stakes selection* (pp. 54–97). New York: Routledge.

Sackett, P., & Shen, W. (2010). Subgroup differences on cognitive tests in contexts other than personnel selection. In J. Outtz (Ed.), *Adverse impact: Implications for organizational staffing and high stakes selection* (pp. 329–352). New York: Routledge.

CHAPTER 23

STRATEGIC EVALUATION OF THE WORKPLACE ASSESSMENT PROGRAM

E. Jane Davidson

Workplace assessment programs require a substantial investment of time, money, and expertise to develop, implement, maintain, and use effectively. A good-quality program will pay for itself many times over; a flawed one could cost the organization dearly in time, money, lost opportunities, and serious legal ramifications.

As with any other major investment, risk management and maximizing return on investment are critically important priorities for any manager or practitioner. This chapter outlines the following topics:

- The evaluation imperative: Why organizations must evaluate important programs, products, services, and strategies and what is in it for those that do
- Evaluation for strategic decision making: How to make sure an evaluation answers the most important strategic questions and does not get lost in the details
- The nuts and bolts of strategic evaluation: What to look at, how to interpret the evidence, and how to weave the findings back into succinct, incisive, and strategically useful answers to important questions

- Challenges and tensions: Getting buy-in, trading off rigor and reality, and dealing with bias issues
- Advice for commissioning or conducting an undeniably worthwhile evaluation that pays for itself many times over

Strategic evaluation of a workplace assessment program is far more than assessment validation. Validation analyses are an important tool for determining the technical quality and legal defensibility of workplace assessment. But strategic evaluation goes much further, answering the all-important question of how valuable and worthwhile the program is as a strategic investment.

The Evaluation Imperative

As a decision maker, you take considerable care in the purchase or development of a good organizational assessment program from reputable people who are well qualified in industrial-organizational (I-O) psychology. You have already evaluated the program in terms of its features and performance claims, as well as the qualifications of those who develop or implement it for you. You may even have talked to managers in other organizations who have used the same system. Surely you can just trust that it will deliver, right? Wrong.

When you buy major products or services, you don't simply assume that they will live up to the hype on the packaging; you check to make sure that they actually do. If performance is not up to reasonable expectations, you call in after-sales service or other expertise to make adjustments (or demand a refund).

Responding Intelligently to the Call for Evidence-Based Management

As organizational interventions and practices become more sophisticated in response to competition and economic challenges, there has been a surge in the call for evidence-based management. For experienced managers, this may sound like a recipe for decision making to get bogged down in science, measurement, and analysis. However, the alternative, using "gut feel" or extremely limited information, is hardly a good option for high-stakes decisions.

An intelligent response to the call for evidence-based management is not to evaluate everything in detail or to evaluate nothing at all. Evaluation-savvy managers make judicious use of well-designed, incisive evaluation to inform key decisions about strategic organizational initiatives.

Having access to the right information at the right time requires managers to take a lead role in setting the evaluative agenda. This means thinking through and communicating clearly which organizational initiatives need to be evaluated, what questions need to be answered about them, to what level of detail, and within what time frame.

Maximizing the Chances of Success on a High-Stakes Investment

There are three ways in which evaluation can help maximize the chances of success for a high-stakes investment such as a workplace assessment program:

- *Helping a new program find its feet.* Often truly innovative ideas work imperfectly when first implemented, and the time it takes to bring the new system up to speed is a cost to the business. A new workplace assessment initiative needs help to find its feet soon after it is implemented so it can start adding value quickly and with minimal disruption. The best way to do this is to have a carefully targeted evaluation running alongside implementation, feeding just-in-time information to allow for timely streamlining and adjustments.
- *Helping mature programs keep up with changing needs.* Even tried-and-true workplace assessment programs cannot be assumed to keep working optimally or be free from opportunities for innovation or improvement. They are perched atop numerous shifting sands: changing labor markets, the economy, consumer needs, the political environment, strategic priorities, and organizational capability and competency requirements. As these realities change, what has worked well in the past may not always work as well in the present or future. Timely, well-focused evaluative feedback can help a good

workplace assessment program stay nimble and responsive to changing organizational needs.

- *Finding out sooner rather than later if something is amiss.* The later you find out that an important program is missing the mark, the more difficult and costly it is to make improvements or replace it. It is extremely important to have some barometer of effectiveness that will let you know early on whether a workplace assessment program (or any other major organizational initiative) is on track. This is especially true for a large or sophisticated program (for example, a global selection system), which may have some aspects working well and others that need improvement.

Documenting Evidence to Respond to Legal Challenges

Tools and systems used to make personnel decisions such as hiring and promotion are inevitably subject to legal challenges from those who object to decision outcomes. Important issues include ensuring that the content of any assessment criteria and tools are directly related to work duties and that both the assessment criteria and the outcomes of their application do not unfairly disadvantage individuals or groups based on gender, race, ethnicity, religion, national origin, disability status, marital status, or sexual orientation.

The best approach to avoiding legal challenges and dealing with them effectively when they arise is to have a plan for ensuring the legal defensibility of the content, design, implementation, and outcomes or impacts of the workplace assessment program. Obviously considerable care is taken during the front-end design phase, including the use of validated measures. However, there is still no substitute for careful evaluation of the actual up-and-running system to ensure adverse impact is not problematic and all elements comply with the law.

Demonstrating Value Added to Key Organizational Stakeholders

Any organizational program or intervention has its champions and its critics, as well as numerous others who have an interest in whether the resources invested can be justified in terms of savings or value generated. Although support for the purchase and implementation of a workplace assessment program may be achieved through arguments of how it will work in theory, ongoing support frequently hinges on having hard evidence of the value added in practice.

As organizational priorities and financial considerations change, different business units are frequently called on to provide justification for continued investment in various initiatives. This is particularly true for programs seen as costly and those that do not visibly generate revenue. Managers overseeing workplace assessment programs would be well advised to have solid, compelling evidence in hand that demonstrates the value and importance of these programs.

Evaluation for Strategic Decision Making

Strategic evaluation is much more than measurement and analysis. It is about finding useful and timely answers to important questions so that strategic decisions can be driven by organizational priorities and relevant evidence rather than by hunches and opinions. Two considerations are important here. First, start with the high-priority strategic concerns of greatest importance to the organization. Second, develop these into a short list of big-picture evaluation questions whose answers you must know. This ensures the evaluation is geared toward getting real answers to important questions and making a practical contribution to the organization's strategic direction.

Keeping the Focus Strategic

"Check the pulse before trimming the nails" (Scriven, 2009, p. iv). In other words, make sure your evaluation goes after the biggest and most important questions first—the ones that hinge on major underlying assumptions—before diving into the details.

A common fault in many evaluations is to head straight for the measurement and detailed analytical tasks such as traditional assessment validation analyses. This assumes that the main potential problems in a workplace assessment program are likely to be technical in nature.

For a more powerful and useful evaluation, start with big-picture questions that are linked directly to organizational strategy. What led to the decision to implement a workplace assessment program in the first place? What was the evidence that it was needed? Why was it seen as a good strategic investment? And is that rationale still justified in hindsight?

Next, make the link to the organization's strategic direction and priorities. Where are we going, what will we need in terms of human resource capabilities to get there, and is the workplace assessment program well designed to deliver on these?

Worthwhile evaluations will also include a strategic lens on the analysis of workplace assessment outcomes. Appropriate validation analyses are obviously important here, but linking to organizational strategy takes this back up to the big-picture level. Is this program helping us get the right mix of people into the right parts of the organization so we can achieve our strategic goals?

Devising 7 ± 2 Big-Picture Questions to Guide the Evaluation

A sound strategic evaluation of a workplace assessment program should cover the following six questions:

1. Was the program needed in the first place? Is it still the best solution?
2. How well do the content and design of the assessment match the current and future strategic and competency needs for the positions and business units it covers? How well does it address other relevant considerations such as legal compliance, person-organization fit, and improving the gender and ethnic balance in key positions? Is it flexible enough to allow "fitting the lock to the key" (Scriven, 1991), that is, modifying the job to allow hiring a particularly talented applicant who may not exactly fit the predetermined mold?
3. How effectively and how widely is the assessment program being implemented within the organization?
4. How valuable are the outcomes of the workplace assessment program, particularly as they relate to strategic priorities?
5. Is (or was) this program worth implementing? Was the value of outcomes greater than the value of resources used?

6. Is this program the best possible use of available resources to achieve selection, promotion, and placement outcomes of the greatest possible strategic value to the organization, its employees, and its customers? Could something else give better value for the investment?

In many cases, one or more of the following additional questions may also be important:

7. What are the barriers and enablers that make the difference between successful and disappointing outcomes or strategic uses of workplace assessment?
8. What else have we learned about how or why the outcomes were caused or prevented, what went right or wrong, which assessment methods work best for which candidates and positions, and are there any lessons for the future?
9. To what extent is the program, or aspects of its content, design, or delivery, likely to be valuable in other settings (for example, in our other business units or in our other locations) or for other candidate populations?

The Nuts and Bolts of Strategic Evaluation

How should we go about answering the six core evaluation questions? This section includes some advice on what to look at, how to interpret the evidence evaluatively, and how to weave the findings back into succinct, incisive, and strategically useful answers.

Identifying What to Look at

For each of the overarching evaluation questions, what evidence should we look at to answer them? How does each source of evidence feed into the evaluation? A brief guide to addressing each of the six core evaluation questions follows.

Was the Program Needed in the First Place? Is It Still the Best Solution?

The logical starting point here is the identified need that led to the purchase and implementation of the program in the first place. What was the problem it was designed to address—for example, concerns about succession planning, poorly targeted training and development, a series of problematic hires or "missed opportunity" nonhires, or a flurry of legal challenges to promotion decisions? Was there a strategic change that led to a new anticipated set of needs—for example, a new line of business, an organizational restructure, a shift in strategic priorities, or a substantial shift in the customer demographic?

What we are looking for here is some retrospective baseline data on outcomes that a workplace assessment program could reasonably be expected to address. So start with the presenting problem as recalled and documented by those who were there, but spread the net wider to uncover other needs that may not have been recognized at the time. This kind of retrospective needs assessment forms an initial basis for determining what outcomes the program should have impacted once implemented.

What Are the Quality and Value of the Assessment Program and Tool Design?

Coverage of this question includes a checklist of assessment program fundamentals, most of which will apply in any case:

- Coverage of the assessment instruments used: full coverage of the competencies, attributes, and experience required on the job; no extraneous content; clear point-to-point correspondence between the instruments used, the job content, and the organizational context; content validity; construct validity
- Soundness or rigor (both psychometric and evaluative) in the design and user friendliness of measurement tools (both qualitative and quantitative)
- Appropriateness for purpose of assessment instruments and strategies—for selection, promotion, or development; the nature of the job; the context; and the diversity of the personnel to be assessed; validation evidence
- Compliance with any legal and legislative requirements
- Consistency with ethical principles and organizational values
- Timeliness, relevance, and user friendliness of the information generated
- Credibility; face validity in the eyes of those being assessed and those using the assessment information on which to base decisions

- Transparency and perceived fairness of the assessment criteria, the assessment methods, and the decision outcomes that result

Further details on what constitutes good-quality design and implementation of workplace assessment for various different sectors and occupations are covered in Parts One and Two of this book. Another useful resource is the comprehensive *Personnel Evaluation Standards* (Joint Committee on Standards for Educational Evaluation, 2009).

In addition to these general criteria, consider the specifics of the organization's needs at the time of implementation and currently. For example, was there a previous system in place that had identified problems—for example, too expensive, too cumbersome, provided information too slowly for timely decision making? Was there an actual or anticipated need for different information, or a system that would apply to a very different class of jobs?

How Effectively Is the Program Being Implemented?

This question is the other half of process evaluation (the first half being content and design). It covers the following issues:

- Appropriateness of administration of instruments, including required training or qualifications of those administering instruments and compliance with guidelines and requirements for valid and appropriate use
- Compliance with relevant standards and professional codes of practice for personnel evaluation
- Efficiency, lack of waste, a streamlined process, and a set of instruments

How Valuable Are the Strategic Outcomes of the Assessment Program?

To identify key strategic outcomes, start with the initial presenting need and the assessment program's primary purpose. If the main use is for succession planning, one would logically expect outcomes such as these:

- All senior and key positions have a strong list of ready or near-ready candidates who could temporarily or permanently step into the role.

- Any vacancies are able to be filled efficiently and with minimal disruption.
- The new incumbents are able to hit the ground running in their new jobs.

At this point, it is helpful to try to categorize outcomes as being short term, intermediate, or long term. This helps plan which outcomes to look at in an early evaluation of the program. Short-term outcomes can give an early sense of whether the program is on track even though it may still be too soon to see the long-term strategic outcomes.

A useful tool for mapping outcomes is a logic model: a diagram that illustrates the theory of change, or program theory, for an intervention (in this case, an assessment program). It is a visual representation of how the program is expected to work and the kinds of outcomes that should be expected along the way.

A sample logic model for a workplace assessment program for succession planning is shown in Figure 23.1. The left-hand column lists some of the front-end inputs and preparations required as groundwork prior to implementation. The second column shows the main components of the workplace assessment program. The other three columns show the short-term, medium-term, and long-term (strategic) outcomes that might be expected for an assessment program designed for succession planning.

Each long arrow in Figure 23.1 represents a proposed cause-and-effect relationship and may be read as an if-then statement. For example, *if* strong lists of qualified candidates are available for each vacant position, *and if* additional lists are available of ready-soon and high-potential candidates, *then* we would expect key vacancies to be filled more quickly and more often from within the organization. *If* this happens, *and if* new incumbents are able to get up to speed fast and perform well on the job, *then* we would expect this to minimize the level of disruption and downtime during the transition. And so on.

There are many ways to draw logic models and many possible theories of change that may be plausible for a particular workplace assessment program. The logic model does not have to be the only depiction of reality; it simply has to be useful. Its main purposes in this context are to build a shared understanding

Figure 23.1. Sample Logic Model for a Workplace Assessment Program for Succession Planning

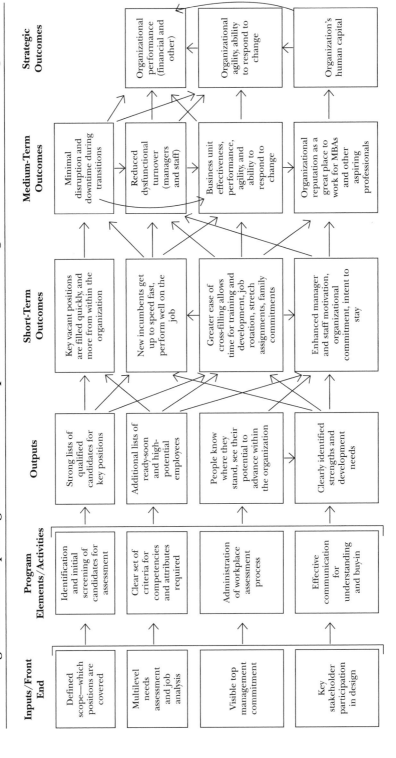

among key stakeholders (and with the evaluators) about what the program is and what it is trying to achieve and to identify those program components and outcomes that should be tracked in an evaluation of the program.

The process of mapping out a logic model with input from key organizational stakeholders, an assessment specialist, and an evaluation expert can be extremely powerful for unearthing any questionable assumptions or disagreements about how or why it is expected to work. Not only can it build a better shared understanding about what the program is and what its intended outcomes are, but points of disagreement can potentially be resolved through reality testing by getting stakeholders to pose inquiry questions and talk about what the answers might look like. For example, what evidence would convince us that the program does or does not work in a particular way?

The logic model also serves as a useful starting point for evaluation planning. The two left-hand columns in Figure 23.1 (inputs and program elements) are what should be covered as part of process evaluation: the evaluation of content or design and implementation. The remaining columns are what can be covered in the outcome evaluation. Depending on budget, it may be prudent to choose a subset of outcomes to track; for a high-cost or high-stakes program, it may be worth covering all outcomes listed.

The evaluation need not be limited to the outcomes identified in the logic model; in fact, an important limitation of logic models is their tendency to focus the evaluation on positive intended outcomes (Funnell & Rogers, 2010). Any good evaluation will include a serious search for side effects (for example, adverse impact). If useful, it might also explore any important positive or negative feedback loops within the system (virtuous cycles and vicious cycles). (Readers interested in the application of systems concepts to evaluation are referred to Williams and Imam's 2007 anthology.)

Is or Was This Program Worth Implementing?

A sound evaluation of any organizational initiative must consider cost. This does not mean simply checking whether the program is within budget. It means asking two questions: Are the costs reasonable? and Do the benefits outweigh the costs?

First, are the costs reasonable? When considering whether the costs are reasonable, two considerations are important. First, how do the costs compare with other offerings available? Is this considered a relatively expensive program by industry standards? A very economical one? About average? Second, was this a reasonable level of expenditure for an organization of this size (given the scope and purpose of the program)? In other words, is it affordable?

The costs of developing and implementing workplace assessment programs can be considerable. The development costs at the front end are substantial, particularly if an off-the-shelf solution is unlikely to deliver for the organization. Not only do assessment tools need to be developed, but so does an information management system that allows secure storage and analysis of results.

Development costs are also ongoing because assessment tools and resources need to be updated, or alternate forms created, to stay up with the field and the organization's needs and priorities. They also need to be refreshed so that candidates are not given too many test items they have done before, which might compromise validity.

Considerable costs are also involved in administering workplace assessment programs, collating the data, evaluative interpretation, ongoing validation analyses to check validity, pass rates, adverse impact, test content datedness, appropriateness of cutoff scores, and so forth. In addition, assessors have to be trained and their work cross-checked for quality assurance purposes.

The second question is whether the benefits outweigh the costs. This question may be answered in one of two ways. One is to translate all costs and benefits into monetary terms, that is, to conduct a cost-benefit analysis or a return on investment (ROI) analysis (Philips & Philips, 2007). Whether a full ROI analysis is feasible depends on the time and resources available for the evaluation itself. In some cases, a partial analysis may suffice. For example, it may be possible to quantify approximately the main benefits for a handful of stand-out success cases and show that those successes alone (in the absence of any serious disaster cases) are enough to justify the total expenditure on workplace assessment. (See the Success Case Method (Brinkerhoff, 2003), for more details on one innovative and highly cost-effective approach.) In other cases, a more detailed analysis of the evidence will be required.

The second way to answer the cost-benefit question is to use informed judgment and a mix of qualitative and quantitative data, without converting everything into monetary terms. This works best in clear-cut cases where the magnitude of the benefits (in evaluative terms, in terms of their significance for the organization) clearly outweighs the value of the resources invested in the program, or vice versa. Even when the quantifiable benefits are not clearly larger or smaller than the quantifiable costs, there are often cases where the intangible benefits have large and obvious payoffs. Common examples include when departures of high-value managers are prevented or when previously overlooked high-potential employees are identified and can be fast-tracked into a role where they can generate value for the business far more effectively than before. These major benefits still need to be documented, but the argument for whether they outweigh the costs of the program is made in qualitative and evaluative terms rather than using a quantitative calculation.

Is This Program the Best Possible Use of Available Resources?

Every dollar, every hour of someone's time, every other cost of a particular workplace assessment program represents resources that could have been spent on something else. This is why good evaluation must consider not just cost-benefit or cost-effectiveness questions, but also the notion of comparative cost-effectiveness. Could resources have been used differently to achieve greater benefits at a similar cost or similar benefits at lower cost?

The obvious place to start is to consider alternative types of workplace assessment programs, including those that might cost a little more but could potentially provide far greater benefits and those that might cost a little less but would deliver the same or very similar benefits. Workplace assessment programs are typically a package of various elements, so it can be useful to ask what the incremental value of each is over and above the others already in the package. Be sure to include a comparison with the single best assessment tool in the kit if used alone versus using it together with everything else.

Comparative cost-effectiveness also requires some more assumption-questioning comparisons. If the workplace assessment program was put in place to support succession planning, for example, one might ask whether a series of succession planning workshops for senior managers could have been just as effective or almost as effective at far lower cost. Or would a more systematic and extensive program of job rotation have been just as (or more) effective for finding out whether employees were ready or nearly ready for particular roles?

Defining How Good Is Good

The discussion has covered the aspects evaluators should examine to evaluate the content, design, and implementation of a workplace assessment program. One additional task remains: defining "how good is good" so that there is some clear basis on which to say whether, for example, the content and design of the program should be considered excellent as opposed to adequate or poor.

This is one of the core activities that distinguish true evaluation from applied research: thinking through in advance the definitions of value before the evidence is collected. This task requires a combination of expertise in evaluation-specific logic and methodology and in workplace assessment design and implementation, as well as an understanding of the organization's needs and strategic priorities. Stakeholder involvement, particularly with those who are most likely to use the information, can be incredibly powerful, not only for getting the evaluation right but for helping the organization think through how they define quality and value, and why.

In evaluation methodology terms, this is referred to as the merit determination step, and a range of practical strategies is available for doing this (Davidson, 2004). One of the best options is to develop a rubric or rating guide that makes explicit what "good" (and other categories) would look like. An example of a generic rubric that can be used or adapted to interpret process or outcome evidence for a wide range of programs (including training programs and workplace assessment programs) is shown in Table 23.1. This version has been condensed to three levels for brevity; however, in many cases, up to six or seven levels can be useful.

Table 23.1. Generic Interpretation Guide for Process and Outcome Evidence

Descriptor	Meaning in Process Evaluation	Meaning in Outcome Evaluation
Excellent	Clear example of exemplary design or delivery for a program at this level (ranks highly alongside some of the best in the world); no weaknesses are apparent	An outstanding outcome that represents having completely met the needs of program participants or the organization, possibly exceeding expectations in some areas
Good	Moderately high-quality design and delivery for a program at this level (compares favorably with average programs internationally); some weaknesses or areas for improvement are evident, though none is very serious	A reasonably valuable outcome that represents having mostly met the needs of program participants or the organization; some gaps or areas for improvement are evident, though none is very serious
Inadequate (or not yet adequate)	Less-than-acceptable quality design or delivery for a program at this level (similar in quality to the weaker programs internationally); one or more very important weaknesses need to be addressed	A minimally valuable outcome that represents having met only minor needs of program participants or the organization; several very important gaps need to be addressed

Note: Drawn from an evaluation report completed by Davidson Consulting Ltd.; client name removed for confidentiality reasons. © Davidson Consulting Ltd.

Involvement of key stakeholders in the process of defining these different levels of performance and in interpreting some of the evidence as part of the evaluation can be extremely powerful as a capacity-building and strategic thinking exercise. It also helps ensure buy-in to the evaluative conclusions and motivation to make any necessary changes. An important question to ask when involving stakeholders is, "Whose voices are at the table?" and, more important, whose are not, and why. Powerful evaluations are those where there is a critical mass of seats at the table for key users of evaluation information and members of underrepresented groups. (For more information about participatory and other utilization-focused evaluation strategies, see Patton, 2002, 2008.)

Packing the Findings Back Together

I recall some advice I received in my early days as an evaluator: one of the most important skills in evaluation is being able to take a fifty-page report and condense it down to two pages without losing any important information. Time after time I have seen evaluation reports with an executive summary that is excessively long and usually looks more like an academic abstract than a summary for managers. Many decision makers read only two pages of the report, so those two pages must contain all the most important information they need to know.

Training in applied psychology and related disciplines does a pretty good job of showing people how to break something down into components and variables and to identify data sources, indicators, and measures. But there is much less guidance about how to pack all of this information back together in a systematic, valid, and transparent way to draw overall conclusions and answer overarching evaluation questions. In evaluation, this is called the synthesis step, and it involves using one or more evaluation-specific methodologies.

We have already touched on one of the most useful synthesis tools available: the rubric or rating guide presented in Table 23.1. This describes what performance at each level looks like based on a range of complementary data sources. The synthesis methodology is based on the broad definitions of overall quality or value contained in the table. There is no mathematical algorithm where you add up scores on indicators and an answer is produced automatically. Instead, deliberation, discussion, and thoughtful judgment are required to determine which picture (performance level) represents the best fit with the evidence. There will not always be complete agreement on where the rating should go, but there should never be disagreement straddling more than two adjacent rating categories.

Several other synthesis methodologies are available, including some that could usefully be applied within assessment programs themselves, for example, to rank or select candidates. The most commonly used for ranking and selection tasks is the simple (but frequently invalid unless it also includes "bars," or minimum acceptable levels, on particular criteria) numerical weight and sum. The strongest alternative is the qualitative weight and sum (Scriven 1991; see also Davidson, 2004).

Various quantitative and qualitative methodologies are also available for evaluations seeking to draw overall conclusions about absolute rather than relative quality or value (for details, see Davidson, 2004). Absolute quality or value is about intrinsic merit or worth, for example: "Should we hire [or promote or develop] this person?" and "Is this program performing well enough to meet our needs?" Relative quality or value pertains to questions about comparative merit and worth like these: "Who are the best three candidates?" and "Is this system better than what we used before?"

Regardless of the synthesis methodologies used, it is important to keep in mind the required end product: incisive answers to the 7 ± 2 overarching evaluation questions. A useful format for the executive summary, then, is to list all of the overarching questions and under each one provide a straight-to-the-point, direct, evaluative answer and a short justification for it.

This turns out to be a far more productive use of the limited space in an executive summary than the long-winded versions often seen in evaluation reports. In fact, an executive summary with clear and direct evaluative conclusions tends to generate a lot more interest in the evidence in the rest of the report and so can be a useful catalyst for important evaluative conversations at a strategic level.

Challenges and Tensions in the Strategic Evaluation of Assessment Programs

Technical and methodological challenges aside, evaluation has always been an intensely political activity that sparks strong emotional reactions and manipulative or subversive behavior. What can be done to get buy-in for evaluation? How can we make intelligent trade-offs between rigor and the reality of the decision-making context? How can we control for general positive bias in evaluation? How should we handle claims of cultural or gender bias in a workplace assessment program?

Getting Buy-In to Strategic Evaluation

"We believe you that it works; why do we need to prove it?" One of the founding fathers of the modern discipline of evaluation, Donald Campbell (1969), described the "overadvocacy trap" as one of the most difficult barriers to getting buy-in for evaluation. Workplace assessment programs are typically marketed and sold to organizations by highly qualified, experienced, and technically competent professionals who work hard to sell the benefits of their products. Well-implemented programs also have a senior, influential sponsor or champion within the organization who does much of the groundwork internally to get support for and utilization of the program.

To even suggest that the program should be evaluated is seen by some as tantamount to an admission that it may not be as good as these people said it would be. To then include an evaluation question about comparative cost-effectiveness is like saying the whole thing might have been a waste of money. Evaluation is seen as politically, financially, and career-wise risky for the program vendors, the internal sponsor or whoever else made the decision to purchase the program, and those who are using it to make decisions that affect people's lives.

The key to getting buy-in is to treat these concerns seriously and act in ways consistent with building an organizational culture where evaluation is used constructively rather than feared. One of the few articles in the literature about managing evaluation anxiety (Donaldson, Gooler, & Scriven, 2002) presents a useful set of guidelines. Drawing on these, suggestions for the evaluation of workplace assessment programs would include:

- Emphasize the synergy of evaluation with the one thing everyone can agree on: that the organization needs a high-quality, fair, valid, efficient, and cost-effective assessment program that gets the right people into the right jobs and development experiences.
- Make sure any objections are not legitimate opposition to bad evaluation; make changes to the evaluation if necessary.
- Discuss why honesty in the evaluation is not disloyalty, and have senior leaders visibly role-model this.
- Encourage involvement in reality testing: if different people have different views about what works well (or not) in the assessment program, encourage them to pose an evaluation question and propose evidence that would convince them one way or the other.

Balancing the Need for Rigor with the Realities of Decision Making

A common challenge is managing the trade-offs between rigor and the reality of organizational decision-making contexts. The default in applied quantitative research is to draw inferences only when a result is 95 or 99 percent certain ($p < .05$ or $p < .01$). Rigorous qualitative research also requires a substantial weight of evidence before drawing any clear conclusions. But the reality of organizational decision-making contexts is that few decisions are ever taken with such a high degree of certainty. As a consequence, decision makers are frequently frustrated when evaluators, using academic standards of proof, conclude there are no effects when something just fails to reach statistical significance or when they conclude that effects exist when they are clearly not practically significant in magnitude.

The standard of proof required varies according to how high stakes the decision is and whether it is likely to be subject to legal challenges. In addition to being rigorous enough, the evidence must be credible, defensible, and persuasive to the various audiences that will see it. More important than statistical significance is practical significance: whether the magnitude of any outcome has any real meaning in the organizational context.

An additional challenge in the evaluation of workplace assessment and other programs is that the questions decision makers ask are often broad, whereas the instruments and measures employed to answer them are most accurate if they are narrow. Remember that it is far more important to be able to provide an approximate answer to an important (and usually broad) question about quality or value than it is to provide a very precise answer to something trivial (for example, about a single, narrow outcome variable).

General Positive Bias

Any external contractor or internal project team wants to be seen as doing a good job in the eyes of whoever commissioned them to do it. How do we know we have done a good job? A strong indicator is client satisfaction. What keeps clients satisfied is the good news that affirms what they already thought. These satisfied clients then hire the same people again for more work and recommend them to others. Dissatisfied clients do in essence kill the messenger: they fire the contractor, fail to hire them again, fail to recommend them, or, worse, speak poorly of them to other potential clients, possibly even sue them for selling and implementing a flawed system.

There are enormous financial and psychological incentives to deliver positive evaluation reports (Scriven, 1991). People are uncomfortable delivering bad news and quite legitimately fear the consequences for themselves and their businesses. The instinct to please the program sponsor is a survival instinct.

The risk of general positive bias is dramatically reduced when the client organization and key people are serious about evaluation and truly look for areas where they can improve, innovate, spend their resources more wisely, and do it better than the competition. But even in highly learning-enabled organizations, there will be advocates and supporters of the workplace assessment program, and they will be keen to have their views supported.

Most managers instinctively see the problems with asking the supplier of a workplace assessment program to evaluate his or her own product. However, any good supplier will have a sound, evaluative quality assurance system in place. This should not be discouraged, but the findings should certainly be complemented with an independent evaluation done by someone without a vested interest in the program.

Investigating Claims of Culture or Gender Bias

Suppose your workplace assessment program is accused of being biased against members of a certain gender or ethnic group. What steps should you take when investigating such a claim, and what evidence should convince you that it is or is not justified?

There are two places to investigate this: process and outcomes. Starting with outcomes, is there any actual evidence of adverse impact? For example, is a smaller proportion of women or minorities being selected, promoted, or classified as having potential? If so, is this simply a reflection of real and performance-relevant differences between men and women or different ethnicities in this population, or is something else going on? For example, is there anything about the assessment process or instruments that actually or potentially makes it unfairly difficult for certain groups to be assessed positively?

Do not limit this investigation to the proportion of those who undertake the assessment that get through; some assessment programs have nomination, prescreening, or other processes that tend to inadvertently include some and exclude others. For example, an assessment program I recently evaluated had a process that in many participating organizations required a candidate to self-identify as someone who aspired to a top leadership position and then to convince his or her chief executive to support the nomination. This required a degree of self-promotion that was considered quite inappropriate behavior in the local indigenous culture, where humility was a fundamental cultural value. So although there were no overt barriers to prevent certain individuals from putting themselves forward, subtle cultural barriers had this effect. These required some serious rethinking if the assessment program was going to support building a more diverse talent pool for senior leadership positions.

Another important place to look is at the assessment instruments and experiences themselves and the way performance is interpreted by assessors. One example I encountered was in an assessment process that included a role play in which the manager was expected to demonstrate performance management skills with a difficult employee. On observing a role play and listening to the assessors discuss their ratings, it became clear that good performance was defined in part as decisive resolution of the issue, with the manager stepping in to take charge of the situation and not letting the employee drive the conversation. One of the candidates who went through the assessment was an Asian woman who took a very different approach. She used a facilitative style to try to get the employee to see the problem and construct a solution. And most important, she was doing it in a way that would allow the employee to save face. The psychologist assessor took a dim view of this approach as being slow moving, weak, and not decisive enough. The senior manager assessor, who was participating in an assessment for the first time, later reported feeling very uncomfortable with the assessment but, being new to the process, had gone along with the judgment and allowed the psychologist to take the lead.

These problems of cultural bias do not only appear in assessment experiences that employ judgment on the part of assessors. In fact, quantitative assessment instruments can be even more deceptive because they carry with them an aura of objectivity that sometimes leads people not to question their content. It is worth remembering that every quantitative assessment item is underpinned by a great many qualitative and evaluative assumptions about what is valued, what is important, and how quality should be defined. As such, they should all be subject to scrutiny with a critical eye—not just for culture and gender bias but also for the validity of those value definitions as a basis for evaluating personnel.

Designing and Conducting Worthwhile Evaluations of Assessment Programs

Four key considerations can make or break strategic evaluation: (1) ensuring that evaluation is geared to the needs of primary intended users of the findings, (2) structuring useful evaluation reports that have impact, (3) quality assurance of the evaluation process and products, and (4) having leaders walk the evaluative talk.

Thinking About Utilization from Start to Finish

There is no point investing resources in an evaluation that is unlikely to be useful or unlikely to be used constructively. What can be done to maximize both utility and use?

The first and most important principle is to insist that evaluation meshes effectively with high-level questions and is timed to provide information at critical decision points. Start by identifying the primary intended users of the evaluation and generating a short list of overarching evaluation questions to which they need the answers. Ask, "Who needs to know what, by when, for what decisions, and to what level of certainty and detail?"

Decision maker involvement in defining the evaluation questions and interpreting some of evidence can be a powerful way of ensuring that they are constructively engaged in the evaluation. This kind of organizational sense making is a valuable process for building shared understanding and ownership of the findings, thereby making it more likely to result in positive action. In my own practice, I have found it extremely worthwhile to have stakeholders take the lead in generating recommendations from an evaluation. People are more likely to act on recommendations they authored and own, as opposed to those suggested by an outsider. After all, what outside expert could possibly be familiar with all the budgetary and political ramifications of whatever course of action he or she suggests?

There is a strong literature on utilization-focused evaluation for readers interested in exploring this further. The most comprehensive treatment of the topic is Patton's *Utilization-Focused Evaluation* (2008). But there is also much of value in Sonnichsen's *High Impact Internal Evaluation* (2000), particularly for those looking to help an internal evaluation unit generate more value for the business.

Drafting a Skeleton Report with an Informative Structure First

Writing an evaluation report is a bit like putting back together a car or motorbike engine: you do not want to have leftover parts with nowhere to go. In mechanics, that could compromise whether the engine will run at all, and if so how well. In evaluation, it is instant evidence of a poorly planned evaluation and wasted informant and evaluator time.

Every piece of data collected for an evaluation must have a home to go to; that is, the evaluator must know where in the report it will go and how it will contribute to the evidence base. To this end, it can be useful to draft a skeleton report during the evaluation planning stage and jot down which sections each piece of evidence will go into. This makes it easier to see if one aspect of the program has been (or was to be) evaluated in a lot of detail at the expense of another equally important aspect for which there is a paucity of good evidence.

One of the best ways to completely ruin a potentially good evaluation is to write it up like a modified master's thesis with an abstract, introduction, literature review, theory, methodology, findings presented separately by source (informant, interviews, surveys, HR data) and type (qualitative and quantitative), discussion, conclusions, references, and appendixes. For a manager, a report like this feels like wading through mud. The reader is faced with page after page of graphs, tables, and interview quotes, but no real explanation of whether or how they were used to answer any of the evaluation questions, if indeed any were listed in the first place. And a report like this takes a long time to get to the point.

So what sort of report structure makes sense to clients? There are many potentially good answers to this question, but the following are some simple guidelines for one structure that has worked particularly well for me:

- Structure the findings part of the evaluation report into 7 ± 2 sections—one for each of the overarching evaluation questions used to frame the evaluation.
- In each section, present a summary of all data pertaining to that question: qualitative, quantitative, interviews, surveys, observations, document analyses, hard data, from different people and perspectives.
- Group the evidence by theme or content rather than by data type or source within each section.
- Interpret the evidence explicitly and evaluatively as it is presented: "How good a result is this? And how do we know?"

Use the rubrics to make evaluative interpretations and support them with the required evidence.

- Weave the diverse types and sources of evidence together to formulate a direct answer to the evaluation question that is the section heading.
- Write a two-page executive summary using the same structure: 7 ± 2 questions with straight-to-the-point and explicitly evaluative answers of one to two paragraphs each.

If the organization's key decision makers had six or seven overarching questions about the program, then the first two pages they read (perhaps the only two pages!) should contain direct answers to those questions. And if any particular decision maker wants to know the basis on which those conclusions were drawn (that is, value definitions, evidence, and evaluative logic), it should be a simple matter to turn to the relevant section of the report and find out.

Who Evaluates the Evaluators?

If the people you are considering hiring to evaluate your workplace assessment program laugh at this question, think twice about hiring them. It is hardly credible to be selling the idea that evaluation is a worthwhile undertaking if those selling it do not actually believe this themselves.

This is not a recommendation to write up a second request for proposal for a full meta-evaluation (i.e., an evaluation of an evaluation), although for a major, high-stakes evaluation, this may well be justified. At the very least, evaluators should deliberately seek out multiple perspectives and vigorous critiques of the evaluation design, the evaluation process, and the products or deliverables, such as reports and presentations or other mechanisms for delivering evaluative feedback. This is all part of the good quality assurance practices that should form part of any serious professional's approach, particularly any serious evaluator.

A range of midsize options is available for getting useful estimates of the cost-effectiveness of the work. These include having an independent evaluation expert and a workplace assessment expert review the evaluation plan, early findings, or the final report. More options have been outlined by Davidson (2004) and are in a range of useful checklists for meta-evaluation, including Stufflebeam's (1999) program evaluation meta-evaluation checklist, available on the Western Michigan University Evaluation Checklist Web site.

Walking the Evaluative Talk

The actions of organizational leaders speak louder than words. Using workplace assessment conveys the message that the organization values sound evidence-based decision making about whom to hire, promote, and invest in for further development.

Leaders who insist on and use strategic evaluation of their workplace assessment programs are conveying another important message: that they are serious about making sure that the assessment program used is fair, valid, useful, and adds enough value to clearly justify the investment.

It follows naturally that other major strategic investments such as organizational restructures and other major change initiatives should also be subject to the same critical analysis. Are they aligned with the strategic goals? Are they well designed and implemented? Do they add enough value to justify the investment? Are they the best possible use of available resources to maximize organizational performance and support the organization's strategic direction?

But there is one really telling sign that leaders are serious about adding value: they deliberately seek out critical feedback on their own performance as leaders, their own strategic value added, their own worth as an investment. Do they subject themselves to the same scrutiny that they apply to their people and the programs and initiatives they ask those people to implement? As Menkes's (2005) extensive research on leadership shows, this is one of the fundamental elements of executive intelligence that all brilliant leaders share.

When strategic evaluation is applied consistently across all of the organization's strategic investments—people, programs, products, policies, systems, and change initiatives—the message is crystal clear: leaders are serious about quality, serious about adding value, and unafraid to ask tough questions, hear disappointing answers, or act decisively on what they learn.

References

Brinkerhoff, R. O. (2003). *The success case method: Find out quickly what's working and what's not.* San Francisco: Berrett-Koehler.

Campbell, D. T. (1969). Reforms as experiments. *American Psychologist, 4,* 409–429.

Davidson, E. J. (2004). *Evaluation methodology basics: The nuts and bolts of sound evaluation.* Thousand Oaks, CA: Sage.

Donaldson, S. I., Gooler, L. E., & Scriven, M. (2002). Strategies for managing evaluation anxiety: Toward a psychology of program evaluation. *American Journal of Evaluation, 23*(3), 261–273.

Funnell, S., & Rogers, P. J. (2010). *Purposeful program theory.* San Francisco: Jossey-Bass.

Joint Committee on Standards for Educational Evaluation. (2009). *The personnel evaluation standards* (2nd ed.). Thousand Oaks, CA: Corwin Press.

Menkes, J. (2005). *Executive intelligence: What all great leaders have.* New York: HarperCollins.

Patton, M. Q. (2002). *Utilization-focused evaluation checklist.* Western Michigan University Evaluation Checklists Project. Retrieved from http://evaluation.wmich.edu/checklists.

Patton, M. Q. (2008). *Utilization-focused evaluation* (4th ed.). Thousand Oaks, CA: Sage.

Philips, J. J., & Philips, P. P. (2007). *Show me the money: How to determine ROI in people, projects, and programs.* San Francisco: Berrett-Koehler.

Scriven, M. (1991). *Evaluation thesaurus* (4th ed.). Thousand Oaks, CA: Sage.

Scriven, M. (2009). Meta-evaluation revisited. *Journal of Multidisciplinary Evaluation, 6*(11), iii–viii.

Sonnichsen, R. C. (2000). *High impact internal evaluation: A practitioner's guide to evaluating and consulting inside organizations.* Thousand Oaks, CA: Sage.

Stufflebeam, D. L. (1999). *Program evaluations metaevaluation checklist.* Western Michigan University Evaluation Checklists Project. Retrieved from http://evaluation.wmich.edu/checklists.

Williams, B., & Imam, I. (2007). *Systems concepts in evaluation: An expert anthology.* Point Reyes, CA: Edgepress of Inverness.

CHAPTER 24

FINAL THOUGHTS ON THE SELECTION AND ASSESSMENT FIELD

Paul R. Sackett

I write this concluding chapter after reading the full set of chapters in this book. I will not take the traditional discussant role of commenting on each chapter in turn; rather, I offer some thoughts on issues facing the selection and assessment field that were prompted by the chapters individually and the book as a whole. The issues highlighted here are largely those where differing perspectives are reflected in various chapters in this book.

The Role of Context

One of this book's great strengths is the presentation of a level of contextual detail not reflected in the typical selection and assessment textbook. The organizing framework of a general introduction to each of the major tools in the assessment repertoire (measures of ability, personality, knowledge and skill, background and experience, and physical performance, for example), followed by chapters dealing with application to specific job domains (sales, technical administrative, supervisory, executive, police and fire) or specific settings (global assessment, succession planning, assessing potential, assessment in the context of organizational change), offers the opportunity to see the same set of basic tools used in different ways that are influenced by contextual features.

These applied chapters illustrate the richness and complexity of effective assessment in organizational settings. For example, newcomers to the selection and assessment field see the issues that surface when developing selection systems in unionized environments (Chapter Nine by Campbell).

They encounter the fact that in many sales settings, the old truism that 20 percent of the sales force produces 80 percent of the sales is true, meaning that one must take highly skewed criterion data into account (see Chapter Eleven by Brown). They find that another old truism, that the best predictor of future behavior is past behavior, carries with it an implicit "in similar settings," a qualifier that becomes significant when making the transition from individual contributor to the dissimilar role of supervisor, as Schmit and Strange note in Chapter Twelve. They encounter the tensions caused when an individual is placed into a position on a temporary basis, performs to the satisfaction of the immediate supervisor, but fails the selection battery when the opportunity to apply for the position on a permanent basis arises (see Chapter Ten by Reed, McCloy, and Whetzell). It is this infinite variety of contextual variation that makes the selection and assessment field a challenging and professionally rewarding field within which to work.

Responding to these contextual complexities requires considerable professional judgment. This implies that the notion that one can or should do selection system development by the book is misguided: there is no one way. Rather, many different bodies of knowledge contribute to effectiveness in this endeavor:

- A strong psychometric foundation for selection and assessment work
- A large scientific literature regarding various aspects of the selection process, containing information about effective methods for analyzing jobs, developing predictor and criterion measures, and developing hypotheses about the types of predictors likely to be useful in a given context
- A body of legal statutes, guidelines, and judicial precedents that can inform decisions

- A literature on business strategy, and on the role of human resources in general and selection systems in particular within this strategy
- A growing literature in the realm of information technology and its use in selection and assessment
- A psychological literature on an array of topics relevant to selection systems, such as decision making and perceptions of justice, among many others

All of these are brought to bear in making judgments about the design and implementation of selection and assessment systems in a given setting. I believe that if one were to perform the conceptual experiment of sending multiple individuals, each consensually regarded in the field as highly qualified, into a setting and having each work independently with the organization to develop a selection system, no two resulting systems would be alike. One implication is that there are many viable solutions in any setting rather than one correct solution. Thus, while we are likely to look at the work done by another colleague and conclude that there are things we would have done differently, we are well served by recognizing that others would look at our work and similarly conclude that they would have done some things differently. Although each of us will quite naturally believe that our approach is the preferable one, it is important to recognize that other approaches are viable.

Differing Perspectives on the Use of Personality Measures in Selection

The use of self-report personality inventories in selection systems remains a source of controversy. This controversy focuses primarily on two related issues: criterion-related validity and the role of faking. Sackett and Lievens (2008) offer several reasons for the interest in personality assessment in the selection context, including the clear relevance of the personality domain for the prediction of performance dimensions that go beyond task performance (such as citizenship and counterproductive behavior), the potential for incremental validity in the prediction of task performance, and the common finding of minimal racial/ethnic group differences, thus offering the prospect of reduced adverse impact. They note some unease about the magnitude of validity coefficients obtained using personality measures. That unease is illustrated in this book in Murphy's Chapter One. Sackett and Lievens noted that what is emerging in the literature is that there are meaningful relationships between variables in the personality domain and important work outcomes but that the pattern of relationships is complex. They suggested that the field "got spoiled" by the relatively straightforward pattern of findings in the ability domain (for example, relatively high correlations between different attempts to measure cognitive ability and consistent success in relating virtually any test with a substantial cognitive loading to job performance measures). In contrast, in the personality domain, several key features complicate matters.

Lack of a Common Specification for Construct Label

We lack a clear specification of key personality constructs. On the one hand, the emergence of the Big Five and its subdimensions has provided a useful start toward a taxonomic structure. On the other, there is considerably less consensus as to the precise definitions of each of these dimensions, such that measures with the same label are not comparable. This is central to Hogan and Kaiser's defense of personality testing in Chapter Four. They document a stronger set of validity findings when focusing on a single personality measure, thereby overcoming the issue of combining similarly named but actually noncomparable measures.

Trait-Performance Relationships Vary Across Jobs and Performance Dimensions

Jobs differ in the personality attributes relevant to various aspects of performance. Extraversion can be important for key aspects of a sales job (see Brown, Chapter Eleven) but irrelevant for a technical job (see Campbell, Chapter Nine). In Chapter Four, Hogan and Kaiser show higher validity when focusing on criterion facets that are conceptually linked to the personality measure of interest. This finding is crucial to the conduct and interpretation of meta-analytic summaries of validity research. It is common to administer a multidimensional personality inventory in validation research and report criterion-related validity results for all dimensions, including those with no conceptual relevance to the criterion of interest. The grand averaging of all available validity coefficients does not really address the research question of interest: How do personality measures relate to conceptually relevant criteria? Our focus should be on analyses that focus on conceptually meaningful predictor-criterion links.

Lack of Clarity as to the "Right" Personality Dimensions

Mean validity coefficients for single Big Five traits are indeed relatively small (the largest corrected validity, for Conscientiousness, is about .20), leading to some critical views of the use of personality measures (Murphy & Dzieweczynski, 2005). However, it is becoming increasingly clear that the Big Five may not be the right level of specificity for the prediction of work outcomes. As Murphy acknowledges in Chapter One, performance is predicted much better by compound traits (contextualized measures, such as integrity or customer service inventories, which share variance with multiple Big Five measures) and composites of Big Five measures. Thus, one fruitful arena is to work with more complex measures rather then seeking purer measures of Big Five traits.

In addition to going broader and examining compound traits, it also appears promising to focus at a more finely grained level than the Big Five. Each of the Big Five dimensions is multifaceted, and we are starting to see evidence that some subfacets are more important than others in predicting work outcomes. I am particularly taken by a study by Dudley, Orvis, Lebiecki, and Cortina (2006) who report a meta-analysis comparing the validity of global measures of Conscientiousness with measures of four conscientiousness facets: achievement, dependability, order, and cautiousness. They found that validity was driven largely by the achievement or dependability facets, with relatively little contribution from cautiousness and order. For some criteria, such as counterproductive work behavior, the narrow facets provided a dramatic increase in variance accounted for over global Conscientiousness measures. Thus, focusing on dependability and achievement may prove more productive in many settings.

While Dudley et al. focused on Conscientiousness, similar work regarding other Big Five dimensions would be most useful. I am intrigued by research outside the work domain by personality psychologists DeYoung, Quilty, and Peterson (2007), who offer empirical support for splitting each Big Five dimension in two. Neuroticism is divided into Volatility (for example, hostility, impulsiveness) and Withdrawal (for example, anxiety, depression); Extraversion into Enthusiasm (for example, friendliness, warmth) and Assertiveness (for example, leadership, proactivity); Agreeableness into Compassion (for example, sympathy, empathy) and Politeness (cooperation, pleasantness); Openness into Intellect (quickness, ingenuity) and Openness to Experience (aesthetics, imagination); and Conscientiousness into Industriousness (self-discipline, achievement striving) and Orderliness (order, perfectionism). (Note that the last nicely dovetails with Dudley et al.'s findings.) Other more finely grained breakdowns of the Big Five also exist, such as the model underlying the NEO-Personality Inventory, which offers six subfacets for each of the Big Five. It will take time for the right level of differentiation to emerge, but this seems a promising avenue to explore.

The Role of Faking

Faking is a clear flash point for the differences in views of the viability of the use of personality assessment for selection purposes. Within this book, readers will see perspectives ranging from Murphy's view in Chapter One that faking is "likely to be a realistic barrier" to the use of personality measures in many settings, to Hogan and Kaiser's argument in Chapter Four that research shows individuals can fake if asked to do so, but do not do so in real employment settings, to the observations of Barrett, Doverspike, and Young in Chapter Fourteen and of Brown in Chapter Eleven that the validity of personality tests found in concurrent studies is substantially reduced, if not eliminated, in applicant settings.

Hogan and Kaiser's claim that faking is not an important issue is based on the assertion that only one study uses a truly informative research design: a comparison of real applicants' initial scores as applicants with their retest scores after not being selected on the first attempt. Hogan, Barrett, and Hogan (2007) used this design with a large sample, and found no change ($d = -.02$). Although it is an interesting research design, I do not view it as definitive. That initial failers did not improve on retesting does not speak to whether some or many of those who passed did so by faking. And because there was incentive to fake on the initial test, score consistency may reflect faking on both occasions. The personality measure was part of a larger test battery, and so "failure" does not mean a low score on the personality measure. In addition to these conceptual issues, other studies using this design produce different findings, with retest improvement of $d = .26$ (Ellingson, Sackett, & Connelly, 2007), $d = .86$ (Landers, Sackett, & Tuzinski, 2009), and $d = 2.8$ (Young, 2003). There is clear variability here, but I view this as strong evidence that faking does occur in at least some applicant settings.

I see no magic bullet but offer two thoughts regarding the faking issue. First, Sackett and Lievens (2008) noted that most research modeling the effects of faking has focused on top-down selection. However, in many operational settings, such measures are used with a relatively low fixed cutoff as part of initial screening. In such a setting, faking may result in an undeserving candidate succeeding in meeting the threshold for moving on to the next stage, but that candidate does not supplant a candidate who responds honestly on a rank-order list, as in the case of top-down selection. Mueller-Hanson, Heggestad, and Thornton (2003) showed that faking reduced the validity of a measure of achievement motivation at the high end of the distribution but not at the low end, suggesting that faking may be less of an obstacle to screen-out uses of noncognitive measures than to screen-in uses. Berry and Sackett (2009) model the use of personality in this screen-out fashion.

Second, Hogan and Kaiser in Chapter Four offer the useful distinction between two views of personality: personality as the inner self and personality as reputation, that is, the way others expect you to behave based on prior observed behavior. Reputation is what we would like to know in work settings, and yet we rely largely on self-report. Alternatives include personality ratings based on interviews, simulations such as assessment center exercises, and ratings by others with extensive prior contact with the individual. Connelly and Ones (in press) offer a meta-analytical synthesis of research on other ratings of personality, which suggests that assessments by others can be a promising approach. Of course, other ratings are also amenable to faking by motivated raters, but this appears to be an underexplored arena.

The Cognitive Ability–Adverse Impact Dilemma

Like the issue of the use of personality inventories, the use of cognitive ability measures is another area where readers will see conflicting messages across chapters. Many chapter authors comment on the sizable mean differences that are quite consistently found by race/ethnicity and on the consistent pattern of validity evidence when such measures are used. As has long been noted, this creates conflict for organizations that value both maximizing performance among those selected and maximizing diversity among those selected. McDaniel and Banks in Chapter Three review the literature on criterion-related validity and predictive bias. They conclude that validity is high relative to available alternatives, the use of cognitive tests does not result in predictive bias by race/ethnicity, and item format is not the cause of group differences.

There are multiple possible responses to the findings McDaniel and Banks summarize. One is to challenge the conclusions, such as challenging the use of the regression-based predictive bias model (Outtz & Newman, 2010) or questioning the conclusion that changing item format is not a viable solution to the problem of group differences (see Outtz's suggestion in Chapter Twenty-Two that item formats that do not require selecting the one best response may prove superior). None of these critiques has yet persuaded the selection field in general, but the field does have a history of considering and evaluating such proposals as they arise.

A second response combines accepting the conclusions from the cumulative body of research to date with a perspective that views maximizing the validity as the fundamental goal of the selection system (though generally acknowledging practical constraints such as limits on testing time or cost). Reducing group differences is not a goal under this approach, in the sense that advocates of this perspective are not willing to sacrifice validity in order to reduce group differences. This does not imply indifference to group differences; in fact, advocates of this approach will draw on everything the field knows about controlling group differences without sacrificing validity. The caricature of this perspective is that its advocates endorse the sole use of top-down selection on cognitive tests as the sole means of selection. In fact, advocates would heartily endorse broadening the selection system to include other predictors with smaller subgroup differences or the exploration of predicting a broader range of criteria—as long as those alternative predictors are demonstrably valid and weighted in a fashion that properly reflects their contribution to prediction of the criterion of interest and as long as criteria are weighted based on their relative contribution to overall effectiveness.

A third response is to accept the accuracy of the conclusions for the cumulative body of research to date, but to adopt selection systems that are less than optimal in terms of maximizing the performance of selected candidates in the interests of other organizational objectives. One of those objectives may be diversity, but it is important to note that departures from performance maximization are often chosen for a range of other reasons, such as cost, speed with which selection decisions can be made, or simplicity in administering a selection process, among others (Kehoe, 2008). Examples illustrated in this book include the use of cognitive measures with cut scores set in a fashion that reduces adverse impact or the use of cognitive tests in conjunction with other measures, although using weights other than the regression weights that optimize the performance criterion given the set of predictors under consideration. Thus, although the perspective outlined in the previous paragraph endorses validity as the fundamental goal of a selection system, this perspective acknowledges the possibility of multiple goals, which may include goals related to diversity.

It is important to note the difference between the bases for advocating one of these three prototypical positions (and there is no claim here that these three are an exhaustive list). The first is a science-based position: it is based on assertions of technical flaws in our conclusions about validity, bias, or other issues. A claim made on the basis of the first position can be rebutted by evidence: it is falsifiable. The second and third are value-based positions. There is no technical or scientific basis for choosing between valuing validity maximization and valuing multiple goals.

In scenarios in which the use of multiple predictors, including measures of cognitive ability, is being considered, a question that surfaces with some frequency is whether the predictors could be combined in some fashion other than by regression weighting, such that the results would be a system with equal, or nearly equal, validity and less adverse impact. I frequently see this examined in technical reports, where various ad hoc weighting schemes are compared with regression weighting in terms of validity and adverse impact. In recent work, my colleagues Wilfried De Corte, Filip Lievens, and I have used tools from the field of multiobjective optimization to develop computer programs that permit a systematic examination of the validity-adverse impact trade-off (De Corte, Lievens, & Sackett, 2007, 2008). For a given set of predictors and a given criterion, the programs answer questions such as, "Relative to the level of validity and adverse impact obtained via a regression-weighted composite, how much of a reduction in adverse impact is attainable if one is willing to accept an X percent reduction in validity (where X takes on a range of values, such as 1, 5, 10, and 20 percent). Using one simple two-predictor example of an ability test in conjunction with a structured interview, using a 10 percent selection ratio with mean validity and adverse impact values drawn from meta-analyses on the topic, we find a black-white adverse impact ratio value of .27 when regression weights are used. We find that increasing the weight given to the structured interview reduces the validity of the composite, but also reduces adverse impact. The adverse impact values corresponding to weighting that reduces validity by 1 percent, 5 percent, 10 percent, and 20 percent, respectively, are .31, .37, .43, and .54."

There are a number of key points about the above illustration. First, it is simply descriptive. It shows what would happen if differing weights were applied; it does not offer prescription as to what weights one should use. Second, in this specific example, the results are such that it is not the case that there is a set of alternative weights that achieve essentially equal validity with markedly less adverse impact. If such were available, advocates of the validity maximization position would presumably accept such an alternative if the difference between the validity resulting from regression weights and the alternative weights were less than what is perceived as a just-noticeable difference. Third, the example shows the adverse impact consequences of 1, 5, 10, and 20 percent reductions in validity, without attaching evaluative labels to these reductions. Descriptively, one can say, "Accepting a 10 percent reduction in validity can raise the adverse impact ratio from .27 to .54." My suspicion is that while some would be willing to insert the adjective *small* in front of "10 percent reduction," others might apply an adjective like *sizable*. Again, whether one finds this validity-impact trade-off acceptable is a matter of values.

As the discussion repeatedly raises the issue of values, it is important to ask, "Whose values determine these choices?" There are settings where organizational values are clear—for example, both validity and diversity are valued, and the trade-off between them is understood. Here the selection system developer is asked to work within constraints set by the organization. In other settings, organizational values are not clearly articulated, and the organization may be unaware of the value issues involved in selection system development. Here the selection system developer might impose his or her own value system or might help organizational decision makers understand the issues such that an organizational value position might emerge and subsequently drive selection system development. I am an advocate of the latter position, believing that the values reflected in a selection system should be the organization's.

Job Analysis and Competency Modeling

A bedrock notion underlying effective assessment and selection work is the need to base the individual characteristics that are assessed as part of the selection system on characteristics of the work role into which individuals are to be selected. Thus, there has been essentially universal agreement that selection system development requires some form of job analysis to identify the knowledge, skills, abilities, and other characteristics (KSAOs) that underlie effective performance on the criterion of interest, and to use this information as the basis for selection system development. Thus, an extensive array of conceptual approaches and data-gathering techniques makes up the domain of job analysis. As Schippmann notes in Chapter Eight, there is a history of tension and semantic confusion between traditional job analysis techniques and a more recent movement toward approaches that fall under the general rubric of competency modeling. Schippmann does a marvelous job of cutting through the confusion and setting forth a path toward clear thinking and effective practice in this area.

In terms of relevance to the development of selection systems, I find it useful to differentiate between process and outcome when it comes to job analysis and competency modeling. "Job analysis" is a catchall label for any of a wide variety of methods for collecting a wide variety of different types of information about a job, ranging from work behaviors, to work context, to the individual attributes linked to effective performance. This data collection process is in the service of different possible outcomes, depending on the purpose for which job analysis is undertaken. Some purposes call for a specification of key job tasks or task clusters, as in the case of job analysis to develop a set of performance appraisal dimensions. Others call for specification of the KSAOs linked to job performance; this is a common use of job analysis in the selection context.

It is here that job analysis and competency modeling intersect, as the emerging consensual meaning of the term *competency* is in many ways virtually synonymous with *KSAOs*. Both terms are reflected in the chapters in this book, with some using "KSAO" consistently (an example is Outtz in Chapter Twenty-Two), others using both terms interchangeably (Reed, McCloy, and Whetzel in Chapter Ten, for example), and others using *competency* consistently (Howard and Thomas in Chapter Thirteen and Paese in Chapter Fifteen). *Competency* as used by the chapter authors seems to refer generically to individual difference characteristics linked to effective criterion performance. At this level, we are talking of nothing more than a semantic change, substituting *competency* for *KSAO*. But the broader process of "competency modeling" is more than an alternate term for *job analysis*. First, job analysis typically focuses on a single job or a family of closely linked jobs. Competency modeling, in contrast, focuses at a much broader level, often the entire organization, identifying competencies that cut across jobs. Second, and following logically from the first, the resulting competencies are far more general than the job-specific KSAOs identified in many job analysis efforts. Sackett and Laczo (2003) offer the example of one firm's set of organizationwide competencies: business awareness, communication, teamwork, resilience, influencing others, critical thinking, managing conflict and change, results orientation, innovation, and functional excellence. Third, as this list illustrates, competency approaches clearly go far beyond the performance of prescribed job tasks. In fact, what is commonly specified in great detail in job analytical approaches is relegated to the catchall competency of "functional excellence." Fourth, the intent of competency modeling is for the model to cut across and integrate all human resource activities. One selects for, designs training activities for, develops appraisal systems for, and rewards performance on the same competencies. Having a common competency framework driving all of these activities would be an enormous step forward from the all-too-common situation in which each of these activities is owned by different units pursuing independent, and sometimes conflicting, agendas. Fifth, although job analysis commonly focuses on studying jobs as they currently exist, competency modeling is commonly forward looking and aspirational. A change in strategic orientation and firm values can mean that an attribute can suddenly become a key part of a firm's competency model.

Schippmann lays out an integrated next-generation approach to competency modeling that addresses some of the tensions between the competency approach and job analysis. A key issue is the high level of generality of many competency models, which simply are not at the level of specificity needed for developing and validating measures of the competencies. Schippmann offers an approach that differentiates between competencies at multiple levels, from organizationwide to business unit-wide to job-level specific. By doing so, an approach emerges that acknowledges the rigor and depth needed for some applications such as selection while still retaining the strength of competency modeling's broader integrative approach.

Komaki's Call to Action

This second part of this book opens with a call to action in which Komaki uses a hypothetical case study to set up a call for conducting and publishing validation work with the goal of making it easier for practitioners to locate selection tools for use in a given context. This case study illustrates quite a number of important issues in the development, validation, and implementation of selection systems. The scenario involves a drugstore chain seeking a valid selection system for store managers in the wake of a legal challenge to an unstructured interview-based system.

First, the decision as to the attributes to be measured in the new selection system appears to be based on a conversation between the narrator and the HR vice president, leading to the conclusion that what is needed is a measure of whether store managers can lead and motivate employees effectively. Selection professionals commonly encounter such a scenario in which a manager asserts that what is needed is a measure of a particular attribute. Selection professionals attempt to guide the manager to see the value of a broader inquiry, incorporating job analysis and competency modeling activities. The case later reveals the presence of other issues, including the closing of a number of stores due to ineffective management. It is not clear that this reflects ineffective employee motivation; only with a more probing inquiry can we determine whether other aspects of managerial performance, such planning and organizing and analytical skills, are as or more important.

Second, the HR vice president imposes severe constraints on our narrator: that only a single test can be used and that it must be cheap. This reflects another common tension: a tendency to focus on up-front costs in considering selection systems. The facts presented in the case offer a basis for a broader perspective. Selection research shows quite compellingly that the return on investment for effective selection systems is high, and in settings where the consequences of managerial failure are substantial and expensive (store closings, for example), selection professionals have the opportunity to make the case for investment in selection systems.

Third, the HR vice president calls for a measure of supervisory leadership skills as the selection device of choice. The narrator expresses dismay at finding evidence for ability and personality measures, but not for stand-alone measures of supervisory leadership. Although I would suggest situational judgment tests as measures that might serve this purpose (Motowidlo, Dunnette, & Carter, 1990, which initiated the resurgence of interest in situational judgment, describes an applied effort to develop and validate a selection tool for managers using criteria including interpersonal effectiveness), the broader issue is that whether to measure the attribute of interest (supervisory leadership) or to measure more fundamental attributes that predict the acquisition and demonstration of the attribute of interest is a fundamental choice to be made in the development of selection systems. In the terminology of Howard and Thomas in Chapter Thirteen, one can choose to measure attributes that permit inferences about future leader behavior or to seek demonstrations of leadership behavior. The two approaches to selection reflect classic distinctions between signs and samples (Wernimont & Campbell, 1968). I do not view one approach as intrinsically superior to the other and instead view both as viable. The sample, or demonstration, approach requires a smaller inferential leap ("a person who can show this skill in a selection setting can show that skill on the job") than the sign approach ("a person with this attribute is shown statistically to be more likely to exhibit the criterion behaviors of interest"). All else equal, minimizing the inferential leap is a good thing, which might lead to a general preference for samples over signs. But all else is rarely equal. The sample approach, for example, assumes that candidates already possess the skills of interest, whereas in many cases, skills are developed in training and on the job. It is also the case that the higher the fidelity of the sample to the job in question, the more its use is dependent on the job's being stable. In fast-paced changing environments, one might offer a general preference for measuring more general attributes. Thus, a careful assessment of the organizational context is an important aspect of the choice of predictors.

Fourth, one of the narrator's criteria for sound validation work is that the validation study use a measure of interpersonal skills, rather than a measure of overall job performance, as the criterion. My take is that both criteria are perfectly acceptable and that there would not be consensus within the selection community if forced to choose between an overall performance criterion and a domain-specific criterion. There are advantages to a domain-specific criterion. Pragmatically, higher correlations can be expected with a domain-specific criterion, all else equal, thus lowering the risk that sampling error will produce an underestimate of the true correlation that falls below a criterion for statistical significance. There are also advantages to an overall criterion, in that it permits the relative contribution of various components of a selection process to be compared on a common metric. And, of course, using both types of criteria permits the best of both worlds. The key point here, though, is to advise against viewing a study as deficient for the use of an overall performance criterion.

Fifth, the quest in the case is for a test for which one form of validity evidence, criterion-related evidence, has been reported elsewhere. It appears that the characters in this case are adopting an often-encountered misbelief about the meaning and role of validation: that validity is a characteristic that a predictor measure either does or does not possess, and that if validity evidence has been gathered in one setting, the predictor measure is thus "validated" and safe for use. In fact, however, the issue is always one of making the case for the validity of the intended test interpretations and uses in the specific selection setting. As McPhail and Stelly outline in Chapter Twenty-One, there are a variety of possible approaches to gathering evidence to support test use in the current organizational setting, some of which do involve reliance on data gathered elsewhere. But transporting validity evidence from another setting requires close correspondence between the scenario in which the original validity study was conducted and the new setting, and thus is far more stringent than looking for whether the test publisher has any criterion evidence available. That said, inquiring about the body of validity evidence gathered by a test's publisher is certainly a useful component of a search for existing measures that may be of potential use.

Finally, Komaki expresses concerns about the lack of available validity evidence, both in general and in the peer-reviewed literature. To add some context, let me make a number of observations about validation studies and the peer-reviewed literature. In general, journals publish validity studies only when a case can be made for a contribution to scientific understanding. For example, the study may involve a new predictor construct or a new way of measuring an established construct, a new criterion construct or a new way of measuring an established criterion construct, or a novel methodological feature. In contrast, journals generally have not been receptive to what are viewed as routine validation studies: the documentation of relationships between a given predictor and a given criterion for a given job in a given setting. In addition, it does not appear to be the case that journal policies are the sole reason for a lack of published validation work. Historically, many decades ago the journal *Personnel Psychology* ran a section labeled "Validity Information Exchange," which was finally cancelled due to a lack of submissions. A more recent effort to revive this idea as a freestanding publication was unsuccessful in drawing enough submissions to be viable. The message here is that looking for validity evidence when considering the purchase of a commercial test is certainly a wise practice, but an expectation that the publisher's validation work has been published would be unrealistic.

Future Prospects for the Selection and Assessment Field

Recently Filip Lievens and I had cause to review the past decade of selection research (Sackett & Lievens, 2008). We opened with a big question: "Can we do a better job of selection today than a decade ago?" Our sense was that we had made substantial progress in our understanding of selection systems. We have greatly improved our ability to predict and model the likely outcomes of a particular selection system as a result of developments such as more and better meta-analyses, better insight into incremental validity, better range restriction corrections, and better understanding of validity-adverse impact trade-offs. Thus, someone well informed about the research base is more likely to attend carefully to determining the criterion constructs of interest to the organization, more likely to select trial predictors with prior conceptual and empirical links to these criteria, more likely to select predictors with incremental validity over one another, and less likely to misestimate the validity of a selection system due to use of less-than-optimal methods of estimating the strength of predictor-criterion relationships. In terms of our ability to develop selection systems with higher levels of criterion-related validity, we concluded that at best we are able to modestly improve validity at the margin.

The field's technical literature tends to define the effectiveness of a selection process primarily in terms of validity, with diversity a second outcome that is also valued by many. My sense is that three additional outcomes also need to be taken into account as we look to the future. These are not new, and each is well represented in this book. The first is the integration of selection systems with other HR activities. Linking selection, appraisal, development, and other activities to a common framework driven by business strategy has the potential for a marked improvement over a series of separate activities that are often unconnected and at times are at cross-purposes (for example, selecting for one set of attributes while rewarding another). The second is seamless information access and flow through various aspects of the selection process and between processes that are precursors to selection (recruiting) and those that follow selection (appraisal and development). Integrative information technology platforms have become important aspects of HR systems (Reynolds & Weiner, 2009).

The third outcome is selection system security. In a great many settings, the value of a selection system is compromised, sometimes to the point of rendering it unusable, if examinees gain advance access to live test items. The importance of this issue has historically varied across settings, with a key feature being the likelihood of information sharing between various parties. In settings where this is high, such as where participants in the process are part of an established community, as in the case of a promotional examination for police officers, there is generally a high degree of concern about item exposure, with items viewed as compromised after a particular degree of exposure. Historically in many instances, the likelihood of information sharing has been viewed as low due to the enormous diversity of selection tools used across settings. Many applicants approach a given employer completely naive as to the process facing them. It is not at all uncommon for an individual to apply for a job and be surprised to be asked to complete one or more tests. This diversity of tools and methods has permitted the successful use of tools that would not be imaginable in an environment with greater visibility. For example, consider testing for college admissions, where the SAT and ACT are widely used and an extensive test preparation industry exists. While predictors in the noncognitive domain such as personality measures may be conceptually relevant to aspects of college performance, it is hard to imagine self-report measures retaining validity once item content is captured and publicized in this environment. My concern is that Internet-related information sharing may change this common scenario of applicants having little information about the content of selection tools used by a given employer. Test users constantly need to become more vigilant and sophisticated in monitoring information sharing about the content of their employment practices.

This multioutcome framework illustrates the breadth of knowledge needed for effective practice in the selection and assessment area. The challenges facing us continue to grow, but they are well worth facing, as talent identification at all levels of the organization continues to be a crucial contribution to organizational effectiveness.

References

Berry, C. M., & Sackett, P. R. (2009). Faking in continuous flow selection systems: Tradeoffs in utility vs. fairness resulting from two cut score strategies. *Personnel Psychology, 62*, 833–861.

Connelly, B. S., & Ones, D. S. (in press). Another perspective on personality: Meta-analytic integration of observers' accuracy and predictive validity. *Psychological Bulletin.*

De Corte, W., Lievens, F., & Sackett, P. R. (2007). Combining predictors to achieve optimal trade-offs between selection quality and adverse impact. *Journal of Applied Psychology, 92*, 1380–1393.

De Corte, W., Lievens, F., & Sackett, P. R. (2008). Validity and adverse impact potential of predictor composite formation. *International Journal of Selection and Assessment, 16*, 183–194.

DeYoung, C. G., Quilty, L. C., & Peterson, J. B. (2007). Between facets and domains: Ten aspects of the Big 5. *Journal of Personality and Social Psychology, 93,* 880–896.

Dudley, N. M., Orvis, K. A., Lebiecki, J. E., & Cortina, J. M. (2006). A meta-analytic investigation of conscientiousness in the prediction of job performance: Examining the intercorrelations and the incremental validity of narrow traits. *Journal of Applied Psychology, 91,* 40–57.

Ellingson, J. E., Sackett, P. R., & Connelly, B. S. (2007). Personality assessment across selection and development contexts: Insights into response distortion. *Journal of Applied Psychology, 92,* 386–395.

Hogan, J., Barrett, P., & Hogan, R. (2007). Personality measurement, faking, and employment selection. *Journal of Applied Psychology, 92,* 1270–1285.

Kehoe, J. F. (2008). Commentary on Pareto-optimality as a rationale for adverse impact reduction: What would organizations do? *International Journal of Selection and Assessment, 16,* 195–200.

Landers, R. N., Sackett, P. R., & Tuzinski, K. A. (2009). *Retesting after initial failure, coaching rumors, and warnings against faking in the use of personality measures for selection.* Manuscript submitted for publication.

Motowidlo, S. J., Dunnette, M. D., & Carter, G. W. (1990). An alternative selection procedure: The low fidelity simulation. *Journal of Applied Psychology, 75,* 640–647.

Mueller-Hanson, R., Heggestad, E. D., & Thornton, G. C. (2003). Faking and selection: Considering the use of personality from select-in and select-out perspectives. *Journal of Applied Psychology, 88,* 348–355.

Murphy, K. R., & Dzieweczynski, J. L. (2005). Why don't measures of broad dimensions of personality perform better as predictors of job performance? *Human Performance, 18,* 343–357.

Outtz, J. L., & Newman, D. A. (2010). A theory of adverse impact. In J. L. Outtz (Ed.), *Adverse impact: Implications for organizational staffing and high stakes selection* (pp. 53–94). New York: Routledge.

Reynolds, D. H., & Weiner, J. A. (2009). *Online recruiting and selection.* Malden, MA: Wiley-Blackwell.

Sackett, P. R., & Laczo, R. M. (2003). Job and work analysis. In W. C. Borman, D. R. Ilgen, & R. J. Klimoski (Eds.), *Comprehensive Handbook of Psychology, Vol. 12: Industrial and Organizational Psychology* (pp. 21–37). Hoboken, NJ: Wiley.

Sackett, P. R., & Lievens, F. (2008). Personnel selection. In S. T. Fiske, A. E. Kazdin, & D. L. Schacter (Eds.), *Annual review of psychology* (pp. 419–450). Palo Alto, CA: Annual Reviews.

Wernimont, P. F., & Campbell, J. P. (1968). Signs, samples, and criteria. *Journal of Applied Psychology, 52,* 372–376.

Young, M. C. (2003, June). *Effects of retesting on a new army measure of motivational attributes: Implications for response distortion, test validity, and operational use.* Paper presented at the annual meeting of the International Public Management Association Assessment Council, Baltimore, MD.

Appendix

Example Assessments Designed for Workplace Application

Jill M. Strange, Michael R. Kemp

This Appendix provides examples of the types of tests and assessments currently available for use in the workplace. To compile the following list, we asked the chapter authors to provide examples of tests associated with their area of focus, conducted online research, and contacted publishers to provide the most up-to-date information regarding relevant assessments.

The list is not intended to be comprehensive, and the authors and editors of this book are not endorsing these measures over other available assessments. Moreover, we did not evaluate these assessments; they are offered only as examples.

Qualified users are encouraged to evaluate the quality and appropriateness of any measure in light of the requirements suggested by the purpose for which they are to be used. Several aspects of assessments are important to consider when evaluating measures for use, such as:

Evidence of:
- Validity
- Reliability
- Fairness and subgroup differences
- Available and relevant norms

Technical documentation describing:
- Appropriate applications
- Target audience

- Administration protocols
- Limitations
- Development methodology
- Technical support for automated delivery systems

This appendix is organized into sections related to four types of assessments: construct oriented, position oriented, management and leadership oriented, and job analysis support. For each entry, the assessment title and publisher are listed with a brief description of the assessment's purpose. Following the description, one or more codes indicate the type of construct(s) covered by the assessment. A key is provided following.

For more information on the properties of various measures, the following resources may be helpful:

Ballack, A. S. (2002). *Dictionary of behavioral assessment techniques.* Clinton Corners, NY: Percheron Press. A well-indexed quick reference guide for a multitude of behavioral assessment tools that provides substantive descriptions and sources of additional information on each test.

Buros Institute for Mental Measurements. *Test Reviews Online* Web site: http://www.buros.unl.edu. Provides a search engine by alphabetical or category listings of test titles or by key word. Information on over twenty-five hundred tests has been critically reviewed by the Buros Institute.

Hammill, D. D., Brown, L., & Bryant, B. R. (1992). *A consumer's guide to tests in print* (2nd ed.). Austin, TX: Pro-ED. Presents objective evaluations and ratings of norm-referenced tests designed for diagnostic and screening purposes. A lengthy narrative section describes measurement principles, reviewers' evaluation methods, and criteria, followed by an alphabetical list of the tests rated according to the criteria. Several appendixes serve as indexes.

Hersen, M. (Editor-in-Chief). (2003). *Comprehensive handbook of psychological assessment.* San Francisco: Jossey-Bass. Four-volume set containing 121 chapters by expert contributors. Some chapters present historical review, theoretical considerations, and cross-cultural factors, while others are on individual tests described in great detail. Extensive bibliographies end each chapter. Volume 1: *Intellectual and Neuropsychological Assessment;* Volume 2: *Personality Assessment;* Volume 3: *Behavioral Assessment;* Volume 4: *Industrial and Organizational Assessment.*

Keyser, D. J. (2009). *Test critiques: 1984–current*. Austin, TX: Pro-ED. These volumes review and critique the most frequently used psychological, educational, and business tests, listing references for further research.

Plake, B. S., & Impara, J. C. (Eds.). (2009). *The mental measurement yearbook: 1938–current*. Lincoln, NE: Buros Institute of Mental Measurements. The aim of the annual publication is to provide critical evaluations of published tests and thereby raise the standards for test construction, validation and use. New editions supplement rather than supersede each other. Information provided includes description of the test, critical evaluations, and references to journal articles and reviews. Beginning with volume 9, the MMY is available online.

Key to Type of Construct Covered

A: Abilities and intelligence   BE: Background and experience

BC: Behavioral competency   JA: Job analysis

K: Knowledge and skills   P: Personality

PP: Physical performance

Construct Targeted

Applicant Profile Matrix, Aon Consulting. Based on competencies shown to predict job performance in key skill areas. The test contains a mixture of item types, including biodata, personality, situational judgment, and cognitive biodata items to assess cognitive ability in an unproctored environment. A, P, BE, BC

■ ■ ■

Bennett Mechanical Comprehension Test, Pearson. A selection tool for industrial and repair jobs covering mechanical aptitude, physical principles, and spatial visualization. The test can be administered online or in paper format, with hiring being the most common purpose of use. A, K

■ ■ ■

California Personality Inventory, Consulting Psychologists Press. A 434-item measure designed to provide a description of personality in clear, everyday language. It can be completed in forty-five to sixty minutes. P

■ ■ ■

Caliper Predictor, Caliper. Measures which candidates are a strong fit for a role through a thirty-minute assessment. Graphical reports indicate how each candidate's personality characteristics compare to those of others who have performed successfully in similar roles. P

■ ■ ■

Caliper Profile, Caliper. Measures over twenty-five personality traits, takes about ninety minutes to complete, and can be taken online or on paper. This assessment is most often used to evaluate an individual's characteristics, potential, and motivation for hiring purposes. P

■ ■ ■

Critical Reasoning Test Battery, SHL. Designed to assess critical reasoning skills at administrative, supervisory, or junior management levels. The battery encompasses three cognitive assessments—Verbal Evaluation, Interpreting Data, and Diagrammatic Series—and has a sixty-minute administration time. A

■ ■ ■

CultureFit, LIMRA Services. Helps reduce turnover by assessing a candidate's match to an organization's unique work culture. The twenty-minute Internet-based assessment is used to describe the organization's work culture, setting scoring benchmarks for key culture dimensions such as achievement orientation, customer orientation, professionalism, and pace. P

■ ■ ■

e-Selex Biodata Predictors, e-Selex.com. Provides a catalogue of over five hundred job-relevant biodata items. Customers have the option of selecting from assessments for nine job families (Administrative, Customer Service, Industrial, Information Technology, Retail, Sales, Telecenter, Tellers, and Loss Prevention) or developing a customized assessment based on important job constructs. These assessments are administered online to identify the most qualified job applicants. B

■ ■ ■

Employee Aptitude Survey, PSI Services LLC. A ten-test series measuring cognitive, perceptual, and psychomotor abilities, including reasoning, numerical, verbal, and special abilities. Uses for the test include preemployment, promotion, training, and development. A

■ ■ ■

General Aptitude Test Battery, U.S. Department of Labor. Used for government-related positions. The battery is used for vocational counseling, rehabilitation, and hiring. Containing twelve subtests, it assesses verbal aptitude, numerical aptitude, spatial aptitude, form perception, clerical perception, motor coordination, finger dexterity, and manual dexterity. A

■ ■ ■

Global Personality Inventory, Previsor. Assesses thirty-seven personality traits. Designed for global applications, the inventory is a multiple-choice test with three hundred items. Development data were collected on all levels of employees across several countries, with a focus on middle managers, professionals, and executives. The inventory is often used for selection, development, and coaching in professional and managerial job levels. P, A

■ ■ ■

Hogan Development Survey, Hogan Assessment Systems. Identifies personality-based performance risks and derailers of interpersonal behavior that are difficult to detect during an interview. The survey contains 168 true-false items and can be completed by online or paper administration for multiple purposes, including hiring and individual development. P

■ ■ ■

Hogan Personality Inventory, Hogan Assessment Systems. A measure of normal personality used to predict job performance. Based on the Five Factor Model of personality, it contains 206 true-false items. The tool is used to strengthen employee selection, leadership development, succession planning, and talent management processes. P

■ ■ ■

Motives, Values, Preferences Inventory, Hogan Assessment Systems. Reveals a person's core values, goals, and interests. This information helps determine the kinds of environments in which the person will perform best and the kind of culture the person will create as a leader. Organizations can use this information to ensure that a newly hired employee's values are consistent with those of the organization. P

■ ■ ■

NEO Personality Inventory, Psychological Assessment Resources. Consists of 240 multiple-choice items designed to assess normal personality based on the Five Factor Model of personality. Measures interpersonal, motivational, emotional, and attitudinal styles. P

■ ■ ■

Nonverbal Personality Questionnaire, Sigma Assessment Systems. The item illustrations in the questionnaire show personality-relevant behaviors by asking respondents to rate the likelihood that they would engage in the type of behavior depicted in the item illustration. The 136-item questionnaire takes approximately twenty minutes to complete and is intended for cross-cultural assessment needs. P

■ ■ ■

Occupational Personality Questionnaire, SHL. Assesses personality on thirty-two scales. Available in thirty languages, the questionnaire is designed to provide consistent assessment across a variety of languages and cultures. It is available in an online format and can be used for both selection and developmental purposes. P

■ ■ ■

Previsor Skill Assessments, Previsor. Previsor's test catalog contains a variety of assessments of job-specific skills. Organized by skills needed for specific jobs such as administrative and clerical, information technology, customer service, contact center, and health care. These assessments are commonly used in selection processes. K

■ ■ ■

Raven's Standard Progressive Matrices, Pearson. A forty-two-minute test of observation skills and clear-thinking ability that offers insight into an individual's capacity to observe, solve problems, and learn; administered online or in hard copy. The nonverbal nature of the test minimizes the impact of cultural or language bias while assessing job candidates for hiring purposes. A

■ ■ ■

SkillCheck Suites, SkillCheck. Fourteen assessment suites based on the SkillCheck tests ranging from basic skills to software skills to legal skills to ensure accurate and reliable assessment of job-related knowledge. K, A

■ ■ ■

Values Arrangement List, Pearson. An online survey used to measure personal values. It can be used in coaching and selection situations to examine and clarify an individual's value system or help define and refine an individual's career and life plans based on his or her value system. P

■ ■ ■

Watson-Glaser Critical Thinking Appraisal, Pearson. Designed to assess how well an applicant will make accurate inferences, recognize assumptions, properly deduce, interpret information, and evaluate arguments for hiring, promotion, development, or succession planning purposes. The assessment can be administered online using the standard form (forty to sixty minutes to complete) or the short form (thirty to forty-five minutes). A

■ ■ ■

Wiesen Test of Mechanical Aptitude, Psychological Assessment Resources. Uses pictures and simple sentences to measure basic mechanical aptitude ability rather than formal schooling or experience. Available online or in paper format, the test is commonly used for hiring. A

■ ■ ■

Wonderlic Personnel Test–Revised, Wonderlic. A short-form test that measures cognitive ability or general intelligence. Most often used in the employee selection process, it helps match people with positions that suit their learning speed and aptitude. A

■ ■ ■

Work Applied Cognitive Ability Test, Y2 Consulting Psychologists. Fifty multiple-choice questions that measure five aspects of cognitive ability—logical reasoning, spatial aptitude, numeric aptitude, verbal aptitude, and clerical perception—available in online and paper formats. Commonly used in the framework of selection processes. A

Position Targeted

Applicant Profile Industrial Suite, Aon Consulting. Designed to assess key competencies that are critical for success in industrial settings. The tests provide information to determine a candidate's job success in either entry-level (level 1 test batteries) or semiskilled/skilled (level 2 test batteries) positions. A, BC

■ ■ ■

Applicant Profile Professional Sales, Aon Consulting. An assessment of key competencies critical to success in sales. It measures sales orientation and drive, reliability and follow-through, adaptability and innovation, interpersonal presence and persuasion, and practical problem solving. High scores have been related to improved job performance, increased revenue, and reduced turnover. BC, P

■ ■ ■

BioData Powered by Pan, Talx. Consists of three assessments: Administrative and Clerical Questionnaire; Managerial, Professional, and Technical Questionnaire; and Manufacturing Operations Questionnaire. Each uses biographical information that relates to job performance to identify individuals with the potential for high-level job performance. B

■ ■ ■

Caliper First Step, Caliper. Measures the basic qualities required for success in sales or service positions. It is a screening instrument designed to measure whether candidates have the empathy, desire to please, and conscientiousness needed to succeed in customer service and similar support positions. P

■ ■ ■

Candidate Physical Agility Test, International Association of Fire Fighters and International Association of Fire Chiefs. A timed test consisting of eight essential activities of a firefighter: stair climb, hose drag, equipment carry, ladder raise, forcible entry, search, rescue, and ceiling breach and pull. The test is most commonly used for selecting among job applicants. PP

■ ■ ■

Career Battery Series, Development Dimensions International. Designed primarily for personnel selection applications. It includes tests designed to predict frequently occurring performance components in several job series. Assessments are available for customer service, sales, manufacturing, and professional job families. Each battery includes situational judgment, biodata, and personality scales. Scores are reported in three areas: making effective judgments and decisions, managing self and getting along with others, and demonstrating personal competence. A, P, BE

■ ■ ■

Career Profile+, LIMRA Services. Helps managers recruit candidates with the highest potential for success selling insurance, pensions, financial services, and more. Managers receive reports about each candidate, including a career profile score. Each report also includes key information about the applicant's attitudes toward the financial services industry and the organization, highlighting issues that should be discussed with the candidate. BE, P, K

■ ■ ■

Comprehensive Examination Battery, FPSI. A series of paper-based exams that measures the skills, abilities, and personal characteristics required of a successful firefighter. Primarily, the battery focuses on cognitive ability, reading ability, and selected personal characteristics. A, K, P, BC

■ ■ ■

Customer Care Ability Test, G.Neil. Predicts an applicant's abilities in the critical areas of customer care by looking at a variety of indicators, including sociability, helping disposition, drive to achieve, teamwork, punctuality, and pride in the quality of work. P

■ ■ ■

Customer Service Skills, Learning Resources. A video-delivered softskills assessment that measures competencies such as face-to-face and phone-based customer service skills that are required to be successful in positions involving customer interaction. The CSR is used for identifying the current competencies and developmental needs of individuals and can be implemented in development, hiring, and promotional situations. BC

■ ■ ■

eSkill Assessment Test Battery, Success Performance Solutions. An online tool to assess necessary skills in office, administrative, and most computer hardware and software applications. The test covers a wide range of topics such as typing, data entry, math and English skills, software Web development, and hardware and networking, among others, and is commonly used for selection purposes. A, K

■ ■ ■

Firefighter/Police Test Preparation Manual Test, FPSI. Assesses critical skills needed to succeed as an entry-level firefighter or police officer. Candidates are given the test preparation manual to study for four to six weeks. They are then administered a multiple-choice test measuring their acquisition and retention of the material in the manual. K

■ ■ ■

Insight Inventory Series, Development Dimensions International. Includes tests for senior sales roles and leadership roles, each assessing an individual's disposition, judgment, and potential effectiveness for future roles within the target job family. Insight inventories can be administered online or in paper format as part of a hiring process or as a way to place current employees into new or existing sales or leadership roles. A, P, BE

■ ■ ■

Mechanical Aptitude Test, Ramsay Corporation. Form 3C of the test assesses an individual's ability to learn or potential to be successful in an apprenticeship or trainee program for maintenance jobs such as maintenance mechanics, industrial machinery mechanics, and millwrights or in production jobs such as machine operators and tool setters. Contains thirty-six multiple-choice items and is used for hiring job applicants. A

■ ■ ■

Office Skills Software Test Battery, Success Performance Solutions. A fully automated, selection solution for office and industrial positions. Tests offered include Data Entry, Grammar, Proof Reading, Math, and Microsoft Office Skills Testing. A, K

■ ■ ■

Office Success Skills, Learning Resources. A video-delivered skills assessment that measures the competencies required to be successful in a wide range of office positions, such as customer relations, organizing and prioritizing, and problem solving. The assessment is used for identifying the current competencies and developmental needs of individuals and can be implemented in development, hiring, and promotional situations. A, BC

■ ■ ■

Performance Skills Index, LIMRA. Designed to identify people who can pass life and health insurance, property and casualty insurance, and Financial Industry Regulator Authority (FINRA) exams. Test scores can be used to provide training advice for applicants who are hired based on their learning style. K, P

■ ■ ■

Physical Ability Test, Firefighter Selection. Assesses a candidate's ability to meet the physical demands required on the job of a firefighter. The assessment is made up of eleven critical and physically demanding tasks every firefighter must be able to perform and is commonly used for evaluating job applicants. PP

■ ■ ■

Practical Skills Test, FPSI. A written test that measures mechanical aptitude and predicts entry-level firefighter academy and job performance. It contains questions assessing applicants' abilities in using, operating, repairing, and maintaining equipment and tools, as well as problem solving, analysis, and decision making related to fire technology and science. A, K, BC

■ ■ ■

Sales Skills, Ramsay Corporation. A forty-eight-item test of sales knowledge with content in prospecting, interpersonal, communication/expressiveness, product knowledge, confidence, listening, persistence, closing, follow-up, negotiating, honesty, and motivation skills. It indicates the degree to which an applicant would be successful at various aspects of sales. BC, P, K

■ ■ ■

Selling Styles Questionnaire, LIMRA Services. A personality assessment that helps to identify individuals with the selling style that best fits an organization's products and markets. It measures key personality components of sales performance such as achievement orientation, self-confidence, leadership, persuasiveness, persistence, and concern for others. These individual component scores are then analyzed to describe the candidate in terms of three fundamental sales styles. P

■ ■ ■

SkillCheck Clerical Office Professional, SkillCheck. Assesses computer-related skills in addition to customer service, telephone, and office management skills. The assessment battery measures twenty-three distinct competencies related to working in a professional clerical role and can be used for both selection and development purposes. A, P, K

■ ■ ■

SPQ-Gold, Behavioral Sciences Research Press. Measures sales call reluctance and tells organizations if sales candidates have the motivation to cold-call. It detects and measures twelve types of call reluctance in the candidates undergoing the test. P

Teller and Financial Service Skills, Learning Resources. A video-delivered skills assessment that measures competencies required by employers for jobs in banking and financial services. The program identifies the current competencies and developmental needs of individuals such as customer relations, soliciting new business, judgment, and identifying customer dissatisfaction. The assessment can be used for developmental, hiring, and promotional situations. A, P

■ ■ ■

Writing Ability Test, FPSI. A written assessment used to measure firefighter and police candidates' proficiency in spelling, grammar, punctuation, and sentence structure specific to the English language. A, K

Managerial and Leadership Targeted

Assessing Talent Series, Development Dimensions International. A collection of assessment center exercises designed to be used for first-line leaders through strategic executives. Exercises are configured to provide a "day-in-the-life" simulation of the target roles. Assessments typically include ability and personality tests as a component of the experience. The assessments may be used for personnel selection, individual development, and succession management. A, P, BC

■ ■ ■

Business Reasoning Test, Aon Consulting. Designed to measure professional and managerial-level candidates' ability to analyze and use information to solve problems. Candidates are required to determine appropriate actions or to draw logical conclusions based on the information provided in several different formats. The test requires forty-five minutes to complete thirty multiple-choice questions related to applying rules and inferential reasoning. A

■ ■ ■

Hilson Management Inventory, IPAT. Aids in identifying a number of personality and behavioral characteristics associated with managerial success. It is used for selection and placement, as well as evaluations of leadership and management potential. BC, P

■ ■ ■

Hogan Business Reasoning Inventory, Hogan Assessment Systems. Evaluates tactical and strategic reasoning using basic business data presented in the form of textual, quantitative, and graphic items. The test is administered online, takes twenty-five to thirty minutes to complete, and provides norms based on managerial samples. A

■ ■ ■

LEADeR Assessment, Aon Consulting. Measures supervisory potential based on a set of competencies related to executive leadership success. It uses a Web-based simulation format with role plays. BC

■ ■ ■

Leadership Inventory Plus—Proctored, Previsor. For selecting effective frontline leaders. It takes sixty minutes to complete, includes both cognitive and noncognitive content, and produces scores on four leadership dimensions. A, BC

■ ■ ■

Manager Selector, Kenexa Manager. Designed to predict performance in beginning to midlevel management positions in all service industries. This questionnaire with one hundred items also provides an individual profile of each candidate's strengths and limitations, along with developmental recommendations and potential interview questions to guide hiring managers. BE, BC

■ ■ ■

Management & Supervisory Skills Online, SHL. A test of knowledge of management and supervisory skills in the following areas: planning, motivating, organizing, communicating, and leadership. This test contains forty items in a multiple-choice format. BC

■ ■ ■

Supervisor Solution, Previsor. Used for job candidates applying to entry-level leadership positions who supervise hourly employees. This assessment is a computerized simulation. BC

■ ■ ■

TalentView of Leadership Transitions, PDI Ninth House. Designed to measure leadership potential based on the key factors for predicting future leadership performance. It is a combined multifactor measure that incorporates separate measures of personality predisposition, career interests, cognitive ability, and leadership experiences. A, BC, BE, P

■ ■ ■

TalentSIM Leadership Assessment, Censeo. An interactive, online leadership assessment using a job simulation approach to measure the competencies and skills of high-potential, entry, and midlevel managers. Candidates are presented with a series of challenging situations and asked how they would react. Once complete, the assessment provides information that helps companies select and develop high-quality leaders. BC

Job Analysis Support

Common-Metric Questionnaire, Personnel Systems and Technologies Corporation. A standardized job analysis questionnaire that focuses on the competencies needed by an individual to be successful in a particular job. The questionnaire is used most often for research purposes. JA

■ ■ ■

Fleishman–Job Analysis Survey, Management Research Institute. Determines the levels of knowledge, skills, and abilities required to perform a wide range of jobs using behaviorally anchored rating scales to determine the relevance of a KSA for a particular job. JA

JobMetrics, APTMetrics. An online job analysis tool that facilitates the identification of the important tasks, KSAOs, competencies, and other qualifications required for successful job performance. This tool, deployed using software as a service model, is intended to establish the foundation for the full range of HR systems: recruitment and selection, performance management, training and development, compensation, promotion, organizational design, and strategic planning. JA

■ ■ ■

Occupational Information Network, U.S. Department of Labor. Provides a list of job requirements for a large and diverse number of jobs. Information provided by O*Net is often considered basic, generic, or initial job analysis data that include physical requirements, education level, and some mental requirements of jobs. Task-based statements describing the work performed were created based on the functional job analysis technique. JA

■ ■ ■

Position Analysis Questionnaire, PAQ Services. A structured job analysis questionnaire that measures job characteristics and relates them to human characteristics. The PAQ is often used to develop compensation models, develop selection criteria for jobs, and by researchers studying the nature of work. JA

■ ■ ■

Success Profiles Navigator, Development Dimensions International. An online tool for conducting competency-based job analyses. The tool provides support for multiple data collection options, including observation, questionnaires, or interviews, to define the essential competencies for success in a particular position. Results may be used to define selection criteria, design development programs, and other HR applications. JA

Name Index

Subject Index